P9-CDW-278

For more than a hundred centuries the Emperor has sat immobile on the Golden Throne of Earth. He is the Master of Mankind by the will of the gods and master of a million worlds by the might of his inexhaustible armies. He is a rotting carcass writhing invisibly with power from the Dark Age of Technology. He is the Carrion Lord of the Imperium, for whom a thousand souls die every day, for whom blood is drunk and flesh eaten. Human blood and human flesh – the stuff of which the Imperium is made.

To be a man in such times is to be one amongst untold billions. It is to live in the cruellest and most bloody regime imaginable. This is the tale of those times.

It is a universe you can live today – if you dare – for this is a dark and terrible era where you will find little comfort or hope. If you want to take part in the adventure then prepare yourself now. Forget the power of technology, science and common humanity. Forget the promise of progress and understanding, for there is no peace amongst the stars, only an eternity of carnage and slaughter and the laughter of thirsting gods.

But the universe is a big place and, whatever happens, you will not be missed...

CONTENTS

DARK MILLENNIUM
In the nightmare future of the 41st Millennium,
Mankind teeters on the brink of extinction. Here you
will find the history of the mighty Imperium and details
of the ravening aliens and heretic rebels that threaten
on all sides.

THE WARHAMMER 40,000 HOBBY
Including a showcase of beautifully painted Citadel
miniatures, tips on collecting and painting an army –
with plenty of examples – plus pages of ideas and
inspiration for creating missions, campaigns and
amazing battlefields.

REFERENCE
In this section are the basic profiles for the majority of
models available to collect. In addition, all the key
tables and charts needed during a battle are collected
here for easy reference.

INTRODUCTION

Welcome to the dark future of Warhammer 40,000.

Warhammer 40,000 is far, far more than just a game. It is an engrossing and fulfiling pastime that allows you to collect and paint armies of Citadel miniatures and then use them to fight tabletop battles.

Warhammer 40,000 is set in a savage future age where Mankind must battle for survival in a galaxy riven by destruction and bloodshed. It is a time when the power-armoured Space Marines and the uncountable numbers of the Imperial Guard must stand against the slavering hordes of alien warriors.

The Warhammer 40,000 game puts you in command of a futuristic army of infantry squads, powerful fighting vehicles, mighty heroes, and even monstrous alien creatures. These armies of miniatures do battle over your tabletop, floor, or any area large enough to contain the warring forces.

You will have realised by now that Warhammer 40,000 differs from normal games. There are unlimited possibilities and players must be prepared to expend time and effort collecting, assembling and painting their models and setting up their battlefields. If all this sounds like hard work, you're right – it is! Glory on the battlefields of the far future is not won lightly.

Creating the magnificent spectacle of a fully painted army is an accomplishment one can be rightfully proud of. Once you've taken part in a tightly contested battle between well-painted miniatures raging across fully modelled terrain you'll be hooked. And you'll be joining a community of thousands upon thousands of gamers across the world. If you are anything like us, you will soon be spending endless hours thinking about what to collect next, deciding how to paint your latest model, and devising game-winning tactics for your next battle.

GETTING STARTED

Newcomers may find this weighty tome and the sheer scope of the game somewhat daunting, but there is no need to worry. Only the first third of the book concerns the rules, and many of those deal with special models or situations that you won't need straight away. The rest of the book will tell you about the 41st Millennium – the beleaguered Imperium of Mankind and the desperate battles it fights against enemies both from without and from within.

Additionally this book will introduce you to the other aspects of the Warhammer 40,000 hobby. We'll take a look at how you can get started collecting and painting an army. The book is packed with showcase miniatures painted by the world famous 'Eavy Metal team, as well as plenty of player's armies for reference and inspiration.

Finally we show you some ways you can take your games further. You'll find lots of information on creating themed battles and awe-inspiring alien battlefields, on how to link your battles together to form a campaign that decides the fate of entire planets, and on how to run a tournament to prove you are indeed the galaxy's best general.

A NOTE TO EXISTING PLAYERS

Those of you who are familiar with previous editions of Warhammer 40,000 can be rightfully excited about the book you now hold. There are dramatic rules changes that add to the challenge, without sacrificing the game play we know and love. Now your warriors can advance more quickly, go to ground, make off-table outflanking moves, and tanks can ram other vehicles. Close assaults are more brutal but missions are more objective-based, so it may not be enough to merely slaughter your foe. You'll also find new background and stories alongside classic history. The book is packed with lavish artwork, battle diagrams, galaxy maps and an extensive time-line of the 41st Millennium.

TO BATTLE

True heroes are recognised not by their medals, but by their scars. So muster your armies and prepare for war – the dark millennium awaits.

Encased in power armour and firing deadly boltguns, Space Marines defend the Imperium of Mankind.

WHAT YOU NEED

① AN OPPONENT

Between you both, you will need the things shown here in order to play Warhammer 40,000.

Tape measure

A tape measure or some other measuring device marked in inches is required to measure movement distances and the ranges of weapons.

Terrain

You can play without terrain, but adding it makes the game even more exciting. We've set up our battlefield with elements from our Citadel terrain range.

Dice

The game uses ordinary six-sided dice to work out combat results. It will be handy to have quite a few, including some that are different colours. In addition, you will need a Scatter dice, which is used to determine random directions. This is explained on page 2.

Rulebook

The rules are also available in a pocket-sized version found in the Warhammer 40,000 Assault on Black Reach boxed set.

Learning the rules

The easiest way to learn is undeniably to have someone show you how to play. If you can get to a Games Workshop store, then the staff will be happy to give you an introductory game. Getting a friend to teach you is another good idea. If neither of these is possible, then have a look at the Overview of Play on page xii and then skim through the first few sections that cover moving, shooting and assaulting (more complicated things like tanks and heroic characters can be added later). After this, we suggest getting stuck in to a battle, looking up things you're unsure of as you play. The goal is to have fun, so don't worry about getting everything exactly right straight away. Even long-time gamers are constantly finding nuances of the rules and different tactics, as well as developing their painting skills and discovering new facets of the background and history of the Warhammer 40,000 universe.

② BATTLEFIELD

This will consist of a table or some other surface, and some terrain. When you are starting out, a few books will work fine as hills, whilst cereal packets or the like will make perfectly good buildings.

TWO ARMIES

To start with, aim to have roughly even numbers on each side. Working out a fair match-up is covered over the page.

Painting your models is a lot of fun, and will make your battles look much more impressive.

Pen and paper

This will be handy to note down damage to vehicles, heroes that have been wounded or any other details that you need to remember during a battle.

Templates and blast markers

Some weapons, such as flame throwers and missiles, affect a large area and can wound many enemy troops at once. These are worked out using templates or blast markers to decide which models are hit.

A fully modelled battlefield, created by an experienced terrain maker, makes for a spectacular game.

HELP ON THE WEB

You'll find information on just about every aspect of Warhammer 40,000 on our website:

www.games-workshop.com

BUILDING AN ARMY

It is time to take your place alongside the defenders of humanity – the mighty Space Marines and the ranks of the Imperial Guard. Or, if you dare risk the wrath of the mysterious Inquisition, join the insidious forces of Chaos – traitors every one. Perhaps you will side with one of the many alien races poised to ravage the Imperium of Man – the barbaric hordes of the Orks that infest the galaxy, the enigmatic Eldar who look to sacrifice other races to save their own, or even the monstrous Tyranids whose voracious swarms consume entire planets.

To play Warhammer 40,000 you will need an army – in other words a collection of Citadel miniatures. An army can be almost any size – from a small force of three or four squads, to a massive horde. It is quite possible to play Warhammer 40,000 with an army that consists of every model you own, even if the warriors are from different races. However, most players soon decide to collect one particular army, such as Space Marines or Orks, because they love the miniatures, the background history, the way they fight, or all three!

CODEXES

Once you have chosen which army to collect, it is a good idea to get hold of the Codex. Each army has a Codex – its own dedicated book, which contains in-depth background details and complete rules for all the models in the force, along with their weapons and wargear. Codexes also contain accounts of great heroes and famous battles, a showcase of miniatures, and an army list that will help you to pick an organised force.

POINTS

Warhammer 40,000 uses a system of points values that allow players to fight evenly matched battles. Each model is given a points cost that reflects its value in the game. For example, a single Ork warrior costs 6 points, while a mighty Space Marine Land Raider tank costs 250 points.

◄ Each army has a large range of troops, characters and vehicles, as well as its own Codex to help you organise your collection into a cohesive fighting force.

PICKING A FORCE FOR BATTLE

When arranging a battle, players agree on a particular points limit for each side – 1,000 for example. This means that a force of powerful, elite models will be quite small, while an army of weaker models will likely outnumber the enemy. Whatever you choose within this total, the battle will be a fair match, decided by good tactics and a little bit of luck.

The army list in each Codex gives the points cost for all the models in that army, as well as the many optional upgrades such as squad leaders, special weapons and other equipment. The army list also provides a structure that helps you to create an effective fighting force. For example, every army must have a leader such as a Space Marine Captain or an Ork Warboss. Within these parameters there is a lot of freedom, and once players have a sizeable collection of miniatures, they have the option of picking exactly which troops to use for each battle. Some gamers really enjoy this process of coming up with new force 'rosters', spending hours working out different combinations and planning cunning tactics before they even reach the battlefield.

With a calculator and a Codex, this Space Marine player plans out an unstoppable battle force.

This Space Marine force has been chosen for a 1,000 point battle.

➤ *These miniatures were left out of the force for this particular game. Having extra models means that you can change your army to try out different tactics and combinations.*

FIGHTING A BATTLE

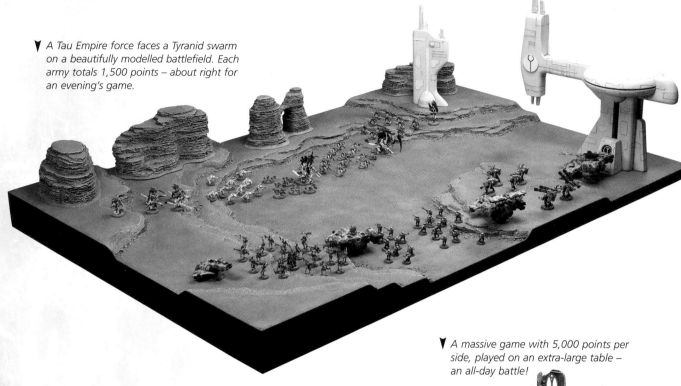

▼ A Tau Empire force faces a Tyranid swarm on a beautifully modelled battlefield. Each army totals 1,500 points – about right for an evening's game.

▼ A massive game with 5,000 points per side, played on an extra-large table – an all-day battle!

SIZE OF GAME

The size of a Warhammer 40,000 battle is determined by three factors – how many models you have to choose from, how much time you can dedicate to the battle, and what type of game or mission you plan on playing.

Generally speaking, in a small game of Warhammer 40,000 each player has an army of between 500-1,000 points. To play out a standard mission for a game of this size will take about an hour. Medium-sized matches of between 1,000-2,000 points usually take an evening to finish. Large battles of over 2,000 points can take all day or even longer.

Very experienced (or plain ambitious) players will even play matches of enormous size with added unique mission rules. These massive battles may last a weekend or longer and will almost certainly require a gaming space where models can be left standing over night!

◄ For your first few games, using a small army will keep things manageable. This small force is composed of a Space Marine Chaplain and a Tactical squad – roughly 250 points-worth.

➤ A multi-player bash, using 1,000 points each. The winner gets free drinks all night!

OVERVIEW OF PLAY

MODEL PROFILES

All models have a profile similar to the one shown below, representing their abilities within the game. The different Characteristics are explained briefly on these pages (see page 6 for more details).

WS Weapon Skill
BS Ballistic Skill
 S Strength
 T Toughness
 W Wounds
 I Initiative
 A Attacks
Ld Leadership
Sv Armour Save

	WS	BS	S	T	W	I	A	Ld	Sv
Space Marine	4	4	4	4	1	4	1	8	3+

WEAPON PROFILES

Weapons also have profiles to tell you their range, Strength, armour piercing value (AP), the number of shots they fire and any special rules they have (see page 27).

	Range	Strength	AP	Special
Boltgun	24	4	5	Rapid fire

Terrain

Terrain can offer cover from enemy fire (see page 21) but also slows movement (see page 13).

TAKING TURNS

Each game is played out over a series of turns, until one player achieves victory and is declared the winner.

Both players alternate taking their turn. First one player moves, shoots and assaults with his army. Once he's finished, the other player does the same with his own army.

THE MOVEMENT PHASE

In the Movement phase, your squads can manoeuvre around the battlefield.

Squads

Models are organised into squads, commonly of 5 or more models. Each member of the squad must stay within 2" of a squad-mate at all times.

Infantry movement

Infantry can move up to 6" in the Movement phase (see page 11).

Independent characters

The Space Marine Captain and Ork Warboss are mighty individuals who do not need to operate in squads (see page 47).

② THE SHOOTING PHASE

In the Shooting phase, models can shoot at enemies they can see. A dice is rolled for each shot to determine the outcome.

Roll to hit

Models use their Ballistic Skill (BS) to determine their chances of hitting. Space Marines have a BS of 4, which means that they always hit on a dice result of 3 or more (see page 17).

Roll to wound and save

Any models hit by shooting have a chance to be wounded, according to the Strength (S) of the weapon and the Toughness (T) of the model hit (see page 19). Models that are wounded normally have a chance to make a 'saving throw', to represent their armour saving them from the shot (see page 20).

③ THE ASSAULT PHASE

In the Assault phase, squads within 6" of the enemy can charge into close combat (see page 33).

Striking blows

In an assault, models from both sides strike in Initiative (I) order using their Attacks value (A) to determine how many times they strike. How easily models inflict hits on each other is determined by comparing their Weapon Skill (WS).

Close combat attacks have a chance to cause wounds according to the Strength (S) of the model striking blows and the Toughness (T) of the model being struck. If wounds are caused, saving throws (Sv) may be taken and casualties removed (see page 39).

CASUALTIES

Each model can take a certain number of Wounds (W) before it is slain and removed from the table. Most models only have a single Wound, although heroic individuals and large monsters may have more (see page 26).

Morale

If a squad takes too many casualties, it must take a Morale test using its Leadership (Ld). If the test is failed, the squad will retreat towards the edge of the board (see page 43).

Dreadnought

Vehicles have different rules to other models (see page 56).

Deffkoptas

Ridden by Orks, Deffkoptas hover over the ground and speed towards the enemy. They use the rules for jetbikes (see page 53 for more information).

THE NEXT TURN

Once the Space Marines have completed their Assault phase, the Orks take their turn, working through the Movement, Shooting and Assault phases in the same way.

THE RULES

This section starts with the basic rules as they apply to the most common type of model – infantry. This means you can learn how to move, shoot and assault with your troops and quickly get playing a battle, without having to read for hours first. As soon as you have a grasp of the fundamentals, you can introduce other types of models, such as speeding jetbikes, ferocious monsters, courageous heroes and mighty battle tanks, looking up the rules as you need them.

This is a dark and terrible era where you will find little comfort or hope.
If you want to take part in the adventure then prepare yourself now.

THE MOST IMPORTANT RULE!

Warhammer 40,000 is an involving game, with many different armies, weapons and possibilities. In a game of this size and complexity there are bound to be occasions where a particular situation lies outside these rules, often when unusual models interact. At other times you may know the rule is covered but you just can't seem to find the right page. Then again you may know the rule, but the reality of exactly where your models are on the table may make it a really close call – measuring assault moves and deciding if a key model is in cover are classic examples.

All of these instances can lead to arguments, so it is important to remember that the rules are just a framework to create an enjoyable game. Winning at any cost is less important than making sure both players – not just the victor – have a good time. If a dispute does crop up then work out the answer in a gentlemanly manner. Many players simply like to roll-off and let the dice decide who is right, allowing them to get straight back to blasting each other to pieces. After the game you can happily continue your discussion of the finer points of the rules, or agree how you will both interpret them should the same situation happen again. You could even decide to change the rules to suit you better (this is known as a 'house rule').

The most important rule then is that the rules aren't all that important! So long as both players agree, you can treat them as sacrosanct or mere guidelines – the choice is entirely yours.

DICE

DICE (D6)

In a Warhammer 40,000 battle you often need to roll dice to see how the actions of your models turn out – how effective their shooting is, what damage they've done to a vehicle, how far they fall back from enemy fire, and so on. Almost all of the dice rolls in Warhammer 40,000 use standard six-sided dice (usually referred to as 'D6').

ROLLING A D3

In rare circumstances you may be told to roll a D3. Since there's no such thing as a three-sided dice, use the following method for determining a score between 1 and 3. Roll a D6 and halve the score, rounding up. Thus 1 or 2=1, 3 or 4=2 and 5 or 6=3.

RE-ROLLS & ROLL-OFFS

Re-rolls

In some situations the rules allow you a 're-roll' of the dice. This is exactly as it sounds – pick up the dice you wish to re-roll and roll them again. The second score counts, even if it means a worse result than the first, and no single dice can be re-rolled more than once regardless of the source of the re-roll. If you re-roll a 2D6 or 3D6 roll, you must re-roll all of the dice and not just some of them, unless the rule granting you the re-roll explicitly specifies otherwise.

Roll-offs

If the rules require players to roll-off, this simply means that each player rolls a dice and the player that scores the highest result wins the roll-off. If the players roll the same result, both dice must be rolled again until one player is the winner.

MODIFYING DICE ROLLS

Sometimes, you may have to modify the result of the dice roll. This is noted as D6 plus or minus a number, such as D6+1 or D6-2. Roll the dice and add or subtract the number to or from the score to get the final result. For example, D6+2 means roll a dice and add 2 to the score, giving a total of between 3 and 8.

You may also be told to roll a number of dice in one go, which is written as 2D6, 3D6, and so on. Roll the indicated number of dice and add the scores together, so a 2D6 roll is two dice rolled and added together for a score of between 2-12. Another method is to multiply the score of a dice by a certain amount, such as D6x5 for a total between 5 and 30. Finally, a combination of methods may be used, such as 3D6-3 giving a total of 0-15.

SCATTER DICE

Some weapons are fairly random in their accuracy and require you to roll a scatter dice to determine where their shots land. The scatter dice is marked on four sides with an arrow, and on two sides with a special 'HIT' symbol. Simply roll the scatter dice near the target point – if an arrow is rolled this shows in which direction the shot has deviated. If a HIT symbol is rolled this means the shot is bang on target. Some weapons may scatter automatically, with no chance of a direct hit, in which case you will find a small arrow on the HIT side to determine the direction.

Reason begets doubt;
doubt begets heresy.

MODELS & UNITS

MODELS

The Citadel miniatures used to play games of Warhammer 40,000 are referred to as 'models' in the rules that follow. Each model is an individual playing piece with its own capabilities. Models represent an enormous variety of troops ranging from Gretchin, the small, weak slaves of the Orks, to noble Space Marines, the protectors of Mankind, to Wraithlords, mighty Eldar constructs containing the souls of the dead. To represent all these differences, each model has its own characteristics profile as described in the next section.

BASES

Citadel miniatures are normally supplied with a plastic base. If so, they must be glued onto their bases before they can be used in the game.

Some players like to mount their models on impressive scenic bases. As mounting your models on different-sized bases might affect the way they interact with the rules, make sure before the game that your opponent does not mind this.

UNITS

Warriors tend to band together to fight in squads, teams, sections or similarly named groups – individuals do not normally go wandering off on their own for obvious reasons! In Warhammer 40,000, we represent this by grouping models together into units.

Units fight in loose groups with gaps between each model. This gives the troopers the freedom to move over difficult terrain quickly, and enables them to take advantage of such things as minor folds in the ground, scrub, and other small features, to shelter from enemy fire. Similarly, artillery batteries consist of large guns and the crew that fire them, vehicle squadrons are made up of a number of vehicles and so on. The different elements of the unit have to stay together to remain an effective fighting force. This is detailed more fully in the Movement section (see page 12).

A unit will usually consist of several models that fight as a group, but it can also be a single, very large or powerful model, such as a battle tank, a monstrous alien creature or a lone hero. In the rules that follow, all of these things are referred to as 'units'. The different types of unit are detailed overleaf.

Thought for the day:

Wisdom is the beginning of fear.

MEASURING DISTANCES

A model is considered to occupy the area of its base, so when measuring distances between two models, use the closest point of their bases as your reference points. For models supplied without a base (like some large vehicles) use the model's hull or body instead.

When measuring distances between two units, use the closest models as your reference points, as shown in the diagram below. So, for example, if any model in a unit is *within 2"* of an enemy unit/model, the unit is said to be *within 2"* of that enemy unit/model.

In general, players are not allowed to measure any distance except when the rules call for it (e.g. after declaring an assault or firing at an enemy, to work out a rule's area of effect, when deploying their forces, etc).

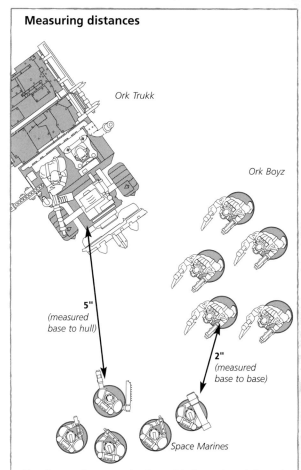

Measuring distances

Ork Trukk

Ork Boyz

5"
(measured base to hull)

2"
(measured base to base)

Space Marines

*The distance between the Space Marine unit and the Ork Trukk is 5 inches. We normally say that the Trukk is **within 5"** of the Space Marine unit.*

*The distance between the Space Marine unit and the Ork unit (i.e. between the two closest models) is 2 inches. The two units are **within 2"** of each other.*

UNIT TYPES

In order to make it easier to learn the basic rules, the first few sections of the book, covering Movement, Shooting, Assault and Morale are written with respect to infantry units, because these are by far the most common unit type in the game. The other types of unit are also defined here and then explained in detail later in specific sections that cover their unique rules. The unit types in Warhammer 40,000 are as follows:

INFANTRY

Infantry units include all types of foot soldiers, whether human or alien. A typical unit of infantry is between five and ten models strong but can be much larger. In rare cases, an infantry unit may comprise only a single model. Infantry are fairly slow moving, but can cross almost any terrain (given enough time) and make the best use of cover to avoid enemy fire. Infantry are the most common and dependable units in Warhammer 40,000 and the bulk of the rules are concerned with them.

Space Marines of the Ultramarines Chapter

BEASTS AND CAVALRY

Consisting of particularly vicious hunting animals or a rider with a living mount, beasts and cavalry are able to swiftly carry the battle to the enemy. Beasts and cavalry have a profile like other infantry, but are able to make use of a special faster move when they assault an enemy unit.

Beast and cavalry units are typically quite rare and small in number. Just like bikers, cavalry riders may not dismount during the game and so have a characteristic profile that takes into account both the beast and rider. We assume that if one is killed, the other is also incapacitated or simply flees the battlefield.

Flesh Hound of Khorne

MONSTROUS CREATURES

Some creatures are just too big to fit into the ordinary infantry unit category. These are towering giants that are capable of crushing a tank – like the Tyranid Carnifex, a creature bio-engineered and evolved to become a living battering ram. While monstrous creatures use many of the infantry rules, their size and destructive capability make them a lot more dangerous. Fortunately for their foes, a monstrous creature unit will usually consist of a single model.

Tyranid Carnifex

Blood Angels
Assault Marine

Ork Zzap Gun and Gretchin crew

JUMP INFANTRY

Jump infantry are equipped with jump packs, jet packs, wings, teleport devices or other means of moving quickly over short distances. They commonly take advantage of these by dropping onto the battlefield in the midst of the enemy – heroically or foolishly depending on your perspective. Jump infantry can move like normal infantry or activate their jump device to make a high-speed move, leaping over intervening terrain and models. Jump infantry tend to be a rare and valuable commodity in most armies.

ARTILLERY

These units represent large weapons and their crews, the gun models themselves being large enough to be treated as small vehicles. Artillery units count as infantry in most respects, but when they are fired at, hits may be scored on the guns themselves, which have vehicle-like characteristics.

BIKES AND JETBIKES

These units are riders mounted on a variety of conventional bikes or jetbikes. They are capable of moving really quickly, and will often have weapon systems built onto their bikes. Both types of bike manoeuvre much faster than infantry and jetbikes are able to glide over obstructions, such as buildings, without being slowed. Their only major weakness is the risk of crashing when moving through terrain. Note that, to keep things simple, riders may not dismount during the game and therefore these models have a combined characteristic profile that factors in both the bike and rider.

Eldar Jetbike

VEHICLES

Vehicle units include all kinds of war machines. Battle tanks, grav-tanks, Monoliths and Dreadnoughts all fall into this category. Most vehicles can move more rapidly than infantry but need to stick to open ground to avoid getting bogged down. Vehicle units are represented by single models in the case of tanks and other large vehicles, or as a group of smaller vehicles. Vehicle crew members – the drivers, commanders and gunners – are assumed to be an integral part of their machine, and if their vehicle is destroyed they are considered to be lost along with it. Note that bikes and jetbikes have their own unit type, and are not counted as vehicles.

Imperial Guard Leman Russ
battle tank

CHARACTERISTICS

In Warhammer 40,000, there are many different types of warriors, ranging from the mighty Space Marines to the brutal Orks, the agile Eldar to the dreaded Tyranids. To represent the different abilities of these creatures in the game, each model has a profile made up of nine numbers that describe the various aspects of their physical and mental make-up. These are called characteristics.

The characteristics are: Weapon Skill (WS), Ballistic Skill (BS), Strength (S), Toughness (T), Wounds (W), Initiative (I), Attacks (A), Leadership (Ld) and Armour Save (Sv).

For all models except vehicles these characteristics are given a value on a scale of 0 to 10 – the higher, the better (except for a model's Armour Save, where the opposite is true!).

Certain pieces of wargear or special rules may modify a model's characteristics positively or negatively, by adding to it (+1, +2, etc.) or even multiplying it (x2, x3, etc.). However no modifier may raise any characteristic above 10 or lower it below 0. Saves can at best be modified to 2+.

WEAPON SKILL (WS)

This characteristic defines how skilled and vicious a warrior is with his weapons in close combat. The higher the score, the more likely the warrior will land blows on a close combat opponent. An average human soldier has WS3, while a genetically-enhanced Space Marine will have WS4 or even WS5.

BALLISTIC SKILL (BS)

Ballistic Skill shows how accurate a creature is with ranged attacks, such as guns, rockets or energy weapons. The higher this score is, the easier a creature finds it to hit when it shoots at something. Some monsters have natural weapons that can be used at range (they may be able to spit venom, for example) and their BS is also used to determine whether they hit or not.

STRENGTH (S)

Strength shows how physically strong a creature is. An exceptionally puny creature may have a Strength of 1, a deadly Wraithlord has S10 and most humans have S3. Strength tells us how hard a creature can hit in close combat and therefore how easily it can hurt an enemy.

TOUGHNESS (T)

Toughness measures a creature's ability to resist physical damage and pain, and includes such factors as the thickness of its flesh, hide or skin. The tougher a creature, the better it can survive enemy blows or shots. A human is T3, while a resilient Ork is T4.

WOUNDS (W)

Wounds show how much damage a creature can take before it either dies or is so badly hurt it can't fight any more. Most man-sized creatures have only a single Wound. Heroes and large monsters are often able to withstand several injuries that would slay a lesser creature, and so have a Wounds value of 2, 3, or more.

INITIATIVE (I)

How alert a creature is and how quickly it reacts is shown by its Initiative. In close combat, faster creatures gain a massive advantage over slower ones because they get to strike first. A normal human is Initiative 3, while an agile Eldar Aspect Warrior is Initiative 5.

ATTACKS (A)

Warriors of exceptional skill and particularly ferocious monsters can unleash a flurry of blows against their opponents. This characteristic indicates the number of dice a model rolls when fighting in close combat. This is normally 1 for most models, but a heroic leader or a large monster can have 3 or even more Attacks. The number of Attacks a creature makes may be increased if it has the added impetus of assaulting into its foes or is fighting using two weapons, for example.

LEADERSHIP (LD)

The Leadership (Ld) of most warriors is around an average value of 7 or 8. A creature with a higher Leadership value is courageous, steadfast, or very well-trained. A creature with a lower value is temperamental, unpredictable or cowardly. Models that represent generals, heroes, sergeants and other such characters often have a high Leadership that allows them to lead others, inspiring them on to greater feats of valour.

ARMOUR SAVE (SV)

A creature's Armour Save (Sv) gives it a chance of avoiding harm when it is struck or shot. Most creatures have an armour save based on what kind of armour they are wearing, so this characteristic may be improved if they are equipped with better armour. Other creatures may receive a natural saving throw from having thick bony plates or a chitinous shell.

VEHICLE CHARACTERISTICS

The Warhammer 40,000 universe is home to all sorts of tanks, war machines and other combat vehicles, both human-built and alien. To reflect the many differences between creatures of flesh and blood and constructs of steel and iron, vehicles have many different rules and their own set of characteristics. Vehicle characteristics are described in the Vehicles section (see page 56).

ZERO-LEVEL CHARACTERISTICS

Some creatures have been given a '0' for certain characteristics, which means that they have no ability whatsoever in that field (the same is also occasionally represented by a '–'). This usually applies to creatures unable to use missile weapons, and so they have a BS of 0, but it might apply to other characteristics too. A defenceless model will have no Attacks whatsoever, while a model with WS0 will be hit automatically by his enemies in close combat. A warrior with an Armour Saving Throw of '–' has no armour save at all.

CHARACTERISTIC PROFILES

Each model in Warhammer 40,000 has a profile that lists the value of its characteristics. At the back of this book, and in the Codex books for each army, you will find profiles for many races and creatures.

Below are the profiles for an Ork Boy and a Space Marine of the Imperium:

	WS	BS	S	T	W	I	A	Ld	Sv
Ork Boy	4	2	3	4	1	2	2	7	6+
Space Marine	4	4	4	4	1	4	1	8	3+

As you can see, they are similar in some respects. They have the same Weapon Skill and the same Toughness value. They both have 1 Wound, which is the norm for man-sized creatures. The Ork has more Attacks in close combat, representing its great ferocity,

but when it comes to BS, S, I, Ld and Sv, the Space Marine is superior. The Space Marine's Ballistic Skill of 4 means that he will hit more often when shooting. In hand-to-hand combat, the greater Strength value gives the Space Marine a better chance of killing the Ork and his superior Initiative means that he gets to strike first. The Space Marine has a Leadership of 8, which is slightly higher than the average. The Space Marine's thicker armour gives him another marked advantage over the Ork, as most shots or blows that hit the Space Marine are deflected on a D6 roll of 3 or more. The Ork instead needs a result of 6 to be saved by its primitive type of armour.

Obviously, an Ork is no match for a Space Marine when fighting one-on-one, but, as Orks are usually found in large numbers, they can be lethal opponents, even for Space Marines!

MULTIPLE MODIFIERS

If a model has a combination of rules or wargear that both add to and multiply one of its characteristics, first multiply the basic value and then add the extra points. For example, if a model with Strength 4 has both '+1 Strength' and 'double Strength', its final Strength will be 9 (4x2=8, 8+1=9).

CHARACTERISTIC TESTS

During a battle, a model might have to take a test on one of its characteristics, commonly its Strength, Toughness or Initiative. For example it might have to test its Toughness to resist the effects of a lethal gas.

In order to take the test, roll a D6. To succeed, you must score equal to or lower than the value of the characteristic involved. Note that if a 6 is rolled, then the model automatically fails the test regardless of the characteristic's value or any other modifier that might apply, and conversely a 1 is always a success.

Of course, if a model has to take a test for one of its characteristics with a value of 0, it automatically fails.

LEADERSHIP TESTS

Tests made against the Leadership characteristic (like Morale checks) are different from other tests. In the case of a Leadership test, roll 2D6 (two dice added together, as explained earlier). If the result is equal to or less than the model's Leadership, the test is passed.

If a unit includes models with different Leadership values, always use the one with the highest Ld value.

Modifiers may apply to the Leadership characteristic in particularly trying circumstances – for example, -1 if the unit suffered wounds from an Ordnance barrage weapon, as described later.

POINTS VALUES

Generally, you'll find characteristic profiles come along with one other piece of information – the model's points value. This represents the relative battlefield value of the creature in question. Points values take into account a number of different factors including characteristics, different races' overall strengths and weaknesses, basic weapons, unit size, rarity and so forth. Choosing forces that are worth a specific points total allows players to organise an evenly matched battle.

For comparison, a Space Marine is worth 15 points, and an Ork is 6 points. This means that an Ork horde would normally outnumber a Space Marine force by more than two to one. It is just as well that Space Marines are really hard!

THE TURN

A tremendous amount of action takes place in a battle: squads are constantly manoeuvring and shooting, tanks rumble into action and artillery fire roars overhead in a torrential downpour of destruction. A game of Warhammer 40,000 represents the ebb and flow of battle but, in order to turn the chaos into a manageable game, players alternate taking turns moving and fighting with their units. So, one player will move and fight with his forces first, then his opponent will move and fight. Then the process repeats with the first player moving and fighting again, and so on until the end of the game.

During his turn, a player can usually move and fight with all of his units. For convenience, moving, shooting and fighting in close combat are dealt with one after the other. This means that you move all of the models you want to first, then you shoot with any who can, and finally you resolve all close combats. This process helps to keep track of what is going on and makes it easier to know when one player's actions are over and his opponent can start his turn.

GAME TURNS AND PLAYER TURNS

In a complete game turn, both players get a player turn, each one divided into Movement, Shooting and Assault phases (see Turn Sequence, below). Exactly what is going to happen in each phase is described in the following sections of this book.

THE TURN SEQUENCE

1 The Movement phase
The player can move any of his units that are capable of doing so. See the Movement rules for more details of how to move your forces.

2 The Shooting phase
The player can shoot with any of his units that can see an enemy. See the Shooting rules for more details about how to resolve this.

3 The Assault phase
The player can move any of his units to assault the enemy if they are close enough. Assaults are bloody, desperate affairs where units are fighting in close combat. This means that both forces can fight in an Assault phase, but only the player whose turn it is can move into an assault. The Assault rules will tell you more about them.

Hence one game turn will comprise two player turns. Whenever a rule uses the word 'turn', both in this rule book and in the Codexes, it means 'player turn', otherwise it will clearly state 'game turn'.

So, for example, in game turn 1 a player will take his player turn 1 and go through his Movement, Shooting and Assault phases. Then the other player will take his player turn 1 and go through his Movement, Shooting and Assault phases, thus ending game turn 1. Game turn 2 will then follow.

WHO GETS THE FIRST TURN?

Which player gets the first turn of the game can be determined in a number of different ways. Normally, both players roll a D6 and the player with the highest score deploys his army first and then takes the first player turn. The mission you are fighting will specify exactly how this works. Fighting a variety of different missions is covered in more detail in the Organising a Battle section, on page 90.

THE END OF THE GAME

The standard missions presented in this book last a random number of game turns (five to seven turns), determined by a dice roll. However the final section of the book includes ideas for creating your own missions, which could end in a number of ways. A battle could last a specific number of game turns, so that both players know when the end is nigh.

Alternatively, players might be able to win a 'sudden death' victory that ends the game immediately – for example, if they destroy the power generator they win straight away. You could also decide to end a battle at a pre-set time if you only have a limited amount of time to play in.

VICTORY

Once the game is finished, the players determine who has won, as dictated by the mission they are playing (see the Organising a Battle section on page 90). For now it is enough to know that Warhammer 40,000 standard missions generally revolve around capturing tactical objectives or inflicting the most damage upon the enemy.

TURN SEQUENCE EXCEPTIONS

There are times when a player is allowed to perform actions during their opponent's turn (fighting in an assault being the most common example). It may also be convenient to interrupt a player's turn because of some event occurring, like a booby trap being triggered. Whatever the reason, after the interruption, the turn sequence always continues as normal.

THE MOVEMENT PHASE

Although the Movement phase is the easiest to perform, it's probably the most tactically important. Getting models into the right position on the battlefield is often the key to victory. For the time being we'll just explain how squads of infantry move, as they are by far the most common units in the game. Vehicles, jump infantry, bikes and certain other units move in different ways to represent their greater mobility, and these will be discussed in detail later.

In his turn, a player may move any of his units – all of them if he wishes – up to their maximum movement distance. Once a unit has completed all of its movement, the player selects another unit and moves that one, and so on, until the player has moved all of the units he wishes to move. Note that a player doesn't have to move all (or indeed any) of his units. A unit that doesn't move is often more effective at shooting, as we will explain later in the rules. Once you have started moving a unit, you must finish its move before you start to move another unit. You may not go back and change the move already made by a previous unit.

MOVEMENT DISTANCE

Infantry move up to six inches (6") in the Movement phase. This represents most creatures moving at a reasonable pace but stopping several times to scan the surrounding landscape for enemies, communicate with their commanders, etc. Even warriors who are moving in a part of the battlefield where no enemies are apparent can only move 6". This is because your units lack your own god-like knowledge that there are no enemies around. It is perfectly fine to measure a unit's move in one direction, and then change your mind and decide to move it somewhere else (even the opposite way entirely!) or decide not to move it at all.

MODELS IN THE WAY

A model may not move into or through the space occupied by another model (which is represented by its base or by its hull) or through a gap between friendly models that is smaller than its own base (or hull) size. A model cannot move so that it touches an enemy model during the Movement and Shooting phases – this is only possible in an assault during the Assault phase. To keep this distinction clear, a model may not move within 1" of an enemy model unless assaulting.

DIFFERENT MOVEMENT DISTANCES IN A UNIT

All of the models in a unit move at the speed of the slowest model.

RANDOM AND COMPULSORY MOVEMENT

Sometimes, a unit may have to move a random distance instead of the usual 6" or be forced to move in a certain way (directly towards the closest enemy, for example). Such situations are discussed later.

TURNING AND FACING

As you move the models in a unit, they can turn to face in any direction, without affecting the distance they are able to cover. Infantry models can also be turned to face their targets in the Shooting phase, so don't worry about which way they are pointing at the end of their Movement phase (although dramatically facing off against their foes is traditional).

MOVING AND CLOSE COMBAT

Units already locked in close combat with the enemy may not move during the Movement phase.

Moving models

When moving models, it's a common mistake to measure the distance and then place the model on the far side of the tape measure. This is incorrect, as it adds the entire length of the model's base to the distance moved. While this is not a huge error on a 25mm base, it makes a considerable difference on a vehicle, in which case it might almost double the move (as shown below). The two diagrams here show examples of the right and wrong way to move your models.

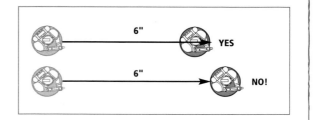

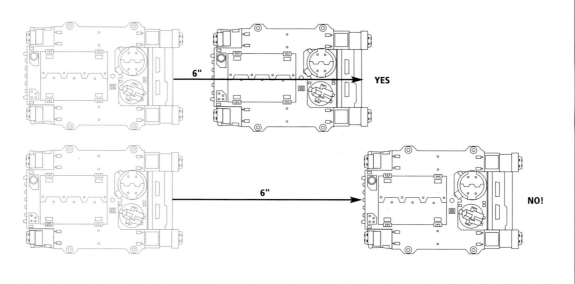

UNIT COHERENCY

When you are moving a unit, the individual models in it can each move up to their maximum movement distance – but remember that units have to stick together, otherwise individual models become scattered as the unit loses its cohesion as a fighting force. So, once a unit has finished moving, the models in it must form an imaginary chain where the distance between one model and the next is no more than 2". We call this 'unit coherency'.

During the course of a game, it's possible a unit will get broken up and lose unit coherency, usually because it takes casualties. If this happens, the models in the unit must be moved in such a way that they restore coherency in their next Movement phase. If the unit cannot move for some reason in its next turn (because they are pinned down by a barrage or sniper fire, for example), then they must move to restore unit coherency as soon as they have the opportunity.

"Follow me if I advance.
Kill me if I retreat.
Avenge me if I die."

Warmaster Solon

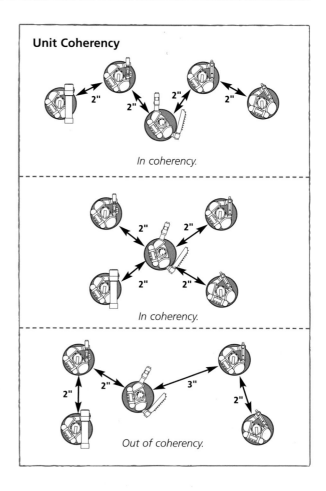

TERRAIN

The galaxy is a vast place with millions of different warzones: ice worlds, desert worlds, hive worlds, feral worlds and many other exotic types of battlefield – if you can imagine it, then it probably exists somewhere. The terrain covering these worlds can vary from broad, empty plains to sky-scraping towers of plexiglass and plasteel, from verdant jungles to barren moonscapes or baking hot deserts. How to represent terrain on the battlefield is discussed later (see page 88 and 230). For now, we're going to discuss terrain only in terms of how infantry move through it.

TERRAIN TYPES

Terrain provides useful cover from enemy fire, but can also impede the movement of your units. Troops can be slowed by pushing through or climbing over barriers and obstructions. There are three general classes of terrain: clear, difficult and impassable.

- **Clear terrain** can be moved across without any penalty, and generally covers most of the battlefield.

- **Difficult terrain** slows down models wishing to move through it, and can sometimes be dangerous to models passing through it.

- **Impassable terrain** cannot be moved across or into.

Guidelines on categorising terrain

It is a relatively simple matter to classify terrain within these four categories, and it is important that you and your opponent agree what class of terrain each feature falls into before starting your game.

- Clear terrain includes open areas, such as fields, moorland, grass, deserts, ash wastes and gentle hills. This could be embellished with the odd tree, shrub or cactus (or alien equivalents) for visual appeal.

- Difficult terrain includes areas of rubble, jungles, woods, ruins, brush and scrub, rocky outcrops, boggy ground, low walls, hedges, fences, razor wire, barricades, steep hills, streams and other shallow water (as well as terrain features that combine several of these types, such as a ruin surrounded by woods). If the terrain feature includes hazards, such as booby traps, carnivorous plants, toxic vents, erupting geysers and the like, then it may be additionally categorised as both difficult and dangerous terrain.

- Impassable terrain includes deep water, lava flows, steep rocky cliffs and buildings that models cannot enter, as agreed with your opponent. Remember that other models, friends and enemies, also count as impassable terrain.

- Buildings that models can enter, like bunkers, bastions and other fortifications.

You will notice that buildings appear in more than one category. Buildings will be treated in detail in their own section, on page 77.

AREA TERRAIN

Sometimes a terrain feature has clearly defined edges, such as a crater, a stream or an intact building. Other times, however, this might be slightly less clear, as in the case of marshes, woods, ruins and other types of rough ground. In reality a wood might be a tangled, overgrown mass of foliage, without a clear edge. If it is represented like this on your tabletop, then it will be very difficult to stand models on it, and it would be difficult to decide if the models are inside or outside it.

For the clarity of the game it is important to be able to tell where the boundary of the terrain feature is, as these pieces normally count as difficult terrain. This is where we need to introduce the concept of 'area terrain'. You can show the boundary of a piece of area terrain by using a flat baseboard, an outline of lichen or sand, or by painting a slightly different colour on your gaming board. Trees, rocks, ruins, or whatever is appropriate for the kind of area terrain you are representing, are usually placed within the boundary of the area terrain's base.

When moving models into this area, you may temporarily remove the rocks, trees, etc. (if they are not glued in place!) to make moving the models easier. Remember, however, to put them back where they originally were (or as close as possible!) after you finish moving, as they may affect the line of sight of models shooting through that area terrain.

You should discuss all such terrain features with your opponent before the game and agree exactly what everything counts as and where boundaries of terrain features lie. When the game is underway, it will be harder to discuss it quite so impartially.

Wobbly Model Syndrome

Sometimes you may find that a particular piece of terrain makes it hard to put a model exactly where you want. If you delicately balance it in place, it is very likely to fall as soon as somebody nudges the table, leaving your beautifully painted miniature chipped or even broken. In cases like this we find it is perfectly acceptable to leave the model in a safer position, as long as both players have agreed and know its 'actual' location. If later on your enemy is considering shooting at the model, you will have to hold it back in the proper place so he can check line of sight.

Of course if you prefer things to be completely clear and exact, then stick to simple, flat terrain!

Both the wood and the ruin are examples of area terrain. As you can see, their bases clearly define their extent on the table top. Both these features are also difficult terrain, and players may agree that the ruin counts as dangerous too.

MOVING THROUGH DIFFICULT TERRAIN

During a game of Warhammer 40,000, there can be two slightly different cases of units moving through difficult terrain.

If any of the models in a unit start their move inside difficult terrain, the unit is affected by the terrain and must take a difficult terrain test. Roll two D6 and select the highest – this is the maximum distance in inches that all of the models in the unit (not just the ones in difficult terrain!) may move.

If a unit starts its move outside difficult terrain, the player must declare if he wants his unit to try to enter difficult terrain as part of their move. If he chooses not to, the unit moves as normal but may not enter difficult terrain. If he chooses that they will do so, the unit must take a difficult terrain test as described above. Even if the distance rolled is too short for any of the models to reach the difficult terrain, the unit is still slowed down as described above. We assume that they are cautiously approaching the terrain, using their sensors to ascertain that no enemy is hiding in there.

If you take the difficult terrain test, you are never compelled to move the models, as you may not have rolled high enough to make it worth moving at all. However, if you roll the dice, the unit is still considered to have moved for the purposes of firing, as detailed later in the Shooting rules.

Note that as part of their move through difficult terrain, models may move through walls, closed doors and windows, and all sort of similarly solid obstacles, unless the players have agreed that a certain wall or obstacle is impassable. This represents the warriors bashing their way past locked doors and windows, using explosives or their weapons to create breaches in light walls, climbing over low obstacles and so on.

DANGEROUS TERRAIN

As mentioned previously, some terrain features will be dangerous to move through. This is represented by the dangerous terrain test. Roll a D6 for every model that has entered, left or moved through one or more areas of dangerous terrain during its move. On the roll of a 1, the model suffers a wound, with no armour or cover saves allowed (wounds and saves are explained in the next section).

IMPASSABLE TERRAIN

Models may not be placed in impassable terrain unless the models concerned have a special rule in their profile granting them an exception (like being able to fly above the terrain) or both players agree to it.

Blessed is the mind too small for doubt.

THE SHOOTING PHASE

As the two armies engage each other, guns thunder ceaselessly with plasma blasts, shells and shrapnel raining down on both sides.

In a Warhammer 40,000 battle, we split up the firing so that each player's force fires during the Shooting phase of his own turn. During the Shooting phase, any and all of your units may fire. You can choose any order for your units to shoot, but you must complete all the firing by one unit before you move on to the next.

Normally each model in a firing unit can fire a single weapon. Some models, including vehicles, may be able to fire more than one weapon, as detailed later.

The shooting process can be summarised in six steps, as described below.

Once you've completed this shooting sequence with one of your units, select another and repeat the sequence. Once you have completed steps 1 to 6 for each unit in your army, carry on to the Assault phase.

The rules for the Shooting phase end with details of the different categories of ranged weapon available to warriors in the 41st Millennium.

DISALLOWED SHOOTING

Certain situations prevent a unit from firing. The most common are:

- Units that are locked in close combat with the foe.

- Units that are running (see overleaf).

- Units that have gone to ground because of enemy fire in the previous turn (see page 24).

In addition to the above, certain types of weapons can only be fired if the unit did not move in the same turn. However, this will only prevent models with that weapon from shooting – not the whole unit.

THE SHOOTING SEQUENCE

1. **Check line of sight & pick a target.**
   Pick one of your units, check its line of sight and choose a target for it. All models in the unit that can see at least one enemy model in the target unit may open fire.

2. **Check range.** At least one target model must be within range of the weaponry of your firing models.

3. **Roll to hit.** Roll a D6 for each shot fired. The model's BS determines what score they must equal or beat to hit their target.

4. **Roll to wound.** For each shot that hits, roll again to see if it wounds the target. The score needed is determined by comparing the Strength of the firing weapons with the Toughness of the target.

5. **Take saving throws.** Each wound suffered may be cancelled by making a saving throw. Saving throws usually derive from the armour worn by each model, from being in cover, or some other piece of wargear or ability. If the target unit includes different types of models, you will first have to allocate the wounds onto specific models.

6. **Remove casualties.** The target unit suffers casualties for any wounds that have not been saved.

RUN!

At times, warriors may have to quickly redeploy, literally running from cover to cover or simply concentrating on movement and giving up their chance to shoot. In their Shooting phase, units may choose to run instead of firing, immediately moving D6" (we find that this is a popular choice for units that have no ranged weaponry or no target!). Running movement is not affected by difficult terrain – it is always simply D6" – but models running through dangerous terrain must test as normal. Units that run in the Shooting phase cannot assault in the following Assault phase.

CHECK LINE OF SIGHT & PICK A TARGET

A firing unit can choose a single enemy unit that is not locked in combat as its target, and may not split its fire among different targets. In order to select an enemy unit as a target, at least one model in the firing unit must have line of sight to at least one model in the target unit. If no models have line of sight then a different target must be chosen.

The player is checking the Space Marine's line of sight by looking from behind the firer's head to the body of the target model.

Line of Sight

Warhammer 40,000 uses what we call 'true line of sight' for shooting attacks. This means that you take the positions of models and terrain at face value, and simply look to see if your warriors have a view to their targets. This is different to other, more abstract systems where terrain is assigned a height value and you have to calculate what warriors can see. We have chosen true line of sight because it makes the game feel much more cinematic and 'real'. There's nothing quite like getting a 'model's eye view' to bring the game to life. Of course, this method does mean that occasionally there are border-line cases when it is quite hard to decide if a model can see a target or not, but sporting players will always be generous and give their opponent the benefit of the doubt.

Line of sight literally represents your warriors' view of the enemy – they must be able to see their foe through, under or over the tangle of terrain and other fighters on the battlefield. Of course your models are made of plastic or metal, so they can't tell you what they can see – you'll have to work it out for them. In some cases it will be obvious – if there is a hill or a tank blocking their view, the enemy may be blatantly out of sight. In other cases two units will be plainly in view of each other, as there is nothing at all in the way. Many times however, it will be more difficult to tell if line of sight is blocked or not, so players will have to stoop over the table for a 'model's eye view'. This means getting down to the level of your warriors, taking in the view from behind the firing models to 'see what they can see'. You will find that you can spot lurking enemies through the windows of a ruined building, and that high vantage points become very useful for the increased line of sight that they offer.

Line of sight must be traced from the eyes of the firing model to any part of the body of at least one of the models in the target unit (for 'body' we mean its head, torso, legs and arms). Sometimes, all that may be visible of a model is a weapon, an antenna, a banner or some other ornament he is wearing or carrying (including its wings and tail, even though they are technically part of its body). In these cases, the model is not visible. These rules are intended to ensure that models don't get penalised for having impressive standards, blades, guns, majestic wings, etc.

OWN UNIT

There is one important exception to the rules for line of sight. Firing models can always draw line of sight through members of their own unit (just as if they were not there), as in reality they would take up firing positions to maximise their own squad's firepower.

WHICH MODELS CAN FIRE?

All models in the firing unit that have line of sight to at least one model in the target unit can fire.

A player may choose not to fire with certain models if he prefers (as some models may have one-shot weapons, for example). This must be declared before checking range, as all of the models in the unit fire at the same time.

CHECK RANGE

All weapons have a maximum effective range, which is the furthest distance they can shoot. If a target is beyond this maximum range, the shot misses automatically. This is why you have to choose your target before measuring the range. Here are some examples of weapon ranges:

Weapon	Maximum Range
Laspistol	12"
Boltgun	24"
Autocannon	48"

When you're checking range, simply measure from each firer to the nearest visible model in the target unit.

Any model that is found to be out of range of all of the models he can see in the target unit misses automatically – his shots simply do not reach.

> "Victory does not always rest with the big guns; but if we rest in front of them, we shall be lost."
> Commander Argentius

Checking Range

Four Orks are found to have a target within the 12" range of their pistols (black lines). The remaining Ork is out of range of the closest visible model (grey line).

MOVING & SHOOTING

Whether a unit has moved or not can make a big difference to its firing. If the warriors hold a position, take up firing stances and aim at their targets properly, some weapons can hit targets further away than if they are firing on the move. Other guns are so heavy that they can only be used if their firers halt completely to brace themselves or set up their weapons on the ground. This is explained in more detail in the Weapons section later, but for the time being it's enough to know that moving can make a difference to a unit's shooting.

The most important thing to remember is that the whole unit counts as moving if any of its models moved in the Movement phase.

ROLL TO HIT

To determine if the firing models have hit their target, roll a D6 for each shot that is in range. Normally troopers will only get to fire one shot each. However, some creatures or weapons are capable of firing more than once, as we'll explain in more detail later. The dice score needed to hit will depend on how accurate the firers are, as shown by their Ballistic Skill characteristic (or BS). The chart below shows the minimum D6 roll needed to score a hit.

Firer's BS	1	2	3	4	5
Score needed to hit	6	5+	4+	3+	2+

For example, if the shooters are a unit of five Space Marines with a BS of 4, you would roll five dice and each roll of a 3 or more would score a hit.

To Hit rolls are easy to remember if you just subtract the BS of the shooter from 7. This will give you the number you need; e.g. a model with a BS of 2 needs to roll a 5 or more (7–2=5).

Note that the minimum roll needed to hit is always at least 2. When rolling to hit, there is no such thing as an automatic hit and a roll of a 1 always misses.

The reward for treachery is retribution

BALLISTIC SKILL OF 6 OR BETTER

Very rarely a model may have a BS of 6 or even more. If a model has a BS of 6 or higher, it gains a re-roll whenever it rolls a 1 to hit with ranged attacks. The second roll has normally a lower chance of hitting, and the number needed is given in the chart below in italics after the slash.

Firer's BS	6	7	8	9	10
Score needed to hit	2/6	2/5	2/4	2/3	2/2

For example, a model with BS 7 fires a shot with its pistol. It rolls a 1, missing, but thanks to its exceptional BS it can re-roll the dice. This time, however it won't hit on a 2, but rather on a 5.

If a model has a special rule that already confers it a re-roll to hit (like a master-crafted weapon, for example), then that re-roll takes precedence and the chart above is not used. Instead the chances to hit on the re-roll are the same as the first shot, depending of the firer's BS. Remember a dice can only ever be re-rolled once!

FAST ROLLING WITH DIFFERENT WEAPONS

When a unit fires, all of its weapons are fired simultaneously, so you should ideally roll all of its To Hit dice together. Sometimes there will be different weapons firing, or firers with different BS in the same unit, in which case we find it easiest to use different coloured dice, so that those shots can be picked out. For example, a squad may include several bolters, a plasma gun and a lascannon, in which case you could use white dice for bolter shots, a green dice for the plasma gun and a red dice for the lascannon. Alternatively, you can simply make separate dice rolls for different weapons or shooters, as long as it is clear which dice rolls represent which shots.

"Let the Orks come by the thousand, or by the tens of thousands; we shall be ready for them. This world is the Emperor's, not theirs, and we shall wash it clean with their blood."

Pedro Kantor, Master of the Crimson Fists

ROLL TO WOUND

Hitting your target is not always enough to put it out of action. The shot might result in nothing more than a superficial graze or flesh wound.

To decide if a hit causes a telling wound, compare the weapon's Strength characteristic with the target's Toughness characteristic. Each weapon has its own Strength value, given in the description of the weapon. Here are some examples of different weapons and their Strength characteristics.

Weapon	Strength
Boltgun	4
Plasma gun	7
Lascannon	9

Consult the chart below, and cross-reference the weapon's Strength (S) with the target's Toughness (T). The number indicated is the minimum score on a D6 needed to convert the hit into a wound. Just like rolling To Hit, roll the dice together and, once again, use different coloured dice to pick out weapons with different Strengths or roll them separately.

Example: a Space Marine with a boltgun shoots at an Ork and hits him. A boltgun has a Strength of 4 and the Ork has a Toughness of 4. Referring to the chart, a score of 4 or more is needed to convert the hit into damage. If the roll is 4 or more, the Ork takes a wound.

MULTIPLE TOUGHNESS VALUES

Quite rarely, a unit will contain models with differing Toughness characteristics.

To keep things simple, roll to wound using the Toughness characteristic that is in the majority in the target unit. If no majority exists, use the highest value in the unit.

For example, in a unit containing Gretchin and an Ork Runtherd, the Gretchin's Toughness of 3 is used for all models. Only if the unit is reduced to two models (the Runtherd and a single Gretchin) at the moment when the enemies roll to wound, must they roll against the Ork's Toughness of 4 for both models.

Speed rolling
You'll soon get used to the system of rolling to hit, to wound and to save. We find it is quickest to pick up the dice that rolled a successful result at each stage and roll them again.

Cocked dice
Occasionally a dice will end up in a crevice in your terrain or in the crack between two sections of board and doesn't lie flat. We call this a 'cocked dice'. Some players use a house rule that if any dice is not completely flat on the table, it must be re-rolled. More common is for players to re-roll the dice only if they can't be sure of the result. Of course, if your gaming surface is very textured and results in a lot of cocked dice (or simply if you prefer a tidy battlefield) you can make all your rolls in a tray or box lid.

Dice on the floor
It is generally accepted that if a dice ends up on the floor, it doesn't count – so you don't need to shine a torch under the sofa to find out if you made your save or not! Most gamers agree that such dice can be rolled again. However, one player we know has a house rule that if your dice misses the table, you have failed the roll – after all, if you can't hit a huge table with a tiny dice, then what chance have your warriors got!

TO WOUND CHART

		Toughness								
Strength		**1**	**2**	**3**	**4**	**5**	**6**	**7**	**8**	**9**	**10**
1	4+	5+	6+	6+	N	N	N	N	N	N
2	3+	4+	5+	6+	6+	N	N	N	N	N
3	2+	3+	4+	5+	6+	6+	N	N	N	N
4	2+	2+	3+	4+	5+	6+	6+	N	N	N
5	2+	2+	2+	3+	4+	5+	6+	6+	N	N
6	2+	2+	2+	2+	3+	4+	5+	6+	6+	N
7	2+	2+	2+	2+	2+	3+	4+	5+	6+	6+
8	2+	2+	2+	2+	2+	2+	3+	4+	5+	6+
9	2+	2+	2+	2+	2+	2+	2+	3+	4+	5+
10	2+	2+	2+	2+	2+	2+	2+	2+	3+	4+

Note that N on the chart means the hit has no effect. A target with the Toughness indicated cannot be harmed by a hit of such puny Strength. Also note that a roll of 1 never scores a Wound, regardless of its Strength.

TAKE SAVING THROWS

Before he removes any models as casualties, the owning player can test to see whether his troops avoid the damage by making a saving throw. This could be because of the target's armour, some other protective device or ability, or intervening models or terrain.

If all the models in a unit are the same, and have a single Wound each, such as a squad of Eldar Rangers or Necron Warriors, then this is a very simple process. You roll all the saves for the unit in one go (as described below), and a model of your choice is removed as a casualty for each failure.

On the other hand, it is common for units to include models with different weapons or wargear and characters with different profiles (and sometimes even different armour). In these cases we need to know exactly who has been wounded, and this requires an extra step in the shooting process. The wounds the unit has suffered must be allocated onto specific models before saving throws are taken. This extra step is explained after the basic rules (see page 25).

ARMOUR SAVES

Most troops wear some sort of protective clothing or armour, even if it's only a helmet! Some creatures may have a form of natural protection, such as a chitinous exo-skeleton or thick bony plates. If a model has a Sv value of 6 or better on its profile, it is allowed a further dice roll to see if the armour stops it being wounded. This is called an armour saving throw.

Roll a D6 for each wound the model has suffered from incoming fire and compare the results to the model's Sv characteristic. If the dice result is equal to or higher than the model's Sv value, the wound is stopped. If the result is lower than the Sv value, the armour fails to protect its wearer and the model suffers a wound. This means that, differently from other characteristics, a Sv value is better if it has a lower number.

The following table shows how the minimum D6 score required varies between three types of armour:

Armour Type	Sv
Ork armour	6
Imperial Guard flak armour	5
Space Marine power armour	3

Example: a Space Marine wearing power armour is hit and wounded. The Space Marine is entitled to a saving throw of 3, so a D6 is rolled resulting in a score of 5. The damage is therefore saved, and the model is unharmed – the shot bounces off his power armour.

Armour piercing weapons

Some powerful weapons are quite capable of punching through even the thickest types of armour. This is shown by a weapon having an Armour Piercing value,

usually referred to as AP. Nearly all weapons have an Armour Piercing value. Some sample AP ratings for different weapons are shown below:

Weapon	AP
Boltgun	5
Heavy bolter	4
Lascannon	2

The AP rating indicates the armour save the weapon can ignore – so lower means more powerful. A weapon shown as 'AP –' has no Armour Piercing value and will never disallow the target's armour save.

- If the weapon's Armour Piercing value is equal to or lower than the model's armour save then it is sufficiently powerful to punch straight through the armour and the target gets no armour save at all. The armour is ineffective against the shot.

- If the weapon's Armour Piercing value is higher than the armour, the target can take his save as normal.

Example: a boltgun with an AP of 5 can pierce armour which has a Sv of 5+ or 6. A heavy bolter has an Armour Piercing rating of 4 so saves of 4+, 5+ or 6 are ignored. A lascannon with its AP of 2 ignores even the best armour it is possible to wear!

INVULNERABLE SAVES

Some warriors are protected by more than mere physical armour. They may be shielded by force fields, enwrapped by mystic energies or have an alien metabolism that can shrug off hits that would put holes in a battle tank. Models with wargear or abilities like these are allowed an invulnerable saving throw. Invulnerable saves are different to armour saves because they may always be taken whenever the model suffers a wound – the Armour Piercing value of attacking weapons has no effect. Even if a wound normally ignores all armour saves, an invulnerable saving throw may still be taken.

"As our bodies are armoured with adamantium, our souls are protected with loyalty. As our bolters are charged with death for the Emperor's enemies, our thoughts are charged with wisdom. As our ranks advance, so does our devotion, for are we not Marines? Are we not the chosen of the Emperor, his loyal servants unto death?"

Chaplain Fergas Nils

COVER SAVES

A position in cover shields troops against flying debris and enemy shots, enabling them to get their heads down or crawl amongst the rocks and (hopefully) avoid harm. Because of this, units in or behind cover receive a cover saving throw. The great thing about cover saving throws is that they are not affected by the Armour Piercing value of the attacking weapon, so units in cover will normally get a saving throw regardless of what's firing at them.

What counts as Cover?

Cover is basically anything that is hiding a target or protecting it from incoming shots. For example, a soft obstacle (like a hedge) that would hide soldiers behind it, but would not even slow down enemy shots, confers a 5+ save, purpose-built fortifications confer a 3+ save, most other things confer a 4+ save. More detail can be found in the Cover chart below. Before deploying their armies, it is a very good idea for players to go through all the terrain pieces on the battlefield quickly and agree what kind of cover each will offer.

COVER CHART

Cover Type	Save
a) Razor wire, Wire mesh	6+
b) High Grass, Crops, Bushes Hedges, Fences	5+
c) Units (friends and enemies), Trenches, Gun pits, Tank traps, Emplacements, Sandbags, Barricades, Logs, Pipes, Crates, Barrels, Hill crests, Woods, Jungles, Wreckage, Craters, Rubble, Rocks, Ruins, Walls, Buildings, Wrecked vehicles	4+
d) Fortifications	3+

When are models in Cover?

When any part of the target model's body (as defined on page 16) is obscured from the point of view of the firer, the target model is in cover. This is intentionally generous, and it represents the fact that the warrior, unlike the model, will be actively trying to take cover (as well as the smoke, explosions and flying debris that are mercifully absent from our tabletop battlefields).

Firers may of course shoot over intervening terrain if they are tall enough or high up on some terrain piece so that their line of sight is completely clear. As usual, check the firers' line of sight by taking a good look from behind their heads, and 'see what they see'.

Intervening models

If a target is partially hidden from the firer's view by other models, it receives a 4+ cover save in the same way as if it was behind terrain.

This does not mean that intervening models literally stop the shots, but rather that they obscure the sight of the firers or otherwise spoil their aim. A successful cover save in this case might mean that the firer has not shot at all, missing the fleeting moment when the target was in its sights. This is because, in the case of intervening friends, the firer would be afraid of hitting his comrades; while in the case of intervening enemies, the firer is distracted by the more immediate threat.

Scenic rocks and other decorative elements that players might have placed on the base of their models are always ignored from the point of view of determining cover (you cannot take your cover with you!).

"If all else fails: duck. As a defensive stratagem it's unreliable, but incredibly reassuring for a moment or two."

Lord Corvis of Petrax

Exceptions

In order to keep the game flowing at a faster pace, we have made a few exceptions to the cover rules given on the previous page, namely:

- **Own unit:** In the same way as they can trace line of sight through members of their own squad, models can always shoot, and be shot at, through members of their own unit without conferring or receiving a cover save.

- **Inside area terrain:** Target models whose bases are at least partially inside area terrain are in cover, regardless of the direction the shot is coming from. This represents their increased chance of diving into or behind a piece of covering terrain.

- **Firing through units or area terrain:** If a model fires through the gaps between some elements of area terrain (such as between two trees in a wood) or through the gaps between models in an intervening unit, the target is in cover, even if it is completely visible to the firer. Note that this does not apply if the shots go over the area terrain or unit rather than through it (see the photographic diagram below).

- **Firing out of area terrain:** Models that are inside area terrain firing out will position themselves with good fields of vision. Therefore they may fire through up to 2" of the area terrain they are occupying without that terrain conferring a cover save to the target. Remember, of course, that models still need to see their target in order to be able to shoot at all.

- **Firing over a barrier:** Models that are in base contact with a linear piece of terrain they can see over, such as a low wall, barricade, tank trap or a fence, can fire at enemies on the other side without the barrier getting in the way of their shots.

Units partially in cover

Sometimes, a unit will only be partially in cover, with some of its models in cover and some not. In this case you must decide if the majority of the unit is in cover. Models that are completely out of sight are considered to be in cover for this purpose.

If half or more of the models in the target unit are in cover, then the entire unit is deemed to be in cover and all of its models may take cover saves.

If less than half of the models in the target unit are in cover, then the entire unit counts as exposed and none of its models may take cover saves.

Of course being in cover or not often depends on the position of the firer as well as the target. If only one model is shooting, it will be easy to tell how many models in the target unit are in cover from the firer's point of view. If multiple models are shooting, you will need to work out how many models are in cover from the point of view of the majority of the firing models that are in range. If the majority of the firers have a clear shot to the majority of the models in the target unit, the unit receives no save. Otherwise it does. This may sound complex, but you will find that in reality in most cases it is quite obvious if a unit is in cover or not.

In situations where it's not obvious whether a unit is in cover or not, the normal solution is to strictly apply the majority rule above, and count how many models are in cover from the point of view of each of the firing models in range. As this process might prove to be rather time-consuming, for a faster (albeit less precise) solution, the players may agree to treat these units as in cover, but with a cover save of one less than normal (for example a 5+ save if partially in cover behind a building or another unit, which normally would offer a 4+ save). See the diagrams opposite for examples of units partially in cover.

Model A is inside the area terrain and so is in cover. Model B is not inside the area terrain, but is between two elements of that area terrain (the same as if it was between two models of an intervening unit), so it is in cover. Model C is not in cover.

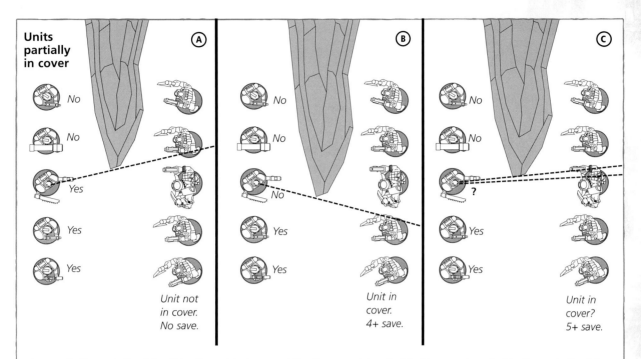

Units partially in cover

A
No
No
Yes
Yes
Yes

Unit not in cover. No save.

B
No
No
No
Yes
Yes

Unit in cover. 4+ save.

C
No
No
?
Yes
Yes

Unit in cover? 5+ save.

In case A, the majority of the firing Space Marine squad (i.e. three models out of five) have a clear shot to the majority of the models in the target unit (i.e. they have a clear shot to three or more Orks out of five). The Ork unit receives no cover save.

In case B, only two out of five Space Marines have a clear shot to the majority of the models in the target unit. The Ork unit receives a 4+ cover save (as rocks are in the way).

In case C, two Space Marines have a clear shot to the majority of the models in the target unit, and two Space Marines do not. The players check from the point of view of the model in the middle of the unit, and decide that is practically impossible to be sure if he has a completely clear shot to at least three Orks. In this case, the players agree to give the Ork unit a cover save of 5+.

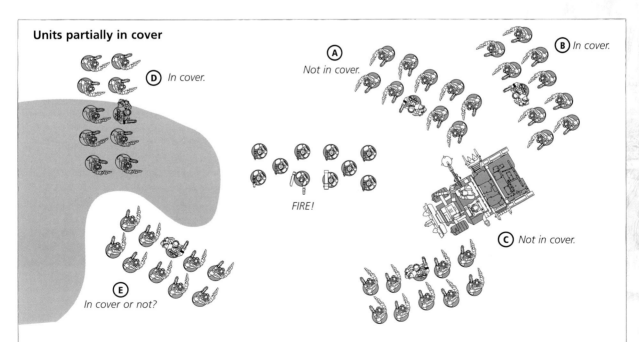

Units partially in cover

D *In cover.*

A *Not in cover.*

B *In cover.*

FIRE!

C *Not in cover.*

E *In cover or not?*

Unit A is entirely in the open and so is the Trukk. The majority of unit C is in the open. The majority of unit B is in cover behind other models and the majority of unit D is in cover inside area terrain. Unit E is a less obvious case. The players can very carefully count the Orks in cover from the point of view of each firer, or give unit E a cover save of 5+ instead of 4+.

GOING TO GROUND

If warriors come under heavy fire, they may decide to keep their heads down and stay alive a little longer while they wait for reinforcements.

After the enemy has rolled to hit and wound against any of your units, but before you take any saves or remove any models, you can declare that the unit is going to ground. To represent this, place a suitable marker next to the unit (you may alternatively want to lay the models down). Models in a unit that has gone to ground immediately receive +1 to their cover saving throws. Units that are not currently in a position that would give them a cover save can still go to ground by diving to the floor (or some other evasion technique) and receive a 6+ cover save.

The drawback of going to ground is that the unit can do nothing until the end of its following turn. At the end of its following turn the unit returns to normal, the marker is removed and the unit is free to act as normal from then on.

Whilst it has gone to ground the unit may do nothing of its own volition, but will react normally if affected by enemy actions (for example, it will take Morale tests as normal). If the unit has to fall back, it will return to normal immediately. If assaulted, the unit will fight as usual, but gains no advantage for being in cover because they are not set to receive the enemy charge (see page 36).

"He that may still fight, heal him.
He that may fight no more,
give him peace.
He that is dead,
take from him the Chapter's due."

– Master of the Apothacarion Aslon Marr

MODELS WITH MORE THAN ONE SAVE

Sometimes, a model will have a normal armour save and a separate invulnerable save – a good example is a Space Marine Chaplain who is protected by both power armour and a Rosarius-generated force field. As if this wasn't enough the model might be in cover as well. In these cases, the model only ever gets to make one saving throw, but it has the advantage of always using the best available save.

For example, if the Chaplain described above was standing in a fortified building and was wounded by an AP3 weapon his power armour would be of no use, as the shot's AP is equal to or lower than his armour save. The force field grants a 4+ invulnerable save. However, the fortified building grants a 3+ cover save. Neither of these saves is affected by the AP of the weapon so the Chaplain uses the cover save to give him the best chance of surviving.

If a unit can benefit from different types of cover, for example being behind a hedge (5+ cover save) and a low wall (4+), the unit uses the best cover save available (in this case 4+).

MAXIMUM SAVE

Some models gain additional benefits from rules that may increase any of their saves by +1 or +2. However, no save (armour, cover or invulnerable) can ever be improved beyond 2+. A roll of 1 always fails.

REMOVE CASUALTIES

For every model that fails its save, the unit suffers an unsaved wound. Of course this also includes wounds against which no save can be attempted, such as those from weapons with very high AP. Most models have a single Wound on their profile, in which case for each unsaved wound one model is immediately removed from the table as a casualty. As long as all the models in the unit have the same profile, special rules, weapons and wargear, the player who owns the unit can choose which of his models is removed.

Note that any model in the target unit can be hit, wounded and taken off as a casualty, even models that are completely out of sight or out of range of all of the firers. This may seem slightly strange, but it represents the fact that the real action on the battlefield is not as static as our models. In reality the warriors, both the firers and the targets, would be moving around and real bullets have a nasty habit of ricocheting or simply going through covering terrain!

Casualties are not necessarily dead – they may be merely knocked unconscious, too injured to carry on fighting or incapacitated in other some way. In any case, they are no longer fit to participate in the battle.

COMPLEX UNITS

The rules for taking saving throws and removing casualties, as presented so far, assume that all the models in the target unit are identical in gaming terms. By this we mean they have the same profile of characteristics, the same special rules and the same weapons and wargear.

Of course many units include different models, and when this is the case an extra step is needed to determine which warriors have been hit by which weapons. This is worked out as follows:

Once the number of wounds caused by the firing unit has been determined, the player controlling the target unit must decide which models have been wounded, allocating the wounds to the warriors of their choice. Remember that any model in the unit can be wounded, not just those in range or in view.

The player must allocate one wound to each model in the target unit before he can allocate a second wound to the same model.

Once all models in the target unit have one wound allocated to them, the process is repeated and the player must allocate a second wound to all models in the target unit before he can allocate a third wound to a model, and so on, until all wounds from the firing unit have been allocated.

We find that the clearest way of doing this is to literally pick up the dice that have scored wounds and place them next to the models that they have wounded. It is still important to know which weapon has caused which wound, because they may negate the target's save, so sticking with the same coloured dice used when rolling to hit will really help.

TAKING SAVING THROWS

Having allocated the wounds, all of the models in the unit that are identical in gaming terms take their saving throws at the same time, in one batch. Casualties can then be chosen by the owning player from amongst these identical models. If there is another group of identical models in the unit, the player then takes all of their saves in one batch, and so on.

Finally, the player rolls separately for each model that stands out in gaming terms. If one of these different models suffers an unsaved wound, then that specific model must be removed. Note that if a model carrying a different weapon to the rest of the unit is killed and removed, his squad-members are not allowed to pick up his gun. We can assume that he was the only one trained to use the weapon, or that the weapon itself has been damaged and is now useless.

The diagram below shows an example of how this process works. You'll find that it is quite intuitive once you have tried it a few times.

Allocating wounds on complex units

This Space Marine Devastator combat squad consists of five models: two Space Marines armed with bolters, two armed with missile launchers and one Veteran Sergeant (who has a different profile and wargear from the rest of the squad). They are hit by a volley from a nearby enemy squad and suffer eleven wounds – ten wounds from weapons whose AP is not high enough to pierce their armour, and one from a weapon that can (e.g. an AP1 meltagun). This amounts to two wounds per model and a single spare wound.

The player controlling the Space Marines picks up the dice that scored a wound and uses them to show how he is going to allocate the wounds (shown above). He allocates one normal wound, the meltagun one (the grey dice) and

the spare wound on a Space Marine with a bolter, and then two normal wounds on every other model. He is trying to minimise the damage by allocating both the worst wound (the meltagun's) and the spare wound on the same model.

He goes on to roll the four saves for the Space Marines with bolters in one go, failing two. He should remove three models (two unsaved wounds plus one wound with no armour save from the meltagun), but as there are only two models in this group of identical models, he just removes them both. Then he rolls the four saves for the Space Marines with missile launchers in one go, failing one and removing one of the models. Finally he takes the two saves for the Veteran Sergeant, passing both.

MULTIPLE-WOUND MODELS

Especially tough and heroic individuals such as Space Marine commanders, or horrendous alien monstrosities such as Tyranid Hive Tyrants, can sustain more damage than ordinary troopers and keep on fighting. To show this, they have more than one Wound on their characteristic profile.

When such a multiple-wound model suffers an unsaved wound, it loses one Wound from its profile. Once the model has lost all of its Wounds, it is removed as a casualty (so a model with 3 Wounds would only be killed after it had been wounded three times). Keep track of how many wounds such models have suffered on a piece of scrap paper, or by placing a dice or marker next to them.

INSTANT DEATH

Even though a creature might have multiple Wounds, there are plenty of weapons in the 41st Millennium that are powerful enough to kill it instantly. If a model suffers an unsaved wound from an attack that has a Strength value of double its Toughness value or greater, it is killed outright and removed as a casualty. It can be imagined that the creature is vapourised, burned to a pile of ash, blasted limb from limb or otherwise mortally slain in a suitably graphic fashion.

Example: a Space Marine Captain is Toughness 4 and has 3 Wounds. Ordinarily, he could survive being wounded twice before being removed as a casualty on the third wound suffered. However, if he were to have the misfortune to be wounded by a krak missile (Strength 8 – normally used for knocking out battle tanks), he would become a casualty immediately because the missile's Strength is double his Toughness.

Some models can gain improvements to their Toughness by using wargear items like bikes, Chaos Marks, etc. When it comes to instant death, such bonuses do not count (ie, riding a bike won't save you from being obliterated by a lascannon blast!). In these cases two values will be shown for the Toughness characteristic of the model, one of which is in brackets. Use the lowest value for working out instant death.

BURN THE HERETIC!

KILL THE MUTANT!

PURGE THE UNCLEAN!

UNITS OF MULTIPLE-WOUND MODELS

Units consisting of models with multiple wounds on their profile, such as Tyranid Warriors and Ork Nobz, are quite rare. Working out how to allocate wounds and remove casualties from such units can be quite complex, so if you don't have any in your army, feel free not to finish reading this page!

If a unit consists entirely of models that are identical in gaming terms and have multiple wounds, then take all the saves for the unit in one go.

If the unit includes different models, first allocate the wounds suffered. Then take saves for identical models at the same time as normal.

Once you have determined the number of unsaved wounds suffered by a group of identical multiple-wound models, you must remove whole models as casualties where possible. Wounds may not be 'spread around' to avoid removing models. Track any excess wounds with a note or a marker as noted above. Multiple-wound models in the unit that are unique are rolled for individually and their unsaved wounds must be recorded separately.

For example, let us examine a unit of four Ork Nobz, which have 2 Wounds each. Three of the Nobz are identical, while one has been upgraded with a better weapon. If the unit suffers nine wounds, the player must allocate two on each model, leaving a spare wound that he will allocate on a normal Nob. The player then takes seven saves for the three normal Nobz, failing three. He cannot put a single wound on each Nob, but must remove one model as well as recording that one normal Nob has suffered a wound. He then takes the two saves for the upgraded Nob and fails one, so he must record that the upgraded Nob has suffered a wound as well. The unit is then fired upon by another enemy and suffers a single wound. This will automatically kill the wounded Nob and cannot be allocated to the remaining healthy Nob.

If amongst the unsaved wounds there are some that inflict instant death, the player must first, if possible, remove one unwounded model for each unsaved wound that causes instant death, and then proceed as normal (this is done for each group of identical multiple-wound models). This rule is designed to stop players avoiding single wounds by putting them on a model that has suffered instant death anyway.

In the example above, if one of the three unsaved wounds on the normal Nobz caused instant death, the player would remove one unwounded Nob for that wound and then another normal Nob for the remaining two unsaved wounds. This would leave only one normal Nob and the upgraded Nob, which suffered one wound.

WEAPONS

By the 41st Millennium, warfare has spawned innumerable weapons, ranging in capability from the simple but efficient laspistol to the barely controllable energies of the plasma cannon. In this section we describe how characteristics and special rules reflect the differences between different weapons.

Every weapon has a profile that consists of several elements, for example:

Name	Maximum Range	Strength	Armour Piercing	Type
Boltgun	24"	4	5	Rapid Fire

MAXIMUM RANGE

Ranges are all given in inches. If the weapon's range is given as 'Template' then the weapon fires using the teardrop-shaped Flamer template (the exact method is explained later).

STRENGTH

As explained in the Shooting rules, when rolling to wound for shooting hits, you use the weapon's Strength rather than the firer's.

ARMOUR PIERCING (AP)

This value shows how good the weapon is at punching through armour. The lower the number, the better the weapon is at piercing armour, cancelling the target's armour save. See the Shooting rules for more on armour saves and AP values.

TYPE

All weapons are classified as either Rapid Fire, Pistol, Assault, Heavy or Ordnance. These rules (found overleaf) are a measure of the weapon's portability and affect the way it can be fired in relation to the model's movement during that turn's Movement phase.

Some weapons such as storm bolters and multi-lasers fire multiple shots. Where this is the case the number of shots a weapon fires is noted after its type. For example, a multi-laser fires three shots in each Shooting phase so its type is noted as Heavy 3.

Remember that the player can decide that any model in a firing unit is not going to fire its weapon. However, if a model does fire, it must do so at full effect and cannot reduce its weapon's firepower (for example, it cannot fire only two shots from its Heavy 3 weapon).

Some weapons may be able to fire in different ways, representing different power settings or different types of ammo. Where this is the case, there will be a separate line in the weapon's profile for each.

ADDITIONAL CHARACTERISTICS

In addition to its type, a weapon may have some additional characteristics that define the way they work. These are added to the weapon type in the weapon's profile, and include characteristics like 'gets hot!' or 'blast'. A weapon may have any number of these characteristics in addition to its type.

> To a Space Marine, the boltgun is far more than a weapon; it is an instrument of Mankind's divinity, the bringer of death to his foes. Its howling blast is a prayer to the gods of battle.

WEAPON TYPES

RAPID FIRE WEAPONS

Rapid fire weapons are very common and usually come in the form of semi-automatic rifles. Their versatility means they can be fired effectively 'from the hip' when a squad is advancing, spraying shots into the enemy whenever they present themselves, or instead used for aimed single shots against targets at greater distances.

Models armed with a rapid fire weapon can move and fire two shots at targets up to 12" away.

If the unit has not moved, models armed with rapid fire weapons may instead fire one shot at targets over 12" away, up to the weapons' maximum range. If such a unit is found to have firing models both within 12" of the target and further away, the firers within 12" will fire two shots, while those further away will fire one.

Models that shoot with rapid fire weapons in the Shooting phase cannot assault into close combat in the ensuing Assault phase.

Example	Range	S	AP	Type
Boltgun	24"	4	5	Rapid Fire

ASSAULT WEAPONS

Assault weapons are fired by warriors as they move forward into the attack. They either fire so rapidly or are so indiscriminate that you don't have to do much more than point and shoot. For example, a flamer is a weapon that fires a fan-shaped gout of burning fuel, so it's just as accurate whether you are moving and firing or not. This means they are very good for moving and assaulting things… hence the name!

Assault weapons shoot the number of times indicated – whether you move or not and regardless of range.

Models carrying assault weapons can fire them in the Shooting phase and still assault into close combat in the Assault phase.

Example	Range	S	AP	Type
Big Shoota	36"	5	5	Assault 3

Look to your wargear!

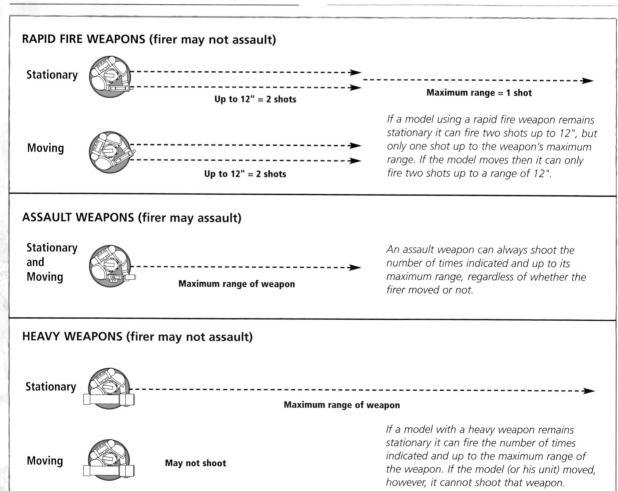

RAPID FIRE WEAPONS (firer may not assault)

Stationary — Up to 12" = 2 shots / Maximum range = 1 shot

Moving — Up to 12" = 2 shots

If a model using a rapid fire weapon remains stationary it can fire two shots up to 12", but only one shot up to the weapon's maximum range. If the model moves then it can only fire two shots up to a range of 12".

ASSAULT WEAPONS (firer may assault)

Stationary and Moving — Maximum range of weapon

An assault weapon can always shoot the number of times indicated and up to its maximum range, regardless of whether the firer moved or not.

HEAVY WEAPONS (firer may not assault)

Stationary — Maximum range of weapon

Moving — May not shoot

If a model with a heavy weapon remains stationary it can fire the number of times indicated and up to the maximum range of the weapon. If the model (or his unit) moved, however, it cannot shoot that weapon.

HEAVY WEAPONS

These are heavy, man-portable weapons, such as missile launchers, or lighter weapons that require reloading between each shot, careful set-up or bracing against their considerable recoil.

If a unit moves then it cannot shoot heavy weapons – they either move or shoot, but not both. Remember that if any models move, their whole unit counts as having moved for that turn, and this will prevent models with heavy weapons from firing even if those specific models stayed still. When shooting, heavy weapons always fire the number of times indicated regardless of range. They are very good for laying down long range supporting fire or taking out tanks and monstrous creatures. Units that fire heavy weapons in the Shooting phase may not assault into close combat in the Assault phase.

Example	Range	S	AP	Type
Lascannon	48"	9	2	Heavy 1

PISTOL WEAPONS

Pistol weapons are light enough to be carried and fired one-handed, but as they often have a less powerful charge, their range is limited. On the plus side, they are handy enough to allow a trooper to fight in close combat with a combination of a pistol and sword, axe or other close combat weapon.

All pistols are effectively Assault 1 weapons with a range of 12" (unless differently specified in their profile). In addition a pistol counts as a close combat weapon in the Assault phase.

Example	Range	S	AP	Type
Bolt Pistol	12"	4	5	Pistol

ORDNANCE WEAPONS

Ordnance weapons are so huge and powerful that they cannot be physically carried by infantry, but must be mounted onto a vehicle or be built into the structure of a bunker or fortress. Their rules are covered in the Vehicles section on pages 58 and 60.

Example	Range	S	AP	Type
Battle Cannon	72"	8	3	Ordnance 1, Large Blast

ADDITIONAL WEAPON CHARACTERISTICS

These extra weapon characteristics are represented by additional rules that are added to a weapon's type.

TEMPLATE

These are particularly indiscriminate short-ranged devices, such as flame throwers, which affect a broad, cone-shaped area represented by a template (see diagram). They are indicated by having the word 'template' for their range instead of a number.

Instead of rolling to hit, simply place the template so that its narrow end is touching the base of the model firing it and the rest of the template covers as many models as possible in the target unit without touching any friendly models. Against vehicles, the template must be placed to cover as much of the vehicle as possible without also touching a friendly model. Any models fully or partially under the template are hit. Against vehicles, use the direction of the firer to determine which armour facing is attacked. Because template weapons bathe the area in burning fuel, cover saves are ignored when resolving wounds, even by models inside area terrain! Wounds inflicted by template weapons do not have to be allocated on the models actually covered by the template, but can be put onto any model in the unit.

Example	Range	S	AP	Type
Flamer	Template	4	5	Assault 1

Multiple template weapons

If a unit is firing more than one template weapon, resolve each shot, one at a time, as described above, determining and recording how many hits are scored by each template. Finally, fire any other weapon in the unit, then add up all of the hits and roll to wound.

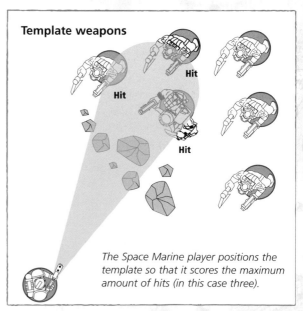

Template weapons

Hit

Hit

Hit

The Space Marine player positions the template so that it scores the maximum amount of hits (in this case three).

BLAST

Blast weapons fire shells, missiles or bolts of energy that explode on impact.

When firing a blast weapon, models do not roll to hit, instead just pick one enemy model visible to the firer and place the blast marker (see diagram) with its hole over the base of the target model, or its hull if it is a vehicle. You may not place the marker so that the base or hull of any of your own models is even grazed by it.

Next, check if the shot has landed on target. If the hole at the centre of the marker is beyond the weapon's maximum range, the shot is an automatic miss and the marker is removed.

If the target is in range, the large area affected by the blast means it's going to be very hard to miss completely. Nonetheless, the shot may not land exactly where it was intended to. Roll the scatter dice and 2D6 to see where the shot lands. If the scatter dice rolls a hit symbol the shot lands on target (ignore the 2D6). If an arrow is rolled, the marker is shifted in the direction shown by the arrow a number of inches equal to the total of the 2D6 minus the firing model's BS (to a minimum of 0).

For example, a BS4 Space Marine fires a frag missile and rolls an arrow result on the scatter dice. The 2D6 roll is a 7, so the blast is moved 3" (7 minus 4) in the direction indicated by the arrow.

Note that it is possible, and absolutely fine, for a scattering shot to land beyond the weapon's range and line of sight, representing the chance of ricochets, the missile blasting through cover and other random chance. In these cases hits are worked out as normal, and can hit units out of range and sight (or even your own troops, or models locked in combat).

If the shot scatters so that the hole in the centre of the marker is beyond the table's edge, the shot is a complete miss and is discarded.

Once the final position of the blast marker has been determined, take a good look at the blast marker from above – all models whose bases are completely or partially covered by the blast marker are hit (as shown in the diagram).

Once the number of hits inflicted on the unit have been worked out, the firer rolls to wound as normal and then the controlling player may allocate these wounds on any model in the unit, not just the ones under the marker.

Example	Range	S	AP	Type
Missile Launcher (frag)	48"	4	6	Heavy 1, Blast

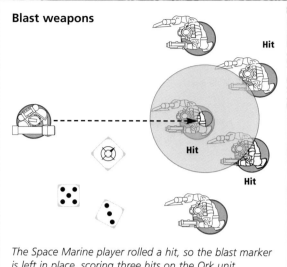

Blast weapons

The Space Marine player rolled a hit, so the blast marker is left in place, scoring three hits on the Ork unit.

Large blasts

There are two sizes of blast marker: the normal one (3" diameter) and the large one (5" diameter). This is clearly indicated in the weapon's profile. Both types of blast marker use exactly the same rules.

Multiple blasts

If a unit is firing more than one blast weapon (for example, four Space Marine Devastators fire four frag missiles at an enemy), resolve each shot, one at the time, as described above, determining and recording how many hits are scored by each blast marker. Finally fire any other weapon in the unit, then add all of the hits together and roll to wound as normal.

Blast weapons and re-rolls

If a model has the ability to re-roll its rolls to hit and chooses to do so after firing a blast weapon, the player must re-roll both the scatter dice and the 2D6.

Scattering blast markers

When rolling a scatter a dice to determine where a shot lands, you may have to move the blast marker several inches away from its intended position. If there are other potential targets nearby (and there often are!), it is quite normal for players to disagree on exactly where the blast marker should end up. This is because sitting at the opposite side of the table tends to give them a different point of view on the relative direction of the arrow on the scatter dice (and the wind always seems to nudge the blast marker slightly towards enemy models...).

To reduce this 'parallax error' we find that it's considerably more practical to roll the scatter dice as close as possible to the target point!

PINNING

Coming under fire without knowing where the shots are coming from is extremely shocking, making troopers throw themselves flat and hug cover as much as possible. Sniper fire and barrages are the most common causes of this.

If a unit other than a vehicle suffers any unsaved wounds from a pinning weapon, it must immediately take a Pinning test. This is a normal Leadership test.

If the unit fails the test, it is immediately forced to go to ground (as described on page 24). As the unit has already taken its saves, going to ground does not protect it against the fire of the pinning weapon that caused the test (or indeed of any other weapon fired by the same unit that phase) – it's too late!

As long as the tests are passed, a unit may be called upon to take multiple Pinning tests in a single turn, but if a unit has already gone to ground, no further Pinning tests are taken.

If the special rules of a unit specify that the unit can never be pinned, the unit always automatically passes Pinning tests. Such units can still choose to go to ground voluntarily.

GETS HOT!

'Gets hot!' represents the penchant of certain unstable weapons for overloading and badly burning their user. Roll to hit as normal, except that you must roll to hit even if the target is found to be out of range. For each result of a 1 rolled on its to hit rolls, the firing model suffers a wound (normal saves apply). Because of their additional cooling systems, weapons on vehicles are not affected by this rule.

Example	Range	S	AP	Type
Plasma gun	24"	7	2	Rapid Fire, Gets Hot!

Gets Hot! and blast weapons

Blast weapons do not roll to hit, so you must always roll a D6 before firing a Gets Hot! blast weapon to check if the weapon overheats. If you roll a 1, the weapon gets hot, it does not fire, and the firing model suffers a wound (normal saves apply). Otherwise the shot is resolved as normal.

Gets Hot! and re-rolls

If a model has the ability to re-roll its rolls to hit (including because of BS 6+), it may re-roll Gets Hot! results of 1 without suffering a wound, unless the result of the re-roll is a 1 as well.

TWIN-LINKED

Weapons are sometimes linked to fire together in order to increase the chances of scoring a hit through the crude expedient of blasting more shots at the target.

A set of twin-linked weapons count as a single weapon of that type, but to represent their fusillade of fire you may re-roll the dice to hit if you miss (including twin-linked blast weapons). In other words, twin-linked weapons don't get more shots than normal ones, but you get a better chance of hitting with them.

Example: A Space Marine Land Raider is firing its twin-linked heavy bolters at an enemy. It gets three shots (as heavy bolters are Heavy 3) and may re-roll any to hit dice which don't score a 3 or higher (which is a hit for a Space Marine's BS of 4) because the weapons are twin-linked.

Twin-linked template weapons

Twin-linked template weapons are fired just like a single weapon, but they can re-roll the dice to wound. When fired against a vehicle, you may re-roll the armour penetration dice instead.

RENDING

In the right circumstances, rending weapons have a chance of piercing any armour with a hail of shots, pinpoint accuracy or diamond-hard ammunition.

Any roll to wound of 6 with a rending weapon automatically causes a wound, regardless of the target's Toughness, and counts as AP2. Against vehicles, an armour penetration roll of 6 allows a further D3 to be rolled, with the result added to the total score.

Example	Range	S	AP	Type
Assault cannon	24"	6	4	Heavy 4, Rending

SNIPER

These deadly weapons can be used to pick out a target's weak or vulnerable points.

Sniper hits wound on a roll of 4+, regardless of the victim's Toughness. In addition, all sniper weapons are also rending and pinning weapons (see above).

Against vehicles, sniper weapons count as Strength 3, which, combined with the rending rule, represents their chances of successfully hitting exposed crew, vision ports, fuel or ammo storage, etc.

Example	Range	S	AP	Type
Sniper rifle	36"	X	6	Heavy 1, Sniper

BARRAGE

Certain weapons launch their shells high up into the air so that they plunge down upon their target, passing over any intervening cover en route and even striking targets that are out of sight.

Note that in older Codex books barrage weapons were identified by having a G (guess) before their range (e.g. Range: G48"). This is the same as having the word 'barrage' under their Type.

All barrage weapons use blast markers and consequently use the rules for blast weapons, with the following exceptions:

- To determine if a unit wounded by a barrage weapon is allowed a cover save, always assume the shot is coming from the centre of the marker, instead of from the firing model. Remember that models in area terrain get their cover save regardless of the direction the shot is coming from.

- Some barrage weapons have a minimum range as well as a maximum range (e.g. Range: 12"- 48"). If the centre of the marker is placed by the firer within the minimum range (before rolling for scatter), the shot misses automatically and is removed.

- Death raining from the sky is a truly terrifying experience, therefore all barrage weapons are pinning weapons as well (see Pinning).

- Barrage weapons can fire at a target they cannot see, but if they do this, the BS of the firer makes no difference and the blast marker scatters a full 2D6" if an arrow is rolled on the scatter dice.

Example	Range	S	AP	Type
Lobba	48"	5	5	Heavy 1, Blast, Barrage

Multiple barrages

If a unit has more than one barrage weapon, they are all fired together in a salvo, as follows:

First place the blast marker for the weapon in the firing unit that is closest to the target. If the target is in range, roll for any scatter as described above.

Once the first marker is placed, roll a scatter dice for each other barrage weapon fired by the unit. If an arrow is rolled, place the marker in the direction indicated so that it is adjacent and touching the edge of the first marker placed (as shown in the diagram). If a hit is rolled, the firing player places the marker so that it touches any part of any marker in the salvo that has already been placed. Note that it is perfectly fine if, through this process, some markers are placed overlapping one another.

Once all of the markers are in place, work out the number of hits scored for each blast marker as usual for blast weapons and then roll to wound as normal.

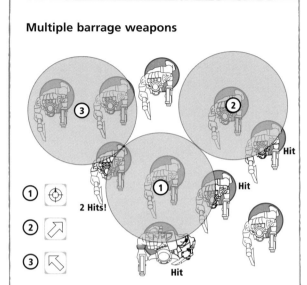

The original marker (1) scores a hit and does not scatter, while arrows are rolled for the second (2) and third (3) markers, which are placed accordingly. The number of hits scored is worked out separately for each marker, and in this case the salvo scores a total of nine hits on the unit! If, for example, a hit had been rolled for the third marker instead, the player could have placed it anywhere in contact with or over markers 1 and 2, even directly on top of the first marker (as long as it causes the most hits on the target). If he did so, the salvo would have caused a total of ten hits instead of the nine caused in the example above.

MELTA

Melta weapons are lethal, short-ranged 'heat rays'. They roll an extra D6 when rolling to penetrate a vehicle's Armour Value at half range or less. If the weapon is more than half its maximum range away, a single D6 is rolled as normal. See the Vehicles rules later for more details on armour penetration.

Example	Range	S	AP	Type
Meltagun	12"	8	1	Assault 1, Melta

LANCE

These weapons fire a coherent, focused beam that can bore through any armour, regardless of its thickness. Due to their unique nature, lance weapons count vehicle Armour Values higher than 12 as 12.

Example	Range	S	AP	Type
Bright lance	36"	8	2	Heavy 1, Lance

THE ASSAULT PHASE

While firepower alone may be enough to drive an enemy back from open ground or lightly held positions, shifting a determined foe from a fortified bunker or ruined settlement will need sterner measures. In an assault, troops storm forward, screaming their battle cries, eager to strike at their foes with knives, claws, bayonets or gun butts in a desperate close combat.

ASSAULT PHASE SUMMARY

1 Move assaulting units
- Pick a unit.
- Declare which enemy unit it is going to assault.
- Move the assaulting unit.
- Pick another unit and repeat the above until all assaulting units have moved.

2 Defenders react
- The opponent picks one of his units that have been assaulted.
- The opponent moves all of the models in the unit into base contact with the enemy, or at least into position to be engaged.
- Pick another unit and repeat until all assaulted units have moved.

3 Resolve combats
- Pick a combat.
- Fight close combat. Engaged models roll to hit and to wound in Initiative order. Their opponents take saving throws as required.
- Determine assault results. Total up wounds inflicted. The side that inflicted the most wounds overall in the combat is the winner.
- Loser checks morale. The loser has to pass a Morale check or fall back. If the loser passes the test, go directly to pile-in.
- Sweeping advances, fall backs and consolidations. Units falling back from close combat must test to see if they successfully break off, if they fail they are destroyed. The winners may then consolidate their position.
- Pile-in! If units are still locked in close combat, then any models not engaged are moved towards the enemy to continue the fight next turn.
- Pick another combat and repeat until all combats have been resolved.

DECLARE ASSAULTS

The maximum distance most units can move during an assault is 6". As you cannot measure the distance to the enemy before declaring the assault, if you misjudge the distance and the unit is unable to reach its target, then the unit does not move and that assault is ignored. Bear in mind that models may have to expend some of their movement to move around impassable terrain or other models in order to reach their enemy.

DISALLOWED ASSAULTS

Units are not allowed to assault if:

- They are already locked in close combat.
- They ran in the Shooting phase (see page 16).
- They have gone to ground (see page 24).
- They shot rapid fire weapons or heavy weapons in the Shooting phase (see page 28).
- They are falling back (see page 45).

In addition to the above, a unit that fired in the Shooting phase can only assault the unit that it shot at – it cannot assault a different unit to the one it previously shot at. However, see the exception over the page for multiple targets.

MOVE ASSAULTING UNITS

Assaulting units must now move into close combat with the unit they have declared an assault against. A player must move all of the models in each assaulting unit before moving on to the next unit. The assaulting player decides the order in which his units will move.

MOVING ASSAULTING MODELS

All of the models in an assaulting unit make their assault move following the same rules as in the Movement phase, with the exception that they may be moved within 1" of enemy models. This means that assaulting models may still not move through friendly or enemy models, may not pass through gaps narrower than their base, and may not move into base contact with enemy models from a unit they are not assaulting.

Assaulting units must attempt to engage as many opposing models as possible with as many of their models as possible – no holding back! Start each assault by moving a single model from the assaulting unit. The model selected must be the one closest to the enemy (going around impassable terrain, friendly models and enemy models in units not being assaulted). Move the model into contact with the nearest enemy model in the unit being assaulted, using the shortest possible route. Roll for difficult or dangerous terrain if necessary, and if the model is killed by a dangerous terrain test, start the assault again with the next closest model. If the closest model is found not to be within move distance to the enemy, that assault does not happen and no model is moved.

If the enemy is within range, then the assault move continues. After moving the first model in the unit, you can move the others in any sequence you desire. There are some constraints on their movement though:

- The most important one is that each model must end its assault move in coherency with another model in its own unit that has already moved.

- If possible, the model must move into base contact with any enemy model within reach that is not already in base contact with an assaulting model.

- If there are no such models in reach, the model must move into base contact with an enemy model that is already in base contact with an assaulting model.

- If a model cannot reach any enemy models, it must try to move within 2" of one of its own unit's models that is already in base contact with an enemy.

- If this is impossible, it must simply stay in coherency.

If you follow this sequence you will end up with all the models in the assaulting unit in unit coherency, having engaged as many enemy models as possible with as many assaulting models as possible.

ASSAULTING MULTIPLE ENEMY UNITS

As you move assaulting models, you may find it is possible to reach other enemy units that are close to the one you are assaulting.

As usual the closest attacking model must be moved to contact the closest model in the enemy unit against which the assault was declared. Then remaining models can assault models belonging to other enemy units, as long as they keep following the rules for moving assaulting models. Remember that the assaulting unit is not allowed to break its unit coherency, and this will obviously limit the potential for this kind of assault.

If the assaulting unit shot in the Shooting phase then it must declare its assault against the unit it shot at, but it can engage other enemies as described here.

DEFENDERS REACT

When their comrades come under attack, the remaining troopers rush forward to bolster the defence.

After all assault moves have been made, the player controlling the units that have been assaulted this turn must move any member of these units that is not yet in base contact with a foe towards the enemy.

These models move up to 6" in an attempt to move into base contact with an enemy. This follows the same rules as moving assaulting models, except that models are not slowed by difficult terrain and do not take dangerous terrain tests. Also, this move may not be used to contact enemy units that are not currently involved in the assault.

FIGHTING A CLOSE COMBAT

How effective creatures are in close combat depends almost entirely on their physical characteristics – in other words how fast, strong, tough and ferocious they are. In close combat, armour remains as useful as ever for warding off blows and shots, but ranged weaponry becomes a secondary consideration – the best gun in the galaxy won't help if your opponent is bashing your brains out with a rock!

In close combat, both players' models fight. Attacks in close combat work like shots in shooting – each attack that hits has a chance to wound. The wounded model gets a chance to save, and if it fails is (generally) removed as a casualty. How many blows are struck and who strikes first is detailed later.

There may be several separate assaults being fought simultaneously in different parts of the battlefield. If this is the case, the player whose turn it is can choose the order in which to resolve the combats, completing each combat before moving on to the next one, and so on until all combats are resolved.

WHO CAN FIGHT?

Close combat is a swirling melee of troops leaping, spinning, hacking and slashing at one another. As well as fighting hand-to-hand, warriors will be firing pistols at point blank range at any target that presents itself.

Units that have one or more model in base contact with enemies are said to be 'locked in combat'. Within such units, the following models are said to be 'engaged' and must fight:

• Models in base contact with any enemy models.

• Models within 2" of at least one model in their unit that is in base contact with any enemy models.

All engaged models will fight in this turn's Assault phase with their full number of Attacks and use any special close combat attack they have. Any models left unengaged because they are too far from an enemy model cannot attack this turn. However, they can still be killed by the enemy, and the result of the combat will still affect them.

Working out which models are engaged in combat is done at the start of the fight, and will not change until its end, but casualties may make it difficult to remember as the fight continues, especially in a large combat. To make the distinction clear, you may find it useful to turn unengaged models so that they are facing away from their opponents. This will help you to remember once the dice start rolling.

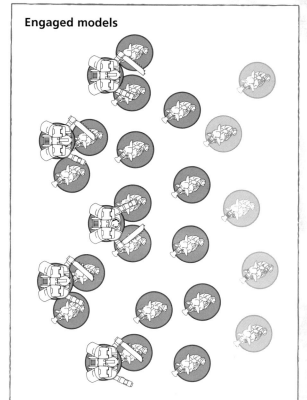

Engaged models

All of the Gretchin in base contact with a Space Marine, and the ones within 2" of an Gretchin that is in base contact with a Space Marine are engaged and can therefore attack. The remaining Gretchin, shown in a lighter tone of grey, cannot attack.

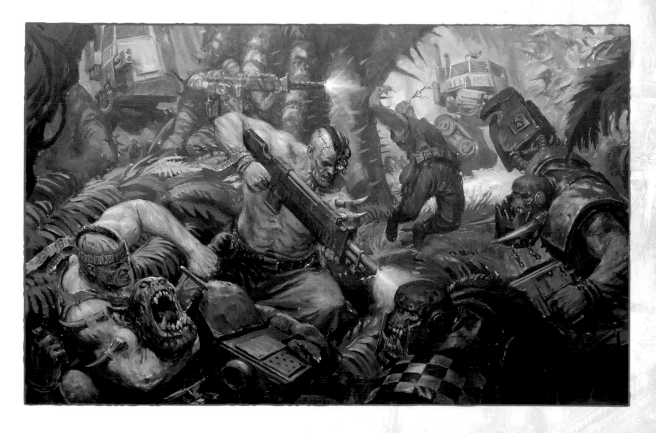

WHO STRIKES FIRST?

It's all in the reflexes when it comes to close combat – slow, lumbering opponents can be dispatched quickly by a faster and more agile foe. Unfortunately, many cumbersome opponents, such as Orks, are tough enough to withstand a vicious pummelling and keep coming back for more.

In close combat, a model's Initiative characteristic determines who attacks first. Work your way through the Initiative values of the models engaged in the combat, starting with the highest and ending with the lowest. Models make their attacks when their Initiative value is reached, assuming they haven't already been killed by a model with a higher Initiative! If both sides have models with the same Initiative value, their attacks are made simultaneously. Note that certain situations, abilities and weapons can modify a model's Initiative.

For example, a squad of Space Marines (Initiative 4) including a Veteran Sergeant with a power fist (which reduces his Initiative to 1) assaults a mob of Orks (Initiative 2). The Space Marines strike first at Initiative 4, followed by the Orks at 2, then the Sergeant strikes last at Initiative 1.

> "Let's stomp some 'umies!"
>
> Ghazghkull Thraka

ASSAULTING THROUGH COVER

If, following the rules for moving assaulting models (see page 34), any model in an assaulting unit will have to go through difficult or dangerous terrain as part of its assault move, the unit must take the relevant terrain test before moving. This has two disadvantages. The first and most obvious is that such tests might cause the assault to fail altogether if the closest model cannot make it into contact with the enemy. Note that if a model stopped 1" away from the enemy in the Movement or Shooting phase, it can Assault even if its unit rolls a double 1 on its difficult terrain test.

The second disadvantage is that warriors who are assaulting through cover are subject to deadly salvoes of close range fire as they slowly struggle to get to grips with their foe and may be ambushed by foes that are ready for them. To represent this, if an assaulting unit had to take a difficult or dangerous terrain test during their assault move, all of its models have their Initiative value lowered to 1 when attacking, regardless of other Initiative modifiers. Remember that assaulting models must try to engage as many enemies as possible – no holding back to avoid the test!

If all of the enemy units assaulted were already locked in combat from a previous turn or had gone to ground, this penalty does not apply as the enemy warriors are not set to receive the charge, and the unit assaulting though cover fights at its normal Initiative.

GRENADES

Grenades in Warhammer 40,000 are generally used as part of an assault. A well-placed barrage of grenades can help immeasurably in the vital last few seconds it takes to overrun an enemy and come to grips. What follows are some of the most common types of grenades used in assaults. Any actual damage done by the grenade is assumed to be taken into account in the unit's attacks in close combat, but the unit using them gains the added benefit described below.

Assault Grenades
(e.g. frag grenades, plasma grenades, and so on)

Assault grenades, like the ubiquitous fragmentation grenades or the more advanced Eldar plasma grenades, can be thrown at opponents in cover to force them to keep their heads down during an assault. The lethal storm of shrapnel (or the delayed plasma blast) from these grenades will drive opponents further under cover for a few precious moments, allowing attackers more time to close in. Models equipped with assault grenades don't suffer the penalty to their Initiative for assaulting enemies through cover, but fight as normal.

Defensive Grenades
(e.g., photon grenades, etc.)

An example of defensive grenades are the photon grenades of the Tau, weapons that blind and disorientate the attacker with multi-spectral light and a sonic burst. Models assaulting against units equipped with defensive grenades gain no Assault Bonus attacks (see opposite). However, if the defending unit was already locked in combat from a previous turn, or had gone to ground, these grenades have no effect and the attackers gain the Assault Bonus attacks as normal.

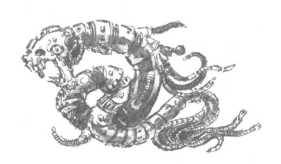

NUMBER OF ATTACKS

As explained earlier, models attack in order of Initiative. When their Initiative value is reached, models with that Initiative who are still alive must attack. It does not matter if all the enemies that they were engaged with have been killed – if a model was engaged at the start the fight (and is still alive when its turn to attack comes) it can still attack.

Each engaged model strikes with the number of Attacks (A) on its characteristics profile, plus the following bonus attacks:

• +1 Assault Bonus: Engaged models who assaulted this turn get +1 attack.

• +1 Two Weapons: Engaged models with two single-handed weapons (typically a close combat weapon and/or pistol in each hand) get an extra +1 attack. Models with more than two weapons gain no additional benefit – you only get one extra attack, even if you have more than two weapons.

• Other bonuses: Models may have other special rules and wargear that confer extra attacks.

Note that bonus attacks are an exception to the rules for characteristics' maximum modifiers and may bring a model's total attacks above 10!

Example 1: A unit of five Space Marines with bolters normally roll five dice for their attacks in close combat. If they were assaulting they would roll ten dice (1 Attack +1 for assaulting = 2 each).

Example 2: A unit of five Orks with two close combat weapons normally roll fifteen dice (2 Attacks +1 for two weapons). If they were assaulting they'd roll twenty (2 Attacks +1 for assaulting +1 for two weapons = 4 each!).

ROLLING TO HIT

To determine whether hits are scored, roll a D6 for each attack a model gets to make. The dice roll needed to score a hit on your enemy depends on the relative Weapon Skills of the attacker and the target. Compare the WS of the attacking model with the WS of the target unit and consult the To Hit chart below to find the minimum score needed on a D6 to hit.

It is worth explaining the mechanic behind the chart, which is as follows: if the target's WS is lower than the the attacker's, he hits on 3+; if the target's WS is equal or up to twice as high as the attacker's he hits on 4+, and if it is more than twice as high he hits on 5+.

Where the same roll to hit is needed, attacks should be rolled together, as this speeds up the game.

In the previous example, the Ork player would therefore roll all of his twenty attacks together.

Units with different WS

A few units in Warhammer 40,000 contain models with different Weapon Skill values. Attacks against such units are resolved using the Weapon Skill of the majority of the engaged models. If there is no majority Weapon Skill, use the highest Weapon Skill of the models engaged.

For example, a mob of 20 Gretchin (WS2) led by an Ork Runtherd (WS4) are all engaged in a combat. Since the Gretchin are in the majority, attacks against the unit are resolved using their WS of 2 – the Runtherd can't prevent the Gretchin getting hit. When the models attack, they calculate their own scores required to hit based on their individual Weapon Skill. So, when the Gretchin and Runtherd attack their enemies, the Gretchin will hit based on a comparison of their WS2 and the enemy's WS, while the Runtherd will compare his WS4 with the enemy's.

TO HIT CHART

Target's Weapon Skill

Attacker's Weapon Skill	1	2	3	4	5	6	7	8	9	10
1	4+	4+	5+	5+	5+	5+	5+	5+	5+	5+
2	3+	4+	4+	4+	5+	5+	5+	5+	5+	5+
3	3+	3+	4+	4+	4+	4+	5+	5+	5+	5+
4	3+	3+	3+	4+	4+	4+	4+	4+	5+	5+
5	3+	3+	3+	3+	4+	4+	4+	4+	4+	4+
6	3+	3+	3+	3+	3+	4+	4+	4+	4+	4+
7	3+	3+	3+	3+	3+	3+	4+	4+	4+	4+
8	3+	3+	3+	3+	3+	3+	3+	4+	4+	4+
9	3+	3+	3+	3+	3+	3+	3+	3+	4+	4+
10	3+	3+	3+	3+	3+	3+	3+	3+	3+	4+

NB. If a model has WS 0, all close combat attacks directed against it will hit automatically.

ROLLING TO WOUND

Not all of the attacks that hit their mark will harm the enemy. They may be parried at the last moment or may merely inflict a graze or flesh wound. As with shooting, once you have scored a hit with an attack you must roll again to see if you score a wound and incapacitate your foe. Consult the chart below, cross-referencing the attacker's Strength characteristic (S) with the defender's Toughness (T). The chart, which is the same as the one in the Shooting section, indicates the minimum value on a D6 roll required to inflict a wound. In most cases, when rolling to wound in close combat, you use the Strength on the attacker's profile regardless of what weapon they are using. Some close combat weapons give the attacker a Strength bonus – this is explained later in Special Close Combat Attacks.

In a unit containing models with different Strength values, roll their attacks separately (they'll quite often have different Initiative characteristics too).

For example, in a unit containing Gretchin and an Ork Runtherd, the Gretchin's attacks are made with their puny Strength of 2, but the Runtherd's attacks use his Strength of 3.

Multiple Toughness values

Quite rarely, a unit will contain models that have different Toughness characteristics. To keep things simple, roll to wound using the Toughness value of the majority of the engaged foe. If no majority exists, use the highest value in the unit.

Know the mutant; kill the mutant.

TO WOUND CHART

		Toughness								
		1	2	3	4	5	6	7	8	9	10
Strength	1	4+	5+	6+	6+	N	N	N	N	N	N
	2	3+	4+	5+	6+	6+	N	N	N	N	N
	3	2+	3+	4+	5+	6+	6+	N	N	N	N
	4	2+	2+	3+	4+	5+	6+	6+	N	N	N
	5	2+	2+	2+	3+	4+	5+	6+	6+	N	N
	6	2+	2+	2+	2+	3+	4+	5+	6+	6+	N
	7	2+	2+	2+	2+	2+	3+	4+	5+	6+	6+
	8	2+	2+	2+	2+	2+	2+	3+	4+	5+	6+
	9	2+	2+	2+	2+	2+	2+	2+	3+	4+	5+
	10	2+	2+	2+	2+	2+	2+	2+	2+	3+	4+

Note that N on the chart means the hit has no effect. A target with the Toughness indicated cannot be harmed by a hit of such puny Strength. Also note that a roll of 1 never scores a Wound, regardless of its Strength.

Allocating wounds

After determining the number of wounds inflicted against a unit at a particular Initiative value, the unit takes saves and casualties are removed as detailed below. Just like in the Shooting phase, if all the models in the unit are the same in gaming terms, you can carry straight on and roll all the saves in one batch. Otherwise, wounds are allocated against the target unit by the controlling player, exactly like the fire of a single enemy unit during the Shooting phase (refer back to page 25).

Either way, all of the models in the target unit can be hit, wounded and killed, including those that are not engaged. This represents the fact that each fighter is contributing his shots and blows to the swirling combat while warriors are rushing forward to replace their comrades that fall under the blows of the enemy. Indeed it is a good tactic to allocate wounds on models that are not engaged, as it will often allow your engaged models to survive long enough to attack back! Remember to use different coloured dice or otherwise mark out the wounds that have different special rules attached to them (like those inflicting instant death or those that ignore armour saves), as you would do in the Shooting phase.

TAKING SAVES

Models struck and wounded in close combat can attempt armour saves to avoid becoming casualties. Models usually get to save regardless of the attacker's Strength, but some especially monstrous creatures and powerful close combat weapons will punch straight through armour. Otherwise, the procedure for taking saves is the same as the one described for Shooting.

Cover does not provide protection in close combat as it does against shooting. This means that models do not get cover saves against any wounds suffered in close combat, and for obvious reasons cannot go to ground.

Remember that even if the rules for a weapon or attack states that no armour save is allowed, an invulnerable save may still be made.

REMOVING CASUALTIES

All of the rules for removing shooting casualties apply in close combat.

If a model becomes a casualty before it has an opportunity to attack, then it may not strike back. When striking blows simultaneously, you may find it more convenient to resolve one side's attacks and simply lay wounded models on their side to remind you that they have yet to attack back.

The Martyr's grave is the
foundation of the Imperium.

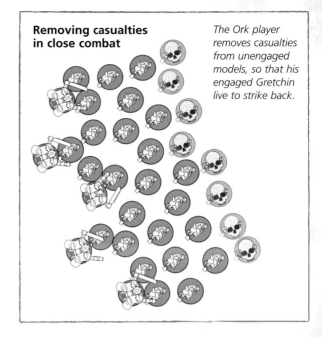

Removing casualties in close combat

The Ork player removes casualties from unengaged models, so that his engaged Gretchin live to strike back.

DETERMINE ASSAULT RESULTS

Assaults are usually decisive, one side or the other quickly gaining the upper hand and forcing back their foe. Good Leadership can keep a side in the fight, but the casualties that each side inflicts are usually the most telling factor. To decide who has won the combat, total up the number of unsaved wounds inflicted by each side on their opponents. The side that caused the most is the winner. The losing side must take a Morale check and will fall back if they fail.

If both sides suffer the same number of wounds, the combat is drawn and continues next turn.

Of course, if one side destroys the enemy it wins automatically, even if it sustained more casualties!

Note that wounds that have been negated by saving throws or other special rules that have similar effects do not count, nor do wounds in excess of a model's Wounds characteristic, only the wounds actually suffered by enemy models (including all of the Wounds lost by models that have suffered instant death). In rare cases certain models can cause wounds on themselves or their friends – obviously these wounds are added to the other side's total for working out who has won.

CHECK MORALE

Units that lose a close combat must take a Morale check to hold their ground, with a penalty depending on how severe the defeat was (see page 44). If they pass, the unit fights on – the combat is effectively drawn and no further account is made of the unit's defeat (apart from some good-natured taunting by the winner!). If they fail, they must abandon the fight and will fall back. Morale checks and falling back are covered in the Morale section on page 43.

SWEEPING ADVANCES

When a unit falls back from combat, the victors make a Sweeping Advance, attempting to cut down the retreating enemies.

Both the unit falling back and the winning unit roll a D6 and add their Initiative value to the result. Always count the Initiative value from the model's profile without any modifiers. In a unit with mixed Initiative characteristics, count the majority value, or the highest if there is no majority.

They then compare their totals.

- If the winner's total is equal or greater they catch the fleeing enemy with a sweeping advance. The falling back unit is destroyed. We assume that the already demoralised foe is comprehensively scattered, ripped apart or sent packing, its members left either dead, wounded and captured, or at best fleeing and hiding. The destroyed unit is removed immediately. Unless otherwise specified, no save or other special rule can rescue the unit at this stage; for them the battle is over.

- If the falling back unit's total is higher, they break off from the combat successfully. Make a fall back move for the losing unit (see page 45). The winners can then consolidate as detailed below.

DISALLOWED SWEEPING ADVANCES

If a victorious unit is still locked in combat with other units that are not falling back, it does not get a chance to execute a sweeping advance and the retreating enemy falls back safely.

Some troops, as detailed in their entries, are not allowed to make a sweeping advance – in such cases the enemy always manage to disengage safely.

PILE-IN!

After the combat been resolved, it might happen that some models from units that did not fall back from the combat are not in base contact with an enemy. These models must make a pile-in move.

Just like when defenders react to being assaulted, these models move up to 6" in an attempt to move into base contact with an enemy or, if not possible, into a position in which they are engaged and will be able to fight. This follows the same rules as moving assaulting models, except that is not slowed by difficult terrain and does not trigger dangerous terrain tests. Also, a pile-in move may not be used to contact enemy units that are not currently involved in the assault.

When making pile-in moves, the player whose turn it currently is moves first. If for some reason (mass carnage, usually), his model's pile-in moves are insufficient to move into base contact with any enemy that was involved in that fight, the player must still move them as close as possible to such enemies. The opponent will then execute his own models' pile-in moves, back into contact with the enemies they were fighting. If both units' pile-in moves combined (that's more than 12" – very unlikely!) would be insufficient to bring the combatants back together, the assault comes to an end and both sides may make consolidation moves instead, as described below.

While a unit is locked in combat it may only make pile-in moves and may not otherwise move or shoot.

CONSOLIDATION

At the end of a combat, if a unit's opponents are all either destroyed or falling back, so that the victorious unit is no longer locked in combat with any enemy, they may consolidate. This means that they may move up to D6" in any direction, as the sudden victory may leave the warriors raring to storm onward or flat-footed and dumbfounded, according to the vagaries of fate.

Units making a consolidate move are not slowed by difficult terrain and do not trigger dangerous terrain tests. A consolidation move may not be used to move into base contact with enemy models, as this can only be done with an assault move. Consolidating models must therefore stop 1" away from all enemy models, including any that might have just fallen back from the combat that the consolidating unit has fought in.

SHOOTING INTO & OUT OF CLOSE COMBAT

Models belonging to units locked in combat may not fire weapons in the Shooting phase. Their attention is completely taken by the swirling melee. Likewise, while especially twisted and soulless commanders may wish their warriors to fire indiscriminately into the middle of close combats in the hopes of hitting the enemy, this is not permitted. The events in a close combat move too quickly and the warriors themselves will be understandably hesitant about firing on their comrades.

While blast markers and templates may not be deliberately placed such that they cover any models locked in combat, they may end up there after scattering and will then hit any models they touch (friends and foes!).

Units that are locked in close combat do not have to take Morale and Pinning tests caused by shooting; they are considered to be much too focused on fighting to be worried about being shot at!

There is no substitute for zeal.

MULTIPLE COMBATS

Combats that involve more than two units are called 'multiple combats' (see the diagram below for an example). Because of the extra complexity, they need some additional rules, which are provided on this page.

DEFENDERS REACT

If a unit that is already locked in combat from a previous turn is assaulted by a new enemy unit, it can react as normal. Its models must be moved into base contact with models from any of the units that they are fighting, not just the enemies that just assaulted them.

ATTACKING

In multiple combats, when it is time for a model to attack, the following extra rules apply:

• Models that were engaged with just one of the enemy units at the beginning of the combat (before any model attacked) must attack that unit.

• Models that were engaged with more than one enemy unit at the beginning of the combat (before any model attacked) may split their attacks freely between those units. Declare how they are splitting their attacks immediately before rolling to hit.

ASSAULT RESULTS

When determining assault results in a multiple combat, total up the number of wounds inflicted by each side to see which side is the winner. Every unit on the losing side has to check their Morale (they all use the same penalty, as described in the Morale section). After all of the losing units have taken their Morale checks, any winning unit that is now free to make a sweeping advance rolls the dice and compares its total with the total of each of the falling back enemy units it was engaged with. Any that it equals or beats are destroyed. Remember that winning units can only sweeping advance if all of the units they were locked with fall back or are wiped out in the fight.

After assault resolution, all units that were involved in that multiple combat must make pile-in moves towards enemies that fought in that combat. If a unit's pile-in cannot reach any such enemies, the unit must move as close as possible to the enemy to allow them to pile-in into contact. If it is impossible, both sides consolidate.

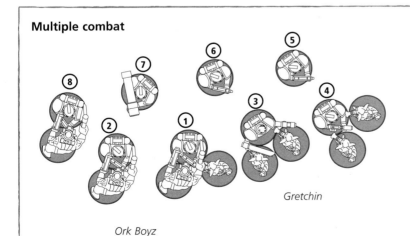

Multiple combat

Ork Boyz

Gretchin

The Space Marines have charged the Orks and Gretchin. Space Marine 1 can choose to attack either the Orks or the Gretchin (or split his attacks). Space Marines 6 and 7 can also choose to fight either enemy unit (or split their attacks), because they are within 2" of a member of their own unit who is in base contact with both enemy units.

Space Marines 2, 3, 4 and 8 can only attack the units they're in base contact with. Space Marine 5 can only attack the Gretchin (as he is only within 2" of members of his own unit that are in base contact with the Gretchin).

CLOSE COMBAT WEAPONS

On the battlefields of the 41st Millennium, close combat remains commonplace – seasoned warriors often bear a deadly array of combat knives and frag grenades, while specialised assault troops take pistols, swords and deadly power weapons into battle. In terms of rules, they are all grouped into either of the following two categories:

NORMAL CLOSE COMBAT WEAPONS

Weapons like chainswords, rifle butts, combat blades, bayonets, etc., do not confer any particular bonus to the model using them. Remember that, in close combat, pistols count as normal close combat weapons and so the Strength and AP of the pistol are ignored.

SPECIAL CLOSE COMBAT WEAPONS

These include more complex and powerful weapons that enhance the wielder's combat skills and confer bonuses, and sometimes penalties, to the models using them. The most widely used are listed below:

Power weapons

A power weapon is sheathed in the lethal haze of a disruptive energy field, which eats through armour, flesh and bone with ease. Models wounded in close combat by the attacks of a model armed with a power weapon are not allowed armour saves.

Lightning claws

Lightning claws are commonly used as matched pairs and consist of a number of blades, each a mini-power weapon, normally mounted on the back of the hand. A lightning claw is a power weapon and it also allows the wielder to re-roll any failed roll to wound.

Force weapons

These psychic weapons are described on page 50.

Poisoned weapons

Poisoned weapons range from blades coated in venom to hypodermic claws. They do not rely on a comparison of Strength and Toughness to wound – they always wound on a fixed number, generally shown in brackets. In most cases this is 4+. Some venoms are so lethal that the merest drop can kill – these may wound on a 3+, or even 2+ (as described in the appropriate Codex). In addition, if the Strength of the wielder is the same or higher than the Toughness of the victim, the wielder must re-roll failed rolls to wound in close combat. These weapons confer no advantage against vehicles.

Power fists

A power fist (or 'power claw') is an armoured gauntlet surrounded by a disruptive energy field. A power fist is a power weapon, and also doubles the user's Strength (up to a maximum of 10). Power fists, however, are difficult and cumbersome to use, so attacks with a power fist are always delivered at Initiative 1 (ignore Initiative bonuses from special rules, wargear, etc.).

Thunder hammers

Thunder hammers release a tremendous blast of energy when they strike. A thunder hammer uses the same rules as a power fist. In addition, all models that suffer an unsaved wound from a thunder hammer and are not killed will be knocked reeling, reducing their Initiative to a value of 1 until the end of the next player's turn. Against vehicles with no Initiative value, whenever a thunder hammer inflicts any damage result, it also inflicts a crew shaken result (see page 61).

Rending weapons

If a model armed with a rending close combat weapon rolls a 6 on any of his rolls to wound in close combat, the opponent automatically suffers a wound, regardless of its Toughness. These wounds count as wounds from a power weapon. Against vehicles, an armour penetration roll of 6 allows a further D3 to be rolled, with the result added to the total score.

Witchblades

These psychically attuned weapons are often carried by Eldar psykers. All hits scored in close combat by models armed with a witchblade inflict wounds on a roll of 2+, regardless of the target's Toughness. Armour saves are taken as normal. Against vehicles, the wielder of a witchblade counts his Strength as 9.

FIGHTING WITH TWO SINGLE-HANDED WEAPONS

Some models are equipped with two single-handed weapons they can use in close combat, with the rules given below for the different possible combinations. Of course, if a model is using a two-handed close combat weapon (such as a rifle's butt or a two-handed battle axe), it may not use it together with another weapon.

Two normal close combat weapons

These models gain one bonus attack (see page 37).

Two of the same special weapon

These models gain one additional attack. All of their attacks, including the bonus attack, use the special weapon's bonuses and penalties.

A normal and a special weapon

These models gain one additional attack. All of their attacks, including the bonus attack, benefit from the special weapon's bonuses.

Power fists, thunder hammers and lightning claws are an exception to this. Only a second power fist, thunder hammer or lightning claw can confer a bonus attack to a model equipped with one of these weapons.

Two different special weapons

When it is their turn to attack, these models must choose which weapon to use that turn, but they never get the bonus attack for using two weapons (such is the penalty for wielding too many complex weapons!).

MORALE

It is a fortunate commander who can always rely on his troops to perform fearlessly. In the chaos and confusion of battle, troops can easily become demoralised, disoriented or simply terrified by the violence unleashed against them. To represent this element of the unknown, your units of troops have to check to see if their morale holds under certain circumstances. As you will have already gathered, particular events will require that your troops take a Morale check, and a unit in particularly dire straits may be forced to take several Morale checks in a single turn.

Morale checks are a specific kind of Leadership test. Note that Leadership tests are used for other functions in Warhammer 40,000, such as using Psychic powers.

MORALE CHECKS

Morale represents the grit, determination, or (sometimes) plain stupidity of warriors in action. Like all other Leadership-based tests, Morale checks (also called Morale tests) are taken by rolling 2D6 and comparing the total to the unit's Leadership value. If the score is equal to or under the unit's Leadership value, the test is passed and the unit does not suffer any ill effects – their nerve has held. However, if the score rolled is higher, then the test is failed and the unit will immediately fall back, as described over the page.

Some units have special rules pertaining to Morale checks that are detailed in the appropriate Codex. For example, some particularly fanatical units may be immune to the effects of morale. Some units always pass Morale checks, while a few others always pass all Leadership tests. This is a subtle but important difference. For example, units that always pass Morale checks will still have to test for Pinning.

"Warriors of Ultramar! This is where we make our stand. If death is to be our fate then we shall meet it with the Emperor's word on our lips and his light in our eyes. If we must die, we will die; but we shall never yield."

Marneus Calgar, Lord Macragge

MORALE CHECK MODIFIERS

Certain circumstances can make Morale checks harder for a unit to pass. This is represented by applying Leadership modifiers to Morale checks, which can reduce the unit's Leadership value by -1, -2 or sometimes even more.

INSANE HEROISM!

Occasionally, warriors will refuse to retreat even when faced with impossible odds or particularly harrowing experiences. Sometimes you can push someone just too far! A score of double 1 on the 2D6 roll always indicates the unit has passed its Morale check, regardless of modifiers.

TAKING MORALE CHECKS

Units normally have to take a Morale check in the following situations:

A) Casualties

A unit losing 25% or more of its models during a single phase must pass a Morale check at the end of that phase, or else it will fall back. Do not count casualties caused by close combat attacks, as they are covered later in C) Losing an Assault.

A unit that is locked in close combat does not have to take Morale checks for taking 25% casualties.

Example: A unit of five troops suffers two casualties from enemy shooting, so it takes a Morale check, which it promptly passes. Next turn, the unit, now three strong, suffers a single casualty from shooting, which is now enough for it to have to take another Morale check.

B) Tank Shock

Units that are overrun by an enemy tank may wisely decide it's time to abandon their position and fall back. If a tank reaches an enemy unit's position then the unit must take a Morale check to see whether or not it falls back. For a more complete explanation of how tank shock works, see the Vehicle rules on page 68.

C) Losing an Assault

Units that lose a close combat (ie, they suffer more wounds than they inflict) must pass a Morale check to hold their ground. If they fail, they must fall back.

Units taking this Morale Check suffer a -1 Ld modifier for each wound their side has lost the combat by.

Example: An Imperial Guard squad has lost an assault. They would normally require a 7 or less to pass the Leadership test, but since they have lost the fight by a difference of 2 Wounds (-2), they now require a 5 or less to hold their ground.

NO RETREAT!

It's not uncommon for units to be immune to Morale checks for losing an assault, or to automatically pass them for some reason (they may have the 'fearless' special rule, be subject to a vow or some other special rule). When such units lose a close combat, they are in danger of being dragged down by the victorious enemy despite their determination to hang on.

These units do not take Morale checks and will never fall back. Instead, these units suffer a number of wounds equal to the number their side has lost the combat by (allocated as normal).

All types of saving throws, except for cover saves, can be taken against these wounds.

For example, after all blows are struck, a fearless unit has lost the fight by a difference of 3. The fearless unit does not take a Morale test, but it immediately suffers three wounds and will take three armour saves.

If none of the enemies involved in the combat against a fearless unit can actually hurt it, the unit does not suffer any wounds if its side is defeated in combat, and simply continues to fight.

"A good soldier obeys without question. A good officer commands without doubt."

Tactica Imperium

FALL BACK!

A fall back move is a fighting withdrawal rather than an out-and-out rout. Sometimes a fighting retreat in the face of overwhelming odds is the only option left. A withdrawal can give troops the chance to retire to a stronger position, to regroup and mount a fresh attack, or to hold back the approaching enemy.

Units make a fall back move immediately upon failing a Morale test. In each subsequent Movement phase, they will make further fall back moves instead of moving normally, until the unit regroups, is destroyed or leaves the table.

Units normally fall back 2D6". Fall back moves are not slowed by difficult terrain, but tests for dangerous terrain are taken as normal.

Each model in the unit falls back directly towards their own table edge by the shortest possible route. If playing a mission where there is no 'own' table edge, models fall back towards the closest table edge instead.

If any model from a unit that is falling back moves into contact with a table edge, the entire unit is removed from the game and counts as destroyed, as it scatters and deserts the battle.

FALLING BACK FROM CLOSE COMBAT

Models falling back from a combat will move through all enemy models that were involved in that combat (these enemies have already missed their chance of catching the falling back unit!). If any models would end their move less than 1" from one of these enemies, extend the fall back move until they are clear.

TRAPPED!

Sometimes a unit will find its fall back move blocked by impassable terrain, friendly models or enemy models (remember they have to stay 1" away from enemy models). The models in the falling back unit may move around these obstructions in such a way as to get back to their table edge by the shortest route, maintaining unit coherency.

If the unit cannot perform a full fall back move in any direction without doubling back, it is destroyed (see diagram below).

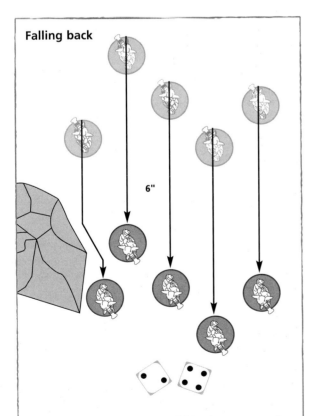

Falling back

6"

The player rolls a 6 on the 2D6 fall back move, so each model is moved 6" directly towards their base edge. The leftmost model has to go around impassable terrain.

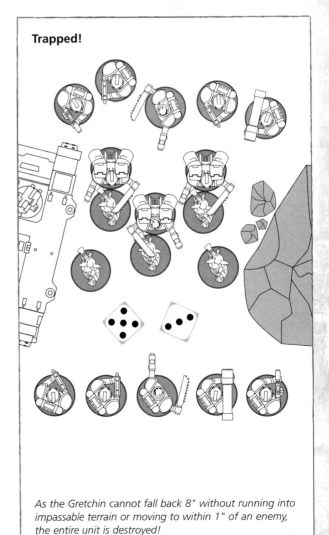

Trapped!

As the Gretchin cannot fall back 8" without running into impassable terrain or moving to within 1" of an enemy, the entire unit is destroyed!

FIRING WHILE FALLING BACK

Units that are falling back may not go to ground and automatically pass Pinning tests.

Troops who are falling back may continue to shoot, but obviously count as moving. They may of course choose to run instead of firing, but if they do so it must be towards their own table edge.

ASSAULTS WHILE FALLING BACK

A unit that is falling back may not launch assaults.

If an enemy unit declares an assault against a unit that is falling back and is found to be in range, the falling back unit must immediately test to regroup (see right). If the test is successful, the unit regroups (without moving), and from then on the fight continues as normal, starting with the enemy moving in his assaulting models. If the test is failed, the unit is destroyed and the assaulting unit does not move at all.

Sometimes a unit that is assaulting an enemy unit that is not falling back can, as part of a multiple assault move, also contact models from a nearby enemy unit that is falling back. As soon as one assaulting model is found to be able to move into contact with the falling back unit, test to regroup as described above. If the test is successful, the unit regroups (without moving) and the assault continues as normal. If the test is failed, the falling back unit is destroyed and the assaulting model must continue its assault move as if the falling back unit was never there.

MORALE WHILE FALLING BACK

Troops who are falling back automatically fail all Morale checks, except those to regroup (see right).

REGROUPING

Just because a unit falls back doesn't mean it is out of the fight. Courageous officers will try to inspire their troops to rally. Warriors might regain their will to fight out of honour, duty or sheer bloody-mindedness.

A unit falling back can attempt to regroup by taking a Regroup test in the Movement phase just before they move. This is a special type of Leadership test, which falling back units cannot attempt if any of the following conditions apply:

- The unit is below half strength.
- There are enemies within 6".
- The unit is not in coherency.

Units that are assaulted while falling back must always attempt this test as soon as the enemy is found to be in assault range, and can do this regardless of any of the above restrictions (the alternative is just too bad!).

If the unit successfully passes its Leadership test, it stops falling back and regroups. The unit can immediately move up to 3" (this move is unaffected by difficult terrain, but dangerous terrain tests must be taken as normal).

Once a unit has regrouped, it cannot otherwise move during that Movement phase, but otherwise it behaves as normal. For example, it can shoot (though it always counts as moving on the turn it regroups) or run, and it can even launch an assault if it gets the chance.

If the unit fails its Leadership test, (or cannot regroup because of the restrictions given above), then it must immediately continue to fall back.

CHARACTERS

Veteran warriors, brilliant officers, possessed prophets and ferocious war-leaders can inspire the troops to great feats of heroism (or fiendish bravery as the case may be) and are often quicker, stronger and more skilled in combat. In Warhammer 40,000 these kinds of powerful individuals are called 'characters'.

CHARACTER TYPES

Warhammer 40,000 armies normally include two types of characters:

- Independent characters are represented by individual models, which fight as units in their own right. One of the most useful abilities of independent characters is to join other units in battle, so that they can move in to bolster the battle line where the fighting is fiercest. If a model is an independent character, it will have its own entry in the appropriate Codex, and its rules will also clearly state that the model is an independent character. Bear in mind that there are other models that only ever fight as units of one model, but are not independent characters.

- Upgrade characters are fielded as part of units from the start of the game, representing a squad leader or unit champion, such as a Space Marine Veteran Sergeant. They do not have an entry of their own and are effectively just another trooper in their unit, with enhanced characteristics and perhaps a wider selection of weapons and wargear choices.

> **'What You See Is What You Get'**
> Character models in particular tend to have a lot of options as to what weapons and wargear they can use – given in the army list of their Codex. The rule is that such equipment must be visually represented on the model so your opponents can clearly see what they are facing. This concept is often referred to as WYSIWYG, which stands for 'what you see is what you get'.
>
> Of course, many gamers enjoy trying out different combinations of wargear in different battles. So, for example, a player might decide that for his next game a model's power sword will simply count as a close combat weapon, but he will also equip the model with melta bombs. While some tournaments may be more strict about this kind of thing, most opponents are happy to accommodate a small degree of one thing counting as another, so long as you explain exactly who has what at the start of the game.

CHARACTERS AS LEADERS

Remember that a unit's Leadership tests are taken using the Leadership of the model with the highest Ld value in the unit (see page 8). As characters normally have a better Ld than other warriors, this means that they make very good leaders for other units in the army.

INDEPENDENT CHARACTERS

MOVING INDEPENDENT CHARACTERS

Independent characters follow the Movement rules for models of their type, be it infantry, jump infantry, bike, etc. In addition, independent characters can move through difficult terrain more quickly and safely than ordinary troops. All independent characters have the 'move through cover' and 'skilled rider' special rules (see pages 75 and 76). This advantage does not extend to any vehicles they may be travelling in.

INDEPENDENT CHARACTERS JOINING & LEAVING UNITS

Independent characters are allowed to join other units. They cannot, however, join vehicle squadrons (see the Vehicles section) and units that always consist of a single model (like most vehicles and monstrous creatures). They can join other independent characters though, to form a powerful multi-character unit!

- In order to join a unit, an independent character simply has to move so that he is within the 2" coherency distance of a friendly unit at the end of their Movement phase. If the character is within 2" of more than one unit at the end of its Movement phase, the player must declare which unit it is joining. If a character does not intend to (or cannot) join a unit, it must remain more than 2" away from it at the end of the Movement phase. This is to make clear to the opponent if the character has joined a unit or not. Note that after a character joins a unit, that unit may move no further that Movement phase.

- Alternatively an independent character may begin the game already with a unit, by being deployed in coherency with them.

- While an independent character is part of a unit, he must obey the usual coherency rules. The combined unit moves and assaults at the speed of the slowest model while they stay together.

- An independent character can leave a unit during the Movement phase by moving out of coherency distance with it.

- If an independent character moves and joins or leaves a unit that did not move, the character counts as having moved in the ensuing Shooting phase, but the unit does not.

- An independent character may not join or leave a unit during the Shooting and Assault phases – once shots are fired or assaults are launched it is too late to join in or duck out!

- An independent character may not join or leave a unit while either he or the unit is locked in combat or falling back.

- If an independent character joins a unit that has gone to ground, he immediately goes to ground as well, and vice versa. He may not leave as long as his unit has gone to ground.

Special Rules

When an independent character joins a unit, it might have different special rules from those of the unit. Unless specified in the rule itself (as in the 'stubborn' special rule), the unit's special rules are not conferred upon the character, and the character's special rules are not conferred upon the unit. In some cases though, the independent character or the unit may lose their special rules as a result of the character joining the unit. For example, if an independent character without the 'infiltrate' special rule joins a unit of infiltrators during deployment, the unit cannot infiltrate (see the Universal Special Rules section for more details).

Retinues

Some Codex books allow you to field characters together with a special unit that they cannot leave during the game (which is normally called a 'retinue', 'bodyguard' or similar). Where this is the case, the character counts as an upgrade character until all of the other members of this unit are killed, at which point it starts counting as an independent character and it will do so for the rest of the game.

INDEPENDENT CHARACTERS & SHOOTING
Shooting at independent characters

In the heat of battle it is often hard to distinguish individuals, and even harder to pick them out as specific targets. Independent characters that have joined a unit are considered part of that unit and so may not be picked out as targets. If the unit they have joined is hit, the controlling player can choose to allocate hits against the characters just like the other members of the unit. This gives you some tricky tactical choices as a character may be able to soak up more damage than the normal troopers, but will be a serious loss if he is killed.

Independent characters that have not joined a unit can be targeted as normal, being separate units. Independent characters that are monstrous creatures can always be picked out as separate targets, unless they've joined a unit of monstrous creatures or a unit with special rules that offer them protection.

Independent characters shooting

All independent characters shoot just like ordinary troopers, although in many cases they will have better Ballistic Skill or exotic weaponry that sets them apart. If they have joined a unit, either roll for them separately or use different coloured dice to differentiate their shooting. However, they must still fire at the same target as the unit they have joined.

INDEPENDENT CHARACTERS & ASSAULTS

In the Assault phase, an independent character on his own can assault into close combat if within range of the enemy as normal.

If a unit that has been joined by an independent character assaults into close combat, the character assaults too, as it is part of the unit. When the attacks are resolved, however, independent characters are always treated as a separate single-model unit (as described under Multiple Combats on page 41), even though they have joined the unit. This is to make them stand out in the fight, as befits such heroic individuals, and it means that they have to be in base contact with the enemy to be able to attack. Be aware, though, that this also means that independent characters can be targeted separately by models that are engaged with them! Once all attacks have been resolved, these characters are once again treated as normal members of the unit they have joined (from determining assault results onwards).

When a unit is reacting to being assaulted, or making a pile-in move, independent characters that have joined the unit must move before other friendly models in order to get into base contact with an enemy if at all possible (otherwise they will not be able to fight). Using their own men as a screen in order to avoid the fight is a cowardly act, one that these great heroes would never consider!

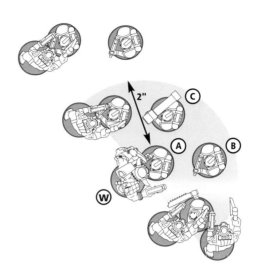

Independent characters in combat

The Ork Warboss (W) is an independent character and so counts as a separate unit. Space Marine (A) can only attack the Warboss. Space Marines (B) and (C) can attack either the Warboss or the Ork unit. All of the other Space Marines can only attack the Ork unit, as they are not engaged with the Warboss.

SPECIAL CHARACTERS

The 41st Millennium is filled with famous characters renowned as legendary heroes or infamous villains – these unique individuals, who stand out from normal characters because they have a personal name and not just a title, are called 'special characters'. Special characters are highly skilled and dangerous heroes who have incredible traits or skills that make them particularly valuable to an army.

For example, Commissar Yarrick is without doubt the most respected Imperial Guard Commissar in the Imperium, his inspiring presence securing the world of Armageddon against two massive Ork invasions within the space of fifty years. An army led by him can expect great benefits in terms of morale and leadership. On the other hand, Khârn the Betrayer, an Exalted Champion of the Blood God, is a mad slaughterer of men, with no thought for anything other than personal combat (at which, it must be granted, he excels).

UNIQUE

Special characters can be either independent or upgrade characters, but each one of them is unique, so the player may not include multiples of the same special character in an army (for example, Marneus Calgar is the Master of the Ultramarines Chapter of Space Marines – you cannot field three of him!).

PSYKERS

Psykers are warriors gifted with awesome mental powers, which enable them to channel the baleful energy of the Warp.

These powers vary from race to race and sometimes from one individual psyker to another. The psychic powers available to our models are not discussed further here, but are described in detail in the Codexes, where you will find complete rules for individual powers. The following general rules explain how psychic powers are employed. Exceptions to these rules are covered in the Codexes.

Psykers can use one psychic power per player turn. To use a psychic power successfully the psyker must pass a Psychic test, which is a normal Leadership test. Note that this test must always be made on the psyker's own Leadership value. Even where Leadership tests would normally be taken on the value of another model, tests for using psychic powers are always taken using the psyker's own Leadership.

PERILS OF THE WARP

If the result of a Psychic test is either a double 1 or double 6 this indicates that something horrible has happened to the psyker. The forces of the Daemon-haunted Warp claw at the psyker's mind and threaten to engulf and destroy him. The psyker suffers 1 wound with no armour or cover saves allowed. Invulnerable saves are allowed, but the power of the Warp is so great that successful saves must be re-rolled. Note that a psyker who rolls double 1 will still use his power, even if he is wounded or killed as a result.

PSYCHIC SHOOTING ATTACKS

Psychic powers that take the form of shooting attacks are very common. Using a psychic shooting attack counts as firing a ranged weapon (an assault weapon, unless specified otherwise). So, for example, the psyker must be able to see his target unit, cannot be locked in combat, or must not have run in the Shooting phase if he wishes to use a psychic shooting attack. In the same way, if a psyker targets a unit with a psychic shooting attack, then he can only assault that unit in the ensuing Assault phase. Even if a psyker has a special rule allowing him to use more than one psychic power per turn, he can use only one psychic shooting attack (as models can fire only one ranged weapon per turn). However, if he is allowed to fire more than one ranged weapon per turn, he can replace the firing of any of the weapons he is allowed to fire with a psychic shooting attack (but still cannot use the same power twice in a turn).

FORCE WEAPONS

Force weapons are potent psychic weapons used exclusively by trained psykers. They have the same effects as power weapons, but also confer to the wielder one additional psychic power, used in close combat, that can instantly extinguish the life force of any opponent.

Roll to hit and wound as normal, allowing any invulnerable saving throws the victim might have. The psyker may then take a Psychic test to use the weapon's power against any one opponent that suffered an unsaved wound by the weapon in that player turn. The normal rules for using psychic powers apply (remember that a psyker may normally use only one power per turn). If the test is passed, the enemy model suffers instant death, regardless of its Toughness value. This power has no effect against vehicles, models that are immune to instant death and any other model that does not have a Wounds value.

UNIT TYPES

The armies of the 41st Millennium are remarkably diverse and include many specialist warriors and exotic creatures.

In this section, you will find the rules for each of these unit types, namely monstrous creatures, jump infantry, bikes & jetbikes, beasts & cavalry and artillery. Note that vehicles are also a different unit type, but they are so vastly different that they have an entire section of the rules devoted to them.

Except for the rules detailed in this section for each unit type, these units follow the same rules as infantry.

MONSTROUS CREATURES

These terrifying monsters tower over their opponents, butchering all the enemies who face them and hurling tanks out of their path. Greater Daemons, Eldar Avatars and Tyranid Carnifexes count amongst their number.

MOVEMENT

All monstrous creatures have the 'move through cover' special rule (see page 75). They simply bash their way through trees and ruins!

SHOOTING

Instead of firing a single weapon, monstrous creatures can fire two of their weapons once per Shooting phase. They must, of course, fire both of them at the same enemy target. In addition, monstrous creatures have the 'relentless' special rule (see page 76).

Unless otherwise specified in their special rules, monstrous creatures cannot go to ground, voluntarily or otherwise. In addition, for a monstrous creature to be in cover, at least 50% of its body (as defined on page 16) has to be in cover from the point of view of the majority of the firing models. Also, standing in area terrain does not automatically confer a cover save to monstrous creatures – the 50% rule takes precedence. Cover for them works exactly as for vehicles (see page 62). As usual, if you cannot clearly tell if 50% of the model's body is covered, modify its cover save by –1.

ASSAULT

All wounds inflicted in close combat by a monstrous creature ignore armour saves, just like those from a power weapon. In addition, monstrous creatures roll an additional D6 for armour penetration (2D6 + Strength) when attacking a vehicle in close combat.

JUMP INFANTRY

Some special troops use devices that allow them to move at great speed across the battlefield, making them especially good at assaulting enemy troops and outflanking their positions. The Space Marines use jump packs, which utilise high powered controlled bursts from turbines to make bounding leaps across the field of battle, jumping over terrain with ease. Other races tend to have their own particular versions, such as Orks, whose Stormboyz use rudimentary 'rokkit packs' to close with the enemy, and Eldar, whose Swooping Hawks soar elegantly on light wings supported by gravitic motors. Sometimes the technology will be more exotic, such as that used by Eldar Warp Spiders, who utilise short-ranged teleport devices for a similar effect.

MOVEMENT

Jump infantry can use their jump packs (or equivalent) and move up to 12" in the Movement phase. This is optional and they can choose to move as normal infantry if they wish. When using jump packs, they can move over all other models and all terrain freely. However, if a moving jump infantry model begins or ends its move in difficult terrain, it must take a dangerous terrain test. Jump infantry models may not end their move on top of other models or impassable terrain, except that they can end their move on top of impassable terrain if it is actually possible to place the models on top of it. If they do that, however, they treat the impassable terrain as dangerous terrain. All jump infantry units may enter the battle by 'deep strike', as explained on page 95.

Fall back moves

Jump infantry fall back 3D6", because they always use their jump packs when doing this. They move over any terrain and models when falling back, but if they end their move in difficult terrain (or on top of flat impassable terrain) they must still take a dangerous

terrain test. They cannot end their move on top of other models, and must alter the direction of their fall back move as little as possible in order to avoid them, just as a normal unit would when falling back on foot. If they cannot do this, they are trapped and destroyed.

SHOOTING

Jump infantry follow the same rules as infantry.

ASSAULT

Jump infantry assault 6" like normal infantry. This move is slowed by difficult terrain in the same way as other infantry, because the unit always covers the last few yards of an assault on foot.

> ### Different Unit Types
>
> *So far the rules have just dealt with troops that move around on foot – infantry. This section covers different unit types, and these not only add new tactical elements to your games, but also more complexity to the rules. These unit types have different rules for the way they move, how terrain affects them, how far they can assault, and so on. You will find that Codexes often add even more changes and exceptions for specific models. In any given situation during a battle, if the Codex doesn't say any different, follow the rules for the appropriate unit type, and if those rules don't say anything different, follow the basic rules for infantry.*
>
> *If you're just starting out, you may find it easier to use just infantry units in your first game or two, while you get used to the basic rules. On the other hand, if you do want to jump straight in, we suggest that you just read those unit type rules that apply to models in your collection.*

JET PACKS

Some jump infantry are equipped with a special type of jump pack, referred to as a jet pack. Jet packs are designed to provide stable firing platforms rather than a means of getting into close combat. The most frequent users of this technology are the Tau. Jet packs differ from jump packs in the following ways:

- In the Movement phase, they only move 6" when using their packs, but are always allowed to move 6" in the Assault phase, even if they don't assault. When jet packers move in the Assault phase and do not assault, they treat difficult terrain just as other jump infantry do in the Movement phase.

- Models with jet packs have the 'relentless' special rule (see page 76).

BIKES

Troops mounted on bikes excel at hit-and-run attacks. They are able to use their high speed to strike deep into enemy territory, complete their mission and escape before an enemy is able to react. A skilled commander will recognise the benefit of having bikes at his disposal, and is able to use them for advanced reconnaissance, as well as to outflank a slower enemy. Indeed, in open ground, bikes are easily capable of outrunning all but the fastest vehicles. Riding through heavy terrain can be somewhat dangerous however, but many riders take great pride in their superior driving skills and daring. These warriors are often regarded as dangerously hot-headed risk-takers, but their effectiveness cannot be denied.

ADDITIONAL PROTECTION

Bikes are large, solid constructions, and are often fitted with protective armour and shields to deflect and absorb incoming fire. Bike riders benefit from the protection offered by their bike, which increases their Toughness characteristic by 1. Note that this increase does not affect the model's Toughness for the purposes of instant death (see page 26).

Hope is the beginning of unhappiness.

MOVEMENT

Bikes can move up to 12" in the Movement phase. Bikes are not slowed down by difficult terrain. However, they treat all difficult terrain as dangerous terrain instead.

Bikes also have the 'turbo boosters' special rule (see page 76).

Fall back moves

As bikes are so fast moving, they fall back 3D6", rather than 2D6". Remember that they treat all difficult terrain as dangerous.

SHOOTING

Bikes cannot run in the Shooting phase.

Bikes have the 'relentless' special rule (see page 76).

Each bike in a unit may fire with one weapon for each rider on the bike. Thus a Space Marine Attack Bike with a driver and passenger in sidecar can fire two weapons.

ASSAULT

Bike assault moves are not slowed down by difficult terrain. However, each model entering or moving through difficult terrain, or assaulting an enemy who is standing in difficult terrain or behind an obstacle, must take a dangerous terrain test.

JETBIKES

Jetbikes are powered by anti-gravitational technology that allows them to hover a few metres above the ground and make powered boosts over obstacles. They are ideal for making raids on unsuspecting enemies, hitting hard and then using their superior speed and handling to escape.

Jetbikes are the same as bikes, with the following exceptions:

- In the Movement phase, jetbikes can move over all other models and all terrain freely. However, if a moving jetbike begins or ends its move in difficult terrain, it must take a dangerous terrain test. Jetbikes may not end their move over other models or impassable terrain, except that they can end their move on top of impassable terrain if it is actually possible to place the models on top of it. If they do that, however, they treat the impassable terrain as dangerous terrain.

- In the Assault phase, jetbikes are treated like normal bikes when assaulting, as they must move close to the ground in order to fight.

- When falling back, jetbikes move over any terrain and models, but if they end their move in difficult terrain (or on top of flat impassable terrain) they must still take a dangerous terrain test. They cannot end their move on top of other models, and must alter the direction of their fall back move as little as possible in order to avoid them, just as a normal unit would when falling back on foot. If they cannot do this, they are trapped and immediately destroyed.

Eldar Jetbikes

The Eldar are the undisputed masters of anti-grav technology, and their jetbikes form swift moving attack forces that are justifiably feared by any who have faced them. Their favourite tactic is to suddenly emerge from cover, open fire and then dive back into cover before the enemy can retaliate.

All Eldar jetbikes (including Dark Eldar ones) are allowed to move 6" in the Assault phase, even if they don't assault. When Eldar jetbikes move in the Assault phase and do not assault, they treat difficult terrain in the same way as other jetbikes do in the Movement phase.

BEASTS & CAVALRY

As well as squads of warriors fighting on foot, and the armoured bulk of vehicles, many armies of the 41st Millennium make use of fearsome predators and beasts, such as Warp Beasts and Flesh Hounds, to augment their forces. Other warriors ride to battle on horses, grunting boar-like monstrosities, daemonic steeds and countless other strange creatures. These unit types are referred to as 'beasts' if they have no rider, or as 'cavalry' if they do. They both, however, follow the rules given in this section.

When closing on their enemies, they are able to move at far greater speeds than warriors on foot, and as such are able to launch deadly charges and counter charges.

MOVEMENT

Beasts and cavalry move like infantry.

Fall back moves

Beasts and cavalry fall back just like infantry, except that they move 3D6" due to their speed.

SHOOTING

Although beasts generally do not shoot, cavalry frequently can. They follow the same rules as infantry when they do so.

ASSAULT

Beasts and cavalry have the 'fleet' special rule (see page 75).

Beasts and cavalry are capable of making an especially fast assault to charge their enemies. When assaulting they move up to 12".

If assaulting through cover, beasts and cavalry are slowed by difficult terrain – roll for the distance they can move just as you would for infantry, but double the result of the highest scoring dice.

Otherwise, they assault just like infantry.

"I have seen war in all its forms. I have seen feral world savages braining each other with stones, and I have seen the death of a whole planet at the hands of a virus bomb. I have seen Space Marines drop to certain death, and win. I have seen Titans crush whole platoons underfoot. But there is no more stirring sight in war than the charge of massed cavalry."

Dravin Gratz

ARTILLERY

Some weapons are so large and powerful that a single man could not hope to carry them by himself. They are more usually mounted on vehicles, but are sometimes utilised by infantry artillery teams, particularly if the battlefield's terrain is not suitable for vehicles. These mighty artillery weapons are mounted on wheeled supports or on anti-grav platforms, as they are simply too heavy to lug across a battlefield.

THE UNIT

Artillery units consist of a number of crewman models and the gun models themselves. These units are quite complex as they include some vehicle models and some infantry models. The gun models are treated as vehicles with an Armour Rating of 10 (see the Vehicles section). Any glancing or penetrating hit will destroy a gun – do not roll on the Vehicle Damage table, the gun model is simply removed. If all the crewman models are killed, the guns are immediately removed as well.

Sometimes the player has the choice of adding leaders or additional models to the crew of an artillery unit. These models are part of the crew in all respects and may operate the guns as normal, even if they are otherwise slightly different from the rest of the crew. Independent characters that join the unit, however, do not count as crew and cannot operate the guns.

MOVEMENT

Artillery units are slowed by difficult terrain like infantry, but gun models must also take dangerous terrain tests when they pass through it. There must be at least one crewman per gun to allow the unit to move – if there are fewer than this, then the unit may not move.

SHOOTING

Unlike other vehicles (see next section), the gun models cannot fire if they moved at all in that turn's Movement phase. Any crewman that is within 2" of a gun in the Shooting phase can fire it. The crewmen firing the guns may not fire any weapons they are carrying, while the other crew members (and any independent character that joined the unit) are free to fire their side arms, and can even shoot against a different unit than the one targeted by the unit's guns. The guns themselves cannot split fire. When firing the guns, there must be a line of sight to the target from both the gun model and the crewman firing it (unless they are barrage weapons, of course). Ranges are measured from the gun model.

When firing against an artillery unit, roll for each hit inflicted: on a 1-4 a gun is hit, on a 5-6 a crewman is hit. Roll to wound the crewmen and to penetrate the guns' armour separately.

If an artillery unit goes to ground, this has no additional protective effect on the unit's guns.

Artillery units cannot run in the Shooting phase.

ASSAULT

Artillery units may not launch assaults as long as they include any gun models.

If they are assaulted, move the assaulting models in base contact with the crew and guns as normal, but from then on the guns are ignored. All engaged enemies roll to hit and to wound against the crew (even if they are only engaged with guns). Engaged crew models can of course fight back, but the guns do not.

MORALE & FALL BACK MOVES

For the purposes of Morale and other Leadership tests, and for combat resolution, always ignore the gun models, as if they were not there. Because they need at least one crewman per gun in order for the unit to move, if an artillery unit does not have one crewman per gun when it is forced to fall back, the gun models without crewmen are abandoned and immediately removed. The rest of the unit then falls back as normal. If an artillery unit is forced to fall back from close combat and the enemy is free to make a sweeping advance, then the artillery unit automatically loses the Initiative roll and is caught and destroyed by the victor.

VEHICLES

Because vehicles do not fight in the same manner as creatures of flesh and blood, their rules differ from other models in a number of ways, detailed here.

VEHICLE CHARACTERISTICS

Vehicles have characteristics that define how powerful they are in a similar way to troops. However, their characteristics are different. Shown here is one example of a vehicle's profile:

Name	Type	Front Armour	Side Armour	Rear Armour	BS
Leman Russ	Tank	14	12	10	3

TYPE

The different types of vehicle are: transport, tank, open-topped, fast, skimmer and walker. These types can be combined to define, for example, a fast skimmer or an open-topped walker, in which case the vehicle has all of the rules for all of its types.

The first part of this section presents the rules common to all vehicles. Then, each of the vehicle types has a separate entry, listing their unique rules and any exceptions to the normal vehicle rules (walkers being by far the most different).

ARMOUR VALUE

The Armour Value of a vehicle tells you how hard it is to damage. Vehicles have separate Armour Values to represent the protection on their front, sides and rear. Armour Values typically range from 10 to 14, depending on which side of the vehicle is being attacked, usually with the lightest armour on the rear to represent vulnerable fuel tanks, engine compartments, etc.

BALLISTIC SKILL

Vehicles have a BS value just like troops and it represents the accuracy of the crew as they blast away at their enemy with the vehicle's weapons.

VEHICLES & MEASURING DISTANCES

As vehicle models do not usually have a base, the normal rule of measuring distances to or from the base cannot be used. Instead, for distances involving a vehicle, measure to or from their hull (ignore gun barrels, dozer blades, antennas, banners and other decorative elements).

There is however a notable exception, a vehicle's weaponry. When firing a vehicle's weapons, ranges are measured from the muzzle of the firing weapon, whilst line of sight is determined from the weapon's mounting point and along its barrel (as explained later).

VEHICLES AND MOVEMENT

The distance a vehicle moves influences the amount of weapons it may fire and how easy a target the vehicle will be if assaulted, as described later.

- A vehicle that remains stationary will be able to bring its full firepower to bear on the enemy.

- A vehicle that travels up to 6" is moving at combat speed. This represents the vehicle advancing slowly in order to keep firing, albeit with reduced firepower.

- A vehicle that travels more than 6" and up to 12" is moving at cruising speed. This represents the vehicle concentrating on moving as fast as possible without firing its guns.

Moving a maximum of 12" may seem relatively slow for a vehicle, but it represents a cross-country speed rather than travelling on a road.

Vehicles can turn any number of times as they move, just like any other model. Vehicles turn by pivoting on the spot about their centre-point, rather than 'wheeling' round. Turning does not reduce the vehicle's move. This means that a vehicle may combine forward and reverse movement in the same turn providing it does not exceed its maximum move. Pivoting on the spot alone does not count as moving, so a vehicle that only pivots in the Movement phase counts as stationary (however, immobilised vehicles may not even pivot). Just like other units, vehicles cannot move over friendly models.

TERRAIN EFFECTS

Vehicles attempting to move through broken terrain are not slowed down like other units, but risk becoming stuck, bogged down or damaged.

Vehicles are not slowed down by difficult terrain, but treat all difficult terrain as dangerous. Roll a D6 for every vehicle that has entered, left or moved through one or more areas of dangerous terrain during its move. A result of 2-6 on the dice means that the vehicle can carry on moving. A result of 1 means that the vehicle halts immediately and suffers an Immobilised damage result, so if it was attempting to enter difficult terrain it stops just outside.

When discussing terrain at the beginning of the game, it is perfectly fine for players to agree that some terrain has different effects on vehicles than it does on other units. For example, players may agree that tank traps are dangerous or even impassable to vehicles, but clear terrain for other units. Similarly, you could agree that vehicles (or just certain vehicle types) treat barbed wire as clear terrain, and so on.

ROADS

Vehicles, with the exception of walkers and skimmers, that move at Cruising Speed following a road for their entire Movement phase may move up to an extra 6".

Crash, bang, wallop

One of the greatest pleasures to be had in the Warhammer 40,000 game is zooming vehicle models about the battlefield, unleashing the firepower of armoured behemoths and, conversely, blowing up those vehicles that belong to the enemy. The destruction of a vehicle is usually a spectacular event that can totally change the course of the game, and vehicle wrecks become important pieces of terrain unto themselves. But how best to represent such high-octane carnage?

Some like to demonstrate their vehicular misfortune by turning a destroyed tank onto its top or side. A few go even further and sculpt battle damage underneath the vehicle to complement this approach. However, many vehicles have delicate parts on top, so players often object to treating their beautifully-painted tanks in such a rough and ready manner, and adopt a different solution. We know several gamers who use cotton wool to represent the smoke billowing from destroyed vehicles, a visually pleasing solution and doubly handy if someone spills their tea.

Battle damage

As you read on you will find that there are some damage results that debilitate rather than destroy vehicle models. Tanks can find themselves immobilised by a thrown track, have their weapon systems crippled or shot off altogether, or be stunned into inactivity for a turn. Marking these events is a little more difficult. Some players leave the weapons and turrets on their models unglued so that they can be carefully removed during battle. This helps with ease of transport and is a great way to represent Weapon Destroyed results – just take the relevant weapon off altogether.

A different approach is to place a dice on or next to the vehicle, showing the number that corresponds with the appropriate damage result. You could even invest in a set of damage markers. These have specific icons for each of the damage results, so you just need to place the relevant marker on or next to the vehicle when damage is inflicted. As with many aspects of the wargaming hobby, there is no 'right answer' – just make sure that your opponent is happy with whatever convention you decide upon.

VEHICLES SHOOTING

When a vehicle fires, it normally uses its own BS characteristic and shoots like other units – all its weapons must fire at a single target unit.

MOVING AND SHOOTING VEHICLE WEAPONRY

The number of weapons a vehicle can fire in the Shooting phase depends on how fast it has moved in that turn's Movement phase, as detailed below.

In addition, the normal penalties of movement on shooting rapid fire and heavy weapons do not apply – when fired from a vehicle, these weapon types always fire as if the firing model had not moved, regardless of whether it actually did or not. Note that vehicles cannot run.

- Vehicles that remained stationary may fire all of their weapons (remember that pivoting on the spot does not count as moving).

- Vehicles that moved at combat speed may fire a single weapon (and its defensive weapons, as explained below).

- Vehicles that moved at cruising speed may not fire.

There are a few exceptions to these rules: ordnance, ordnance barrage, defensive and optional weapons.

Defensive weapons

Any vehicle weapons of Strength 4 or less (or with no Strength value) are classified as 'defensive' weapons.

A vehicle that moved at combat speed can fire all of its defensive weapons in addition to the single weapon it is usually allowed to fire.

Optional weapons

Some vehicles have, among the options of their army list entry, the possibility of buying additional weapons, such as one-shot missiles and pintle-mounted guns. Firing one of these additional weapons counts as firing one of the vehicle's normal weapons (unless they are defensive weapons, as described above).

Ordnance weapons

Firing a massive ordnance weapon requires the attention of all the gunners of the vehicle, so no other weapons may be fired that turn (not even defensive weapons!). In return, they are better at penetrating armour (see page 60). Unless their profile specifies otherwise, all ordnance blast weapons use the large blast marker.

Ordnance Barrage weapons

Differently from other unit types, vehicles carrying ordnance barrage weapons can choose to fire them either directly or as a barrage – declare before you fire.

If fired directly at the target, they are treated exactly like normal ordnance weapons (ignoring the minimum range in the weapon's profile).

Alternatively, the vehicle may fire these weapons as an ordnance barrage. In this case, the crew must carefully calculate the firing trajectory, so only vehicles that remained stationary may fire an ordnance barrage weapon (and may, of course, fire no other weapons that turn).

Just like normal barrages, ordnance barrages may have a minimum range (see their profile), they cause Pinning tests, and their targets work out their cover save as if the shot came from the centre of the blast marker. If fired at a target that is out of sight, the BS of the firer makes no difference and the blast marker scatters a full 2D6 if an arrow is rolled on the scatter dice. In addition, ordnance barrages are even more terrifying than normal ones – Pinning tests caused by ordnance barrages are taken with a -1 Ld modifier.

VEHICLE WEAPONS & LINE OF SIGHT

Just like infantry, vehicles need to be able to draw a line of sight to their targets in order to shoot at them. When firing a vehicle's weapons, point them against the target and then trace the line of sight from each weapons' mounting and along its barrel, to see if the shot is blocked by terrain or models. If the target unit happens to be in cover from only some of the vehicle's weapons, then work out if the target gets cover saves exactly as if each firing weapon on the vehicle was a separate firing model in a normal unit.

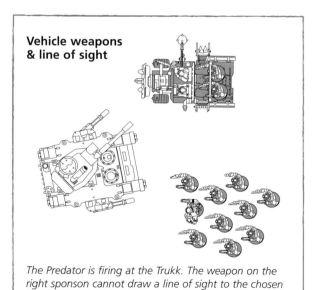

Vehicle weapons & line of sight

The Predator is firing at the Trukk. The weapon on the right sponson cannot draw a line of sight to the chosen target, and so it cannot be fired.

The Emperor asks only that you obey.

On some models it will be actually impossible to literally move the gun and point it towards the target, because of the way the model is assembled or because the gun has been glued in place. In this case, players should assume that the guns on a vehicle are free to rotate or swivel on their mountings. In order to make clear how much any gun is supposed to rotate, refer to the vehicle's entry, where each weapon has been classified as either turret-mounted, pintle-mounted (or 'bolt-on'), sponson-mounted or hull-mounted. Then apply the following guidelines:

- Turret-mounted weapons can usually rotate 360°, together with the entire turret, unless the design of the model prevents this.

- Hull-mounted weapons can fire in a 45° arc from their mounting point (see diagram).

- Sponson-mounted weapons vary greatly, as some can cover the full 180° of the flank they are mounted on (or even slightly more), while others are more limited. This is determined by the shape and position of the sponson's mounting (see diagrams).

- Pintle-mounted (or bolt-on) weapons can either fire in a 360° arc, if they are mounted on the vehicle's turret; or can fire in a 45° arc from their mounting point, if they are mounted on the vehicle's hull.

In the rare cases when it matters (your tank might be targeting a sniper high up in a bell tower), assume that guns can swivel vertically roughly by 45°, even if the barrel on the model itself cannot physically do that!

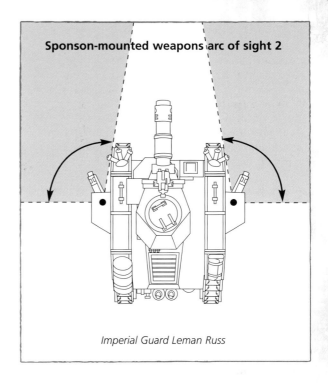

Sponson-mounted weapons arc of sight 2

Imperial Guard Leman Russ

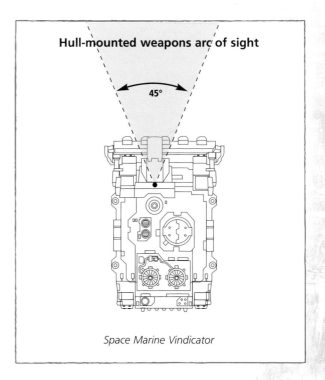

Hull-mounted weapons arc of sight

45°

Space Marine Vindicator

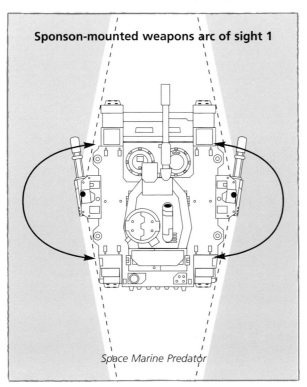

Sponson-mounted weapons arc of sight 1

Space Marine Predator

"What I cannot crush with words I will crush with the tanks of the Imperial Guard."

Lord Solar Macharius

SHOOTING AT VEHICLES

When a unit fires at a vehicle it must be able to see its hull or turret (ignoring the vehicle's gun barrels, antennas, decorative banner poles, etc.). As the whole unit must fire at the same target, often this means that some of their weapons can't damage the target vehicle, so we assume that the other members of the squad are providing covering fire, bringing forward ammunition for heavy weapons or simply keeping their heads down.

If the target vehicle is in range, roll to hit as normal. If any hits are scored, roll for each to see if they penetrate the vehicle's Armour Value, as explained next.

VEHICLE FACING AND ARMOUR VALUES

Not all vehicles are equally armoured. Some massive tanks are protected by countless layers of reinforced adamantium and ceramite plates, while other lighter vehicles rely more on their speed to avoid incoming fire. As such, each different type of vehicle will have different Armour Values, representing not just the thickness and slope of its armour, but also how difficult a target it is because of its size and speed, how tough and numerous its crew are, and so on. Armour Values for individual vehicles also vary depending on which facing of the vehicle the shot comes from – its front, sides, or rear, as explained in the diagram.

If a unit has firing models in two different facings of a target vehicle (some models in the front and some in the side, for example), shots are resolved separately for the two facings.

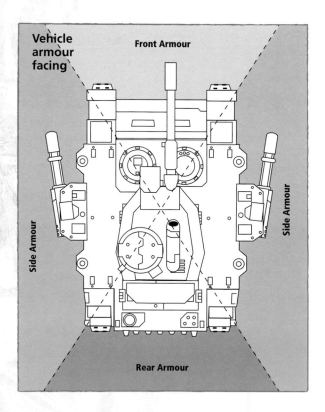

ARMOUR PENETRATION

Hitting a vehicle is no guarantee that you will actually damage it. Once a hit has been scored on a vehicle, roll a D6 and add the weapon's Strength to it, comparing this total with the Armour Value of the appropriate facing of the vehicle.

- If the total is less than the vehicle's Armour Value, the shot has no effect.

- If the total is equal to the vehicle's Armour Value, the shot causes a glancing hit.

- If the total is greater than the vehicle's Armour Value, the shot scores a penetrating hit.

Example: A lascannon shot hits the front of a Space Marine Predator (Armour Value 13). Rolling a D6, the player scores a 4, and adds this to the lascannon's Strength of 9, for a total of 13. Because this equals the Predator's Armour Value, it inflicts a glancing hit.

Ordnance weapons and Armour Penetration

Ordnance weapons (including Ordnance Barrage) hit with such force that the target's crew are turned to mush. When you roll to penetrate a vehicle's armour with an ordnance weapon, roll two dice instead of one and pick the highest result!

Template and Blast weapons against vehicles

If a vehicle is even partially under a template weapon, it is hit on the Armour value the firer is facing.

When firing a blast weapon against a vehicle, place the marker with the hole over any part of the vehicle's hull and then roll for scatter as normal. In the case of multiple blasts, place the hole in the centre of the first marker on the vehicle's hull. If the markers scatter so that they're not over the vehicle at all, then obviously the vehicle is not affected. If a marker ends over the vehicle, it makes a big difference if the hole in the centre of the marker is over the vehicle or not:

- **The centre of the blast marker ends over the vehicle's hull.** In this case the shell or missile has hit the vehicle and exploded on it. The armour penetration roll is resolved against the Armour value facing the firer, regardless of the position of the marker, using the full Strength of the weapon. Hits from barrage weapons, however, always hit the vehicle's side armour (representing its top armour).

- **The centre of the blast marker ends outside the vehicle, but part of the marker covers its hull.** In this case the shell or missile has missed the vehicle, and only some shrapnel clanks against the vehicle's armour. The armour penetration roll is resolved against the Armour Value facing the centre of the marker, regardless of the position of the firer, and the weapon's Strength is halved (round down).

DAMAGE ROLLS

A hit on a vehicle can have a variety of results. A vehicle's armour could be completely pierced, yet merely result in giving the crew a nasty shock. Alternatively, a lucky shot could detonate ammunition held within the vehicle, resulting in an explosion of titanic proportions. If a vehicle's armour is breached, you need to determine what damage is caused. Roll a D6 for each shot that glanced or penetrated the vehicle's armour, apply any appropriate modifiers (they are all cumulative) and look up the result on the Vehicle Damage table below.

Glancing hits

If the shot has only caused a glancing hit, the damage to the vehicle will not be so severe. Apply a -2 modifier to the dice result.

'AP–' weapons

While some weapons are especially good at cutting through heavily armoured targets, others lack the penetrating power to destroy a vehicle easily. Penetrating and glancing hits inflicted by a weapon shown as 'AP–' suffer a modifier of -1 to the roll on the Vehicle Damage table.

'AP 1' weapons

Some weapons are so destructively powerful that they can penetrate a vehicle's heavily armoured hull with ease. If an AP 1 weapon, such as a multi-melta, scores a glancing or penetrating hit, add a modifier of +1 to the roll on the Vehicle Damage table.

Other modifiers

Specific weapons and vehicles may have special rules that apply further modifiers to the damage roll. For example, hits on open-topped vehicles receive a +1 modifier, as explained on page 70.

VEHICLE DAMAGE TABLE

D6	RESULT
1 or less	Crew – Shaken
2	Crew – Stunned
3	Damaged – Weapon Destroyed
4	Damaged – Immobilised
5	Destroyed – Wrecked.
6 or more	Destroyed – Explodes!

Modifiers:

Glancing hit	-2
Hit by 'AP–' weapon	-1
Hit by 'AP1' weapon	+1
Target is open-topped	+1

DAMAGE RESULTS

1   Crew – Shaken
The vehicle is rocked by the attack, but no serious damage is sustained (or perhaps the crew have decided that it is time to quickly relocate). The vehicle may not shoot until the end of its next player turn.

2   Crew – Stunned
The vehicle's crew is knocked about by the attack, or perhaps all of the vehicle's targeting and steering systems are temporarily scrambled (or maybe the crew have decided to temporarily bail out and take cover somewhere nearby). The vehicle may not move nor shoot until the end of its next player turn.

Note: Additional stunned and shaken results are not cumulative, so if a vehicle is shaken three times it is still only unable to fire in its next Shooting phase, not its next three Shooting phases!

3   Damaged – Weapon Destroyed
One of the vehicle's weapons (chosen by the attacker) is destroyed – ripped off by the force of the attack. If a vehicle has no weapons left, treat this result as an 'immobilised' result instead. This can include vehicle upgrades that function as weapons, such as pintle-mounted storm bolters or hunter-killer missiles.

4   Damaged – Immobilised
The vehicle has taken a hit that has crippled a wheel, track, grav plate, jet or leg. It may not move for the rest of the game. An immobilised vehicle may not turn in place but its turret may continue to rotate to select targets, and other weapons retain their normal arc of fire. Further 'immobilised' results count as 'weapon destroyed' instead.

Note: A vehicle that suffers either Damaged result when it has no weapons left and is already immobilised treats the result as 'Destroyed – Wrecked' instead.

5   Destroyed – Wrecked
The attack critically damages the hull and internal systems – the vehicle is destroyed. The model is left in place and becomes a wreck (see page 62).

6   Destroyed – Explodes
The vehicle is destroyed, as its fuel and ammo detonate, ripping it apart in a spectacular explosion. Flaming debris is scattered D6" from the vehicle, and models in range suffer a Strength 3, AP– hit. The vehicle is then removed and is replaced with an area of difficult ground representing scattered wreckage or a crater (if you have one).

Note: Vehicle drivers, gunners and other crew are killed if their vehicle suffers either Destroyed results.

WRECKS

Wrecked vehicles are left on the table and effectively become a piece of terrain, counting as both difficult and dangerous terrain, and providing cover. Players must clearly mark that a vehicle has been wrecked in any way they consider suitable. For example, they can turn the vehicle or just its turret upside down (and not sideways to gain extra cover!), place a marker or cotton wool on it to represent smoke and flames, and so on.

VEHICLES AND COVER – OBSCURED TARGETS

Vehicles do not benefit from cover in the same way as infantry – their sheer size and bulk mean they cannot take advantage of cover as well as infantry and other smaller, more agile troops. They can, however, position themselves in such a way as to make it harder for the enemy to hit them in a vulnerable location. The difference from the way cover works for other models is represented by the following exceptions to the normal rules for cover:

- At least 50% of the facing of the vehicle that is being targeted (i.e. its front, side or rear) needs to be hidden by intervening terrain or models from the point of view of the firer for the vehicle to claim to be in cover. If this is the case, the vehicle is said to be obscured (or 'hull down'). If a squad is firing at a vehicle, the vehicle is obscured only if it is 50% hidden from the majority of the firing models (do not count models that cannot hurt the vehicle). Just like with units of several models, if you're not sure whether the vehicle is 50% in cover or not, simply modify its save by −1.

- Vehicles are not obscured simply for being inside area terrain. The 50% rule given above takes precedence.

- Obviously, vehicles cannot go to ground, voluntarily or otherwise.

If the target is obscured and suffers a glancing or penetrating hit, it may take a cover save against it, exactly like a non-vehicle model would do against a wound (for example, a save of 5+ for a hedge, 4+ for a building, 3+ for a fortification, and so on). If the save is passed, the hit is discarded and no roll is made on the Vehicle Damage table.

If a special rule or a piece of wargear confers to a vehicle the ability of being obscured even if in the open, this is a 4+ cover save, unless specified otherwise in the Codex.

It may rarely happen that the firing unit cannot see any part of the facing they are in (front, side or rear), but they can still see another facing of the target vehicle. In this case they may take the shot against the facing they can see, but to represent such an extremely angled shot, the vehicle receives a 3+ cover save.

Picture 1: more than 50% of the Rhino's side is hidden by the building – the Rhino is obscured.
Picture 2: less than 50% of the Rhino's side is hidden by the building – the Rhino is not obscured.

SMOKE LAUNCHERS

Some vehicles have small launchers mounted onto them that carry smoke canisters (or a more sophisticated equivalent in the case of some alien vehicles). These are used to temporarily hide the vehicle behind concealing clouds of smoke – especially useful when moving out into the open.

Once per game, after completing its move, a vehicle with smoke launchers can trigger them (it doesn't matter how far it moved). Place some cotton wool or other suitable marker on or around the vehicle to show it is obscured. The vehicle may not fire any of its weapons in the same turn as it used its smoke launchers, but will count as obscured in the next enemy Shooting phase, receiving a 4+ cover save.

After the enemy's Shooting phase, the smoke disperses with no further effect. Note that a vehicle may still use smoke launchers even if its crew are shaken or stunned.

It is worth pointing out that some armies might use different versions of smoke launchers, which have slightly different rules. As normal, the rules in the Codex take precedence.

VEHICLES AND ASSAULTS

Vehicles can be both very dangerous and very vulnerable at close quarters. On one hand, massively armoured vehicles can scatter infantry before them, as no one in their right mind would wish to be caught beneath the tracks of an eighty-tonne tank bearing down on them! On the other hand, a stationary vehicle can often be very easily destroyed, as individuals clamber over it, attaching all manner of grenades and shooting into vulnerable spots.

ASSAULTING VEHICLES

Infantry can pose a grave threat to vehicles if they get close enough. They can wreck a vehicle by shooting through vision slits, planting explosives on fuel tanks, tearing open hatches to attack the crew or committing some other equally imaginative act of mayhem.

Launching an assault

A unit can assault a vehicle in the Assault phase. The assault move is conducted just the same as assaulting other enemy units. As normal, all engaged models will attack.

Rolling to hit against vehicles

As the vehicle has no WS, the score needed for a hit depends on the speed of the target, as follows:

Target	D6 roll needed
Attacking a vehicle that is immobilised or was stationary in its previous turn.	Automatic hit
Attacking a vehicle that moved at combat speed in its previous turn.	4+
Attacking a vehicle that moved at cruising speed in its previous turn.	6

Note: when assessing how far a vehicle has moved, only take into account the actual distance covered from its original position. Moving backwards and forwards or driving around in circles does not help!

Armour penetration in close combat

Armour Penetration is worked out in the same way as for shooting (D6 + the Strength of the attacker). In close combat, however, all hits are resolved against the vehicle's rear armour, to represent the chance of attacking a vulnerable spot.

Combat results

Combats against vehicles are very different from those among other unit types. For a start, whilst vehicles can be assaulted, they cannot be locked in combat.

At the conclusion of a round of close combat against a vehicle there is no combat result, and so there are no sweeping advances, no pile-in and no consolidation moves. The vehicle and the enemy remain where they are and are free to simply move away in future turns. In a multiple fight including enemy vehicles and other unit types, the result of the fight is worked out as normal against the latter, ignoring the vehicles.

Successive turns

If a vehicle that has been assaulted, and has survived, does not move in its successive Movement phase, enemy models will still be in base contact with it during its Shooting and Assault phase. Enemy models that are in base contact with a vehicle are not locked in combat and can therefore be shot during the Shooting phase.

If the vehicle pivots on the spot (to shoot at its attackers for example), move these models out of the way as you shift the vehicle and then place them back into base contact with the vehicle.

Units that still have models in base contact with a vehicle in its Assault phase may attack it again, just as in a normal ongoing combat (including all models that would count as engaged in a normal assault).

GRENADES

A well-placed grenade can often achieve a kill on a vehicle. Specialist tank-hunting troops are frequently equipped with krak grenades (a special type of high-explosive grenade designed to stop vehicles in their tracks) or even melta bombs (fusion based charges that can reduce a battle tank to a burnt-out wreck in milliseconds).

Grenades have to be clamped or placed so as to inflict enough damage, so each model using them can only ever make one attack, regardless of the number of Attacks on their profile and any bonus attacks. Against vehicles, grenades have the following armour penetration:

Defensive and assault grenades	4+D6
Krak grenades	6+D6
Melta bombs	8+2D6

VEHICLES AND MORALE

Vehicles never take Morale checks for any reason. It is assumed that in all cases the vehicle's crew has unshakeable faith in their vehicle and their orders. Any occasional lapses that do occur are represented by crew shaken and stunned results on the Damage table.

UNITS OF VEHICLES – SQUADRONS

Most vehicles fight as individual units and are represented by a single model. However, some small vehicles, like Ork Warbuggies and Eldar Vypers, operate in units of more than one vehicle, known as squadrons. These follow the rules for normal units, with the following exceptions:

MOVEMENT PHASE

When a squadron moves, all of its vehicles move at the same speed (i.e. they all move at combat speed, at cruising speed, etc.). All of its vehicles have to maintain coherency, just like ordinary units, but vehicles in a squadron need only to remain within 4" of each other to be in coherency, rather than within 2".

SHOOTING PHASE

When shooting, a squadron of vehicles fires all of its available weaponry at a single enemy unit. Like other units, vehicles in squadrons can see and shoot through members of their own unit, just as if they were not there. This represents the vehicles manoeuvring around each other in a well-practiced battle formation.

When a squadron of vehicles is fired at, roll to hit and for armour penetration against the squadron's common Armour Value (which is normally the same for all facings, and in most cases is 10). If the vehicles in the squadron have different Armour Values on different facings, use the Armour Value of the facing of the closest visible vehicle.

Once all of the armour penetration rolls have been made, the player controlling the squadron allocates the glancing and penetrating hits to squadron members as he would allocate wounds to members of a normal unit. Then he takes any cover saves available to the squadron – use the rules for vehicles to determine if each squadron member is in cover (ignoring other members of the squadron, as if they were not there), and then the rules for normal units to work out if the entire squadron is in cover or not. After cover saves are taken, make the damage rolls for any remaining glancing and penetrating hits. The effects of damage results on vehicle squadrons are slightly different than on normal vehicles, as described below.

DAMAGE RESULTS AGAINST SQUADRONS

The mutual support of vehicles in squadrons makes them resilient to damage results affecting the crew. On the other hand, the crews are under strict orders to abandon immobilised vehicles and disable them, not to leave them as spoils of war for the enemy.

To represent this, treat all immobilised results as destroyed (wrecked) and all stunned results as shaken. If a squadron consists of a single vehicle when an enemy unit fires at it, it reverts to the normal rules for vehicle damage results.

For example, a squad of Space Marine Devastators opens fire against a squadron of three Eldar Vypers, scores several hits, and rolls for armour penetration against the squadron's Armour Value of 10. This results in three penetrating hits and three glancing hits. The Eldar player allocates two penetrating hits on one Vyper, two glancing hits on another and one penetrating and one glancing hit on the last Vyper. He then takes the cover saves for his Vypers (4+, for example), saving one of the glancing hits and one of the penetrating hits. Finally the opponent rolls for damage for the two glancing and two penetrating hits that are left, and the results are immediately applied on the Vypers that suffered them.

ASSAULT PHASE

When engaged in close combat against a squadron, enemy models roll to hit and for armour penetration against the squadron as a whole. Damage results have the same effect as described above, and are allocated against the squadron at each Initiative value, in the same way as a normal combat. As usual for combats against vehicles, there is no defenders' reaction, combat resolution, pile-in moves, consolidation, etc.

VEHICLE TYPES

Transport vehicles
Transport vehicles are designed to carry infantry squads around the battlefield. They offer to the warriors either the protection of an armoured hull to shield them from anti-personnel fire or a much higher movement speed, or might even combine both advantages, as in the case of Eldar transports.

Tanks
Tanks are a common sight on the battlefields of the 41st Millennium. Most races field some kind of heavily armed and armoured vehicle, from the huge and lumbering Leman Russ battle tanks of the Imperial Guard, to the sleek and sophisticated grav-tanks of the Eldar. Tanks are often fitted for multi-role capability, which will commonly include troop transportation, tank-hunting and infantry support.

Open-topped vehicles
Some vehicles are not fully enclosed, but expose their crews to a hostile universe. There are many reasons for this – to give reconnaissance units a clear field of vision, to make embarking and disembarking passengers easier, or it may simply be impractical to enclose the crew. While crews and embarked passengers on open-topped vehicles have more freedom of movement and better arcs of vision, the lack of an enclosed crew space inevitably means that the vehicle is more vulnerable to incoming fire.

Fast vehicles
As the name suggests, fast vehicles are significantly quicker than most. Many fast vehicles are also skimmers, however, a few wheeled or tracked vehicles are also capable of high speeds, mostly due to either their light weight or extremely powerful engines. This type of vehicle has the additional advantage of being able to fire weapons while moving at higher speeds.

Skimmers
While most vehicles travel across the ground on wheels, tracks or legs, some advanced machines are fitted with jets or anti-gravity drives that enable them to swoop and hover a few metres above the battlefield. This is not true flight, but rather a limited version of it. Often skimmers will also be categorised as fast vehicles but this is not always the case.

Walkers
On any battlefield, there are places where conventional vehicles cannot go – built-up areas, dense forests, narrow tunnels, and so on. For this reason, many armies use vehicles that are propelled by two, or sometimes more, mechanical legs. These vehicles are usually capable of carrying as many weapon systems as a tank on a significantly smaller and lighter chassis. They combine the resilience of a tank with the manoeuvrability of an infantryman.

TRANSPORT VEHICLES

Some vehicles can carry infantry across the battlefield, providing speed and protection. Of course if the transport is destroyed, the passengers risk being burnt alive in the explosion.

Transports have several additional characteristics: Transport Capacity, Fire Points and Access Points.

TRANSPORT CAPACITY

Each transport vehicle has a maximum passenger capacity, which can never be exceeded.

A transport may carry a single infantry unit and/or any number of independent characters (as long as they count as infantry), up to a total of models equal to the vehicle's transport capacity. The entire unit must be embarked on a transport if any part of it is – a unit may never be partially embarked or spread across multiple transport vehicles.

Only infantry models may embark in transports (it is worth specifying that this does not include jump infantry), unless a Codex book states otherwise.

Some larger infantry models may count as more than one model for the purposes of taking up a transport's capacity, and this will be specified in the transporting vehicle's rules (for example, each Space Marine Terminator counts as two models).

Sometimes, there will be constraints on which types of models can embark on a particular vehicle, and this will be specified in the vehicle's entry. Space Marine Terminators, for example, cannot embark on a Rhino or Razorback, although they may be transported by a Land Raider.

FIRE POINTS

A transport vehicle may have a number of fire points defined in its entry. A fire point is a hatch or gun slit from which one or more passengers inside the vehicle can fire (or use a psychic power).

Unless specified differently in the vehicle's entry, a single passenger may fire out of a fire point and the other transported models may not fire. Ranges and line of sight are measured from the fire point itself.

Models firing from a vehicle count as moving if the vehicle moves, and may not fire at all if the vehicle moved at Cruising speed that turn.

ACCESS POINTS

Each vehicle capable of carrying passengers will have a number of access points defined in its entry. These are the doors, ramps and hatches that passengers use to get in and out of the vehicle. Models can embark or disembark within 2" of an access point.

EMBARKING AND DISEMBARKING

Models can only voluntarily embark or disembark in the Movement phase, and may not voluntarily both embark and disembark in the same player turn. However, they may embark and then be forced to disembark if their transport is destroyed.

Embarking

A unit can embark onto a vehicle by moving each model to within 2" of its access points in the Movement phase. The whole unit must be able to embark – if some models are out of range, the unit must stay outside. When the unit embarks, it is removed from the table and placed aside, making a note or otherwise marking that the unit is being transported (we find that placing one of the unit's models on top of the transport works well!). If the players need to measure a range involving the embarked unit (except for its shooting), this range is measured to or from the vehicle's hull.

- If the vehicle moved before its passengers got aboard, it may not move any further (including pivoting on the spot).

- If the vehicle has not moved before its passengers got aboard, it can move as normal.

Only in death does duty end.

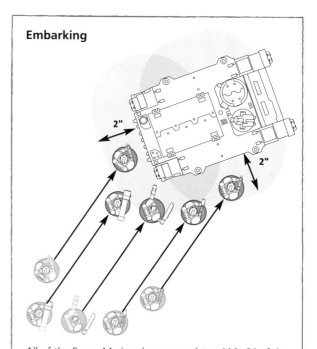

Embarking

All of the Space Marines have moved to within 2" of the transport's access points. The squad may embark.

Disembarking

A unit that begins its Movement phase aboard a vehicle can disembark either before or after the vehicle has moved. When the unit disembarks, each model is deployed within 2" of one of the vehicle's access points, and within unit coherency. Models cannot disembark within 1" of an enemy. If any models cannot disembark because of enemies or because they would end up in impassable terrain, the unit can perform an 'emergency disembarkation' – the models are deployed anywhere within 2" of the vehicle's hull, but the unit can't do anything else for the rest of the turn. If even this disembarkation is impossible, they can't disembark.

- If the vehicle has already moved (including pivoting on the spot), the passengers may disembark, but not move any further in that Movement phase. Once the models have disembarked, the vehicle may not move any further (including pivoting on the spot). After disembarking, these models may shoot (counting as moving), but may not assault.

- If the vehicle has not yet moved, then the passengers may disembark and move normally. The vehicle can also then move normally. The disembarked models may shoot (counting as moving), and may assault as normal.

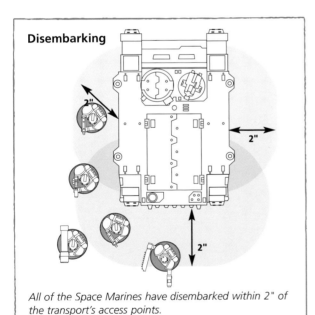

Disembarking

All of the Space Marines have disembarked within 2" of the transport's access points.

Independent characters embarking and disembarking

If an independent character (or even more than one) and a unit are both embarked in the same vehicle, they are automatically joined, just as if the character was within 2" of the unit. If either an independent character or a unit is already in a vehicle, the other may join them by embarking too (assuming, of course, that there is enough space left).

The unit and the independent characters may, in a later Movement phase, disembark together as a single unit. They can also disembark separately by either the unit or the characters disembarking while the others remain onboard, or even disembarking at the same time using different access points (but they must end their move more than 2" away from each other). If the vehicle has yet to move, both unit and characters can disembark together and in coherency, but then the characters can leave the unit as they move, as normal.

EFFECTS OF DAMAGE RESULTS ON PASSENGERS

Crew shaken & crew stunned

Passengers may not shoot from the vehicle in their next Shooting phase, but are otherwise unaffected.

Weapon destroyed & immobilised

These results have no effect on passengers.

Destroyed – wrecked

The passengers must immediately disembark and then take a Pinning test. Any models that cannot disembark are destroyed. After this, the vehicle becomes a wreck.

Destroyed – explodes!

The unit suffers a number of Strength 4, AP– hits equal to the number of models embarked, treated just like hits from shooting. The surviving passengers are placed where the vehicle used to be and then take a Pinning test.

Note: remember that all models in a single unit fire simultaneously, so a squad cannot take out a transport with its lascannon and then mow down the occupants with their bolters. However, if a transport is destroyed (either result) by a ranged attack, the unit that shot it may assault the now disembarked passengers, if it is allowed to assault according to the assault rules.

DEDICATED TRANSPORTS

Sometimes a unit entry in a Codex will include a transport option, allowing a vehicle to be selected together with the unit. These 'dedicated transports' do not use up a slot on the force organisation chart. Other vehicles may also have a transport capacity, but they are chosen separately as normal and occupy a force organisation chart slot of their own (for example, the mighty Space Marine Land Raider).

The only limitation of a dedicated transport is that when it is deployed it can only carry the unit it was selected with (plus any independent characters). After the game begins, it can then transport any friendly infantry unit, subject to transport capacity and other special exclusions, as explained in the vehicle's entry (it might not be able to transport Terminators, for example).

TANKS

Tanks are the most common vehicle type found on the battlefields of the 41st Millennium, where their armour and firepower are an invaluable asset for any army.

Tanks follow the normal rules for vehicles, with the additions and exceptions given below.

TANK SHOCK!

Tanks may decide to use their mass as a weapon, driving right into and through densely packed enemies. This often throws the opposing battle line into disarray, as having some monstrous metal behemoth coming straight at you is unnerving for anybody.

When moving a tank, the player can declare that the vehicle is going to attempt to make a tank shock attack instead of moving normally. This is an exception to the rule that enemy models cannot be moved through.

Remember, though, that friendly models still cannot be moved through, so a tank shock cannot be attempted if friendly models are in the way. Also, tank shock cannot be attempted against enemy units that are locked in combat, as the risk of harming friends in the swirling melee is too high.

To make this kind of attack, first turn the vehicle on the spot in the direction you intend to move it and declare how many inches the vehicle is going to move. The vehicle must move at least at combat speed. Note that because pivoting on the spot does not count as moving, this is not enough for a tank shock.

Once the vehicle has been 'aimed' and the speed declared, move the vehicle straight forward until it comes into contact with an enemy unit or it reaches the distance declared – no other changes of direction are allowed during a tank shock. If no enemy unit is reached, just move the vehicle straight ahead for the distance declared and no special attack takes place.

If an enemy unit other than another vehicle is reached (including any model in an artillery unit), the unit must take a Morale check and will immediately fall back if it fails it. If the test is passed the unit will simply let the tank move through, as if it was not there. Regardless of the result of the test, the vehicle keeps moving straight on, possibly tank shocking more enemy units until it reaches its final position. If the tank accidentally moves into contact with a friendly model or comes to within 1" of an enemy vehicle, it immediately stops moving.

If some enemy models in the enemy unit would end up underneath the vehicle when it reaches its final position (it makes no difference whether the unit is falling back or not), these models must be moved out of the way by the shortest distance, leaving at least 1" between them and the vehicle and maintaining unit coherency.

If the tank moved slowly enough during the tank shock attack, it may fire as normal in the Shooting phase.

My armour is contempt.

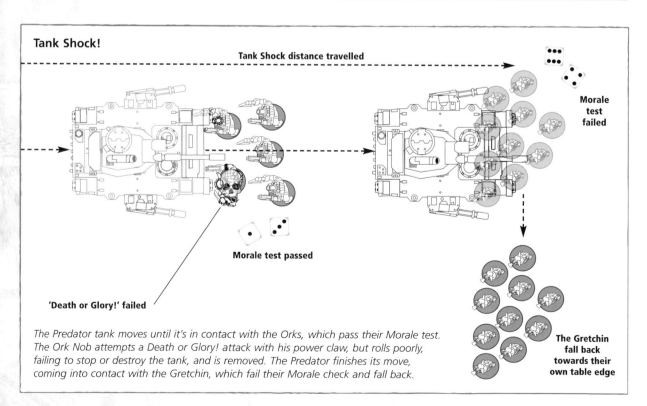

Tank Shock!

Tank Shock distance travelled

Morale test failed

Morale test passed

'Death or Glory!' failed

The Gretchin fall back towards their own table edge

The Predator tank moves until it's in contact with the Orks, which pass their Morale test. The Ork Nob attempts a Death or Glory! attack with his power claw, but rolls poorly, failing to stop or destroy the tank, and is removed. The Predator finishes its move, coming into contact with the Gretchin, which fail their Morale check and fall back.

Death or Glory!

If a unit that has been attacked by tank shock passes its Morale test, one of its models in the vehicle's path can stand and attempt to destroy it rather than move out of the way (this is potentially a rather suicidal thing to do!). The model nominated for this heroic duty makes a single attack against the incoming tank. Even if the weapon used is assault 3, for example, or the model is normally allowed more than one attack, only one attack is ever resolved in this case. The attack can be either a shot from a weapon carried by the model, or a single close combat attack using any weapon carried, including grenades. Whatever form it takes, the attack hits automatically, so resolve the hit against the vehicle's front armour (using the front armour even if the model uses a close combat attack), and immediately apply any damage results.

If the model successfully managed to stun, destroy or immobilise it, the vehicle grinds to a halt directly in front of the heroic individual (or blows up there!).

If the attack fails to stop the vehicle, then the tank shock continues as normal, except that the brave (but perhaps rather foolish) glory seeker is crushed by the vehicle grinding over him – the model is removed, regardless of Wounds, saves (invulnerable or not), or any other clever way of staying alive they can think of.

Artillery units may attempt a Death or Glory! as well, with either a crewman (resolved as above) or a gun model. If a gun model does this and fails to stop the tank, both the gun and one crewman are removed.

RAMMING

Ramming is a rather desperate manoeuvre and means that the tank must concentrate on moving at top speed towards one enemy vehicle. This means that it may not shoot in that turn's Shooting phase, making it an attractive choice for vehicles that have no armament left, or are shaken.

Ramming is a special type of tank shock move and is executed the same way, except that the tank must always move at the highest speed it is capable of. Units other than vehicles in the way of a ramming tank are tank shocked as normal. However, if the ramming tank comes into contact with an enemy vehicle, the collision is resolved as follows.

Each vehicle immediately suffers a hit against the armour facing where the other vehicle has impacted (so the rammer always uses its front armour). The Strength of the hits will often be different for different vehicles, and is calculated as follows for each vehicle:

- **Armour.** Each point of armour   +1
  above 10 on the point of impact:

- **Speed.** Each full 3" moved that turn   +1
  by the rammer before impact:

- **Mass.** If the vehicle is a tank: +1

For example: a Land Raider rams an Ork Trukk, hitting it in the side. The Land Raider has a front armour of 14 (4 points over 10, for a total of +4), has moved 10" before reaching the Trukk (for an extra +3) and is a tank (+1). The total is 4+3+1, which means that the Trukk suffers a Strength 8 hit against its side armour. At the same time, the Land Raider suffers a Strength 3 hit against its front armour (+0 for the Trukk's side armour of 10, +0 because the Trukk is not a tank and +3 for the Land Raider's own speed).

Both players roll for armour penetration against their enemy vehicle and any result is immediately applied. If the vehicle that is rammed is not removed, the rammer halts. However, if the rammed vehicle is removed because it suffers a 'destroyed – explodes!' damage result, the rammer continues its move, until it reaches its maximum move distance or another enemy (which it will tank shock or ram again!).

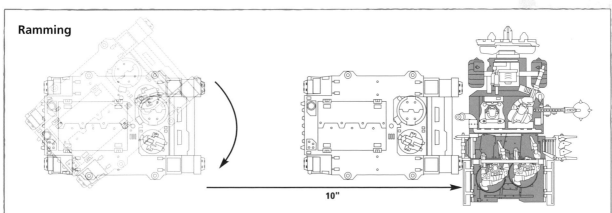

Ramming

10"

The Rhino pivots towards the Trukk and moves 10 full inches before hitting the Trukk. As the Rhino's front armour is 11, the total is 5 (+1 for armour, +3 for speed and +1 for being a tank), so the Trukk suffers a Strength 5 hit on its side armour (which is 10). In return, the Rhino suffers a Strength 3 hit on its Front Armour.

OPEN-TOPPED VEHICLES

Some vehicles are much less armoured than tanks. This means they are more vulnerable to damage because of their lightweight construction and the fact that their crew is exposed to enemy fire. However, passengers can fire out and disembark much more easily than normal. Typical examples of open-topped vehicles are Ork Trukks and Dark Eldar Raiders. Open-topped vehicles follow the normal vehicle rules, with the additions and exceptions given below.

OPEN-TOPPED TRANSPORT VEHICLES

Open-topped vehicles do not have specific fire points. Instead, all passengers in an open-topped vehicle may fire, measuring range and line of sight from the hull of the vehicle. Open-topped vehicles do not have specific access points. Models can embark or disembark within 2" of any point of the vehicle. The passengers of open-topped vehicles may assault, even if the vehicle has moved before their disembarkation. As it is much easier to bail out from an open topped transport, the Strength of hits inflicted on passengers by exploding open topped transports is one point lower than it would be in a normal transport (i.e. Strength 3).

DAMAGING OPEN-TOPPED VEHICLES

Whenever a damage roll is made against an open-topped vehicle, add +1 to the result.

FAST VEHICLES

Some vehicles are markedly faster then the more ponderous tanks, because of the combination of their lighter construction and more powerful engines.

Fast vehicles follow the normal rules for vehicles, with the additions and exceptions given below.

MOVING FAST VEHICLES

Fast vehicles are capable of a third level of speed, called 'flat out'. A fast vehicle going flat out moves more than 12" and up to 18". This represents the fast vehicle moving at top speed, without firing its guns and is treated in all respects exactly the same as moving at cruising speed for a vehicle that is not fast (except where noted otherwise). For example, a fast vehicle moving flat out on a road may move up to 24".

FAST VEHICLES FIRING

Fast vehicles may move and fire more effectively than other types of vehicles.

Fast vehicles that move at combat speed may fire all of their weapons, just like other types of vehicles that have remained stationary (including ordnance barrage weapons, which cannot usually be fired on the move).

Fast vehicles that move at cruising speed may fire a single weapon (plus all defensive weapons, just like other types of vehicle moving at combat speed).

Fast vehicles moving flat out may fire no weapons.

ASSAULTING FAST VEHICLES

Fast vehicles that moved 'flat out' in the previous turn and are not immobilised are hit on a 6 in assaults (exactly as if moving at cruising speed).

FAST TRANSPORT VEHICLES

Passengers may not embark onto or disembark from a fast vehicle if it has moved (or is going to move) flat out in that Movement phase.

"Why do we ride atop these elegant craft? The better to hear the screams of our prey as we ride them down, to savour the fear etched on their faces, to taste the tantalising tang of their blood in the air as an appetiser before the feast. But most of all we ride them so that the slaughter may begin as soon as possible."

Dhariaq Bladetongue, Kabal of the Pierced Eye

SKIMMERS

Some highly advanced vehicles are fitted with anti-gravity drives that allow them to skim swiftly over rough terrain and intervening troops.

Skimmers follow the normal rules for vehicles, with the additions and exceptions given below.

MEASURING DISTANCES

Unlike other vehicles, skimmers have transparent 'flying bases' under their hull. As normal for vehicles, distances are measured to and from the skimmer's hull, with the exceptions of the vehicle's weapons, access points and fire points, which all work as normal. The skimmer's base is effectively ignored, except when assaulting a skimmer, in which case models may move into contact with the vehicle's hull, its base or both.

MOVING SKIMMERS

Skimmers can move over friendly and enemy models, but they cannot end their move on top of either. Note that a skimmer must be set down on the table and left in place at the end of its move – it cannot be left hovering in mid-air!

Skimmers can move over all terrain, ignoring all penalties for difficult terrain and tests for dangerous terrain. However, if a moving skimmer starts or ends its move in difficult or dangerous terrain, it must take a dangerous terrain test. A skimmer can even end its move over impassable terrain if it is possible to actually place the model on top of it, but if it does so it must take a dangerous terrain test.

A skimmer that is also fast and is moving flat out can move up to 24".

SHOOTING AT SKIMMERS

Skimmers moving at high speed are very difficult to hit. A skimmer that is not immobilised and has moved flat out in its last Movement phase counts as obscured (cover save of 4+) when fired at.

On the other hand, having your engines stall when flying at high speed has its consequences, so a skimmer that is immobilised immediately crashes and is destroyed (wrecked) if it moved flat out in its last turn. If it moved slower, it suffers an immobilised result as normal.

If a skimmer is immobilised or wrecked, its base is removed, if possible. If this is not possible (the base might have been glued in place, for example), don't worry about it. The skimmer's anti-grav field is obviously still working and an immobilised skimmer will simply remain hovering in place, incapable of any further movement (including turning on the spot); a wrecked one is now a floating, burning wreck. Note that it is not permitted to remove the flying stand other than in the two cases above, as normally skimmers cannot land in battle conditions.

RAMMING A SKIMMER

Skimmers may try to dodge out of the way of tanks attempting to ram them (as long as the ramming tank is not also a skimmer). The ramming tank stops in contact with the skimmer as normal, but then, if the player controlling the skimmer wants to dodge, he rolls a D6. On a 1 or 2 the collision proceeds as normal. On a 3+ the skimmer avoids the tank, neither vehicle suffers any damage, and the ramming tank stops in its tracks (literally!), its crew confused and disappointed.

"Listen not for the approach of the Eldar, nor look to the skies for their coming. Their craft are silent as midnight, swift as dawn, and bring naught but death to the enemies of that forlorn race."

Inquisitor Czevak, Admonitions and Portents

WALKERS

Walkers are a very unusual type of vehicle. Instead of wheels or tracks they have mechanical limbs that allow them to stride forward, ploughing through densely packed terrain with ease in order to bring their weapons to bear. Because of this they use some of the rules for normal infantry.

ADDITIONAL CHARACTERISTICS

Walkers have a Weapon Skill, Strength, Initiative and Attacks value, representing their ability in close combat and reaction speed, in the same way that they do for models that aren't vehicles. Shown here is an example:

| | | | | | Armour | | | | |
	Type	WS	BS	S	F	S	R	I	A
Dreadnought	Walker	4	4	6	12	12	10	4	2

MEASURING RANGES

If a walker has a base, measure ranges and distances to and from its base, as you would for an infantry model. If a walker does not have a base (like the Chaos Defiler), measure to and from its hull (including its legs and other limbs), as normal for vehicles. Firing the walker's own weapons is an exception to this, as explained later on this page.

MOVING WALKERS

While other vehicles can only move in the Movement phase, walkers can also run in the Shooting phase and assault in the Assault phase, just as infantry can.

Walkers move in exactly the same way as infantry, so they can move up to 6" in the Movement phase and assault up to 6" in the Assault phase.

Difficult terrain affects walkers just as it does infantry. Difficult terrain only counts as dangerous terrain for walkers if it would do so for infantry. If walkers fail a dangerous terrain test, they are immobilised.

Unlike infantry, a walker has a facing, which influences where it can fire (see below) and its Armour Value when fired at.

WALKERS SHOOTING

Walkers can move and fire all of their weapons, just like a stationary vehicle.

Alternatively, they can choose to run like infantry, and this prevents them from firing and assaulting that turn, as normal (though they can still trigger their smoke launchers, if they have any). Obviously they cannot run if they are stunned or immobilised.

When firing a walker's weapons, pivot the walker on the spot so that its guns are aimed at the target (assume that all weapons mounted on a walker can swivel 45°, like hull-mounted weapons) and then measure the range from the weapon itself and line of sight from the mounting point of the weapon and along its barrel, as normal for vehicles. This pivoting in the Shooting phase does not count as moving and represents the vastly superior agility of walkers in comparison with other vehicles. Keep in mind however that the walker will probably remain facing in this direction until its next Movement phase, so its facing will determine where its rear armour is going to be when the enemy returns fire!

SHOOTING AT WALKERS

When firing at a walker, work out which of its Armour Values to use as you would for any other vehicle, based on the position of its body. Walkers that are locked in combat cannot be shot at.

> "We pray for our brethren who pilot the Dreadnoughts. Though they take new form, their souls, and their weapon mounts, remain pure."
>
> Marneus Calgar

WALKERS AND ASSAULTS

Walkers assault like infantry models, meaning that they make assault moves and can be locked in combat with enemy units. Walkers can make an assault even if they fired heavy or rapid fire weapons. However, like normal infantry, they can still only assault the unit they fired at.

In close combat, walkers fight like infantry models. However, any hits scored against them must roll for armour penetration and damage as for a vehicle. Models hitting a walker in close combat always roll for penetration against its front armour. This is because the walker is not a static target like other vehicles and rampages through the melee, turning to face its enemies. Consequently a walker is quite capable of tearing apart its foe in close combat, while only the specially armed (or monstrously powerful) will have any hope of destroying a walker up close.

Grenades and melta bombs can be used against a walker. A model will only manage to score a hit with a grenade against a walker on the roll of 6. However, if a walker is already stunned or immobilised at the start of the Assault phase, the attackers roll to hit based on the normal comparison of WS. Remember that models using grenades against vehicles only make one attack.

Immobilised and/or stunned walkers fight in close combat with one less attack than usual (to a minimum of 1), but otherwise attack normally, no matter how many immobilised and stunned results they suffered.

Shaken damage results do not affect the way a walker fights in close combat.

Each roll made on the Vehicle Damage table against a walker counts as a single wound for the purposes of working out who won the combat.

Defeated walkers do not take Morale checks and are not affected by the No Retreat! rule.

Walkers make sweeping advances, pile-in moves and consolidations unless they are stunned or immobilised.

RAMMING A WALKER

If a walker is rammed by a tank, it can choose to either brace itself for the impact, in which case the collision is resolved as normal for a vehicle, or it can attempt a 'Death or Glory!' attack in the same way as infantry (it cannot do this, however, if it is rammed in its rear arc).

If it chooses 'Death or Glory!' and its attack fails to stop the ramming tank, the walker will not be ready for the impact and is hit on its rear armour in the collision.

SQUADRONS OF WALKERS

Squadrons of walkers follow all normal rules for vehicle squadrons, except in assaults. They assault and react to being assaulted in the same way as units of infantry, moving to engage their attackers before attacks are rolled. Damage results are resolved as described for vehicle squadrons, however, and they attack back, perform sweeping advances, pile-in moves and consolidations like walkers (see Walkers and Assault).

DREADNOUGHT CLOSE COMBAT WEAPONS

Walkers are often armed with huge close combat weapons – hammers, wrecking balls, claws, etc. A Dreadnought close combat weapon is a power weapon and doubles the walker's Strength in close combat (up to a maximum of 10).

If the walker suffers a weapon destroyed result and the player chooses the close combat weapon, the walker loses the bonuses conferred by the Dreadnought close combat weapon (and any other weapon built into the same arm).

If a walker is armed with two or more close combat weapons, it gains one bonus attack for each additional weapon over the first. If one of its additional weapons is destroyed, one bonus attack is lost.

VEHICLE MOVING & SHOOTING SUMMARY CHART

	Stationary	Combat Speed	Cruising Speed	Flat Out
All (except Fast & Walkers)	All Weapons	1 Weapon*	No Weapons	N/A
Fast	All Weapons	All Weapons	1 Weapon*	No Weapons
Walker	All Weapons	All Weapons	N/A	N/A

*plus all defensive weapons.

UNIVERSAL SPECIAL RULES

Many units of models in Warhammer 40,000 have unique special rules. There are, however, quite a few special rules that are shared by several units, even across different Codex books. These are called 'universal special rules' and are listed in this section for ease of reference.

As this is just a summary, if any of the Codexes include one of these special rules and the rule is different, the one in the Codex takes precedence (representing how the general special rule applies to that specific race).

The special rules marked with an asterisk (*) are automatically lost by an independent character joining a unit that does not have the same special rule. These rules are also lost by a unit that is joined by an independent character that does not have the same special rule.

COUNTER-ATTACK

Troops with this skill believe that attack is always the best form of defence. If assaulted, they will spring forward themselves and ferociously counter-attack the charging enemy.

To represent this, when a unit with this rule is assaulted by the enemy it must take a Leadership test. If the test is successful all models in the unit get the +1 assault bonus to their attacks, exactly as if they too had assaulted that turn.

This rule cannot be used if, when assaulted, the unit was already locked in combat from a previous turn.

ETERNAL WARRIOR

The model is immune to the effects of the Instant Death rule.

FEARLESS

Fearless troops automatically pass all Morale and Pinning tests they are required to take, and will never fall back. They can however go to ground voluntarily. This special rule is gained by any independent character joining a fearless unit. However, as long as a fearless character stays with a unit that is not fearless, he loses this special rule. If a unit that is falling back suddenly gains this rule, it will automatically regroup at the beginning of its next Movement phase, regardless of all normal restrictions on regrouping.

FEEL NO PAIN

Some warriors are so blood-frenzied or tough that they can ignore injuries that would incapacitate even a battle-hardened Space Marine. If a model with this ability suffers an unsaved wound, roll a dice. On a 1, 2 or 3, take the wound as normal (removing the model if it loses its final Wound). On a 4, 5 or 6, the injury is ignored and the model continues fighting. This ability cannot be used against wounds from weapons that inflict instant death (by having a high enough Strength or a special rule to that effect; even if the model is an eternal warrior). Neither can it be used against wounds from AP1 and AP2 weapons, power weapons and any other wound against which no armour save can ever be taken (like wounds from power fists, Dreadnought close combat weapons, rending weapons that roll a 6, Perils of the Warp, failed dangerous terrain tests, etc).

FLEET*

There are many variants of this rule: Fleet of Foot, Fleet of Claw, even Fleet of Hoof. Title aside, all models with these abilities are treated the same. A unit with this rule may assault in the same turn in which it has run.

FURIOUS CHARGE

Models with this skill are known for the wild ferocity of their assaults. In a turn in which they assaulted into combat they add +1 to both their Initiative and Strength characteristics when attacking in close combat (note that this has no effect on the Initiative tests for sweeping advances).

HIT & RUN*

Units with this ability that are locked in combat may choose to leave close combat at the end of the Assault phase. The unit using the hit & run ability must take an Initiative test. If the test is failed nothing happens and the models remain locked in the fight. If the test is passed, the unit breaks from combat and immediately moves up to 3D6" in a straight line in any direction, ignoring the units they are locked with. No sweeping advance rolls are made. Enemy units that are no longer locked in combat may consolidate. A hit & run move is not slowed by difficult terrain, but is affected by

dangerous terrain. It may not be used to move into contact with the enemy. If there are units with this rule on both sides, roll-off to determine who goes first and then alternate disengaging them. If the last of these ends up no longer in combat, it consolidates instead.

INFILTRATE*

In the right circumstances, stealthy troops have the ability to work their way into a forward position on the battlefield or outflank enemy lines.

Units with this special rule are deployed last, after all other units (friends and foe) have been deployed. If both sides have infiltrators, the players roll-off and the winner decides who goes first, and then alternate deploying these units. Infiltrators may be set up anywhere on the table that is more than 12" from any enemy unit, as long as no deployed enemy unit can draw a line of sight to them. This includes inside a building (see page 83), as long as the building is more than 12" from any enemy unit. Alternatively, they may be set up anywhere on the table that is more than 18" from any enemy unit, even in plain sight.

If a unit with this ability is deployed inside a transport vehicle, it cannot infiltrate. Infiltrate also confers a special outflank move to units of infiltrators that are kept in reserve (see page 94).

MOVE THROUGH COVER*

Some units of infantry are especially adept at moving through difficult terrain. Units with this rule roll an extra D6 when rolling to move through difficult terrain. In most circumstances this will mean that they roll three D6 and pick the dice with the highest score.

NIGHT VISION/ACUTE SENSES

Warriors in certain parts of the galaxy have developed nocturnal tendencies by fighting in perpetual night, or perhaps carry equipment that gives them such abilities. When the Night Fighting mission special rule is in use, such models may choose to re-roll the test to determine how far they can see, but must abide by the new result. Characters with this rule confer it onto any unit they join, as long as they are part of the unit. Units with this rule confer it onto any characters joining them, as long as they are part of the unit.

PREFERRED ENEMY

Some warriors are able to predict the moves of the enemies they are used to fighting. In close combat, they have developed special techniques that enable them to counter such enemies more effectively. Such troops can always re-roll their rolls to hit in close combat against their preferred enemy. This ability does not work when attacking vehicles without a Weapon Skill characteristic.

RAGE

Some warriors are little more than mindless killing machines, incapable of rational thought and only interested in getting to grips with the enemy as soon as possible. In the Movement phase, units subject to rage must always move as fast as possible towards the closest visible enemy. In the Shooting phase, they are free to decide whether to run, but if they do they must run towards the closest visible enemy. In the Assault phase they must always consolidate towards the closest visible enemy. Whilst falling back, embarked on a transport, or if no enemy is visible, they ignore this rule.

RELENTLESS

Unlike common infantry, some powerful warriors like monstrous creatures, jet packers and bikers can advance while firing their weapons at full capacity. Relentless models can shoot with rapid fire and heavy weapons counting as stationary, even if they moved in the previous Movement phase, and are also allowed to assault in the same turn they fire them.

Note that a relentless independent character must still abide by the assaulting limitations of any unit it has joined, if the unit is not itself relentless.

SCOUTS*

Scouts are used to reconnoitre ahead and are always in the vanguard of the army. To represent this, after both sides have deployed (including infiltrators), but before the first player begins his first turn, any scouts may make a normal move. This is done exactly as in their Movement phase, except that during this move, scouts must remain more than 12" away from any enemy.

If both sides have scouts, the players roll-off and the winner decides who goes first, and then alternate moving these units.

If a unit with this ability is deployed inside a dedicated transport vehicle, it confers the scout ability to the transport too.

This rule also confers a special outflank move to units of scouts that are kept in reserve (see page 94).

SKILLED RIDER

The rider is highly practiced at moving though perilous warzones. It may re-roll the dice for failed dangerous terrain tests as long as its unit type is bike or cavalry.

SLOW AND PURPOSEFUL

Models with this special rule are relentless (see above). However, they always count as moving through difficult terrain (including in assaults). Remember that a slow and purposeful independent character will cause any

unit he joins to move at his speed (and vice versa) as units have to move at the speed of the slowest model.

STEALTH

The ability to make maximum use of available cover has saved many a warrior from discovery and death. All of the unit's cover saves are improved by +1.

STUBBORN

Stubborn resistance against impossible odds is a feature of some races. When taking Morale tests, stubborn units always ignore any negative Leadership modifiers. Independent characters that are stubborn confer the ability onto any unit that they join.

SWARMS

Swarms represent creatures that are too puny to be an individual threat on the battlefield, but when operating as a sea of dozens of creatures they can destroy much larger enemies. All swarms have the 'stealth' and 'vulnerable to blasts/templates' special rules. In addition, intervening swarms never offer any cover save to monstrous creatures or vehicles.

TANK HUNTERS

Tank hunters are especially skilled at finding and exploiting weaknesses in the armour of enemy vehicles. They add +1 to their armour penetration rolls whenever they hit a vehicle (both at range and in close combat). In addition, they automatically pass Morale checks caused by tank shock.

TURBO-BOOSTERS*

Units mounted on bikes and jetbikes may utilise turbo-boosters to move at extreme speed. When using their turbo-boosters they may move up to 24" in the Movement phase. Controlling their bike at such speeds takes all their concentration and skill, however, so they cannot move through difficult terrain, shoot, launch assaults or execute any other voluntary action in the same turn. In the following enemy Shooting phase, the bike benefits from a cover save of 3+ to represent the difficulty of hitting such fast-moving targets. In that enemy Shooting phase, however, bikers lose the ability of going to ground, and automatically pass Pinning tests. A unit using turbo-boosters must end its move at least 18" away from its starting point to claim this cover save, as it relies on flat-out speed.

VULNERABLE TO BLASTS/TEMPLATES

Some units are especially vulnerable to blast weapons and template weapons. If the unit is a vehicle, then each hit counts as two hits. If it is not a vehicle, each unsaved wound is doubled to two wounds.

BUILDINGS AND RUINS

The buildings of the Warhammer 40,000 universe range from the small, primitive structures built by tribesmen on feral planets, through to huge futuristic skyscrapers, crystalline spires, hardened adamantium bunkers or glistening biostructures. In addition, many of the structures on a battlefield have been reduced to ruins. Coping with this variety of different structures, or even the rather smaller number of types you are likely to see on the average wargames table, can cause problems. Generally at the most inopportune moment, when the battle is raging at its fiercest, a player will discover his opponent had an entirely different take on how the rules apply to a particular building. To help you deal with these problems, and hopefully confine the bloodshed to the tabletop, we've put together the following guidelines.

DEFINING BUILDINGS AND RUINS

As with any type of tabletop terrain, it is worthwhile discussing with your opponent what effect each different structure will have before the battle begins. This need not be a time consuming process; in fact it will probably only take a few minutes, and each structure can be as complicated or as straightforward as you and your opponent wish it to be. There is no right or wrong way to choose how your buildings and ruins work – they can even behave differently in different games!

BUILDINGS

This category includes all those intact buildings in which players cannot physically place their models, because they are solid pieces of terrain. This includes military buildings like bunkers and barracks, but other intact structures as well, such as the hardened control centres at a spaceport, for example. On the battlefield, intact buildings can be used not only as cover to hide behind, but you can imagine your models entering them and using them as a firing position from which to repel the enemy. Buildings use aspects of the transport vehicle rules allowing squads from both sides to occupy and fire from them, or try to destroy them.

Impassable buildings

Some buildings in your terrain collection may look impossible for models to enter (fortifications with barred doors, solid metal cubes, imprisonment facilities, etc.) or that it makes no earthly sense for models to enter (gas storage silos, white-hot smelting cauldrons, thermonuclear reactors, etc.). Any of these buildings can be deemed impassable terrain.

RUINS

These structures have taken a hammering from shells, explosions and rampaging war machines. They are normally composed of badly damaged walls sitting amongst piles of broken rubble. Ruins can also have one or more floors partially intact. As they are often lacking large chunks of walls and roof, ruins are the easiest for gaming purposes. Players can place their models inside and move them around to show their position. No abstractions are required – both players will be able to see the models for themselves.

This Space Marine command post is built to withstand attack – it could be a treated as a building.

This Tau power relay is bursting with radioactive hazards – it is best considered impassable terrain.

This battered administratum structure is a perfect example of a ruin.

BUILDINGS

The bloody battles of the 41st Millennium often envelop cities, towns, defence lines, research outposts, hab blocks, pumping stations, army barracks, mining colonies, space ports, tribal forts, ancient tombs, sacred shrines and countless other types of building. In the middle of a war zone, such structures are generally deserted, and as such they can be used as defensive positions for troops from either side. Depending on their size, buildings can house anything from a small squad to an entire army.

Not all buildings need be designed with a military purpose in mind – they merely need to be intact structures (preferably with thick walls and good arcs of fire) that troops can use as a defensive position against an oncoming foe.

Which pieces in your terrain collection count as buildings is up to you and your opponent, but they can range from unprepossessing wooden shacks to stone dwellings and ceramite bunkers to ancient alien hab-complexes and battle fortresses.

A shrine of the Adepta Sororitas.

Buildings of all types use aspects of the transport vehicle rules. The main difference between them and actual vehicles is that they can't move, and units from either side can go inside.

Some bunker or bastion models may be fitted with their own weapons. These weapons cannot be used to shoot unless previously agreed with your opponent, or unless there are special rules for that terrain piece or the mission you intend to play that specifically say otherwise. It is generally a good idea to assume that these weapons were abandoned long ago, and that they no longer work.

IMPASSABLE BUILDINGS

There are times when a player's collection may include buildings that makes no sense for warriors to enter – huge storage tanks, vast solid monuments and the like. In game terms we refer to these structures as impassable buildings.

Impassable buildings and movement

If a building is agreed to be impassable at the start of the game, it follows the normal rules for impassable terrain, and models cannot go inside it for any reason. This is not to say that models will not interact with the building – it will of course block line of sight and provide cover for models sheltering in its lee.

Remember that if it is possible to physically place models on top of an impassable building, jump infantry, jetbikes and skimmers are allowed to end their move there, treating it as dangerous terrain. As usual, a brief discussion with your opponent about the building before the game begins is well worthwhile.

What sort of game?

Warhammer 40,000 players like many different things about the game. Some see it as a purely competitive, tactical exercise, some prefer to focus on telling an exciting story as the battle unfolds, while others just love writing their own rules – devising new missions, creating special characters or even changing the main rules of the game! Obviously, players that meet regularly, at someone's house or a club, quickly learn what sorts of games their friends like to play. However, when you are gaming against someone new, it's always worth spending a few minutes before the battle talking about the game.

For example, if you have any ruins, you should agree exactly how to use them. One player may prefer to treat them simply as area terrain so that he can concentrate on his grand plan, while another may like the additional story-telling that is created if models cannot move through solid walls or climb up levels without stairs or ladders. Yet another player may have written a house rule where an elevator is activated if you also have models next to the power generator on the other side of the table! No single approach is right or wrong, as long as both players have agreed before the game.

OCCUPYING BUILDINGS

Models can enter or exit a building through a doorway or other opening that the players have agreed to treat as an access point. Players should decide what the access points are before deployment, in order to avoid any possible confusion on this matter. This aside, moving into or out of a building works the same as embarking or disembarking from a vehicle (including emergency disembarkations).

All of the normal rules apply, so only one infantry unit (plus any independent characters that joined them) may occupy a building at one time. The 'transport' capacity of a small bunker might be ten models, while a large bastion could hold any number of models from a single unit. Again, this can vary according to what you and your opponent agree on before the game begins. Often, a Codex specifies that a certain infantry unit made of rather large models may use transports, but will count as more than a single model (Space Marine Terminators, for example, count as two models each). These rules should also be used whenever such units enter a building (so, to continue our former example, up to five Terminators could occupy a bunker that the players have agreed to have a capacity of ten models).

Models entering a building are removed from the table – you can either note down where they are on a piece of paper or use another suitable reminder. Units of jump infantry, jetbikes and skimmers cannot land on a building that is occupied by enemy units.

You'll find that some structures won't have obvious doors or stairs allowing access, but you wish to use them as buildings, rather than impassable terrain. For example, we've got some Orky buildings that include little watchtowers – unfortunately they lack any visible method for actually getting up to the watchtower! In cases like this the players can simply agree to assume that there are internal doors or ladders which allow access to the building.

FIRING FROM BUILDINGS

Just like some transport vehicles, buildings have fire points that allow units inside to fire out. These could be the fire slits on bunkers and bastions or the windows on other buildings. Players should agree beforehand where these fire points are. Unless the players agree otherwise, up to two models may shoot through each fire point of a building. Note that all of the models in a unit firing from a building can only target a single enemy unit, as normal.

ATTACKING BUILDINGS

The best way to kill enemy troops in a fortified position is usually just to destroy the fortified position. Units may shoot at or assault an occupied building just as if it was a vehicle. Units inside a building may not be attacked directly, but will be affected in the same

All Space Marines in the squad have moved to within 2" of the building access point, so that the unit can 'embark' into it.

manner as units inside a transport vehicle should the building be damaged, and so may suffer damage and/or be forced to 'disembark'.

Bunkers and bastions have an Armour Value of 14 all around. The Armour Values of other buildings may vary between 9 and 13 (see the chart below for some examples). The players must agree at the start of the game on the Armour Value of all buildings in use.

When shooting at a building, roll to hit and for armour penetration normally (in close combat they are hit automatically, just like stationary vehicles). Buildings treat stunned, immobilised and weapon destroyed results as shaken results instead (weapon destroyed may work as normal if you have agreed to use the weapons mounted on the building, of course). Wrecked buildings are treated in the same way as a wrecked vehicle, and therefore become difficult and dangerous terrain. If one is available, players may like to put down a ruin in its place. Buildings that explode can be replaced with an area of rubble or a crater.

BUILDINGS ARMOUR CHART

Building	Armour Value
Bastion or bunker	14
Stone-walled palace	13
Concrete city building	12
Brick house	11
Log cabin	10
Corrugated iron or wooden shed	9

Template weapons

Template weapons such as flamers are designed to attack enemies hidden behind defensive terrain, and can attack models even if they are inside a building.

To represent this, if one or more of the fire points on a building fall under a template, the unit occupying the building suffers D6 hits from the template weapon. The building itself also suffers one hit, as normal.

The Ork is hitting the unit occupying the building by firing his burna at the fire point.

PARAPETS AND BATTLEMENTS

Many buildings are constructed so warriors can be positioned on the roof and fire from behind fortified parapets or battlements. This allows extra models from the unit to fire, but leaves the building more vulnerable to attack. If any models from the unit are placed on a parapet, they can fire in addition to those using firing points. They still count as being in the building though, so cannot be shot or assaulted directly. However, if a Damage roll is made against the building while some occupiers are on the roof, add +1 to the result.

Use your imagination!

Some players may want to use a very large building, such as a fortress, which could include towers, battlements, bunkers and so on, each with different capacities and Armour Values. You may simply want to deploy a unit inside a building and another on the roof. You may even want to come up with rules for jump packers assaulting enemies on parapets. Inventing extra rules like this is great fun, and will make for a very different game. Players will have to agree before the game how will models move between two adjoining elements, and other details. You may even want different elements of a fortress to be treated as several types of structure – perhaps one section is ruined, another impassable, whilst the rest is treated as one or more buildings – see opposite for an example. As with most other things that we have discussed in this section, the only limits are the buildings you own and your imagination.

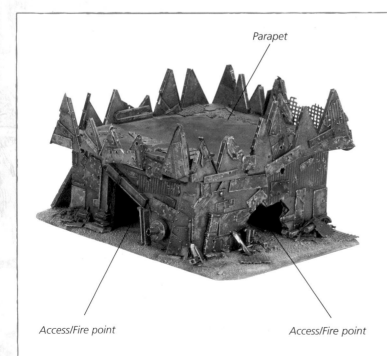

Parapet

Access/Fire point

Access/Fire point

Example:

From appearances, this Ork hut might be considered a corrugated iron shed. However, we're assuming that an Ork Mekboy has "fixed it up good an' propa" by welding scavenged armour throughout its primitive frame. Accordingly, it has been assigned an Armour Value of 12 – as much as a concrete building!

We've assigned the structure a capacity of thirty – enough for a big mob of Ork Boyz to take shelter.

There is a jagged doorway on every side of the building (we decided to treat each one as both an access point and a fire point) while the wide roof will allow plenty of extra Boyz to shoot.

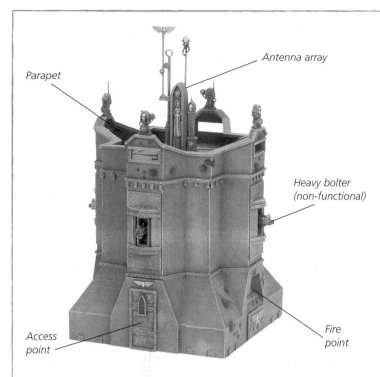

Parapet

Antenna array

Heavy bolter
(non-functional)

Access
point

Fire
point

Example:

This bastion is a hardened structure, purpose built for war, and so has been assigned an Armour Value of 14. It's literally as tough as they come.

The bastion has only a single access point, but several fire points – one on each facing. As it is a large structure with multiple floors, we've decided that the bastion can hold a unit of any size.

There are several fixed-mount heavy bolters on the bastion, but we've assumed that they are too ancient and decayed to do much else than look menacing. Of course players could agree that the heavy bolters can be fired. Similarly, we consider the antenna array on the roof to be purely decorative, but in some games you could allow a bonus to reserve rolls for the side that occupies the building. Bear in mind that if you did use the heavy bolters and antenna array, then the side occupying the bastion would gain a considerable advantage, and it would likely become the focus of fierce fighting in your battles.

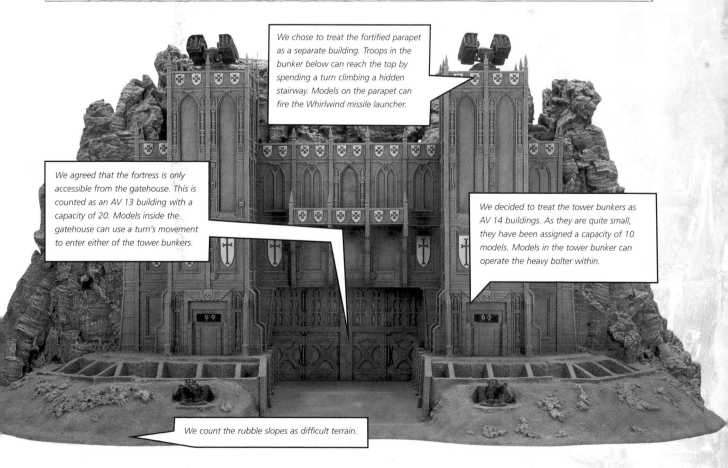

We chose to treat the fortified parapet as a separate building. Troops in the bunker below can reach the top by spending a turn climbing a hidden stairway. Models on the parapet can fire the Whirlwind missile launcher.

We agreed that the fortress is only accessible from the gatehouse. This is counted as an AV 13 building with a capacity of 20. Models inside the gatehouse can use a turn's movement to enter either of the tower bunkers.

We decided to treat the tower bunkers as AV 14 buildings. As they are quite small, they have been assigned a capacity of 10 models. Models in the tower bunker can operate the heavy bolter within.

We count the rubble slopes as difficult terrain.

This glorious building is an extreme example of the fun you can have with the rules for buildings. While such a structure is complicated and likely to dominate any game it appears in, it'll certainly give you a battle to remember!

RUINS

This section concentrates on ruins – the ones that players can actually place their models inside. The extra height and multiple levels of ruins require some extra clarifications to explain how certain rules work. For example, it is useful to explain how unit coherency, and blast markers and templates work in this environment.

These rules are based on the height and area of the plastic Warhammer 40,000 city ruins. They will work just as well with ruins of your own creation, so long as their dimensions are roughly similar.

RUINS: THE BASICS

All ruins are area terrain (providing a 4+ cover save) and difficult terrain. Players may also agree at the beginning of the game to treat some ruins as dangerous terrain as well, representing unstable structures on the verge of collapsing or that are still on fire. Of course, the nature of ruins means that the boundaries of the area terrain can be somewhat indistinct. The best way to counter this is to ensure that both players are clear on the limits of each ruin before the game begins.

Ruins with bases

A ruin may be mounted on a base, decorated with rubble, collapsed walls and other debris, in which case it is best to treat the base exactly the same as the upper floors – as area terrain (providing a 4+ cover save) and difficult terrain.

Ruins without bases

If the ruin has not been mounted on a base, then the ground floor is not counted as either difficult terrain or area terrain. Of course, units will still have to take difficult terrain tests if they move through the walls or if they climb to the upper floors (see opposite).

COPING WITH DIFFERENT HEIGHTS

With units in ruins you will often need to measure weapon ranges between models on different levels and at different heights. Measure the distance from base to base, holding your tape measure at an angle as necessary. Sometimes a wall of rubble or an exposed stanchion will get in the way and you'll find it difficult, or impossible, to accurately measure the distance. Should this happen, it's more than acceptable to estimate based on what you can measure.

UNIT COHERENCY

In the course of movement, it is possible that several models from the same unit may end up spread across two or more levels of a ruin. When this happens, the models in the unit maintain unit coherency as long as any part of the body of a model on a lower level is within 2" of the base of a model that is higher up. This means that you measure up 2" from the head of a model on one level to the base of the model on the next level up, and so on. Players should be generous when measuring for very short models, like swarms, which otherwise may be unable to spread over several levels of a ruin (give them a break – they're only little!).

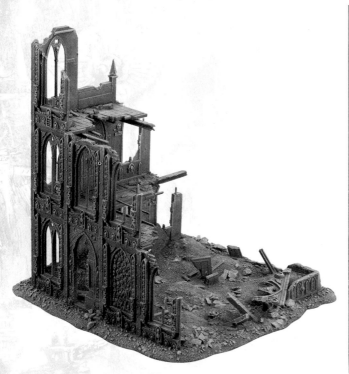

An example of a two-storey ruin mounted on a base.

The Space Marines in this squad are in unit coherency.

MOVING WITHIN RUINS

Only certain troops are capable of clambering to the upper levels of ruins. Accordingly, only infantry, jump infantry, jetbikes, monstrous creatures and walkers may move on the upper levels of a ruin – and only if the model can physically be placed there. Other units may only move on the ground level of the ruin.

Infantry, monstrous creatures and walkers

Even though different building models can vary in this respect, we assume that every level of a ruin is 3" tall. A model moving on foot in a ruin therefore needs 3" of its movement to go up or down a level. As ruins are difficult terrain, this means that if a 1 or 2 is rolled, a model may not make any vertical movement (but may still move horizontally on its level). If a 3 is rolled, the model can either move up to 3" horizontally or simply go up or down a level without any horizontal movement. If a 4 or 5 is rolled, a model can either move horizontally up to the maximum rolled or go up/down a level as well as moving its remaining 1" or 2" horizontally. On a result of 6, the model will be able to go up/down two levels if it does not move horizontally at all, or move one level up/down and horizontally for the remaining 3".

Jump infantry and jetbikes

Remember that jetbikes, and jump infantry that are using their packs, are not hindered by difficult terrain, and may move over any terrain as part of their move without penalty.

However, if these models start or end their move in difficult terrain (such as a ruin!), they must take a dangerous terrain test. All surviving models are then simply placed within 12" of their starting point, including on a different level of a ruin (as shown in the diagram on the right).

Walls, doors, ladders and lateral thinking

Should troops be able to move through walls if there is no door? That's really down to what you and your opponent decide. It's perfectly acceptable to assume the combatants on both sides have brought plenty of cutting tools, acidic disintegrators or naked ferocity to muscle their way through any wall so foolish as to block their path. Indeed, the normal rules for moving through difficult terrain allow you to do just this. Equally you could decide that models can only pass from one side of a wall to the other if they walk around, or if there is a door, window, grate or similar handy opening.

The same is true of ascending and descending levels within a ruin. It's just as valid to assume that the combatants should be able to climb the few feet from one floor to the other as it is to disallow models from climbing higher in a ruin that has no ladders. Just remember that the more involved your rules for ruins are, the longer the game will take.

The Space Marine's difficult terrain roll of 5 allows him to move 2" horizontally and one level up (3").

The jetbike has passed its dangerous terrain test and can therefore move up to 12" through the ruin.

"A fortress is a living thing: the commander its brain, the walls its bones, the sensors its eyes and ears, the troops its blood, their weapons its fists. This tells us two things: If one organ fails, the whole dies. And if the whole dies, no single organ can survive alone."

Mordin Barr

TEMPLATE AND BLAST WEAPONS

Multi-level ruins require certain conventions and clarifications to ensure that template and blast weapons behave in a consistent fashion, and to keep the game moving.

When firing template or blast weapons at models in a ruin, it can be tricky to physically place the marker or template over the models in question. The best way to gauge which models are actually under the template is to simply hold the template above the entire ruin, and look down through it. This is illustrated below.

The method for placing templates and markers over ruins requires a degree of trust between players, especially when intervening floors obscure your view of the affected models.

Remember that once you have used the template or blast marker to work out how many models are hit, casualties can be removed from anywhere in the squad, including models completely out of the firer's sight.

Blast weapons

When firing a weapon with a blast marker into a ruin, declare which floor you are aiming at, and continue as normal. If a blast weapon scatters, it can still only hit models on the level declared as the target.

The Space Marine player has declared that he is targeting the Genestealers on the ground level, and so those on the higher levels are unaffected, even though they are beneath the marker.

It is easiest to hold blast markers and templates above the ruin and look down.

> "There can be no bystanders in the battle for survival. Anyone who will not fight by your side is an enemy you must crush."
>
> Scriptorus Munificantus

The Tau Empire player declares that his Hammerhead tank is targeting the Genestealers on the first level. The shot scatters, and although there are still models under the marker, none are on the level declared as the target, so no hits are scored.

Barrage weapons

Barrage weapons work by lobbing munitions high into the air, bringing death to the enemy from above. The advantage of these indirect fire weapons is that they can be used to engage targets beyond the limited lines of sight. The disadvantage is that they explode the moment they strike a structure, meaning warriors can shelter deep within the ruin.

Barrage weapons always strike the highest level that is under the hole in the centre of the marker. Only models on this level and under the template are actually hit.

Template weapons

When targeting a unit in a ruin, template weapons (such as a flamer) may only affect models under the template on a single level. This can be on the same level as the firer, or one level higher or lower. The firer must declare which level is being targeted before placing the template.

A skimmer, jump infantry or jetbike model that fires a template weapon may target models on any single level of the ruin.

RUINS AND ASSAULTS

Once an assault begins, both friendly and enemy models can end up scattered all over the ruin. For the sake of simplicity, the same principle described for unit coherency is used to determine which models are engaged in an assault. That is to say, distances between models on different levels are measured between the heads of the models on the lower level to the bases of the models on the upper levels (see page 82).

In some cases the ruin might genuinely be unstable or uneven, or the space could be very limited on a particular level, making it impossible to move assaulting models into base-to-base contact with the unit they wish to assault. When this happens, it is perfectly acceptable to place models as close to their foe as is safely possible, including the level below or above, providing that you place the assaulting models as close as possible to their opponents and you make clear to your opponent which of your models are in base-to-base contact with his models. We find that directly below or above works well, representing them charging up or down a flight of stairs.

"There will be no retreat from Hades Hive. We will fight to the end."

Commissar Yarrick

As the hole in the marker hits the upper level first, only one model is hit by the barrage weapon.

The middle level is declared as the target of the flamer and therefore only two Genestealers are hit. Note that the top level is not a valid target as it is too high up.

All of the models in the picture are engaged and can fight except for models A and B, which are not within 2" of a member of their unit that is in base contact with the enemy.

ORGANISING A BATTLE

Now that you've learned the rules for moving, shooting and fighting with your army, we'll look at how to organise a game of Warhammer 40,000, including how to choose your forces, how to set up the battlefield and how to select a mission to play.

ORGANISING A BATTLE

1 **Agree points limit & choose forces**

2 **Prepare the Battlefield**

3 **Select a Mission**

4 **Deploy Forces**

5 **Start the game!**

AGREE POINTS LIMIT & CHOOSE FORCES

A game of Warhammer 40,000 can use as many models as you can collect. The army lists included in the Warhammer 40,000 Codex books specify the precise characteristics and abilities of each troop type, detail the maximum and minimum size of each unit and provide a points value for each model. The better a combatant is, the more points it will cost. Normally a soldier will have a basic cost, which is then increased if you upgrade his equipment or abilities.

The most popular approach to playing a game of Warhammer 40,000 involves both you and your opponent selecting forces to a previously agreed points limit. A limit of 1,500 or 2,000 points per side produces a well-balanced game that can be concluded in a few hours. A 500 points game is still very entertaining, feeling like a clash of patrols, and normally lasts less than an hour. Larger games take proportionally longer, and you might expect a 3,000 points game or more to take the entire day – perfect for a rainy Sunday!

As you build up your armies and become more comfortable with the rules, you will no doubt crave opportunities to get your entire figure collection onto the battlefield and play with bigger points values. Don't be in a mad rush to play huge points-limit games. It is easier to start small and gain familiarity with the rules rather than trying to master everything at once. You will inevitably forget things in your first few games, so it will help to play a number of small, quick games to learn the ropes before moving up to a larger battle.

The first thing players need to do when arranging a game is to decide what points limit they are going to use. For example, they may agree to play a 1,000 points game, in which case the total value of all models in each player force must come to 1,000 points or less (it will often be a few points short, but it still counts as a 1,000 points game).

FORCE ORGANISATION

Once they have agreed a points limit, the players will pick their forces. The best way to do this is to use the full army lists in the relevant Codex book for each army, but players just starting out can use any models that they have in their collection. As detailed in each army's Codex, all the forces you can use are categorised broadly by categories that tell you something about the role they play in the army. These roles are normally: HQ, Troops, Elites, Fast Attack and Heavy Support. Occasionally, a Codex might introduce new categories or give them alternative names, which better reflect their role in the army in question, but such exceptions will be clearly explained in the Codex's army list section.

HQ

A Headquarters unit might be a single heroic commander or fearsome monster. These models are amongst the most powerful in the game, as leaders will generally have access to more special equipment than everyone else. They are not invincible, but can provide a powerful spearhead for an attacking army, and a strong core for a defensive one. Every army contains at least one Headquarters unit to command it.

Troops

These represent the most commonly available soldiers in an army. This does not mean they are poor fighters though; the category includes such troops as Space Marines and Ork Boyz, both formidable adversaries. These are the warriors that make up the bulk of an army, and every army will have at least two such units. These units' main tactical role is that of consolidating the gains of the army and defending the objectives that have been taken by the army's more specialised units.

Elites

Elite units are normally powerful but expensive. They are the best soldiers an army has to offer, but there are never enough of them. In some cases they will be specialists, while at other times they will be more experienced versions of the regular soldiers.

Fast Attack

Fast Attack units are generally (surprise, surprise!) faster than their comrades and are masters at manoeuvre. Often they are responsible for reconnaissance and scouting, while at other times they are assault troops relying on speed to strike at the heart of the enemy.

Heavy Support

Heavy Support units are literally the big guns of the army. In this section you will find the heaviest items of equipment and the toughest creatures. However, these units are also very expensive in points, so an over-reliance on them might leave you badly outnumbered.

FORCE ORGANISATION CHART

The minimum and maximum numbers of each of these types of unit for each army are detailed on the force organisation chart of each army Codex book. Shown on this page is an example of one such chart, which is the one used by most armies for standard missions (i.e. the three missions presented later in this section).

One box on the chart allows you to make one selection from that part of your army list. Dark boxes are compulsory selections. As you can see, normally you will have to take at least one HQ selection and two Troops selections. These compulsory choices ensure that whatever else you select, your force will have a core within it that is representative of that army. This is rarely a disadvantage and many players often use the maximum number of Troops selections.

Sometimes a single choice on the force organisation chart will allow you to select more than one unit. This will always be explained in the appropriate Codex, so be sure to read it carefully.

Dedicated transports

Dedicated transport vehicles sit outside the Force Organisation structure, as they are attached to the unit they are bought for. When this distinction is called for (for example in some missions or deployment types), dedicated transport vehicles count as being from the same force organisation category as the unit they were bought for. For example, a Rhino bought for a Space Marine Tactical Squad (Troops) counts as a unit of Troops, but if it was bought for a unit of Veterans (Elites) it counts as Elites.

Other exceptions

Quite a few Codex books include units that, much like dedicated transports, are not part of the army's force organisation chart. This may be because they are too puny, specialised support units, or simply not part of the main fighting forces of that race. Often labelled with terms such as 'supernumerary' or 'insignificant', these units normally do not count towards the number of choices the player can make from the force organisation chart and have rules that will clearly tell the player how many can be included in his force.

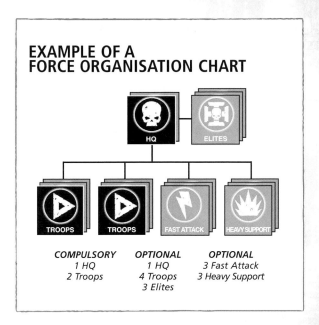

EXAMPLE OF A FORCE ORGANISATION CHART

COMPULSORY	OPTIONAL	OPTIONAL
1 HQ	1 HQ	3 Fast Attack
2 Troops	4 Troops	3 Heavy Support
	3 Elites	

Multiple detachment games

As your collection of miniatures grows, the urge to use them all at once will become hard to resist. Above a total of 2,500 points, the force organisation chart deliberately becomes a very limiting factor. The chart allows you to build the minimum sized force that can reasonably be expected to complete a mission. On a larger scale, an army will consist of many such detachments, each performing separate missions. If you want to play an especially large game then, as well as agreeing a points limit, you should also agree a maximum number of detachments. Each detachment will be a separate army, using its own force organisation chart.

Non-standard missions

Players may of course make up their own missions, varying the way units are deployed, the victory conditions, the terrain, or even adding their own mission special rules to represent artillery barrages, volcanic eruptions, alien teleportation devices or anything else you can think of. They may also decide to vary the force organisation chart, to represent different forces, more suitable to their missions. They may want to change the compulsory/optional units, or increase, decrease or remove altogether one kind of unit (no Heavy Support and two compulsory Fast Attack units, representing a rapid insertion force, for example). More examples of non-standard missions can be found on page 266 and in other Warhammer 40,000 supplements (explained on page 274 and 278).

PREPARE THE BATTLEFIELD

THE GAMING SURFACE

Standard missions are designed to be played on a 6'x4' gaming surface, with each player sitting behind one of the long table edges ('his own' table edge, see diagram below). The concept of 'own' table edge is important, because when units fall back, they will always fall back towards 'their own table edge'. We assume this is in the direction of their base of operations. The remaining two edges of the gaming surface are referred to as the two 'short table edges', which do not belong to any player, as shown in the diagram below.

If you are playing a game with a very large or small points limit, you may want to consider larger or smaller gaming surfaces. Whatever the size and shape of your table, it is important to establish the different table edges as described.

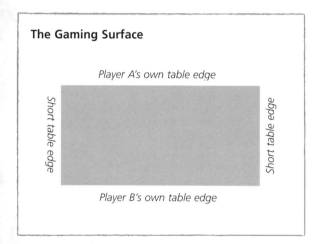

The Gaming Surface

Player A's own table edge

Short table edge

Short table edge

Player B's own table edge

SETTING UP TERRAIN

Setting up a well-modelled, interesting battlefield will enhance the enjoyment that you get from playing a game of Warhammer 40,000. Many players will collect several armies before considering the possibility of investing in some good terrain. This is a shame, as a new set-up for your games can breathe fresh life into the most heavily played armies and missions. Adapting your tactics from fighting in rolling woodland to capturing buildings, ruins and other heavily defended positions is both challenging and fun.

It is best if the players place the terrain together, ensuring that the set-up is acceptable to them both. Alternatively, you may ask a third person to set up the terrain in a fair manner. A third common way of setting up the terrain is for the player hosting the game (or arriving first at the club) to set the terrain up, and for the other player to automatically win the roll to choose who deploys first (see missions). In tournament play, terrain will normally be pre-set by the organisers.

HOW MUCH TERRAIN?

As a general rule in Warhammer 40,000, the more terrain, the better the gaming experience. If you use too little terrain, games will be short and not very satisfactory, with too much advantage going to the player who gets to shoot first. For a balanced game, where close combat troops have a chance to get into contact with the enemy without being completely blown away in a couple of turns, we expect that about a quarter of the total playing surface should have terrain on it. The assumption here is that if terrain pieces are roughly 12" by 12", then six or seven pieces are needed to fulfil the 25% recommendation on a standard 6'x4' table (of course these dimensions are approximate and terrain features like woods should not be square, as irregular features look much better!).

In your terrain collection there should be a good mixture of types. An equal division between terrain which interferes with line of sight and provides cover (such as woods or ruins), terrain which provides cover, but does not block line of sight (such as barricades, craters, scrubland and low rubble) and terrain which blocks line of sight completely (such as hills, rocky outcrops, buildings, etc.) makes for good tactical play. It is best to build your terrain collection with this in mind, otherwise the game balance could be seriously affected. Terrain that completely blocks line of sight is particularly important. Too much of it and your ranged firepower will be seriously impaired favouring assault troops; too little and the game will turn into a shooting match, with very little movement or tactical choices.

DEFINE THE TERRAIN

Before continuing, you should agree with your opponent how to define each piece of terrain you are using (see pages 13 and 77 for more details). This doesn't take more than a few minutes, but it is important to do before the battle starts – otherwise it has a tendency to cause confusion and arguments in the middle of the game. Of course if you are playing with your usual adversary on the same terrain that you always do, this will be as simple as saying "Just like last time, okay?" However with a less familiar opponent, or if you are playing over some new terrain, remember to clarify the following:

- Which terrain pieces are **area terrain**, **difficult terrain** or **dangerous terrain** (or a combination)?

- Which terrain pieces are **impassable terrain**?

- Which terrain pieces are **ruins**?

- What **cover saves** do different terrain pieces confer?

- Which buildings are **impassable**?

- What are the **Armour Values**, **fire points**, **access points** and **capacity** for any buildings?

EXAMPLE BATTLEFIELDS

Wilderness outpost

The battlefield on the right has been based around the wargaming terrain staples – woods and hills – with the addition of some other elements to provide the Warhammer 40,000 flavour. The players have taken turns to place the 'wilderness' elements of the terrain, and because neither knows yet where his army will be deploying, they have both taken care to ensure there is an even spread over the table. This means that wherever their forces end up, there will be some cover nearby.

The use of a bastion makes it clear that the battle is set in the 41st Millennium. Because whichever side occupies this building will have a useful advantage, the players have agreed to place it in the centre of the table – the armies will have to fight to gain its protection. The road will allow vehicles to cross the board quickly, in order to transport passengers or contest objectives themselves – plus it really adds to the look of the battlefield.

A fortified bastion is sure to be the focus of fierce fighting.

Hills provide good vantage points for shooting.

Woods allow troops to advance in cover.

Vehicles can move faster on a road.

Small squads can shelter from enemy fire within craters.

Large piles of rubble break up the line of sight across the table.

War-torn settlement

In the example on the left, one player has set up all the scenery, arranging it to represent a small settlement, blasted and ruined by years of war. His opponent will then get to decide whether to deploy first or second, thereby choosing the best angle of attack.

The various ruins will block models' views across the table, forcing units to manoeuvre and advance on the enemy. Of course models in the upper levels of the ruins will have a great vantage point, so these structures will be tactically important – especially if objectives are placed within them. The piles of rubble and barricades provide cover for warriors, as do the craters. Squads that run from one piece of terrain to the next will be able to stay protected from enemy fire.

Barricades will offer protection while troops close with the foe.

Upper levels of the ruins provide great firing positions.

Serve the Emperor today, tomorrow you may be dead.

SELECT A MISSION

Missions define how to work out which side has won, dictating the tactics that the players will have to employ during the battle. The three standard missions in this section are the most common way Warhammer 40,000 battles are played. They are relatively simple, and do not require an army that is designed specifically towards a single style of play. You can either agree with your opponent which mission to play, or roll D6 and consult the chart below:

STANDARD MISSIONS CHART

D6	Mission
1-2	Seize Ground
3-4	Capture and Control
5-6	Annihilation

ENDING THE GAME

Standard missions last a random number of game turns – between five and seven. At the end of game turn 5, a player must roll a dice. On a 1-2 the game ends immediately, on a 3+ game turn 6 is played. If this is the case, a player will roll another dice at the end of game turn 6, and this time on a 4+ the game continues and game turn 7 is played. At the end of game turn 7, the game ends automatically.

In standard missions, as soon as the game ends and before working out victory conditions, all units that are falling back are removed and count as destroyed.

WIPEOUT!

Regardless of the victory conditions, if at the end of any standard mission your enemy has no units left on the table, you win the game!

SCORING UNITS

During a military campaign the most powerful and specialised units assault the objectives and take them. They then forge ahead to the next objective, engaging the enemy with lightning-fast assaults and irresistible armoured thrusts. It is left to the grunts, the squads making up the bulk of any fighting force, to dig in and consolidate any territorial gains, defending the objectives from any enemy counter-attack.

The concept of scoring units is central to the first two standard missions, which are won or lost by controlling more objectives than the enemy (see those mission's victory conditions), and only scoring units can do that.

An army's scoring units are all the units that come from its **Troops** allowance. The presence of other units may deny an objective to the enemy, but only Troops can control it. There are a few exceptions, however, when a unit of Troops does not count as scoring:

- If it is a vehicle.

- If it has the Swarm special rule.

- If it has a special rule specifying it never counts as a scoring unit.

Unit of Troops embarked in a transport can control objectives (measure the distance to their vehicle's hull).

SEIZE GROUND

The battlefield is strewn with discarded equipment, wounded comrades, supplies and other detritus of war that, for various reasons, you wish to recover. You must fight off the enemy while scouring the field to secure as many of these vital objectives as you can.

Victory Conditions

Before deciding deployment zones (see next section – Deploy Forces), the players must determine the position of D3+2 objectives. The winner of a roll-off chooses a point on the table to be an objective (by placing a counter on it, choosing a detail of a terrain feature, or any other method that is equally clear). Then the opponent does the same, and the players alternate choosing a point on the table until the position of all the objectives has been determined.

These objectives may not be in impassable terrain, nor within 12" of a table edge or another objective.

After positioning the objectives, deployment of the forces begins, as described in the type of deployment being used.

At the end of the game you control an objective if there is at least one of your scoring units, and no enemy unit (any unit, whether scoring or not), within 3" of it. As different objectives vary in shape and size, it is important to agree at the beginning of the game exactly where this distance will be measured from.

The player controlling the most objectives wins. If the players control the same number of objectives, the game is a tactical draw.

CAPTURE AND CONTROL

Both sides are attempting to capture the enemy base of operations or another similarly vital objective, whilst defending their own.

Victory Conditions

After deciding deployment zones, but before deploying any unit (see next section – Deploy Forces), starting with the player that will deploy first, each player chooses a point in his own deployment zone to be an objective (by placing a counter on it, choosing a detail of a terrain feature, or any other method that is equally clear). These objectives may not be in impassable terrain or within 24" of the other objective.

After positioning the objectives, deployment of the forces begins, as described in the type of deployment being used.

At the end of the game you control an objective if there is at least one of your scoring units, and no enemy unit (any unit, whether scoring or not), within 3" of it. As different objectives vary in shape and size, it is important to agree at the beginning of the game exactly where this distance will be measured from.

The player controlling the most objectives wins. If the players control the same number of objectives, the game is a tactical draw.

ANNIHILATION

Some battles are fought with only one goal – find your enemy, crush him utterly and take away his means to mount further resistance.

Victory Conditions

At the end of the game, each player receives 1 'kill point' for each enemy unit that has been completely destroyed.

If a character has a retinue, the character and his unit are worth 1 kill point each.

The player with the highest total of kill points wins. If the players have the same total, the game is a tactical draw.

"Strike fast and suddenly. Attack without warning. Secure victory before the foe is aware of the danger.

Remember always, a war is easily won if your enemy does not know he is fighting."

Maxims of Lord General Solar Macharius

DEPLOY FORCES

Sometimes battles occur between forces that have been in place for weeks, carefully preparing their positions, while at other times a skirmish between patrols escalates into a major engagement, with reserves pouring in from other sectors. You can either agree with your opponent which type of deployment to use for your armies, or roll a D6 and consult the chart:

DEPLOYMENT TYPE CHART

D6	Deployment type
1-2	Pitched Battle
3-4	Spearhead
5-6	Dawn of War

A NOTE ON SECRECY

To keep things fair, you should always allow your opponent to read your force roster after a game. In the same spirit, always make clear to your opponent which squads are embarked in which transport vehicle. However, before starting to deploy their armies, it is a good idea for players to agree whether or not they can read the opponent's force roster before and during the game. Some players prefer full disclosure (which is the norm in tournaments, for example), as they want to concentrate on outmanoeuvring the enemy rather than springing a secret trump card on them. Others prefer to leave a feel of secrecy around their lists, as bluffing can make a game really entertaining. The choice is yours!

MISSION SPECIAL RULES

All standard missions and deployment types use the following mission special rules, detailed on pages 94 and 95: 'reserves' and 'deep strike'.

INFILTRATORS AND SCOUTS

In all three types of deployment, the sequence is the same. First the players deploy their forces (apart from any unit left in reserve or that chose to use their 'infiltrate' special rule). Then they deploy their infiltrators (as described on page 75), and finally they move units with the 'scouts' special rule (see page 76).

MULTIPLE UNIT CHOICES

Note that occasionally the Codexes allow the player to include several units in his army at the cost of a single force organisation slot (like dedicated transports, etc.). Apart from being bought as a single choice, these units operate and count as separate units in all respects.

SEIZE THE INITIATIVE!

In war, no plan survives contact with the enemy. In any standard mission, just before the player that should go first begins his first turn, the opponent can decide to try to steal the initiative, catching the enemy flat-footed. If he decides to do so, he rolls a dice. On a result of a 6, he will go first instead, immediately beginning his first turn (and no, the opponent cannot then try to seize the initiative back again!).

PITCHED BATTLE – Long Table Edges

In the most classic style of engagement, the two opposing forces deploy in battle formation and advance head-to-head, guns blazing.

The table is divided lengthways into two halves, by drawing an imaginary line through the middle of the short table edges. For example, a 6'x4' table would have two 6'x2' halves.

The players roll-off, and the winner chooses to go first or second. The player that goes first then chooses one of the long table edges to be his own table edge. He then deploys his force in his half of the table, with all models more than 12" away from the table's middle line (this is his 'deployment zone'). His opponent then deploys in the opposite half.

Deploy any infiltrators and make any scout moves.

Start the game! Once deployment has finished, the player that chose his deployment zone first starts game Turn 1 with his first player turn.

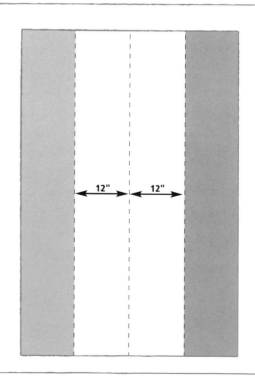

SPEARHEAD – Table Quarters

Both armies are trying to outflank the enemy, when contact is made and battle erupts.

The table is divided into four quarters, formed by drawing two imaginary perpendicular lines through the centre point. So a 6'x4' table would have four 3'x2' quarters.

The players roll-off, and the winner chooses to go first or second. The player that goes first then chooses one of the long table edges to be his own table edge. He then deploys his force in one of the two table quarters on his side the table, more than 12" away from the centre of the table (this is his 'deployment zone'). His opponent then deploys in the diagonally opposite quarter.

Deploy any infiltrators and make any scout moves.

Start the game! Once deployment has finished, the player that chose his deployment zone first starts game Turn 1 with his first player turn.

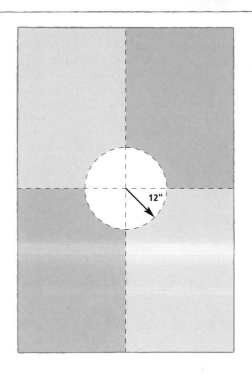

DAWN OF WAR – Table Halves

A clash of patrols escalates into a major engagement as the sun rises and reinforcements begin to pour in.

The table is divided lengthways into two halves.

The players roll-off, and the winner chooses to go first or second. The player that goes first then chooses one of the long table edges to be his own table edge. He then can deploy up to two units from his Troops selections and up to one unit from his HQ selections in his half of the table (this is his 'deployment zone'). His opponent then does the same in the opposite half, but must position his three units more than 18" from enemy units.

Troops and HQ units that can infiltrate, can do so, as long as at the end of deployment the player still has a maximum of one HQ and two Troops units on the table. Lastly, players make any scout moves.

Start the game! Once deployment has finished, the player that chose his deployment zone first starts game Turn 1 with his first player turn.

All units that were not deployed, and were not declared to be in reserve during deployment, must enter the game in the Movement phase of their first player turn by moving in from their own table edge, just like units moving in from reserve.

During game Turn 1 the Night Fighting mission special rule is in effect.

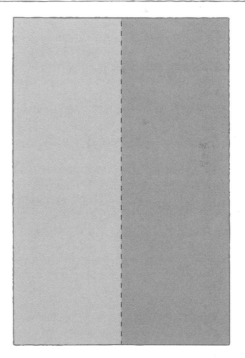

Example: player A wins the roll-off and deploys an infantry unit from his Troops and one monstrous creature from his HQ, in his half of the table. He also declares that a second infantry unit from his Troops will use its Infiltrate ability. In his half of the table, player B then deploys a unit of Troops, already embarked into their dedicated transport (which is his second unit of Troops). He then deploys an independent character from his HQ, joining the unit embarked in the transport. Finally, player A deploys his infiltrating unit.

MISSION SPECIAL RULES

The 'reserves' and 'deep strike' special rules given here are used in all standard missions. 'Night fighting' is used with the Dawn of War deployment type.

Of course, players may like to add other special rules and design their own own when creating new missions (more on this can be found on page 266).

RESERVES

Reserves are forces in the same sector as the units on the battlefield who can be called in to reinforce them at relatively short notice.

Preparing reserves

When deploying their army, players may choose not to deploy one or more of the units in their army and instead leave them in reserve. Units in reserve will become available in later turns of the game.

During deployment, when declaring which units are left in reserve, the player must clearly explain the organisation of his reserves to the opponent.

First he must specify to the opponent if any of his independent characters left in reserve are joining a unit, in which case they will be rolled for and will arrive together, or not in which case they will count as a separate unit when rolling for reserves.

Similarly, the player must specify if any transport vehicle in reserve is carrying any of the infantry units and/or independent characters in reserve. If they do, the unit and the transport will be rolled for together and will arrive together. Remember that a dedicated transport can only be deployed, and consequently can only be kept in reserve, either empty or transporting the unit it was selected with (plus any independent characters).

If units in reserve have the 'deep strike', 'scout' or 'infiltrate' special rule, the player must declare to his opponent, during army deployment, whether they are going to use their special rules to deep strike/outflank or they are going to enter from his own table edge when they will become available (see Arriving from Reserve). This decision may not be changed later.

Rolling for reserves

At the start of each of his Movement phases except the first, before moving any unit, the player must roll a dice for each of his units in reserve. Depending on the turn in question, a certain result will mean that the unit has arrived. For example, on Turn 1 no reserves arrive, on Turn 2 the player needs a 4+ for a unit to arrive, and so on until Turn 5, when any units left will arrive automatically (see the Reserves table on this page).

Once all of the units have been rolled for, the player picks any one of the units arriving and deploys it, moving it onto the table as described later. Then he picks another unit and deploys it, and so on until all

RESERVES TABLE

Turn	Unit arrives on a roll of:
1	N/A
2	4+
3	3+
4	2+
5+	Automatic

arriving units are on the table. The player may then proceed to move his other units as normal.

Note: you must roll for reserves as soon as possible and must bring them onto the table as soon as they are available. You may not delay making the dice rolls or keep the reserves hanging around off-table until you decide you need them!

Arriving from reserve

When a reserve unit arrives, it must move onto the table from the controlling player's own table edge (unless it's deep striking or outflanking). Each model's move is measured from the edge of the battlefield, as if they had been positioned just off the board in the previous turn and moved as normal. This means it is incorrect to place a model on the board touching the edge and then move it – this would mean it moved too far, especially in the case of large vehicles.

If a unit has a special rule forcing it to move in a specific direction (such as 'rage', for example) or that could stop it from moving, the rule is ignored in the phase when it arrives from Reserve.

Certain rare units are permanently immobile. If a unit like this cannot be deployed (for example in the Dawn of War deployment), or the player decides to keep it in reserve, it will enter the game by deep strike. This represents the immobile unit being airdropped or teleported into battle.

Outflank

During deployment, players may declare that units with the 'scout' or 'infiltrate' special rules are attempting to outflank the enemy. This means they are making a wide sweeping move to come at the foe from an unexpected direction. When an outflanking unit arrives from reserve the controlling player rolls a dice: on a 1-2 the unit will come in from the short table edge on the player's left; on a 3-4 they will come from the right, on a 5-6 the player can choose left or right. Models move onto the table as described for other reserves, above. Note that if such units are picked from their army list together with a dedicated transport, they may outflank with their transport, but if they do so they must move onto the table embarked in it.

DEEP STRIKE

Some units' special rules allow them to enter play via tunnelling, teleportation, flying, or some other extraordinary means. If you wish to use this 'deep strike' option, then the units in question must begin the game in reserve (even if you are playing a special mission where the 'reserves' special rule is not being used). Roll for arrival of these units as specified in the rules for reserves and then deploy them as follows.

First place one model from the unit anywhere on the table, in the position you would like the unit to arrive, and roll the scatter dice. If you roll a hit the model stays where it is, but if an arrow is shown this determines the direction the model is scattered in. If a scatter occurs, roll 2D6 to see how many inches the model moves away from the intended position.

Once this is done, the unit's remaining models are arranged around the first one. Models must be placed in base contact with the original model in a circle around it. When the first circle is complete, a further circle should be placed with each model touching the circle inside it. Each circle should include as many models as will fit.

Models arriving via deep strike treat all difficult terrain as dangerous terrain.

In the Movement phase when they arrive, these units may not move any further, other than to disembark from a deep striking transport vehicle. Units deep striking into ruined buildings are placed on the ground floor. They may not deep strike directly inside a transport vehicle or a building, which will count as impassable terrain as normal.

In that turn's Shooting phase, these units can fire (or run) as normal, and obviously count as having moved in the previous Movement phase. Vehicles count as having moved at cruising speed.

In that turn's Assault phase, however, these units may not launch an assault (even if they have the 'fleet' special rule), unless clearly stated in their special rules – they are too disrupted by their deep strike move.

Note that some units always have the option to deep strike, while others may only arrive in this way in missions where the deep strike special rule is used. Of course all the standard missions presented here do use deep strike, so normally you won't need to worry about this distinction.

Even a man who has nothing can still offer his life.

Deep strike mishaps

Teleporting or dropping onto a crowded battlefield may prove extremely dangerous, as one may arrive miles away from the intended objective or even inside solid rock! If any of the models in a deep striking unit cannot be deployed because they would land off the table, in impassable terrain, on top of a friendly model, or on top or within 1" of an enemy model, something has gone wrong. The controlling player must roll on the deep strike Mishap table and apply the results.

DEEP STRIKE MISHAP TABLE

D6   Effect

1-2   Terrible accident! Teleporting troops are lost in the Warp, deep striking jump infantry are shot down with their transport, or some other suitably dramatic event occurs. The entire unit is destroyed!

3-4   Misplaced. Were the coordinates slightly inaccurate, or has the enemy jammed your instruments? Your opponent may deploy the unit anywhere on the table (excluding impassable terrain, but including difficult terrain, which of course counts as dangerous for deep striking units!), in a valid deep strike formation, but without rolling for scatter.

5-6   Delayed. Because of mechanical failure or enemy action, the reinforcements are delayed. The unit is placed back in reserve. If the unit is unlucky enough to roll this result in turn 5 or later and then the game ends while it is still in reserve, it sadly counts as destroyed.

NIGHT FIGHTING

It is much harder to accurately identify enemy units at night; warriors must be sure of their targets before opening fire, and tend to be more cautious than normal. After selecting a target, but before a unit fires, a check needs to be made to see if the firers can clearly spot their target through the darkness. Roll 2D6 and multiply the result by 3, then measure the distance between the two units (remember that distances to/from vehicles are measured to/from their hull, and not their guns). If the distance between the firing unit and their target is higher than the total rolled, the unit cannot fire at all in this Shooting phase, as they search the dark for a target that never appears.

Barrage and ordnance barrage weapons can still fire at targets in the dark, but if they do and fail to roll a hit, they add an extra D6" to the distance scattered.

DARK MILLENNIUM

For 10,000 years, the galaxy spanning Imperium of Mankind has endured, surviving disasters, heresies and invasions from alien races intent on the extinction of humanity. The tide of the Emperor's enemies is only held back by the vigilance of the Imperial fleets and the weapons of humanity's armies. Millions of soldiers fight over a thousand worlds against every conceivable type of foe: from the all-consuming Hive Fleets of the Tyranids and the rampaging invasions of the warmongering Orks to rebellion and insurrection from within.

To be a man in such times is to be one amongst untold billions. It is to live in the cruellest and most bloody regime imaginable. This is the tale of those times.

THE IMPERIUM OF MAN

It is the 41st millennium and Mankind stands on the brink of extinction.

From the palaces of Holy Terra, the High Lords of the Imperium watch as their domain crumbles. Armies and fleets fight on with the valour of heroes, calling for reinforcements that do not exist. In shattered cathedrals on a million worlds, Imperial citizens pray with the desperation of the damned, begging their immortal Emperor for a salvation they shall never see. As the lines of battle draw ever closer to Terra, the light of the Emperor fades and darkness swallows all.

THE EMPEROR

This is the time of the Emperor, the Age of the Imperium. It is an epoch of war already ten thousand years old. In this war mere survival is justly hailed as a victory. Defeat can only lead to the irrevocable end of humanity and to the destruction of the very fabric of the universe. It is a war waged across the galaxy – in the darkness of space, on a million worlds, and within the depths of every human soul. There can be no peace, only the stillness of oblivion.

Four hundred centuries have passed since man stepped out into the cold of space. Forty thousand years. An age so long that its history lies shrouded in legend. Who knows how Mankind came to be scattered across a million disparate worlds? Who remembers the wars that split the Earth asunder and dragged humanity down to the level of brute beasts? Who would recognise the names of Earth's ancient ruins, of nations destroyed and peoples long since crumbled to dust? To these questions there can be no answers. From those times come only whispers of horror and death.

Over one hundred centuries ago the Great and Beneficent Emperor of Mankind ascended to the Golden Throne of Earth. Legends hint darkly at the terrible wars of the Horus Heresy, of the battles that raged across the galaxy, and of the final victory of the Emperor over the thrice-damned Horus and the forces of Chaos. The truth lies buried under millennia of superstition, submerged beneath myth and locked behind adamantine doors sealed with ancient runes of power. The only man who might remember those far-off days is the Emperor himself, and none can guess what thoughts revolve inside his undying skull.

Ten thousand years ago the Emperor lived and breathed as a mortal man, but his physical life has long since ended, crushed out of him by Horus, the Great Enemy, in the final battle for Earth. Today, as for the last ten thousands years, the Emperor lives only by the force of his supreme will. His broken and decayed body is preserved by the stasis fields and psi-fusion reactors of the Golden Throne. His great mind endures inside a rotted carcass, kept alive by the mysteries of ancient technology. His immense psychic powers envelop and protect Mankind across the entire galaxy. His consciousness wanders through Warp space, warring against the Daemons that inhabit it, keeping closed the doors between this world and the next.

If the Emperor fails then the Daemons of Chaos will flood into the galaxy. Every living human will become a gateway for the destruction of Mankind and the stuff of Warp space will submerge the galaxy. There will be no physical matter. No space. No time. Only Chaos.

The spiritual heart of the Imperium is ancient Terra, cradle of the human race. Terra is a sprawling hive of towering metal spires, gothic cathedrals and ancient ruins. Untold billions shuffle through the polluted air, mindlessly eking out their miserable existence beneath the empty gaze of gargoyles and weeping angels. Numberless scribes toil by the candlelight of vaulted scriptoria, collating crucial verities and statistical bibelots of times long since past for reasons long since lost.

Masses of pilgrims arrive each day. Many have travelled their entire lives to set foot upon Terra. Many are trampled to death by their fellows during the journey from shrine to shrine, others are executed by the grim judges of the Adeptus Arbites for straying into restricted areas. Those that survive can expect only a future of penury and wasting death, for the Imperium wastes no resources on those who refuse to help themselves. Yet still the pilgrims come, believing it better to die within sight of the Imperial Palace than to live anywhere else.

Even on a world choked by gothic structure and arcane spires, the Imperial Palace dominates the skyline. It is a sprawling complex of cathedrals, fortresses and palaces, where petty functionaries of all ranks scurry to perform the business of empire. Ten thousand heroes guard the approach to the Imperial Palace's walls, ten thousand statues as colossal in stature as they are in memory. To speak their names is to invoke the greatest moments in human history. Dorn the Unwavering, Maldorus the Pure, Dracos the Conqueror – the list goes on. In another time and place these men would have been gods, for their deeds delivered Mankind from the blackest of days. Here they are retainers, watching over in death the Emperor they served in life.

THE ADEPTUS TERRA

The Emperor has not spoken nor moved since his incarceration in the arcane mechanism of the Golden Throne. His material body is to all intents dead, and his psychic mind is wholly preoccupied within Warp space, fighting for the preservation of Mankind. All that is left of the Emperor is consciousness divorced from the material world, incapable of ordinary communication with his billions of devoted servants.

The Imperium is ruled in the Emperor's name by the incalculably vast Adeptus Terra, the ancient Priesthood of Earth, whose masters are the High Lords of Terra. The Adeptus Terra numbers billions upon billions of individuals on Earth alone. Its offices span the galaxy and its powers extend to every human world. No man is free from its influence or from the strictures of its rule. The Emperor has become a god and saviour to sprawling Mankind. Superstition and dogma have become the rituals of worship.

The Adeptus Terra is a huge and multi-faceted organisation. It is divided and subdivided into countless subordinate organisations, millions of offices each with awesome powers over the common man. Indeed, the Adeptus Terra is so vast that no one can say with certainly how many divisions work under its banner, nor what their purpose may be. Ten thousand years of endeavour has built an edifice that reaches into the heart of human society. Information is gathered; facts are accumulated; taxes are levied. Like an ancient and ponderous clock, the wheels of bureaucracy grind slowly forward, carried by their own momentum, without thought or consideration. Only a very few of the most important of these vast organisations are known to the average citizen – it is doubtful anyone knows the full extent of the Adeptus Terra.

So vast is the Imperium, so colossal are the distances and delays in communication between branches of the labyrinthine hierarchy that centralised rule and accurate census are impossible. Billions of citizens die every day, tiny embers lost against the backdrop of the stars, their passing unnoticed for a thousand years or perhaps not even noted at all. Orders issued by the High Lords must run the gauntlet of the Imperium's ponderous bureaucracy, passing down through Segmentum commanders, sector and sub-sector administrators before reaching planetary governors who must enact those edicts. Such communications are prone to alteration, so the orders a governor receives will often bear little resemblance to those that were issued. Pleas for aid or clarification may not be acted upon for centuries, whilst the request plies its uncertain path to a functionary senior enough to take action. Indeed, it is not uncommon for fleets and armies to arrive at a war zone to discover the conflict they were despatched to wage has long since concluded. So it is that some worlds fall into anarchy or are abandoned to a terrible fate through simply being forgotten, having slipped through the cracks of the Imperial bureaucracy.

AN EMPIRE AMONG THE STARS

The Imperium of Man comprises a million inhabited worlds, stretching from the furthest reaches of the Eastern Fringe to the distant Halo Stars. Although this is a huge number of planets, it is as nothing when compared to the immense size of the galaxy itself. The Imperium is spread very thinly across space: its worlds are dotted through the void and divided by hundreds, if not thousands of light years. It is therefore wrong to think of the Imperium in terms of a territory which extends across the galaxy. The truth is far more complex. The Imperium's holdings are scattered far and wide by the vagaries of Warp travel and spatial drift. One inhabited system may be separated from its nearest neighbour by alien civilisations, unstable Warp storms, dimensional cascades or unexplored space. Indeed, Mankind's ignorance of his environs far exceeds his meagre knowledge, for humanity has yet to explore much of the galaxy. Who knows what ancient secrets lie undiscovered and undisturbed amongst the stars?

The pattern of human settlement throughout the galaxy owes much to the nature of space travel. All interstellar travel is undertaken using Warp drives that launch a spacecraft into the alternative dimension of Warp space. Within Warp space a ship can cover the equivalent of many thousands of light years within a relatively short time, dropping back into real space far away from its starting point. The unpredictable and turbulent nature of Warp space means that some parts of the galaxy are harder to reach than others. Some zones are eternally isolated by swirling Warp storms,

dichotomic turbulence and violent currents within the ether. Other areas can only be reached by difficult and dangerous routes, or are accessible only during lulls in the fierce fluctuations of the Warp. Some parts of Warp space act as dimensional vortices, ensnaring spacecraft and tearing them apart with impossible forces. In others, time flows disjointedly with the material realm. Days become nanoseconds, minutes stretch into years, and the future spirals into the past.

"You might as well throw a traveller into a sea of sharks and tell him to swim home as send him through the Warp unprotected."

Fra Safrane, 5th aide to Navigator Da'el

The Imperium's mastery of Warp space is born of three factors. The first is the maintenance of ancient technology by the Adeptus Mechanicus – the Tech Priests of Mars who preserve the lore of ancient science on behalf of the Adeptus Terra. Without the technological advantage of efficient Warp engines it would be impossible for the Imperium to defend its scattered planets. The second factor is the existence of human mutants known as Navigators – a race apart which traces its origins to the uncertain times of the Dark Age of Technology.

Warp space is an alternative dimension composed of energy, as opposed to the physical matter of the material universe. There are dangers within the Warp which can wreck spacecraft and carry them off course, unexpected turbulence, Warp storms and dimensional loops that can trap a ship for eternity. These perils, though calamitous, are as nothing compared to the profound and unimaginable dangers that lurk in the Warp.

To understand these dangers it is necessary to realise two important facts about the nature of the Warp. Firstly, Warp space is composed entirely of emotion and psychic energy. Indeed, it is the same psychic energy which a human psyker draws upon to use his powers, to send telepathic messages hurtling from world to world, or to propel a psychic bolt of energy against a foe. Secondly, Warp space is not empty, but inhabited by many strange and dangerous beings, the most dangerous of which are the Great Gods of Chaos and their terrible legions of Daemons.

Daemons lust after the flesh and blood of living creatures. They want only to destroy Mankind, to drag the souls of men back to their shadowy realm, to obliterate the material universe and engulf it within the roiling energy of Warp space. Fortunately, this is not easy quest to accomplish. Daemons cannot exist for long in the material universe and they need to find psychic gateways in order to leave the Warp. Such gateways exist – they are rare, but not so rare that their threat can be ignored. The most vulnerable portals of all are the souls of psykers. A psyker's powers open up a path between reality and the Warp, a path which a Daemon may discover and follow to the mind of the psyker himself.

Such are the dangers of the Warp – at once a boon and protector, and an unimaginable horror. Without the ability to travel through Warp space, the Imperium would certainly collapse and Mankind would fall victim to the thousand perils that threaten to destroy it. Without psykers, the whole system of astro-telecommunication would be utterly non-existent. It would be impossible to guide the Imperium's armies and fleets against its many enemies. For these reasons at least, Warp space is essential to the Imperium's very existence. Yet at the same time, Warp space harbours terrors so great, dangers so profound, that much of the Imperium's effort is spent in combat against them.

Only a Navigator can pilot a ship through Warp space. His swollen cranium houses a mind which is sensitive to the tides and currents of the Warp, enabling him to guide his ship through Warp space to its eventual destination. The third factor which makes Warp travel possible is the immeasurably powerful beacon of the Astronomican. Broadcast from holy Terra by a choir of psykers and guided by the Emperor's Will, this beacon reaches out through Warp space, where Navigators follow its guiding light. It is the Astronomican that allow Navigators to use their powers to the full. Without it, not even the most powerful of their number could pilot his ship over the immense voyages required in service to the Imperium.

Without command of Warp space and the ability to manoeuvre its military forces across the gulf of space, the Imperium would be unable to function as a whole. It would wither and die, torn apart by internal uprising and alien aggression.

Everywhere, the foes of humanity stand poised to exploit weakness and infirmity. Some are traitors from within – rebel governors and corrupt commanders who have turned from the Emperor's mercy for their own selfish ends. Other foes are alien in thought and deed. Barbarous Orks descend upon world after world, plundering and destroying, leaving death and destruction in their wake. Long dormant Necrons stir in the dust of a thousand dead worlds, implacable of will and merciless in nature. Voracious Tyranids sweep though the galaxy like a plague of locusts, laying bare whole star systems before moving ever onwards. The upstart Tau press upon the Imperium's boundaries, their deceptive and iniquitous ideals of common cause as dangerous as their military advance. From their wondrous Craftworlds in the void, the enigmatic Eldar cast meddlesome influence across all, tugging at the fate of other races to assure their own survival.

Yet even these foes are as nothing beside the horrors that lurk beyond the veil of the material universe. From the shifting seas of the Warp come Daemons, entities whose bodies are fashioned not of flesh and blood but unadulterated power, whose food and drink is the terror and ambition of man. Creatures that draw hatred and greed for breath, and that will not rest whilst a single man lives.

THE GATHERING DARK

Though the Imperium is surrounded and alone in the hostile galaxy, it is far from defenceless. The superhuman Space Marines, the innumerable Imperial Guard, the star-conquering vessels of the Imperial Navy and the mighty machines of the Titan Legions, all stand as a bulwark against threats both within and without, combating the encroaching darkness with fire and courage. Yet the Emperor's light grows dim and his domain dwindles, planet by planet and system by system. The enemies of Mankind gather like carrion and a time of endless night presses in. There is no peace, no respite, no hope of victory.

There is only war.

THE HIERARCHY OF TERRA

THE INQUISITION

The eye that
sleepeth not.

**THE HIGH LORDS
OF TERRA**

They govern the
destiny of Mankind.

THE EMPEROR

The living god,
the saviour of humanity.

THE ADEPTUS ARBITES

They are judge, jury
and executioner.

**THE ADEPTUS
CUSTODES**

They guard our past,
our present, our future.

**ADEPTUS
ASTRA TELEPATHICA**

The Emperor's voice
amongst the stars.

**THE ADEPTUS
ASTARTES**

The Angels of Death.

THE IMPERIAL GUARD

The Hammer of
the Emperor.

**THE ADEPTUS
MECHANICUS**

Disciples of the Omnissiah,
keepers of arcane lore.

The Masters
of Earth. Their
will be done.

ADEPTUS MINISTORUM

Vessels of the will,
defenders of the faith.

THE ADEPTUS
TERRA

ADEPTUS
ADMINISTRATUM

Without them, disorder.
Upon them turn the
wheels of governance.

ADEPTUS ASTRONOMICA

Bearers of light in the
darkness of the Warp.

OFFICIO ASSASSINORUM

Ask not for whom they
seek, lest it be thyself.

PLANETARY LORDS

They rule in His name.

IMPERIAL FLEET

They bind the
stars together.

MANIFEST GLORY OF THE EMPEROR

SCIONS OF THE IMPERIUM

The Emperor is the strength of Mankind, and Mankind is the strength of the Emperor.

The Imperium is home to countless billions of lost souls. The teeming masses of humanity throng the stars, but few have time to appreciate the majesty of the heavens. For the greater part of the human race, their only concern is a desperate struggle for survival.

All servants of the Imperium have a vocation that defines their existence, often allotted before they are even born. Pallid citizens toil day and night at thankless and futile tasks forced upon them by uncaring superiors, blind to the terrible truths that threaten Mankind from the void. Oblivious, they sacrifice their dreams on the altar of false hope, giving their all for the continuing survival of a decaying civilisation that cares not if they thrive or if they are ground to dust.

In the hab-complexes of the civilised worlds, the shuffle of sore-ravaged feet and the scratch of thermoquil upon vellum is punctuated by the thunder of distant war. Hunchbacked factotums and aged lickspittles slave endlessly under the unforgiving vigilance of Judiciar-Prelates and Titheproctor Superians. Only a few hours' sleep is permitted each night, and even that is plagued by the grind of constant industry, for the incessant wars of the Imperium demand a heavy price. Drooling Ideosavants trade gibberish with Pendanticum, Dataslave and Stasis Clerk in a babel tongue which none truly understand. Even death is no escape; the remains of the faithful are reincarnated as servo-skulls so that they might serve the Imperium for eternity.

In the streets outside the hab-blocks and manufactorums, the Arbitrators enforce their unforgiving rule upon the desperate and homeless. Feral children fight over the dead flesh of the fallen, their struggles lit only by flickering luminas set into crumbling masonry. Scapegoats, lepers, and pilgrims press and push in great queues that will last a lifetime, desperate in their quests for absolution they will never receive. Through this sickly gruel of flesh stride the privileged few, untouched by disease or the ravages of acidic rain. It is they who maintain the status quo for their own hidden ends, they who guide humanity itself. Some are pure of intent, some embody the corruption at the heart of the Imperium, but one thing is true of all - they care not for the fate of the common man.

No army is big enough to conquer the galaxy. But faith alone can overturn the universe.

In the blazing furnace of battle we shall forge anew the iron will of a yet stronger race.

Only those that follow the guiding light of the Emperor may save their souls.

All hail the martyrs! On their blood is our Imperium founded, in their remembrance do we honour ourselves.

They who feast today do so in ignorance of their mortality. Tomorrow they must die or change.

BY THE EMPEROR

Thou shalt attend to thy work at the appointed hour.

Thou shalt seek no reward but the satisfaction of thy Master.

Thou shalt know thy Duties.

Thou shalt Obey thy Master in all matters.

Thou shalt rejoice in thy Service.

Thou shalt be grateful of thy Master's Favour.

Thou shalt not make improper use of thy Master's comm-links, nor his las-lines, nor his opticon either.

Thou shalt be glad of thy Master's Punishment, for it is deserved and it improves thee.

Thou shalt not speak but Praise of thy Master.

Thou shalt not look upon the works of the Heretic nor speak of them.

Ecclesiarchal Proscriptions MCXVII.IV

We must be as unsleeping in vigilance, swift in judgement, merciless in deed.

The Priesthood of Mars maintain our Emperor's throne. Thusly do they underpin the Imperium entire.

What fear of death have we who know there is immortality in the great and noble deeds of men?

THE ENEMY WITHIN

A destiny unfolding, marred by weakness and mutation

Despite the constant alien assaults and incessant wars wracking the Imperium, the greatest threat to the survival of the human race comes from within. Mutation sweeps across the Imperium like a galaxy-wide plague, twisting body and soul into ever more deviant forms. Mankind is on the verge of an evolutionary change tens of thousands of years in the making. If humanity can survive the birth trauma, the mundane shackles of its current form will be thrown off and a new epoch of wonderment and psionic mastery ushered in. That Mankind will survive is by no means certain. In all but a very small handful of cases, mutants are a danger to the wider Imperium. Feared and shunned for their deviances and deformities, mutants swiftly become an underclass far from the sight of 'ordinary' folk, destined to be hunted with steel and purged through fire.

Widespread and calamitous though mutation of the body may be, the mind of man has ever been more dangerous than ought else at his command, and of a mutated mind this is doubly true. Psychic mutants, such as precognistics, telepaths, pyrocasters, projectors, sunderers and the like, are far more dangerous than those whose aberrations are purely of the body.

Most psykers are innocent of the scope and implication of their abilities, but there are some blessed or cursed with awareness of their gift. A few even actively court the dreadful attentions of Warp entities, tempting the most terrible of fates for morsels of knowledge and power. In so doing these psykers inevitably damn themselves, and all who associate with them, to a grisly end. For Mankind is but a nascent power and easy prey for old and hungry spirits.

The most deviant mind is often concealed in an unblemished body.

The minds of psykers appear as bright flames in the ether of the Warp, ripe sweetmeats for a pandemonium of planeshifters, enslavers, Daemons and other astral predators. An untrained psyker's only chance of survival lies in going unnoticed – he cannot hope to defend himself against a hungry Warp presence.

If ensnared, a psyker is gradually transformed into a portal through which streams of Warpspawn begin to manifest. This begins slowly, but each entity that transits the portal forces the gateway a little wider, granting passage to ever greater numbers of Warp-fiends. Needless to say, this process is quite fatal to the luckless psyker who is consumed in both body and spirit. He is normally only the first amongst countless billions of such deaths. Horrific otherworldly creatures rampage across the world in search of fresh souls, their mere presence destabilising the structure of all actuality. The Imperium has to be ever vigilant, lest the hellish denizens of the Warp overrun real space at Mankind's unconscious beckoning.

Such is the true threat of the enemy within.

In the search for acceptance and protection, mutants of all kinds often fall prey to the honeyed promises of the secret and devolved cults hidden amid the strata of Imperial society. Some cults are trivial things, their members little more than rabble-rousers and panjandrums railing ineffectually against the confines of Imperial dictat. More deadly and iniquitous by far are those cults driven by madness and ambition to acquire power and enslave their fellow men.

In their quest for dominance many such cults turn to the worship of the Chaos Gods, sacrificing their untainted and immortal souls for ephemeral power. So do cults of Chaos spring into life on world after world. Millions upon millions of humans – mutant and 'normal' alike – driven into damnation's embrace through hatred, jealousy and fear. Organisations of this kind reach into all levels of the Imperium, counting adjudicators, military commanders and even planetary governors amongst their number.

The rewards of tolerance are treachery and betrayal.

THE WORLDS OF THE IMPERIUM

A million worlds, unnumbered souls, perils beyond counting.

In the 41st Millennium, Mankind is spread throughout space, each planet separated from the next by the void and a history of regression and rebuilding. Many human worlds form loose alliances for trade and mutual defence. Others have become primitive and barbarous, often as a result of periodic isolation. New human worlds are discovered all the time, and there are an unknown number which have lain forgotten for hundreds, if not thousands of years. Even so, these human worlds represent only a tiny proportion of the stellar systems in the galaxy.

HIVE WORLDS

Hive worlds such as Armageddon, Vanaheim and Minea are the production centres and priniciple manufactorums of the Imperium. Centuries of industrial production have left a hive world's surface inhospitable, with toxic fumes and parched soil. Each hive world is home to many hundred billion citizens, crammed into towering urban conglomerations, known as hives, and working to provide the Imperium with much-needed ores, alloys and mass produced items. So vast are their populations that few hive worlds are self-sufficient, and often subsist on colossal imports of food and water from other worlds.

AGRI WORLDS

Agri worlds are given over entirely to hydroponics, animal breeding and crop cultivation. Small human populations work thousands of acres of farmland and battery farms, to feed the countless billions who toil on barren and diseased hive worlds, or serve with deep space fleets. Without the verdant fields of Kabaal II, Delphenia, Chiros and a thousand others, the Imperium would starve.

FERAL AND FEUDAL WORLDS

These worlds are broadly considered to be backward planets, separated mostly by a mastery (or lack thereof) of gunpowder weaponry. Such a world is easily dominated, as strength of arms has long replaced any civilised structure of governance and the regressive inhabitants are normally cowed by any display of advanced technology. Though feral and feudal planets are generally poor worlds monetarily, the warrior skills bred on them more than compensate for the paucity of tithes. Attila, Trysia and Fenris in particular have proven fertile recruiting grounds for the Adeptus Astartes and other military units, although there is always an element of culture shock to be overcome before draftees can function in their new environment.

MINEA
Imperial Reference 1342056/gbc/54032.11.2/K
[ha class hive world, Ultima Segmentum]

Cross-reference: Armageddon, Avellorn, Ichar IV, Kado, Lastrati, Vanaheim

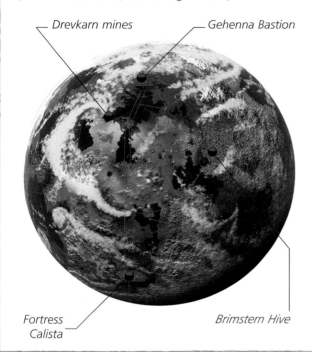

Drevkarn mines — Gehenna Bastion

Fortress Calista — Brimstern Hive

Population:	154 billion
Approx. number of hive worlds in the Imperium:	3.238×10^4

MILITARY AND GOVERNANCE

Aestimare (strategic value):	D146
Imperial Fleet Presence:	Moderate
Governor's Capital:	Brimstern Hive
Planetary Garrisons:	Fortress Calista Gehenna Bastion
Imperial Garrison Strength:	2,000,000 men
Planetary draft:	1,249,000 per annum
Closest Space Marine Chapter:	Crimson Scions
Prefix Inquisitoria:	Stable

PRODUCTION

Tithe Grade:	Exactis Extremis
Chief exports:	Banedax Ore, Phosgene Gas
Average Warp Travel duration from Terra:	35 months

Information believed accurate 798.M41

ARTIFICIAL WORLDS

The Imperium maintains many orbital stations, asteroidal emplacements and other constructed facilities. These range from listening posts and research laboratories to military space stations and doomsday bastions.

QUARANTINED WORLDS

Sometimes a world proves too difficult or dangerous for settlement, but the potential for exploitation is too high to become subject to an Exterminatus order. This is true of the dead cities of Proxima Trantor, the artificial moons of Jagram and the hollow world of Haxan Prime. For now the secrets are out of reach, wreathed in acidic vapours that can dissolve adamantium in seconds, eldritch auto-defences or chronal fluxes. These worlds are placed under blockade to prevent intruders getting in or the secrets they contain getting out, until such a time that the Imperium can properly exploit them.

FORGE WORLDS

Mars, Goethe Majoris, Lucius and their sister planets are all forge worlds, the sovereign domains of the Adeptus Mechanicus. Forge worlds are planet-wide factories, home to closely guarded technological secrets and essential for the supply of mundane or arcane equipment for the Imperium's combat forces. A forge world's every process and system is watched over and repaired by shuffling Tech Priests and adepts who intone the blessings of the Omnissiah with every strike of the hammer or turn of the wrench.

GHOST WORLDS

These were once thriving planets, but now have minimal or non-existent life as a result of ecological catastrophe, unchecked warfare, Imperial Exterminatus or some other, unknown cause. Most ghost worlds are of limited value to the Imperium, but can make for excellent military training grounds, providing whatever killed the original population does not arise once again.

DEATH WORLDS

Death worlds are planets deemed too dangerous to support widespread human settlements. Such worlds are nearly impossible to colonise, but have some intrinsic value – either strategic or mineral – that necessitates the provision of outposts or other facilities. The exact nature of a death world's threat varies from planet to planet. Catachan is infamous for its continent spanning jungles and myriad forms of carnivorous life, while Praxeti is a barren and blasted rockscape, riven with ion storms that strike with enough force to shatter rocks. Other death world threats are stranger still – the living planet of Croatoa, the psychic storms of Sycorax or Kragadam's indestructible crystalline fauna, to name but a few. From the endless deserts of Luther Macintyre to the burning sulphur fields of Jjojos, any population able to scratch out an existence on a death world will have to overcome threats far beyond the imagination of most Imperial citizens. Such hard-bitten folk are ideal recruits for the Imperial Guard, a detail that more than justifies the settlement of a death world regardless of other factors.

IMPERIUS DOMINATUS

The Age of Battle has begun.

The fires of war burn brightly from star to star. Everywhere the fortresses of Man are steeped in blood and ancient enemies appear from the darkness. Sensing weakness they gather for the kill. They know as we know that night approaches and all mortal life shall be extinguished. We know, as they cannot, that there shall be a new dawn and a new day when we will rise and they will be driven into the darkness forever.

INDOMITABLE WRATH
Emperor Class Battleship

Hundreds of mighty craft, such as the Indomitable Wrath, prowl the inky blackness of the void, ready to dispense swift death.

BINARY SYSTEM 'CABULIS'

CABULIS
Dying star

CELESTRA
Parasite star

CRUX
Capital World
Munitions Core

BOONHAVEN
Agri-world

GLORIAM
Weapons
Testing Facility

TEMPERIS
Hive World

EMELE
Maiden World
Forbidden Zone

Cabulis, primarily a munitions tithe zone, is a typical example of a binary system. One of its suns is a parasitic star that has reduced its partner to little more than a stellar skeleton. The entire Cabulis system has been plunged into a desperate war of attrition with the seemingly unstoppable Waaagh! Gragnatz.

SEGMENTUM PACIFICUS

HOLY TERRA
Blessed in his authority,
here dwells the most beneficent Emperor.

Imperial Primus Palace

Scholastica Psykana

Hall of the Astronomican

Ecclesiarchal Palace

The Cathedral of the Emperor Deified

The Halls of Judgement

Orbital Defence System

Terra is the slow-beating heart of the Imperium, a sacred world of power and majesty that has become legend. It is the site of the Golden Throne; the demesne of the Immortal Emperor of Mankind. The breathtaking architecture of its soaring buildings strike awe into the hearts of the supplicants below. Forbidding statues of angels and Primarchs loom down from their eyries, their sightless stare driving out all thoughts of heresy. Truly it is such a blessing to set foot upon Glorious Terra that most pilgrims never leave.

SEGMENTUM OBSCURUS

HALO STARS

SCARUS SECTOR

CALIXIS SECTOR

FINIAL SECTOR

THE EYE OF TERROR

Cypra Mundi

Mordian

Naogeddon

Dimmamar

STORM OF TH
EMPEROR'S WR.

GOTHIC SECTOR

Valhalla

Chinchare

Belis Corona

Piscina

Cadia

Fenris

Molov

Hydraphur

Armageddon

Elysia

SEGMENTUM SOLAR.

Terra

Prospero

Golgotha

Lastrati

Ryza

Catachan

THE MAELSTROM

Gathalamor

Necromunda

Badab

Macharia

Krieg

Luther McIntyre

Tallarn

Nocturne

Chiros

Ophelia

UHULIS SECTOR

V'run

Aleusis

Solstice

SEGMENTUM TEMPESTUS

REDUCTUS SECTOR

Bakka

Antagonis

Ag

Illustris

Gryphonne IV

THE VEILED REGION

PLEURIC SYSTEM, VAN REILAC BELT

Murchad

Pleuris

Liethe Prime

Elevoc

Gleiros

Anaro

Zindleschlitz

Ghast

The Pleuric System appeared from nowhere on the millenial cusp of M.41. It was not documented in any Imperial records or star charts and, being largely habitable, was almost immediately consumed by wars between rival houses of Rog... ...ers. Whether the system has always been hidden within the Van Reilac bel... ...s born of the Warp is open to speculation.

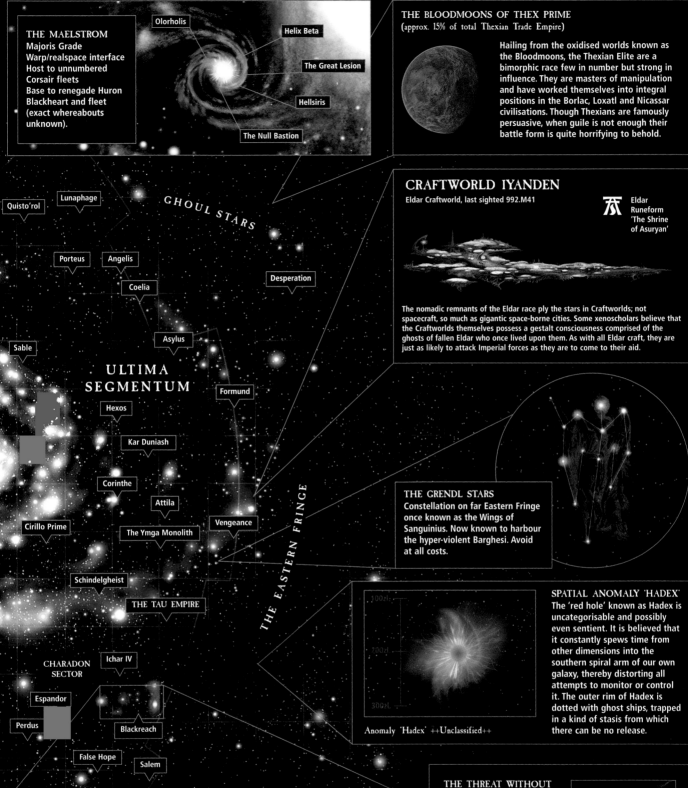

THE MAELSTROM
Majoris Grade
Warp/realspace interface
Host to unnumbered
Corsair fleets
Base to renegade Huron
Blackheart and fleet
(exact whereabouts
unknown).

Olorholis

Helix Beta

The Great Lesion

Hellsiris

The Null Bastion

THE BLOODMOONS OF THEX PRIME
(approx. 15% of total Thexian Trade Empire)

Hailing from the oxidised worlds known as the Bloodmoons, the Thexian Elite are a bimorphic race few in number but strong in influence. They are masters of manipulation and have worked themselves into integral positions in the Borlac, Loxatl and Nicassar civilisations. Though Thexians are famously persuasive, when guile is not enough their battle form is quite horrifying to behold.

GHOUL STARS

Quisto'rol

Lunaphage

Porteus

Angelis

Coelia

Desperation

Asylus

Sable

ULTIMA SEGMENTUM

Formund

Hexos

Kar Duniash

Corinthe

Attila

Cirillo Prime

Vengeance

The Ymga Monolith

Schindelgheist

THE TAU EMPIRE

THE EASTERN FRINGE

Ichar IV

CHARADON SECTOR

Espandor

Perdus

Blackreach

False Hope

Salem

CRAFTWORLD IYANDEN
Eldar Craftworld, last sighted 992.M41

Eldar Runeform 'The Shrine of Asuryan'

The nomadic remnants of the Eldar race ply the stars in Craftworlds; not spacecraft, so much as gigantic space-borne cities. Some xenoscholars believe that the Craftworlds themselves possess a gestalt consciousness comprised of the ghosts of fallen Eldar who once lived upon them. As with all Eldar craft, they are just as likely to attack Imperial forces as they are to come to their aid.

THE GRENDL STARS
Constellation on far Eastern Fringe once known as the Wings of Sanguinius. Now known to harbour the hyper-violent Barghesi. Avoid at all costs.

SPATIAL ANOMALY 'HADEX'
The 'red hole' known as Hadex is uncategorisable and possibly even sentient. It is believed that it constantly spews time from other dimensions into the southern spiral arm of our own galaxy, thereby distorting all attempts to monitor or control it. The outer rim of Hadex is dotted with ghost ships, trapped in a kind of stasis from which there can be no release.

Anomaly 'Hadex' ++Unclassified++

THE REALM OF ULTRAMAR

MACRAGGE
UL01.01
Orb. Dist. 2.01AU
Adeptus Astartes Chapter Planet
Tithe Grade: Aptus Non
Aestimare: D0
Population: 400,000,000
Defeat of Hive Fleet Behemoth
(qf: BattleMacragge 745.M41)

Home of the Ultramarines Chapter, Ultramar is an Empire of beautiful and highly developed civilised worlds that stand as an indomitable bulwark against the encroaching darkness of the Eastern Fringe.

THE THREAT WITHOUT
The majority of the Tyranid Hive Fleets thus far encountered have originated from the galactic east. Several tendrils of Hive Fleet Behemoth and Hive Fleet Kraken have been engaged and neutralised at great cost in life, but many tendrils remain. Worse still, many xenologisticians believe that the vast majority of the Tyranid race is watching and waiting in the cold void.

Known advance of the Eastern Hive Fleets. 998.M41

AN EMPIRE UNDER SIEGE

There is no mercy amongst the stars, only an eternity of war in the Emperor's name.

The Age of the Imperium is an epoch of total war. Mankind's every deed is focussed on a never-ending struggle for survival against the most terrible odds. Only by force of arms and unnumbered daily acts of desperate valour is the Imperium held together, for the threats that assail Mankind are as multitudinous as they are widespread.

A DIMINISHING EMPIRE

The sheer scale of the Imperium means that no method of control can ever be foolproof. Worlds inevitably fall into disorder through neglect, forgotten by the massive inertia of the Administratum and left to fend for themselves in a hostile galaxy. More troublesome are those worlds that purposefully deny the will of the Emperor. Many are the paths to heresy of this kind: greed, pride, alien influence, worship of dark and terrible gods. Such traitors and malcontents are amongst the gravest threats to the security of the Imperium. This is not because of what they themselves can achieve – a dozen planets, more or less, makes little difference to a realm of a million worlds. The threat lies is their perfidious example.

Thousands of worlds teeter on the brink of anarchy, maintained only by the ineluctable truth that they survive only with the protection of the wider Imperium. To successfully confront this truth and endure is to encourage others and fan the flames of rebellion. A single breakaway planet left unchallenged sparks a broader secession. Each planet that secedes then increases the number of psykers freed from the righteous restraints placed upon them, which in turn feeds the burgeoning psychic turbulence of anarchy. If unchecked, the building psychic emanations of the frenzied population will draw forth the gaze of Daemons and so doom not only that world, but bring untold suffering onto the entire region.

> "Some may question your right to destroy ten billion people.
> Those who understand realise that you have no right to let them live."
>
> In Exterminatus Extremis

Such drastic threats require drastic solutions, and so to raise even the slightest dissent with Imperial decree is to invite a swift and brutal response. This may seem unnecessarily harsh, but the 41st Millennium is no time for half measures. If millions must be sacrificed to preserve the lives of billions, then so be it.

THE ALIEN MENACE

Mankind is not the only race to tread the stars. There are dozens, perhaps hundreds, of civilisations whose destinies cross those of humanity amid the star-strewn pathways of the galaxy, and countless other rising cultures whose threat is contained only through Imperial might. Some of these races are ancient beyond Mankind's reckoning while others are nascent powers, reaching forth their grasp for the first time. All must be fought tooth and nail, for the Imperium learnt long ago that an accord with outsiders is worthless unless forged through the threat of a vast and bloody retribution. The actions of aliens throughout the galaxy have reinforced that most ancient of lessons: nature abhors frailty – the strong prosper and the weak are devoured.

Of the galaxy-spanning foes, the ancient Eldar are the most enigmatic. Their technological and societal attainment far outstrips that of humanity, yet they are capricious and vexatious beyond belief, as likely to side with Mankind as they are to inflict murder and devastation upon it. For the moment, the Imperium

mostly refrains from aggressive action against the Eldar. This is partly because the Eldar are numerically amongst the smallest galactic threats, partly because they are allies almost as often as enemies, but largely because the last Imperial assault on an Eldar Craftworld ended with the disaster of Blood Nebula and the loss of an entire sector fleet. It is better to fend off a single wasp than to provoke the entire nest.

> "Contact with alien races always renews one's faith in Humanity. It is my belief that foreign travel narrows the mind wonderfully."
>
> Helem Bosch

Orks are an all-pervasive alien threat. They cannot be bargained with, for they do not wage war for territory, wealth or glory – the fight is its own reward. Mercifully, the power of the Orks waxes and wanes. A single rampaging Ork Waaagh! has the power to bring ruin upon countless systems but, given time, inevitably collapses into several violently squabbling factions, allowing time for an opponent to regroup and strike back. Should the Orks ever truly unite, they will sweep all before them in a tide of unremitting slaughter.

Both Orks and Eldar are ancestral foes that have besieged humanity since it first took to the stars. But the alien menace has intensified without precedent over the last millennium, with more territory lost each year. In the galactic east, Tyranid Hive Fleets descend upon world after world, devouring everything in their path and growing stronger with every battle. The sepulchral Necrons, long believed extinct, are stirring once more on a thousand worlds.

A threat growing in strength is that of the rapidly rising younger races. Worlds that once trembled before Imperial wrath are casting off their shackles and looking to carve their own empires among the stars. The Draxian Hegemony, the Tau Empire, the Worldweave of the Noisome Reek, the Uluméathic League, the Church of Dracolith – the list goes on. Individually these upstarts cannot hope to challenge humanity's dominance, but if their encroachments are taken as a whole then their containment promises to drain valuable military resources.

Throughout the Imperium, priests and zealots preach that the rise of so many alien foes is Mankind's punishment for heresy, for straying from the Emperor's light. Elsewhere, in darkened chambers and scriptoria, Inquisitors and their peers express a deeper fear; Mankind's time is drawing to a close, and these new powers have risen to fill the inevitable void that the Imperium will leave behind.

DEFENDERS OF THE IMPERIUM

United by faith, proud heroes do battle for Mankind's survival.

Thousands of years of constant warfare have honed Mankind's military might to the galaxy-wide struggle for survival. An Imperial commander can call on many diverse organisations in his pursuance of the Emperor's Will, and each of the Imperium's military forces brings its own tactical specialisation to the ever-lasting war effort. Some organisations, such as the mighty Space Marines, the stalwart Imperial Guard or the pious battle-sisters of the Adepta Sororitas are paraded as heroic saviours, their efforts lauded and praised by the common man. Others, such as the shadowy operatives of the Officio Assassinorum, dwell in the darkness, proponents and practitioners of more sinister arts.

The Imperium draws great advantage from the unbelievably huge weight of manpower it can bring to bear. Indeed, the soldiers of the Imperial Guard outnumber the entire population of most alien empires all by themselves. Yet the Imperium also draws upon the strengths of machinery and arcane technology – the mighty Titans of the Adeptus Mechanicus and the gargantuan star-treading vessels of the Imperial Navy amongst them. It is undeniable that the Imperium's diversity of military forces is its greatest strength.

Though the forces of the Imperium are myriad and diverse, they all work to a single shared goal: enforcing the Emperor's divine will, and thus ensuring the continued survival of Mankind.

THE IMPERIAL GUARD

The Imperial Guard is the galaxy's largest cohesive fighting force, comprising planetary defence forces, militia units and colossal armies of conquest. Relying on devastating firepower first and attrition second, the Imperial Guard fights wars for decades if it must, throwing ever more bloody grist into the mill of warfare until victory is achieved.

THE SPACE MARINES

What the Imperial Guard cannot overwhelm, the Space Marines destroy. If the Imperial Guard are the shield of Mankind, the Space Marines are the sword, carrying the fight to the foe with precision, skill and terrifying swiftness. Though they are few in number, the valour and dedication of the Space Marines is as without measure as the superhuman might they wield – without them humanity would have long since fallen into darkness.

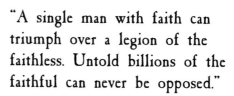

"A single man with faith can triumph over a legion of the faithless. Untold billions of the faithful can never be opposed."

The Sermons of Sebastian Thor, Vol. XI, Chapter IV

THE SISTERS OF BATTLE

The Adepta Sororitas, or the Battle Sisters of the Orders Militant as they are otherwise known, are the mainstay of the Adeptus Ministorum armies. Utterly dedicated to the protection of the Imperium, the Battle Sisters are trained and equipped to the highest standards. Wherever there are foes of the Emperor, the Sisters of Battle will be found fighting to the last.

There are three major Orders of Adepta Sororitas, the fighting strength of each numbering several thousand warriors, as well as many lesser sisterhoods comprised of around a hundred or so Battle Sisters. An Order's warriors rarely fight as a unit, but instead are commonly spread throughout the galaxy in various battle zones. Nevertheless, the Sisters of Battle rank amongst the Imperium's most trusted defenders, for their unshakeable faith can overcome all but the most terrible foes.

THE GREY KNIGHTS

The Grey Knights are a Space Marine Chapter like no other, and the Imperium's foremost defence against the daemonic threat. Working in close co-operation with the Ordo Malleus, the militant arm of the Inquisition, the Grey Knights can be found wherever the daemonic forces of Chaos wax strong, combating unimaginable horrors with resolute faith, unshakeable determination and the finest weapons the Imperium can produce.

> "For every battle honour a thousand heroes die alone, unsung and unremembered."
>
> Proverb

THE OFFICIO ASSASSINORUM

A single death can prevent a war that would claim a billion lives. Such is the credo of the Officio Assassinorum, the Imperium's shadowy brotherhood of assassins. Imperial Assassins are the ultimate tool of destruction and diplomacy, able to quell rebellions, silence demagogues and change the course of history with a few well chosen murders. Alien warlords, traitorous heretics, ambitious officials and misguided separatists: none are safe from an assassin's knife.

THE ADEPTUS MECHANICUS

The Adeptus Mechanicus are the keepers of ancient knowledge. It is these Tech Adepts who construct the awesome technologies that feed the Imperial armouries, who preserve the operations of the Emperor's Golden Throne, and operate the forge worlds that supply an ever-hungry Imperium. Through mystic rites, intricate invocations and arcane ceremonies, the Tech Priests maintain the Standard Template Construct systems that allow the mass production of vital tools, mechanisms and war machines. Without the Adeptus Mechanicus, Mankind would swiftly fall once more into a technological dark age, and the Imperium would collapse soon after.

THE TITAN LEGIONS

A Titan is a towering mechanical behemoth with an armoured carapace that shelters a devastating array of weapons. The pinnacle of Imperial battle-technology, Titans are emblematic of the Imperium's military might; cumbersome perhaps, but nigh unstoppable. Titans are manufactured on forge worlds, utilising arcane technology from earlier times. There are many patterns of Titan, from the agile Warhounds to the earth-shaking Warlords. Many Titans have proud histories, sometimes stretching back to the beginning of the Age of the Imperium. Such leviathans are revered as much for their long service and past deeds as they are for the apocalyptic fury they unleash upon the foe.

THE INQUISITION

The mysterious Inquisitors are utterly ruthless in their defence of Mankind. They seek and annihilate the enemies of the Emperor whether they can be found – without, within or beyond. No conspiracy or rebellion of mind or body is beyond the purview of an Inquisitor, no matter its scale or form, its allies or its defences. Though the Imperium is the greatest stellar realm ever known, no being – man or alien – can evade the stern gaze of the Inquisition, nor evade the stern judgement it metes out. Inquisitors are ceaseless, unfailing and untiring, thought by many to be the mortal embodiment of the Emperor's rationality and wisdom.

Each Inquisitor is a peer of the Imperium, one of a finite elite who hold ultimate authority over Mankind. As such, an Inquisitor can recruit any military or civilian force in the pursuit of Imperial duties, from hive world security details through to entire Space Marine Chapters, Titan Legions and vessels of the Imperial Navy. Yet the Inquisitor has in his arsenal one weapon like no other: Exterminatus, an orbital bombardment of cataclysmic proportions that employs virus bombs, cyclonic torpedoes and seismic missiles to scour all life from a planet, leaving it a dead and ruined shell.

THE AGES OF MANKIND

DARK AGE OF TECHNOLOGY

Mankind realises its destiny amongst the stars, colonising world after world at a rapacious pace. Warp space is tamed and the first alien races subjugated. An age of expansion and plenty begins. Psykers emerge amid the race of Man, and the attention of the dread powers is drawn towards humanity.

DARK AGE OF TECHNOLOGY
c.M18 – c.M23

AGE OF STRIFE

c.M31 THE GREAT CRUSADES

The Emperor emerges from the anarchy of sundered Terra and creates the first Space Marines. Through campaigns unnumbered and strife untold the Emperor's legions unite Mankind under his beneficent leadership. So is born the Imperium of Man.

AGE OF STRIFE

A time of barbarism and collapse. Mankind's holdings are fragmented and isolated by Warp storms of unprecedented ferocity. Brother wars against brother for the control of humanity's dominions. Weakened through over-reliance on technology, civilisation collapses into anarchy. Mankind is mercilessly beset. Untold thousands of planets and colonies are destroyed by Daemons or subjugated by aliens.

AGE OF THE IMPERIUM

Humanity endures through the Emperor's sacrifice. Psykers, traitors and mutants arise in ever greater numbers, and only eternal vigilance preserves Mankind from annihilation. The Astronomican, a great psychic beacon steered by the Emperor's immortal mind, allows Mankind to harness Warp travel once again, and many worlds are reunited with the Imperium. However, all is not well in humanity's domain. Without the Emperor to guide them, the children of Terra quarrel amongst themselves and must be restrained and defended in equal measure by the High Lords of Terra.

Survival is no birthright, but a prize wrested from an uncaring galaxy by forgotten heroes.

Proverb

AGE
OF THE
IMPERIUM

c.M30 onwards

c.M31 THE HORUS HERESY

The Emperor's most trusted servant, the Warmaster Horus, marches upon Terra with a third part of the hosts of the Imperium which he had seduced to his purpose. Horus is slain, but the Emperor is mortally wounded and reigns evermore from the life-giving Golden Throne.

TIME OF ENDING

As the dark days close in, Mankind stands before the precipice. Now is the time of judgement, where faith shall be tested in fire, and courage put to its very limits. Secession and rebellion are rife in all corners of the Imperium. Sensing weakness, alien empires close in from all sides. The Space Marines and Imperial Guard are at war as never before, defending humanity from threats within, without and beyond. This is humanity's darkest hour.

THE AGE OF THE IMPERIUM

.M31 THE HORUS HERESY

.M31 THE SCOURING
The campaign of vengeance in which those traitors who survived Horus' fall are driven into the Eye of Terror. For a time the Imperium knows peace from the corrupted followers of the Dark Gods.

077.M33 THE WAR OF THE CONFESSOR

313.M33 SIEGE OF ETERNITY'S GATE

615.M33 THE BLADE OF INFINITY
The pre-Heresy cruiser, the *Blade of Infinity*, emerges from the Warp, twenty thousand years after its departure.

544.M32 THE BEAST ARISES

831.M33 THE YEAR OF GHOSTS
The honoured dead rise up to defeat the terrors of the Warp.

910.M32 THE FIRESTORM

THE AGE OF REBIRTH
The Imperium arises from the ashes of the Horus Heresy. The Codex Astartes and other doctrines are drawn up and implemented, in the hope of ensuring that large-scale military rebellion will never again be possible.

THE FORGING
The Golden Age of the Imperium. The Adeptus Terra begins an ambitious project to bring the most important systems in the Imperium under its direct control. Astropath choirs are established on Armageddon, Bakka, Macragge and a thousands others. Long-lost Standard Template Constructs are unearthed amid the ruins of the Cana system, slowing the decline of Imperial technology. The borders of the Imperium expand to a point almost on par with the successes of the Great Crusade. Chaos Renegades and Xenos are purged from the galaxy in phenomenal numbers, and countless rebel systems are brought to heel.

NOVA TERRA INTERREGNUM
The time of twin Empires. The Ur-council of Nova Terra denounce the High Lords and claim rule of the Segmentum Pacificus. For nine centuries the Imperium becomes a realm split in twain.

546.M32 THE BEHEADING
The internecine politics of the Imperium take a calamitous turn when the High Lords of Terra are slain to a man at the orders of Drakan Vangorich, the Grand Master of the Officio Assassinorum. A Space Marine retribution force drawn from the Halo Brethren, Imperial Fists and Sable Swords Chapters tracks the Grand Master to an Assassinorum temple. The commander of the strike force is assassinated as soon as he makes planetfall, but the Brother Marines commence their attack nevertheless. Within the temple they are assailed by a hundred Eversor Assassins. A single Space Marine survives to reach the Grand Master and deliver the Emperor's judgement with his boltgun. The Imperium descends into anarchy.

265.M33 THE LAST VOYAGE OF ADMIRAL USURS
Admiral Usurs is cast down by the High Lords of Terra. He is too powerful to execute without inviting civil war, so is instead despatched on an explorator mission to the intergalactic gulf beyond. For the following decade, Usurs' reports reach Terra, detailing the conquering of new systems for the glory of the Emperor. After two decades, the communiqués cease. Contact is never made with the systems mentioned in Usurs' reports.

401.M34 THE HOWLING
Black Templar Space Marines end the Catelexis Heresy by executing the Cacodominus, an alien cyborg whose formidable psychic presence allowed it to control the populace of thirteen hundred planetary systems. Alas, the Cacodominus' death scream echoes and amplifies through the Warp, burning out the minds of a billion astropaths and distorting the signal of the Astronomican. Millions upon millions of ships are lost in the resulting upheaval and entire sub-sectors slide into barbarism without the dictats of the Adeptus Terra to guide them.

888.M32 THE ASTROPATH WARS

975.M35 THE CATACLYSM OF SOULS

The Ecclesiarchy begins to rebind the sundered Imperium as a religious state that transcends political differences. Millions die in religious wars when the Ur-council of Nova Terra reject the Ecclesiarchy's teachings.

.M36 THE REIGN OF BLOOD

Goge Vandire, Ecclesiarch and High Lord of the Administratum, falls from the Emperor's light and sparks a civil war that lasts for seven decades. Only when loyal citizens rally to the banner of the preacher Sebastian Thor is the strife ended. Though Vandire's blood has long since been washed away, his memory stains the Emperor's Palace still.

310.M36 THE PLAGUE OF UNBELIEF

020.M37 THE GREAT CULL

In their mercy, the High Lords of Terra begin a systematic extermination.

034.M38 THE BLOODTIDE AWAKENS

"A man may die yet still endure if his work enters the greater work, for time is carried upon a current incepted by forgotten deeds.

As all men must thank progenitors obscured by the past, so we must endure the present that those who come after may continue the greater work."

– The Chime of Eons
Garbo Mojaro
Technomagos of the Adeptus Mechanicus

THE AGE OF APOSTASY

Zeal eclipses reason, and misrule reigns supreme. The word of the Emperor is subverted by corrupt idealogues. The strong prey upon the weak like jackals.

THE AGE OF REDEMPTION

In which the sins of apostasy are purged in blood and tears. The Imperial cult grows in power as never before. Heretic pyres burn day and night on a thousand worlds as the populace of the Imperium mortify their sins through the flesh of others. Crusade after crusade is launched to recapture the squandered wealth of the Imperium. The fervour peaks and thousands of worlds are left with inadequate defences as sector fleets, Space Marine Chapters and Imperial Guard Regiments are drawn into longer and more terrible crusades.

THE WANING

With the Imperium's military exhausted by the Redemption Crusades, world after world and system after system fall to Ork invasion, Chaos insurgence or internal strife. Anarchy is rife. Ever more systems are turned over to direct governance by Space Marine Chapters to bring war-torn...

321.M37 THE ABYSSAL CRUSADE

The judgement of Saint Basillius. Thirty Space Marine Chapters are found wanting. The guilty embark upon a crusade into the Eye of Terror, to purge those worlds stolen by the birth of the Dark Prince.

956.M37 HEAVENFALL MASSACRES

550.M37 THE OCCLUSIAD

The north western fringe is ravaged by the Apostles of The Blind King, rogue Tech Priests who view humanity as an affront to the Machine God. The Apostles uncover wondrous artefacts lost in the Dark Age of Technology that allow the creation of supernovae from the hearts of living suns. Constellations are forever changed as the Apostles purge the outer Segementum Obscuris. War rages for a decade, until the Navigator Joyre Macran discovers the palace-warship of the Blind King hidden in a fold of Warpspace. Escaping with his knowledge, Macran guides the Emperor-class battleship *Dominus Astra* to the palace's location. The Blind King is killed when the *Dominus Astra's* lance batteries pierce the palace-warship's hull, and without his prescience the Apostles are swiftly overcome.

995.M40
THE MACHARIAN CONQUESTS

Lord Commander Solar Macharius musters the greatest army the galaxy has even seen. In five years Macharius reconquers a thousand worlds on the western reaches, and his glory carries him into the darkest sectors, places where the Emperor's light had never before been seen. Upon his death, the whole Imperium weeps for the fallen commander, but Macharius' territories soon collapse into rivalry and war. The Macharian Heresy, as this time has come to be known, lasts for seventy years and is only ended through the combined efforts of one hundred Space Marine Chapters.

THE TIME OF ENDING

The Emperor's light is fading, yet Mankind shall not pass quietly into damnation.

Dating Code	Events
744.M41	Taggarath, the Seer of Corrinto, proclaims the approach of the End Times. He prophesies a time of unprecedented upheaval, in which even the light of the Emperor is swallowed in darkness. Taggarath is swiftly executed for heresy.
745.M41	The Tyranids enter the galaxy and the Tyrannic Wars begin. Hive Fleet Behemoth destroys the Imperium-held Tyran and Thandros systems. Later that year, Hive Fleet Behemoth descends upon the realm of Ultramar, laying waste to several planets and decimating the Ultramarines. The threat of Hive Fleet Behemoth is finally ended under the guns of two entire Imperial battlefleets. Imperial commanders across the Ultima Segmentum look at their borders with increasing unease.
757.M41	First recorded incidence of the Zombie Plague occurs on Hydra Minoris. Quarantine is imposed, trapping 23 billion uninfected Imperial citizens alongside a rising tide of the undead.

766.M41	Several Imperial listening posts in the Catachan and Ryza systems are attacked by Eldar pirates under the command of Prince Yriel.
783.M41	Eldrad Ulthran, Farseer of Ulthwé, foresees an Imperial explorator fleet unwittingly awakening a Necron tomb complex on the dead world of Maedrax. Striking swiftly, the Eldar destroy the Imperial ships before descending on Maedrax to purge the Necron presence. As the Eldar withdraw, they are brought into conflict with Space Marines of the Blood Angels Chapter dispatched to investigate the disappearance of the explorator fleet.
795.M41	An uprising in the Krandor system is put down by the Cadian 23rd.

THE MARCH OF TIME

This timeline is expressed using the dating system of the Imperium, though it should be expressed that the events themselves may go unrecorded – or recorded with considerable bias – within the Imperial archives. Indeed, Imperial records on different worlds may vary greatly in their representation of the facts. The dates and events noted here can be considered to be 'true' insofar as such things are possible.

An Imperial date is a date 'Anno Domini', but expressed in different terms to those we are used to. The most noticeable change is the suffix 'M' followed by a number. This is the millennium number. In Imperial terms any date between 2001 and 3000 would be suffixed by M3. The current millennium in the Warhammer 40,000 mythos is the forty-first or M41. Incidentally, this suffix is normally emphasised by a full stop for clarity. A typical dating code, such as you will find in this book, is 0150935.M41. The M41 means we are dealing with a forty first millennium date. The other numbers tell us the year, the fraction of the year and the accuracy of the date.

Year: The last three digits are the year within the millennium running from 001-000 (one thousand). 0150930/M32 is the year 930 of the thirty-second millennium, described as the year 31930AD. When referring to a year in general terms, and where it is not necessary to include the year fraction or check number, it is acceptable to write 'year 930/M32'.

Year Fraction: For administrative purposes the standard year is divided into 1000 equal segments; 001-000. This is a purely administrative convention and not part of everyday usage.

Check number: The first digit in the sequence is the dating reference or check number. This check number is necessary due to temporal distortions which affect ships in Warp space as well as worlds which are remote, or isolated, from Earth. Its presence qualifies the accuracy of the date given in each case. Note that as this timeline is a record of absolute fact, rather than a presentation of Imperial records, there is no check number on entries – the following is therefore appended out of completeness and for the satisfaction of curiosity.

797.M41 The Siege of Zalathras. Marneus Calgar, Chapter Master of the Ultramarines, holds the gate alone against the greenskin horde for a night and a day.

801.M41 An unprecedented flicker in the Astronomican throws thousands of ships off course, dooming them to destruction in the Warp.

822.M41 The Chaos Warmaster Abaddon raids the Maiden world of Ildanira. He is ultimately driven off by forces from Alaitoc Craftworld.

849.M41 All contact is lost with outposts on Birmingham, the Black Planet. Subsequent investigations of the massacre indicate it to be the work of Dark Eldar raiders.

850.M41 Ordo Xenos Inquisitor Lok leads his expedition to the Anphelion system.

863.M41 The Saint Cyllia Massacre. The Adamant Fury Titan Legion turn away from the Emperor and fall to Chaos. They turn their guns on loyalist regiments of the Planetary Defence Force before making their escape.

888.M41 The Crusade of Wrath. The Black Templars Space Marine Chapter inflict heavy losses on the Word Bearers Chaos Space Marine Legion and reclaim several systems in close proximity to the Maelstrom.

891.M41 The Long Midnight. The worlds of the Persya sector suffer countless attacks from Eldar pirates. Using ancient technology, the raiders swathe their targets in utter darkness and then pillage and slaughter at will. The vicious raids continue for half a year until Imperial Patrol Praxion arrives to drive off the raiders.

897.M41 The fortress-convent Sanctuary 101, and all Sisters of Battle within, is destroyed by the Necrons. There are no survivors and few tangible proofs of the perpetrators.

901.M41 Lugft Huron, master of the the Astral Claws chapter, declares himself the Tyrant of Badab and announces the system's secession from the Imperium. Eleven years of inter-system war follows, wreaking havoc on shipping lanes and embroiling more than a dozen Space Marine Chapters. Huron is eventually defeated, but escapes into the Maelstrom.

913.M41 Disciples of the Chaos Sorcerer Ahriman sack the Librarium on Jollana.

920.M41 Eldar pirates attack the troopship Emperor's Faithful as it exits Warp space in the Thanas system. The ship is boarded and then disappears, taking with it a complement of 5,000,000 Imperial Guardsmen and 200,000 men of the Imperial Navy.

Prefixes 1 to 8 indicate widening 'grey areas' of a given item of data's surrounding the origins . Prefix 9 is slightly different. It's used when, for instance, a source reporting from a world that doesn't use Imperial dating, needs to make a reference to that world's history. The historical date would carry the prefix 9.

0/1 Earth standard date. Referring to an event which happened within the Sol system.

2 Direct. Source in direct psychic contact with Earth when date reference was made.

3 Indirect. The source is in direct psychic contact with a class 2 source, but not Earth.

4 Corroborated. The source is in direct psychic contact with a class 3 source, but not a class 0/1 or 2 source.

5 Sub-corroborated. The source is in direct psychic contact with any corroborated source.

6 Non-referenced 1 year.0 No psychic contact with a class 1-5 source when the reference is made. The reference does belong to a sequence beginning or ending with a date with a class 1-5 source. The unsourced time period is less than 1 standard year.

7 Non-referenced 10 years. This is an unsourced date in the same way as a class 6 date, but with an unsourced period of 1-10 years.

8 Non-referenced more than 10 years. This is an unsourced date as for 7, but for an unsourced sequence of more than 10 years.

9 A approximated date with no fixed coordinates at either end of a sequence, or a date drawn from non-Imperially dated references.

Example: **0, 150, 935.M41,** (or the year 40,935 AD)

Check Number ——— Year fraction   Year

925.M41 Contact is lost with eighteen planets in the Vidar sector, including the forge world Lentrel Prime.

926.M41 The Vaxhallian genocides. In less than a month, Chaos renegades, known as the Purge, slaughter fourteen billion Imperial citizens.

928.M41 Arha and Karandras, opposed Phoenix Lords of the Striking Scorpions, duel for seventeen days amongst the shattered ruins of ancient Zandros.

937.M41 Inquisitor Pranix leads five companies of the Space Wolves Chapter as well as units of the Cadian 301st and the Tallarn 14th in an attempt to reclaim the nine Hollow Worlds from the vile clutches of Huron Blackheart and the traitorous Red Corsairs.

941.M41 Waaagh! Ghazghkull descends upon Armageddon. The Orks are defeated only by the extreme stubbornness of the defenders and the combined might of three Space Marine Chapters. Thought dead by his foes, Ghazghkull himself escapes into space.

944.M41 Commissar Yarrick, hero of the Battle for Armageddon, hears rumours that the Ork Warlord Ghazghkull still lives. Leaving retirement, Yarrick sets off in pursuit of his nemesis, vowing to bring Ghazghkull to justice.

963.M41 The Ultramarines clash with a Tau expeditionary fleet for control of the cursed planet of Malbede. When the conflict awakens the Necron Tombs hidden on Malbede, the Ultramarines and the Tau join forces to defeat the emerging Necrons. In the wake of the battle, Marneus Calgar initiates Exterminatus on Malbede, but generously allows the Tau to evacuate before the planet is destroyed.

969.M41 The plagueship Terminus Est is reported in the Cando system. The Zombie Plague sweeps across the system in the following months.

971.M41 The Ork outlaw Wazdakka Gutsmek sets in motion his plan to create an interstellar supa 'eyeway through the Warp. His intent is to ride his kustomised bike from one side of the galaxy to the other, slaughtering everything he finds on the way.

975.M41 The Bloodthirster Skarbrand materialises on the Cadian fortress-planet of Lutoris Epsilon. His berserk rage infects the garrison and soon the fortifications are knee-deep in blood as the Guardsmen tear each other apart in crazed bloodlust.

985.M41 Rumours abound in the Underhives of Cathoria II concerning shadowy warriors that steal away gangs and families. Broken Eldar weapons are discovered. Word reaches the upper levels of the hive and a punitive force of several hundred of the Imperial Commander's personal guard is sent to deal with the elusive invaders. None of the hive ruler's men return.

989.M41 Waaagh! Snagrod rampages across the Loki sector, culminating on a devastating assault on Rynn's World that leaves the Crimson Fists Chapter battered and bloodied.

995.M41 Tau fleet units strike at the shrine world of Ghola's Hope.

992.M41 Raiders from Ulthwé Craftworld strike at Cadian holdings on Aurent, only to be utterly defeated through the genius of Lord Castellan Ursarkar Creed.

993.M41 The Ultramarines quash rebellion on the industrial world of Ichar IV, only to find themselves in the forefront of a desperate defence against Hive Fleet Kraken. Elsewhere, the Eldar Craftworld Iyanden is ravaged by other tendrils of the Kraken. Two Space Marine Chapters – the Scythes of the Emperor and the Lamentors – are all but wiped out and hundreds of Imperial worlds are lost to the Tyranids before the incursion is blunted.

995.M41 Pirates of the Red Corsairs capture the Space Wolves cruiser 'Wolf of Fenris'.

138997.M41 The twin tendrils of Hive Fleet Leviathan strike at the underbelly of the Imperium, cutting a swathe of destruction through Segmentums Tempestus, Ultima and Solar.

221997.M41 The Imperial world of Piscina IV is invaded by Orks under the joint leadership of Ghazghkull Thraka and Nazdreg. Master Belial of the Dark Angels defends the planet until reinforcements can arrive and end the Ork threat.

509997.M41 Elements of the Ultramarines and Mortificators Space Marine Chapters make a stand against one spur of Hive Fleet Leviathan on the world of Tarsis Ultra. The defenders defeat this tendril with a biological plague, but the remainder of Hive Fleet Leviathan rampages on unabated.

601997.M41 Commissar Yarrick and Warlord Ghazghkull finally come face to face on the battlefields of Golgotha. Yarrick is captured, but ultimately released by Ghazghkull as the Warlord is planning to invade Armageddon once more, and wants a good fight.

622997.M41 Dark Eldar raiders slaughter Golgothan refugees on the moon of Jagdor.

977997.M41 The Tau Empire begins a third phase of expansion. They capture several Imperial worlds on the Eastern Fringe and show no sign of slowing.

757998.M41 Ghazghkull returns to Armageddon at the head of a new, even greater, Waaagh! Imperial commanders, having learnt from the previous invasion, do not hesitate to commit ever greater numbers of troops to this new battle for Armageddon. Several months into the siege, Ghazghkull grows bored with the grinding stalemate and, leaving his generals to continue the fight, begins the conquest of nearby worlds. Upon learning of the Warlord's departure, Commissar Yarrick joins a Black Templars crusade to finally end the menace of Ghazghkull.

718999.M41 Hive Fleet Leviathan invades the Ork empire in the Octavius system. War between Tyranid and Greenskin rages on with no sign of stopping. It remains to be seen if the victor will emerge stronger than ever, and an even greater threat to the Imperium.

975999.M41 The light of the Astronomican grows dimmer. Contact is lost with Ultima Macharia, and is intermittent at best with Macragge and Cypra Mundi.

978999.M41 Dark Eldar raiders cripple the Imperial Navy's moorings at Bakka.

980999.M41 A massive Chaos Space Marine fleet, under the command of Huron Blackheart, emerges from the Maelstrom and brings the Chogoris, Kaelas and Sessec systems under siege.

982999.M41 The Great Awakening. A ripple of psychic activity passes through the Imperium, awakening the dormant powers of latent psykers. The resulting backlash creates innumerable Warp rifts and a thousand worlds are lost to daemonic incursions.

986999.M41 Tech Priests of the Adeptus Mechanicus discover failures in the mechanisms of the Golden Throne that are far beyond their ability to repair.

987999.M41 Necron raids strike the Cypra Segentus system – the first activity of its kind within 2,000 light years of Terra.

989999.M41 The Ultramarines 3rd company liberate the Lagan system from the Tau Empire.

990999.M41 Eldar from the Biel Tan and Saim Hann Craftworlds devastate Imperial and Ork-held worlds surrounding the Octavius system with the intent of denying crucial bio-resources to Hive Fleet Leviathan.

992999.M41 The Night of a Thousand Rebellions. Uprising and discord strikes countless planets across the Imperium, including the supposedly secure worlds of Enceladus, Darkhold and Minisotira Contact is lost with large swathes of Segmentum Pacificus.

995999.M41 Warmaster Abaddon launches his 13th Black Crusade. The armies of Chaos invade Cadia and many surrounding worlds. Imperial forces counterattack, but there appears to be no end to the forces of the Dark Gods.

THE SPACE MARINES

They are the Adeptus Astartes, the Angels of Death, the Saviours of Mankind.

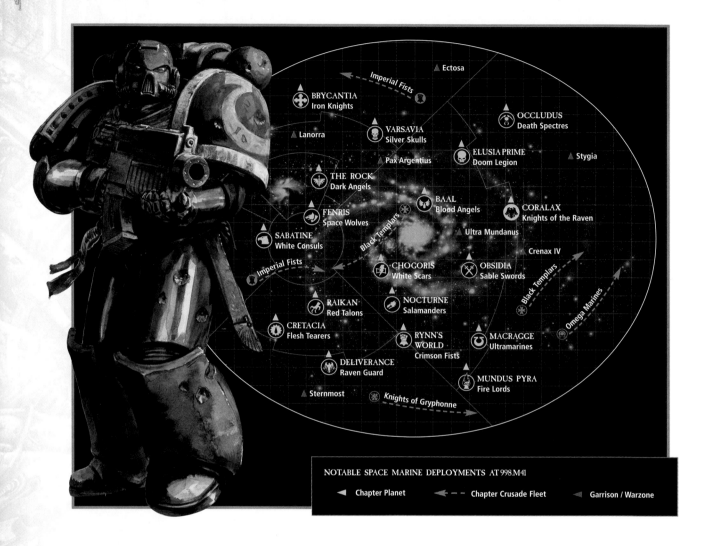

BRYCANTIA
Iron Knights

Lanorra

VARSAVIA
Silver Skulls

Pax Argentius

THE ROCK
Dark Angels

FENRIS
Space Wolves

SABATINE
White Consuls

Imperial Fists

RAIKAN
Red Talons

CRETACIA
Flesh Tearers

DELIVERANCE
Raven Guard

Sternmost

Imperial Fists

Ectosa

OCCLUDUS
Death Spectres

ELUSIA PRIME
Doom Legion

Stygia

BAAL
Blood Angels

CORALAX
Knights of the Raven

Ultra Mundanus

Crenax IV

Black Templars

CHOGORIS
White Scars

OBSIDIA
Sable Swords

NOCTURNE
Salamanders

Black Templars

Omega Marines

RYNN'S
WORLD
Crimson Fists

MACRAGGE
Ultramarines

MUNDUS PYRA
Fire Lords

Knights of Gryphonne

NOTABLE SPACE MARINE DEPLOYMENTS AT 998.M41

◄ Chapter Planet   ◄--- Chapter Crusade Fleet   ◄ Garrison / Warzone

The Adeptus Astartes are the most powerful of all human warriors. In many respects they are not really human at all, but superhuman beings forged by genetic modification, arduous training and the rigours of strict discipline. Space Marines are the embodiment of the Emperor's will – their roaring boltguns bring death to the enemies of Mankind, their presence in battle the difference between life and death. They are the Angels of Death, and none can stand against them.

Space Marines are organised into independent armies, called Chapters, of which there are roughly one thousand spread throughout the galaxy. Each Chapter has its own ships, its own heraldic uniforms and its own distinct identity and traditions. Unlike other military formations within the Imperium, a Space Marine Chapter is entirely self-sufficient, with its own forges, warships and support facilities.

Most Chapters operate from a Chapter Planet – a world within the Imperium, owned and governed by the Space Marines that maintain a base there. Some Chapters are not planetbound at all; their base of operations can be a vast space fleet, an orbital asteroid or a space station. As some Chapters rule entire planets, systems or sub-sectors, a Space Marine Chapter Master may act as the head of government as well as a marshal of war.

All the Space Marines in a Chapter belong to its warrior cult. These warrior cults preserve traditions and practices that date back to the earliest days of the Emperor's reign. Space Marines from a single Chapter are therefore spiritual brothers as well as brothers-at-arms. This dual existence as physical and spiritual warriors is what forges the Space Marines into such dedicated and determined warriors.

Although there is less than one Space Marine for every planet in the Imperium, they are sufficient to the task. The superhuman abilities of the Space Marines allow them to fight with a tenacity that lies far beyond the capabilities of lesser men, laying down a lethally accurate hail of bolter fire until the foe lies broken and beaten. The Battle-Brothers of the Adeptus Astartes cannot rest behind walls or fortifications – this they leave to the Imperial Guard. Seek, strike, secure – this is the combat doctrine of the Space Marines. They conduct the most dangerous and crucial of assaults, leading lightning raids behind enemy lines, seizing vital positions and slaying enemy warlords to render opposing troops leaderless.

ORBITAL ASSAULT

A Space Marine attack is heralded by the screaming approach of Drop Pods – armoured capsules launched from near orbit at speeds impossible to track or intercept. Supplied with coordinates by Space Marine Scouts, the Drop Pods deploy squad after squad of power armoured warriors into the very heart of the foe.

While Tactical, Assault and Devastator Squads secure the initial beachhead, Thunderhawk Gunships swoop low over the battlefield, deploying Land Raider or Predator tanks to the fray. Nigh inviolable in their Terminator armour, veteran Space Marines teleport onto key objectives, shredding enemy soldiers with assault cannon fire and smashing tanks apart with their power fists.

Such offensives are normally over in mere hours, for few armies can contend with the full fury of the Space Marines. On those rare occasions when an assault stretches out into days or weeks, the Space Marines press the assault with valour and determination, carrying bolter, chainsword and lascannon against the enemy long after lesser men would have given up hope. Only when the foe is beaten, when the cratered ground is hidden beneath a carpet of enemy dead and the area secured, do the Space Marines move on.

It may take one, two or a dozen such strikes to bring a campaign to a victorious end, but victory is never in doubt. Whilst a Space Marine draws breath he will fight, and whilst a Space Marine fights, triumph remains within his grasp. A half-company of fifty Space Marines is sufficient to end the rebellion of thousands, while a full Chapter of a thousand or so battle brothers can decide the fate of an entire sub-sector. Many foes have underestimated the sheer determination and valour of the Adeptus Astartes, but not one has survived to repeat that grave mistake.

With victory won, the Space Marines remain planetside until fresh units of the Imperial Guard and local defence forces arrive. Scarcely is the battlezone secured when the Space Marines embark once more on fresh campaigns. They are the saviours of the Imperium, made strong through faith and refined in the crucible of war. For such heroes there can be no rest – only an eternity of battle in the Emperor's name.

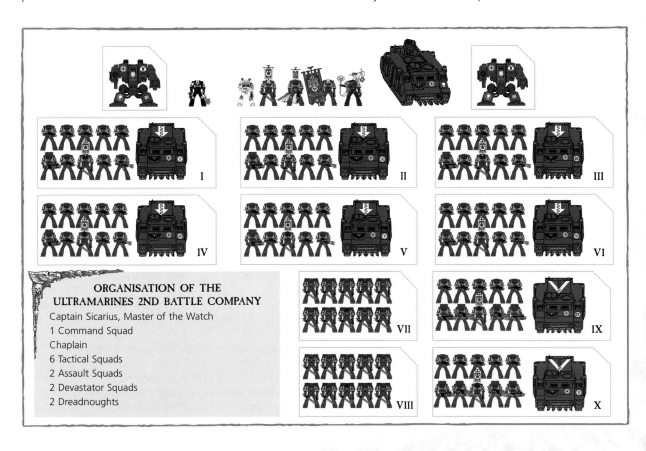

ORGANISATION OF THE ULTRAMARINES 2ND BATTLE COMPANY

Captain Sicarius, Master of the Watch

1 Command Squad

Chaplain

6 Tactical Squads

2 Assault Squads

2 Devastator Squads

2 Dreadnoughts

CHAPTERS OF THE SPACE MARINES

One thousand bastions of strength and valour, fighting for the survival of mankind.

Tactical Marine,
Ultramarines 2nd Company

Shoulder plates bearing squad
and Chapter markings

Ultramarines Chapter banner

ULTRAMARINES

First Founding

The Ultramarines are the exemplars of the Space Marines, the purest and noblest of all of the Adeptus Astartes. It was the founding Primarch of the Ultramarines, Roboute Guilliman, who established the Codex Astartes, the august tome that laid the foundation for the Space Marine Chapters. Many hold the Ultramarines to be the rightful heirs not only of Guilliman, but of the Emperor himself.

> "We are the Ultramarines, the Sons of Guilliman. Whilst we draw breath, we stand. Whilst we stand, we fight. Whilst we fight, we prevail. Nothing shall stay our wrath."
>
> – Marneus Calgar
> Chapter Master of the Ultramarines

Tactical Marine
Blood Angels 3rd Company

Assault Marine
Blood Angels Death Company

BLOOD ANGELS

First Founding

The Blood Angels strive for absolute perfection in all things. Their martial disciplines are practiced unceasingly over long and vigorous lives, their rituals and doctrines as flawless in execution as they are wondrous to behold. Yet for all their outward nobility, the Blood Angels are deeply marred. Each carries a curse within his blood, a dormant flaw that inevitably awakens to madness and blood rage. This is the legacy of their Primarch, Sanguinius, and it has doomed the Blood Angels to be feared and mistrusted by those they protect.

Grey Hunter
Space Wolves 2nd Company

Blood Claw
Space Wolves 2nd Company

SPACE WOLVES

First Founding

Made feral in thought and appearance by their genetic heritage, the Space Wolves are the most ferocious of all Space Marines. They are are also the most unorthodox, having forsaken the Codex Astartes in favour of the Teachings of their own Primarch.

The Space Wolves have little patience with the fawning superstitions of other men, preferring the ancient warrior-traditions of their home planet, Fenris. Each strives to perform great deeds worthy of song, calling upon the Emperor only to witness the living and to judge the slain.

IMPERIAL FISTS
First Founding

The Imperial Fists have earned battle honours against many major alien races and been instrumental in holding the Imperium together through the bleakest of times. They also performed a pivotal role in the defence of the Emperor's palace during the dark days of the Horus Heresy.

DARK ANGELS
First Founding

The Dark Angels stand first amongst the Space Marine Chapters, as they have done since their very inception. Theirs is a proud Chapter, with traditions and rituals that date back to the earliest days of the Imperium.

SALAMANDERS
First Founding

Born out of darkness and fire, the battle brothers of the Salamanders Chapter are tenacious in the extreme, refusing to yield battle even when other Space Marines would fall back.

WHITE SCARS
First Founding

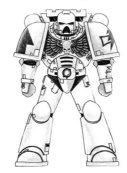

White Scars are the proven masters of reconnaissance and of the hit-and-run attack. They are hunters and raiders without peer in the armed forces of Imperium.

FLESH TEARERS
Second Founding (Blood Angels Successors)

The Flesh Tearers are subject to a terrible blood-rage, driven to win victory in close assault where they can sunder the foe with chainsword and power fist. Such is their bloodlust that many other forces of the Imperium are wary of calling upon the Flesh Tearers in all but the direst need.

CRIMSON FISTS
Second Founding (Imperial Fists Successors)

The Crimson Fists are a Chapter on the edge of extinction. Yet they fight on, bearing the blows of a cruel fate with a stoicism that has become legend across the Imperium.

SILVER SKULLS
Unknown Founding

The Silver Skulls believe that the Emperor guides their purpose. They take to the battlefield only when portents demand it, fighting with valour that has won them great renown across the Imperium.

BLACK TEMPLARS
Second Founding (Imperial Fists Successors)

The fanatical Black Templars have no Chapter Planet. They are a fleet-based Chapter, divided into many Crusades. The Black Templars have modified the Codex Astartes, and each Crusade is led by a Marshall whose ad hoc company is assembled to pursue a particular goal.

ASSAULT ON BLACK REACH

Two months after the invasion of Waaagh! Zanzag, salvation came to Black Reach. At Ghospora Hive, Orkish attacker and Imperial defender alike turned their eyes towards the wailing skies as the Ultramarines' strike cruiser *Valin's Revenge* began its bombardment. Plasma blast after plasma blast rained down from orbit, detonating amid the Ork lines with the fury of an exploding sun. Orks died by the thousand, rendered unto ash by the onslaught. Thousands more were knocked sprawling by the shockwave, their Battlewagons and Buggies sent tumbling into fiery oblivion as the ground shook and roared under the strike cruiser's guns. Before the echoes had fully died away, Drop Pods slammed into the cratered earth, their hulls glowing red from the heat of re-entry. The Ultramarines' Second Company had arrived, and there would be a reckoning.

Five thousand, ten thousand, perhaps even twenty thousand Orks fell to the wrath of the Ultramarines that day, and when the story was recounted on Black Reach in future years the number would grow ever larger with each fresh telling. The Orks fought with all the maddened fury of their race, but the Ultramarines fought like heroes born. Never once did they falter, though the enemy outnumbered them two hundred times and more. With boltgun and chainsword they scoured the Greenskins from Ghospora's walls, but still

the Orks came on. With lascannon and missile they destroyed Battlewagon and Stompa, but still the Orks came on. Ten thousand lesser men could not have hoped to prevail against the tide of rage that ebbed and flowed before the walls of Ghospora that day, but the Ultramarines stood firm. They fired until their guns ran dry, then cast themselves at the Orks with blades and fists, never once falling back, never once despairing at the odds.

Wherever the Orks threatened to overcome their disorder, wherever a Warboss rallied his warriors, there could Captain Sicarius be found. No blade tasted more blood that day than his, for Sicarius met the fury of the Orks and matched it with his own. The Captain and his entourage cut a bloody swathe through the Greenskin lines, his blade severing heads and limbs even as his eyes sought the Warlord whose will drove this conquering Waaagh!

There, finally, amid the breached walls of Ghospora, did Sicarius find his prey. With the Terminators of Squad Helios to his left and the unstoppable Dreadnought that was Brother Ultraxes to his right, the Ultramarines Captain hurled himself into battle with Zanzag's retinue. Only one could walk away from that terrible struggle – the victor would dictate the final fate of Black Reach and all who dwelled upon it.

SPACE MARINE DREADNOUGHTS

When a Space Marine suffers mortal harm, the like of which even his physique cannot endure, his body is borne from the battlefield with reverence. Most die swiftly from their wounds, or receive the Emperor's Mercy from one of the Chapter's Apothecaries. But the mightiest fallen, those within whom the spark of life and honour still burns bright though their body be rent and torn, are preserved from final rest. For such a man the battle is not yet done. His skills, his wisdom and his fighting spirit must continue to serve the Emperor, even if it must do so in another form. The hero's crippled body is installed in the cyborganic web of an armoured sarcophagus, his dimmed senses bound to electro-fibre implants. So does he cast off a frail mortal frame for something greater and more difficile. So does he become a Dreadnought.

A Dreadnought is a truly massive fighting machine, weighing several tons and standing two or three times the height of a man. As the Dreadnought strides into battle, incoming fire spatters like rain off his towering adamantium and ceramite hull. Fiery death roars from his weapons and his great metal fists churn through all who stand before him.

THE IMPERIAL GUARD

The Conqueror, the Unstoppable, the Hammer of the Emperor.

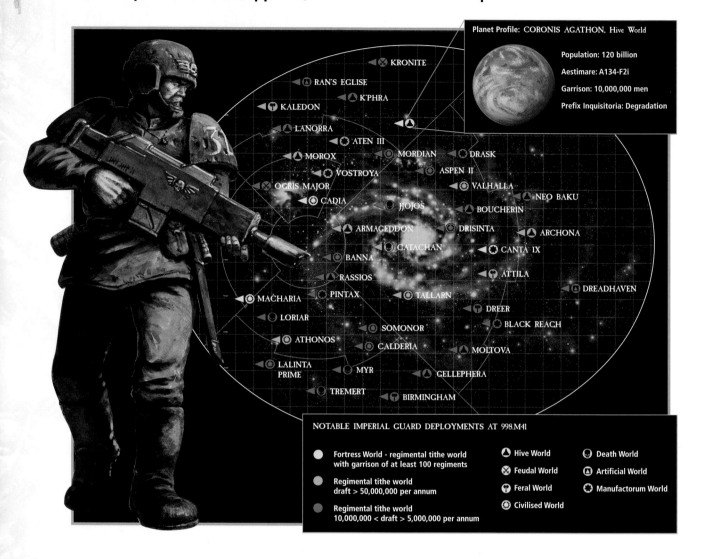

Planet Profile: CORONIS AGATHON, Hive World

Population: 120 billion

Aestimare: A134-F2i

Garrison: 10,000,000 men

Prefix Inquisitoria: Degradation

KRONITE
RAN'S EGLISE
K'PHRA
KALEDON
LANORRA
ATEN III
MOROX
MORDIAN
DRASK
VOSTROYA
ASPEN II
OGRIS MAJOR
VALHALLA
CADIA
NEO BAKU
JJOJOS
BOUCHERIN
ARMAGEDDON
DRISINTA
ARCHONA
CATACHAN
CANTA IX
BANNA
RASSIOS
ATTILA
PINTAX
DREADHAVEN
MACHARIA
TALLARN
LORIAR
DREER
SOMONOR
BLACK REACH
ATHONOS
CALDERIA
MOLTOVA
LALINTA PRIME
MYR
GELLEPHERA
TREMERT
BIRMINGHAM

NOTABLE IMPERIAL GUARD DEPLOYMENTS AT 998.M41

⬤ Fortress World - regimental tithe world with garrison of at least 100 regiments

⬤ Regimental tithe world draft > 50,000,000 per annum

⬤ Regimental tithe world 10,000,000 < draft > 5,000,000 per annum

🜨 Hive World

❌ Feudal World

⊕ Feral World

◉ Civilised World

☻ Death World

Ⓐ Artificial World

✲ Manufactorum World

The Imperial Guard is Mankind's primary and most numerous defence. It is the Hammer of the Emperor, numbering billions upon billions of soldiers divided into millions of regiments. Even the Departmento Munitorium has no idea of the number of troops under arms, as the continuous toll of casualties and influx of recruits may run to millions in a single day. With thunderous barrages and crackling volleys of las-fire, the Imperial Guard attacks in endless waves until victory is won. It is warfare at its most brutal, where individual soldiers are irrelevant and only the mettle of countless forgotten soldiers decides a world's fate.

An Imperial Guardsman can never possess the battle prowess of a Space Marine, but there are millions of such Guardsmen for each Space Marine, sufficient that they can be expended for the smallest of goals or committed to the most desperate of defences. Where the Space Marines can be likened to a surgical blade, striking swiftly and precisely, the onslaught of the Imperial Guard is akin to a sledgehammer, cumbersome but unstoppable. Its doctrines focus on training soldiers to aim steady and stand firm when faced with the foe.

REGIMENTS OF THE GUARD

Each world of the Imperium is obliged to raise Regiments of Imperial Guard, and these are shipped all across the galaxy to conduct endless wars in the Emperor's name. The size of these regiments is by no means fixed. Indeed, depending on the population of the world from which it is raised, the number of men in a new regiment can range from a few hundred to several tens of thousands. Troops regard themselves as belonging first and foremost to their regiment, which consists of comrades from the same world who speak the same dialect and practice the same customs.

Many Imperial Guard regiments are recruited from the savage urban environments of hive worlds, such as Moltova, Armageddon or Coronis Agathon, planets where family or corporate-based warfare is endemic. Such troops are battle-hardened long before they are drafted into the Imperial Guard and are regarded as the best raw material for a fighting regiment; although summary executions and whippings are often needed to instill a little discipline, of course.

Other favourite recruiting grounds are worlds such as Kaledon, Shodrax and Kanak – the feral or medieval planets where warrior castes and martial brotherhoods thrive. Primitive recruits are not discouraged from native practices such as head-hunting, the taking of scalps and other such trophies. These customs are regarded as perfectly acceptable for the battle-spirit they awaken in the troops and for the fear provoked in the foe. Such warriors must be trained to use modern tools of war, although the weapons employed by the Imperial Guard are deliberately straightforward and durable to ensure that even the most backward members of the human race can wield and maintain them.

Once a regiment has been raised, it is shipped to its posting, often receiving further training in transit. While regiments are normally posted straight to the heart of a conflict, they are occasionally assigned to a world that borders a warzone, both to reinforce that outpost's defences and to give the inexperienced guardsmen sight and smell of the enemy. Sometimes a regiment will be posted to a newly conquered or liberated world, inevitably leading to conflict with lingering pockets of

resistance. More often than not, the new garrison will find itself consolidating control of an entire planet from little more than an initial dropzone. This is very much a baptism of fire, forging a hardened fighting unit from the raw troops or damning them to certain death on the beachhead.

THE WEAPONS OF WAR

Imperial Guard regiments vary enormously across the galaxy, and include disciplined ranks of infantry, glorious cavalry, fearsome artillery as well as earth-shaking tanks and war engines. Each Imperial Guard regiment is largely uniform in its composition. An infantry regiment will contain nothing in the way of heavy artillery, whilst an artillery regiment will contain little else. As a result, the Imperial Guard are at their strongest when formed into an army drawn from several regiments. This is a deliberate organisational procedure set in place to prevent large scale rebellion occurring – one of many painful lessons the Imperium learnt in the dark days of the Horus Heresy.

The cruel truth is that manpower is the cheapest of the Imperium's myriad currencies. Commanders of the Guard spend the lives of their men in the search for victory as carelessly as other armies expend ammunition. It is through this, the inexorable and overwhelming application of power onto a single strategic point, that the Imperial Guard wins its bloody victories. Though ponderous, it can field an unending tide of infantry, supported by armoured vehicles and artillery. It is a strategy of attrition, and few foes can endure its mighty onset.

IMPERIAL GUARD REGIMENTS

The nameless heroes who live and die so that the Imperium might endure.

CADIAN SHOCK TROOPS

Cadia has always been a fortress world, charged with guarding a narrow corridor of space known as the Cadian gate – the one and only safe passage between the Daemon worlds of the Eye of Terror and Earth. Cadia itself is therefore one of the most strategically important planets in the galaxy, and its defence is vital to the survival of the Imperium. As a result of this, Cadia is a fortress, first, last and always. Its entire population is destined for a military life. The birth rate and recruitment rate are synonymous, and the death rate is not so very far separated.

Cadian Regiments are swift to deploy, with excellent morale and unswerving loyalty. Such is the heroism the Cadians display that even the superhuman Space Marines hold these guardsmen as important allies. Cadian commanders believe that it is discipline, and discipline alone, that makes a good soldier. While this view is perhaps a little narrow, it is impossible to argue with the impressive honours lavished on the Cadian high command by a grateful Imperium. Such is the reputation of the Cadians that many other regiments utilise the same pattern equipment, although specific fighting styles and regimental credos may differ.

CATACHAN JUNGLE FIGHTERS

The planet Catachan is a death world on which the climate, animal life and plant life is all inimical to humanity. On Catachan, daily survival requires skill and courage undreamt of on other worlds. It is not surprising therefore that the men forming the Catachan Regiments are tough, resourceful and uncompromising warriors, as deadly from afar with mortar and lascannon as they are from ambush with lasgun and flamer.

In the jungle, Catachan warriors are unsurpassed. Each is easily worth five men from any other regiment, and those skills learnt in the jungle are easily adapted to other war zones. Indeed, most Catachans claim that even the most suicidal of military engagements are as nothing to a day in the lethal jungles of their homeworld. This gung-ho enthusiasm is often mistaken for bravado by Guardsmen from other regiments. The fact remains that Catachan jungle fighters remain the most uncomplaining, determined and valourous soldiers of the Imperial Guard, whether assigned to drudgerous garrison duties or a hopeless assault upon an impregnable fortress.

MORDIAN IRON GUARD

The Mordian Iron Guard are superbly drilled and accoutred soldiers from a world bathed in perpetual night and cursed with the attentions of Chaos.
In battle, the Iron Guard present a solid wall of brightly-uniformed, flawlessly-formed troops, cutting down the foe with precisely timed volleys from behind a hedge of polished bayonet points.

TALLARN DESERT RAIDERS

The Tallarn are guerrilla fighters, evasive and opportunistic. They are especially renowned for hard-fighting Sentinel squadrons and reconnaissance operatives. Every Tallarn is an accomplished rider, and they will often use riding beasts to move from battle to battle, or to charge into the thick of the fray where knives and hunting lances can do their wicked work.

VALHALLAN ICE WARRIORS

Regiments raised in the frozen hive cities of Valhalla have a formidable reputation for unwavering courage when in defence. Normally the only way to capture ground held by Valhallans is to wipe them out to the last man. When attacking, the Ice Warriors combine massed artillery barrages with endless infantry wave assaults – few foes can withstand such tactics.

ARMAGEDDON STEEL LEGIONS

Fully mobile in their Chimera transports, the Steel Legions are able to overrun the enemy lines with swift-moving infantry formations. Recruited from the great industrial hives of Armageddon, Steel Legion ranks are thick with conscripted Armageddon hive gangers – a fact that goes a long way to explain the fabled brutality of the Steel Legions.

ATHONIAN TUNNEL RATS

Governance of Athonos is vied for by a dozen rival families. The resultant gang warfare – fought in the streets and sewers of the hydroponic gardens – is brutal and unending. Such is the recruiting ground for the Athonian Tunnel Rats. They are masters of urban combat and amongst the most determined close-quarter fighters of the Imperial Guard.

VOSTROYAN FIRSTBORN

Vostroya's regiments are conscripted from the first born sons of every family on the planet. The arms and armour of Firstborn regiments are directly supplied from the clamourous manfactorums of their smog-shrouded homeworld. Each weapon is a family heirloom, passed down from Firstborn to Firstborn, and worth considerably more than the man who carries it.

THE DEATH KORPS OF KRIEG

Krieg was laid to waste when rebellion led to a 500 year campaign of atomic purging. The Death Korps now seek to make amends for their earlier heresy by martyring themselves to the Imperial cause. The Death Korps fight without fear of death, grinding their enemies down in battles of attrition, disdaining retreat and surrender whilst victory is still in sight.

KALEDON HUNTERS

The complex warrior clans of Kaledon are an invaluable recruiting ground for the Imperial Guard and contribute several of the toughest, if least disciplined, regiments in the Imperium. Each regiment is drawn from a single clan and Kaledoni regiments inevitably fight all the harder to prove their superiority over a regiment recruited from a different clan.

THE KIELDAR OFFENSIVE

A rebellion systematically crushed beneath the weight of the Imperial Guard.

The Kieldar rebellion of 956.M41 began with a declaration of independence and flagrant rejection of the Imperial Creed. Shortly thereafter all those deemed a threat to the newly 'independent' Fortress world – including representatives of the Ecclesiarchy and military advisors from nearby Cadia were executed.

Unbeknownst to the rebels, an Astropath attached to the Cadian delegation was able to send warning of Kieldar's uprising. Fearing that misrule would spread – especially to the nearby, and vital agri worlds of the Dinorwyc cluster, an Imperial Guard task force was assembled and ordered to crush the Kieldar rebellion.

DAYS 1 to 7

Three attempts to secure a drop site on the northern continent are defeated. The fourth drives the enemy from the beach-head.

Casualties inflicted:
Moderate
Casualties sustained:
Severe

Dauntless
Imperial Navy Battlegroup

DAY 18

Blitzkrieg assault on outer defence line.
Thunderbolt fighters provide air cover.

Estimated casualties inflicted: Heavy
Infantry casualties sustained: Light
Fighting vehicles casualties sustained: Moderate

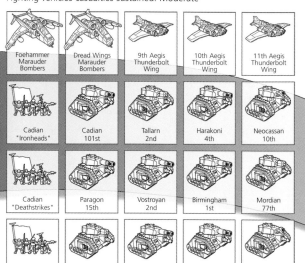

Cadian 10th Light	Morox 1st Recon	Cadian 2nd Recon
Cadian 11th Light	Loriar 2nd Drop	Elysia 5th Drop	Cadian 3rd Recon	Cadian 77th Recon
Cadian Whiteshields	Cadian Whiteshields	Cadian 7th Drop	Elysia 50th Recon	Elysia 12th Recon
Elysia 3rd Drop	Elysia 4th Drop	Cadian 15th Light	Elysia 9th Recon	Catachan 4th Recon

Foehammer Marauder Bombers	Dread Wings Marauder Bombers	9th Aegis Thunderbolt Wing	10th Aegis Thunderbolt Wing	11th Aegis Thunderbolt Wing
Cadian "Ironheads"	Cadian 101st	Tallarn 2nd	Harakoni 4th	Neocassan 10th
Cadian "Deathstrikes"	Paragon 15th	Vostroyan 2nd	Birmingham 1st	Mordian 77th
Cadian "Marauders"	Jjojos 3rd	Pintax 33rd	Pintax 28th	Cadian 8th

TACTICA CONTROL

Regimental commanders of the Imperial Guard are expected to lead their men from the front; to enforce discipline and set an example to the common soldiers. By contrast, officers who oversee the wider strategies of the battlegroup are too valuable to be commonly exposed to the volatile theatres of operation. A high commander of this kind directs the bombardments, entrenchments and assaults of their numberless soldiers from the relative safety of a Proteus-class command bunker or orbiting starship. Here a coterie of aides, servitors and astropaths keep him abreast of battlefield developments, and an ever-vigilant Lord Commissar ensures that his duties are discharged correctly and without weakness.

THE LEMAN RUSS

The Leman Russ is the chief battle tank of the Imperial Guard. Over the many centuries the design has been in use there have been many fundamental changes in construction and even in appearance, but the capabilities of the vehicle have changed very little. The Leman Russ' rugged construction has proved time and again that it can inflict and sustain heavy damage. No other tank – human or alien – of the Leman Russ' size can match its firepower. At the same time the solid and durable design the tank to endure a variety of lethal environments, as well as the field modifications of often less-than-expert crews and repair teams.

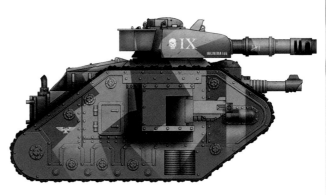

Cadian 14th Light

Cadian 9th Mech

Athonos 56th Recon

DAYS 20-24

Recon elements destroyed whilst cutting enemy supply lines. Reports point to captured guardsmen having been ritually sacrificed.

Estimated casualties inflicted: Light
Casualties sustained: Heavy
Strategic Impact: Heavy

Cadian 37th Heavy

Cadian 38th

Cadian 211th

Mordian 2nd Penal

Mordian 133rd

Vostroyan 4th Artillery

Cadian 9th Artillery

Cadian 34th

Cadian 8th

Cadian 4th

K'phrani 11th Artillery

"Thundergod" Super Heavy Company

Cadian 77th Recon

Vostroyan 2nd Recon

Mordian 11th Artillery

Cadian 7th Artillery

"Boneheads" Ogryns

Cadian 8th

Cadian 4th

Rassiosan "Levellers"

Catachan 18th

Bannan 1st

Rassiosan "Light"

Vostroyan 2nd

DAYS 25 to 40

Taskforces Ironwind and Steel Hammer engage in pyrrhic sieges of outlying enemy-held cities and trenchlines. The mission goal is that the taskforces should die slowly enough to prevent the enemy reinforcing his stronghold. Presence of Daemons reported, but not independently verified.

Estimated casualties inflicted: Moderate
Casualties sustained: Moderate - estimated at 70,000

DAYS 60 TO 93

The Siege of Darkridge. The Darkridge Hold fortifications are reduced to rubble by thirty days of continuous bombardment. Kieldar rebel defence units fall back before infantry advance. Taskforce Ironwind cuts enemy line of retreat.

Casualties inflicted: Severe
Casualties sustained: Heavy

DAYS 41 to 63

Flank March. Unexpected victory by taskforce Ironwind allows seizure of the Krokorax bastion from Chaos Renegade agitators. Taskforce Ironwind advances upon enemy positions in the Kieldar Darkridge.

Estimated casualties inflicted: Light
Casualties sustained: Heavy
Forced march casualties: Moderate

Cadian 2nd

Cadian 34th

Cadian 101st

Cadian 89th

Cadian 1st Penal

Catachan 10th

Catachan 11th

Catachan 12th

Harakoni "Hunters"

Paragon 1st

Neocassan 4th

Neocassan 9th

Cadian 2nd

Catachan 2nd Recon

Cadian 3rd Recon

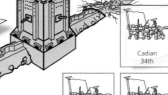

Cadian 34th

Cadian 101st

Harakoni "Reavers"

Catachan 10th

Catachan 11th

Neocassan 9th

Catachan 34th

CHAOS SPACE MARINES

Cruel Marauders, Ruthless Overlords – Traitors all.

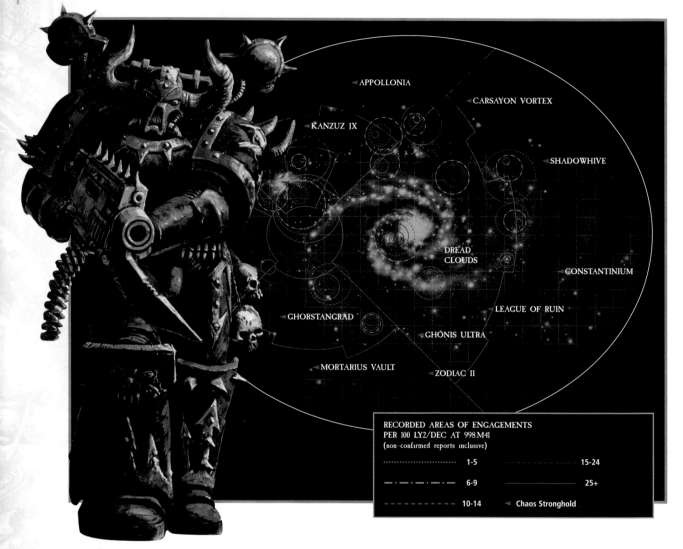

APPOLLONIA

CARSAYON VORTEX

KANZUZ IX

SHADOWHIVE

DREAD CLOUDS

CONSTANTINIUM

LEAGUE OF RUIN

GHORSTANGRAD

GHONIS ULTRA

MORTARIUS VAULT

ZODIAC II

RECORDED AREAS OF ENGAGEMENTS
PER 100 LY2/DEC AT 998.M41
(non-confirmed reports inclusive)

.... 1-5	--------- 15-24
— · — · — · — 6-9	————— 25+
– – – – – – – 10-14	◄ Chaos Stronghold

The Chaos Space Marines wage war for glory, for adulation, for the joy of battle, for worldly power and spiritual release; and for other reasons too dark for the faithful to comprehend. Chaos Space Marines were once the Imperium's greatest defenders but are now deadly warriors bent on anarchy and destruction. They serve nothing but their own desires and the Gods of the Warp that grant them the power to fulfil their depraved ambitions. A warrior of the Chaos Gods holds allegiance only to those more powerful than he is.

Chaos Space Marines are gene-engineered behemoths of war, clad in formidable power armour and wielding weapons forged from human technology and blessed by daemonic patronage. Along with their physiques and unparalleled battlecraft, the Chaos Space Marines are blessed with the gifts of the Dark Gods, and many have otherworldly abilities and strange mutations.

TRAITORS AND RENEGADES

Throughout the war-torn history of the Imperium, Space Marines have strayed from their service to the Emperor and turned to the Chaos Gods. Such a betrayal caused the cataclysmic events of the Horus Heresy at the birth of the Imperium. Entire Legions of Space Marines, tens of thousands-strong, betrayed the Emperor. The Traitor Legions have since broken into hundreds of roving warbands. As well as these warriors, individual Space Marines, squads, companies and whole Chapters have turned renegade and sworn themselves to Chaos. These are the most loathed of all the Emperor's enemies, for they are traitors who have forsworn their oaths of allegiance and turned their backs on duties held dearer than life. The Chaos Lords are the most powerful of these warriors, capable of welding together coalitions of these disparate forces long enough to enslave and despoil.

HIDDEN LAIRS

At the heart of the Imperium lies the twisting morass of the Eye of Terror Warp storm. Here, starships cannot easily forge their way through the swirling energies of the Warp, and so within the Eye are found the greatest fastnesses of Chaos, preserved from Imperial retribution by the power of their dark masters. Yet the Eye of Terror is also a prison, for its tempestuous energies trap the Chaos Space Marines within.

Time flows strangely within the Eye of Terror. While a month or day passes in the material universe, an hour or a century may pass amid the swirling Warp rifts of the Eye. Thus the Chaos Space Marines erupt forth on sporadic raids as the chance flows of energy allow, rampaging across worlds and star systems before returning to their strongholds. Occasionally the Eye of Terror opens fully, allowing the multitudinous hordes of Chaos to burst forth in devastating incursions known as the Black Crusades.

Chaos renegades and Traitor Legionnaires dwell not only in the Eye of Terror, but also within other Warp storms such as the Maelstrom and the Well of Shadows. Warbands stalk their prey from the wilderness space between Imperial sectors aboard starships, on hidden moonbases and within drifting space hulks; there is no target beyond the reach of the Chaos Space Marines and no world that does not feel their coming.

DEADLY WARRIORS

The Chaos Space Marines are highly trained and motivated by greed, lust and glory. Many have decades, centuries or even millennia of combat experience, won on countless corpse-riddled battlefields. All are highly skilled in every manner of weapon and war. Heavy weapon squads known as Havocs lay down blistering covering fire, while jump pack-equipped Raptor squads swoop down on their enemies. The most fearsome and experienced warriors advance clad in archaic Terminator armour. Some renegades dedicate their lives to a single god and a single purpose, wholly surrendering their humanity for the glories of their patron. Foremost amongst such warriors are the Khorne Berzerkers, who are gripped by a bloodthirsty battlelust and hurl themselves at their foes with pistols and chain-axes, and the Plague Marines of Nurgle, dedicated to spreading pestilence and decay.

A few Chaos Space Marines allow Daemons to possess their bodies, exhibiting destructive Warp-based powers that consume their host as surely as they do his foes. The mysterious Obliterators have made strange pacts with the Ruinous Powers and are capable of transforming their bodies into living weapons. These warriors fight alongside war machines that have seen ceaseless battle for centuries on end; icon-encrusted battle tanks, psychopathic Dreadnoughts and Daemon-possessed Defilers. Such are the forces of the Chaos Space Marines. Such is the doom of Mankind.

THE FALL OF VILAMUS

The piratical band of renegade Space Marines known as the Red Corsairs regularly raid the Imperium from lairs within the Warp storm known as the Maelstrom. Most of these attacks target shipping, but there are some raids, those led by the dread commander Huron Blackheart, that go much further in their daring, and the Fall of Vilamus was one such attack. In the last years of the 41st Millennium, Huron set out to steal a large amount of gene-seed – the raw genetic material his Apothecaries require to make more Space Marines. Vilamus was the fortress-monastery of the Marines Errant Space Marine Chapter. It was a formidable target, protected by the greatest warriors of the Imperium, throbbing power shields to prevent teleporting, and armoured bastions equipped with lasers capable of blasting targets out of orbit. The first of these defences, the Space Marines, was relatively straightforward to negate. Over the course of two years the Red Corsairs performed ever more daring attacks on shipping in the sector, drawing more and more of the Marines Errant out on patrol and counter-piracy missions. Eventually, this left Vilamus garrisoned by only 120 Space Marines, supported by numerous Chapter serfs.

Night Lords Veterans

Huron struck a deal with several warriors of the Night Lords Legion, infamous for their ambushes and sneak attack tactics. These Night Lords formed a vanguard. Having been dropped onto the world under cover of a cosmic storm, they infiltrated the defences of Vilamus via poorly defended ventilation shafts and maintenance tunnels. Once inside the fortress-monastery they disabled the generatorum, shutting down the teleport field and defence lasers.

Terminator Assault

With the defence lasers out of commission, Huron's cruisers and strike craft were able to enter low orbit. From here, Huron's Terminators – highly experienced and heavily-armoured warriors – were able to teleport directly into Vilamus. Their main target was the power relays that still fed energy to the defence bastions. Once these were severed, the Terminators diverted their attack to the apothecarion where the Chapter's gene-vault was to be found.

Huron's Victory

With Vilamus' automated defence turrets deprived of power and the fortress-monastery's garrison combating the Terminators, Huron delivered the killing blow. He led an assault against the main chapel, which contained many of the Chapter's most prized artefacts. Torn between protecting their gene-seed and their Chapter relics, the Marines Errant were divided, and thus easily conquered. Huron escaped with nearly all of the Chapter's gene-seed, dooming the Marines Errant to a slow demise.

THE ANTECANIS MASSACRE

Perhaps the greatest of all the bloodthirsty warlords of Chaos is Abaddon, Warmaster of the Black Legion. It was during Abaddon's 9th Black Crusade that the world of Antecanis felt his ire. At the start of the 37th Millennium it was a heaving hive world with a population in the tens of billions. Its principal export was people, most of whom were sent to labour in the nearby Naval dockyard of Cancephalus or to crew the warships built there. Knowing that the Imperial Navy docks were heavily defended, Abaddon chose to strike at its most vulnerable point – the world from which its workers came. Without a supply of millions of labourers, Cancephalus' manufactories and shipyards would fall silent.

Abaddon promised great riches and countless slaves to his warriors, making pacts with the frenzied Space Marines of the World Eaters, the darkly zealous Word Bearers, renegades from the Purge and the Apostles of Minthras, and dozens of smaller warbands. The might of the Black Legion and their allies fell upon Antecanis in 165.M37. A space battle erupted around the orbital defences, but the defence monitors and Imperial Navy space stations could do little against the battle barges, grand cruisers and battleships of Abaddon's fleet. After seven days, fusion bombs and vortex torpedoes rained down from the heavens onto the towering citadels of Antecanis' hives. Millions died as glistening towers toppled under the orbital barrage. In the wake of this devastation, dropships poured onto the surface, disgorging hundreds of ruthless killers.

Abaddon's lieutenants and allies had divided the spoils and set about attacking their targets. Abaddon focussed upon Monarchive, the seat of the Imperial Commander. At the vanguard of Abaddon's attack strode Dhar'Leth, a Daemon Prince who had fought for the Night Lords during the Horus Heresy, but who now swore allegiance to the Warmaster. Dhar'Leth's assault was relentless; for sixteen days the Daemon Prince and his Black Legionnaires burned and butchered their way through the lower levels of Monarchive. Refugees fled in the tens of millions, but still columns of slaves hundreds of kilometres-long trudged across the wastes to the Black Legion's landers.

When the Chaos Space Marines attacked, Astropaths had broadcast warnings and calls for aid. Space Marines of the Silver Skulls Chapter were the first to respond. They harried the Chaos fleet with daring hit-and-run attacks that robbed the warriors on the surface of orbital support. The Silver Skulls were but the first warriors in the Imperium's response as the Departmento Munitorum gathered forces and raised regiments for all-out war. Abaddon knew that once the limitless numbers of the Emperor's armies were committed, Antecanis would become a cauldron of battle from which there would be no escape. He resolved to swiftly end the siege of Monarchive.

Abaddon led the final assault on the capital, attacking with his bodyguard of Black Legion Terminators. They slaughtered squads of Adeptus Arbites, whole platoons of planetary defence troopers and the elite Oath Wardens of the Imperial Commander's personal guard. The sacrifices of the defenders were in vain, for it took Abaddon a mere two days to breach the final defence line and storm the inner sanctum of the Imperial Commander. With Monarchive now under his control, Abaddon sent his forces to kill or capture as many of the hive's populace as possible. Those too old or too infirm to slave for the Warmaster were executed, while millions of others were transported to captured haulage and merchant ships waiting in orbit.

When Abaddon received word that the first Imperial Guard transports had broken from Warp space, he ordered his lieutenants to quit Antecanis. To his allies, he gave no warning, knowing that they would be forced to fight and would delay Imperial pursuit. With the holds of his ships crammed full of loot and slaves, Abaddon departed Antecanis, dropping a dozen cyclonic warheads onto the ruins of Monarchive as a last contemptuous gesture. Breaking through the cordon of Silver Skulls warships, the Black Legion moved on to their next target.

Imperial Guard regiments from Cadia, Lostak and Second Hubris arrived at Antecanis in the following weeks and months, and the Chaos Space Marines left behind fought grimly. Some escaped the tightening Imperial noose, others fought to the last in battles marked more by bloody slaughter and defiance than tactical acumen. As Abaddon had planned, Cancephalus gradually stopped its construction works and within a year was unable to refit even the smallest naval warships. Unmolested by the Imperial navy, Abaddon's fleets were able to ravage the sector at will.

For seventeen years, battles continued for possession of Antecanis, from which the world never recovered. The ruins of its hives loom darkly over the ash wastes like the skeletons of gargantuan beasts.

CHAOS DAEMONS

Scions of the Warp, Doom Given Form, the Children of Madness.

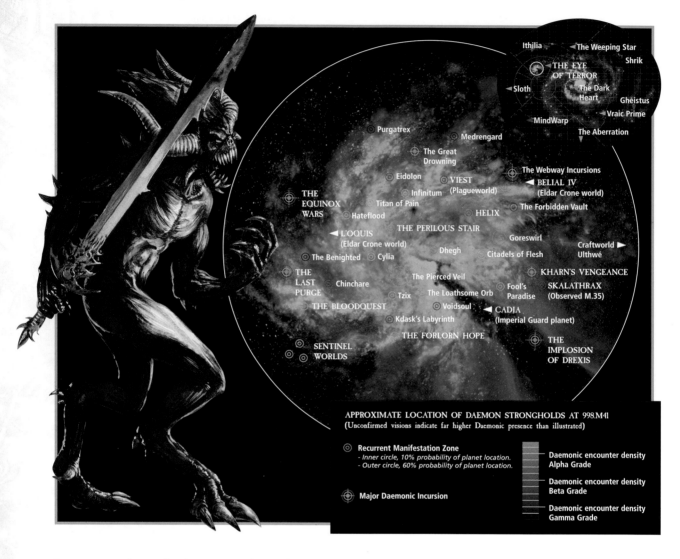

Ithilia · The Weeping Star
Shrik
THE EYE OF TERROR
Sloth
The Dark Heart
Gheistus
Vraic Prime
MindWarp
The Aberration

Purgatrex
Medrengard
The Great Drowning
Eidolon · VIEST (Plagueworld)
The Webway Incursions
Infinitum
BELIAL IV (Eldar Crone world)
THE EQUINOX WARS
Titan of Pain
The Forbidden Vault
Hateflood
HELIX
L'OQUIS (Eldar Crone world)
THE PERILOUS STAIR
Goreswirl
Dhegh
Craftworld Ulthwé
The Benighted · Cylia
Citadels of Flesh
THE LAST PURGE
KHARN'S VENGEANCE
Chinchare
The Pierced Veil
SKALATHRAX (Observed M.35)
Tzix
The Loathsome Orb
Fool's Paradise
THE BLOODQUEST
Voidsoul
CADIA (Imperial Guard planet)
Kdask's Labyrinth
THE FORLORN HOPE
SENTINEL WORLDS
THE IMPLOSION OF DREXIS

APPROXIMATE LOCATION OF DAEMON STRONGHOLDS AT 998.M41
(Unconfirmed visions indicate far higher Daemonic presence than illustrated)

◎ **Recurrent Manifestation Zone**
- Inner circle, 10% probability of planet location.
- Outer circle, 60% probability of planet location.

⊕ **Major Daemonic Incursion**

Daemonic encounter density Alpha Grade

Daemonic encounter density Beta Grade

Daemonic encounter density Gamma Grade

Daemons are destruction incarnate. When a daemonic army is on the march, anarchy is rife, reason collapses and carnage consumes whole planets. All fear the Daemons of the Chaos Gods, for their mere presence can permanently alter reality itself.

The Warp is a perversion of the material dimension, a bottomless mirror-pool hidden only by the delicate veil of sanity. Within the Warp dwell unholy terrors formed of purest malevolence and murderous intent. They watch the material world from another plane of existence, tirelessly searching for a weakness in the barrier between planes that will allow them access to the mortal realm. These vile denizens are manifestations of all that is twisted and dark in the human psyche. They are hatred and violence given form, twisted lust and perfidious envy come to life.

Hidden within the shifting tides of the Warp, the Daemons watch the realms of humanity, their souls burning with an eternal thirst that can only be quenched in blood and havoc. It is the Daemon's sole desire to possess and pervert the works of man. Though there are many factions amongst the Daemons of the Warp, they are all united in a single quest: to make the mortal plane a playground for their hateful needs and to slaughter and punish every living creature they can find.

DAEMONIC ASSAULT

There are many ways for the Daemon to invade reality. The psyker's gift, most common of the Daemon's means of entry, thins the walls of reason and allows otherworldly assailants to penetrate the veil. Whilst traversing the Warp, many an Imperial crew will watch in horror as their ship's protective shields collapse, and when the vessel eventually drifts from the fickle tides of the Immaterium it is filled with fiends instead of men. Sometimes a stellar trauma will tear the fabric of reality itself, leaving a permanent lesion from which daemonic invasions of unprecedented size spill forth. There are even those planets that have been consumed by arcane power, transformed into Daemon worlds that defy reason to better echo the whims of their mad lords. Whatever its source, once a Warp rift is fully open, the doom of any nearby worlds is nigh.

THE HOSTS

Daemons are an extension of the will of their parent deity, splinters of the Ruinous Powers made sentient. Each Daemon resembles its vile progenitor, at least in part, and when the hosts march to war they do so as a coruscating cavalcade of unreason that can unravel the mind of a mortal man. Unimaginably sickening Plaguebearers shuffle and plod toward their foes, noxious slime pooling in their deliquescent wake as they drone monotonous catalogues of disease. Iridescent Horrors cackle and cavort, wreaking mutation and ruin with hysterical glee. Bloodletters stalk forward, long black tongues flickering around hell-forged blades in their eagerness to claim more skulls. No less deadly are those known as Daemonettes, the writhing handmaidens of Slaanesh, their hypnotic movements alone enough to beguile a man. Yet these are but the most common of the abhorrent forms in the daemonic host; those closest to the comprehension of mankind.

Amongst the ranks of the Daemon soldiery are entities far more exotic and terrifying. When the rift in space has dilated sufficiently the host's war-beasts will attack, creatures possessed of animalistic intelligence but hideous strength. Scaled hounds the size of stallions and sinuous Daemon-steeds race alongside brass-armoured behemoths and swooping terrors of the sky.

But within the ranks of the daemonic legions none are more powerful than those known as Greater Daemons. These monstrosities epitomise all that is unholy, looming over their nightmarish minions as a mighty predator towers over its young. A blow from a Greater Daemon can tear apart a platoon, shred a tank, even split open a duralium vault. To stand in defiance against a Greater Daemon is to risk an eternity of torture and damnation. At their whim, reality is reforged. At their command, the Daemon armies punish and slaughter the populations of entire systems.

WAR WITHOUT END

Though Daemons can be driven back to the Warp with unremitting force and a will of steel, ultimately this hellish grotesquerie can only be slowed, not halted. The destruction of a Daemon's physical form will banish it, but not put an end its existence. The malefic presence will gradually reform in the Warp, nursing its grudge over long and painful decades. When it gets a chance to return to the material plane, its revenge will be bloody indeed. Worse still, once a breach in space has allowed a daemonic host to bleed through, it remains a weak point in reality that may split open again without warning. As more and more individuals dabble with the Warp, so does the power and frequency of daemonic assault increase. Though the common man knows little of such things, those who have studied the Daemon believe it the greatest of all enemies, for they are the doom that comes from within.

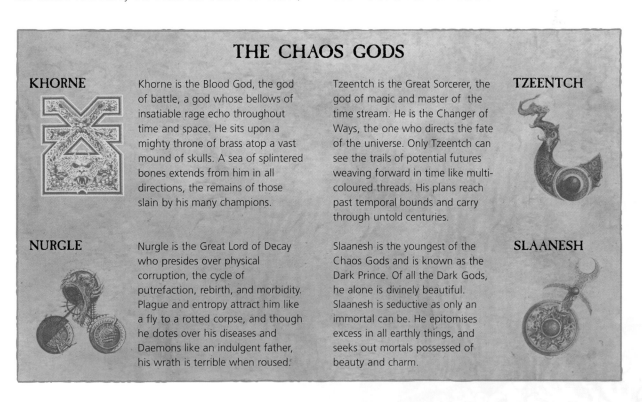

THE CHAOS GODS

KHORNE

Khorne is the Blood God, the god of battle, a god whose bellows of insatiable rage echo throughout time and space. He sits upon a mighty throne of brass atop a vast mound of skulls. A sea of splintered bones extends from him in all directions, the remains of those slain by his many champions.

NURGLE

Nurgle is the Great Lord of Decay who presides over physical corruption, the cycle of putrefaction, rebirth, and morbidity. Plague and entropy attract him like a fly to a rotted corpse, and though he dotes over his diseases and Daemons like an indulgent father, his wrath is terrible when roused.

Tzeentch is the Great Sorcerer, the god of magic and master of the time stream. He is the Changer of Ways, the one who directs the fate of the universe. Only Tzeentch can see the trails of potential futures weaving forward in time like multi-coloured threads. His plans reach past temporal bounds and carry through untold centuries.

TZEENTCH

Slaanesh is the youngest of the Chaos Gods and is known as the Dark Prince. Of all the Dark Gods, he alone is divinely beautiful. Slaanesh is seductive as only an immortal can be. He epitomises excess in all earthly things, and seeks out mortals possessed of beauty and charm.

SLAANESH

THE GHEISTOS CATACLYSM

In the early years of .M41, upon the agri-world of Gheistos, an abattoir worker no older than a dozen summers began to suffer from crippling headaches. Though he had been schooled by the quadrant's Proctor about the dangers of harbouring the unholy, the youngster was reluctant to report the migraines to his overseers, or the strange voice that accompanied them. He knew full well that if he confessed to what the voice had been suggesting he would be taken from the agri-complex, perhaps for good.

One day, the boy was taken to the abattoir by the shiftmaster, and beaten severely for failing to attend the bloodmachines with proper diligence. The boy, in the thrall of a particularly severe headache, lashed out with a strange curse that even he did not understand. For a moment, reality buckled and split, and his words coalesced into thousands of fat-bodied flies.

Within seconds both of mortals were beset. The flies shrouded the boy and lifted him off the ground. The shiftmaster choked as dozens slimy and bristled insectoid bodies forced their way into his throat and lungs. In their panic, neither victim noticed that each of the flies had the boy's face, nor realised that their

maddening buzz was a droning prayer to Nurgle. With a sickening popping of bone, the farmhand opened up like a gory flower. Something terrible began to push its way through from the Warp.

THE BLACK POX

The gurgling screams coming from the barn brought many of the older labourers running. They were greeted by a repulsive sight. Greenish-grey Daemons were pulling their way out of the mewling womb-thing that was once the young worker, chanting ceaselessly in a maddening monotone as the flies swarmed around them. Though most of the workers turned tail and ran, their fate was sealed. Each had been touched by a Daemon-fly. Each had been infected with the Black Pox.

Within a matter of hours, the victims began to putrefy and severe bouts of coughing brought up not only dark phlegm, but also more daemon-flies. They returned to their hab-blocks in panic, and the Black Pox spread, taking a terrible toll. Before dawn, much of the quadrant's livestock had withered away to black sludge, and the workers and their families had been replaced by disease-ridden parodies of their former selves. The footsoldiers of Nurgle were on the march.

A DARK REVENGE

Due to the vigilance and efficiency of a local Arbites patrol, the infected agri-complex was quickly quarantined. Hundreds of Planetary Defence Troopers were scrambled to combat the emergent menace, along with a detachment of pure-hearted Adepta Sororitas from the local Ecclesiarchy garrison. Eventually, with flame and faith, the Imperial soldiery drove back the Daemons and reduced much of the infected complex to ash.

Father Nurgle was not pleased by this turn of events. Wrathful and with a desire for vengeance wracking his fetid heart, Nurgle, petitioned his brother gods for aid against the upstart defenders of Gheistos. Though subtle Slaanesh declined and inscrutable Tzeentch ignored the Plaguefather's plea, Khorne the Blood God was only too pleased to join the excess of slaughter that Nurgle had in mind.

Combining their power, the gods forced the nascent Warp rift wider until a glowing portal had opened within the ruins of the agri-complex. This time, the Daemons that pushed through the Warp rift came by the dozen rather than in ones and twos. This time, gore-hungry Bloodletters marched toward the Imperial barracks alongside pustulent Plaguebearers and chattering Nurglings. The butchery that ensued was the worst that Gheistos had ever seen and the trenches soon ran red and black with infected blood. But the planet's nightmarish fate had yet to fully unfold.

With the agents of disease abroad, it was not long before Gheistos was in the grip of the Black Pox once more. Maggots swarmed through the blood-slicked streets. Shored up in his airtight dome-fortress, the Planetary Governor ordered his Astropath to send out a hymnal of distress. The governor was fortunate indeed, for the message was received by the Vorpal Swords Space Marine Chapter.

The Adeptus Astartes attack struck like lightning, but for the populace it was too late. The world was riddled with infection. Reality shimmered and split in dozens of locations, leaking pustulent matter that congealed into more of Nurgle's dreadful children. Worse still, to ensure his plans came to fruition, the Father of Plagues had reached an accord with Slaanesh.

Despite their initial victories the Space Marines were met by a daemonic horde of terrifying size. The battle raged for days and both sides suffered horrendous casualties. Despite the heroism of the Astartes troops and the unrelenting fury of the daemonic host, neither side could gain the advantage.

THE FLOOD OF GORE

Khorne was incensed that Nurgle had turned to fickle Slaanesh for aid. In his rage, the Blood God took up his legendary blade and slashed a mighty wound in the skies above Gheistos. Through the wound came a gushing torrent of boiling blood, a tidal wave of crimson that swept away Daemon and defender alike. Only the scions of Khorne and the Adeptus Astartes stood true.

The once-peaceful planet of Gheistos began to resemble a slaughterhouse as more and more of Khorne's footsoldiers poured onto the planet. A hail of skulls plummeted from red-hued clouds, screaming in praise of the Blood God as they hammered down. Those few natives who survived the deluge quickly lost their minds under this fell barrage, clawing at their eyes in horror and desperation.

The Vorpal Swords, suffering casualties at an untenable rate, called for reinforcements. Three weeks later, the Grey Knights, daemonhunters beyond compare, had added their might and expertise to the battle consuming Gheistos. The Daemons of Khorne began to lose ground, their blood-hungry frenzy shrivelling under the flames of the Grey Knights' fury.

Though Gheistos was eventually cleansed of daemonic presence, it was judged tainted beyond all hope, and the Inquisitors of the Ordo Malleus were left no choice but to enact Exterminatus. At the behest of the Inquisition the strike cruisers of the Grey Knights scoured the planet clean with an unrelenting barrage of cyclonic torpedos.

Though a mere matter of months had passed since the original Warp rift had opened, Gheistos was no more. Nurgle was most displeased, for he had been denied the breeding ground for his newest plague, and both Khorne and Slaanesh felt they had been cheated of victory. Tzeentch, the Great Schemer, watched his brother gods squabbling and fighting amongst themselves and smiled.

THE ELDAR

Wielders of Fate, Lords of the Void Above, First Amongst the Stars.

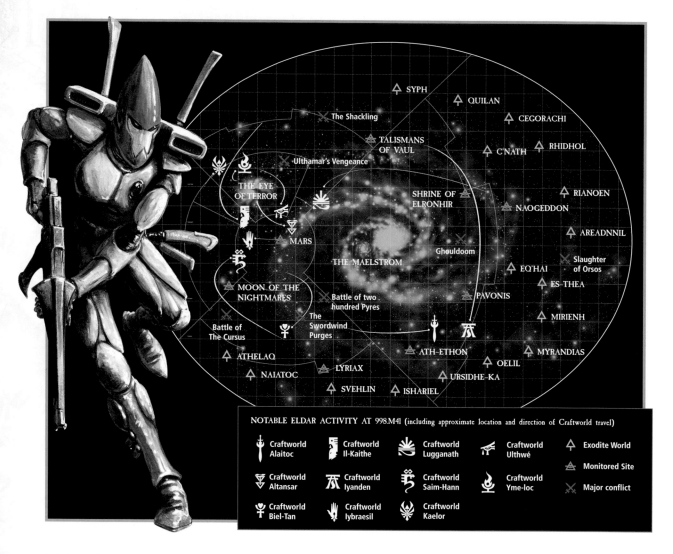

SYPH

QUILAN

The Shackling

CEGORACHI

TALISMANS
OF VAUL

C'NATH

RHIDHOL

Ulthamar's Vengeance

THE EYE
OF TERROR

SHRINE OF
ELRONHIR

RIANOEN

NAOGEDDON

MARS

AREADNNIL

Ghouldoom

THE MAELSTROM

Slaughter
of Orsos

EQ'HAI

ES-THEA

MOON OF THE
NIGHTMARES

Battle of two
hundred Pyres

PAVONIS

MIRIENH

Battle of
The Cursus

The
Swordwind
Purges

ATHELAQ

ATH-ETHON

MYRANDIAS

OELIL

NAIATOC

LYRIAX

URSIDHE-KA

SVEHLIN

ISHARIEL

NOTABLE ELDAR ACTIVITY AT 998.M41 (including approximate location and direction of Craftworld travel)

Craftworld Alaitoc	Craftworld Il-Kaithe	Craftworld Lugganath	Craftworld Ulthwé	Exodite World
Craftworld Altansar	Craftworld Iyanden	Craftworld Saim-Hann	Craftworld Yme-loc	Monitored Site
Craftworld Biel-Tan	Craftworld Iybraesil	Craftworld Kaelor		Major conflict

Subtle and mysterious, the Eldar are enigmatic aliens possessed of incredible skill. Before Mankind's ancestors had even crawled from the cold womb of the Terran seas, the shining constellations of the Eldar empire already spanned the galaxy. The whims of the Eldar moulded history, and the greatest amongst them created worlds and quenched suns.

The Eldar's pride ultimately proved to be their undoing. Their civilisation was ripped apart by a terrible cataclysm that permanently scarred the heavens themselves. Now the Eldar race is all but extinct, the last fragments of its shattered civilisation in a constant battle for survival.

The Eldar are at first glance physically similar to humans, though they are all slender-limbed and dextrous, possessing fine features and an ethereal grace. It is in their extraordinary minds that the true

differences lie. The Eldar mind is innately psychic, possessing a capacity for experience and thought that scales heights of ecstasy unthinkable to a human or Tau. This potential for joy is equalled by their capacity to feel anger, bloodlust and even hatred. No creature, not even an Eldar, can taste such rich fruits in an uncontrolled way without consequence. For an Eldar to yield absolutely to his desires would destroy him. Such was the fate of the ancient Eldar, whose depravities brought about the birth of a vicious and obscene god, and the fall of the Eldar race itself.

THE TRUE PATH

Since the dark days of the Fall, those few Eldar who survived struck out upon a different path. They became isolationist and cautious in the extreme, flitting like ghosts within great spacefaring cities called Craftworlds. Fearful of falling into the same spiritual malaise as their forefathers, the Eldar practice but one discipline at a time to the exclusion of all others. Their focus is so intense that each skill becomes a complete way of life, a sphere of experience that they explore completely before adopting a different path. In this way, the Eldar master dozens of facets of existence during their centuries-long lives.

In the dark days of the 41st Millennium, the most renowned path is that of the Warrior. This path in turn is subdivided into several facets called Aspects. Each of these warrior factions is modelled after an aspect of the Eldar war god Khaine, and each shrine has its own cultures, wargear and supernatural skills. The Aspect Warriors are feared throughout the galaxy, for none can match them in their chosen fields of battle. The Path of the Warrior is dangerous for the soul as well as the body, for all the branches of the Warrior path lead to the same dark place – a twilight existence where the spirit becomes unable to escape from the bonds of its own rage. It is there that the Exarchs dwell, those who are trapped forever upon the Path of the Warrior in an eternal cycle of bloodshed and strife.

THE WAY OF VIOLENCE

Despite all they have lost, the Eldar wield technology so advanced that, to the uncivilised races, even their militia appear as masters of powerful magics. A small force of Eldar is capable of methodically destroying a far larger army without the loss of a single drop of Eldar blood. This is due in part to the manner in which the Aspect Warriors fight. The sharpened skills of each unit interlock and complement those of their comrades, weaving individual acts of battle into a symphony of destruction. The orchestrators of the Eldar war efforts are the Autarchs, those warriors who have worshipped at the Aspect shrines for centuries and yet never succumbed to the deadly fate of the Exarchs, and the Farseers, who divine all possible futures to better guide their people to success.

The elite infantry of the Eldar armies, though integral to the survival of their race, are but one facet of a much larger war machine. They march to battle alongside elegant bipedal war walkers and arcane artillery platforms capable of tearing apart reality. Above the warhost the sleek prows of grav-tanks glide gracefully through the air, casting their distinctive shadows over darting strike forces of Guardians. Heavily-armed Jetbikes speed around the flanks of the Eldar warhost in blurs of bright colour. At the heads of the armies march the immortal Phoenix Lords and the incandescent Avatar, a god of war incarnate. Their numbers are few, though, and for all its pageantry and pride the grand warhost still bears the mark of the Eldar's plight. Alongside the living march the ghost warriors, the dead heroes of yesteryear wrenched from their rest and compelled to fight again. Such are the acts the Eldar are forced to commit in order to ensure the survival of their dwindling race.

THE FALL OF THE ELDAR

The doom of the Eldar, when it came, took a form far more subtle and dangerous than civil war or alien invasion. The Eldar's pursuit of perfection in all things led them down the path of decadence until their society fell to a terrible sickness of the soul.

Some heeded the portents that haunted their dreams, building great Craftworlds on which to flee to safety. Most glutted themselves on the pursuits of the depraved. Before long, brother fought brother and sadistic killers stalked the shadows.

Amidst the swirling psychic energy of the Empyrean, the corruption of the Eldar became manifest. What an unimaginably foul and sickening being it was that the Eldar raised unknowingly in the Warp. No creature was ever birthed that was as terrible or perverse as the Chaos God Slaanesh, She Who Thirsts, the Doom of the Eldar incarnate.

With a howl of raw power Slaanesh rose into supernatural life, and a psychic implosion tore at the universe. The epicentre lay within the gilded heart of the Eldar realms, leaving a pulsing afterbirth of raw Chaos in its place. Within the space of a single breath the Eldar had become a doomed people, knowing that their nemesis had been born and that it would hunt them for the rest of eternity.

THE LAST HOPE

GUARDIANS

The Eldar Guardians are those who do not follow the path of the Warrior or Seer, but who take up arms to ensure their race's survival. Such is the level of Eldar technology that they are potent combatants nonetheless.

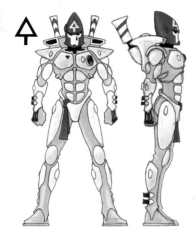

▲ Shuriken Catapult

AUTARCHS

The Autarchs are the commanders of the Eldar warhost, gifted in strategy as well as in personal combat. They take their wargear from the Aspects that they have mastered over centuries of battle.

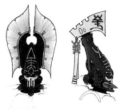

▲ Helm variants from the Iliaq Insurrection

◄ Dire Avenger Aspect Armour

Banner of the ➤ Sable Helm Shrine

▲ Avenger Shuriken Catapult

DIRE AVENGERS

The Dire Avengers embody the Aspect of Khaela Mensha Khaine as noble warrior, and are the most common of all the Aspect Warriors in the Craftworlds.

They are armed with the deadly shuriken catapult, the weapon that most readily characterises the Eldar at war. The shuriken catapults of the Dire Avengers are the pinnacle of their kind, and are far more advanced than those entrusted to the Guardians.

STRIKING SCORPIONS

The Striking Scorpions are the strongest and most violent of the Aspect Warriors. They excel in rugged terrain, silently stalking the shadows to spring ambushes on their prey. The mandiblasters built into their helmets fire deadly energy charges, making the Scorpions much-feared close assault specialists.

▲ Scorpion chainsword, Oex pattern

◄ Striking Scorpion Aspect Armour

Striking Scorpion ➤ Exarch Armour incorporating sensor mane and 'Scorpion's Claw' Exarch artefact.

▲ Shuriken pistol

FIRE DRAGONS

The Fire Dragons embody the wanton destruction left in the wake of the Eldar war god. Clad in armour the colour of flame, they carry fusion guns that can reduce even the heaviest battle tanks to piles of molten slag. Fire Dragons are highly aggressive and nothing less than the total annihilation of their enemy will suffice. If a squad of Fire Dragons manages to close with an enemy fortification it will be destroyed, either by fusion gun or melta bomb.

▲ Fire Dragon Aspect Armour

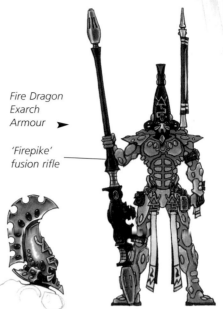

Fire Dragon Exarch Armour ➤

'Firepike' fusion rifle

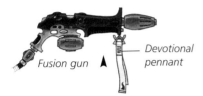

Fusion gun ▲ — Devotional pennant

Exarch war helm, Battle of Blood Dawn ➤

HOWLING BANSHEES

Predominantly female, Howling Banshees are swift and highly mobile troops who excel at close quarter fighting. They derive their name from a legendary spectre whose call heralds the death of those who hear it. The Banshees emulate this call, using psychosonic amplifiers contained in their Banshee masks. Those who are exposed to this psychic scream suffer almost total paralysis, making them easy prey.

▲ Banshee Power Sword, Assyri Devastation

▼ Howling Banshee Aspect Armour

▲ Shuriken pistol

▼ Exarch mask 'Hegscream'

ELDAR WRAITHLORDS

The towering Eldar 'Ghost Warrior' constructs are crewed by the spirits of dead Eldar heroes. None can stand before their might and survive.

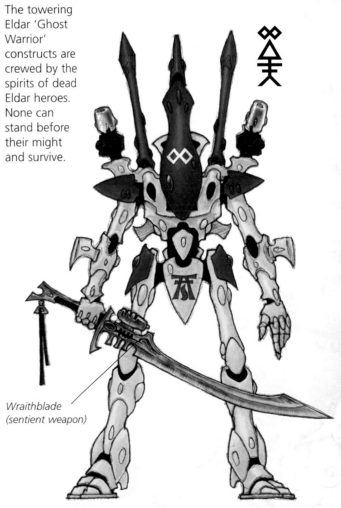

Wraithblade (sentient weapon)

Craftworld Lugganath, the Light of Fallen Suns

THE ORKS

The Beast, the Star-savages, the Wrathful Green Tide.

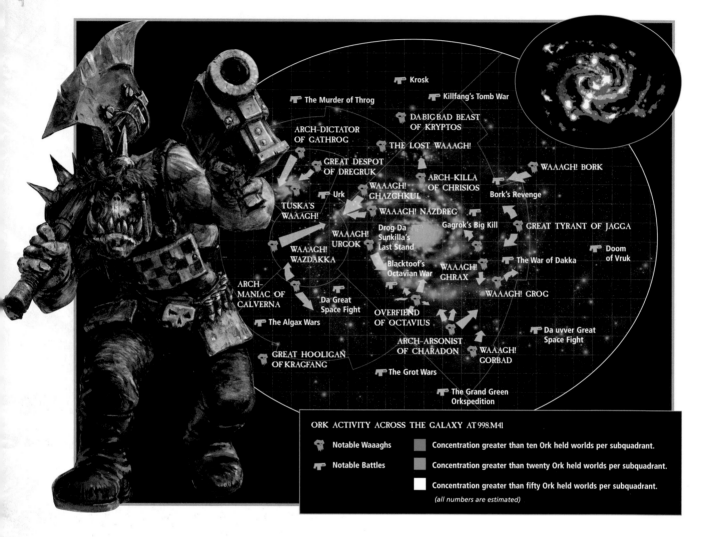

Krosk

The Murder of Throg

Killfang's Tomb War

DA BIG BAD BEAST OF KRYPTOS

ARCH-DICTATOR OF GATHROG

THE LOST WAAAGH!

GREAT DESPOT OF DREGRUK

WAAAGH! BORK

ARCH-KILLA OF CHRISIOS

WAAAGH! CHAZGHKUL

Bork's Revenge

Urk

WAAAGH! NAZDREG

TUSKA'S WAAAGH!

Drog Da Sunkilla's Last Stand

Gagrok's Big Kill

GREAT TYRANT OF JAGGA

WAAAGH! URGOK

Doom of Vruk

WAAAGH! WAZDAKKA

Blacktoof's Octavian War

The War of Dakka

WAAAGH! GHRAX

ARCH-MANIAC OF CALVERNA

WAAAGH! GROG

Da Great Space Fight

OVERFIEND OF OCTAVIUS

The Algax Wars

Da uvver Great Space Fight

ARCH-ARSONIST OF CHARADON

WAAAGH! GORBAD

GREAT HOOLIGAN OF KRAGFANG

The Grot Wars

The Grand Green Orkspedition

ORK ACTIVITY ACROSS THE GALAXY AT 998.M41

Notable Waaaghs   Concentration greater than ten Ork held worlds per subquadrant.

Notable Battles   Concentration greater than twenty Ork held worlds per subquadrant.

Concentration greater than fifty Ork held worlds per subquadrant.

(all numbers are estimated)

The Orks are a barbaric and brutal alien race that infest the galaxy from end to end. Green of skin and violent of temperament, they live only to fight, kill and conquer.

Orks are hulking creatures that have more in common with a great savage ape than a man. They have long, slab-muscled arms that end in powerful taloned hands perfect for throttling and gouging. Their fang-toothed maws gape and snarl when they bark out their guttural language, and their porcine eyes glower from sunken hollows in their thick skulls. An Ork's skin is wrinkled and tough, covered in pock-marks, battlescars and colonies of parasitic grubs.

Orks prefer to dwell in filth and squalor, saving their energy for their killing sprees. A numerous race, the Orks are never truly beaten, for when an Ork is finally killed he releases thousands of spores that settle in dank places and eventually mature into yet more Orks.

A CULTURE OF VIOLENCE

All greenskins are naturally violent creatures, from the bulkiest Ork warrior to the scrawniest Gretchin slave. They need conflict just as human beings needs food and drink. Stranger still, they become physically larger and more powerful every time they assert their dominance. An Ork is never happier than when he is maiming, burning, or killing.

Should all the warbands, clans and tribes of the Orks ever truly unify, they would drown the galaxy in a torrent of mindless violence. But the Orks' unquenchable need for battle is their downfall as well as their strength. They will frequently indulge in bloody wars with their own kind just for the thrill of battle. In this way the Orks establish their own hierarchy, for they firmly believe that might makes right. The largest and most belligerent Orks rise to the status of Nob, Boss or even Warlord, bullying and stealing from anyone smaller than them with impunity. Similarly, the most powerful tribes subsume smaller warbands until they become barbaric hordes that number in the hundreds of thousands or even millions.

THE GREAT WAAAGH!

The warbands and clans of the Orks spend most of their time fractured and disorganised, warring amongst themselves to ensure that only the strongest survive. When an Ork population has swelled to untenable proportions, it reaches a kind of critical mass. By this time the strongest and most dominant Ork will have fought his way to the top of the horde, enforcing his rule with an iron fist to keep a semblance of control over his bellicose kin.

On occasion, this Ork will be a visionary aflame with plans of galactic conquest. He imparts his vision to his followers, usually via the medium of repeated blows to the head with a blunt object. As word travels, the Ork tribes put aside their differences and begin to unite. Great war machines are built from scrap metal, often in the image of the warlike Ork gods. Nearby planetary populations are enslaved to provide ammunition and war materiél for the coming conflict.

As the excitement of imminent conquest reaches fever pitch, the Warlord at its heart attains the status of prophet and warmonger. Other tribes flock to fight under the ascendant Warlord's banner, eager for a piece of the action and the chance to excel in the eyes of their brutal deities. When the Orks can wait no more, they take to the stars in great ramshackle fleets, roaring towards their unwitting victims in a great armada of surpassingly ugly attack craft. This crusade of violence is known as a Waaagh!; a holy war that gains a terrible momentum until it drowns whole star systems in a tide of anarchy and bloodlust.

THE STORM BREAKS

When the Orks make planetfall upon the worlds they invade, a great muster takes place. Thousands upon thousands of growling vehicles and tanks belch poisonous fumes into the atmosphere, their grilles painted to resemble fierce animals from the Ork home worlds. Solidly-built walkers clank into position, great mobs of Killa Kans and Deff Dreads supported by cathedral-sized Gargants, metal-skinned effigies whose tread shakes the earth like the footfall of the gods themselves. Great hordes of Ork warriors take up their position, blackening the horizon from end to end with their numbers, their warcries audible for miles around. Batteries of Big Gunz, bizarre energy weapons and force field generators crackle and buzz amidst the green throng. Speed Freeks impatiently rev their engines, and the Boyz at the heart of each army fire their guns into the air. Here the power of the Waaagh! is palpable as a wave of raw aggression. With an almighty bellow the Orks surge forwards, and another world is plunged into unending war.

IORNIS
Agri-world
left aflame.

Waaagh!
Kogtoof

Gragnatz's Boyz

ANTARIS

Waaagh!
Biglug

HALEX MINING COLONIES
Kogtoof captures heavily
mined asteroid belt and
convert largest asteroids
into space-borne fortresses.

Azgra the Slasher's
warband devoured
by errant
Void Whale.

Azgra's Boyz

Waaagh!
Gragnatz

Waaagh!
Kogtoof
(Asteroid fleet)

GEMIN PRIME
Civilised world.
Protracted war due to
presence of Hawk Lords
Chapter. Ork
force depleted.

Waaagh!
Gragnatz

Waaagh!
Gragnatz

Space Hulk 'Killteef'
captured and guided
into Warprift
'Hellfury' aka 'Da Big
Swirly Fing'.

Waaagh!
Gragnatz

Bograt's Blitz
Boyz join
Waaagh!
Gragnatz.

Bograt's
Blitz Boyz

THE CONQUEST OF VORSK

This is a star chart depicting the progress of
Waaagh! Gragnatz, an Ork crusade that
devastated the Vorsk subsector in M41*.
Gragnatz's invasion force began as a few
hundred thousand Orks besieging the agri-
world of Iornis. Rival Warbosses split off to
launch their own Waaaghs! with varying
degrees of success. Meanwhile, the progress
of Gragnatz's own Waaagh! was slowed by
the presence of the Warprift 'Hellfury', but

emerged bolstered by the presence of
Kogtoof's Ork fleet, encountered on the
fringes of the rift. By the time Gragnatz's
Grand Armada reached the Vorsk sector its
numbers were further swelled by the
Big Bosses of Orguk, forming a
galactic onslaught capable of crushing
several systems at once.

*Star systems, planets and phenomena not to scale.

Da Big
Orgu...
diff...

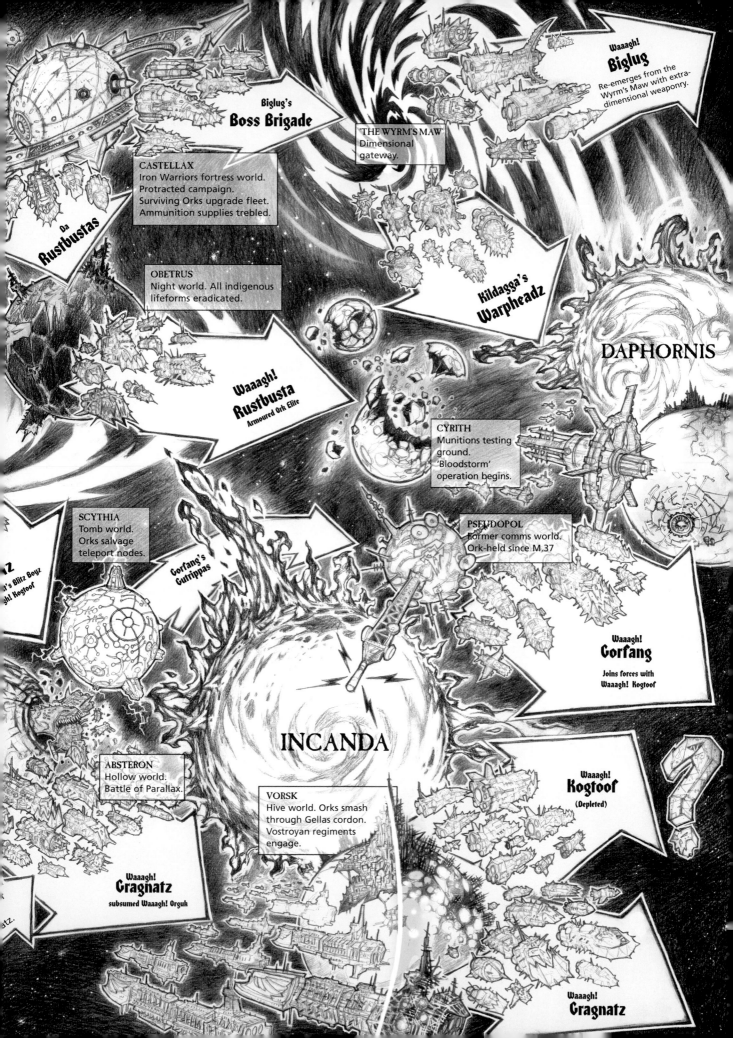

Waaagh!
Biglug
Re-emerges from the Wyrm's Maw with extra-dimensional weaponry.

Biglug's
Boss Brigade

'THE WYRM'S MAW'
Dimensional gateway.

CASTELLAX
Iron Warriors fortress world. Protracted campaign. Surviving Orks upgrade fleet. Ammunition supplies trebled.

Da
Rustbustas

OBETRUS
Night world. All indigenous lifeforms eradicated.

Kildagga's
Warpheadz

DAPHORNIS

Waaagh!
Rustbusta
Armoured Ork Elite

CYRITH
Munitions testing ground. 'Bloodstorm' operation begins.

SCYTHIA
Tomb world. Orks salvage teleport nodes.

Gorfang's
Cutrippas

PSEUDOPOL
Former comms world. Ork-held since M.37

z's Blitz Boyz
gh! Kogtoof

Waaagh!
Gorfang

Joins forces with
Waaagh! Kogtoof

INCANDA

Waaagh!
Kogtoof
(Depleted)

ABSTERON
Hollow world. Battle of Parallax.

VORSK
Hive world. Orks smash through Gellas cordon. Vostroyan regiments engage.

Waaagh!
Gragnatz

subsumed Waaagh! Orguk

Waaagh!
Gragnatz

THE LAST HOURS OF VORSK

The snowstorm had given the Orks cover enough to close the distance, and the promise of slaughter hung heavy in the air. Gragnatz da Killa licked his blackened lips in anticipation, his foul-smelling breath frosting as he took a moment to assess the battlefield anew. Hundreds of corpses littered the arctic wasteland, human and Ork in equal number, and the blanket of snow underfoot was stained with violent streaks of gore. Ahead, the Imperial troops were formed up into neat lines in the ice-choked pass, denying the Orks the advantage of superior numbers. Blistering volleys of las-fire flickered out into the greenskin ranks. Undaunted, a horde of Boyz crunched along behind Gragnatz's mob, gathering speed as they reached firmer ground. Gragnatz didn't like the fact that the pass was still occupied by the runty humans and their precious tanks. It made him mad.

'Oi! Zogdeg!' he shouted, firing his slugga into the air to get his rival's attention, 'tell yer pansy mates ter keep up, we shoulda been up to our guts in blood by now!' He turned back, grinning savagely as he heard the stream of crude invective coming from Zogdeg's direction, and led his Boyz in a loping run towards the enemy position.

A low grinding filled the air and squinting, Gragnatz could just about make out a column of Imperial artillery rumbling into place behind the human infantry. He spat a curse as the first of the artillery shells began to hammer into the Ork ranks. The ear-splitting detonations sent vast plumes of icy water into the air, each impact killing dozens of Orks and sending many more to their death in the freezing waters below. Still the greenskins came on.

Around the flanks of the chanting, stomping Ork infantry, a ramshackle fleet of Warbuggies careened and skidded across the pack ice. Volleys of Ork rokkits corkscrewed into the air, some even hitting the Imperial tank squadrons ahead. Behind the Warbuggies came a group of six giant Battlewagons, their chain-wheeled tyres and spiked dethrollas biting great chunks out of the ice. The ground shook as the gun-beasts returned fire with their killcannon, incandescent explosions breaking apart the Imperial battle tanks ahead. As if in reply, more and more Imperial artillery thundered into the howling mobs of Warbikers leading the charge. Gragnatz barked a guttural laugh as one of the bikers blossomed into a fireball and slewed into a snowbank with a hiss.

The human battle line was within reach and Gragnatz flexed his claws as he strode forward. The Ork footsoldiers in his wake opened fire with their own weapons, scything down the human defenders in a storm of solid slugs. To their credit, the Imperials held

their ground. The fusillade of las-fire aimed towards Gragnatz's mob was becoming too intense to ignore. Occasionally one of the greenskins dropped, felled by a clean head shot. Enough is enough, thought Gragnatz. It's killing time.

Throwing back his head, the Ork Warboss bellowed his warcry at the top of his lungs. A great 'Waaagh!' went up from the Ork horde, drowning out all but the crack-boom of the Imperial artillery. The roars of the greenskin horde seemed to intensify as Gragnatz's pet Weirdboy joined in, magnifying the noise threefold until the very valley itself seemed to shake with elemental rage. With majesterial slowness, a hundred thousand tonnes of snow sloughed away from the upper reaches of the pass ahead, silencing the Imperial artillery beneath.

Gragnatz lowered his horned helmet and charged, closing the last few metres with the human battleline at a headlong sprint. The sheer force of the giant Ork's charge bowled over the Imperial Guardsmen arrayed to stop him. Sharp bayonets punched into his belly and neck, which just made Gragnatz even angrier. The Warboss swung his great chain-axe in wide, decapitating arcs, kicking out with his steel-capped boots at any who got inside his reach. Behind him the Boyz were also getting stuck in. Spittle, blood and ice water filled the air as the Orks tore apart their prey in a berserk frenzy.

Without warning, the thunder of iron-shod hooves announced the Imperial cavalry's counter-charge from their hiding place behind an icy escarpment. A well-aimed las-round caught Gragnatz in the chest, and he tossed the human soldier he had been pounding into the ice to one side, squaring up against the new threat. Ahead, a fur-clad rider was charging straight at him with a long, explosive-tipped lance lowered.

Gragnatz dropped, uppercutting the human's mount with such force that both rider and beast collapsed onto the ice in a tangle of limbs and entrails. Gragnatz hauled the beast up by its reins and swung it bodily into the line of Guardsmen charging him, jumping over the horse's flailing limbs to plough into the rest of the startled humans. The Guardsmen fell back in disarray, caught off guard by the sudden violence of the Ork Warboss's attack

'Stand and fight, ya runts!' screamed Gragnatz, his chain-axe rising and falling in gory arcs, 'I got plenty for the lot of ya!'

THE TYRANIDS

The Great Devourer, the Star-Swarms, the Hive Mind Incarnate.

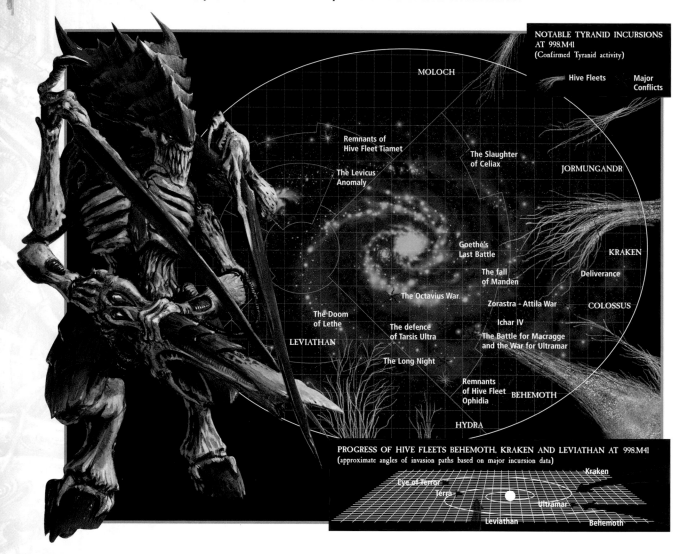

NOTABLE TYRANID INCURSIONS
AT 998.M41
(Confirmed Tyranid activity)

Hive Fleets   Major Conflicts

MOLOCH

Remnants of
Hive Fleet Tiamet

The Slaughter
of Celiax

JORMUNGANDR

The Levicus
Anomaly

Goethé's
Last Battle

KRAKEN

The fall
of Manden

Deliverance

The Octavius War

The Doom
of Lethe

Zorastra - Attila War

COLOSSUS

The defence
of Tarsis Ultra

Ichar IV

The Battle for Macragge
and the War for Ultramar

LEVIATHAN

The Long Night

Remnants
of Hive Fleet
Ophidia

BEHEMOTH

HYDRA

PROGRESS OF HIVE FLEETS BEHEMOTH, KRAKEN AND LEVIATHAN AT 998.M41
(approximate angles of invasion paths based on major incursion data)

Kraken

Eye of Terror

Terra

Ultramar

Leviathan

Behemoth

Beyond the range of human spacecraft and the most strident astrotelepathy lies the unspeakable cold of the intergalactic void. It is the great barrier that divides galaxy from galaxy, a place where vistas of time and space conspire to hold the stars apart with inconceivable distances.

Yet the void is not empty. An immeasurably ancient and implacable intelligence moves through the darkness, its many eyes fixed on a galaxy rich in life. The Great Devourer drifts between the stars, hungering for the warm flesh of all who lie before it. This great organism, this monstrous entity, men know as the Tyranid race.

THE GREAT DEVOURER

The Tyranids are the most alien of races to infest Imperial space, for they come from the void itself. Their chitinous bio-ships drift from star system to star

system in brooding silence. Behind the Hive Fleets lie the barren husks of a dozen galaxies already consumed. Once the remorselessly hungry shoals of bio-ships detect the presence of a prey world, they begin to teem with life, closing upon their target like a set of impossibly large jaws. There can be no escape from their fatal embrace. For this reason the Tyranids are known as the Great Devourer.

THE HIVE MIND

The Tyranid race is highly psychic, linked by a dread sentience known as the Hive Mind. On the battlefield, the leader-beasts of the Tyranid swarm channel the Hive Mind's raw psychic power, strengthening the lesser Tyranid organisms and sapping their prey's will to fight. It is the Hive Mind that guides the invading Tyranid armies, nightmarish tides of many-limbed horrors that have evolved purely to kill. Every organism in the swarm is a separate Tyranid, from the microscopic spores that choke the planet's air to the symbiotic gun-beasts used by the larger warrior organisms. Regardless of size or function they are united as one by the Hive Mind's hunger to subjugate and devour. Though the individual beasts can be killed, the Hive Mind is immortal, for it exists outside of space.

THE SHADOW IN THE WARP

Each Hive Fleet has a smothering psychic signature known to Imperial Astropaths as the Shadow in the Warp. It is as if the darkness of the void has been made incarnate, bleeding into the consciousness of all who lie before it and causing even the strongest minds to unravel with despair. Worst of all, the Shadow in the Warp is capable of blotting out even the sacred guiding light of the Emperor himself; the Astronomican. Thus do the Hive Fleets isolate and destroy all in their path.

The Hive Fleets devour worlds just as a human might consume a meat-beast. The process is swift and grisly. At first, the Tyranid presence consists of feeder-probes whose role it is to detect centres of biomass. Should the world be rich in prey, these assassin-scouts will send psychic signals into space. Slowly, a tendril of the Hive Fleet will advance, its billions of component entities hyperactive with an alien hunger that will not be denied.

INVASION

Once the prey world has been prepared for consumption the Tyranid assault begins in earnest. Gigantic hunks of gristle and cartilage known as mycetic spores plummet through the skies like a living hailstorm, splitting open to reveal broods of ferocious weapon-beasts. Swarm after swarm of chittering scythe-limbed aliens flow together into a living tide, falling upon the enemy defences in an avalanche of unremitting violence guided by the immortal Hive Mind. Each brood has evolved the ideal tools to butcher their prey, from diamond-hard talons to weapon-symbiotes that spit acid or burrowing feeder-beasts. Roaring alien behemoths batter against the enemy defences, breaking down fortifications so their brethren can slaughter any prey inside.

The final horror of a Tyranid invasion is only realised once the planet's defenders have been overrun. The lifeforms of the prey world are harvested by billions of feeder organisms, rendered down into a thick genetic gruel and channelled back to the bio-ships. The planet's entire biomass is then used to create even more advanced Tyranid organisms. In this way the Tyranids constantly evolve and replenish their innumerable hordes. Unrelenting and all but unstoppable, the Tyranid race represents the eventual doom of every other species that inhabits the galaxy.

THE DEVOURER OF WORLDS

When a Tyranid invasion begins in earnest they attack in great waves, each more terrible than the last. Though these may seem like discrete armies unto themselves they usually bleed into each other in a great mass of killing machines that falls upon the foe in a stabbing, tearing frenzy.

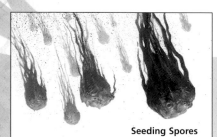

Seeding Spores
The bio-fleet releases spores into the atmosphere to encourage growth of native flora and pervert the atmosphere into toxic fog before the full-scale deployment of attack beasts.

ELAPSED CHRONOSEGMENTS
0.0 (rough estimate) averaged over 26 recorded invasions

Vanguard Attack
Scout organisms, usually Genestealers and Lictors, emerge from hiding and attack enemy command centres.

Genestealer

2.0 ▶

Lictors absorb information about their prey using feeder tendrils, and summon attack swarms to enemy strongpoints using a pheromone trail.

4.0 ▶

Total War
When a Tyranid invasion is in full swing, the prey world is transformed into a nightmarish landscape under a tortured, lightning-wracked sky. Nowhere is safe from the living tides of attack beasts that hunt out every last pocket of resistance, reinforced by massive assault beasts that plough into enemy fortifications like living battering rams.

Assault Beasts
Where the enemy resistance is strongest, the Tyranids will deploy line-breaker forces such as mighty Carnifexes or even the colossal terrors known as bio-titans.

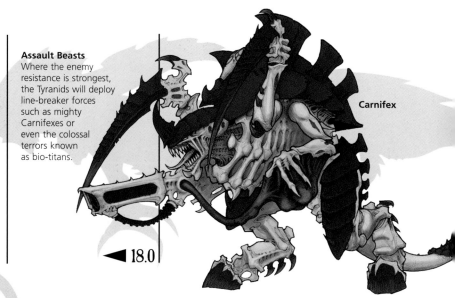

Carnifex

◀ 18.0

22.0 ▼

Ravener

Death from Below
If the enemy has holed up in fortresses or underground lairs then the Tyranids will employ burrowing broods such as Raveners and Trygons, sensitive to vibration and each capable of butchering an entire platoon.

24.0 ▶

Digestion Pools
Towards the latter stages of invasion, mycetic spores full of bilious acid burn into the planet's crust, forming 'digestion pools' that act much like external stomachs for the bio-ships. The bodies of defenders and invaders alike are gathered up and plunged into the digestion pools that they may be rendered down into biological gruel and fed back to the Hive Fleets.

26.0 ▶

28.0 ▶

> "There is a cancer eating at the Imperium. We have given the horror a name to salve our fears; we call it the Tyranid race. If it is aware of us at all it must know us only as Prey."
>
> Inquisitor Czevak

Terror Tactics

The main Tyranid swarms are preceded by flocks of Gargoyles that work in conjunction with the Tyranid vanguard organisms, corralling the planet's defenders and sowing panic and discord in their wake. When the full horror of the swarm is revealed, many stricken souls despair completely and lose their sanity on the spot.

8.0 ▶

The Endless Swarm

Countless mycetic spores rain down from orbit, deploying billions of minor attack organisms whose function is to deplete enemy resources, identify centres of resistance and engage the front line of defence.

Termagant

10.0 ▶

12.0 ▼

Tyranid Warrior

Weapon-symbiotes

Synapse creatures such as the Tyranid Warrior are often armed with complex bio-weapons, allowing them to engage massed enemy infantry and armour at range.

Synapse Control

The innumerable swarms of Tyranid weapon-beasts are controlled by synapse creatures, larger Tyranid leader-beasts that channel the imperatives of the Tyranid Hive Mind into the animalistic brains of the swarm. In this way the entire Tyranid invasion force attacks as one, each component fulfilling its own role with unthinking obedience.

◀ 16.0

◀ 14.0

Consumption

Once the enemy has been encircled and overcome the process of consumption will begin. This is largely executed by great living carpets of voracious devourer organisms known as Rippers.

Ripper

Death of a World

When every last trace of biomass has been devoured and drawn from the prey world into the Hive Fleets, the Tyranids will withdraw, leaving nothing but barren earth, twisted spires and ruined rockcrete in their wake.

34.0 ▶

30.0 ▶

DARK MILLENNIUM: The Tyranids   **169**

THE TAU

Children of the Greater Good, Vibrant Upstarts, Sparks of Life in a Dying Galaxy.

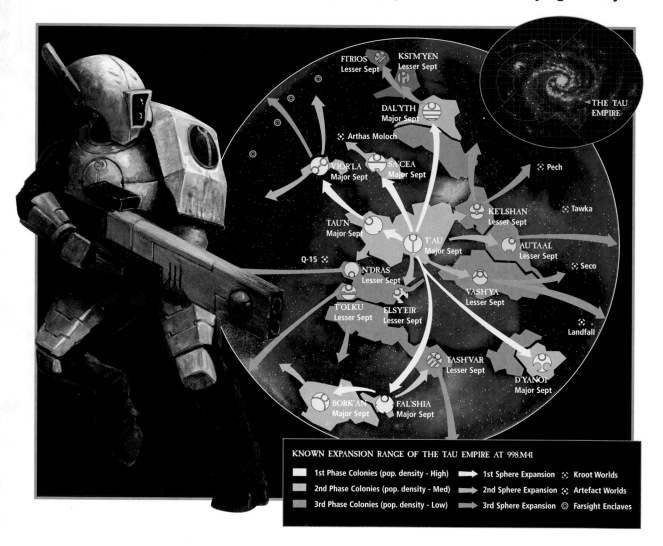

FI'RIOS
Lesser Sept

KSI'M'YEN
Lesser Sept

THE TAU
EMPIRE

DAL'YTH
Major Sept

◇ Arthas Moloch

VIOR'LA
Major Sept

SA'CEA
Major Sept

◇ Pech

KE'LSHAN
Lesser Sept

◇ Tawka

TAU'N
Major Sept

T'AU
Major Sept

AU'TAAL
Lesser Sept

Q-15 ◇

N'DRAS
Lesser Sept

◇ Seco

VASH'YA
Lesser Sept

T'OLKU
Lesser Sept

ELSY'EIR
Lesser Sept

Landfall

TASH'VAR
Lesser Sept

D'YANOI
Major Sept

BORK'AN
Major Sept

FAL'SHIA
Major Sept

KNOWN EXPANSION RANGE OF THE TAU EMPIRE AT 998.M41

▪ 1st Phase Colonies (pop. density - High)	➡ 1st Sphere Expansion ◇ Kroot Worlds
▪ 2nd Phase Colonies (pop. density - Med)	➡ 2nd Sphere Expansion ◇ Artefact Worlds
▪ 3rd Phase Colonies (pop. density - Low)	➡ 3rd Sphere Expansion ◎ Farsight Enclaves

The aliens known as the Tau inhabit an area of space near the eastern fringe of the galaxy. A dynamic and inquisitive race, the Tau utilise highly advanced technology in all fields, from medicine to warfare. Though less than two thousand years old, this fledgling empire is rapidly expanding into space and encountering the elder races of the galaxy.

The Imperium's explorers encountered the Tau just prior to the Age of Apostasy, finding a race little more than savannah-roaming primitives and a world ripe for cleansing and colonisation. Yet, the Imperium's seeding ships were all lost upon arrival in the region, the dense cluster boiling with tumultuous energies. These storms raged for long millennia, the Tau undergoing drastic change all the while. When the storms subsided, the Tau had evolved beyond recognition. Within centuries, a newborn Empire was expanding across the stars.

Tau civilisation is based upon a rigid system of castes, each forming a distinct sub-species within the race. Each relates to one of the four elements of nature – fire, water, air and earth – and each dictates a Tau's particular role within society, be it warrior, bureaucrat, pilot or worker. The members of the Ethereal Caste bind the other castes together; the inviolate commands of the Council of the Highest guiding the entire empire.

The Tau Empire is underpinned by the concept that the individual must set aside personal desires and work for the Greater Good. Most Tau are short lived compared to other races, with a lifespan of around forty years being the norm. It has been noted however that key individuals have attained greater age, as if their lifespans were linked to the manifest destiny of the race itself. It may be said that the Tau's boundless energy is the direct result of such a short lifespan, as if the race were compelled to expand and drive onwards in ever wider phases of advancement, to achieve the greatest amount possible in the comparatively short time allotted. The Tau mature quickly; infirmity comes suddenly, and death soon after, so that none linger overlong at the end of a life fully lived. The fruits of a Tau's labour will be known only to the next generation. To burn brightly, yet briefly, is the purest essence of the Greater Good.

THE TAU AT WAR

Tau military doctrine dictates a highly mobile style of warfare, in which overwhelming fire superiority is brought to bear where and when it is most effective.

The basic military unit used by the Tau is the cadre, a combined arms force able to face enemies several times its numerical superior. But the Tau style of warfare bears little resemblance to that of any other army, for each cadre is a supremely flexible force, its members able to change roles and equipment as the situation dictates. Each cadre maintains a large stock of vehicles, weapons and other equipment, meaning it can be fielded in greatly varying roles, from covert infiltration to armoured breakthrough.

It is the Fire Warriors of the Fire Caste that provide the fighting strength of the Tau military. These stoic individuals are exceptionally well disciplined and well-versed in the use of sophisticated battlefield weapons systems. Foremost amongst these are the various types of battlesuit, piloted more than worn by the most experienced Fire Warriors. Tau battlesuits range from the lightweight Stealth Suits, each of which contains a powerful stealth field generator, to the awesome XV-88 Broadside suits, each carrying a pair of mighty rail guns. The mainstay battlesuit is, however, the XV-8 'Crisis' suit, a highly versatile system capable of being fitted with a wide variety of weapons and support equipment. Crisis suits can be configured to engage any foe, from massed hordes of Tyranids to lumbering armoured vehicles.

THE EMPIRE

Unlike many alien races, the Tau are not overtly hostile, though their armies will fight fiercely to protect those territories claimed. The sheer dynamism of the race is pushing the empire further into occupied areas of the galaxy and this has inevitably brought conflict with both humans and other races. As the Tau Empire expands outwards, new and previously unknown races are inevitably encountered, and to each an offer of allegiance is made. There are many aggressive, arrogant and selfish races in the galaxy, and first contact often, sadly, results in nothing more than another bloody war. There are other races, however, who readily accept the message of the Greater Good. The Carnivore Kindreds of the mercenary Kroot frequently fight alongside Fire Warriors, as do the Stingwings of the insectoid Vespid. The warriors of many such races have found a place in the Tau military, fighting with honour and skill beside the warriors of the Fire Caste.

THE MANTLE OF THE HERO

Each Tau battlesuit carries a number of weapons systems, dependent upon its role and class. Lighter suits, such as the XV-17 and XV-26, sacrifice firepower for speed or agility while heavy fire support models, such as the Broadside, are ponderous, yet carry weapon systems equivalent to those of a tank.

In addition to its weapons and armour, a battlesuit may carry an array of support systems. Some, such as shield generators, drone controllers and target locks, are common to all variants. Others, such as the ablative 'integrated interface armour' fitted to the space-going XV-86 are unique to the role in which the suit is intended to function.

The pilot of a battlesuit is protected by armour made from dense, nanocrystalline structured metals. In durability, such materials exceed the armour of many other races, and are often many times lighter. Each model of battlesuit is a perfect balance between offensive capability, armoured protection, speed, agility and utility. It is therefore little wonder only the most skilled of Fire Warriors are promoted to the rank of battlesuit pilot, to wage war from the very leading edge of the Wars of Expansion.

THE CYTHERIAN ANNEXATION

In the Tau Empire's Third Sphere Expansion, an expeditionary force was assembled and dispatched from the Bork'an Sept, tasked with the annexation and colonisation of the world of Cytheria. Expecting stiff resistance, the force was amply supplied for a hard-fought and taxing campaign.

An outlying Imperial world, Cytheria's rugged dry plains were interspersed by dense alien jungle. Although sparsely populated, the planet was home to a valuable Adeptus Mechanicus research facility. As a result, Cytheria's defences were reinforced by seven regiments of the Catachan Imperial Guard; three standard infantry, two veteran light infantry, and two armoured.

The Tau's landing sites were cleared by Stealth Teams and spearheaded by Battlesuits. Despite initial success, the operation took heavy casualties. Phase two was the eradication of enemy armour, which was highlighted by the destruction of the entire Catachan 97th Armoured Regiment by Tau Hammerhead 'Elimination Groups' on the third day of the invasion. As the Tau gained the upper hand, the Catachans withdrew to the jungles for a protracted guerrilla war. In the third phase of the campaign the Fire Warriors quickly found themselves outclassed in the dense terrain. Sensing a loss of momentum, Tau Ethereals redirected the attack to the Herzen Ridge research and communications zone, ultimately forcing the Catachans to give battle.

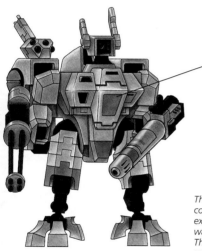

Note individual armour segments painted the turquoise blue of the Bork'an Sept.

The 'Brightwind' configuration was used extensively by the first wave assault cadres. The battlesuits' manoeuvrability, speed and weapons fit out-matched even the ace Sentinel squadrons of the Catachan XXVI.

'Brightwind' configuration
XV8 Crisis Battlesuit
Desert pattern camouflage

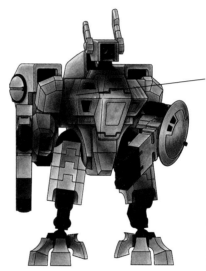

Blast damage, indicative of the dangerous nature of close range anti-armour tactics.

The 'Fire Knife' configuration was utilised by Crisis teams in support of the Armour Elimination Groups. Though successful, the Crisis teams sustained high casualties in these crucial battles.

'Fireknife' configuration
XV8 Crisis Battlesuit
Modified desert pattern camouflage

Markings indicate a team leader of a first wave Insertion Group.

XV25 Blacksun Filters, used in all night time landings.

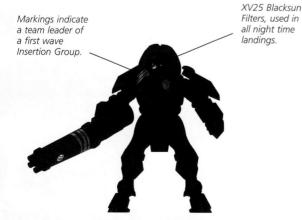

XV25 Stealth Battlesuit
Passive mode

Armour surface is matte black in passive mode, and adopts chameleonic pattern in active mode. Sept colours and other markings are only visible in passive mode.

Each Hammerhead in the group bears the symbol of the Bor'kan Sept. Each bears text that reads 'For the Greater Good', a common slogan on Tau vehicles.

Armour Elimination Group K22
28 confirmed armour kills

COMMANDER ALO'RRA

Leading the Fire Caste's assault on Cytheria was Commander Alo'rra ('Cold Shadow'). Having only recently completed his fourth Trial by Fire, Alo'rra had much to prove. It was during the fourth and final assault on Herzen Ridge that Alo'rra earned his place in the histories of the Fire Caste of Bor'kan.

The Commander led the frontal assault that overran the Catachan headquarters and then held the position against desperate, but ultimately futile counterattacks.

Bor'kan Fire Warrior
Planetary Assault Cadre
Desert camouflage
Fire Warriors fighting in the plains bore standard desert camouflage and carried the long ranged pulse rifle in preference to the pulse carbine.

Bor'kan Fire Warrior
Upland Jungle Suppression
Cadre Specialised camouflage
Teams fighting in the upland jungles utilised a red camouflage scheme appropriate to the alien flora and carried pulse carbines.

Fal'shia Fire Warrior
Strategic Reserve Cadre
Desert camouflage
The Fal'shia Sept provided a number of cadres to the expedition, all of which saw action in the fighting to secure the primary landing zones.

Bor'kan Pathfinder
Preliminary Observation Cadre
Desert camouflage
Pathfinder teams were inserted up to five months prior to the invasion, reconnoitring over 300 potential landing zones.

IMPERIUM FORCES ON CYTHERIA

Jungle Fighter
Catachan XXVI 'Lurking Cobras'
This trooper wears the standard issue Catachan battledress. The Lurking Cobras who held the line long enough for the bulk of the Catachans to redeploy into the jungle following the collapse on the plains.

Jungle Fighter Sniper
Catachan LI 'Black Vipers'
This regiment's snipers took a fearsome toll on the Tau of the first assault wave. Although not confirmed, it is claimed one sniper killed a Tau Ethereal.

Jungle Fighter
Catachan LVI 'Sidewinders'
The Sidewinders were successful at holding up superior numbers and firepower for several weeks. The entire regiment was issued rebreathers as the deep jungles periodically erupted in poisonous sporepod blooms.

The Herzen Ridge battles broke the last organised Imperial defence and afterwards Cytheria became largely pacified. Transport of materials and personnel for colonisation is now well underway, and on schedule for the expansion of the Empire.

Scattered remnants of the Catachan forces still mount sporadic guerrilla attacks on vulnerable targets, in the hope of eventual reinforcements. However, regular hunter patrols scour the jungles for these misguided humans who stubbornly resist the Greater Good.

DARK ELDAR

The Lost, Shadows of Slaughter, Nightstalkers.

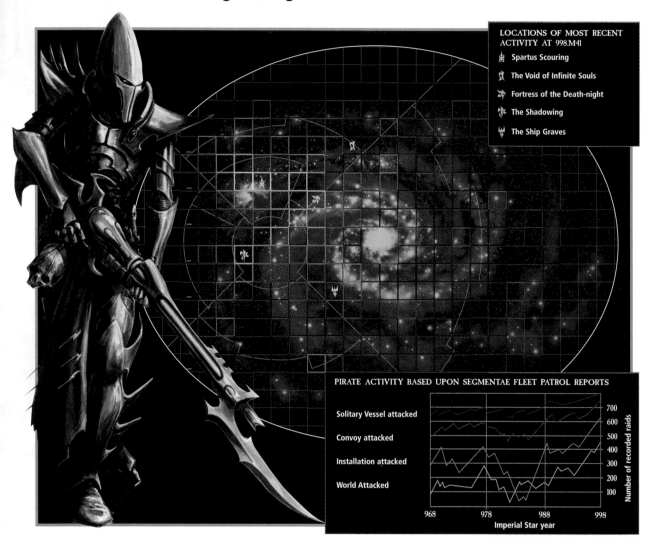

LOCATIONS OF MOST RECENT
ACTIVITY AT 998.M41

- Spartus Scouring
- The Void of Infinite Souls
- Fortress of the Death-night
- The Shadowing
- The Ship Graves

PIRATE ACTIVITY BASED UPON SEGMENTAE FLEET PATROL REPORTS

Solitary Vessel attacked

Convoy attacked

Installation attacked

World Attacked

Number of recorded raids

968   978   988   998

Imperial Star year

A shadowy terror prowls the chill darkness between the stars. None can predict their attacks and few survive them. The Dark Eldar are expert at locating the vulnerable and the weak, and their devastating raids steal away entire generations and leave worlds devastated beyond recovery. These bloodthirsty corsairs care nothing for territorial gain or strategic positioning; their pirate fleets exist purely to bring slaughter and misery, stealing what they can and enslaving any being they encounter.

The Dark Eldar arose back in the distant reaches of time, during the cataclysm of the Fall that all but destroyed the Eldar race. Possessed of the worst traits of selfishness and immorality, Dark Eldar are an embodiment of the debauchery and excess that laid low the once great Eldar race.

In the Dark Eldar exists the need to torture, maim and humiliate all other creatures. There is no pleasure other than that which is at the expense of others. There is no goal for the Dark Eldar that is not accomplished without pain and suffering for their prey. Grief and bloodshed are ends in their own right for the evil pirates of Commorragh.

PIRATICAL RAIDS

To survive the Fall, the Dark Eldar fled material space into the webway; a labyrinthine network of Warp tunnels that exists neither within realspace nor within the Warp. The Dark Eldar use the webway to move unseen across the galaxy, travelling where no fleet, no patrol, no listening stations can detect them. With warships appearing suddenly in low orbit and warriors emerging directly from the webway onto the surface of their target world, the Dark Eldar strike with absolute surprise. As well as raiding worlds, the Dark Eldar prey upon ships and convoys in the depths of space, and have even been known to strike at vessels lying under the watchful guns of a dockyard. The speed and viciousness of a Dark Eldar raid swiftly overwhelms any hasty defence and eludes any counter-attack. The Dark Eldar take what they want, slaying and slaving in a vicious whirlwind, before disappearing as quickly as they arrive, leaving nothing in their wake but ravaged corpses and mourning families.

AN ALLIANCE OF DEATH

Dark Eldar society has given rise to all manner of warriors and strange weapons of war. Most Dark Eldar Warriors wield the terrifying splinter rifle, which shreds skin and flesh with a hail of razor-sharp barbs. Others wield weapons of arcane power, born of an ancient and twisted heritage. Alongside these warriors battle the Wyches, raised as stunningly skilled gladiatorial fighters in the arenas of death. For power and prestige, the callous and insane Haemonculi concoct exotic combat drugs and lead squads of twisted, altered creatures created in hellish laboratories.

The principle vehicle of the Dark Eldar is the Raider; a swift anti-grav skiff that carries a force of ruthless killers into the heart of the enemy. Ravager anti-grav tanks bristling with weaponry support the Raiders, along with lightning-fast Reaver Jetbikes and howling Hellions riding aboard soaring skyboards. With precision strikes, the Dark Eldar slay commanders, cut off reinforcements and isolate their quarry.

TERROR AND POWER

It is a constant fight for survival and power that drives the Dark Eldar to their depraved acts. Hidden in the depths of the webway lies the city of Commorragh, where most of the Dark Eldar make their lair. Here, and in scattered enclaves throughout the webway, the Dark Eldar try to outdo each other in power, wealth and ruthlessness. Only absolute power guarantees absolute survival, so Dark Eldar band together into organisations known as Kabals.

Many Kabals are simply a captain and his crew, or one of the violent street gangs that terrorise the docks of Commorragh where the fleets arrive. Some Kabals, however, are powerful indeed. Through war, intimidation and alliance, the Greater Kabals have influence that stretches into every aspect of Dark Eldar society. The largest Kabals extort taxes from the pirate fleets, sponsor Wych Cults and bargain with strange creatures such as the sinister, cannibalistic Mandrakes and the winged mercenaries of the Scourge Eyries. For the Dark Eldar, there is one simple tenet:

The strong survive; the weak perish.

The Port of Lost Souls, Gateway to Commorragh

NECRONS

Eternal warriors, Souless Echoes of Hatred, the Inevitable Ones.

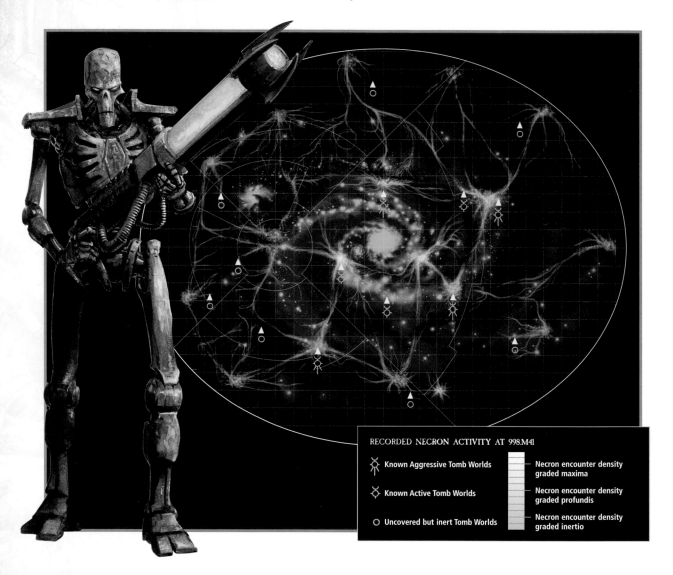

RECORDED NECRON ACTIVITY AT 998.M41

☥ **Known Aggressive Tomb Worlds**	**Necron encounter density graded maxima**
☥ **Known Active Tomb Worlds**	**Necron encounter density graded profundis**
○ **Uncovered but inert Tomb Worlds**	**Necron encounter density graded inertio**

The Necrons are ancient beyond imagining. Long have they slept in stasis, hidden beneath the surface of silent tomb worlds, their alien consciousnesses transferred from weak and brittle flesh and preserved against the ravages of time within immortal mechanical bodies. So long and deep did the Necrons sleep that for centuries the Explorators of the Imperium thought the civilisation extinct, a colossal star-spanning empire brought to dust by the weight of aeons.

Of those Necron tombs that survived, some have been damaged by tectonic shifts, plundered by younger races or suffered catastrophic failures of their stasis systems. Most of those that remain are cut off from one another, for the ancient relays that allowed Necron worlds to communicate across the vast gulf of space have been destroyed or cannibalised by other races.

Now the Necrons have awakened from slumber to find the galaxy greatly changed and degenerate life forms squatting amidst the ruins of their empire. They do not like what they see.

Necrons are skeletal parodies of the living, with preservative fluids oozing from mechanical joints and baleful emerald wychfires blazing in lifeless eyes. Although Necrons can differ according to rank and function, all have sophisticated auto-repair systems coursing through their exoskeletons, allowing recovery from all but the most crippling of damage. Should irreparable damage occur, the Necron 'phases out'. Body and consciousness are teleported to the nearest tomb complex, where they remain in storage until such time as repairs can be effected or a new form can be forged. Such seeming inviolability is not without its limitations, and each act of transference exacerbates any weaknesses in the Necron's engrams. A Necron that has 'died' several hundred times will often be little more than a shambling automaton, with no memory of the creature it once was. Such Necrons have no free will. Hard-wired programming drives their instincts and their only goals are those set by Necron Lords.

The Necron Lords are the driving force behind the awakening. Of as high a rank in death as they were in life, the Necron Lords benefit from more sophisticated artificial bodies and stasis tombs than their vassals, allowing them to sleep through the millennia unplagued by the slow decay that has taken a terrible toll from others of their kind. As a result, Necron Lords retain the personality and memory denied to their minions. Even so, not all have survived the great sleep unscathed. Filled with bitter resentfulness of other life, some Necron Lords lead their minions on bloody harvests, murdering millions in an attempt to quench their rage. Others have been driven utterly insane by the weight of aeons. Believing themselves to be the reincarnations of ancient gods, these Necron Lords have their consciousnesses grafted into ever newer and more grandiose forms as they embark on campaigns of conquest and destruction.

A tomb world restored to full operation will have many hundreds of Necron Lords, each dedicated to a particular role. Some are builders and shapers, responsible for the endless swarms of Tomb Spyders

and Scarabs that maintain the tomb complex. Others are programmed to unearth and awaken buried starships, defend the tomb world from interlopers or scour nearby planets for mineral resources. If the tomb complex has been damaged, and many Necron Lords lost to stasis failure, the resulting imbalance will shift the behaviour of the entire tomb. There are worlds in the Imperium that suffer Necron raids at precisely regular intervals, simply because the function of the ranking Tomb Lord is to gather resources. That the Lord's followers are always wiped out in the pursuit of this goal doesn't matter. As soon as the tomb creates new bodies for the fallen, the attacks begin again. On some worlds this has given rise to myth, on others it is simply welcomed as part of a military training cycle so regular that chronometers can be set to it.

Necrons often strike without warning, issuing forth from tombs hidden far beneath a planet's surface or teleporting directly to their target. They are implacable foes, remorseless in advance and practically impervious to enemy fire. Conventional defence lines and bastions are almost useless before a Necron onslaught. Flawless command of ancient technology allows the machine warriors to phase through the most heavily defended obstacles, or to tear fortress and flesh asunder with gauss cannon and particle whip. Glittering phalanxes of Necron Warriors and eldritch machine constructs stalk silently through the ruins, unfeeling harbingers of death that leave nothing but blackened corpses and scorched rubble in their wake.

THE FALL OF DAMNOS

One world brought to ruin by the waking Necron menace.

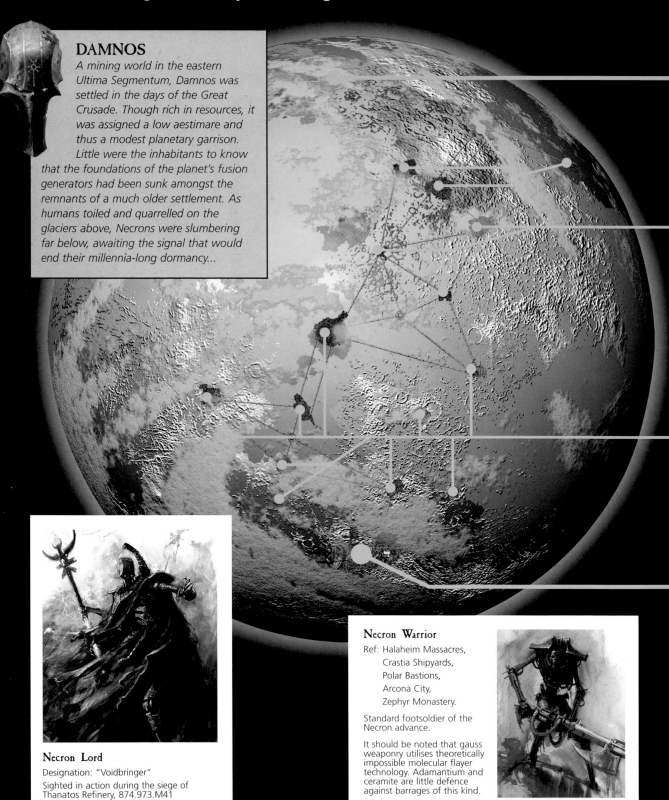

DAMNOS

A mining world in the eastern Ultima Segmentum, Damnos was settled in the days of the Great Crusade. Though rich in resources, it was assigned a low aestimare and thus a modest planetary garrison.

Little were the inhabitants to know that the foundations of the planet's fusion generators had been sunk amongst the remnants of a much older settlement. As humans toiled and quarrelled on the glaciers above, Necrons were slumbering far below, awaiting the signal that would end their millennia-long dormancy...

Necron Lord

Designation: "Voidbringer"

Sighted in action during the siege of Thanatos Refinery, 874.973.M41

Necron Warrior

Ref: Halaheim Massacres,
　　 Crastia Shipyards,
　　 Polar Bastions,
　　 Arcona City,
　　 Zephyr Monastery.

Standard footsoldier of the Necron advance.

It should be noted that gauss weaponry utilises theoretically impossible molecular flayer technology. Adamantium and ceramite are little defence against barrages of this kind.

274.973.M41 RUINS DISCOVERED

The geothermic fusion stations of Mandos Prime suffer a series of critical failures following seismic activity of unprecedented strength. In the course of repairs, exofabricators discover a series of ancient ruins buried beneath the permafrost. Representatives from the Adeptus Mechanicus immediately lay claim to the discovery. Unable to gain entry, the Tech Priests nonetheless retrieve several alien mechanisms from the site and bring them to the forge world Goethe Majoris for study.

779.973.M41 THE MENACE STIRS

Phalanx after phalanx of Necrons emerge from the ruins under the cover of terrible storms and descend upon the manufactorums of Damnos Prime. A shroud of comms-interference precedes the Necron advance, preventing the manufactorums from sending for help or alerting others to their fate. Unprepared for so sudden an assault, the defenders are overrun in a matter of hours. As the complexes fall silent, reconnaissance Thunderbolts from Damnos Secundus are sent to investigate. None return.

850.973.M41 THE ONSLAUGHT CONTINUES

The comm-shroud moves south over the Tyrrean Ocean to Damnos Secundus. The Necrons follow in its wake, silencing every refinery, mining complex and outpost in their path. Imperial Guard recon companies reach the manufactorums of Damnos Prime. They find the structures largely intact, but no sign of either attackers or defenders. As the battlezones creep ever south, reports confirming the nature of the enemy finally reach the Planetary Governor, who immediately mobilises every regiment under his command. He also sends a desperate request for aid to the nearby Ultramarines before gathering his advisors and retreating to a Proteus-class command bunker. The battleship Nobilis adopts a geostationary orbit above the planetary capital, Kellenport, and prepares to bombard the oncoming Necrons.

020.974.M41 NECRONS TRIUMPHANT

The Necrons assault Kellenport. Thanks in no small part to a melta torpedo bombardment from the orbiting Nobilis, the battle initially goes well for the Imperial defenders, but triumph swiftly turns to disaster. A compressed energy pulse pierces the atmosphere and destroys the Nobilis. As burning debris spirals through the dawn sky to smash into Damnos, phalanxes of Necrons teleport behind the walls and slaughter the Guardsmen in their own bunkers. The governor is killed when his bunker complex is breached by tunnelling Scarabs and Tomb Spyders. When units of the Ultramarines 2nd Company arrive shortly thereafter, they launch a series of daring raids to rescue the few survivors of the Necron onslaught and withdraw to deep space. Damnos now belongs to the Necrons.

THE WARHAMMER 40,000 HOBBY

This section of the book showcases the full glory of collecting and painting armies of Citadel miniatures, and playing out hard-fought battles on amazing terrain. First there is an extensive gallery of beautifully painted models from every army, followed by some basic tips and advice to help beginners get started. We look at how to set up your battlefield using readily available scenery pieces as well as expert, purpose-built tables. You will find a multitude of ideas to add even more variation to your games, such as inventing your own missions and including an exciting campaign that allows the result of one battle to have an effect on the next in an ongoing story. At every stage, the section is illustrated with players' armies, as well as models painted by the world famous 'Eavy Metal team.

There is no peace amongst the stars, only an eternity of carnage and slaughter and the laughter of thirsting gods.

COLLECTING, PAINTING AND PLAYING BATTLES

Warhammer 40,000 is more than just a tabletop wargame. It is a completely self-contained hobby, with a vast community of players the world over. All gain something different from their pastime, whether it is playing, collecting, painting, terrain building or any combination of the limitless possibilities on offer.

This section of the book is all about providing a glimpse into the experience of Warhammer 40,000. Whether you are a relative beginner or a seasoned veteran, you will find a rich seam of inspiration within these pages. There is plenty of advice, tips and techniques for collecting, painting, modelling and gaming. In each case, we'll provide an overview of the subject, followed by actual examples of the 'theory put into practice'. So varied and wide in scope is the subject of the Warhammer 40,000 hobby that we have broken this section down into a number of topics.

SHOWCASES
An array of Citadel miniatures from the different armies in the Warhammer 40,000 universe are shown here in all their glory.

COLLECTING AN ARMY
This section provides advice on putting together your forces, with three players' armies that have been chosen for very different reasons.

The large Ork army bears the black and white markings of the Goff clan - a group that is considered brutal and bloody-minded even by Ork standards.

This battlefield features craters, hills, ruins and trees – providing vital cover for the battling warriors.

PAINTING

Here you will get an idea of the different things to consider when painting your own army – from the individual models to the look of the force as a whole. Included are ideas on inventing your own colour schemes as well as information on established uniforms and heraldry. You will also find more beautifully painted example armies.

BATTLEFIELDS

The next section focuses on creating a tabletop battlefield on which to play your games. A range of examples are shown, from set-ups using terrain readily available in Games Workshop hobby centres and independent stockists, all the way to scenery made entirely from scratch.

BATTLE REPORT

This section describes a real game of Warhammer 40,000, covering how the players chose their armies, their battle plans and tactics, as well as what they learnt and intend to do differently next time!

LINKING YOUR BATTLES

It is a lot of fun to fight out a series of battles, creating an ongoing war, or campaign. We have provided a simple campaign that you can play through, linking the different standard missions together.

INVENTING YOUR OWN MISSIONS

Some gamers enjoy coming up with their own missions, representing anything from ambushes to last stands. We've come up with a range of examples you can take inspiration from or use as presented.

EXPANSIONS TO THE GAME

In this section we take a look at the Cities of Death and Apocalypse expansion books, both of which allow you to play your games in new and exciting ways.

AND...

We finish the section with information about the Warhammer 40,000 community and all the various ways of getting involved.

These armies are playing out an Annihilation standard mission, using the Pitched Battle deployment.

The Space Marines are one of the most tactically flexible armies available – equally strong in attack or defence.

SPACE MARINES

Space Marines go into battle protected by power armour and armed with boltguns.

Captain with thunder hammer.

Space Marine squads are led by Sergeants.

Devastator with heavy bolter.

Scouts infiltrate behind enemy lines.

Assault Marines use jump packs to close quickly with the enemy.

Bearer of the Ultramarines Chapter Standard.

Dreadnoughts are massive, armoured fighting machines capable of ripping apart enemy tanks.

Chaplain with jump pack.

The heaviest armour a Space Marine can wear is known as
Tactical Dreadnought armour, or 'Terminator' armour.

Techmarines tend to the machine spirits
of the Chapter's vehicles.

Marneus Calgar,
Chapter Master of the Ultramarines.

Chaplain in Terminator armour.

The Angels of Death descend from the sky into the midst of the enemy.

The sinister Space Marines of the Dark Angels Chapter pursue their foes without mercy.

Dark Angels Veteran.

Dark Angels Captain.

The 1st Company of the Dark Angels is known as the Deathwing.

Dark Angels Terminator Librarian.

The Dark Angels Ravenwing hunts down enemies of the Chapter.

Commander Dante, Lord of the Blood Angels.

The Blood Angels Chapter is known across the Imperium for its aggressive tactics in battle.

Brother Corbulo, Sanguinary High Priest

The Baal Predator is named after the Blood Angels' home world.

The Space Wolves Chapter is organised into Great Companies, each led by a Wolf Lord.

Space Wolves Rune Priest.

The Black Templars attack the enemies of the Imperium from space-going crusade fleets.

High Marshal Helbrecht.

Chaplain Grimaldus.

Space Marines of the Ultramarines Chapter defend an Imperial edifice.

A White Consuls combat squad.

White Scars Sergeant.

Crimson Fists Assault Marine.

Angels of Sanguinius Veteran.

Devastator of the Mentor Legion.

Brazen Claws Sergeant.

Salamanders Assault Marine with flamer.

The Imperial Fists Chapter is steeped in glory.

Hawk Lords Tactical Marine.

Captain Shrike of the Raven Guard.

Doom Eagles Assault Marine

Blood Ravens Space Marine with an auspex scanner.

Iron Hands Sergeant, with bionic implants.

THE IMPERIAL GUARD

Cadian Shock Troops are renowned for their discipline and valour in battle.

Catachan Jungle Fighters are tough and resourceful warriors.

*Commissar Yarrick –
Saviour of Hades Hive.*

Cadian Senior Officer.

Catachan Sergeant.

*Ursarkar E. Creed,
Lord Castellan of Cadia.*

Cadian heavy weapon team with mortar.

A Vostroyan officer and his command squad.

Each team consists of two men – a gunner and a loader.

Valhallan Ice Warrior.

Mordian Iron Guard.

Vostroyan Sniper.

Techpriest Enginseer.

Ogryns use the fearsome ripper gun,
which doubles as a sturdy club.

Sentinel walkers act as scouts,
harrying the enemy's flanks.

A Cadian infantry squad advances alongside a Leman Russ, the mainstay battle tank of the Imperial Guard.

FORCES OF
THE IMPERIUM

The zealous Battle Sisters of the Adepta Sororitas form the armies of the Holy Ecclesiarchy of Terra.

Saint Celestine – The Living Saint.

A Canoness leads each convent.

The Seraphim are the most devout of the Sororitas.

Inquisitor of the Ordo Hereticus.

Crusader.

Acolyte.

Imperial Navy pilot.

The Inquisition roots out enemies of the Imperium.

Penitent Engine.

Sage.

Inquisitor Lord Coteaz of
the Ordo Malleus.

Vindicare Assassin.

Eversor Assassin.

Callidus Assassin.

Death Cult Assassin.

The Grey Knights purge the daemonic with nemesis force weapon and incinerator.

Grey Knights Brother-Captain Stern.

CHAOS SPACE MARINES

Alpha Legion Chaos
Space Marine.

'The Cleaved' Chaos
Space Marine.

Khorne Berzerker.

Plague Marine.

An Aspiring Sorcerer leads a squad of Thousand Sons.

Raptor of the
Blood Disciples.

Icon bearers summon
daemonic allies.

Possessed Space Marines
are hosts to Daemons.

Obliterators can morph
different weapons.

The fate of many champions is to become
a gibbering, mutated Chaos Spawn.

Chaos Lord with lightning claws.

The most dedicated servants of Chaos wear suits of tainted Terminator armour.

Black Legion
Aspiring Champion.

Deathmongers
Chaos Space Marine.

Renegade from
Hakanor's Reavers.

Possessed of
the Red Corsairs.

Defilers are infernal war machines powered by the essence of a Daemon from the Warp.

CHAOS DAEMONS

*Pink Horror –
Lesser Daemon of Tzeentch.*

*Plaguebearer –
Lesser Daemon of Nurgle.*

*Daemonette –
Lesser Daemon of Slaanesh.*

*Bloodletter –
Lesser Daemon of Khorne.*

Daemonette champion.

Flamer of Tzeentch.

Bloodletter champion.

Plaguebearer musician.

Fiend of Slaanesh.

Bloodcrusher of Khorne.

Beasts of Nurgle smother their victims in corrosive slime.

Lord of Change – Greater Daemon of Tzeentch.

Epidemius keeps a tally of the many splendid diseases of Nurgle, and their unfortunate victims.

A daemonic Soul Grinder strides to war alongside Daemonettes and Bloodletters.

THE ELDAR

Dire Avenger
Aspect Warrior.

Howling Banshee
Aspect Warrior.

Swooping Hawk
Aspect Warrior.

Warp Spider
Aspect Warrior.

Striking Scorpion Aspect Warriors stalk their prey through
the shadows.

Fire Dragon
Aspect Warrior.

Dark Reaper
Aspect Warrior.

Autarchs lead the Eldar forces in battle.

Farseers scry the paths of fate.

Eldrad Ulthuan –
Farseer of Ulthwé Craftworld.

Citizens of the Craftworlds fight as Guardians.

Rangers are unrivalled scouts and marksmen.

The Harlequins are warrior-dancers of the Laughing God.

Warlock with singing spear.

Wraithlords are wraithbone constructs animated by the souls of long-dead Eldar heroes.

Jetbikes of the Saim-Hann Craftworld, accompanied to battle by a Wave Serpent and two Vypers.

ORKS

Orks live for war, charging into battle with a variety of brutal and noisy weapons.

Meganob armed with kombi-shoota and power claw.

An Ork Warboss must be large, loud and cunnin'.

Weirdboys seethe with the power of the Waaagh!

Big Meks construct all manner of strange wargear, from kustom force field generators to shokk attack guns.

Piloted by Ork Boyz, Deff Dreads clank forward, armed with power claws and big shootas.

Boss Zagstruk, leader of the Vulcha Squad.

Painboyz patch up injured Boyz.

Gretchin are spiteful but cowardly Greenskins who stick together in large numbers on the battlefield.

Runtherds keep the Gretchin in line.

An Ork Trukk races eagerly to battle, flanked by Warbikes and a Skorcha.

THE TAU EMPIRE

Pathfinder with rail rifle.

Fire Warriors, equipped with advanced weapons and armour, form the bulk of Tau armies.

The Ethereals inspire unquestioning devotion in the Tau.

Ethereal with honour blade.

XV25 Stealthsuit.

The warlike Commander Farsight.

Commander Shadowsun, leader of the Third Phase Expansion.

XV8 Crisis Battlesuit.

Fire Warriors disembark from their Devilfish transport.

The Tau Empire includes other alien races, such as the Kroot.

Kroot Carnivore.

Sniper Drone Team and Fire Warrior.

Vespid Stingwing.

Kroot Hound.

Piranha light skimmer.

Krootox Rider.

TYRANIDS

Termagants are agile and bear gruesome symbiotic weapons.

Hormagaunts are blisteringly fast, their scythe-like claws able to eviscerate the hardiest of foes.

Tyranid Warrior.

A Hive Tyrant directs the swarm, accompanied by his Tyrant Guard.

Gargoyle.

Raveners burst upon the enemy from
beneath the ground.

A Carnifex is a living engine
of destruction!

Genestealers infiltrate prey-worlds ahead of the Hive Fleets.

Ripper Swarm.

For many prey, a Lictor is the first and last they will see of a Tyranid invasion.

Zoanthrope.

DARK ELDAR

The Dark Eldar are raiders, assassins and slavers from the impossible shadow-realm of Commorragh.

Wyches are masters of gladiatorial combat.

Dark Eldar Archon.

Incubi – elite bodyguard to the Archon.

Grotesque.

Mandrake.

Haemonculus.

Reaver jetbikes raid a Tau outpost.

The Talos is fuelled by the death spasms of its victims.

NECRONS

Necron Warriors awake from dusty tombs in which their race has slept for uncounted aeons.

Necron Lord.

Immortals carry heavy gauss weaponry.

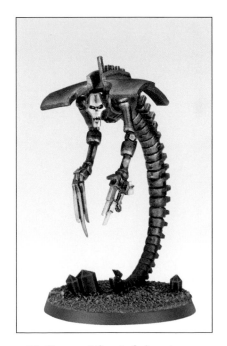

Wraiths can shift out of phase to pass through solid objects.

Serried ranks of Necrons emerge to begin harvesting the population.

COLLECTING AN ARMY

CHOOSING YOUR ARMY

Players are drawn to collect their armies for a huge variety of reasons – as many reasons as there are gamers, in fact. It could all start with the release of a new and exciting miniature, the reading of a passage of background or perhaps a special tactic the army can perform on the battlefield. Often it's a combination of elements that draw player and army together.

Miniatures

At the centre of the Warhammer 40,000 hobby are Citadel miniatures. Many players are drawn to their army by the sheer character of the miniatures, regardless of the playing style, background or any other consideration. Each range has its own individual look and feel, whether it's the technologically advanced Tau or the hordes of slavering beasts that make up a Tyranid army.

Background

Each army has a wealth of character and background to inspire the collector. The Space Marines are the elite defenders of Mankind, while the Orks are barbaric aliens bent on destruction and bloodshed. Background material is presented in the 'Codexes', and also appears in White Dwarf magazine and on the website.

Gaming

Every army has its own style of play on the tabletop. The Eldar are fast and manoeuvrable yet delicate, while Necrons are slower, but able to absorb huge amounts of damage. There are many possible combinations of speed, toughness, close combat ability and firepower, and there's an army to fit each one.

Many players find themselves particularly suited to a specific style of play, perhaps enjoying more success with a close combat army than with a ranged, firepower based one.

That certain something

There is one last reason to choose an army over all the others, best summed up as "just because". Many players feel an attraction to a particular army that transcends the possibilities discussed previously. There is often a certain, indefinable pull exerted on certain gamers by certain armies, as if the player really was the general leading his army to war.

FIRST STEPS

There are plenty of ways to collect your army. One of the simplest (and most exciting!) is to collect the miniatures you are most attracted to first, and then fill out the other units later. There is nothing like the thrill of fielding your favourite new model in its first game.

Other people take a very different approach, drawing up their army list in minute detail. Having decided upon its composition, they buy the entire army in one go.

Many players collect their armies in small chunks. That way, they can purchase a squad set and then assemble and paint it before moving on to another. Furthermore, it may help if you concentrate on the most common or representative troop types in your army. If you were collecting Space Marines, you might start with the Tactical Squads before moving on.

There really is no single right way to do things, so go with whatever suits you best.

Every Warhammer 40,000 army has its own Codex. Each one is the definitive guide to collecting and fielding that army, including the full background, making it an essential purchase once you have chosen your force.

This Ork collection began with the Warhammer 40,000 Assault on Black Reach boxed set. The Warboss, two Boyz Mobz and a squadron of Deffkoptas come in at 350 points, and amount to an HQ, two Troops and a Fast Attack choice. Such an army is the perfect size to paint in a short time, and to get to know how the units work on the tabletop.

The second chunk of the army adds some much needed hitting power, as well as bulking out the army. The Deff Dreads and Killa Kans are hard hitting in close combat, while the extra Boyz will swamp the enemy with sheer weight of numbers!

The third chunk adds in some elite units and additional firepower. The Warbikes and Skorcha are fast moving, while the Big Mek and Burna Boyz are capable of inflicting fearsome damage with their weapons. This chunk takes the army up to 1,500 points.

ULTRAMARINES STRIKE FORCE

Most collections build and develop for a combination of reasons, as demonstrated here by Matt Hutson's Space Marine Strike Force.

Matt is an experienced Warhammer 40,000 player, Space Marines and Chaos Space Marines being his favourite armies. When starting this army, he decided that his goal would be to collect an entire battle company. But Matt wanted to start with a balanced force that was able to take on a variety of foes.

The first units painted were the Captain and the Tactical Squads, giving a solid core that could be fielded straight away. Matt enjoyed applying the bold colours and distinctive iconography, carefully following the reference material in the Codex to ensure all the markings were correct.

After a few small games, Matt decided to add Rhinos to the Tactical squads. The transports made the squads ideal for capturing objectives. Matt also found that a squad of Space Marines piling out of a Rhino to unleash close range bolter fire can take care of most opponents.

In no time at all, Matt was almost half way to his goal of collecting an entire company. His collection enables him to field a variety of army types, depending on the mission and enemy. Turn to page 244 to see 1,500 points of Matt's army in battle against the Eldar of his old adversary, Phil Kelly.

The black banding on the shoulder guards indicates that Matt's force belongs to the 5th Company of the Ultramarines.

Matt painted his Dreadnought as a 'reward' for completing the third of his Tactical squads.

Matt's Predator adds some mobile heavy firepower to his force.

The Techmarine keeps the army's many vehicles battle-ready.

TYRANID ASSAULT SWARM

It was the background that inspired this beautiful Tyranids army. Warhammer 40,000 publications are packed full of such inspiration, so get reading!

Dave Taylor is the sort of hobbyist who likes to collect background-driven armies. The spark could be provided by a piece of art, a detail in a story, a passage in a unit description or any other source from a Codex to a White Dwarf article. In this case, Dave was inspired by the paragraph below, recounting the attack on the Eldar Craftworld of Iyanden by the Tyranids of Hive Fleet Kraken.

The halls and passageways of Iyanden were soon overrun with the foul Tyranids, the twin waves engulfing the craftworld in a tide of chittering, screaming death. Battle was joined in every imaginable arena. Amongst the treetops of the ancient and holy Forests of Silence, Swooping Hawks fought a deadly aerial dance with dark flocks of bat-winged Gargoyles. Striking Scorpions sliced their way through the massed Termagants blocking the arterial passageways. Falcons hunted massive Carnifexes as they smashed apart the beautiful and complex sculpture-bastions of the Fortress of Tears. On the hallowed steps of the Shrine of Asuryan, Dire Avengers fought close and bloody battles with seemingly infinite numbers of Hormagaunts. But all fell to the sheer numbers of attackers, their lives sold at a great cost to the Tyranid hordes. It was not enough.

Extract from 'Doom of the Eldar'

The army is led by a fearsome Hive Tyrant – one of its many victims lies broken at its feet.

The bases of all the models have been modelled and painted as the surface of the craftworld.

The Tyranids of Hive Fleet Kraken overwhelm the Eldar defenders of Craftworld Iyanden.

The Gargoyles' flying bases have been designed to resemble the wraithbone treetops of the Forests of Silence.

Dave has used small pieces from various Eldar kits on the bases of the Tyranids, to show the destruction they have wrought during the Craftworld invasion.

TAU ATTACK CADRE

This Tau army belongs to accomplished tournament player Paul Scott. Like many, Paul chooses his army based upon its tactics and how it performs on the tabletop.

Paul is a big fan of the Tau, and has collected a large and impressive army. He also enjoys entering tournaments and leagues, relishing the combined test of generalship, sportsmanship and painting, as well as the chance to meet new gamers. When playing in such events, Paul draws on his larger collection of Tau to field a small, yet highly tuned and flexible force that has the tools to deal with most of the armies he is likely to face in a tournament.

Paul finds that the Tau army suits his style of play very well. The key is its manoeuvrability, which Paul uses to bring his units' formidable, if relatively short ranged, firepower to bear. By focusing the attentions of several of his units upon isolated enemy squads or vehicles, Paul's army can devastate an opponent in short order. Paul says this approach works well against most enemies, though he does admit that it's the Necrons that give him the most trouble.

1,500 POINT TOURNAMENT ARMY

HQ
Shas'el Commander: 97 points
Plasma rifle, fusion blaster, targeting array, hard-wired multi-tracker.

Shas'el Commander: 97 points
Plasma rifle, fusion blaster, targeting array, hard-wired multi-tracker.

ELITES
Crisis Battlesuit Team Leader: 67 points
Plasma rifle, missile pod, hard-wired multi-tracker.

Crisis Battlesuit Team Leader: 67 points
Plasma rifle, missile pod, hard-wired multi-tracker.

TROOPS
Fire Warriors Team: 66 points
6 Fire Warriors with photon grenades

Kroot Carnivore Squad: 100 points
10 Kroot, 5 Kroot Hounds

Kroot Carnivore Squad: 100 points
10 Kroot, 5 Kroot Hounds

FAST ATTACK
Pathfinder Team: 167 points
6 Pathfinders. Devilfish with targeting array, multi-tracker.

Pathfinder Team: 167 points
6 Pathfinders. Devilfish with targeting array, multi-tracker.

HEAVY SUPPORT
Hammerhead Gunship: 165 points
Railgun, burst cannons, multi tracker, decoy launchers.

Hammerhead Gunship: 165 points
Railgun, burst cannons, multi tracker, decoy launchers.

3 Sniper Drone Teams: 240 points

Paul's Crisis Battlesuits carry a mix of anti-infantry and anti-tank weaponry. As each of the four Battlesuits is a one-model unit, enemies can only target one at a time.

The Kroot are great for holding important objectives, especially in wooded terrain.

The Pathfinders use their 'scouts' special rule to threaten the enemy from Turn 1.

1. Crisis Battlesuits have access to a wide range of weaponry, allowing them to engage both infantry and vehicles.

2. After firing, the Battlesuits leap back into cover, and out of range of enemy reprisals.

Objective

3. The Kroot assault any survivors of the Battlesuits' shooting, eliminating the threat.

Tau tactics centre around the combined use of manoeuvrability and firepower to overwhelm the foe. The ability of Crisis battlesuits to leap back into cover after firing makes them a tricky foe to get to grips with!

PAINTING

There's nothing quite like the glorious sight of two painted armies squaring off against one another for a tabletop battle.

LEARNING TO PAINT

Painting miniatures is an enjoyable hobby in its own right and information on painting and different techniques could fill several books. If you've never painted before, the best way to get started is to just get stuck in and give it a try. There is plenty of help to hand – particularly in White Dwarf magazine and on the Games Workshop website. If you are lucky enough to live near a Games Workshop store then stop by – they will be very happy to give you introductory painting lessons. More extensive advice is available in the How to Paint Citadel Miniatures book.

GAINING EXPERIENCE

The best way to get better at painting is to practice. Even the top painters of the 'Eavy Metal team started out as beginners. If you're new to painting, or trying out a new technique, you might want to start off with some core troops. As your experience grows, you can look back with pride as you achieve even better results. When you feel ready for it, try your best efforts on a leader, special character, or favourite model.

PAINTING AN ARMY

When you are first learning, painting a single model at a time is best. For players trying to amass an entire army, however, this technique will take a long time. By working on a batch of models at a time, you can

Detailed painting tips for beginners and experts alike can be found in How to Paint Citadel Miniatures.

greatly speed up your painting. With an assembly line-style process, you can use one colour to paint the same area on a series of models. By the time you're ready for the next stage, the first model in the line will be dry.

Some people want to get an army out on the table straight away and choose the simplest of paint jobs. Others spend hours and hours, shading and highlighting each model to create a masterpiece. Between these two poles there are the rest of us – gamers who love to fight battles with model soldiers and for whom painting an army is a satisfying and challenging part of the hobby.

Space Marines give painters an opportunity to try their hand at heraldic colours, insignias and squad markings.

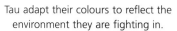

Orks are green, and usually bear distinctive clan colours and markings. These clan markings can be found in a host of places, most often on body armour or wargear.

Tau adapt their colours to reflect the environment they are fighting in.

There are a wide variety of different Imperial Guard regiments but all bear distinctive militaristic uniforms and many make use of camouflage.

Necrons are metallic and monochrome.

Eldar are distinguished either by their Craftworld colours or by their Aspect. Regardless, all feature bright, crisp colours.

Chaos Space Marine Renegades have distinctive colours, textures and symbols.

A FINISHED SQUAD

This squad of Red Corsairs Chaos Space Marines features the colours and iconography detailed in Codex Chaos Space Marines. The models were painted as a single batch, starting with the red of the armour.

Each miniature was primed with Chaos Black spray. The red areas are Mechrite Red, highlighted first with Blood Red and finally with Blazing Orange.

In order to set the Aspiring Champion apart from the rest of the unit, he has been assembled using the bare head.

Metal areas were a given wash of black ink before being highlighted.

The Red Corsair iconography was painted freehand onto the shoulder pad.

The bases have been coated in PVA glue and then dipped in sand. Once dry, they were painted in neutral tones to blend in on different terrain.

A FINISHED ARMY

Here you can see the same squad as part of a larger army. The models all bear the Red Corsairs' colours, applied in different combinations.

The same palette has been used to paint the black, red and gold of all of the Chaos Space Marines in the army, as well as the Predator tank. This gives the army a coherent feel, but at the same time isn't as regimented as their Imperial brethren the Space Marines. Huron Blackheart really stands out, and the most attention has been lavished upon this centrepiece model.

CHAPTERS, REGIMENTS AND CLANS

Warhammer 40,000 is a universe of endless variety, presenting numerous choices when it comes to deciding how you will paint your army.

Plenty of people decide to paint their new army in the colour that appeals to them the most, but others look for an established scheme to follow or to take inspiration from. What colours will your army bear to battle? What insignia will its members wear? What rank markings will make its leaders stand out? Such issues are addressed in the Codexes, and you will find more information and inspiration in White Dwarf magazine, on the Games Workshop website and in the books of the Black Library and Forge World.

Many races are divided into different groups. The Space Marines have over a thousand different Chapters, while there are innumerable Imperial Guard regiments. This means that there are many different colours you could paint your army, depending on which appeals to you the most.

While some armies use one basic scheme across all its units, with subtle variation between squad types, others are a riot of different styles. A Chaos Space Marine force might feature squads from different Legions, or an Ork army might gather mobs from many clans.

Iconography and banner designs, from Codex: Dark Angels.

Harlequin patterns from White Dwarf magazine.

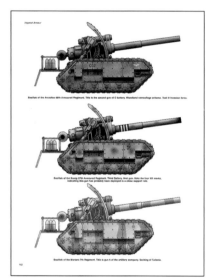

Basilisk camouflage, from Forge World's Imperial Armour Volume One.

Codex Chapters, from the Black Library's Insignium Astartes.

INVENTING YOUR OWN

Some players like to invent their own Space Marine Chapter, Imperial Guard Regiment, Tau Sept World or Tyranid Hive Fleet. They name their force, devise their own colour scheme, badge and iconography, and some even create a background story for their army.

An easily accessible starting point is a variation on an established colour scheme. To use Space Marines as an example, Successor Chapters bear heraldry derived from an existing Chapter, providing fertile ground for inventive painters. The Dark Angels Chapter for instance, has dark green as its main colour, accented with bone white, black and red.

You could invent a Successor Chapter of the Dark Angels that swaps around the main and accent colours, using them in different proportions to the parent chapter.

For those who want to go the whole way and create their own colour scheme and iconography from scratch, the sky really is the limit. The entire Citadel paint range is there to be used, and inspiration can be found throughout Games Workshop's publications and beyond. Films, books, TV shows and history all provide rich pickings for the player looking to create a truly unique army.

CUSTOMISING YOUR MINIATURES

Some collectors like to make changes to the models they have bought, to make their army completely unique. Such personalisation ranges from simply combining parts from two or more kits, to more ambitious 'scratch-built' projects.

This Veteran Sergeant has a spare head from the Space Marine Commander set – a simple but effective conversion.

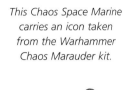

This Chaos Space Marine carries an icon taken from the Warhammer Chaos Marauder kit.

An Ork Nob equipped with an 'uge choppa made from metal and plastic components, and some plastic tubing.

An Ork Deffkopta, scratch-built from spare components and bits of plasticard.

Using plasticard and two part epoxy putty (sometimes called 'green stuff') this Tau Broadside has been dramatically reposed.

This conversion was done by a Chaos Space Marine player who wanted his Sorcerer to have a jump pack with more of a Chaotic feel to it.

A Sister of Battle Canoness, remodelled with extensive use of Green Stuff putty.

ALAITOC CRAFTWORLD ELDAR

Some painters like to invest such attention in their army that every model is a masterpiece. John Shaffer is such a painter, as shown by his stunning Eldar army.

John's decision to paint an army from the Alaitoc Craftworld was inspired by the patterned blue armour the warriors and vehicles bear. Once his technique for this visually striking effect was worked out, John devised a system for painting his units in a production line, allowing him to paint each unit quickly.

This philosophy carried forward to army selection. The force contains a lot of large models, whether War Walkers, Wraithlords or grav tanks. The primary reason for the inclusion of these models in the army was the fact that they represented a chance to apply the stippled blue patterning across large areas.

John gave hoods and cloaks to one of his squads of Guardians using plastic parts from a Warhammer Wood Elf kit.

John achieved the characteristic Alaitoc colour scheme by stippling various shades of blue onto the surface using a large brush. Stippling is achieved by dabbing the brush onto the miniature, twisting it as you go for a random, blotchy effect.

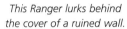

This Ranger lurks behind the cover of a ruined wall.

Extensive conversion work has been done to make all the characters unique.

John has assembled his Wraithlord to give the impression it is stalking forward, hunting the enemy.

SERVANTS OF KHORNE

Every miniature in Andrew Taylor's Chaos Space Marine army has been lavished with detail, from the daemonic faces painted on each model's armour, to the lava effect used on the bases.

Andrew Taylor is one of those hobbyists who revels in every aspect of Warhammer 40,000. He regularly participates in Grand Tournaments, and is well known for the quality of the armies he brings along. This army represents a Chaos Space Marine warband entirely given over to the worship of the Chaos God Khorne.

It is a great example of a collection that has been personalised within the established character and background of the army. The red and bronze of the

god of war is used throughout, as are skulls and Khornate icons, making it unmistakably an army of the Blood God. The creativity and imagination of its owner are stamped clearly upon it for all to see.

The most striking element Andrew has used to really make the army his own are the leering daemonic faces applied to every surface of armour. Although intricate, the faces were applied in only four stages. They did take a fair amount of patience and a steady hand though!

Each miniature in the army has been assembled in a dynamic pose, covered in glowing runes and daemonic faces, while bubbling lava has been modelled and painted on the bases.

On this model a piece of chain has been added to connect the axe to a wicked looking meat hook.

A piece from the Ork Boyz kit has been used to make the business end of this chain glaive.

The power of the Warp lifts this Berzerker in the air as he is possessed by a Daemon.

The daemonic faces that adorn the armour of Andrew's models are painted in stages, using progressively finer lines, and brighter colours.

Even as the planet breaks apart, the servants of Khorne rampage on in a frenzy of blood-letting.

Warped and mutated by the Daemons inside them, these Possessed are probably the most dangerous unit in the warband.

BATTLEFIELDS

Throughout the galaxy wars rage across cratered wastelands, seething hive cities, asteroid mining outposts and deadly alien jungles. Creating a modelled battlefield will make your games look amazing, as well as adding tactical challenges.

Having a decent amount of terrain will really improve your Warhammer 40,000 battles. Not just because it gives your warriors vital cover to shelter in or behind, but because laying out the terrain in different ways means that every battle will be completely different to the last.

Terrain also sets the scene. Instead of moving around a flat board, your troops are advancing fearlessly through shattered buildings. They are hacking their way through dense alien jungle or launching a gruelling assault against an impenetrable enemy defence line.

There is plenty of Citadel terrain available with which you can build an impressive battlefield – such as those pieces shown here. Many gamers also like to build their own terrain, representing the various war zones of the 41st Millennium. Some examples of this approach are shown on the following pages.

Blasted War Zone

The battlefield shown here is a blasted wasteland that has suffered desperate warfare, with craters from bombardments, shattered buildings, blackened trees and a fortified outpost.

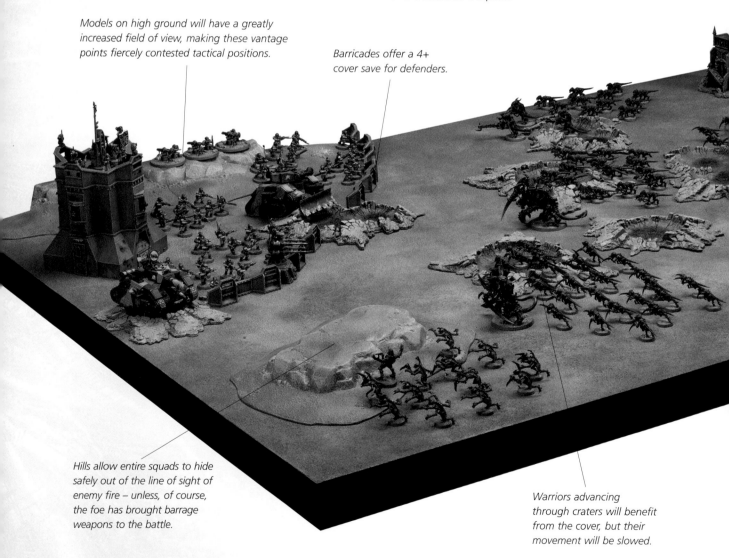

Models on high ground will have a greatly increased field of view, making these vantage points fiercely contested tactical positions.

Barricades offer a 4+ cover save for defenders.

Hills allow entire squads to hide safely out of the line of sight of enemy fire – unless, of course, the foe has brought barrage weapons to the battle.

Warriors advancing through craters will benefit from the cover, but their movement will be slowed.

An Imperial gun line is breached by Tyranids.

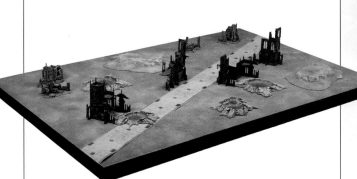

Ruined Settlement

With the addition of some larger City Ruins and a road, we have created the remains of an Imperial settlement. A battle played across this table will be a close quarter and bloody affair, as short-ranged gunfights and desperate assaults erupt amidst the ruins.

Ruined buildings block line of sight and offer the protection of a cover save. Many armies will look to place snipers or units bearing heavy weapon in upper stories.

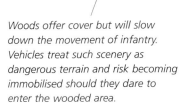

Contested Ground

This battlefield has been set up as the crater-strewn area between two armies. The centre has little terrain other than the craters themselves, but a competent commander will make good use of every scrap of cover.

Woods offer cover but will slow down the movement of infantry. Vehicles treat such scenery as dangerous terrain and risk becoming immobilised should they dare to enter the wooded area.

Unexplored Wilderness

This region is more distant from the front lines, and so more trees have been used and the craters left out. The arcane monolith makes a great centrepiece, while the crashed shuttle suggests a previous mission gone horribly wrong.

CITADEL TERRAIN

As well as miniature warriors, Citadel produces a wide range of terrain which can be used on your Warhammer 40,000 tabletop. Many of these versatile kits can be assembled in a variety of ways, meaning no two set-ups need look alike.

Manufactorum

Sanctum Imperialis

Ruins

The City Ruins kits are fully modular, allowing you to construct a vast range of different structures. Each of the three kits are entirely interchangeable, so you can make your own unique structures. Although they need little more than drybrushing to look great on the table, each of the City Ruins is covered in detail that can be picked out should you wish.

In the game, ruins serve to provide cover, to break up movement and block line of sight. Using just one on your tabletop will make your game more dynamic, as units seek to take advantage of the cover and height afforded. Adding two or three more will make for a very different game, as the large structures create narrow fire lanes and deadly killing grounds.

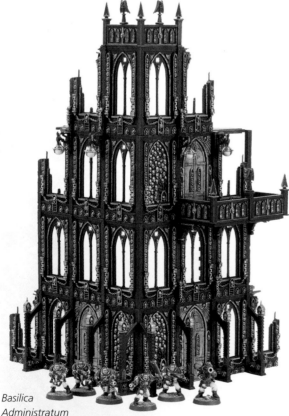

Basilica Administratum

Barricades and Walls

The Barricades and Walls set provides lots of low level cover behind which troops can shelter.

Craters

Craters can occupy a large area of the table surface, providing cover without blocking lines of sight.

Arcane Ruins

The Arcane Ruins set makes a great centrepiece on any tabletop. The ruins could be used as a temple where the fell powers of Chaos are worshiped, or even as the remnants of a long-extinct civilisation.

Battlefield Accessories

Crammed full of crates, barrels, tank traps and more, these items provide extra detail to your battlefield. They also make great objectives, as shown on page 253.

THE RUINS OF AROTHA

Annihilated by wars past, the remains of this Imperial city are slowly being submerged in the drifting sands. Now, conflict rages across the dunes as an ancient alien race awakens, the slumber of aeons disturbed by a trespassing foe.

Once this desolate moon was a thriving green planet. To create the impression that the drifting sands are slowly claiming the ruined remains, each terrain piece was mounted on a specially built, hardboard base. The base was built up with polystyrene that was carved to shape, and then covered in sand. This is a good example of customising Citadel Terrain pieces to suit your own needs and tastes.

More sand was added to the upper stories of the ruins, as if blown there by the incessant desert winds.

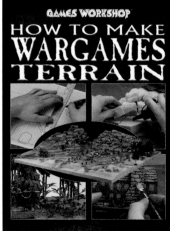

Implacable Necrons rise from the sands to ambush the Eldar trespassers.

For more terrain making tips, pick up How to Make Wargames Terrain.

VULCRON MINING FACILITY

Mined to destruction, the planet of Vulcron is cracking apart, the magma beneath the surface spewing onto the battlefield. The lava channels may prove deadly to any troops that attempt to cross.

This board is made from a large sheet of insulation board (polystyrene also works well for this sort of project). The lava streams have been cut into the surface of the board to create a three-dimensional effect. Fully modelled battlefields such as this look more realistic, and even allow you to build up dramatic contours in the landscape if you wish.

The rock piles and mining station buildings can be moved around between games to vary the battlefield.

Only skimmers and troops equipped with jump packs can cross the lava channels without risk.

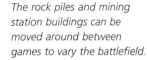

The lava counts as both dangerous terrain and difficult terrain, making it incredibly perilous for troops to cross.

Ultramarines and Chaos Space Marines clash amongst the hellish landscape of Vulcron.

FI'RIOS COLONY OUTPOST

As their Empire expands, the Tau quickly colonise newly conquered territory.

Fi'rios is similar to the Tau home world in climate and terrain type – arid deserts and savannahs.

A drop-down mesa terrain piece, made from layered polystyrene and painted to match the table.

The centrepiece of this terrain set is the outpost's control centre, with landing pad and long-ranged communications array.

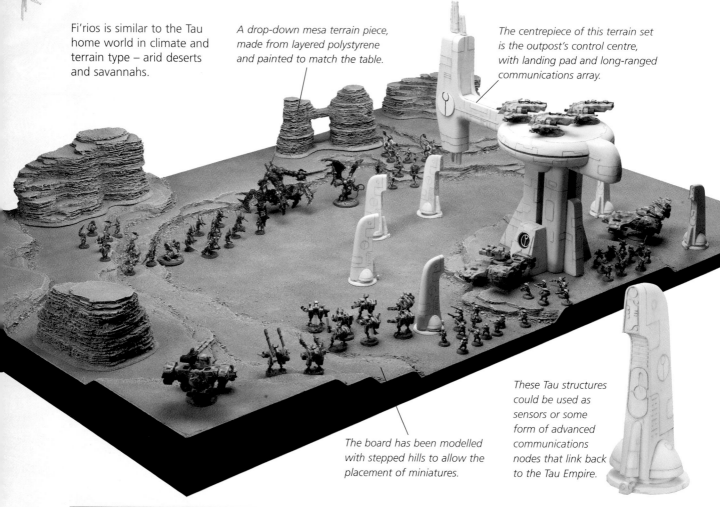

The board has been modelled with stepped hills to allow the placement of miniatures.

These Tau structures could be used as sensors or some form of advanced communications nodes that link back to the Tau Empire.

The Tau defend their colony.

MAIDEN WORLD KAILITH

Deep within the jungles of Kailith lies a distantly remembered webway portal.

Ancient Eldar ruins, carved to shape from polystyrene.

Smaller pieces can be rearranged from one game to the next.

Areas of jungle made from plastic jungle plants mounted on hardboard bases.

FORT BORKRULL

Warboss Borkrull gathers Boyz and gear in his fort, ready to launch his Waaagh!

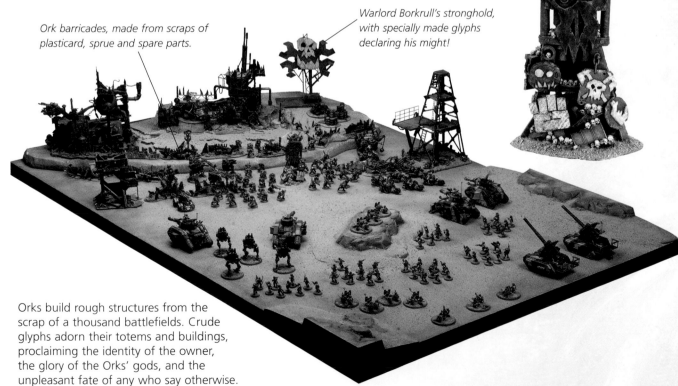

Ork barricades, made from scraps of plasticard, sprue and spare parts.

Warlord Borkrull's stronghold, with specially made glyphs declaring his might!

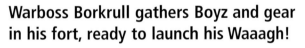

Orks build rough structures from the scrap of a thousand battlefields. Crude glyphs adorn their totems and buildings, proclaiming the identity of the owner, the glory of the Orks' gods, and the unpleasant fate of any who say otherwise.

RESEARCH STATION B8400761

Somewhere in the Eastern Fringe, hidden on a barren moon, the augurs and sensors of this isolated outpost gather information and watch for signs of invasion.

Space Marines of the Dark Angels Chapter protect the research station.

The tower provides an ideal position for snipers.

A battlefield such as this instantly suggests a variety of gaming ideas, from daring raids, to desperate last stands! On page 270 we have used this board as the basis for a special mission in which an Adeptus Mechanicus Genetor must escape from the station before it is overrun by the enemy.

The research station is constructed from various Warhammer 40,000 terrain kits and other spare parts. The base is mounted upon a rock formation, made from sections of tree bark.

The landing pad makes an ideal objective for troops to fight over.

Any attackers assaulting the main structure from the landing pad can expect to take heavy losses as they dare to cross the open bridge.

A lot of the table is open ground, meaning any attackers approaching the research station need to move quickly if they are not to be picked off at range. Models without transport vehicles will make good use of the Running rule.

IMPERIAL PALACE

When the shrine world of Arkost was invaded by Chaos Space Marines, the Imperial palace in the capital city became a rallying point for the defenders.

Within the wreckage-strewn ruins, bold defenders of the faith fight to repulse the forces of darkness.

Devastators defend the main doors of the cathedral.

The mighty Blood Angels stand ready to crush the hated Chaos Renegades.

The walkways and crypt provide different levels for models to fight over.

Inside the palace limited lines of sight, piles of rubble, and collapsed floorways ensure that battles become desperate and bloody close combat affairs.

The open ground around the cathedral is strewn with craters.

A Defiler crashes through into the interior of the building.

BATTLES

Warhammer 40,000 offers possibilities limited only by your imagination. From the standard missions to lengthy campaigns, sudden ambushes, desperate cityfights and apocalyptic clashes, the hobby can take you anywhere.

Wherever your journey through the hobby ultimately takes you, the starting point will almost certainly be the standard missions. By playing these missions against a number of opponents, you will soon learn both the full capabilities of your own army, and get a taste of all the others armies out there. You will amass glorious victories talked of for years to come, and ignominious defeats best kept quiet. Friendly rivalries will develop amongst your regular opponents as your armies clash on the tabletop. Adversaries will hurl challenges against one another in an effort to settle old scores. New tactics will be attempted, or entirely new armies may be started in an effort to earn victory.

As you and your gaming group explore the hobby, you may find yourselves gravitating towards particular types of play. Some will enjoy the no-holds-barred approach of tournament-style games, relishing every test of generalship and nuance of the rules. Others use their battles to tell stories, enjoying above all the chance to engage with the background.

Some people develop this sense of history and background depth further, by playing campaigns – a series of missions, linked by an overall story and rules, with the result of one battle having a bearing upon the next. At the end of the campaign the player who made the best of his wins will be the victor, but all players involved will have had the satisfaction of playing in a truly memorable gaming event.

Others decide to alter the standard missions to suit their own themes or storylines. Those who try this will soon be inventing entirely new missions, perhaps designed specifically for the armies and terrain they use the most.

All this is covered in the Battles section, so if you've ever wanted to write your own missions, host a campaign, or run a league, this section is for you. Here, you will find a range of useful and inspirational gaming material, geared towards taking your games from the standard missions and beyond.

BLOOD IN THE DESERT

In this battle report, two old adversaries face off across the gaming table. Each is a long-time Warhammer 40,000 player and each has a string of victories to his name. Read on for an account of a hard-fought but extremely enjoyable game!

THE ULTHWÉ HOST

HQ

Farseer Ariniae
Spirit Stones, Runes of
Witnessing, and the Doom and
Fortune psychic powers   **140pts**
3 Warlocks   **75pts**
Avatar of Khaine   **155pts**

ELITES

8 Howling Banshees
including Exarch Mieqo with the
Exarch power War Shout,
wielding an Executioner   **155pts**
Wave Serpent 'Windstriker'
twin-linked starcannon   **125pts**

TROOPS

10 Dire Avengers
including Exarch Ul'uric
with the Exarch power
Bladestorm, a shimmershield
and a power weapon   **162pts**
10 Guardian Defenders
including a bright lance platform,
led by Warlock Raelothi with a
Singing Spear   **138pts**
10 Storm Guardians
including two fusion guns,
led by Warlock Ithilis with the
psychic power Enhance and
a Singing Spear   **135pts**
3 Guardian Jetbikes   **66pts**

HEAVY SUPPORT

5 Dark Reapers
including Exarch Lhoix with the
Exarch power Fast Shot   **207pts**
Wraithlord T'laric
with bright lance and
wraithblade   **140pts**

GRAND TOTAL 1,498pts

ANCIENT RIVALRY

Phil: Matt and I have been regular opponents for over eight years now. Though Matt enjoys frustrating me with his flukey power armour saves and my sneaky Eldar tactics sometimes get on his wick in return, we both really enjoy playing each other. Our games are a great mix of well-established rivalry and good-natured fun.

My original Eldar force was designed purely to kill tough-as-nails Space Marines, but over the years I have drifted towards using far more balanced tactics. My Ulthwé armies now include lots of Guardians and psykers, backed up by iron-hard combat machines like the Avatar and Wraithlord. It's a tried and tested combination. Because we had agreed to play a Capture and Control mission (see page 91), my plan is to distract Matt's men in blue with a frontal assault whilst my Guardian Jetbikes, Howling Banshees and Storm Guardians dart round the flank. With any luck, my frontal assault will hit home hard and clear the way for my flankers to claim the enemy objective. Meanwhile, my shooty units (the Guardian Defenders, Dark Reapers and Dire Avengers) will hold the fort, picking off any of Matt's forces that attempt a flank attack on my own home objective.

Phil has faced Matt with his Eldar army many times before!

Battle Reports, published in Games Workshop's monthly magazine 'White Dwarf', showcase nail-biting games of Warhammer 40,000 using the awesomely painted Studio armies.

Beginners and veterans alike consider the monthly battle reports to be one of the finest features of White Dwarf magazine. As well as telling a good story, battle reports give plenty of opportunities to pick up new tactics, devious tricks and inspiration. It is also a great chance to see the newest armies and models 'doing their thing' on a beautifully made battlefield. The most popular elements are often the parts written by the players themselves; pre-game introductions and post-game conclusions that give us an insight into their army selection and battle plan.

PREFERRED ENEMY

Matt: I've been playing games against Phil for longer than I care to remember. Over the years I've taken him on with several Space Marine Chapters, the majority of which were Black Templars, but lately the Ultramarines have been my weapon of choice.

In the past my Space Marine forces have always been assault-orientated, but this time I've gone for a force based around Tactical squads, because this gives me several units capable of holding objectives. My plan is to hold my objective with a fire base consisting of a Tactical squad, the Devastators, the Dreadnought and a Predator. These will try to destroy anything big and nasty from afar. The rest of the Tactical squads, led by Captain Octavius, will sweep around the flank avoiding any enemy units advancing up the centre – the fire base should have them under control. The Assault squad will protect the other flank, or at least delay any enemy coming that way, and the Scouts will hopefully give them something else to think about. Game on...

Matt and Phil's traditional pre-game handshake. "May the best man win!"

ULTRAMARINES 5TH COMPANY

HQ
Captain Octavius
Lightning claw and plasma pistol.
125 points

ELITES
Dreadnought
with assault cannon. **125 points**

TROOPS
5 Scouts
All armed with bolters. **90 points**
10 Tactical Space Marines
including a flamer and
missile launcher.   **170 points**
Rhino   **50 points**
with a hunter-killer missile
10 Tactical Space Marines
including a flamer and
missile launcher.   **170 points**
Rhino   **35 points**
10 Tactical Space Marines
including a flamer and
heavy bolter.   **170 points**

FAST ATTACK
10 Assault Space Marines
including Veteran Sergeant with
a power fist.   **235 points**

HEAVY SUPPORT
10 Devastator Space Marines
including 2 lascannons and 2
multi-meltas.   **245 points**
Predator
with autocannon and 2 heavy
bolters.   **85 points**

GRAND TOTAL 1,500pts

THE BATTLE RAGES

The duel in the desert started slowly but steadily built to a bloody climax. The scene below is midway through the game, with both players attempting to penetrate the other's defence and steal their objective from the opponent's grasp.

The advanced firepower of the Eldar gave Phil an early advantage. Matt's overall strategy was to ride this incoming fire out and hit back where it hurt, concentrating on destroying Phil's Troops choices. His intention was to rob the Eldar of scoring units so they could not claim either objective. On the other hand, Phil launched his close combat units headlong into the Ultramarines' battle line, hoping to distract Matt with a central feint as the real threat closed in on his left flank.

The Dark Reapers, deployed in a commanding position on the hill, took a heavy toll on the Space Marine infantry in the early game.

HEAVY DUTY
The Predator Destructor cut down swathes of Eldar infantry, even crushing a Guardian under its tracks with a successful Tank Shock!

OBJECTIVE

DUEL TO THE DEATH
In the hard-fought centre of the battlefield, the Wraithlord charged through the Dreadnought's volleys of fire and engaged it in combat. This allowed a dramatic duel between the leaders of the two armies to take place – Farseer versus Space Marine Captain in mortal combat.

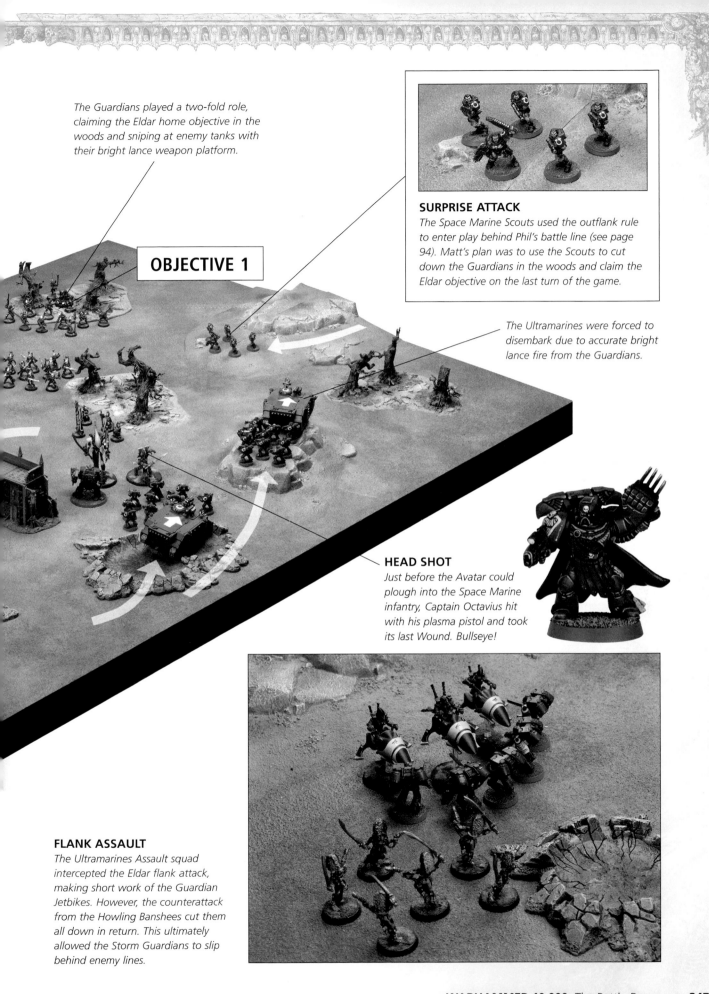

The Guardians played a two-fold role, claiming the Eldar home objective in the woods and sniping at enemy tanks with their bright lance weapon platform.

OBJECTIVE 1

SURPRISE ATTACK
The Space Marine Scouts used the outflank rule to enter play behind Phil's battle line (see page 94). Matt's plan was to use the Scouts to cut down the Guardians in the woods and claim the Eldar objective on the last turn of the game.

The Ultramarines were forced to disembark due to accurate bright lance fire from the Guardians.

HEAD SHOT
Just before the Avatar could plough into the Space Marine infantry, Captain Octavius hit with his plasma pistol and took its last Wound. Bullseye!

FLANK ASSAULT
The Ultramarines Assault squad intercepted the Eldar flank attack, making short work of the Guardian Jetbikes. However, the counterattack from the Howling Banshees cut them all down in return. This ultimately allowed the Storm Guardians to slip behind enemy lines.

THE DUST SETTLES...

After six turns of edge-of-the-seat gaming, the Eldar emerged bloody but victorious. They had Troop units within 3" of both of the objectives, and the remaining Space Marine models were just too far away. Matt made a credible assault upon Phil's home objective with his two Rhinos and his Scouts, but the Eldar bright lance platforms stopped the Rhinos in their tracks, forcing the Space Marines to disembark in front of Phil's Avatar and Wraithlord. Matt dealt with the Avatar using lascannons and his Captain's plasma pistol, but this still left Phil his Farseer unit and Wraithlord with which to stop Matt's advance.

PSYKER POWER

From the very start, the lynchpin of Phil's force was his Farseer. The ancient psyker used his Fortune and Doom psychic powers to bolster the Eldar at critical points, somehow beat the enemy Force Commander in a duel, and still found time to charge the Space Marines trying to outflank the Eldar. Not bad for an oldster.

Despite Matt's successful interception of the Jetbikes with his Assault Marines, the Howling Banshees were able to deal with the jump infantry quickly enough to redeploy. Matt's Devastators put paid to the Howling Banshees' plans, taking out their Wave Serpent, and the deadly warrior women were subsequently cut down without mercy by the rest of Matt's force. Meanwhile, the humble Storm Guardians were able to advance, using the damaged Predator as cover – even when it ran one of them over with a successful Tank Shock! Despite taking a lot of punishment it was the Guardians who carried the day – the Storm Guardians drove off the Space Marine squad on Matt's objective whilst the Guardians held the objective in the woods.

NEVER UNDERESTIMATE AN ELDAR

Phil: Well, things didn't go quite according to plan, but on the whole my feint in the centre distracted Matt's main force, so I was able to capitalise on that in the latter turns of the game. I had far more luck than I had any right to expect (this is normally Matt's forte) but sometimes the dice are just good to you.

Still, the key to winning with the Eldar is to use each unit at the battlefield role for which it is designed, and I think I did that pretty well. The Dark Reapers were very effective early on – those guys killed about sixteen Space Marines between them over the course of the game. Though my Avatar took a lot of fire it did mean that my Wraithlord was almost untouched when he hit home. The combination of Farseer and Warlock bodyguard backed up by the Wraithlord allowed me to

stop Matt's advance for good, which in turn saved the unit of Guardians defending my objective from being mown down in a hail of bolter fire. Using your units to support each other like this is the key to victory in games of Warhammer 40,000.

The game had some priceless moments, and as usual with these games the best times came from when we tried something unusual or risky (just what was my Dire Avenger Exarch doing up a tree again?). Matt's Tank Shock on my Guardians could have swung the game, as could his outflank attack with the Scouts. The real irony was the fact that when Matt saw that I had taken Storm Guardians he asked if I was mad – and it was those little fellas that carried the game! Just goes to show, never underestimate the pointy-eared ones...

DOWN BUT NOT OUT

Matt: Despite the final result, that was actually quite a tense game – up until the final couple of turns it could have gone either way. On the whole, my battle plan worked quite well. The fire base downed the Avatar early, the Assault Marines dealt with the annoyingly fast jetbikes and the Howling Banshees got nowhere near my fire base. The Dire Avengers also died in a shower of bolter shells – very satisfying.

The one unit that really cost me were the Dark Reapers. They almost single-handedly stopped my assault on the Eldar's objective. I just couldn't focus enough long-range firepower on their position, which left them pretty much free to kill whatever they wanted.

Next time I play Phil there's a few things I will do differently. I will definitely deploy my fire base further back, so that it will be out of range of the Dark Reapers. I will also take more tanks, as Phil's army was definitely lacking in heavy weapons, and a Vindicator or two would add a lot of bite to my force. A Librarian and his psychic hood could make it difficult for the Eldar to use their psychic powers, closing down Phil's Farseer, which he maintains is the lynchpin of his force.

I would still ignore the Guardians, as they can't do that much damage to Space Marines; it's their Aspect Warrior brethren that usually do all the damage. You can learn a lot from a close-fought game.

Next time Phil won't be as lucky...

TACTICAL TIP – COMBAT SQUADS
The ability for 10-man Space Marine Tactical, Assault, Devastator and Scout squads to split down into two 5-man squads is a real advantage. It gives the Space Marines twice as many scoring units as well as giving them the flexibility to direct their firepower at different targets in the same turn.

ROAD TO GLORY CAMPAIGN

Having tried your hand at the standard missions, why not play several battles in a row, linked to form an ongoing campaign.

LINKING YOUR BATTLES

A campaign is a series of battles linked together in some way. Over the course of the games, a story evolves, and your army develops a history as it fights from one battle to the next. Campaigns often add extra rules, so that the result of one game has a knock-on effect in the next. How long a campaign takes is up to you – some people like to pack as many games as possible into a weekend, while others like to spread them over the course of a few weeks.

If you like the sound of playing in a campaign but you aren't sure where to start, read on for an example that you can play through with an opponent.

At the end you'll find an account of how two gamers fared when they played through the campaign, followed by ideas on how you might add extra detail and variation. This last section is ideal for those who have played in a campaign before and want to jump right in at the deep end.

ROAD TO GLORY

In this campaign there are five battles. The missions are all standard ones drawn from the main rules section. However, success in one mission will secure an advantage in the next, giving a feeling of continuity .

In order to make the campaign accessible to players of all armies, we haven't given it a specific setting or background story. This is for you to concoct if you get the urge. You could simply set the campaign within one of the many larger wars being fought across the galaxy and beyond, or you could make up an extensive background history all your own.

The overall situation is that two armies have been fighting for many years, neither able to break the bloody deadlock, until a new commander (you!) is shipped in, assigned, spawned or fights his way to the top, to tip the balance and win the war.

The glory of your race depends upon you!

PLAYING THE CAMPAIGN

Playing this campaign is straightforward. The five battles should be played in the order presented. Think of each battle as a snap-shot of a far larger ongoing war.

Battle 1 kicks off the action, but its implications won't be revealed until the end of the campaign, when the victorious forces return on the eve of the final battle. In Battle 2, the forces seek to dominate no-man's-land, each looking to find a weak point in the other's defences. Having found a crack in the line, the winner of Battle 2 will attempt to consolidate his position in Battle 3, while the defender will launch a hurried counter-attack. The war will then escalate in Battle 4 and ultimately leads to an assault upon the enemy headquarters in Battle 5.

THE BATTLES

Each battle presents all the information you need to play, addressing the following points:

Battle Briefing

A summary of the game, along with any significance the battle has in the ongoing campaign.

Playing the Battle

Which of the standard missions is to be played, and which deployment is to be used. In addition, as each battle takes place in an ongoing war, the winner of the previous game may have an advantage, as described here.

Objective

Notes on where objectives should be placed and what they represent, where appropriate.

Terrain

The terrain over which each battle is fought is described here. This is intended as guidance only, and should of course be tailored to your own collection. By assembling a fairly basic terrain set, you will have sufficient scenery for the entire campaign. You can of course undertake special modelling projects for specific locations if you wish.

THE WINNER

The campaign ends in climactic fashion with Battle 5. The winner of that game is the winner of the entire campaign, having crushed his foe utterly.

> In any army, balance is the key to success. A commander who puts his faith in heavy weaponry alone will be outmanoeuvred. A commander who relies on close combat without support will lose his force to enemy fire. Each element must work in harmony, so that the effectiveness of the army is greater than the sum of its parts.
>
> The Tactica Imperium.

CAMPAIGN OVERVIEW

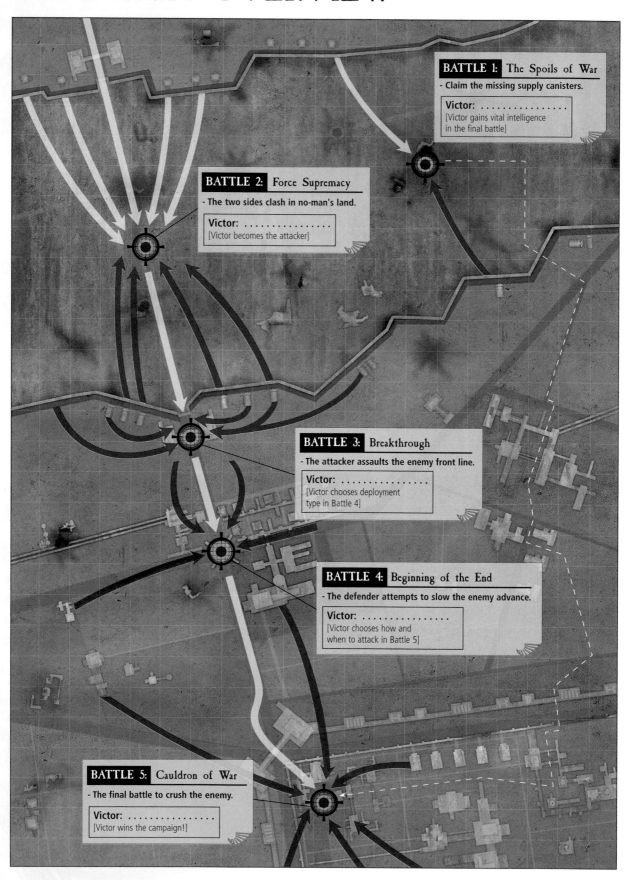

BATTLE 1: The Spoils of War

- Claim the missing supply canisters.

Victor: . . . .
[Victor gains vital intelligence in the final battle]

BATTLE 2: Force Supremacy

- The two sides clash in no-man's land.

Victor: . . . .
[Victor becomes the attacker]

BATTLE 3: Breakthrough

- The attacker assaults the enemy front line.

Victor: . . . .
[Victor chooses deployment type in Battle 4]

BATTLE 4: Beginning of the End

- The defender attempts to slow the enemy advance.

Victor: . . . .
[Victor chooses how and when to attack in Battle 5]

BATTLE 5: Cauldron of War

- The final battle to crush the enemy.

Victor: . . . .
[Victor wins the campaign!]

BATTLE 1 – THE SPOILS OF WAR

As both armies build up their forces for the new campaign, a vital re-supply mission is intercepted, its cargo lost somewhere in the deserted ground between front lines. Both sides speedily dispatch forces to claim the spoils of war.

Battle Briefing

This battle forms a 'prologue' to the campaign, taking place before the main offensive gets underway. Both sides have dispatched a force to recover the supplies lost by the ill-fated re-supply mission. Crucially, neither knows for sure what is in each supply container. It won't be until the containers have been delivered to high command, just before the last battle, that their contents will be revealed.

Playing the Battle

Battle 1 is a Seize Ground mission, and uses the Dawn of War deployment. Details of both can be found in the Organising a Battle chapter.

Objective

The objectives represent the supply containers, and are placed as described in the Seize Ground mission.

Terrain

The supplies are scattered in a sector of the warzone that has seen little fighting in recent months. The table could be set up to represent a wilderness area, using whatever hills, woods and such terrain as you have available.

Before committing your forces, examine the situation. Review your own strength, and that of your enemy. Remember your own objectives, and try to anticipate those of your opponent. He who fights without understanding the battle he is fighting places himself at a disadvantage.

Collects of War

OBJECTIVE MARKERS

Above left is a canister from the Battlefield Accessories set. This makes an ideal objective marker in a Seize Ground mission. Above right is an objective marker constructed from a spare Space Marine banner.

The ammo crate from the Battlefield Accessories set.

Eldar Guardians protect the precious remains of a Revenant Titan.

BATTLE 2 – FORCE SUPREMACY

Enemy forces clash in the crater-strewn wasteland between front lines. Each seeks to dominate the warzone, locate a weak point and overwhelm the foe.

Battle Briefing

This battle represents the armies probing one another's positions while seeking to control ground. The victor will gain an advantage in the campaign ahead.

Playing the Battle

Battle 2 is a Capture and Control standard mission, using the Dawn of War deployment.

Objective

Each objective represents a key point in the lines. This might be a communications array, forward headquarters, Hive node or any such position. Each is equally valuable to the enemy, who will attempt to capture the enemy's position whilst protecting his own.

Terrain

The battlefield is the blasted waste between frontlines. Appropriate, characterful terrain to represent it include craters, barricades and single-storey ruins. All of these provide cover, yet rarely obstruct lines of sight, making the battlefield a truly deadly killing ground. Units attempting to capture an objective must make use of every scrap of cover available if they are to prevail.

Gaining an Advantage

The player who wins Battle 2 has gained the strategic advantage, and is referred to for the rest of the campaign as the **attacker**. The other side is referred to from now on as the **defender**. The attacker may choose who goes first in the next battle.

The Daemons close in on their objective – the Vostroyans' command post

BATTLE 3 – BREAKTHROUGH

Having found a weakness, one side launches a full scale assault. The enemy immediately counter-attacks, stopping at nothing to stem the tide of attackers.

Battle Briefing

Battle 3 represents the winner of Battle 2 having broken through the other side's front line, and looking to consolidate their gains by taking defensible positions from which to make subsequent attacks. The other army will not be sitting around idly of course, and will be launching an all-out counter-attack to prevent the positions falling to the enemy for good.

Playing the Battle

This battle is fought as a Seize Ground standard mission using the Pitched Battle deployment with the following exceptions. The defender must deploy his entire army first and then the attacker may decide who gets the first turn.

Objective

The objectives are key positions both sides have been ordered to secure. Instead of placing counters each player must nominate terrain features such as buildings, barricades, hills or anything else you have available, as the objectives that are to be fought over.

> Do not strike until you are ready to crush the enemy utterly, and then attack without mercy, destroy every vestige of resistance, leave no-one to work against you.
>
> Tactica Imperium

Terrain

The battlefield should be set up to represent one side's front line. This means it could feature intact buildings, roads, communications trenches, bunkers and ammo dumps as well as the craters and barricades used in Battle 1. The more small pieces of terrain, the better.

Gaining an Advantage

The winner of the third battle may choose the deployment type used for the next game. This represents the winner gaining strategic advantage.

The Black Templars fight valiantly to prevent the Tyranids taking their position.

BATTLE 4 – BEGINNING OF THE END

The attacker has reached the perimeter of the defender's main base, but he must strike the decisive blow. The defender must repel the invaders.

Battle Briefing

The attacker has now gained a solid enough advantage that he can launch a major thrust towards his enemy's centre of power. The defender has marshalled his forces to hold back the invaders and block the advance.

Playing the Battle

Battle 4 is fought as a Capture and Control standard mission, apart from the objectives and terrain set up, as detailed below in the Terrain section. The winner of the previous battle may choose the deployment type.

Objective

The objective in the attacker's deployment zone might represent his forward command post, while that in the defender's deployment zone could be a lynchpin position in the defence of the entire sector. When placing the objective in his own deployment zone, each player may place an additional terrain piece, such as a crater, building or barricade, to represent this location.

Terrain

As this battle occurs at the edge of the defender's base, terrain should be set up so that buildings, bunkers and barricades are placed on the defender's side, and such features as hills and craters are placed on the attacker's side. This means that the terrain will dictate each player's table edge, rather than choosing as normal.

Gaining an Advantage

The winner of the fourth battle may once again choose deployment type in the next game but also has a further advantage as detailed in the next mission.

Mission Special Rule – Minefields

In an attempt to slow down the attacker, the ground before the defender's position is strewn with deadly mines. The attacker's advance will be reduced to a painfully slow crawl under the guns of the enemy, unless he can negotiate the lethal minefields.

- The defender may place D3+3 minefields anywhere outside of the attacker's deployment zone.

- For each minefield, place a small marker. The mines extend 3" from the marker in all directions.

- Minefields count as difficult and dangerous terrain, and any units that suffer casualties from them must test for pinning.

A simple minefield marker made from spare components and mounted on a 40mm base.

CITY OF DEATH

If you have the Cities of Death expansion (see page 274), then you could consider playing this game as a cityfighting mission. With the war having reached the defender's capital, using the Cities of Death rules is highly appropriate. The battle will become a desperate street-to-street, building-to-building, man-to-man fight over the ruins of the defender's base. If you take this route, adhering to the terrain guidance above rather than that given in Cities of Death will result in a very different, and challenging game.

"I salute you! For though our path has been long and bloody, you have served our lord with unflinching courage and the honour of true warriors. We have seen many fall today and must remember, even as we die, that our blood too is welcome..."

Harkan Ironfist

The roadblock consists of barricades and tank traps.

The perimeter defence line is made from urban barricades, providing cover for the defender's warriors.

The defender's objective is the attacker's forward command post, hastily established in this crater. A wise attacker will leave troops behind to defend such a vital position.

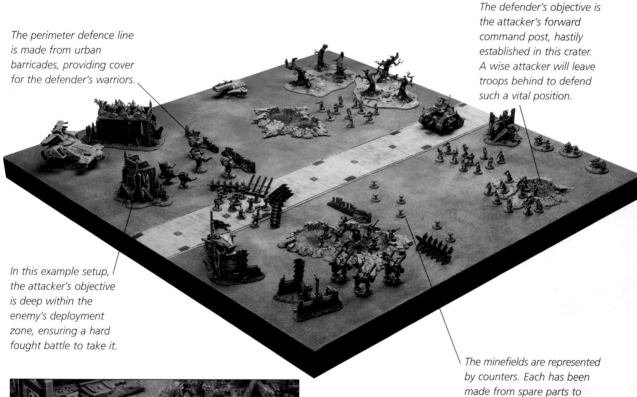

In this example setup, the attacker's objective is deep within the enemy's deployment zone, ensuring a hard fought battle to take it.

The minefields are represented by counters. Each has been made from spare parts to match the Tau defenders.

Cadian Shock Troopers negotiate a deadly Tau minefield.

In this example, the Cadians are attempting to retake an Imperial city lost to the alien Tau. The Tau have placed a roadblock across a major route, and thrown up a line of defences at the edge of the city. The attacker will have to cross the open ground in order to close in upon the defender's lines. The craters will provide cover saves, but the Guardsmen will have to negotiate the minefields to reach the enemy.

BATTLE 5 – CAULDRON OF WAR

The defender is cornered, his back to the wall. It falls now to his forces to mount one last, heroic defence. The commanders of both armies take to the field, leading from the front. One way or another, the war will be won or lost this day.

Battle Briefing

The last battle takes place at the heart of the defender's territory, the attacker having broken through every defence put in place. Both sides are fielding their very finest warriors, throwing every last resource into the final conflict. Both leaders have taken to the field in person, leading from the very front or supervising the final defence first hand. The winner of this battle will be crowned saviour, or conqueror. He will hold the honour of having repulsed a mighty invasion and saved an entire planet, or of breaking the enemy's hold on it once and for all.

Playing the Battle

The battle is an Annihilation standard mission.

The winner of Battle 4 may choose deployment type. He may also decide whether or not the night fighting special rule is in play throughout the entire game, representing him dictating the timing of the final battle.

Objective

The objective in an Annihilation mission is simple - wipe out your foe!

Terrain

The defender sets up the terrain in Battle 5. The character of the terrain can be varied depending on the army, but it should be dense, and very, very war-torn! Whatever you choose to use, keep it in mind that the defender is manning his last bastion, headquarters or most sacred site. You could even take the opportunity to construct a piece of terrain to represent a command bunker, mighty cathedral, daemonic throne, sacred altar or pulsing Hive node!

THE APOCALYPSE!

If you have the Apocalypse expansion book (see page 278), you might want to use the guidelines and Strategic Assets described therein. This battle should have a dramatic, end-of-the-world feel to it with both sides throwing everything into the cauldron of war. The skies should burn with orbital bombardments and the ground shake at the passing of mighty war machines, all of which is possible using the Apocalypse rules.

The Final Twist!

Even as the two armies close for the final confrontation, a ragged patrol, long assumed lost, staggers in to the headquarters. It is the warriors sent to retrieve the supplies in the wastes at the beginning of the offensive. Within the canisters was intelligence vital to defeating the enemy – so vital, that the patrol has fought long and hard to bring it to high command. The intelligence reveals the secrets to beating the enemy, describing in detail his weak points and deficiencies.

The player that won Battle 1 may nominate a number of units equal to the number of games he has won in the campaign so far. These units gain the Preferred Enemy and the Tank Hunters universal special rules, as they know the weaknesses of their foe.

Mission Special Rule - Preliminary Bombardment

The attacker's final offensive is preceded by a thunderous artillery barrage, designed to soften up enemy forces before the assault.

- After both armies have deployed but before the first turn, the attacker rolls a D6 for every enemy unit and terrain piece (excluding buildings and ruins as detailed below) on the tabletop. On a roll of 6, the unit or terrain piece is hit.

- A squad takes D6 Str 5 AP4 hits that cause pinning. Cover saves are allowed if the majority of the unit is within area terrain or behind barricades. Vehicles struck do not take damage, but will suffer a Stunned Driver result instead.

- Vehicles in a squadron are rolled for individually.

- Units that start the game in reserve will not be hit by a Preliminary Bombardment.

- How terrain is effected is not so straightforward. Small terrain pieces, such as sections of razorwire, tank traps or barricades are removed automatically if hit – replace with a crater if you have one. Area terrain is more a judgement call - players could agree that a small wood will be removed and replaced with a crater while marshy ground would be unaffected.

- Buildings and ruins are not effected by the Preliminary Bombardment, nor are any units within.

As the Red Corsairs launch their final assault, only the Eldar stand in their way.

The leaders of each army clash in deadly combat at the height of the final battle.

CAMPAIGN REPORT

Andy Hoare and Matt Toones played through the Road to Glory campaign using their own armies. Here's how Matt's Orks fared against Andy's Imperial Guard.

IMPERIAL GUARD 'TASK FORCE KANE'

Andy's Imperial Guard collection is large and varied enough for him to field many different types of army, so for this campaign, he put together a force tailored for fighting against Orks. One advantage of playing in campaigns is that both players get the opportunity to focus their army selection on the enemy they will face. Never quite knowing what fiendish trick your opponent will come up with next, and how you will counter it, is a great part of the campaign experience.

Andy decided there were two weapons he could not do without – missile launchers and flamers. The former would pound the big mobs from a distance, safe in the knowledge that even shots that scattered had a decent chance of killing some of the numerous Orks. The flamers would be just as lethal, but a little trickier to use, being far shorter ranged. Andy decided these would be ideal in the hands of counter attacking units, or those disembarking from a Chimera.

GRIMTOOF BLUDGUTZ' ORKS

Matt's Orks started as a cityfighting force, as he was inspired to collect a new army by the Cities of Death supplement (see Matt's entire greenskin army on page 276). Soon he'd played quite a few missions and wanted to expand the force and the campaign gave him the perfect excuse to do so. Knowing that he would be playing against Imperial Guard, Matt decided the best (and most Orky) tactic would be to swamp his enemy with choppa-wielding Boyz supported by Deff Dreads and Killa Kans.

One thing the players were both excited about was the opportunity presented by the campaign to add character to their forces. Matt decided to paint a new Looted Wagon, using the same colours Andy uses for his tanks. This gives the impression that the wagon has been looted from the Imperial Guard following a victory on the battlefield. Matt even used the same basing technique on his miniatures that Andy had on his, linking the two armies together.

THE CAMPAIGN

Matt and Andy invented some background for the campaign to fit their own armies. The Orks would be the leading edge of a mighty Waaagh! heading into the Imperium's domains. Only the hurried deployment of the Imperial Guard's Mordant 22nd had saved the world of Sorlax from being overrun in a matter of days. As the front stabilised, both sides committed ever-greater resources into achieving a decisive breakthrough. Now,

the Imperial Guard and the Orks both seek to crush their foe, to defeat him once and for all.

Battle 1 - Patrol Beta 22

Matt and Andy decided that Battle 1 would be best fought as a small game, as this would represent the small search teams sent into no-man's-land to recover the lost supplies. Both armies were 500 points, making for a tense but bloody game that was played over the course of an hour. The Mordant Imperial Guard were victorious, their missile launchers and grenade launchers accounting for the majority of the Orks killed.

Battle 2 - Grimtoof's Glory

Battle 2 was fought for control of the wastes between the two armies' lines. The players brought along armies of 750 points each. This allowed the inclusion of a Leman Russ and a Chimera in Andy's army, and a newly painted Nobz mob in Matt's. The game was as hard fought as the last. Despite the flamers in his command squad taking out an entire mob of Boyz, Andy's Imperial Guard failed to stem the green tide, and Matt was victorious. The Orks had won the victory they needed to get their offensive rolling!

Andy's missile launcher-armed Imperial Guard, collected especially for the campaign.

Battle 3 - Breaking the Kyo Rin Line

Pleased with his victory and eager to field his entire army, Matt finished painting his new Deff Dread for Battle 3. His army smashed through the Imperial Guard's lines, to score a convincing win and break through into the Imperium's rear zone...

Battle 4 - Battle for Block 440

Battle 4 had the option of being fought as a Cities of Death game, and both agreed straight away to play it as such. A spectacular urban warscape was assembled, inspired by the examples in the expansion book. The action was as brutal as you would expect a close-in fight between Imperial Guard and Orks to be, and Andy's massed flamers took a fearsome toll on Matt's army, earning Andy a victory.

Battle 5 - Kane's Last Stand

Both players agreed to make Battle 5 a suitably big game. Andy used his entire Imperial Guard collection, around 6,000 points, and recruited a friend to help field it. Matt joined up with another Ork player to make a mighty Ork coalition. Fortunately for the Imperial Guard, Andy had won Battle 1, and so his side benefited from intelligence that would allow them to target the Orks' (admittedly few) weak points. The battle raged over the course of eight hours (including snack breaks), and saw eighteen Imperial Guard tanks crash into almost two hundred Ork Boyz. When the smoke cleared, victory was Matt's, and the campaign had reached a highly memorable ending.

Andy's tanks saw heavy fighting throughout the campaign. Andy decided to keep track of the kills his Leman Russ earned by adding kill markings. These clan icons are from the Ork transfer sheet. The fact that dead Ork units were tracked with their own markings was a cruel blow to greenskin morale.

Not to be outdone, Matt decided to adorn his Looted Wagon with kill markings too, taunting the Imperial Guard with reminders of their losses.

TAKING THE CAMPAIGN FURTHER

For those who would like a little more detail in their campaign, here are some additional ideas to get the creative juices flowing.

As the Road to Glory campaign has been made deliberately simple to play, this page offers some ideas on how you might alter the campaign or add a little more complexity. Perhaps you've played it through once and want to mix things up a bit, or perhaps you've played in campaigns before and want to add in an additional layer of detail straight away.

Adding Extra Battles

It was mentioned earlier that the battles should be thought of as snap-shots of a much larger war. It's perfectly sensible then to add in extra battles. You might do so because the evolving narrative suggests an ideal extra battle, such as an improvised counter-attack or the landing of much-needed reinforcements. The map on page 252 might also provide some inspiration – you could add in a mission to blow up the pipeline supplying the defender's forward base, or fight out some of the battles fought as the men carrying vital information from Battle 1 try to sneak through enemy territory. Extra battles such as these will also help your units gain experience if you are using the Veteran Abilities rules opposite.

Adding More Players

You may find that once word gets out that you are playing a campaign, every player and his pet grox wants to take part. The easiest way to accommodate extra players is to assign them to one of two teams. Games can be played with more than one player per side, each controlling a part of the army, or you could add in extra battles for these players to fight.

Using Supplements

If you're the sort of player who likes to add lots of detail to your campaigns, there are a number of 'expansions' that are an excellent source of inspiration and character. Each takes your games of Warhammer 40,000 into a new, challenging setting. You could use the Cities of Death supplement for every battle, representing the campaign being fought within an urban war zone, or Apocalypse to take the scale of the battles to a whole new level. See pages 274 to 278 for more details of Cities of Death and Apocalypse.

Creating Your Own Missions

A campaign is the perfect setting to experiment with designing your own missions. As the story progresses you may well find particular scenarios suggesting themselves to you. Perhaps one side dispatches a small, elite force to assassinate a powerful enemy leader. Maybe you will attempt a daring raid against vital enemy supplies. The next chapter deals with the subject of inventing your own missions, so why not give it a go?

Mission Special Rules

The standard missions use a number of mission special rules, such as night fighting and deep strike to add in extra detail to a game. Campaign games give you an opportunity to take things much further, adding special rules appropriate to the narrative and the armies facing each other. There are a selection of mission special rules used in the next section, many of which would be entirely appropriate for use in this campaign. Perhaps the attacker will be ambushed by hidden troops in Battle 2. Perhaps you will set your entire campaign on a world with no atmosphere, or low gravity.

Using such special rules, or any of your own invention, will require both players to agree how they will be put into practice. Neither side should feel unfairly disadvantaged, but keep in mind that this is a campaign, in which many games will be played – although it's cool to be the winner, the best tales told are often those of the glorious last stand or the desperate rear guard action.

If the enemy comes on in a great horde, as Orks are wont to do, then try to direct them into a narrow defile or enclosed space, such that their numbers work against them. Crowded together, those at the front will impede those behind, whilst the push from the rear will prevent those at the front from retreating or finding a better path.

Tactica Imperium

VETERAN ABILITIES

As your warriors gain in experience, so their ability, courage and reliability will increase. Seasoned warriors learn even from defeat, but a string of victories will see your troops go from green recruits to experienced veterans able to face any terror the galaxy has to throw at them.

Gaining Experience

At the end of each game, nominate a unit in your army that you believe performed well, deserves a medal or has the eye of the gods upon it. This unit must not have been wiped out at the end of the game. Choose an appropriate table from those on the right and roll on it to see what ability the unit gains. The winner may nominate two such units, and the loser one. If the game was a draw, both players nominate one.

The units will benefit from a new veteran ability for the rest of the campaign. It is possible for a single unit to gain multiple veteran abilities in this way, but it may not take duplicates of the same skill. If you roll a duplicate on a second or subsequent roll, you may choose which ability the unit gains. In addition, once a unit has received an ability from one of the tables, all its future rolls must be on the same table. This reflects the specialisation that comes with experience.

There is a downside though. If a unit with a veteran ability ends a game below half strength or having fled the battlefield, it will lose one veteran ability. If it ends the game wiped out, it will lose two.

D6	Fieldcraft Veteran Ability
1	Infiltrate
2	Move Through Cover or Skilled Rider
3	Stealth
4	Scouts
5	Fleet
6	Fearless

D6	Melee Veteran Ability
1	Feel No Pain
2	Furious Charge
3	Counter-attack
4	Hit & Run
5	Preferred Enemy
6	Fearless

D6	Gunnery Veteran Ability
1	Night Vision/Acute Senses
2,3	Relentless
4,5	Tank Hunters
6	Fearless

D6	Vehicle Crew Veteran Ability
1	+1 BS
2,3	Can re-roll dangerous terrain test
4,5	Ignore Shaken results
6	+1 AV all facings (max 14)

OTHER TYPES OF CAMPAIGN

What you have just read is just an example of one type of campaign. There are many variations, some straightforward, others fiendishly detailed.

The Road to Glory campaign is a linear series of battles between two players. There are countless other types of campaign, such as map-based, narrative or tree campaigns. They can involve just two players or dozens. A campaign can be as simple as two battles played in a row, or as complex as a sprawling map that plots out continent-spanning army deployments, off planet support, supply lines and reinforcements.

Games Workshop periodically runs worldwide campaigns in which thousands of gamers enter their battle results onto a website to determine the army that has done best overall. These events are not just a great excuse to play more games, but it is also entertaining to read and follow the campaign progress as a spectator.

As campaigns help to create more of a story than a single battle, they often inspire players to customise their armies or their terrain in some way. If your Khorne Berzerkers decimate a squad of Eldar Guardians for example, you might model Eldar helmets mounted on spikes upon the Berzerkers' Rhino as a grizzly trophy of that victory. This will remind your opponent of his crushing defeat in every subsequent game!

The best thing about campaigns is the real sense of history that evolves with every game you play. You will find yourself naming your squad leaders and characters, and really caring about them surviving a battle. No longer will your models be mere choices from an army list – they will take on a life all their own!

Example Tree Campaign

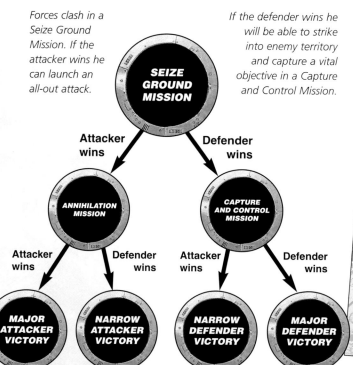

Forces clash in a Seize Ground Mission. If the attacker wins he can launch an all-out attack.

If the defender wins he will be able to strike into enemy territory and capture a vital objective in a Capture and Control Mission.

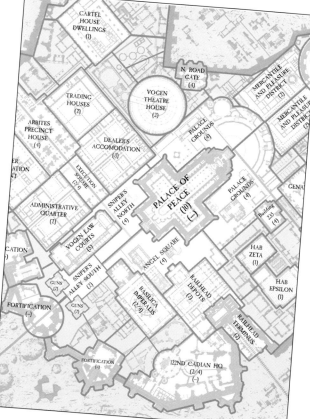

In a tree campaign, battles are organised by a pre-drawn flow diagram. Each time a battle is fought, the diagram will tell you which mission to fight next by following the correct path. The longer the campaign, the larger the diagram will be.

In a map campaign, each battle determines the occupation of a region on a map. The winner is usually the first to control a certain number of areas, or the player that controls the most after a set number of turns. The above map was made for the Vogen campaign, a brutal struggle for an Imperial city.

1. Ork Rok Drop Sites

2. Heliopolis Bridge

2a. Heliopolis Bridge North

2b. Heliopolis Bridge South

3. Victorinius Spaceport

4. Ibis Reef Harbour

5. Nadala Gorge Ore Mine

6. Valkyrie Bay Refinery

7. Jabiru Quay

8. Phoenix Island Mineral Storage Facility

Node campaigns are a combination of tree and map types. In essence, the tree is superimposed over a map, with strategically important points on the map forming the nodes over which battles are fought. Sometimes, particular missions or special rules are assigned to each node - perhaps based on the terrain or environmental features. To win the overall campaign, a certain number of nodes must be captured by winning battles.

A campaign booklet and website told the story and rules for a previous global campaign.

INVENTING NEW MISSIONS

In the Warhammer 40,000 universe anything is possible, and the same is true on the tabletop, especially if you take some time to design your own missions.

A game of Warhammer 40,000 can be played out and won according to the standard missions presented in the Rules section of this book. But what if you want to try a different set-up, fight over different objectives or decide your game using different victory conditions?

Standard missions represent 'encounter' battles – conflicts in which neither side has an inherent advantage, neither is defined as attacker or defender, and each is responding to the battle as it unfolds. The advantage of the standard missions is that they place both players in the same tactical situation and each knows what to expect. You could walk into any Games Workshop store in the world, and play an exciting game against a complete stranger and know what to expect with no extra preparation or organisation at all.

Outside of a tabletop wargame, battles are much more complex, uneven and unpredictable affairs! One side might be lurking in ambush, or perhaps both find themselves at the mercy of the environment they are fighting in. They are forced to contend with not just the enemy, but with adverse weather or hostile terrain. And what if three armies come into contact with each other at the same time?

Each of the missions that follow has been written to illustrate a particular inspiration. The first is inspired by a background story, the second by a tactical situation,

the third by a setting, and the fourth by the need to adapt the Warhammer 40,000 rules to accommodate not two sides, but three. You can play them as presented, using any combination of forces, or you can alter them as much as you like.

We hope that the examples provided will serve as a jumping off point for you to invent your own. You'll find it's not hard to come up with more ideas. The best place to start is with a situation or story, then work out what changes to the standard missions will fit your idea.

When writing your own missions, the simplest ideas are often the best – one or two changes may be all you need for a great game. The hardest part is working out the victory conditions to ensure both sides have a fair chance of winning. It's fine if one side is outnumbered 3:1, so long as his objective is achievable.

Try playing the scenario from both sides, so you can experience both attacking and defending. This way you can enjoy the challenge of trying to outdo your opponent in the exact same tactical situation, seeking to succeed where he may well have failed!

YARRICK'S STAND

This mission is inspired by the tale of Commissar Yarrick leading the defence of Hades hive during the second war for Armageddon.

When the Orks invaded the hive world of Armageddon, Commissar Yarrick offered its leader, von Straab, the benefit of his unique insight into the Orks' way of war. But von Straab would not listen to the Commissar's counsel, and banished Yarrick to Hades, a sprawling hive complex far from the seat of government. As it happened, this was probably the best decision von Straab made during the whole war.

The Ork assault was swift and seemingly unstoppable. Von Straab's armies were by no means small or poorly equipped, but they could not stand before the brutal Ork advance. Only when the Orks reached Hades did the surging tide come to a halt before the well ordered defences the Commissar had quickly put into position, Even so, the initial Ork attack led by Warlord Ugulhard would have swept away human resistance were it not for Yarrick's presence.

The Ork Warlord glimpsed the Commissar across the battlelines and drove his forces directly to where Yarrick stood. With a barbarous roar, the Ork threw himself upon the Commissar. He swung his snapping battle claw at Yarrick and severed the Commissar's right arm at the elbow. The Warlord's bellow of victory was cut short as Yarrick, fighting the pain and shock as no normal man could, swung his chainsword in a crimson arc and severed Ugulhard's bony head from his

shoulders. The Ork's body collapsed to the ground whilst the head continued to sneer and curse until the creature's extraordinary metabolism finally conceded that it was dead.

Yarrick calmly reached down and tore the battle claw from the Ork's twitching body. He held it aloft so that all the green-skinned warriors could see it and know their leader had suffered defeat. A hush fell over the battlefield as man and Ork gazed in silence upon the gnarled old man brandishing the bloody claw. Then the humans cheered and the Orks wailed in horror, and all at once the defenders leapt upon the aliens with indomitable vigour.

Only when the Orks had been beaten from Hades hive did Yarrick allow himself the luxury of passing out.

"Heroes of Armageddon! You have withstood the evil savagery of the Orks, and they have nothing left for you to fear. So raise high the black banners of vengeance – now is our time."

Last transmission of Commissar Yarrick

DEPLOYMENT
Pitched Battle.

OBJECTIVE
In order to win the game, the leader of one army must have killed the leader of the other army. If this has not happened, you can call the battle a draw or, alternatively, use victory points to determine who can claim a moral victory (see page 300).

If a leader is killed in a sweeping advance, this will only count as a win if the other leader was the sole model running him down.

Both players should agree on a points limit for their leaders, such as 200 points. Or, you could decide there will be no limit! Obviously, at the start of the battle, each player needs to make it clear to his opponent which model is his leader.

MISSION SPECIAL RULES
Deep Strike, Reserves, and use the Standard Mission Game Length.

Bitter Enemies: Both Yarrick and Ugulhard are figures of awe to their warriors, and when the two clash in mortal combat, the hatred Orks and Men hold for one another is unleashed. In any turn in which the two leaders are engaged in an assault against one another, every model on the table gains the preferred enemy universal special rule. Should one side's leader be killed in an assault, every unit in the defeated leader's army must take a Morale check.

AMBUSH

As a convoy passes through close terrain, an attacker launches a deadly ambush. The defender must fight his way clear or be destroyed!

In an ambush situation, the challenge comes from the defender having little or no idea where the attacker will deploy. In our example the attacker deploys an 'ambush marker' for each of his infantry units, and a number of 'dummy markers' to add to the defender's confusion. The defender will therefore have to guess whether a marker represents a waiting foe about to unleash destruction or simply a false return on an auspex, a shadow, or leaves rustling in the wind. When the defender identifies a target, or the hidden unit fires, the marker is replaced with the actual models. This hidden element adds a certain amount of second guessing and bluffing to the game - more challenges for 41st millennium commanders to overcome!

Although any armies can play this scenario, here are a few classic match-ups:

Tyranids ambush a column of Imperial Guard reinforcements as they make for the front line.

Catachan Jungle Fighters ambush an Ork army, seeking to pit stealth against brute force.

Eldar Pathfinders intercept Chaos Space Marines who dare set foot upon a isolated Maiden World.

Finding itself ambushed amidst the ruins, the Imperial Guard column has no choice but to gun its engines and push through to safety!

In an ambush it is a wise defender who remembers his objective instead of just getting bogged down into a firefight.

It is possible to use coins or scraps of paper but the modelled markers add to the flavour of the ambush mission.

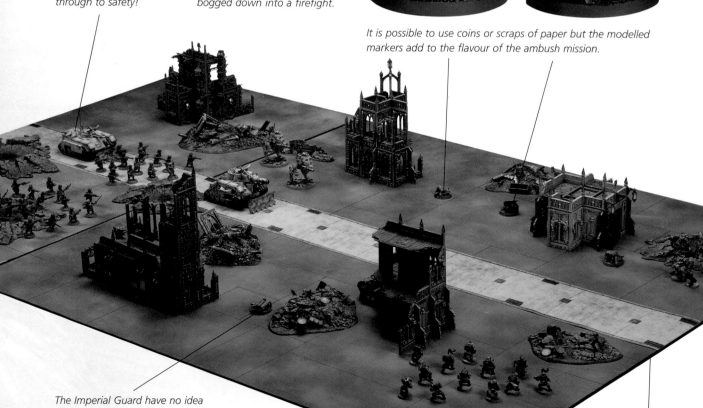

The Imperial Guard have no idea whether this marker represents an insignificant Grots mob, a mighty Nobz mob, highly feared Tankbustas, or nothing at all!

To gain safety, the Imperial Guard column must get as many units as possible with 12 inches of this table edge

DEPLOYMENT

Decide which player is conducting the ambush; he will be the attacker and the other player will be the defender. This scenario is best played on a rectangular table, 6'x4' being ideal.

The table is set up in a mutually agreeable manner, but after all terrain is placed, the attacker may move two pieces of his choice, and choose which of the short board edges will be his table edge. The opposite table edge belongs to the defender.

The defender deploys his army on up to half of the table (measuring from his table edge). The attacker then deploys according to the Hidden Set-up rule opposite, anywhere on the table more than 12" from a defending model. Any non-infantry models in the attacker's army must be held in reserve. The attacker gets the first turn.

OBJECTIVE

The objective of an ambush is to catch the foe unawares and destroy him utterly. The target must push through the ambush and reach safety.

The defender wins if, at the end of the game, he has more scoring units within 12" of the attacker's table edge than are further away from it. In any other event, the attacker wins.

MISSION SPECIAL RULES

Deep Strike, Reserves, and use the Standard Mission Game Length.

Hidden set-up: For each Infantry unit starting the game in ambush, the attacker gets a single 'ambush marker'. In addition to these markers, the attacker gets D3+3 'dummy markers'. It is these markers, rather than the units they represent that are deployed at the start of the game.

Hidden Movement: Markers may move around the table, moving as infantry, until they are revealed as described below. Markers are subject to the slow and purposeful universal special rule, representing the ambushing units sneaking around.

Detecting Ambushers: Whenever a defending unit wishes to fire on or assault a marker, you must first test to see if the unit can detect the ambushers. Make a night fighting roll, and if the marker is within the distance rolled, it is removed if a dummy, or the unit placed if it is not a dummy. At least one of the ambushing models must replace the marker, with the rest in unit coherency and further away from the spotting enemy than the marker.

Ambushers Shooting or Assaulting: Should the ambushing unit shoot or launch an assault, markers are removed and the unit they represented set up.

These ambush markers have all been modelled to represent troops hiding or sneaking about.

Ambush markers can be as simple as small scraps of paper, or they could take the form of modelled counters as shown on this page. The undersides are marked with a tick or a cross, determining which are dummies and which represent the actual unit.

These markers have been modelled to represent 'blips' on a scanner readout. The upper surfaces are marked with the number of the unit they represent.

EVACUATION

On a lonely station in a forgotten frontier system, valiant but outnumbered Space Marines face the advancing tendrils of a Tyranid Hive Fleet.

Inspired by the research station set on an airless moon (page 238), we decided to make some rules for fighting in low gravity and vacuum. On top of these simple environmental effects, we decided that an alien attack on the isolated base would be an exciting and characterful game to play. The landing pad suggested an evacuation, perhaps of an important individual, and so that would become the objective of the game.

We decided to play this game between Space Marines and Tyranids, perhaps representing one of the early battles of the First Tyrannic War, when the Imperium had little idea of the horrifying enormity of Hive Fleet Behemoth. A model was converted to represent a high-ranking Adeptus Mechanicus Genetor, whose survival is key to the ongoing fight against the invaders. Of course, if you want to try this mission, you don't have to make a special model – you could use any suitable miniature from your collection.

Furthermore, this scenario could be played between any two armies. Imperial Guardsmen might be issued rebreathers when fighting in a near or total vacuum, while races such as Orks are so hardy it can be imagined that they can go several hours in such conditions with no ill effects. As ever, the limits are set only by what possibilities you can dream up!

Battle rages across the Imperium and beyond, from hive worlds of soaring gothic towers, to planets with atmospheres so corrosive they would strip an unprotected warrior to bones in seconds.

Such settings make ideal inspiration for your games. By creating your own Mission Special Rules and objectives, your battle can take place in any setting in the galaxy.

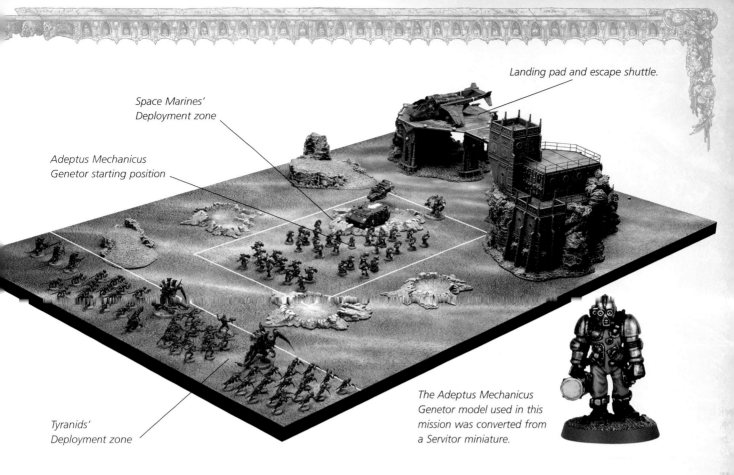

Space Marines'
Deployment zone

Adeptus Mechanicus
Genetor starting position

Landing pad and escape shuttle.

Tyranids'
Deployment zone

The Adeptus Mechanicus
Genetor model used in this
mission was converted from
a Servitor miniature.

DEPLOYMENT

The defender sets up his entire army in the centre of
the table, anywhere more than 18" from any table
edge. Place a suitable model to represent the escape
shuttle, or simply indicate a departure point using a
marker of some sort. The model representing the
Genetor is placed more than 24" from the shuttle.

The attacker then places his army, within 8" of the
opposite table edge from the shuttle. The defender
has the first turn.

OBJECTIVE

Kill points are used to determine the victor, as per
the Annihilation Mission (page 91). The real focus
revolves on the fate of the Genetor. The defender
earns 3 kill points if the Genetor gets into base
contact with the shuttle (where he instantly makes
good his escape). The attacker earns 3 additional kill
points if the Genetor is removed as a casualty.

	WS	BS	S	T	W	I	A	Ld	Sv
Genetor	2	3	3	3	1	2	1	7	4+

The Genetor has the following profile.

Special Rules:
Slow and Purposeful, Independent Character.

MISSION SPECIAL RULES

Deep Strike, Reserves, and use the Standard Mission
Game Length.

Low gravity: Fighting in a low gravity environment
is a dangerous undertaking, for while troops may be
able to leap great distances, they can easily wound
themselves on landing, or become entangled in
dense terrain.

Infantry models may move over terrain in the same
manner as jump infantry (though they are still
limited to 6" of movement). Any such movement
that ends within area terrain will result in a
dangerous terrain test. Models that run must roll an
additional D6 and pick the highest result, but if a
double is rolled, every model in the unit must make
a dangerous terrain test.

Vacuum: Combat in a vacuum is a lethal affair, for
even glancing strikes may puncture air-tight suits and
cause explosive decompression before self-repair
systems can contain the damage.

Models with more than 1 Wound on their profile
lose not one but D3 Wounds when they suffer an
unsaved wound. All attacks, both shooting and close
combat, use the Rending rule.

BROKEN ALLIANCE

The leaders of three separate armies are meeting under truce when negotiations break down - violently!

The Warhammer 40,000 rules accommodate two opposing sides, and it is normally assumed that if you have extra players, you will assign them to one team or another. However, it is possible to play with three (or more!) different sides, with only a slight modification to the rules.

Why would you want to do such a thing? Well, playing a three-way multiplayer battle can be enormously fun, as it opens up a whole range of opportunities for impromptu alliances, backstabbing and ganging up. The game will be chaotic and tense, especially if you use a system for randomly determining the order of play each turn, as we have in this example scenario.

The scenario could represent an alliance gone bad, or three opposed forces fighting over the same objective. In the case of a broken alliance, the leaders of the three armies have come to blows whilst meeting, and before anyone knows what's going on angry curses are filling the air and the bullets start flying. Meanwhile, each army is in its camp, not expecting there to be any

trouble. There will be a moment of confusion while troops reach for weapons and crews rush for their vehicles, before the battle really gets underway.

If you enjoy the rules for playing a multiplayer game, you could also try adapting any of the standard missions presented in the main rules section to incorporate extra sides.

A three-player battle could be fought with any combination of forces, but we thought the scenario leant itself well to a fight between three armies of the same race. There are several races that, according to their background, are just as likely to fight one another as the enemy. The most obvious ones are the Orks, Chaos Space Marines, and Dark Eldar, but you could take inspiration from the background to justify almost any such internecine battle.

DEPLOYMENT

Place a marker or piece of terrain in the exact centre of the table. This represents the meeting place.

Each player must place a marker terrain piece to represent his base camp. No base camp may be placed within 18" of the centre of the table, or within 30" of another base camp. To determine the order in which base camps are placed, each player rolls a D6. The player that rolls highest places his base camp first, followed by the other players in order of their die rolls. In the same order, each player takes it in turn to place an HQ unit within 6" of the centre of the table. The unit may not include a transport vehicle.

Using the same order again, each player takes it in turn to deploy their armies, within 12" of their camp marker. Models must be placed more than 24" of an enemy. Units may be kept in reserve, entering play in the normal way, from the point on the table edge closest to their base camp.

OBJECTIVE

With the unexpected eruption of violence, each army finds its encampment under threat. In order to win the day, they will have to protect their own camp, whilst destroying those of their enemies. The marker in the centre of the table, and the camp markers of each army, must be controlled. At the end of the game, you control a marker if there is at least one of your scoring units, and no enemy units (whether scoring or not), within 3" of it. The player controlling the most markers wins.

MISSION SPECIAL RULES

Deep Strike, Reserves, and use the Standard Mission Game Length.

Confusion: The warriors of each army are initially unprepared for the sudden battle. All units must roll a D6 at the start of their first turn. Those that roll a 4+ can act normally, but those that fail this roll cannot move, shoot, assault or use psychic powers until their second turn (although they can fall back and will fight normally if assaulted by an enemy).

Three player rules: To determine the order of play in game Turn 1, all three players roll off. Play goes in order from the player who rolled highest to the lowest. In subsequent game turns, the player that went first in the previous game turn goes last, with the other two players rolling off for first go.

Play proceeds as it would in a normal game of Warhammer 40,000. When it comes to the Assault phase, only those assaults involving the player whose player turn it is are fought. Assaults may not be launched against ongoing combats involving the warriors of both other armies, so three way close combat is not possible.

Shooting into close combat: In the shooting phase, a player may fire into an assault that does not include his own units. To do this, nominate the target unit as normal. Having rolled to hit, you will need to determine which of the units engaged in the swirling melee are actually struck. Roll another dice for each hit. Each dice that rolls 4+ results in a hit against the target unit, while any other result means the target's opponents are hit instead.

CITIES OF DEATH

In the nightmare future of the 41st Millennium armies battle one another to annihilation amid the ruins of shattered cities. Cities of Death allows you to take your gaming into the deadly confines of the urban warscape!

A NEW SETTING

Cities of Death is an expansion book for the game of Warhammer 40,000, showing you how to take your games into the corpse-strewn cities of the far future. Cities of Death expands the game by presenting new rules and missions, all designed to get the most out of this most blood-soaked of warzones.

Setting a game in a ruined city is an exciting challenge. You will find yourself utilising entirely new tactics, and fielding your army in ways you never have before. Densely packed city ruins restrict lines of sight and concentrate ranged fire into deadly killing zones. Troops hug the cover as they close in on their foes, desperate firefights breaking out around vital objectives. Often, the possession of a building comes down to a bold charge into close combat, though making such a move will be costly for the attacker. You will soon discover that cityfighting is a bloody business. By the time the dust is settled and the battle is over, both victor and vanquished will have paid a terrible price in the lives of their warriors.

TERRAIN

Every cityfight is dominated by ruins, and all of the rules presented within Cities of Death interact with them in some manner. Ruins affect how armies move and fight and therefore how games are played, but you don't need a whole city's worth to fight a battle.

Cities of Death is designed to make the most out of Citadel's range of plastic Warhammer 40,000 buildings. With these highly detailed and versatile terrain kits, you can quickly and easily construct your very own ruined city. One or two of these ruins will see plenty of use in conventional games of Warhammer 40,000, but collect more and you will soon have an entire city sector to defend or smash asunder as you see fit.

A table set up for a cityfighting mission will feature a number of city ruins, clustered in the centre of the battlefield. Many missions focus on capturing the ruins themselves, ensuring a close fought and extremely bloody game.

The upper levels of ruins can provide excellent firing positions – unless line of sight is blocked by other ruined buildings.

A cunning commander will protect his infantry by making use of all the ruins, rubble, and craters around in an urban environment.

Bits of rubble and smashed machinery add extra detail to a model's base.

This Terminator's base is modelled to represent the ruins of an Imperial city.

WARBOSS BLUDGUTZ' CITYFIGHTERZ

Although any army can be used in a cityfighting mission, many players like to pick their units specially, and paint and model them to fit the setting.

Matt Toone is a huge fan of the Cities of Death setting, so when he decided to collect his new Ork army, he took the opportunity to focus on using it in cityfighting missions. Every aspect of the army collecting process was geared towards making the army a great cityfighting force, from the choice of units to the way each model is painted and based.

Starting with an army list of 1,500 points, Matt considered the dense terrain of a Cities of Death battlefield. He knew that the ruins would force him to make less use of vehicles and a lot more of infantry. Therefore, the army's core is made up large mobs of Ork Boyz, supported by Deff Dreads and Killa Kans.

Matt painted his miniatures to stand out strongly on the urban battlefield, while his grey bases are designed to blend in to the setting. When dry-brushing the final highlight with Fortress Grey, Matt carried the brush work up the legs, to give the Boyz the appearance of being covered in concrete dust.

Matt's favourite tactic is to make use of the sewer rats stratagem, a special rule usable in cityfighting missions. This allows his force to enter play via a number of sewer entrance markers. Both the Burna Boyz and the Tankbustas are particularly effective in this role, emerging from the sewers to wreak havoc on enemy infantry and tanks.

The tops of the models have grey bases and chunky bits of sand and rock to better fit in on an urban battlefield.

Burnas are deadly in a ruined city, because they negate cover saves.

In the dense terrain of a city Tankbustas can more easily close with enemy armour.

Matt has made 'sewer rats' stratagem markers, modelled to match his army. When strategically placed, these markers allow units in Reserve to deploy onto key locations, offering potentially game-winning counterattacks.

Matt uses his Looted Wagon to punish any foe that strays into the open.

APOCALYPSE

Apocalypse allows you to take your games of Warhammer 40,000 to a whole new level. In an Apocalypse game, you are not limited to leading a single detachment into combat - instead you will lead hundreds of warriors, dozens of tanks, and the mightiest of war machines to battle against your foes.

Apocalypse is an expansion for the Warhammer 40,000 game, providing everything you need to know in order to fight really huge battles. The expansion has been written to cater for those gamers who just can't stop collecting models and love nothing more than the spectacle of a huge force deployed for battle.

Apocalypse describes how to set up and run games in excess of 3,000 points per side. In addition, the book provides a number of 'legendary units', such as the mighty Baneblade super-heavy tank and 'battle formations' such as the Space Marine Masters of the Chapter. These are units of such awesome power that

they would dominate a normal game of Warhammer 40,000. They are ideal for use in large games though, where they will face other such units and not unduly unbalance the game.

Lastly, and perhaps most importantly, the expansion provides lots of practical advice on running really large games. Everything is covered, from organising your game beforehand, to playing a huge 'floor war'. You may not get to play such large battles every week, or even every month, but you can be assured that when you do, they will be amongst the most memorable and exciting games you will ever play!

The Apocalypse supplement contains lots of useful advice on setting up the huge tables needed to play such enormous battles.

Apocalypse allows you to field all your infantry, all your tanks, all your special characters – literally your entire collection.

Large models such as the Baneblade or even massive Titans are the natural stars of an Apocalypse game. Despite this, don't be fooled into thinking that troops aren't useful – it is the lowly infantry that are essential for holding onto objectives and winning games.

This battle-worn Baneblade has been painted up to match its owner's urban camouflaged Imperial Guard – the fightin' Cadian 72nd.

Forge World make large Warhammer 40,000 resin models like this mighty Warhound Titan and ground-shaking Ork Squiggoth.

TOURNAMENTS

Many players like to test their gaming mettle by pitting their generalship against others in a tournament. If you've ever considered running such an event for your gaming group, here are a few useful pointers.

At a tournament, players come together for a single day or a whole weekend of their favourite wargame. At the end of the event, one of their number will stand victorious having earned the highest number of wins throughout the rounds. For many, such events are the pinnacle of their hobby. They are a great way to meet new players, face new armies and really challenge their knowledge of their own and their opponents' army and of the subtleties of the game.

A tournament does not have to be a huge event run by others – you can easily host one yourself. All you need is a group of players and a little organisation!

The most commonly used tournament format is the 'Swiss system'. The best thing about this system is that it allows everyone taking part to play the same number of games, and after the first round, everyone is matched up against someone of roughly the same ability as themselves.

A Swiss tournament is played in a number of rounds, dependent on how much time is available and how many players are taking part. Bearing in mind that a decent sized game of Warhammer 40,000 is likely to take a few hours, about five rounds over the course of a weekend is a common number.

What tabletop commander doesn't aspire to placing an award next to his all-conquering army? Nothing puts a spotlight on your tactical genius like a hard-earned battle trophy. Such a monument to greatness is sure to draw the respect of your comrades in arms (and also their petty and jealous ire!).

In the first round, players are drawn against one another at random. A number of points are awarded for a victory, less for a draw and less still for a loss. In subsequent rounds, players are paired up according to their running total score, the player in first place against the player in second place, the player in third place against the player in fourth place, etc. Once all the games have been played, some tournaments add additional points for such things as painting, sportsmanship, army composition and the like. This ensures that the overall winner is truly a prince amongst gamers, having excelled himself in every aspect of the hobby.

LEAGUES

Not everyone has the time to put aside a whole weekend to attend or run a tournament. Instead, you can always use the Swiss system to run a league. This is done in exactly the same manner as described above, except the games are spread over a period of weeks. Many gaming stores and clubs run such leagues, and keep track of them on results boards. Such leagues really keep the players on their toes, and provide a focal point for the store or club's activities.

If a league has a large number of people wanting to sign up, they often divide their players into subdivisions. Some even organise play-offs between the winners of each subdivision, resulting in a single player being awarded a truly memorable, and hard-fought title.

One of the winners at a Warhammer 40,000 Tournament.

Most tournaments are organised by small clubs or groups of friends simply arranging to play on the same day. The events pictured here, however, are formal Grand Tournaments that can have hundreds of gamers battling it out for fame and renown.

In some tournaments, players score extra points for having well painted armies. Many players credit the looming date of upcoming tournaments as providing the impetus for getting their entire army painted.

GETTING INVOLVED

One of the best things about Warhammer 40,000 hobby is the community that has sprung up around it. There are a host of events and activities where like-minded enthusiasts can meet to game, or just talk about the hobby.

Warhammer 40,000 can be a very involving hobby and over the years the popularity of the game has soared. Indeed, it can be reliably said that Warhammer 40,000 enthusiasts are everywhere and come from all ages and all walks of life. Whether you are just getting starting out or are a long-time hobbyist, it's always fun to meet, game and talk with other enthusiasts. Here are some great ways to get more involved.

LOCAL GAMES SHOPS

One of the best places to learn more about the game is at your local Games Workshop store. You can find Warhammer 40,000 miniatures, books and essential hobby supplies there. You'll also find that our stores are staffed by experienced gamers who can offer advice if you have any questions or wish to take part in an introductory game. Our stores are also excellent places to meet other hobbyists. As most will have played other Games Workshop games, they're a good starting point if you're new to the hobby.

You can also find Warhammer 40,000 miniatures and books in a larger network of independent toy, hobby and game retailers across the world. Many of these stores offer modelling advice in addition to stocking the Warhammer 40,000 range.

GAMING CLUBS

Gaming is a sociable hobby and you will not be surprised to hear that there are many clubs that cater for gamers of all ages and tastes. Of course, you don't need to be part of a club to enjoy gaming, but there are plenty of advantages, and it is nice to meet people who share your own passion for gaming.

Being in a club means you will never be short of an opponent for a battle, and in addition, there's always someone willing to show you how to play a new game or improve your painting or modelling skills. Some clubs band together to produce huge and ambitious terrain projects and to organise exciting campaigns.

Clubs come in all shapes and sizes. Even just three or more hobbyists who meet regularly to enjoy a game count as a club. If there isn't a club near you, why not consider starting your own? All you need is a group of like-minded friends and a place to meet. From humble beginnings many a large gaming club has grown.

TOURNAMENTS

Warhammer 40,000 tournaments take place in most countries at some time in the annual calendar. Some of the most prestigious events are organised by Games Workshop, under the banner of the Grand Tournament. There are, however, countless other competitions run not only by our own staff but by other enthusiasts and fans of the game. Tournaments are about testing your mettle against other tabletop generals; they also encourage you to show off your painted army and meet other players. Tournaments are not for the faint hearted, but they are open to all with the tenacity and desire to conquer – and they all reward you with a chance to hang out in the company of other players after the duelling is done.

CAMPAIGNS

Competition for competition's sake is not for everyone. With this in mind, it's also possible to take part in a variety of events that are all about creating a story through the gaming exploits of a group of players. Many of these are organised as weekend or one-day events by clubs, our staff, or independent stockists. Yet, it doesn't stop there: campaigns sometimes grow into enormous affairs, and sometimes even boil over to engulf the entire globe, such as with the Fall of Medusa V campaign that took place in 2006.

GAMES DAYS

Each year across the globe Games Workshop hosts a series of Games Day events to showcase the whole of the hobby, including not only Warhammer 40,000 but our other games, miniatures and more cool stuff too. Each event is unique, reflecting the style and scope of the hobby in the country that hosts it, providing massive, spectacular battles to take part in, terrain and models to marvel at, and new ideas to explore. One of the many highlights of each Games Day is the prestigious Golden Demon painting competition, where the best painters in the world show off their talents and compete for the coveted top prizes.

FINDING OUT MORE

WHITE DWARF MAGAZINE

White Dwarf magazine is Games Workshop's monthly hobby supplement, an essential publication for everyone who is interested in any aspect of the Games Workshop hobby. Modelling, painting, terrain building, new rules, scenarios and more can be found within its hallowed pages. White Dwarf has loads of articles based on different aspects of Warhammer 40,000 so you can get the most out of your games, including:

- **News on forthcoming releases.**
- **Exciting and informative battle reports.**
- **Advice on painting and assembling your models.**
- **In depth tactics articles.**
- **A complete list of Games Workshop stockists in your region.**
- **New missions to fight.**
- **Campaigns.**
- **Terrain building.**
- **Showcase armies.**

BATTLE REPORTS

For many years, one of the most popular series of White Dwarf articles has been the battle report. These articles offer blow-by-blow accounts of battles. The action in question could be an important historic battle from the universe of Warhammer 40,000 or it could be a competitive grudge match between two masterful tabletop generals.

Battle reports offer invaluable tactical advice for the beginner and veteran alike. They provide a rare insight into a commander's head during a battle, and make for action-packed reading to boot!

WARHAMMER 40,000 ON THE WEB

Perhaps one of the best ways to find out more about Warhammer 40,000 is to access the Games Workshop website. This vast reservoir of information has pictures of every Warhammer 40,000 miniature currently available, painting guides, sample army lists, getting started information and lots more. You can also find additional articles, assembly guides, scenarios, previews of upcoming new releases and a library of fantastic hobby projects you can build yourself.

The Games Workshop website also has a store locater allowing players to find the Games Workshop store or independent retailer that is nearest to their home or travel destination. If no shops are nearby you can find the full range of products on our safe and secure online store.

www.games-workshop.com

INTO THE FAR FUTURE

If you have made it thus far, then you are nearing the end of the book. However, your visit to the 41st Millennium is, we hope, just beginning. You may have mastered all the rules, but there are always more cunning tactics, devious opponents and hard-fought campaigns and tournaments to challenge you. You may have read every word of history in this tome, but each Codex is packed with even more background, famous characters and events. For those looking for even more epic tales, the Black Library publishes dozens of novels set in the universe of Warhammer 40,000. You may have painted a force and decked out your battlefield, but you can never have enough reinforcements, allies or even whole armies, and building terrain is an art-form in its own right. You may have played all the missions printed here, but every expansion presents a new setting that changes how the game plays, and there is endless scope for writing your own scenarios, campaigns and house rules.

Here at the Games Workshop Design Studio our staff are constantly exploring this Dark Millennium. In the Games Development department Alessio is devising his army list for the next Grand Tournament, Phil is trying to finish enough Ork Boyz for a mighty Waaagh! while our resident tread-head Andy is painting the 26th vehicle in his tank army. In the Hobby department, Neil is expanding his city-fighting Space Marine army into a full battle company, Jonesy is finishing the latest hideous addition to his Nurgle horde and Dom is writing his own experimental rules for his new army. The 'Eavy Metal painters are planning their entries for next year's Golden Demon competition, while over in the White Dwarf bunker Matt is working on his ninth power-armoured army and Christian's second Baneblade takes his Chaos army up to 11,000 points! A small group is preparing the next Studio campaign, including new missions and unexpected events, and everyone is plotting revenge on their old rivals. And this is all just in our spare time, quite apart from all of the Codexes, expansions, articles, web campaigns and other secret projects we are working on in our 'day jobs'.

We trust you are inspired to carry on the adventure – if you are anywhere near as enthusiastic as us, you won't be able to help yourself. So look to your wargear and advance into battle. A galaxy of endless war awaits!

Games Developer Alessio Cavatore oversees playtesting.

> "Come forth you mighty warriors, gather under the bloodstained banners and grisly trophies of conquest."
>
> Warmaster General Solar Macharius

The staff of Games Workshop 'hard at work' on the new game.

REFERENCE

Within these final pages you will find statistics for every troop type for each of the armies in Warhammer 40,000. Although the entries in this section are correct at the time of printing, the Warhammer 40,000 game system is constantly growing and developing. As such, in the event of any contradiction between this section and any of the individual codexes, the codexes always take precedence. We have also included rules for victory points. For players that want to use them, these provide a tiebreaker in the event of a draw, or a more detailed measure of which side has destroyed more of the enemy. At the back are summaries of the Movement, Shooting and Assault phase and the most commonly used charts for easy reference during battle.

The universe is a big place and, whatever happens, you will not be missed...

SPACE MARINES

SPACE MARINES

	WS	BS	S	T	W	I	A	Ld	Sv
Apothecary	4	4	4	4	1	4	2	9	3+
Attack Bike	4	4	4	4(5)	2	4	2	8	3+
Captain	5	5	4	4	3	5	3	10	3+[4+]
Chaplain	4	4	4	4	2	4	2	10	3+[4+]
Company Champion	5	4	4	4	1	4	2	9	3+
Honour Guard	4	4	4	4	1	4	2	10	2+
Librarian	5	4	4	4	2	4	2	9	3+
Scout	4	4	4	4	1	4	1	8	4+
Scout Biker	4	4	4	4(5)	1	4	1	8	4+
Scout Sergeant	4	4	4	4	1	4	2	8	4+
Servitor	3	3	3	3	1	3	1	8	4+
Space Marine	4	4	4	4	1	4	1	8	3+
Space Marine Biker	4	4	4	4(5)	1	4	1	8	3+
Techmarine	4	4	4	4	1	4	1	8	2+
Terminator	4	4	4	4	1	4	2	9	2+[5+]
Veteran Sergeant	4	4	4	4	1	4	2	9	3+

BLACK TEMPLARS

	WS	BS	S	T	W	I	A	Ld	Sv
Castellan	5	5	4	4	2	5	3	9	3+
Cenobyte	4	3	3	4	1	3	1	8	4+
Emperor's Champion	6	4	4	4	2	5	2	10	2+[4+]
Initiate	4	4	4	4	1	4	1	8	3+
Marshal	5	5	4	4	3	5	3	10	3+
Neophyte	3	3	4	4	1	4	1	7	4+

BLOOD ANGELS

	WS	BS	S	T	W	I	A	Ld	Sv
Death Company	4	4	4	4	1	4	2	9	3+

DARK ANGELS

	WS	BS	S	T	W	I	A	Ld	Sv
Chaplain	5	5	4	4	2	5	3	9	3+[4+]
Company Master	5	5	4	4	3	5	3	10	3+[4+]
Interrogator-Chaplain	5	5	4	4	3	5	3	10	3+[4+]
Librarian	5	5	4	4	2	5	3	9	3+
Ravenwing Biker	4	4	4	4(5)	1	4	1	8	3+
Veteran	4	4	4	4	1	4	2	9	3+

SPACE WOLVES

	WS	BS	S	T	W	I	A	Ld	Sv
Wolf Guard Battle Leader	5	5	4	4	2	5	4	9	3+
Blood Claw	3	3	4	4	1	4	1	8	3+
Blood Claw Biker	3	3	4	4(5)	1	4	1	8	3+
Fenrisian Wolf	4	0	4	4	1	4	2	8	6+
Grey Hunter	4	4	4	4	1	4	1	8	3+
Iron Priest	5	5	4	4	2	5	3	9	2+
Long Fang	4	4	4	4	1	4	1	9	3+
Pack Leader	4	4	4	4	1	4	1	9	3+
Rune Priest	5	5	4	4	2	5	4	9	3+
Thrall	3	3	4	5	1	1	1	8	5+
Wolf Guard	4	4	4	4	1	4	2	9	3+
Wolf Lord	5	5	4	4	3	5	4	10	3+
Wolf Priest	5	5	4	4	2	5	4	10	3+[4+]

[4+] Indicates a 4+ Invulnerable Save.

[5+] Indicates a 5+ Invulnerable Save.

VEHICLES

	Front	Side	Rear	BS
	Armour			
Drop Pod	12	12	12	2
Land Raider	14	14	14	4
Land Raider Crusader	14	14	14	4
Leman Russ Exterminator	14	12	10	4
Land Speeder	10	10	10	4
Predator	13	11	10	4
Razorback	11	11	10	1
Rhino	11	11	10	4
Vindicator	13	11	10	4
Whirlwind	11	11	10	4

DREADNOUGHTS

	WS	BS	S	Front	Side	Rear	I	A
				Armour				
Dreadnought	4	4	6(10)	12	12	10	4	2
'Furioso' Dreadnought	4	4	6(10)	12	12	10	4	2(3)
Space Wolf Venerable Dreadnought	5	5	6(10)	12	12	10	4	3

WEAPONS

	Range	S	AP	Type
Assault cannon	24"	6	4	Heavy 4, Rending
Autocannon	48"	7	4	Heavy 2
Bolt pistol	12"	4	5	Pistol
Boltgun	24"	4	5	Rapid Fire
Deathwind	12"	5	6	Heavy 1, Large Blast
Demolisher	24"	10	2	Ordnance 1, Large Blast
Flamer	Template	4	5	Assault 1
Heavy bolter	36"	5	4	Heavy 3
Heavy flamer	Template	5	4	Assault 1
Hunter-killer missile	n/a	8	3	Heavy 1
Lascannon	48"	9	2	Heavy 1
Meltagun	12"	8	1	Assault 1, Melta
Missile Launcher*				
Frag	48"	4	6	Heavy 1, Blast
Krak	48"	8	3	Heavy 1

	Range	S	AP	Type
Multi-melta	24"	8	1	Heavy 1, Melta
Plasma pistol	12"	7	2	Pistol, Gets Hot!
Plasma gun	24"	7	2	Rapid Fire, Gets Hot!
Plasma cannon	36"	7	2	Heavy 1, Blast, Gets Hot!
Shotgun				
Solid shot	12"	3	-	Assault 2
Manstopper	12"	4	-	Assault 2
Sniper rifle	36"	X	6	Heavy 1, Sniper, Pinning
Storm bolter	24"	4	5	Assault 2
Typhoon missile	48"	5	5	Heavy 1, Blast, Twin-linked
Whirlwind**				
Vengeance	G12-48"	5	4	Ord. 1/Large Blast
Castellan	G12-48"	n/a	n/a	Ord. 1/Large Blast
Incendiary Castellan	G12-48"	4	5	Ord. 1/Large Blast, Ignores Cover

IMPERIAL GUARD

	WS	BS	S	T	W	I	A	Ld	Sv
Commissar	4	4	3	3	2	4	2	10	5+
Conscript	2	2	3	3	1	3	1	5	5+
Guardsman	3	3	3	3	1	3	1	7	5+
Hardened Veteran	3	4	3	3	1	3	1	8	5+
Hardened Veteran Sergeant	3	4	3	3	1	3	2	8	5+
Heroic Senior Officer	4	4	3	3	3	4	3	9	5+
Junior Officer	3	3	3	3	1	3	2	8	5+
Ogryn	4	3	5	4	3	3	2	8	5+
Ogryn Bone 'ead	4	3	5	4	3	3	3	9	5+
Priest	3	3	3	3	2	4	2	8	–
Ratling	2	4	2	2	1	4	1	6	5+
Sanctioned Psyker	2	2	3	3	1	3	1	8	5+
Senior Officer	4	4	3	3	2	4	3	8	5+
Veteran Sergeant	3	3	3	3	1	3	2	8	5+
Storm Trooper	3	4	3	3	1	3	1	8	4+
Storm Trooper Veteran Sergeant	3	4	3	3	1	3	2	8	4+
Tech-Priest Enginseer	3	3	3	3	1	3	1	8	3+

VEHICLES

	Armour			
	Front	Side	Rear	BS
Basilisk	12	10	10	3
Chimera	12	10	10	3
Demolisher	14	13	11	3
Hellhound	12	12	10	3
Leman Russ	14	12	10	3

				Armour				
	WS	BS	S	Front	Side	Rear	I	A
Sentinel	3	3	5	10	10	10	3	1

Weapons	Range	S	AP	Type
Autocannon	48"	7	4	Heavy 2
Battle cannon	72"	8	3	Ord. 1, Large Blast
Boltgun	24"	4	5	Rapid fire
Bolt pistol	12"	4	5	Pistol
Demolisher	24"	10	2	Ord. 1, Large Blast
Earthshaker	120"	9	3	Ord. 1, Large Blast
Flamer	Template	4	5	Assault 1
Grenade launcher*				
Frag	24"	3	6	Assault 1, Blast
Krak	24"	6	4	Assault 1
Heavy bolter	36"	5	4	Heavy 3
Heavy flamer	Template	5	4	Assault 1
Heavy stubber	36"	4	6	Heavy 3
Hellpistol	12"	3	5	Pistol
Hellgun	24"	3	5	Rapid fire
Hunter-killer missile	n/a	8	3	Heavy 1
Inferno cannon**	24"	6	4	Heavy 1, Template
Lasgun	24"	3	–	Rapid fire
Laspistol	12"	3	–	Pistol
Lascannon	48"	9	2	Heavy 1
Meltagun	12"	8	1	Melta, Assault 1
Missile launcher*				
Frag	48"	4	6	Heavy 1, Blast
Krak	48"	8	3	Heavy 1
Mortar	G48"	4	6	Heavy 1, Blast
Multi-laser	36"	6	6	Heavy 3
Multi-melta	24"	8	1	Melta, Heavy 1
Plasma cannon	36"	7	2	Gets Hot, Heavy 1, Blast
Plasma gun	24"	7	2	Gets Hot, Rapid Fire
Plasma pistol	12"	7	2	Gets Hot, Pistol
Ripper gun	12"	4	6	Assault 2
Shotgun	12"	3	–	Assault 2
Sniper rifle	36"	–	6	Sniper, Pinning, Heavy 1
Storm bolter	24"	4	5	Assault 2

    * May fire either frag or krak missiles/grenades.

  ** Place flamer template on target. Roll to hit. If you hit, all models touched by template are hit. If you miss, they are hit on a 4+.

FORCES OF THE IMPERIUM

AGENTS OF THE IMPERIUM

	WS	BS	S	T	W	I	A	Ld	Sv
Arco-flagellant	4	0	4	5	1	4	1/D6	8	– 4+
Crusader	4	3	3	3	1	3	1	8	4+4+
Daemonhost	4	4	6	4	4	4	D6	9	– 4+
Death Cult Assassin	5	4	4	3	2	5	2	8	– 5+
Henchman	3	3	3	3	1	3	1	8	6+
Imperial Assassin	5	5	4	4	2	5	3	10	– 4+
Inquisitor	4	4	3	3	2	4	2	8	4+
Inquisitor Lord	4	4	3	3	3	4	3	10	3+
Priest	3	3	3	3	2	4	2	8	–
Storm Trooper	3	4	3	3	1	3	1	8	4+
Warrior Henchman	3	4	3	3	1	3	1	8	4+

GREY KNIGHTS

	WS	BS	S	T	W	I	A	Ld	Sv
Grand Master	5	5	4	4	3	5	4	10	2+5+
Grey Knight	5	4	4	4	1	4	1	8	3+
Brother-Captain	5	4	4	4	1	4	3	10	2+5+
Grey Knight Terminator	5	4	4	4	1	4	2	10	2+5+
Justicar	5	4	4	4	1	4	2	9	3+

4+ *Indicates a 4+ Invulnerable Save.* 5+ *Indicates a 5+ Invulnerable Save.*

BATTLE SISTERS

	WS	BS	S	T	W	I	A	Ld	Sv
Battle Sister	3	4	3	3	1	3	1	8	3+
Canoness	4	5	3	3	3	4	3	10	3+
Celestian	4	4	3	3	1	4	1	9	3+
Celestian Superior	4	4	3	3	1	4	2	9	3+
Mistress	4	4	3	3	1	4(5)	2(3)	10	4+
Palatine	4	5	3	3	2	4	2	9	3+
Seraphim	4	4	3	3	1	4	1	9	3+
Seraphim Superior	4	4	3	3	1	4	2	9	3+
Sister Repentia	4	4	3(6)	3	1	3	1	6	4+
Sister Superior	3	4	3	3	1	3	2	9	3+

VEHICLES

	Armour Front	Side	Rear	BS
Chimera	12	10	10	3
Exorcist	13	11	10	4
Immolator	11	11	10	4
Land Raider	14	14	14	4
Land Raider Crusader	14	14	14	4
Rhino	11	11	10	4

VEHICLES (cont.)

	WS	BS	S	Armour Front	Side	Rear	I	A
Dreadnought	5	4	6(10)	12	12	10	4	2
Penitent Engine	4	2	5(10)	11	11	10	3	D6

Weapons	Range	S	AP	Type
Assault Cannon	24"	6	4	Heavy 3
Boltgun	24"	4	5	Rapid fire
Bolt pistol	12"	4	5	Pistol
Exorcist missile	48"	8	1	Heavy D6
Flamer	Template	4	5	Assault 1
Heavy bolter	36"	5	4	Heavy 3
Heavy flamer	Template	5	4	Assault 1
Hellpistol	12"	3	5	Pistol
Hellgun	24"	3	5	Rapid fire
Incinerator	Template	5	4	Assault 1; no Inv. or Cover Saves
Inferno pistol	6"	8	2	Pistol; melta
Laspistol	12"	3	–	Pistol
Lascannon	48"	9	2	Heavy 1
Meltagun	12"	8	1	Melta, Assault 1
Multi-laser	36"	6	6	Heavy 3
Multi-melta	24"	8	1	Melta, Heavy 1
Needle pistol	12"	–	6	Pistol; wounds on 4+
Psycannon* *May be fired as an assault or a heavy weapon.	18"	6	4	Assault 3; ignores Invulnerable Saves
	36"	6	4	Heavy 3; ignores Invulnerable Saves
Shotgun	12"	3	–	Assault 2
Storm bolter	24"	4	5	Assault 2
Stake crossbow	24"	3	5	Assault 2; wounds psykers on 2+ with no Save.

ORBITAL WEAPONS	S	AP	Notes
Barrage bomb	6	4	Ord blast
Lance strike	10	1	Ord blast
Melta torpedo	8	3	Ord blast; 2D6 Armour Pen
Psyk-out	9	1	See Codex: Witch Hunters

NEMESIS FORCE WEAPON BONUSES

Rank	Strength bonus	Power weapon	Force weapon
Grey Knight	+2	No	No
Grey Knight Brother-Captain	+2	Yes	No
Grey Knights Grand Master	+2	Yes	Yes
Grey Knight Justicar/Terminator	+2	Yes	No

CHAOS SPACE MARINES

	WS	BS	S	T	W	I	A	Ld	Sv
Aspiring Champion	4	4	4	4	1	4	2	10	3+
Aspiring Sorcerer	4	4	4	4	1	4	2	10	3+⁴⁺
Berzerker	5	4	4	4	1	4	2	9	3+
Berzerker Skull Champion	5	4	4	4	1	4	3	10	3+
Chaos Biker	4	4	4	4(5)	1	4	1	9	3+
Chaos Biker Aspiring Champion	4	4	4	4(5)	1	4	2	10	3+
Chaos Lord	6	5	4	4	3	5	3	10	3+⁵⁺
Chaos Space Marine	4	4	4	4	1	4	1	9	3+
Chaos Spawn	3	0	5	5	3	3	D6	10	-
Chosen Chaos Space Marine	4	4	4	4	1	4	1	10	3+
Noise Marine	4	4	4	4	1	5	1	9	3+
Noise Marine Champion	4	4	4	4	1	5	2	10	3+
Obliterator	4	4	4	4	2	4	2	9	2+⁵⁺
Plague Marine	4	4	4	4(5)	1	3	1	9	3+
Plague Marine Champion	4	4	4	4(5)	1	3	2	10	3+
Possessed	4	4	5	4	1	4	2	10	3+⁵⁺
Raptor	4	4	4	4	1	4	1	9	3+
Sorcerer	5	5	4	4	3	5	3	10	3+⁵⁺
Space Marine Daemon Prince	7	5	6	5	4	5	4	10	3+⁵⁺
Summoned Greater Daemon	8	0	6	6	4	4	5	10	-⁴⁺
Summoned Lesser Daemon	4	0	4	4	1	4	2	10	-⁵⁺
Terminator	4	4	4	4	1	4	2	10	2+⁵⁺
Terminator Champion	4	4	4	4	1	4	3	10	2+⁵⁺·
Thousand Sons Marine	4	4	4	4	1	4	1	9	3+⁴⁺

⁴⁺ *Indicates a 4+ Invulnerable Save.*

⁵⁺ *Indicates a 5+ Invulnerable Save.*

VEHICLES

	Armour			
	Front	Side	Rear	BS
Chaos Land Raider	14	14	14	4
Chaos Predator	13	11	10	4
Chaos Rhino	11	11	10	4
Chaos Vindicator	13	11	10	4

				Armour				
	WS	BS	S	Front	Side	Rear	I	A
Chaos Dreadnought	4	4	6	12	12	10	4	3
Defiler	3	3	6	12	12	10	3	3

Weapon	Range	S	AP	Type
Autocannon	48"	7	4	Heavy 2
Battle cannon	72"	8	3	Ord.1, Large Blast
Blastmaster*				
Varied frequency	36"	5	4	Assault 2, Pinning
Single frequency	48"	8	3	Heavy 1, Blast, Pinning
Bolt pistol	12"	4	5	Pistol
Boltgun	24"	4	5	Rapid Fire
Demolisher	24"	10	2	Ord. 1, Large Blast
Doom siren	Template	5	3	Assault 1
Flamer	Template	4	5	Assault 1
Havoc Launcher	48"	5	5	Heavy 1, Blast, Twin-linked
Heavy bolter	36"	5	4	Heavy 3
Heavy flamer	Template	5	4	Assault 1
Lascannon	48"	9	2	Heavy 1
Meltagun	12"	8	1	Melta, Assault 1,
Missile launcher**				
Frag	48"	4	6	Heavy 1, Blast
Krak	48"	8	3	Heavy 1
Plasma Cannon	36"	7	2	Heavy 1, Blast, Gets Hot!
Plasma Gun	24"	7	2	Rapid Fire; Gets hot
Plasma Pistol	12"	7	2	Pistol, Gets hot!
Reaper Autocannon	36"	7	4	Heavy 2, Twin-linked
Sonic blaster	24"	4	5	Assault 2 or Heavy 3***

* *May fire either at a single or varied frequency.*
** *May fire either frag or krak missiles.*
*** *May fire either Assault 2 or Heavy 3*

"I murdered thousands for the Emperor and he gave me nothing except his damning silence. Now his lapdogs yap for every life I take, while the gods promise me the galaxy."

Svane Vulfbad

CHAOS DAEMONS

	WS	BS	S	T	W	I	A	Ld	Sv*
Beast of Nurgle	3	0	4	5	2	2	D6	10	—5+
Bloodcrusher	5	0	5	5	2	4	3	10	4+5+
Bloodletter	5	0	4	4	1	4	2	10	—5+
Bloodthirster	10	4	7	6	4	5	5	10	4+3+
Daemon Prince	7	5	5	5	4	5	4	10	—5+
Daemonette	4	0	3	3	1	6	3	10	—5+
Flesh Hound	4	0	4	4	1	4	2	10	—5+
Fury	3	0	4	4	1	3	2	10	—5+
Great Unclean One	6	1	6	6	5	2	4	10	—4+
Keeper of Secrets	8	4	6	6	4	10	6	10	—4+
Khorne Herald	6	3	4	4	2	5	3	10	—5+
Lord of Change	5	5	6	6	4	5	3	10	—3+
Nurgle Herald	4	3	4	5	2	3	2	10	—5+
Nurglings	2	0	3	3	3	2	3	10	—5+
Pink Horror	2	3	3	3	1	3	1	10	—4+
Plaguebearer	3	0	4	5	1	2	1	10	—5+
Screamer	3	0	4	4	1	3	1	10	—4+

	WS	BS	S	T	W	I	A	Ld	Sv*
Seeker	4	0	3	3	1	6	4	10	—5+
Slaanesh Fiend	3	0	4	4	2	5	3	10	—5+
Slaanesh Herald	5	3	3	3	2	7	4	10	—5+
Tzeentch Flamer	2	4	4	4	1	3	2	10	—4+
Tzeentch Herald	2	4	3	3	2	4	2	10	—4+

3+ Indicates a 3+ Invulnerable Save.

4+ Indicates a 4+ Invulnerable Save.

5+ Indicates a 5+ Invulnerable Save.

VEHICLES

	WS	BS	S	Front	Side	Rear	I	A
				Armour				
Soul Grinder	3	3	6(10)	13	13	11	3	4

Weapon	Range	S	AP	Type
Mawcannon				
vomit	template	6	4	Assault 1
tongue	24"	10	1	Assault 1
phlegm	36"	8	3	Assault 1, large blast
Harvester	24"	4	5	Assault 6

TYRANIDS

	WS	BS	S	T	W	I	A	Ld	Sv
Biovore	3	3	4	4	2	1	1	5	6+
Broodlord	6	3	5	5	3	7	4	10	4+
Carnifex	3	2	9	6	4	1	2	10	3+
Gargoyle	3	3	3	3	1	4	1	10	6+
Gaunt	3	3	3	3	1	4	1	5	6+
Genestealer	6	0	4	4	1	6	2	10	5+
Hive Tyrant	5	3	5	6	4	5	3	10	3+
Hormagaunt	4	3	3	3	1	4	2	5	6+
Lictor	6	0	6	4	2	6	3	10	5+
Ravener	5	3	4	4	2	5	3	10	5+
Ripper Swarm	3	1	3	3	3	2	3	10	6+
Spore Mine	0	0	1	3	1	1	0	5	—
Tyrant Guard	5	3	5	6	2	5	3	10	3+
Warrior	4	2	4	4	2	4	2	10	5+
Zoanthrope	3	3	4	4	2	4	2	10	2+6+

6+ indicates a 6+ Invulnerable Save.

Weapon	Range	S	AP	Type
Barbed strangler	36"	S-1	5	Assault 1/large blast, pinning, Max Str 8
Deathspitter	24"	S+1	5	Assault 1 Blast, Max Str 7
Devourer	18"	S-1	–	Assault 2X, Max Str 6
Fleshborer	12"	S+1	5	Assault X, Max Str 6
Spinefist	12"	S	5	Assault X, Max Str 6 Twin linked
Venom cannon*	36"	S+2	4	Assault X

*Maximum Strength = 10. Can only cause glancing hits against vehicles that are not open-topped.

S indicates that the Strength of the weapon is the same as the Strength of the model firing it. This is sometimes modified by a number written next to S, and/or has a maximum value.

X indicates that the rate of fire of the weapon is equal to the Attacks value of the model firing it (this is sometimes multiplied by a number written next to X).

Note: if a Tyranid Monstrous Creature fires two identical weapons, it counts as firing a single twin-linked weapon.

ELDAR

	WS	BS	S	T	W	I	A	Ld	Sv
Autarch	6	6	3	3	3	6	3	10	3+[4+]
Avatar	10	5	6	6	4	6	4	10	3+
Dark Reaper	4	4	3	3	1	5	1	9	3+
Death Jester	5	4	3	3	1	6	2	9	–
Dire Avenger	4	4	3	3	1	5	1	9	4+
Exarch	5	5	3	3	1	6	2	9	3+*
Farseer	5	5	3	3	3	5	1	10	–
Fire Dragon	4	4	3	3	1	5	1	9	4+
Guardian	3	3	3	3	1	4	1	8	5+
Guardian Jetbike	3	3	3	3(4)	1	4	1	8	3+
Harlequin	5	4	3	3	1	6	2	9	–
Howling Banshee	4	4	3	3	1	5	1	9	4+
Phoenix Lord	7	7	4	4	3	7	4	10	2+
Ranger	3	4	3	3	1	4	1	8	5+
Shadowseer	5	4	3	3	1	6	2	9	–
Shining Spear	4	4	3	3(4)	1	5	1	9	3+
Striking Scorpion	4	4	3	3	1	5	1	9	3+
Swooping Hawk	4	4	3	3	1	5	1	9	4+
Troupe Master	5	4	3	3	1	6	3	10	–
Warlock	4	4	3	3	1	4	1	8	–
Warp Spider	4	4	3	3	1	5	1	9	3+
Wraithguard	4	4	5	6	1	4	1	10	3+
Wraithlord	4	4	10	8	3	4	2	10	3+

[4+] *Indicates a 4+ Invulnerable Save.*

VEHICLES

	Armour			
	Front	Side	Rear	BS
Falcon	12	12	10	3
Fire Prism	12	12	10	4
Vyper	10	10	10	3
Wave Serpent	2	12	10	3

				Armour				
	WS	BS	S	Front	Side	Rear	I	A
War Walker	3	3	5	10	10	10	4	2

"Ask not the Eldar a question, for they will give you three terrifying answers, all of which are true and terrifying to know."

Inquisitor Czevak

WEAPON

	Range	S	AP	Type
Avenger shuriken catapult	18"	4	5	Assault 2
Bright lance	36"	8	2	Heavy 1, Lance
D-cannon*	G24"	X	2	Heavy 1, Blast
Deathspinner	12"	6	–	Assault 2
Dragon's breath flamer	Template	5	4	Assault 1
Exarch deathspinner	12"	6	–	Assault 4
Firepike	18"	8	1	Assault 1, Melta
Flamer	Template	4	5	Assault 1
Fusion gun	12"	8	1	Assault 1, Melta
Fusion pistol	6"	8	1	Pistol, Melta
Hawk's talon	24"	5	5	Assault 3
Lasblaster	24"	3	5	Assault 2
Laser lance	6"	6	4	Assault 1, Lance
Eldar missile launcher				
Krak	48"	8	3	Heavy 1
Plasma	48"	4	4	Heavy 1, Blast, Pinning
Prism cannon* (focussed)	60"	9	2	Heavy 1, Blast
Prism cannon* (dispersed)	60"	5	4	Heavy 1, Large Blast
Pulse laser	48"	8	2	Heavy 2
Ranger long rifle*	36"	X	6	Heavy 1, Sniper, Pinning
Reaper launcher	48"	5	3	Heavy 2
Scatter laser	36"	6	6	Heavy 4
Singing spear*	12"	X	6	Assault 1
Shadow weaver	G48"	6	–	Heavy 1, Blast
Shrieker cannon	24"	6	5	Assault 3, Pinning
Shuriken cannon	24"	6	5	Assault 3
Shuriken catapult	12"	4	5	Assault 2
Shuriken pistol	12"	4	5	Pistol
Spinneret rifle	18"	6	1	Assault 1, Pinning
Star lance	6"	8	4	Assault 1, Lance
Starcannon	36"	6	2	Heavy 2
Sunrifle	24"	3	5	Assault 6, Pinning
Tempest launcher	G36"	4	3	Heavy 2, Blast
Triskele	12"	3	2	Assault 3
Vibro cannon*	36"	4	–	Heavy 1, Pinning
Wraithcannon*	12"	X	2	Assault 1

* These weapons have additional rules. See the Eldar Wargear section.
** May fire either plasma or krak missiles.

DARK ELDAR

	WS	BS	S	T	W	I	A	Ld	Sv
Archon	6	6	3	3	3	7	3	9	5+
Beastmaster	4	4	3	3	1	6	1	8	6+
Dracon	5	5	3	3	2	6	2	9	5+
Grotesque	4	0	4	3	2	3	2	5	n/a
Haemonculus	4	4	3	4	2	4	2	8	5+
Hellion	4	4	3	3	1	6	1	8	5+
Hellion Succubus	4	4	3	3	1	6	2	8	5+
Incubi Master	5	4	3	3	1	6	3	8	3+
Incubi	5	4	3	3	1	5	1	8	3+
Mandrake	4	4	3	3	1	5	1	8	5+
Reaver	4	4	4	4	1	6	1	8	4+
Reaver Succubus	4	4	4	4	1	6	2	8	4+
Scourge	4	4	3	3	1	5	1	8	5+
Sybarite	4	4	3	3	1	5	2	8	5+
Talos	5	3	7	7	3	4	D6	n/a	3+
Warrior	4	4	3	3	1	5	1	8	5+
Warp Beast	4	0	4	3	1	5	3	3	6+
Wych	4	4	3	3	1	6	1	8	6+
Wych Archite	6	6	3	3	3	8	3	9	6+
Wych Dracite	5	5	3	3	2	7	2	9	6+
Wych Succubus	4	4	3	3	1	6	2	8	6+

VEHICLES

	Armour			
	Front	Side	Rear	BS
Raider	10	10	10	4
Ravager	11	11	10	4

WEAPON

Range	S	AP	Type
Blaster	12"	8	2	Lance, Assault 1
Dark lance	36"	8	2	Lance, Heavy 1
Destructor	Template	4	D6	Assault 1
Disintegrator*				
Maximum	36"	7	2	Heavy 1, Blast
Sustained	24"	4	3	Heavy 3
Shredder	12"	6	–	Assault 1, Blast
Splinter cannon	24"	4	5	Assault 4
Splinter pistol	12"	3	5	Pistol
Splinter rifle	24"	3	5	Rapid Fire
Stinger**	12"	n/a	6	Assault 1, Wounds on 2+
Terrorfex***	12"	n/a	n/a	Assault 1, Blast
Talos sting	24"	4	5	Assault 6

*May fire either at maximum or sustained.
**If target killed, place Blast marker over it. S = target's T.; AP = target's Armour Save.
***Only roll to hit. If 1+ models hit, their unit must make a Pinning test.
  -1 modifier if unit under half strength;
  -1 modifier per model hit if more than one model is hit.

ORKS

	WS	BS	S	T	W	I	A	Ld	Sv
'Ard Boy	4	2	3	4	1	2	2	7	4+
Big Mek	4	2	4	4	2	3	3	8	6+
Burna Boy	4	2	3	4	1	2	2	7	6+
Dethkopta	4	2	3	4(5)	2	2	2	7	4+
Flash Gitz	4	2	4	4	2	3	3	7	4+
Gretchin	2	3	2	2	1	2	1	5	-
Kommando	4	2	3	4	1	3	2	7	6+
Loota	4	2	3	4	1	2	2	7	6+
Meganob	4	2	4	4	3	2	3	7	2+
Mek	4	2	3	4	1	2	2	7	6+
Nob	4	2	4	4	2	3	3	7	6+
Ork Boy	4	2	3	4	1	2	2	7	6+
Painboy	4	2	4	4	2	3	3	7	6+
Runtherd	4	2	4	4	2	3	3	7	6+
Stormboy	4	2	3	4	1	2	2	7	6+
Tankbusta	4	2	3	4	1	2	2	7	6+
Warbiker*	4	2	3	4(5)	1	2	2	7	6+
Warboss	5	2	5	5	3	4	4	9	6+
Weirdboy	4	2	4	4	2	3	3	7	6+

VEHICLES

	Armour			
	Front	Side	Rear	BS
Battlewagon	14	12	10	2
Looted wagon	11	11	10	2
Trukk	10	10	10	2
Warbuggy/WarTrak/Skorcha	10	10	10	2

				Armour				
	WS	BS	S	Front	Side	Rear	I	A
Deff Dread	4	2	5(10)	12	12	10	2	3
Killa Kan	2	3	5(10)	11	11	10	2	2

WEAPON

	Range	S	AP	Type
Big shoota	36"	5	5	Assault 3
Boomgun	36"	8	3	Ordnance 1, Large Blast
Burna	Template	4	5	Assault 1
Deffgun	48"	7	4	Heavy D3
Grot blasta	12"	3	–	Assault 1
Grotzooka	18"	6	5	Heavy 2, Blast
Kannon*				
Frag	36"	4	5	Heavy 1, Blast
Shell	36"	8	3	Heavy 1
Killkannon	24"	7	3	Ordnance 1, Large Blast
Kustom Mega-Blasta	24"	8	2	Heavy 1 Gets Hot!
Lobba	G48"	5	5	Heavy 1, Blast
Rokkit launcha	24"	8	3	Assault 1
Shokk Attack Gun	60"	2D6	2	Ordnance, Heavy 1 Large Blast
Shoota	18"	4	6	Assault 2
Skorcha	Template	5	4	Assault 1
Slugga	12"	4	6	Pistol
Zzap gun**	36"	2D6	2	Heavy 1

* See Codex: Orks for more details.
** See Codex: Orks for more details. Zzap guns do not roll to hit.

"I'm da hand of Gork and Mork. Dey sent me to rouse up da boyz to crush and kill 'cos da boyz forgot what dere 'ere for.

I' da profit of the Waaagh 'an whole worlds burn in my boot prints."

Ghazghkull Mag Uruk Thraka

TAU EMPIRE

	WS	BS	S	T	W	I	A	Ld	Sv
Broadside Shas'ui	2	3	5	4	2	2	2	8	2+
Broadside Shas'vre	3	3	5	4	2	3	2	8	2+
Crisis Shas'el	3	4	5	4	3	3	3	9	3+
Crisis Shas'o	4	5	5	4	4	3	4	10	3+
Crisis Shas'ui	2	3	5	4	2	2	2	8	3+
Crisis Shas'vre	3	3	4	3	1	3	2	8	3+
Ethereal	4	3	3	3	2	3	3	10	–
Fire Warrior Shas'la	2	3	3	3	1	2	1	7	4+
Fire Warrior Shas'ui	2	3	3	3	1	2	2	8	4+
Gun Drone	2	2	3	3	1	4	1	7*	4+
Kroot	4	3	4	3	1	3	1	7	–/6
Kroot Hound	4	0	4	3	1	5	2	7	–/6
Krootox Rider	4	3	6	3	3	3	3	7	–/6
Marker Drone	2	2(3)	3	3	1	4	1	n/a	4+
Shaper	4	3	4	3	3	3	3	8	6
Shield Drone	2	2	3	**	1	4	1	n/a	**/4+
Sniper Drone	2	2(3)	3	3	1	4	1	7	4+
Spotter	2	3(4)	3	3	1	2	1	8	4+
Stealth Shas'ui	2	3	4	3	1	2	2	8	3+
Stealth Shas'vre	3	3	4	3	1	3	2	8	3+
Strain Leader	3	3	3	4	1	5	1	9	5+
Vespid Stingwing	3	3	3	4	1	5	1	6	5+

*Gun Drones' Leadership is only applicable when operating in independent squadrons.
**Shield Drones share the Toughness and save of the model they accompany. They also have a 4+ Invulnerable Save.

VEHICLES

	Armour			
	Front	Side	Rear	BS
Devilfish Troop Carrier	12	11	10	3
Hammerhead Gunship	13	12	10	3(4)
Piranha Light Skimmer	11	10	10	3
Sky Ray Missile Defence Gunship	13	12	10	3

WEAPON

	Range	S	AP	Type
Burst cannon	18"	5	5	Assault 3
Flamer	Template	4	5	Assault 1
Fusion blaster	12"	8	1	Assault 1, Melta
Ion cannon	60"	7	3	Heavy 3
Kroot gun	48"	7	4	Rapid Fire
Kroot rifle*	24"	4	6	Rapid Fire
Markerlight*	36"	n/a	n/a	Heavy 1
Missile pod	36"	7	4	Assault 2
Plasma rifle	24"	6	2	Rapid Fire
Pulse rifle	30"	5	5	Rapid Fire
Pulse carbine	18"	5	5	Assault 1, Pinning
Pulse pistol	12"	5	5	Pistol
Railgun (solid shot)	72"	10	1	Heavy 1
Railgun (submunition)	72"	6	4	Heavy 1, 5" Blast Hammerhead only
Rail rifle	36"	6	3	Heavy 1, Pinning
Seeker missile*	Unlimited	8	3	Heavy 1
Smart missile system*	24"	5	5	Heavy 4
Vespid neutron blaster	12"	5	3	Assault 1

*These weapons have additional rules.
See the Tau Vehicle Upgrades and Wargear sections in Codex: Tau Empire.

NECRONS

	WS	BS	S	T	W	I	A	Ld	Sv
Flayed Ones	4	4	4	4	1	4	2	10	3+
Necron Destroyer	4	4	4	5	1	2	1	10	3+
Necron Immortal	4	4	4	5	1	2	1	10	3+
Necron Lord	4	4	5	5	3	4	3	10	3+
Necron Warrior	4	4	4	4	1	2	1	10	3+
Necron Wraiths	4	4	6	4	1	6	3	10	– 3+
Pariahs	4	4	5	5	1	3	1	10	3+
Scarab Swarm	2	0	3	3	3	2	3	10	5+
The Nightbringer	6	4	10	8	5	4	5	10	– 4+
The Deceiver	5	3	9	8	5	5	4	10	– 4+
Tomb Spyders	2	2	6	6	2	2	3	10	3+

4+ *Indicates a 4+ Invulnerable Save.*

3+ *Indicates a 3+ Invulnerable Save.*

VEHICLES

	Armour Front	Side	Rear	BS
Monolith	14	14	14	4

WEAPON

	Range	S	AP	Type
Gauss blaster	24"	5	4	Assault 2, Gauss
Gauss cannon	36"	6	4	Heavy 3, Gauss
Gauss flayer	24"	4	5	Rapid Fire, Gauss
Gauss flux arc	12"	5	4	Heavy D6 per unit within 12", Gauss
Heavy Gauss cannon	36"	9	2	Heavy 1
Particle whip	24"	9	3	Ordnance1, Large Blast
Staff of Light	12"	5	3	Assault 3

VICTORY POINTS

Sometimes a mission ends in a draw, whether it be on objectives, kill points, or other victory conditions in missions of your own design. While most gamers will be happy to know that on this occasion they were equally matched, more competitive players may like to have a 'tiebreaker' to determine which side has done marginally better. Alternatively, you might have inflicted so much damage on the enemy army that you would like to be able to claim at least a moral victory!

This may also be useful in tournaments, where the organisers need a better spread of results among the players, so some finer degrees of victory may be useful. To cover these situations, players may agree to calculate victory points (VPs). VPs are gained by inflicting damage on enemy units, as follows.

Units destroyed

At the end of the game every unit that has been destroyed is worth an amount of VPs equal to its points cost (including the cost of all its extra wargear, vehicle upgrades, etc). Units that end the game falling back or off the battlefield count as destroyed.

For example, a 260 point Land Raider would be worth 260 VPs to the opponent if he managed to destroy it by the end of the game.

Units at half strength

At the end of the game every enemy surviving unit that has lost half of its initial models or more is worth an amount of VPs equal to half its points cost (including the cost of all its extra wargear, vehicle upgrades, etc), rounded down. In the case of units that start the game as a single model (independent characters, monstrous creatures, etc), they are worth half their points cost in VPs if they have lost half or more of the Wounds on their profile. In the case of vehicles, they are worth half their points cost in VPs if they are suffering from the effects of any Damaged result at the end of the game.

For example, a squad of Space Marines starts the game at 10 models strong (costing 190 points) and ends the game with only 5 models left. Such a squad is worth 95 VPs to the opponent.

Moral victory?

Each player adds together all of the VPs he has scored by damaging enemy units, then the two totals are compared to find the difference in VPs. A difference of less than 10% of the game's points limit (i.e. 150 VPs in a 1,500 point battle) means you really were evenly matched. A bigger difference would show that one side has seriously maimed the enemy's force, even though it failed to best them on objectives, and that player has at least earned the bragging rights.

QUICK REFERENCE SHEET

TURN SEQUENCE
1 The Movement Phase
2 The Shooting Phase
3 The Assault Phase

SHOOTING SEQUENCE
1 Pick one of your units, check its line of sight and choose a target for it.
2 Check range.
3 Roll to hit.
4 Roll to wound.
5 Take saving throws.
6 Remove casualties.

ASSAULT PHASE
1 Move assaulting units
2 Defenders react
3 Resolve combats

ROLL TO HIT (SHOOTING)
Firer's BS	1	2	3	4	5
Score needed to hit	6	5	4	3	2

MORALE CHECKS
A unit takes a Morale check:
- If it takes 25% or more casualties in a single phase (close combat casualties do not count) – test at the end of the phase.
- If an enemy tank performs a Tank Shock attack on them – test once the tank has moved into contact.
- If it is defeated in close combat in the Assault phase – test once combat results are established. The unit's Leadership is modified by -1 for every point their side has lost the combat by.

DIFFICULT TERRAIN – EFFECTS ON MOVEMENT
Unit Type	Slowed by difficult terrain?	Dangerous Terrain test required?
Infantry	Yes	No*
Bikes	No	Yes
Jetbikes	No	Only if move starts/ends in the terrain
Monstrous creatures	Yes	No*
Jump Infantry	No	Only if move starts/ends in the terrain
Artillery	Yes	No for crew*. Yes for gun models.
Beasts & Cavalry	Yes	No*
Vehicles – Walkers	Yes	No*
Vehicles – Skimmers	No	Only if move starts/ends in the terrain
Vehicles – Other	No	Yes

* unless terrain is also categorised as dangerous

RESERVES TABLE
Turn	Unit arrives on
1	N/A
2	4+
3	3+
4	2+
5+	Automatic

COVER CHART
Cover Type	Save
• Razor wire, Wire mesh	6+
• High Grass, Crops, Bushes, Hedges, Fences	5+
• Units (friends and enemies) Trenches, Gun pits, Tank traps, Emplacements, Sandbags, Barricades, Logs, Pipes, Crates, Barrels, Hill crests, Woods, Jungles, Wreckage, Craters, Rubble, Rocks, Ruins, Walls, Buildings, Wrecked vehicles	4+
• Fortification	3+

RESOLVING COMBATS
1 Pick a combat.
2 Fight Close Combat. Engaged models roll to hit and to wound in Initiative order. Their opponents take Saving throws as required.
3 Determine Assault Results. Total up wounds inflicted. The side which inflicted the most wounds overall in the combat is the winner.
4 Loser Checks Morale. The loser has to pass a Morale check or fall back. If the loser passes the test, go directly to Pile In.
5 Sweeping Advances, Fall backs and Consolidations. Units falling back from close combat must test to see if they successfully break off, if they fail they are destroyed. The winners may then consolidate their position.
6 Pile In. If units are still locked in close combat, then any models not engaged are moved 6" towards the enemy to continue the fight next turn.
7 Pick another combat and repeat until all combats have been resolved.

TO HIT CHART (Assault)
Opponent's Weapon Skill

Attacker's Weapon Skill	1	2	3	4	5	6	7	8	9	10
1	4+	4+	5+	5+	5+	5+	5+	5+	5+	5+
2	3+	4+	4+	4+	5+	5+	5+	5+	5+	5+
3	3+	3+	4+	4+	4+	4+	5+	5+	5+	5+
4	3+	3+	3+	4+	4+	4+	4+	4+	5+	5+
5	3+	3+	3+	3+	4+	4+	4+	4+	4+	4+
6	3+	3+	3+	3+	3+	4+	4+	4+	4+	4+
7	3+	3+	3+	3+	3+	3+	4+	4+	4+	4+
8	3+	3+	3+	3+	3+	3+	3+	4+	4+	4+
9	3+	3+	3+	3+	3+	3+	3+	3+	4+	4+
10	3+	3+	3+	3+	3+	3+	3+	3+	3+	4+

TO WOUND CHART
Toughness

Strength	1	2	3	4	5	6	7	8	9	10
1	4+	5+	6+	6+	N	N	N	N	N	N
2	3+	4+	5+	6+	6+	N	N	N	N	N
3	2+	3+	4+	5+	6+	6+	N	N	N	N
4	2+	2+	3+	4+	5+	6+	6+	N	N	N
5	2+	2+	2+	3+	4+	5+	6+	6+	N	N
6	2+	2+	2+	2+	3+	4+	5+	6+	6+	N
7	2+	2+	2+	2+	2+	3+	4+	5+	6+	6+
8	2+	2+	2+	2+	2+	2+	3+	4+	5+	6+
9	2+	2+	2+	2+	2+	2+	2+	3+	4+	5+
10	2+	2+	2+	2+	2+	2+	2+	2+	3+	4+

WEAPON TYPE SUMMARY
(not for vehicles)

Weapon Type	Moving and Firing	Firing and Assaulting
Pistol	Can move and fire once	May fire once in the Shooting phase and then assault the same enemy unit in the Assault phase. Counts as an additional weapon in close combat.
Rapid Fire	Fire twice at up to 12", or remain stationary and fire once up to maximum weapon range.	Unit may not assault if the weapon was fired in the Shooting phase (unless allowed to by a special rule).
Assault	Can move and fire normally.	May fire in the Shooting phase and then assault the same enemy unit in the assault phase.
Heavy	Cannot move and fire.	Unit may not assault if the weapon was fired in the Shooting phase (unless allowed to by a special rule).

VEHICLE DAMAGE TABLE

D6	Result
1	Crew – Shaken
2	Crew – Stunned
3	Damaged – Weapon Destroyed
4	Damaged – Immobilised
5	Destroyed – Wrecked
6	Destroyed – Explodes!

Modifiers:

Glancing Hit	-2
Hit by 'AP–' weapon	-1
Hit by 'AP1' weapon	+1
Target is open-topped	+1

DEEP STRIKE MISHAP TABLE

D6	Effect
1-2	Terrible accident! The entire unit is destroyed!
3-4	Misplaced. Your opponent may deploy the unit anywhere on the table (including inside difficult terrain, which of course counts as dangerous for Deep Striking units!), in a valid Deep Stike formation, but without rolling for scatter.
5-6	Delayed. The unit is placed back in reserve. If the unit is unlucky enough that the game ends while it is still in reserve, it counts as destroyed.

VEHICLES' MOVING & SHOOTING SUMMARY CHART

	Stationary	Combat Speed	Cruising Speed	Flat Out
All (except Fast & Walkers)	All Weapons	1 Weapon*	No Weapons	N/A
Fast	All Weapons	All Weapons	1 Weapon*	No Weapons
Walker	All Weapons	All Weapons	N/A	N/A

*plus all defensive weapons.

INDEX

ROLL OF HONOUR

The Warhammer 40,000 game first came into existence over 20 years ago in the Games Workshop Studio in rain-sodden Nottingham, England. The toiling Tech-Priest who wrote its first Standard Template Construction blueprint was Rick Priestley. The dark and gothic artistic vision came from John Blanche. Countless contributions and admonishments were brought to bear by Alan Merrett. Throughout the writing of this edition of the game we often had to fire up the arcane support machineries that (mostly) keep this revered trinity stabilised. Their advice has been invaluable.

Written by: Alessio Cavatore (main rules), Mat Ward, Andy Hoare, Graham Davey, Phil Kelly, Gav Thorpe, Adam Troke, Robin Cruddace, Jervis Johnson, Jeremy Vetock. **Cover Art:** Alex Boyd, Dave Gallagher, Nuala Kinrade. **Illustration:** John Blanche, Alex Boyd, Paul Dainton, Dave Gallagher, Nuala Kinrade, Robin Carey, Karl Kopinski, Adrian Smith, Roberto Cirillo, Ian Miller. **Miniature Design:** Alexander Hedström, Aly Morrison, Brian Nelson, Colin Grayson, David Thomas, Juan Diaz, Mark Harrison, Martin Footitt, Michael Anderson, Seb Perbet, Tim Adcock, Neil Langdown,

Chris Catton, Dale Stringer, Jonny Ware, Tom Walton, Jes Goodwin, Trish Morrison. **'Eavy Metal:** Neil Green, Keith Robertson, Kirsten Williams, Darren Latham, Fil Dunn, Anja Wettergren, Joe Tomaszewski. **Hobby Team:** Dave Andrews, Mark Jones, Chad Mierzwa. **Graphic Elements:** Neil Hodgson, Paul Rudge. **Graphic Design, Layout and Production:** Pete Borlace, Markus Trenkner, Sean Turtle, Tim Vincent, John Michelbach, Carl Dafforn, Kris Jaggers, Rachel Ryan, Chris Eggar, Simon Burton, Marc Elliott, Chris Ward, Sean Cutler, James Shardlow, Kris Shields, Madeleine Tighe. **Photography:** Stuart White, Ian Strickland, Glenn More, Kenton Mills. **Additional Hobby Content:** Matt Hutson, Dave Taylor, Paul Scott, John Shaffer, Andrew Taylor, Matt Toone, Dave Cross. **Sub-Editing:** Andrew Kenrick, Mark Latham, Talima Fox. **Thanks to:** Everyone who provided feedback and playtested the rules.

Several Astropaths, Servo-scribes and Tech-adepts were lost to the Dark Powers during the making of this product (they will be remembered).

Copyright © Games Workshop Ltd 2008. Assault on Black Reach, Games Workshop, the Games Workshop logo, GW, Citadel and the Citadel device, 'Eavy Metal, Eldar symbol devices, Eye of Terror, Warhammer, Warhammer 40,000, the Warhammer 40,000 device, the Double-Headed/Imperial Eagle device, 40K, Battle for Macragge, the Chaos factions and associated logos, Space Marine, Space Marine Chapters and Space Marine Chapter insignia, Eldar, Tyranid, Genestealer, Golden Demon, the Tau caste designations, Tau, Fire Warrior, Kroot, Necron, Ork, Ork devices, Chaos and all associated marks, the 'In the Grim Darkness of the Far Future' tagline, names, races and race insignia, characters, vehicles, locations, units, illustrations and images from the Warhammer 40,000 universe are either ®, TM and/or © Games Workshop Ltd 2000-2008, variably registered in the UK and other countries around the world. All Rights Reserved. 'Scatter' dice are UK registered design no. 2017484.

British Cataloguing-in-Publication Data. A catalogue record for this book is available from the British Library.

UK	US	Australia	Canada	Japan
Games Workshop	**Games Workshop**	**Games Workshop**	**Games Workshop**	**Games Workshop**
Willow Rd, Lenton	6721 Baymeadow Drive	23 Liverpool Street	2679 Bristol Circle,	Willow Rd, Lenton
Nottingham	Glen Burnie	Ingleburn	Units 2&3,Oakville	Nottingham
NG7 2WS	Maryland, 21060-6401	NSW 2565	Ontario, L6H 6Z8	NG7 2WS, UK

Great Depression and New Deal
Primary Sources

Great Depression and New Deal Primary Sources

Sharon M. Hanes
and
Richard C. Hanes
Allison McNeill,
Project Editor

Southern Sr. High Media Center
Harwood, Maryland 20776

402 32171221

Detroit • New York • San Diego • San Francisco • Cleveland • New Haven, Conn. • Waterville, Maine • London • Munich

THOMSON
GALE

Great Depression and New Deal: Primary Sources

Sharon M. Hanes and Richard C. Hanes

Project Editor
Allison McNeill

Permissions
Lori Hines

Imaging and Multimedia
Dean Dauphinais, Christine O'Bryan, Robert Duncan

Product Design
Pamela Galbreath, Cynthia Baldwin

Composition
Evi Seoud

Manufacturing
Rita Wimberley

©2003 by U·X·L. U·X·L is an imprint of The Gale Group, Inc., a division of Thomson Learning, Inc.

U·X·L® is a registered trademark used herein under license. Thomson Learning™ is a trademark used herein under license.

For more information, contact:
The Gale Group, Inc.
27500 Drake Rd.
Farmington Hills, MI 48331-3535
Or you can visit our Internet site at
http://www.gale.com

ALL RIGHTS RESERVED
No part of this work covered by the copyright hereon may be reproduced or used in any form or by any means—graphic, electronic, or mechanical, in-cluding photocopying, recording, tap-ing, Web distribution, or information storage retrieval systems—without the written permission of the publisher.

For permission to use material from this product, submit your request via Web at http://www.gale-edit.com/permis-sions, or you may download our Permis-sions Request form and submit your re-quest by fax or mail to:

Permissions Department
The Gale Group, Inc.
27500 Drake Rd.
Farmington Hills, MI 48331-3535
Permissions Hotline:
248-699-8006 or 800-877-4253, ext. 8006
Fax: 248-699-8074 or 800-762-4058

Cover photographs reproduced cour-tesy of the Library of Congress ("Mi-grant Mother," Dust storm); and cour-tesy of the Franklin D. Roosevelt Library (Roosevelt mural).

While every effort has been made to en-sure the reliability of the information presented in this publication, The Gale Group, Inc. does not guarantee the ac-curacy of the data contained herein. The Gale Group, Inc. accepts no payment for listing; and inclusion in the publication of any organization, agency, institution, publication, service, or individual does not imply endorsement by the editors or publisher. Errors brought to the atten-tion of the publisher and verified to the satisfaction of the publisher will be cor-rected in future editions.

LIBRARY OF CONGRESS CATALOGING-IN-PUBLICATION DATA

Hanes, Sharon M.
    Great Depression and New Deal. Primary sources / Sharon M. Hanes and Richard C. Hanes ; Allison McNeill, editor.
        p. cm.
    Summary: Presents an overview of the Great Depression through the words and writings of the time: more than twenty-five excerpts from speeches, poems, fic-tion and non-fiction works.
    Includes bibliographical references and index.
        ISBN 0-7876-6535-5 (hardcover)
    1. United States–History–1933-1945–Sources–Juvenile literature. 2. United States–History–1919-1933–Sources–Juvenile literature. 3. Depressions–1929–Unit-ed States–Sources–Juvenile literature. 4. New Deal, 1933-1939–Sources–Juvenile literature. [1. United States–History–1933-1945–Sources. 2. United States–Histo-ry–1919-1933–Sources. 3. Depressions–1929–United States–Sources. 4. New Deal, 1933-1939–Sources.] I. Hanes, Richard Clay, 1946- II. McNeill, Allison. III. Title.
E806 .H317 2002
973.917–dc21

2002015354

Printed in the United States of America
10 9 8 7 6 5 4 3 2 1

Contents

Introduction

Embedded within the timeline of a nation's history are certain extraordinary events that spur rapid change within the society and impact the political life and thinking of the people for decades thereafter. In the timeline of the United States, such events include the American Revolution (1775–83), the Civil War (1861–65), World War II (1939–45), and perhaps the Vietnam War (1954–75). Aside from wars, other momentous and highly influential events include the industrial revolution (roughly nineteenth century), the civil rights movement of the 1950s and 1960s, and the Great Depression (1929–41). The Great Depression was the longest and worst economic crisis in U.S. history. It was not only economically devastating for millions, but was a personal tragedy for Americans from the very young to the very old.

What could cause such a dramatic economic downturn in the United States? To most Americans it seemed the prosperity of the "roaring" 1920s would go on forever. Yet, throughout the 1920s economic difficulties in certain segments of the American economy began to surface. Industrialization, that is, the development of industries that mass-pro-

duced consumer goods such as washing machines and automobiles, dramatically affected the United States. Rolling off assembly lines at ever increasing rates, goods were touted by advertisers who encouraged consumers to borrow money to buy the goods, a practice known as buying on credit. In the 1920s American values of thrift and saving money increasingly gave way to accumulating debt as Americans bought the latest products on "credit" just as soon as the products appeared in the stores. Banks eagerly made loan after loan. However, by 1929 this buying had slowed. It seemed consumers could only buy so much.

The major share of wealth in the nation rested in the hands of a tiny percentage of individual families. The very wealthy could not sustain enough buying power to make up for the slowdown in buying by the rest of the population. Goods began to accumulate on store shelves forcing factories to slow down production and lay off workers.

Another sector of the U.S. economy experiencing difficulty was the agriculture sector. Farmers had been overproducing since the end of World War I (1914–18), even after the drop in overseas demand for their products. The glut of farm products had driven farm prices so low that farmers could barely earn a living much less buy consumer goods. Farm families still accounted for 25 to 30 percent of the U.S. population, so a significant number of Americans were already struggling.

Although these various signs of economic trouble began emerging in the 1920s, hardly anyone paid attention. The majority of Americans were enjoying prosperity as never before. So, when in October 1929 the U.S. stock market crashed, the American public was shocked. They suddenly realized the economic health of the nation was not as good as it had seemed. Billions of dollars were lost and small investors were wiped out. Although the stock market crash was only one of a number of factors leading to the Great Depression of the 1930s, in the public's mind it has always marked the start of the worst economic crisis in U.S. history. By 1932 twelve million workers, amounting to over 25 percent of the workforce, were jobless. Industrial production had dropped to 44 percent of the average in the 1920s. For those who kept their jobs, incomes dropped an average of 40 percent between 1929 and 1932.

For the first time many citizens questioned the U.S. system of democracy and capitalism (an economic system in which goods are owned by private businesses and price and production is decided privately). They also questioned the notion of individualism, the American belief that people can successfully make their own way in society without government intervention. The prevailing mood of the nation moved from opportunity to despair; from progress to survival. A philosophical tug of war raged between big business, who wanted to work out the country's economic woes voluntarily, and those who wanted government to begin regulating business. President Herbert Hoover (served 1929–1933) was unable to halt the economic slide.

The inauguration of Franklin D. Roosevelt as the thirty-second president of the United States in March 1933 signaled the beginning of a new relationship between Americans and their government. For the first time in U.S. history the people began to look to the government to aid in their economic well-being. For many Americans, President Roosevelt's introduction of an incredible variety of social and economic programs, known as the New Deal, brought hope again. People believed they had a leader who actually cared about their welfare and establishing economic safety nets. The New Deal programs were designed to first bring relief (food, clothing, monetary payments) to Americans hardest hit by the Depression. Next came the recovery and reform programs to stimulate the economy and put into place plans that would lessen the danger of future depressions. Government became intricately involved in business regulation, labor organizations, public support of the arts, social security, resource conservation, development of inexpensive and plentiful energy sources, stock market reform, farming reform, photodocumentary journalism, housing reform, public health programs, and increasing the number of minorities and women in public life. Business leaders and the well-to-do despaired that the atmosphere of *laissez-faire* (les-a-fair) government (in which industries operated free of government restraint) was over. Government regulations and higher taxes ended the long tradition of industry voluntarily regulating itself.

As the Depression lingered on through the 1930s, various segments of American society were affected differently. Those in the middle classes learned to "make do," creating

meals from simple ingredients, making their own clothes, finding entertainment at home with board games and listening to the radio, and helping other family members who had lost their jobs. The extreme competitiveness and consumption-oriented values of the 1920s gave way to cooperativeness and neighborly help. Those Americans already considered poor or part of a minority group suffered mightily during the Depression. In contrast America's wealthiest families, for the most part, seemingly ignored the Depression and continued their luxurious lifestyle.

Roosevelt's New Deal did not lead directly to major economic recovery for the United States. By the mid to late 1930s President Roosevelt hesitated to spend the amount of money necessary to push the economy into complete recovery. While the New Deal programs did not stop the Depression, they did end the dramatic plunge in the economy and gave food and shelter to those most in need. The Great Depression did not fully end until 1941, as the United States prepared for World War II. The mobilization of industry to manufacture massive quantities of war materials and the growth of the armed forces at last ended the Great Depression.

The extraordinary event of the Great Depression brought major change in how Americans view government. Historically the federal government was viewed as detached from the everyday activities of Americans. The severity of the Depression made Americans consider, even demand, that the federal government act to enhance and insure the well-being of its citizens. At the beginning of the twenty-first century debate continues over how far the government should go in guaranteeing the financial security of its citizens. Debates still rage over government regulation of business, individualism versus cooperation for the common good, and over specific issues such as the Social Security system, the role of labor unions in business, and the welfare system providing aid to the nation's poorest.

Sharon M. Hanes and Richard C. Hanes

Reader's Guide

The Great Depression, which took place between 1929 and 1941, was the deepest and most prolonged economic crisis in United States history. It is a story of great human suffering for many and the inspiring rise of some to meet the challenge. President Franklin D. Roosevelt introduced a diverse series of new federal programs, known collectively as the New Deal, that revamped the nation's governmental system. From the strife came the modern bureaucratic state providing economic safeguards for its citizens. America emerged as a profoundly different nation by 1941 than it had been in 1929. The New Deal did not end the Great Depression and lead to full economic recovery, but it did end the dramatic economic plunge, gave those most affected food and shelter, and reestablished hope in the future and faith in the U.S. economic system.

Great Depression and New Deal: Primary Sources tells the story of the Great Depression in the words of the people who lived it. Thirty full or excerpted documents provide a wide range of perspectives on this period in history. Included are excerpts from presidential press conferences, inaugural speeches, addresses to Congress, and radio addresses; later re-

flections by key government leaders; oral histories of those who experienced the economic crisis, including youth who rode the rails; lyrics of songs derived from the Great Depression experience; and reflections by photographers who recorded the poverty and desperation of the time.

Format

The excerpts in *Great Depression and New Deal: Primary Sources* are divided into eight chapters. Each of the chapters focuses on a specific theme: Crisis of the Great Depression; A New Deal For Americans; Sampling of Key New Deal Legislation; Everyday Living; On the Farm; Women's Voices; Youth Riding the Rails; and Literature and Songs of the Great Depression. Every chapter opens with a historical overview, followed by reprinted documents.

Each excerpt (or section of excerpts) includes the following features:

- **Introductory material** places the document and its author in a historical context.

- **Things to remember while reading** offers important background information about the featured text.

- **Excerpt** presents the document in its original spelling and format.

- **What happened next...** discusses the impact of the document and/or relevant historical events following the date of the document.

- **Did you know...** provides interesting facts about the document and its author.

- **Consider the following...** poses questions about the material for the reader to consider.

- **For More Information** offers resources for further study of the document and its author as well as sources used by the authors in writing the material.

Other features of *Great Depression and New Deal: Primary Sources* include numerous sidebar boxes highlighting interesting, related information. Sixty black-and-white photos and maps illustrate the text. In addition, each excerpt is accompanied by a glossary running in the margin alongside the

reprinted document that defines terms, people, and ideas. The volume begins with a timeline of events and a "Words to Know" section, and concludes with a general bibliography and subject index of people, places, and events discussed throughout *Great Depression and New Deal: Primary Sources.*

Great Depression and New Deal Reference Library

     Great Depression and New Deal: Primary Sources is only one component of the three-part U•X•L Great Depression and New Deal Reference Library. The other two titles in this set are:

- *Great Depression and New Deal: Almanac* (one volume) presents a comprehensive overview of the period in American history known as the Great Depression in sixteen chapters, each geared toward offering an understanding of a single element of the crisis; from the crash of the U.S. stock market in October 1929 to the end of the Depression in 1941 that came as a result of mobilization for World War II (1939–45).

- *Great Depression and New Deal: Biographies* (one volume) presents the life stories of twenty-nine individuals who played key roles in the governmental and social responses to the Depression. Profiled are well-known figures such as Franklin D. Roosevelt, Eleanor Roosevelt, Will Rogers, Frances Perkins, and Woody Guthrie, as well as lesser-known individuals such as Hallie Flanagan, head of the Federal Theatre Project, and Mary McLeod Bethune, educator and the first black American to head a federal agency.

- A cumulative index of all three titles in the U•X•L Great Depression and New Deal Reference Library is also available.

Advisors

     A note of appreciation is extended to the *Great Depression and New Deal: Primary Sources* advisors who provided invaluable suggestions when the work was in its formative stages:

     Frances Bryant Bradburn
     Director of Educational Technologies
     North Carolina Public Schools
     Raleigh, North Carolina

Elaine Ezell
Media Specialist
Bowling Green Junior High School
Bowling Green, Ohio

Dedication

To our son, Dustin, who endured numerous discussions and debates of New Deal policy and Great Depression issues over dinner and during car trips.

Special Thanks

Catherine Filip typed much of the manuscript. Much gratitude also goes to the advisors who guided the project throughout its course.

Comments and Suggestions

We welcome your comments on *Great Depression and New Deal: Primary Sources* and suggestions for other topics to consider. Please write: Editors, *Great Depression and New Deal: Primary Sources,* U•X•L, 27500 Drake Rd., Farmington Hills, Michigan 48331-3535; call toll-free: 1-800-877-4253; fax to (248) 699-8097; or send e-mail via http://www.gale.com.

Text Credits

Following is a list of the copyright holders who have granted us permission to reproduce excerpts from primary source documents in *Great Depression and New Deal: Primary Sources*. Every effort has been made to trace copyright; if omissions have been made, please contact us.

Copyrighted excerpts reproduced from the following periodicals:

Fawcett, John E. "A Hobo Memoir, 1936." *Indiana Magazine of History* v. XC (December 1994): pp. 346–364. Reproduced by permission.

Roosevelt, Eleanor. "In Defense of Curiosity." *Saturday Evening Post* (August 24, 1935): pp. 8, 9, 65, 66. Reproduced by permission.

Copyrighted excerpts reproduced from the following books:

Bethune, Mary McLeod. From "National Youth Administration," in *Building a Better World*. Indiana University Press, 1999. Copyright © 1999 by Indiana University Press. All right reserved. Reproduced by permission.

Davis, Kingsley. In *Youth in the Depression*. University of Chicago Press, 1935. Copyright © 1935 by University of Chicago Press. All rights reserved. Reproduced by permission.

Federal Writers' Project Works Progress Administration, Regional Staff. From "Till the River Rises" in *These Are Our Lives*. The University of North Carolina Press, 1939. Copyright © 1939 by The University of North Carolina Press, renewed 1967. All rights reserved. Reproduced by permission.

Hoover, Herbert. From "the President's News Conference of February 3, 1931" in *Public Papers of The Presidents of the United States, Herbert Hoover.* United States Government Printing Officer, 1976. Copyright © 1976 by United States Government Printing Officer. All rights reserved. Reproduced by permission.

Lumpkin, Katharine DuPre and Dorothy Wolff Douglas. From "Children on the Market," in *Child Workers in America*. Robert M. McBride & Company, 1937. Copyright © 1937 by Robert M. McBride & Company. All rights reserved. Reproduced by permission.

Perkins, Frances. From "Social Security," in *The Roosevelt I Knew*. The Viking Press, 1946. Copyright © 1946 by Frances Perkins, © renewal 1974 by Susanna W. Coggeshall. All rights reserved. Reproduced by permission of Viking Penguin, a division of Penguin Putnam Inc.

Perkins, Frances. From "Labor Under the New Deal and the New Frontier," in *Two Views of American Labor*. University of California, 1965. Copyright © 1965 by University of California. All rights reserved. Reproduced by permission.

Roosevelt, Franklin D. From "Annual Message to the Congress. January 3, 1938," in *The Public Papers and Addresses of Franklin D. Roosevelt, 1938 Volume, The Continuing Struggle for Liberalism*. The Macmillan Company, 1941. Copyright © by Franklin Delano Roosevelt. All rights reserved. Reproduced by permission.

Roosevelt, Franklin D. From "'I Pledge You—I Pledge Myself—to a New Deal for the American People.' The Governor Accepts the Nomination for Presidency, Chicago, Ill., July 2, 1932," in *The Public Papers and Addresses of Franklin D. Roosevelt, Volume One, The Genesis of The New Deal 1928–1932.*

Random House, 1938. Copyright © by Franklin Delano Roosevelt. All rights reserved. Reproduced by permission.

Roosevelt, Franklin D. From "Recommendation for Legislation to Provide Assistance for Repairing and Construction of Homes. May 14, 1934," in *The Public Papers and Addresses of Franklin D. Roosevelt, Volume Three, The Advance of Recovery and Reform 1934.* Random House, 1938. Copyright © by Franklin Delano Roosevelt. All rights reserved. Reproduced by permission.

Roosevelt, Franklin D. From "The First 'Fireside Chat'—An Intimate Talk with the People of the United States on Banking. March 12, 1933," in *The Public Papers and Addresses of Franklin D. Roosevelt, Volume Two, The Year of Crisis 1933.* Random House, 1938. Copyright © by Franklin Delano Roosevelt. All rights reserved. Reproduced by permission.

Steinbeck, John. From "Chapter Nineteen," in *The Grapes of Wrath.* The Viking Press, Inc., 1939. Copyright © 1939 renewed ©1967 by John Steinbeck. Reproduced by permission of Viking Penguin, a division of Penguin Putnam, Inc.

Terkel, Studs. From "Oscar Heline," in *Hard Times, An Oral History of the Great Depression.* Pantheon Books, 1970. Copyright © 1970 by Studs Terkel. Reproduced by permission of Donadio & Olson, Inc.

Van Amber, Rita. In *Volume II, Part I, Stories and Recipes of the Great Depression Of the 1930's.* Van Amber Publishers, 1993. Copyright © by Library of Congress. All rights reserved. Reproduced by permission.

Copyrighted excerpts reproduced from the following songs:
"Brother, Can You Spare a Dime?," by E.Y. Harburg and Jay Gorney. © 1932 (Renewed) Glocca Morra Music (ASCAP), Gorney Music (ASCAP), and Warner Bros. Inc. Rights For Extended Renewal Term in The United States Controlled by Glocca Morra Music and Gorney Music Publishers administered by Next Decade Entertainment, Inc. All rights reserved. Used by permission of Next Decade Entertainment, Inc. and Warner Bros. Publications U.S. Inc., Miami, FL 33014.

"Happy Days Are Here Again," by Jack Yellen and Milton Ager. © 1929 (Renewed) Warner Bros. Inc. All rights reserved. Used by permission of Warner Bros. Publications U.S. Inc., Miami, FL 33014.

"Over the Rainbow," by Harold Arlen and E.Y. Harburg. © 1938 (Renewed 1966) Metro–Goldwyn–Mayer Inc. © 1939 (Renewed 1967) EMI Feist Catalog Inc. All rights reserved. Used by permission. Warner Bros. Publications U.S. Inc., Miami, FL 33014.

"Pastures of Plenty," "Roll On, Columbia," "Storm Disaster," and "I Ain't Got No Home," words and music by Woody Guthrie, TRO © copyright 1960 and 1963, Ludlow Music, Inc., New York, N.Y.

"We're in the Money," by Al Dubin and Harry Warren. © 1933 (Renewed) Warner Bros. Inc. All rights reserved. Used by permission. Warner Bros. Publications U.S. Inc., Miami, FL 33014.

Great Depression Timeline

January 17, 1920 The Eighteenth Amendment, known as Prohibition, goes into effect, banning the sale and manufacture of all alcoholic beverages in the United States.

1921–1932 With every passing year, Prohibition is ignored more and more while the gangsters of organized crime become immensely wealthy from "bootlegging" illegal alcohol.

1923 The value of stocks on the U.S. stock market begins a six-year upward climb.

1928 "Amos 'n' Andy," a radio program, premieres and becomes the most popular radio show through the 1930s.

November 1928 Republican Herbert Hoover is elected president of the United States. His policies would prove ineffective in fighting the Great Depression that struck in October 1929.

October 24, 1929 Known as "Black Thursday," a record-breaking crash on the New York Stock Exchange be-

Thousands are left penniless after the October 1929 stock market crash. *AP/Wide World Photo.*

gins several weeks of market panics. Many investors lose vast sums of money when the value of stocks plummets. Approximately 12.8 million shares of stock are sold in one day, most at prices far below their values only a few days earlier.

October 29, 1929 Known as "Black Tuesday," the value of stocks on the New York Stock Market continues its dramatic decline. Approximately 16,410,000 shares, a record number, are sold. The nation's economy steadily erodes into the Great Depression, the worst economic crisis in U.S. history.

1930–1932 Gangster movies are at their height of popularity.

1930 Hostess food manufacturer creates the Twinkie, an inexpensive treat for economy-minded Americans.

1930 Congress authorizes construction of Hoover Dam, known as Boulder Dam during the New Deal, on the Colorado River. Construction begins in 1930 and is completed in 1936. The project provides thousands of jobs.

1931–1932 More than 3,600 banks suspend operations as the Depression deepens and thousands lose their jobs and incomes.

1931 Sales of glass jars for preserving food at home increases dramatically. Preserving food decreases a family's food expenses.

1931 A drought begins in the Eastern states during the summer and quickly spreads to the Midwest and Great Plains. The drought will continue throughout the decade resulting in "dust bowl" conditions.

1931 New York City reports ninety-five cases of death by starvation as the number of unemployed and those going hungry increases.

October 24, 1931 Alphonse Capone, the nation's most notorious gangster, receives an eleven-year prison sentence for income tax evasion.

1932 Jigsaw puzzles are mass-produced for the first time and provide inexpensive entertainment.

Dust storms ravage the Midwest throughout the 1930s. *Library of Congress.*

1932 Prices for farm produce hit bottom as farmer unrest rises.

1932 Sixty percent of the U.S. population still faithfully pay the few cents it costs to attend movies.

1932 The Depression spawns cuts in educational budgets affecting teacher salaries and programs offered and leads to school closures, especially in rural areas.

January 22, 1932 Congress establishes the Reconstruction Finance Corporation to provide federal financial support to the banking system.

July 2, 1932 Franklin Delano Roosevelt delivers a speech accepting the Democratic nomination for president pledging "a new deal for the American people."

July 28, 1932 Thousands of unemployed and financially strapped World War I veterans and their families, known as the Bonus Army, march on Washington, DC, seeking early payment of previously promised bonus pay, but are denied by Congress. Violence erupts, reflecting badly on the Hoover administration.

November 1932 Roosevelt handily wins the presidential election over incumbent Republican Herbert Hoover but will not be inaugurated until March 4, 1933.

1933–1935 Midwestern outlaws rob banks and kills citizens on wild rampages through the nation's heartland.

1933 Unemployment reaches 25 percent of the nation's workforce.

1933 Estimates reveal that well over one million Americans are homeless and almost one-fourth are riding the railroads in search of work or aimlessly drifting. Youth comprise 40 percent of that number on the rails.

1933 The number of marriages declines 40 percent from the 1920s level as couples, unable to earn a living wage, postpone marriage.

1933 The number of lynchings of black Americans in the United States during the Great Depression peaks at twenty-eight.

Striking farmers demand a solution to low prices paid for goods. *©Minnesota Historical Society/CORBIS.*

Many World War I veterans are in serious financial trouble during the Depression. *AP/Wide World Photo.*

As first lady, Eleanor Roosevelt champions the causes of women and children. *Franklin D. Roosevelt Library.*

Franklin D. Roosevelt prepares to deliver the first "fireside chat." *AP/Wide World Photo.*

1933 Membership in teachers' unions such as the American Federation of Teachers (AFT) increases rapidly in reaction to budget and staff cuts due to the Depression.

1933 Big, splashy musicals become hit movies taking Americans' minds off the hard economic times.

1933 Child actress Shirley Temple is introduced to movie audiences.

1933 The Chicago World's Fair opens.

March 4, 1933 With the U.S. banking system all but paralyzed, Franklin D. Roosevelt is inaugurated as president declaring "there is nothing to fear but fear itself."

March 6, 1933 At 1:00 A.M. President Roosevelt orders a nationwide "bank holiday" from Monday, March 6 through Thursday, March 9, and then extends it through March 12.

March 6, 1933 First Lady Eleanor Roosevelt begins her weekly news conferences open only to women journalists.

March 9, 1933 Congress begins a special session to approve legislation aimed at economic relief and recovery. Congress passes the Emergency Bank Act in a successful effort to restore public confidence in the banking system.

March 12, 1933 President Roosevelt delivers his first radio "fireside chat," explaining to the American people what has happened in the U.S. banking system.

March 13, 1933 Most U.S. banks successfully reopen.

Mid-March 1933 President Roosevelt begins the first of his informal and informative presidential news conferences.

March 31, 1933 The Civilian Conservation Corps (CCC) is established providing jobs in conservation activities for young Americans replanting forests, soil conservation, and flood control.

May 12, 1933 Congress passes the Agricultural Adjustment Act (AAA), designed to raise farm prices by encouraging farmers to reduce production.

May 12, 1933 Congress passes the Emergency Farm Mortgage Act to provide loans to farmers in heavy debt.

May 12, 1933 Congress passes the Federal Emergency Relief Act (FERA), providing funds to assist state relief programs helping the unemployed, aged, and ill.

May 17, 1933 The Tennessee Valley Authority (TVA) is created to bring economic development to the Southeast through construction of numerous dams and hydropower plants.

May 27, 1933 Congress passes the Federal Securities Act, requiring companies and stockbrokers to provide full information about new stocks to potential investors.

June 13, 1933 Congress passes the Home Owners' Refinancing Act, which creates the Home Owners'Loan Corporation (HOLC) to provide loans to homeowners facing the loss of their homes because they cannot make payments.

June 16, 1933 Congress passes the Farm Credit Act. It formalizes the earlier-created Farm Credit Administration, which established a system of banking institutions for farmers.

June 16, 1933 Congress passes the Banking Act, also known as the Glass-Steagall Act, establishing the Federal Deposit Insurance Corporation (FDIC) insuring individual bank accounts against loss.

June 16, 1933 Congress passes the National Industrial Recovery Act establishing codes of fair practice for industry and business and creating the National Recovery Administration (NRA).

June 16, 1933 The Public Works Administration (PWA) is created to distribute almost $6 billion between 1933 and 1939 for public works projects, including construction of roads, tunnels, bridges, dams, power plants, and hospitals.

June 16, 1933 Congress finishes the special session, an intensive period of lawmaking that becomes known as the First Hundred Days.

Young boys living at a Washington, D.C., Hooverville. *Corbis Corporation.*

Dust Bowl migrants in search of work and shelter. *Library of Congress.*

The Civil Works Administration temporarily provides work for many of the jobless in winter 1933–34. *AP/Wide World Photo.*

November 9, 1933 Roosevelt establishes the Civil Works Administration (CWA) to assist unemployed workers through the winter months.

December 5, 1933 The thirtieth state ratifies the Twenty-first Amendment ending Prohibition, which banned the sale of all alcoholic beverages.

1934–1935 J. Edgar Hoover's Special Agents of the Federal Bureau of Investigation (FBI) capture or kill all of the famous Midwest outlaws and restore confidence in U.S. law enforcement.

January 31, 1934 Congress passes the Farm Mortgage Refinancing Act providing $2 billion in loans to refinance farm loans.

June 6, 1934 Congress passes the Securities Exchange Act that prohibits certain activities in stock market trading, sets penalties and establishes the Securities Exchange Commission (SEC) to oversee stock market trading.

June 18, 1934 Congress passes the Indian Reorganization Act (Wheeler-Howard Act) establishing the cornerstone of New Deal Indian policy.

June 19, 1934 Congress passes the Communications Act that creates the Federal Communications Commission (FCC) to oversee the nation's mass-communications industry.

June 28, 1934 Congress passes the National Housing Act, creating the Federal Housing Administration (FHA) to assist homeowners in buying a new house in hopes of spurring the construction industry. This act is the last piece of legislation passed under the First New Deal that began with legislation in March 1933.

1935 Warner Brothers' sensational hit movie *G-Men* immortalizes J. Edgar Hoover as America's number one cop, made his "government men," later known as FBI agents, famous, and helped restore a general respect for law enforcement.

1935 In one week people buy twenty million Monopoly games, providing inexpensive entertainment.

1935 More than 500,000 men are enrolled in 2,600 Civilian Conservation Corps camps across the United States.

April 8, 1935 Congress passes the Emergency Relief Appropriation Act creating the Works Progress Administration (WPA) and providing almost $5 billion for work relief for the unemployed for such projects as construction of airports, schools, hospitals, roads, and public buildings. This act marks the beginning of the Second New Deal

April 27, 1935 Congress passes the Soil Conservation Act establishing the Soil Conservation Service (SCS) to aid farmers suffering drought and massive soil erosion.

April 30, 1935 Roosevelt creates the Resettlement Administration (RA) to help poor farmers either improve the use of their lands or move to better lands. The agency's Historical Section begins a major photodocumentary project of the Depression.

May 11, 1935 Roosevelt creates the Rural Electrification Administration (REA) to bring inexpensive electricity to rural areas.

May 27, 1935 In one of several rulings against New Deal programs, the U.S. Supreme Court in *Schechter Poultry Corporation v. United States* rules the National Industrial Recovery Act is unconstitutional thus removing legal protections for labor unions. This day becomes known as "Black Monday."

June 26, 1935 Roosevelt creates the National Youth Administration (NYA) to provide part-time jobs to high school and college students and other unemployed youth.

July 1, 1935 The Federal Deposit Insurance Corporation (FDIC) begins operation providing stability to the banking system by insuring bank deposits.

July 5, 1935 Congress passes the National Labor Relations Act, better known as the Wagner Act, to support the right of workers to organize and bargain collectively with employers over working conditions, benefits,

Many unemployed men are given paying jobs upon enrolling in the Civilian Conservation Corps.
Corbis Corporation.

Thousands of wandering youth are given training or jobs as part of the National Youth Administration.
National Archives.

Franklin D. Roosevelt signs the Social Security Act into law. *AP/Wide World Photo.*

Eleanor Roosevelt and Lorena Hickok are key in shaping New Deal policies. *Franklin D. Roosevelt Library.*

and wages. The act also bans certain unfair business practices.

August 2, 1935 Created as part of the WPA, the Federal One program is established to provide jobs for the unemployed in music, theater, writing, and art.

August 14, 1935 Congress passes the Social Security Act establishing a program of social insurance to aid the unemployed, the elderly in retirement, needy children and mothers, and the blind.

August 23, 1935 Congress passes the Banking Act strengthening the Federal Reserve System.

August 30, 1935 Congress passes the Wealth Tax Act creating higher tax rates for the wealthy and corporate and inheritance taxes.

November 1935 The Federal Surplus Commodities Corporation is established to continue distributing food to the needy.

November 9, 1935 Labor leader John L. Lewis establishes the Committee of Industrial Organizations to represent semi-skilled and unskilled laborers of the mass production industries.

1936 Mary McLeod Bethune is named head of the Division of Negro Affairs of the National Youth Administration becoming the first black American to head a government agency.

January 6, 1936 The U.S. Supreme Court in *United States v. Butler* rules the Agricultural Adjustment Act is unconstitutional.

June 16, 1936 Congress passes the Flood Control Act in response to massive floods in the Ohio and Mississippi River areas.

November 1936 Franklin Roosevelt wins a landslide reelection capturing a record 61 percent of the vote.

December 30, 1936 Sit-down strikes shutdown seven General Motors plants in Flint, Michigan. The company will give in to worker demands by February 11, 1937.

1937 Roosevelt appoints attorney William Hastie as the first black American federal judge in U.S. history.

1937 Author Erskine Caldwell and photographer Margaret Bourke-White publish *You Have Seen Their Faces.*

1937 Kraft introduces the "instant" macaroni and cheese dinner and Hormel introduces Spam meat. The low cost of both items helps feed families who are on a tight budget.

February 5, 1937 Roosevelt introduces a proposal, known as the "court packing plan," to reorganize the U.S. Supreme Court. The plan attracts substantial public opposition.

The Bankhead-Jones Farm Tenancy Act helps tenant farmers purchase their own land. *Library of Congress.*

May 24, 1937 The U.S. Supreme Court upholds the constitutionality of the Social Security Act.

July 22, 1937 Congress passes the Bankhead-Jones Farm Tenancy Act making low interest loans available to tenant farmers, farm laborers, and small landowners, many of whom are victims of the Dust Bowl, to purchase or expand their own lands.

August 20, 1937 The Bonneville Power Act establishes the Bonneville Power Administration to market public power in the Pacific Northwest.

September 1, 1937 Roosevelt creates the Farm Security Administration, absorbing the Resettlement Administration including the photography project.

September 3, 1937 Congress passes the National Housing Act, known as the Wagner-Steagall Housing Act, creating the U.S. Housing Authority to oversee construction of low-cost housing.

October 1937 An economic "recession" begins as industrial production and farm prices fall and unemployment rises. In hopes of never again using the term "depression," President Roosevelt coins the term "recession."

"Migrant Mother," by FSA photographer Dorothea Lange. *Library of Congress.*

February 16, 1938 Congress passes the new Agricultural Adjustment Act providing new price supports for farmers and promoting conservation practices.

June 24, 1938 Congress passes the Food, Drug, and Cosmetic Act.

June 25, 1938 The Fair Labor Standards Act places legal protections over child labor, minimum wages, and maxi-

A scene from the 1940 movie, *The Grapes of Wrath*. *Corbis Corporation.*

Woody Guthrie composed around twenty Dust Bowl ballads in the late 1930s. *Library of Congress.*

mum hours. This act is the last legislation of the Second New Deal.

October 30, 1938 Orson Welles' *Mercury Theatre of the Air* broadcasts a radio adaptation of H.G. Wells' 1898 novel *The War of the Worlds* causing widespread panic.

1939 Eighty percent of American households own radios.

1939 The Golden Gate International Exposition opens in San Francisco and the New York World's Fair opens in New York City.

1939 The Federal Writers Project publishes *These Are Our Lives* and John Steinbeck publishes *The Grapes of Wrath*.

1939 Drought comes to an end as rains return to the Great Plains in the fall.

1939 Reporter Edward R. Murrow broadcasts from London, England, during the German bombing raids on the city shifting public concerns away from domestic economic issues to foreign issues.

1939 World famous American opera singer Marian Anderson is denied the opportunity to perform in a private concert hall in Washington, DC, because she is black, leading to a major public backlash against racism.

May 16, 1939 The Food Stamp program begins.

August 10, 1939 Congress passes the Social Security Act Amendments adding old age and survivors' insurance benefits for dependents and survivors.

1941 Roosevelt signs an executive order prohibiting racial discrimination in the defense industry, the first such proclamation since Reconstruction in the 1870s.

1941 Author James Agee and photographer Walker Evans publish *Let Us Now Praise Famous Men*.

July 9, 1941 President Roosevelt announces extensive preparations in case of U.S. entrance into World War II.

December 7, 1941 Japan bombs U.S. military installations at Pearl Harbor, Hawaii, leading the United States to enter World War II in both Europe and the Pacific.

January 16, 1942 The War Production Board is established to direct war mobilization.

April 1942 The War Manpower Commission is created to help allocate manpower to industries and military services.

April 12, 1945 Franklin Roosevelt suddenly dies at sixty-three years of age from a cerebral hemorrhage.

Franklin D. Roosevelt was the cornerstone of New Deal relief and recovery.
Franklin D. Roosevelt Library.

Words to Know

A

abstinence: A voluntary decision not to drink alcoholic beverages.

activist: One who aggressively promotes a cause such as seeking change in certain social, economic, or political conditions in society.

amortize: To allow a loan to be repaid with stable monthly payments that include both principal and interest; amortizing mortgages allow buyers to gradually repay the principal balance until the loan is paid back in full .

appraisal: The set value of a property as determined by the estimate of an authorized person.

appropriations: Money authorized by Congress to an agency for a special purpose.

atomic bomb: A bomb whose explosive force comes from a nuclear splitting-apart of atoms releasing a large amount of energy.

attorney general: The chief law officer of a state or country and head of the legal department. In the United States, the person is head of the U.S. Department of Justice and is a member of the president's cabinet.

B

bank holiday: The legal suspension of bank operation for a period of time.

bank run: A sudden demand to withdraw deposits from a bank; bank runs occurred after the stock market crash of 1929, when depositors feared that their banks were unstable.

benefits: Financial aid (such as insurance or retirement pension) in time of sickness, old age, or unemployment. Also holidays, vacations, and other privileges provided by an employer in addition to hourly wages or salary.

big business: Large and influential businesses such as industries or financial institutions.

Black Cabinet: An informal organization of black Americans serving in various federal positions that advised President Franklin Roosevelt on black issues through the late 1930s.

bootlegger: A person who illegally transports liquor.

boycott: A refusal by a group of persons to buy goods or services from a business until the business meets their demands.

breadlines: During the Depression, long lines of unemployed people waiting to receive a free meal of soup and a chunk of bread from a charity or soup kitchen.

broker: One who buys or sells a stock for an investor and charges a fee for the service.

budget: The amount of money a person or family has to spend on food, clothing, shelter, and other necessities.

buying on margin: The purchase of stock by paying some cash down and borrowing the rest of the purchase price.

C

cabinet: An official group of advisors to the U.S. president including the heads of the various major governmental departments such as Department of Commerce.

capital: Money invested in a business and used to operate that business. Capital is the amount banks owe their owners.

capitalism: An economic system in which goods are privately owned and prices, production, and distribution of goods are determined by competition in a free market.

chain gangs: Groups of convicts chained together while working outside the prison.

collective bargaining: Negotiation between representatives of an employer and representatives of labor, with both sides working to reach agreement on wages, job benefits, and working conditions.

collectivism: Shared ownership of goods by all members of a group; a political or economic system in which production and distribution are controlled by all members of a group.

commercial bank: A bank that offers checking accounts, savings accounts, and personal and business loans.

communism: A theory calling for the elimination of private property so that goods are owned in common and available to all; a system of government in which a single party controls all aspects of society, as in the Union of Soviet Socialist Republics (U.S.S.R.) from 1917 until 1990.

conservation: The planned management of natural resources, such as soil and forests.

conservative: A person who holds traditional views and who seeks to preserve established institutions; a con-

servative approach to education, for example, stresses traditional basic subject matter and traditional methods of teaching.

cooperative: A private, nonprofit enterprise, locally owned and managed by the members it serves and incorporated (established as a legal entity that can hold property or be subject to lawsuits) under state law.

corporate volunteerism: To encourage business to support a public program or goal through voluntary actions rather than by government regulation.

craft union: A type of union that represents workers having a particular skill, regardless of their workplace.

cutting lever: The device on rail cars that can uncouple or detach rail cars from each other.

D

default: Failure to meet the payment terms of a legal contract, such as failure to make payments to repay a home loan; in cases of default, lenders may begin foreclosure proceedings to regain their losses.

dependents: People who must rely on another person for their livelihood; generally applied to children age eighteen and younger.

deportation: The removal of immigrant noncitizens from a country.

desegregation: To stop the practice of separating the races in public places such as public schools.

direct relief: Money, food, or vouchers given to needy people by the government for support. This term is not commonly used in the United States anymore; the current term is "welfare."

dividend: A payment made from a corporation's profits to its stockholders.

documentary literature: Articles or books describing actual events or real persons in a factual way.

documentary photograph: A photographic image in black and white or color that is realistic, factual, and useful as a historical document.

domestic goods: Goods related to home life; also, goods produced within the nation as opposed to foreign-made goods.

drought: A long period of little or no rainfall.

drug trafficking: Buying or selling illegal drugs; drug dealing.

E

electrification: The process or event in which a house, farm, industry, or locality is connected to an electric power source.

entrepreneur: An individual willing to take a risk in developing a new business.

eviction: To force a tenant from their home by legal process.

executive order: A statement written and issued by the president that uses some part of an existing law or the U.S. Constitution to enforce an action.

exposure: Being unsheltered and unprotected from the harsh weather elements, such as wind, rain, or cold, to an extent leading to illness or death.

F

foreclosure: A legal proceeding begun by a lender, usually a bank, to take possession of property when the property owner fails to make payments; in a home or farm foreclosure the lender seizes and auctions off the borrower's property to pay off the mortgage.

G

genre: A category of entertainment, such as radio comedy, drama, news, or soap operas.

H

hobo: A tramp, vagrant, or migratory worker.

holding companies: A company that controls one or more other companies through stock ownership.

Hoovervilles: "Towns" of shacks and other crude shelters put up by homeless people; sarcastically named after President Herbert Hoover, whom many felt did nothing to help Americans devastated by the Great Depression.

hopper cars: Rail cars that can readily dump their loads out the bottom.

humanitarian: One who helps others improve their welfare.

hydroelectric power: Electricity generated from the energy of swift-flowing streams or waterfalls.

I

immigration: Legal or illegal entry into a country by foreigners who intend to become permanent residents.

incentives: Something that encourages people to take action such as a guarantee of substantial profits for business leaders.

industrial mobilization: To rapidly transform or change an industry from one manufacturing household or peace-time goods to production of war materials in the time of war for government service.

industrial union: A union that represents all workers, skilled and unskilled, in a particular workplace.

infrastructure: Basic facilities and developments that form a foundation of an economic system including roads, airports, power plants, and military installations.

installment buying: Purchasing items on credit; making a down payment and, after taking possession of the item, paying off the rest of the cost with monthly payments.

interest: Money paid to a lender (in addition to the principal amount borrowed) for use of the lender's money.

L

labor leader: An individual who encourages workers to formally organize so as to more effectively negotiate better working conditions and wages from the employer.

labor movement: The collective effort by workers and labor organizations to seek better working conditions.

labor unions: Employee organizations established to seek improved working conditions and wages from employers.

laissez-faire (les-a-fair): A French term that describes the general philosophy of a government that chooses not to intervene in economic or social affairs; in French the term means "let people do as they choose."

leftist: A person promoting radical or socialistic politics in the form of liberal reform or revolutionary change.

lobby: A group of persons attempting to influence lawmakers.

lynching: The murder of an individual, most commonly a black American by a mob of white Americans, with no legal authority, usually by hanging.

M

making do: Using items on hand to stretch a budget. For example, sewing one's own clothes instead of buying them at a store, or using leftovers and other simple ingredients to spread meals over several days.

maldistribution: An uneven distribution of income or wealth; if the distribution is too unbalanced, it can cause general economic problems.

mass media: Various means of communication such as radio, movies, newspapers, and magazines that reach large numbers of people.

migrant workers: Laborers who travel from place to place to harvest farm crops for various farmers as the crops mature through the seasons.

missions: A place to aid the needy and preach the gospel, often located in poorer city areas.

mobilization: Preparations for war, including assembling of materials and military personnel.

mortgage: A legal document by which property is pledged as security for the repayment of a debt; when a buyer takes out a loan from the bank to purchase a home, the buyer pledges the home as security; if the buyer defaults on the loan, the bank takes the home to pay the debt.

municipal: A local government of a town or city.

mural: A painting applied directly onto a permanent wall.

N

New Dealers: Influential members of President Roosevelt's administration who promoted economic and social programs designed to lead the nation to economic recovery.

newsreels: Short films presenting current events.

O

old-age insurance: Assurance of cash payments, generally made monthly, to retired workers; also called a pension plan.

oral history: The memories of an event or time, captured in the words of the person who lived it.

organized crime: A specialized form of crime carried out by loosely or rigidly structured networks of gangs with certain territorial boundaries.

P

principal: The original amount of money loaned; a buyer must repay the principal and also pay the lender interest for the use of the money.

private sector: Businesses not subsidized or directed by the government but owned and operated by private citizens.

productivity: The rate at which goods are produced.

progressive tax: Taxing the income of wealthy individuals at a higher rate than those with lower incomes.

Prohibition: The period from 1920 to 1933 during which a legal restriction against the manufacture, sale, or distribution of alcoholic beverages was in effect in the United States. Officially known as the Eighteenth Amendment.

proletarian literature: Writing about the working class largely for working class consumption.

public utility: A government-regulated business that provides an essential public service, such as electric power.

public works projects: Government funded projects often for providing jobs for the unemployed such as construction of roads, bridges, airfields, and public buildings.

pump priming: Federal government spending designed to encourage consumer purchases; during the Depression the federal government spent money to create jobs through work relief programs, reasoning that if enough people received wages and began buying goods and services, the economy would improve.

R

racketeering: A person who obtains money through fraud or bribery. In the 1930s, gangsters worked their way into positions of authority in regular labor unions and then stole money from the union's pension and health funds.

recession: A slump in the economy; another term for "depression."

reclamation: A program of converting land unsuited for farming to agricultural production by providing water through irrigation systems.

refinance: To set up new terms for repayment of a loan that are beneficial to the borrower.

relief: Easing the strife of the needy by providing food, money, shelter, or jobs. (See also direct relief and work relief.)

reservations: Tracts of public land formally set aside for exclusive use by American Indians.

retrenchment: Cutbacks in school budgets, including cuts in teacher salaries, number of classes, and number of teachers.

run: Unexpected numerous withdrawals from a bank by depositors fearful of the soundness of the bank.

S

scab: A person who refuses to join a strike and fills the job of a striking worker.

school board: A local committee in charge of public education in their area.

school district: A region or locality within which the public schools share an overall budget and common leadership through a school board.

securities: Stocks or bonds.

sharecroppers: **Farmers who rent the land that they work and who use the landowner's tools; sharecroppers give part of the harvest to the landowner.**

shysters: Lawyers who use questionable or unprofessional methods.

sit-down strike: A refusal to work conducted by laborers who stay at their workstations and block employers from replacing them with other workers.

slum: An overcrowded urban area characterized by poverty and run-down housing.

social insurance: A broad term referring to government-sponsored social well-being programs, such as old-age pensions, unemployment support, workers' compen-

sation for those injured on the job, and health care programs.

social legislation: Laws that address social needs such as assistance for the elderly, retirement payments, unemployment support, workers' compensation, and health care programs.

social reconstructionism: A radical philosophy in education that calls for a new, more equitable social order to be established through classroom instruction in public schools.

soup kitchen: A place where food is offered free or at a very low cost to the needy.

speakeasy: A place where alcoholic beverages were sold illegally during Prohibition.

speculation: Buying stocks and/or other high-risk investments with the assumption that they can always be sold at a higher price.

standard of living: The level of consumption by individuals or a society as reflected by the quality of goods and services available.

strike: An organized effort by workers to gain official recognition, better working conditions, or higher wages by refusing to work.

suburb: A community on the outskirts of a city.

suffrage: The right to vote.

survivor benefits: Monthly cash benefits paid to the surviving family members of a worker who has died. Survivors may include a spouse, dependent children under eighteen years of age, and a dependent parent age sixty-two or older.

syndicate: An association or network of groups that cooperate to carry out certain business or criminal activities.

syndication: An agency that buys articles or photographs and sells them for publication at the same time in numerous newspapers.

T

temperance: Moderation or abstinence in the use of alcoholic beverages.

tenant farmers: Farmers who rent the land they work but who use their own tools; tenant farmers give part of the harvested crops to the landowner.

tenement: A large housing structure containing apartment dwellings that barely meet minimum standards of sanitation, safety, and comfort.

trade unions: Labor unions in which the workers share a common craft in contrast to general labor unions in which workers share a common employment in a common industry.

transient: A person traveling around, usually in search of work.

U

underworld: The world of organized crime.

unemployment insurance: Cash payments made for a limited period of time to workers who involuntarily lose their job; workers must be able and willing to work when a new job is available.

union: An organized group of workers joined together for a common purpose, such as negotiating with management for better working conditions or higher wages.

U.S. Mint: The place where U.S. money is produced.

V

vocational education: Providing instruction or training for a particular trade.

W

welfare: The health and prosperity of an individual or group; also financial assistance to those in need.

white-collar workers: Professional workers whose jobs do not normally involve manual labor.

work relief: A government assistance program that provides a needy person with a paying job instead of money, food, or vouchers (known as direct relief). Different from the twenty-first-century welfare-to-work program, work relief involves government-sponsored projects; the "work" in welfare-to-work is in the private sector. The term "work relief" is not commonly used anymore in the United States.

workers' compensation: A system of insurance designed to provide cash benefits and medical care to workers who sustain a work-related illness or injury.

Great Depression and New Deal Primary Sources

Crisis of the Great Depression

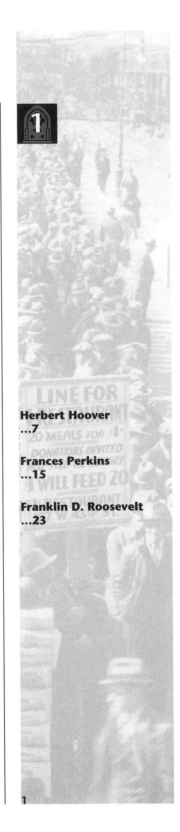

Exciting, fascinating, entertaining, prosperous—all these terms describe the decade of the 1920s, commonly known as the Roaring Twenties. The U.S. population was entering a new era and enjoying a new lifestyle. U.S. soldiers had just helped the Allies win World War I (1914–18), which had been dubbed "the war to end all wars." Women had gained the right to vote. Henry Ford (1863–1947) made the amazing gasoline automobile affordable for many Americans. For the most part, Americans were employed and busy purchasing the array of new goods that flowed out of factories at an ever faster rate. City homes were being supplied with electricity, which enabled families to use laborsaving electric appliances such as washing machines and vacuum cleaners and to replace the ice box with an electric refrigerator. More and more Americans brought radios into their homes, and the silent moving pictures (movies) captivated audiences in extravagant movie houses. Stock speculation gripped the country. (Stock speculation is the practice of buying stocks, often using borrowed money, with the expectation that the stocks' value will rise and make vast profits for the investor. Stocks are shares in the ownership of a corporation.) Stock values had increased

Causes of the Depression

The Great Depression began in October 1929 with the crash of the U.S. stock market, located on Wall Street in New York City. A common misconception is that the crash was the cause of the Great Depression. Actually, historians recognize a number of causes, and it is impossible to pinpoint which was the most important cause. The causes historians have identified include the following:

- The agricultural industry was overproducing farm products, and the surplus caused prices to drop. In addition, the European market did not need American farm goods as much as it had during World War I (1914–18).

- Manufacturing industries had produced more consumer goods than Americans could buy. By 1929 stores and warehouses bulged with goods, so manufacturers began cutting back production and laying off workers.

- Roughly 75 percent of Americans had no money to save after purchasing necessities. Most of America's wealth was in the hands of a very few. The very wealthy spent money on luxury items, but this spending could not counteract the increasing lack of spending on the part of the majority of people. Additionally, after the stock market crash in October 1929, the very wealthy, in

throughout the 1920s, going on a wild upward swing between 1926 and October 1929. Because of speculative buying, the price of a company's stock was often far above the real value of the company. For example, stock of Radio Corporation of America (RCA) sold for $94.50 a share in March 1928. By September 1929 it cost $505.00 to buy one share.

Despite the apparent economic boom, all was not well with the U.S. economy in the 1920s. Although largely ignored by the general public and politicians alike, ominous storm clouds were on the horizon. American farmers had been beset with economic troubles since the end of World War I, when demand for farm products declined as the European nations were again able to produce food for themselves. The farming families represented one-third of the U.S. population. Acutely affected by the farmers' lack of income, thousands of small rural banks had been forced to close. These rural bank closures were symptomatic of an overall weaken-

order to conserve their riches, quit investing in businesses and manufacturing industries.

- The U.S. banking system was weakening as thousands of small, rural, undiversified banks failed when farmers could not repay loans. The Federal Reserve (America's central bank) took little action.

- Holding companies had become a common part of U.S. business. These companies produced no real product, instead only managing other businesses. Americans who invested in holding companies were at risk, because such companies could collapse more easily in this "house of cards" structure.

- Investors were buying stocks with loaned money and assuming the stocks' value would continue to go higher and higher. For example, if an investor wanted to buy a $100 stock certificate, he could buy it with $10 of his own money and $90 borrowed from a stockbroker. If the stocks price increased to $120, the investor could sell, pay back the broker $90, and have $30 to reinvest. However, if the stock's value dropped to $80, the investor would have to come up with $10 of his own money just to pay back the broker. Of course, in reality, investors deal in hundreds, even thousands, of stock certificates, greatly multiplying the problem.

ing in the U.S. banking system. Manufacturing industries had overproduced consumer goods by 1929. Stores and warehouses bulged with more goods than Americans could buy, and factories had begun cutting back production and laying off workers. Even though many Americans still believed they could "get rich quick," in reality only a tiny percentage of Americans were truly wealthy. The top 0.1 percent of American families had a total income equal to the total income of the bottom 42 percent of the population. Nearly 78 percent of American families had almost nothing left over to put in savings after buying necessities.

All of these factors came together in October 1929 to create an uncontrollable slide of the U.S. stock market. The slide signaled the beginning of the Great Depression, the severest economic crisis in the history of the United States. Although the Depression lingered until the early 1940s, when the United States began preparing for World War II

(1939–45), the worst years were from 1929 to 1933. Investors lost fortunes in the Wall Street crash. (The U.S. stock market was located on Wall Street in New York City.) The very wealthy acquired most of their money through decades of involvement in the banking industry and ownership of manufacturing companies, not in the stock market run-up of the 1920s. Although they did not lose all of their investments with the stock market crash as new investors had, they did guard their assets and quit investing in businesses and factories. Those businesses and factories, already suffering from an overstock of goods, began massive layoffs, leaving many families with no cash to buy necessities. Unemployment rose rapidly between 1929 and 1933. Less cash in peoples' hands led to less demand for goods that led to more layoffs. It was a vicious downward spiral. Those who managed to keep their jobs saw their salaries decrease—on average about 40 percent. Many Americans could no longer keep up with payments on bank loans they had accumulated in the good times of the 1920s. As a result, bank after bank collapsed. Depositors made "runs" on banks, demanding all their money at once, which caused even more banks to fail. With no jobs and little cash available, people became desperately hungry. They stood in city breadlines that snaked for blocks for a meal of bread, soup, and coffee.

Herbert Hoover (1874–1964) was inaugurated as president of the United States in March 1929, only a half year before the crash. Hoover (served 1929–33) held tightly to his belief that Americans should be self-reliant and not depend on government to solve their economic difficulties. Hoover viewed the Depression as a downturn in a regular business cycle of ups and downs. He called meetings of business and industry leaders, urging them to voluntarily cooperate to solve the economic woes. He urged people to be more optimistic and to be confident in the U.S. economy. Hoover repeatedly told them that the economy would turn upward within days or at worst a few months. He asked Americans to donate generously to private charities as people had historically done when the United States went through difficult times. In a news conference on February 3, 1931, the first excerpt of the chapter, later published as **"Public vs. Private Financing of Relief Efforts"** in *Public Papers of the Presidents of the United States: Herbert Hoover, 1931,* Hoover reaffirmed his

belief that relief for the needy should be handled by each local community and funded by individual donations to private charities. Hoover did break new ground in government assistance by establishing a federal loan program for farmers and federally funded construction programs designed to relieve unemployment.

By 1932 and early 1933 the whole economy, including business, manufacturing, banking, and agriculture, continued to slide. Approximately one-quarter of the U.S. workforce was unemployed. The second excerpt in this chapter is from the famous **"Roots of Social Security"** speech given in 1962 by Frances Perkins (1880–1965), who had served as the secretary of labor throughout President Franklin D. Roosevelt's administration (1933–45). In the early part of the speech Perkins vividly recalled what had happened to Americans in the early 1930s.

Hoover's reliance on voluntary cooperation and his federal support programs failed to improve the economy. Desperate for new leadership, Americans elected Democrat Franklin D. Roosevelt (1882–1945) to the presidency by a landslide in November 1932. By the time he took office in March 1933, the public was exhausted. Many had lost homes and farms and had used up their lifetime savings. On the morning of Roosevelt's inauguration, the U.S. banking system was paralyzed. Thousands of bank failures across the United States had occurred over the past few years. By March 2, 1933, twenty-one states had declared "bank holidays," or suspension of bank operations. In the early hours of inauguration day the governors of two of America's most populous states, Illinois and New York, also declared statewide bank holidays.

On the campaign trail in July 1932, Roosevelt had pledged to Americans a "new deal." The third excerpt, Roosevelt's **"Inaugural Address,"** delivered in his reassuring manner on the gray morning of March 4, 1933, gave Americans their first glimmer of hope in three years. The speech was later published in 1938 in *The Public Papers and Addresses of Franklin D. Roosevelt: Volume Two, 1933*. In the speech, Roosevelt proposed immediate government assistance to bring relief and recovery to the country. The government programs he instituted to accomplish this task became known as the New Deal.

Herbert Hoover

Excerpt from "Public vs. Private Financing of Relief Efforts"

Delivered in a press conference on February 3, 1931
Reprinted from *Public Papers of the Presidents*
of the United States: Herbert Hoover, 1931
Published in 1976

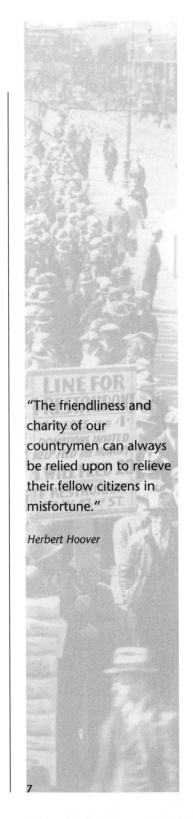

"The friendliness and charity of our countrymen can always be relied upon to relieve their fellow citizens in misfortune."

Herbert Hoover

Herbert Hoover's presidential philosophy was based on voluntary cooperation and business self-regulation. Hoover believed that Americans would always answer the call for contributions to support local charity organizations and national groups such as the American Red Cross. He strongly believed that federal involvement in aiding the needy would stifle individual donations and lead to the dismantling of the nation's many charitable organizations. He pointed out that far more funding came from such organizations than what the federal government proposed to spend on relief for the poor. Reliance on government charity, Hoover feared, would decrease Americans' sense of responsibility toward their fellow citizens. However, as long as charitable efforts were in place, Hoover was willing to authorize some government funding to support private and local efforts.

In his press conference, Hoover acknowledged two distinct situations that required relief efforts at that time: the drought (little or no rainfall for an extended period of time) in the eastern United States and the growing unemployment in cities. To support relief efforts in the drought areas, he asked

Congress to establish a program for government loans to farmers to restore the parched agricultural lands. Hoover also made plans for construction of public works (roads, dams, schools, government buildings) to provide employment in rural areas. However, he pointed out that the American Red Cross refused any funding help from the federal government because it believed it had adequate local organization and enough money and resources that had been donated from private sources to take care of drought relief efforts. To tackle unemployment in the cities, Hoover urged private industry to maintain wages, increase construction activity, and cooperate to equally distribute and stabilize employment. He pledged to greatly increase funding for government construction projects to aid business efforts. At the same time, Hoover strongly reasserted his faith in the tradition of Americans coming to the aid of one another.

Things to remember while reading the excerpt from "Public vs. Private Financing of Relief Efforts":

- Raised in Iowa and Oregon, Hoover was immersed in the Quaker tradition of self-reliance and cooperation. He strongly believed that helping one's neighbors in troubled times was the proper approach for solving problems.

- In the United States, responsibility for aiding the poor in economic hard times had historically rested with private charities and local government.

- Even though he believed volunteerism and self-help were fundamental to the U.S. democratic way of life, Hoover was also a humanitarian. He was interested in the well-being of all Americans and deeply disturbed by the country's growing poverty.

Excerpt from
"Public vs. Private Financing of Relief Efforts"

This is not an issue as to whether the people are going hungry or cold in the United States. It is solely a question of the best

*method by which hunger and cold can be prevented. It is a question as to whether the American people on the one hand will maintain the spirit of **charity** and of **mutual self-help** through voluntary giving and the responsibility of local government as distinguished on the other hand from **appropriations** out of the Federal Treasury for such purposes. My own **conviction** is strongly that if we break down this sense of responsibility, of individual generosity to individual, and mutual self-help in the country in times of national difficulty and if we start **appropriations of this character** we have not only **impaired something infinitely valuable** in the life of the American people but have **struck at the roots of self-government**.*

*And there is a practical problem in all this. The help being daily extended by neighbors, by local and national agencies, by **municipalities**, by industry, and a great multitude of organizations throughout the country today is many times any **appropriation** yet proposed. The opening of the doors of the Federal Treasury is likely to **stifle** this giving and thus **destroy far more resources than the proposed charity from the Federal Government**.*

*The basis of successful relief in national distress is to mobilize and organize the **infinite number** of agencies of self-help in the community. That has been the American way of relieving distress among our own people and the country is successfully meeting its problem in the American way today.*

We have two entirely separate and distinct situations in the country—the first is the drought area [in the eastern states]*; the second is the unemployment in our large industrial centers* [these are the two areas presently needing relief efforts]*.*

*Immediately upon the appearance of the drought last August, I **convoked** a meeting of the Governors, the Red Cross and the railways, the bankers and other agencies in the country and laid the foundations of organization and the resources to stimulate every degree of self-help to meet the situation which it was then obvious would develop. The result of this action was to attack the drought problem in a number of directions. The Red Cross established committees in every drought county, **comprising** the leading citizens of those counties, with instructions to them that they were to prevent starvation among their neighbors, and, if the problem went beyond **local resources**, the Red Cross would support them.*

*To reinforce this work, at the opening of Congress I recommended large appropriations for loans to **rehabilitate agriculture** from*

Charity: Helping the needy.

Mutual self-help: Helping each other.

Appropriations: Funds.

Conviction: Belief.

Appropriations of this character: Funding charity efforts from the federal government's treasury.

Impaired something infinitely valuable: Damaged the valuable tradition of Americans helping Americans.

Struck at the roots of self-government: Undermined the responsibility of local communities to work out their own problems.

Municipalities: Towns and cities.

Appropriation: Funding from government sources.

Stifle: Halt.

Destroy far more resources…: More help was available privately and locally than would be available through the federal government.

Infinite number: Large number.

Convoked: Called together.

Comprising: Made up of.

Local resources: The ability of the local communities to help.

Rehabilitate agriculture: Restore the land.

A long line of jobless and homeless men wait in the cold to receive a free dinner at a New York City soup kitchen in early 1932.
AP/Wide World Photo. Reproduced by permission.

the drought and provision of further large sums for **public works and construction** in the drought territory which would give employment in further relief to the whole situation. These Federal activities provide for an expenditure of upward of $100 million in this area and it is in progress today.

The Red Cross has always met the situations which it has undertaken.... They have refused to accept Federal appropriations as

Public works and construction: Projects that benefit the public, such as building roads, public buildings, and dams.

A storekeeper fills a Red Cross order for a family of four, including coffee, flour, canned goods, and lard. *Courtesy of the Library of Congress.*

*not being **consonant** either with the need or the character of their organization.*

*In the matter of unemployment outside of the drought areas important economic measures of mutual self-help have been developed, such as those to maintain wages, to distribute employment **equitably**, to increase construction work by industry, to increase Federal construction work from a rate of about $275 million a year prior to the depression to a rate now of over $750 million a year, to expand State and municipal construction—all upon a scale never before provided or even attempted in any depression. But beyond this to assure that there shall be no suffering, in every town and county voluntary agencies in relief of distress have been strengthened and created and generous funds have been placed at their disposal. They are carrying on their work efficiently and sympathetically.*

*But after and **coincidentally with** voluntary relief, our American system requires that municipal, county, and State governments shall use their own resources and credit before seeking such assistance from the Federal Treasury.*

Consonant: Being in agreement.

Equitably: Equally.

Coincidentally with: Along with.

*I have indeed spent much of my life in fighting hardship and starvation both abroad and in the Southern States. I do not feel that I should be charged with lack of human sympathy for those who suffer, but I recall that in all the organizations with which I have been connected over these many years, the foundation has been to summon the maximum of self-help ... I am confident that our people have the resources, the initiative, the courage, the **stamina** and kindliness of spirit to meet this situation in the way they have met their problems over generations....*

I am willing to pledge myself that if the time should ever come that the voluntary agencies of the country, together with the local and State governments, are unable to find resources with which to prevent hunger and suffering in my country, I will ask the aid of every resource of the Federal Government because I would no more see starvation amongst our countrymen than would any Senator or Congressman. I have the faith in the American people that such a day will not come.

*The American people are doing their job today. They should be given a chance to show whether they wish to preserve the principles of individual and local responsibility and mutual self-help before they **embark** on what I believe is **a disastrous system**. I feel sure they will succeed if given the opportunity.* [Hoover, pp. 49, 50–53]

What happened next...

The drought that Hoover spoke of only worsened. It moved west and enveloped the Great Plains area from the Dakotas south to Texas. Dust storms, which are clouds of topsoil blown thousands of feet into the air, blew across the Plains, destroying wheat farms and killing livestock. The problem became much too widespread and severe for the American Red Cross to keep up with.

In the cities, unemployment continued to rise, and people went hungry as local and private relief agencies were overwhelmed with the demand for assistance. For example, in late 1931 the city of Philadelphia, Pennsylvania, began a drive to raise $5 million to help its 230,000 residents who were out of work. The fund drive was successful, but the $5

Stamina: Endurance.

Embark: Start.

A disastrous system: Turning to the federal government for aid.

million was used up in only three months. Seeing that local government efforts and private agencies were not meeting the needs of the unemployed and the hungry, Hoover signed the Emergency Relief and Construction Act in July 1932. It provided $2 billion for public works projects and $300 million in loans to states for direct cash payments to the poor. Many believed these actions, although late and too little, prevented a complete collapse of the U.S. economy. Nevertheless, a majority of Americans blamed Hoover for the Depression. In the 1932 presidential election Democratic candidate Franklin D. Roosevelt (1882–1945) won by a landslide.

Did you know...
- Despite the ineffectiveness of Hoover's efforts to relieve the hardships brought on by the Great Depression, his programs marked an important new trend in the federal government's involvement in domestic economic affairs. For the first time in U.S. history, the federal government set up loan programs to aid Americans and established public works projects to provide temporary employment.

- Although he had been a successful businessman and humanitarian in the 1920s, Hoover was uncomfortable in front of crowds. His shyness made him seem insensitive, cold, and uncaring. Few people knew that he donated his entire presidential salary to charity.

- Since the public came to blame Hoover for the country's economic troubles, his name spawned a new vocabulary. Shantytowns, concentrations of make-shift shacks on vacant lots or outskirts of towns, were homes to the poorest Americans and were called "Hoovervilles." Hoboes on trains were hitchhiking rides and not paying for tickets. They were called "Hoover tourists." "Hoover blankets" were newspapers used by the homeless for warmth because they had no blankets. Campfires were "Hoover heaters."

Consider the following...
- Do you think that if Hoover had taken more steps and acted earlier, his actions might have had more impact on the severity of the Depression?

- After leaving office, Hoover remained quiet for two years but reemerged in 1935. Given Hoover's beliefs, do you think he reemerged as a supporter or a critic of President Roosevelt's New Deal? Give your reasons.

- In what various ways do you think Americans who had always worked for a living responded to accepting charity or government handouts?

For More Information

Books

Holford, David M. *Herbert Hoover.* Berkeley Heights, NJ: Enslow Publishers, 1999.

Hoover, Herbert C. *Public Papers of the Presidents of the United States: Herbert Hoover, 1931.* Washington, DC: U.S. Government Printing Office, 1976.

Nash, George H. *The Life of Herbert Hoover.* 3 vols. New York, NY: W. W. Norton, 1966–88.

Web Sites

Herbert Hoover Presidential Library and Museum. http://hoover.nara.gov (accessed on August 26, 2002).

Frances Perkins

Excerpt from "The Roots of Social Security"

Reprinted from the Social Security Administration Web site, available at http://www.ssa.gov/history/perkins5.html

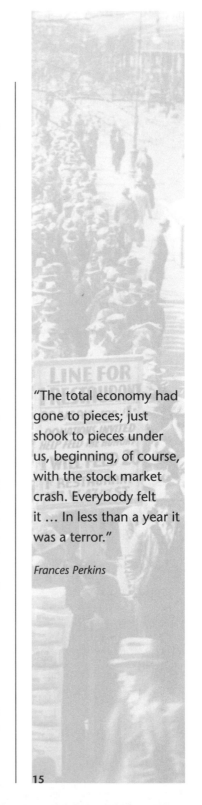

O n October 23, 1962, eighty-two-year-old Frances Perkins (1880–1965) went to the Social Security Administration headquarters in Baltimore, Maryland, and delivered a riveting, lengthy speech on how the Social Security Act of 1935 came into being. Early in the speech she described the situation and conditions facing Americans in the earliest, worst years of the Great Depression, 1929 to 1933. According to Perkins, as quoted in "The Roots of Social Security," the whole U.S. economy "had gone to pieces; just shook to pieces under us, beginning, of course, with the stock market crash.... In less than a year it was a terror." Pay close attention to Perkins's words as she describes hunger, loss of homes, apple sellers, wandering boys, and unemployment.

> "The total economy had gone to pieces; just shook to pieces under us, beginning, of course, with the stock market crash. Everybody felt it ... In less than a year it was a terror."
>
> *Frances Perkins*

Things to remember while reading the excerpt from "The Roots of Social Security":
- Typical middle-class Americans in 1931 and 1932 were shocked and discouraged and fearful of what the future would bring.

- In late 1932 and early 1933, business failures, bank closures, and unemployment rates peaked, and many Americans struggled just to feed their families.

- Frances Perkins watched the first years of the Great Depression unfold in New York. There she was serving as the industrial commissioner of the Department of Labor under Franklin D. Roosevelt, who was governor of the state at that time. From her New York vantage point Perkins saw up close the desperation of the unemployed.

Excerpt from "The Roots of Social Security"

When we came to the problem of doing something for the "poorer kind of people" (as John Garner [1868–1967; the vice president of the United States during Roosevelt's first two terms in office] called them) in 1933 after the Roosevelt administration took office, we, of course had had a very recent experience with poverty. Since 1929 we had experienced the short, sudden drop of everything. The total economy had gone to pieces; just shook to pieces under us, beginning, of course, with the stock market crash. A banking crisis followed it. A manufacturing crisis followed it. Everybody felt it. In less than a year it was a terror.

*People were so alarmed that all through the rest of 1929, 1930, and 1931, the **specter** of unemployment—of starvation, of hunger, of the wandering boys, of the broken homes, of the families separated while somebody went out to look for work—stalked everywhere. The unpaid rent, the **eviction notices**, the furniture and bedding on the sidewalk, the old lady weeping over it, the children crying, the father out looking for a truck to move their belongings himself to his sister's flat or some relative's already overcrowded **tenement**, or just sitting there bewilderedly waiting for some charity officer to come and move him somewhere. I saw goods stay on the sidewalk in front of the same house with the same children weeping on top of the blankets for three days before anybody came to relieve the situation!*

These were the years in which developed, you remember, in New York City—and later in other cities—the pattern of the apple

Specter: Haunting vision.

Eviction notices: Orders to leave a residence after failure to pay rent.

Tenement: Apartment in a slum area.

An unemployed man tries to earn a living by selling apples on the street during the Great Depression.
Corbis Corporation.
Reproduced by permission.

UNEMPLOYED
BUY
APPLES
5¢ EACH

sellers. Some kindhearted man who had a surplus of apples—be-cause the farmers were in this depression, too—thought of getting rid of his apples (which he couldn't sell) by giving them to the un-employed to sell. So they got them every morning somewhere down in the market. Nobody asked them to prove they were unemployed. I'm sure they were because no man in his right mind would have taken a big basket of apples to try and sell at five cents apiece in a poverty-stricken community—out of which he would make just a lit-

tle bit of pocket money—unless he had been out of work, out of wages, out of money, out of everything....

The wandering boys were a source of terror. But it was the most natural thing in the world for a great big grownup boy 14 to 17 years old to go wandering. Consider the case of a boy who found himself in a family where the **breadwinner** was unemployed, where there were other children around, where his mother was distracted by the lack of anything to buy food with, and to feel himself, not unwanted, but one more mouth to feed, and a great big mouth at that.

"I ate so much," one boy said to me, "I couldn't stand it. The kids, the little children were hungry. So I went out to find a job, and I went out of town."

This is what the boys did—not a few of them—thousands of them. They wandered around the country and were a problem to every charity and relief organization, to every State aid or Federal-and-State relief station, and the railroads were terrified of them. These boys, following the road, would steal a ride under the bumpers, and the railroads were frightened all the time that there would be accidents; that somebody would be killed; and I believe some were. It's a dangerous business to ride the **rods**. I remember I went out to see some of the boys. They finally gathered them in— the railroaders did. They sort of herded many of them into the St. Louis yards, and let them pitch a camp. Well, there they lived in the camp—in the St. Louis railroad yards—a hazard to the community—picking up whatever they could. I'm sure some of them learned to steal. Some of them learned to be **panhandlers**. All kinds of things happened. These were really alarming situations. They were alarming because of the **demoralization** and because of the general hazards to the community and to the total economy.

But everything was down. Nobody could get a job. The grocer didn't employ the young boys to deliver goods any more. He couldn't afford to. The grocer himself finally went bankrupt and closed up. He had **given too much credit**. I mean the people who were out of work had credit at the grocery store at first and they could eat; but they couldn't pay their bills, and finally, the grocer couldn't pay his bills; and eventually somebody came and sold him out. It went on like that all the time. One thing led to another, and we began to realize how cruel, how very deep, how almost **irreversible** this situation had come to be. This was the situation which faced people who began to be aware of the problem early as 1930....

Breadwinner: The person bringing in the main, often only, source of income in a household.

Rods: Trains.

Panhandlers: Beggars.

Demoralization: Loss of spirit; giving up.

Given too much credit: Allowed customers to take out goods with a promise to pay later.

Irreversible: Impossible to turn around.

Unemployment was mentioned as a great and outstanding problem of the United States in the year 1932, and the Democratic Party platform included a clause which said it was a problem. They promised to study the causes of unemployment—as though anybody hadn't studied them in years.

They promised to have a committee to study the causes of unemployment, and to study and look into the whole matter.... Most of the committee members seemed to be determined that there should be nothing said about unemployment that would frighten people away from the Democratic Party.

But, you may remember, it didn't frighten the people at all. Actually, nothing frightened them. They would have voted for anybody who was running, and for any platform because they wanted change. Everybody was depressed; every industry was depressed; so every individual had some sort of stake in the situation. Thus, we got the first public mention and the first public commitment to do something or other about unemployment—at least to study it....

At any rate, that was the situation when Roosevelt was elected and we went to Washington. [Perkins, pp. 3–5, 10]

A young man, wandering the country by railroad, leans against a freight car doorway. *National Archives and Records Administration.*

What happened next...

Before Frances Perkins "went to Washington," she met with president-elect Roosevelt. Roosevelt had inquired whether she would consider taking the position of secretary of labor within his cabinet, but before accepting the appointment Perkins had some questions to ask. She informed Roosevelt

that she would pursue an extensive agenda, including unemployment insurance, old-age insurance, minimum wages and maximum hours, and passage of legislation preventing child labor. Roosevelt assured her he would not stand in her way. If she thought she could do it, he promised he would authorize her to push forward. With that, Perkins accepted the position.

By the time Perkins went to Washington, D.C., in the early 1930s, she had accumulated roughly thirty years of experience as an advocate for working people, children, women, and the poor. She had worked in the male-dominated world of labor negotiations, and she had a talent for getting things done in politically challenging situations. After Roosevelt's inauguration on March 4, 1933, Perkins and the rest of the Roosevelt administration set about creating new pieces of legislation to bring economic relief, recovery, and reform to the country.

Did you know...

- Frances Perkins was the first woman to serve in a presidential cabinet.

- Perkins served as secretary of labor for twelve years and three months.

- Throughout Roosevelt's presidential years, Perkins remained his closest adviser on social legislation. Her two proudest achievements were passage of the Social Security Act of 1935 and the Fair Labor Standards Act of 1938.

Consider the following...

- Frances Perkins was the first woman cabinet member in U.S. history. What do you suppose her first few days in the Department of Labor were like? What qualities must she have possessed to be successful in that post?

- When Perkins speaks of "the wandering boys," for what reason does she seem to believe many of the boys left home?

- Perkins quotes Roosevelt's vice president, John Garner, when she refers to America's "poorer kind of people." Who do you think was included in this group in 1933?

For More Information

Books

Pasachoff, Naomi E. *Frances Perkins: Champion of the New Deal.* New York, NY: Oxford University Press, 1999.

Perkins, Frances. *The Roosevelt I Knew.* New York, NY: Viking Press, 1946.

Schlesinger, Arthur M., Jr. *The Coming of the New Deal: The Age of Roosevelt.* Boston, MA: Houghton Mifflin, 1988.

Web Sites

Perkins, Frances. "The Roots of Social Security." *Social Security Administration.* http://www.ssa.gov/history/perkins5.html (accessed on August 26, 2002).

Franklin D. Roosevelt

Excerpt from "Inaugural Address, March 4, 1933"

**Reprinted from *The Public Papers and Addresses
of Franklin D. Roosevelt: Volume Two, 1933*
Published in 1938**

"I pledge you—I pledge myself—to a new deal for the American people. Let us all here assembled constitute ourselves prophets of a new order of competence and of courage. This is more than a political campaign; it is a call to arms. Give me your help, not to win votes alone, but to win in this crusade to restore America to its own people." Franklin D. Roosevelt made this speech in acceptance of the nomination to be the Democratic candidate for president in 1932. His words are recorded in *The Public Papers and Addresses of Franklin D. Roosevelt: Volume Two, 1933.*

Roosevelt was elected to the presidency in November 1932, but he would not be inaugurated until March 1933. The Twentieth Amendment to the U.S. Constitution, which changed the inauguration date to January, was in the process of ratification (being voted on by the states) and would not take effect until the 1936 presidential election and inauguration. Considering the complexity and array of problems that existed in the United States at the end of 1932, Roosevelt knew he could not wait until March 1933 to tackle them. With more businesses and banks failing daily and people losing their jobs,

> "So, first of all, let me assert my firm belief that the only thing we have to fear is fear itself."
>
> *Franklin D. Roosevelt*

homes, and farms, Roosevelt assembled a group of brilliant advisers known as the Brain Trust to begin formulating the "new deal." He also created task force groups to deal with specific problems such as those affecting agriculture. Never before had such activity taken place before the inauguration.

President-elect Roosevelt, the Brain Trust, and the task forces defined the areas that demanded attention first, and on inauguration day Roosevelt told the American people his general plan for leading the country back to economic health. The following excerpt from Roosevelt's speech was published as "Inaugural Address, March 4, 1933" in *The Public Papers and Addresses of Franklin D. Roosevelt.* In this speech Roosevelt spoke honestly about the paralyzing situation of the U.S. economy, and he used perhaps the most famous and most quoted phrase of his entire presidency: "The only thing we have to fear is fear itself." He briefly reviewed the state of the nation, then scolded bankers who had been reckless or dishonest with people's money.

Turning to his plan for economic relief, Roosevelt noted that the first task was putting people to work. He also spoke of raising farm produce prices and halting the foreclosures of homes (banks taking possession of property when loan payments are not made). Suggesting that private relief agencies were overwhelmed, he proposed centralization of relief activities. Finally, Roosevelt urged courage for the difficult days ahead. He closed by reaffirming his faith in the democratic principles of the United States.

Things to remember while reading the excerpt from "Inaugural Address, March 4, 1933":

- Bank holidays had been occurring across the United States in 1932 and early 1933. To avoid running out of cash, banks would suspend operation and close for business for a period of time. In the early-morning hours of inauguration day, the banks in Illinois and New York went on "holiday." The U.S. banking system was paralyzed when Roosevelt began his speech.

- The nation was at the depth of the Depression when Roosevelt took the oath as the thirty-second president of the United States.

- In contrast to departing president Herbert Hoover's cool mannerisms, Roosevelt always spoke in a warm, confident, and reassuring manner. Americans believed what Roosevelt said and believed that what he proposed to do was in their best interest.

Excerpt from "Inaugural Address, March 4, 1933"

*I am certain that my fellow Americans expect that on my **induction** into the Presidency I will address them with a **candor** and a decision which the present situation of our Nation impels. This is **preeminently the time** to speak the truth, the whole truth, frankly and boldly. Nor need we shrink from honestly facing conditions in our country today. This great Nation will endure as it has endured, will revive and will prosper. So, first of all, let me assert my firm belief that the only thing we have to fear is fear itself—nameless, unreasoning, unjustified terror which paralyzes needed efforts to **convert retreat into advance**. In every dark hour of our national life a leadership of frankness and **vigor** has met with that understanding and support of the people themselves which is essential to victory. I am convinced that you will again give that support to leadership in these critical days.*

*In such a spirit on my part and on yours we face our common difficulties. They concern, thank God, only material things. Values [of all assets—stocks, real estate property, material goods] have shrunken to fantastic levels; taxes have risen; our ability to pay has fallen; government of all kinds is faced by serious curtailment of income; **the means of exchange are frozen in the currents of trade**; the withered leaves of industrial enterprise lie on every side; farmers find no markets for their produce; the savings of many years in thousands of families are gone.*

More important, a host of unemployed citizens face the grim problem of existence, and an equally great number toil with little return. Only a foolish optimist can deny the dark realities of the moment....

Compared with the perils which our forefathers conquered because they believed and were not afraid, we have still much to be

Induction: Ceremonial swearing into office.

Candor: Honesty.

Preeminently the time: The most important time.

Convert retreat into advance: Find solutions and move forward.

Vigor: Energy.

The means of exchange are frozen in the currents of trade: Banking and exchange of money has halted.

Languishes: Is lacking.

Rulers of the exchange…: Bankers.

Abdicated: Evaded their responsibility.

Practices of the unscrupulous money changers: Business practices of dishonest bankers.

Indicted: Charged with wrongdoing.

Credit: Lending money.

Stripped of the lure…: People were promised unending profits, but with the stock market crash, profits ended.

Exhortations: Appeals.

Temple: Bank system.

Ancient truths: Honest ways of doing business.

Direct recruiting by the Government itself: The government itself creating jobs for people.

Power to purchase…: Farmers will have more money to buy goods manufactured in cities.

Foreclosure: Banks taking possession of property when loan payments were not made.

Speculation: Reckless investing.

thankful for. Nature still offers her bounty and human efforts have multiplied it. Plenty is at our doorstep, but a generous use of it **languishes** *in the very sight of the supply. Primarily this is because* **rulers of the exchange of mankind's goods** *have failed through their own stubbornness and their own incompetence, have admitted their failure, and have* **abdicated. Practices of the unscrupulous money changers** *stand* **indicted** *in the court of public opinion, rejected by the hearts and minds of men.*

True they have tried, but…faced by failure of **credit** *they have proposed only the lending of more money.* **Stripped of the lure of profit by which to induce our people to follow their false leadership,** *they have resorted to* **exhortations,** *pleading tearfully for restored confidence. They know only the rules of a generation of self-seekers. They have no vision, and when there is no vision the people perish.*

The **money changers** *have fled from their high seats in the temple of our civilization. We may now restore that* **temple** *to the* **ancient truths.** *The measure of the restoration lies in the extent to which we apply social values more noble than mere monetary profit.*

This Nation asks for action, and action now.

Our greatest primary task is to put people to work. This is no unsolvable problem if we face it wisely and courageously. It can be accomplished in part by **direct recruiting by the Government itself,** *treating the task as we would treat the emergency of a war, but at the same time, through this employment, accomplishing greatly needed projects to stimulate and reorganize the use of our natural resources* [such as dams to control water usage and flooding]….

The task can be helped by definite efforts to raise the values of agricultural products and with this the **power to purchase the output of our cities.** *It can be helped by preventing realistically the tragedy of the growing loss through* **foreclosure** *of our small homes and our farms…. It can be helped by the unifying of relief activities which today are often scattered, uneconomical, and unequal. It can be helped by national planning for and supervision of all forms of transportation and of communications and other utilities which have a definitely public character. There are many ways in which it can be helped, but it can never be helped merely by talking about it. We must act and act quickly.*

Finally, in our progress toward a resumption of work we require two safeguards against a return of the evils of the old order: there must be a strict supervision of all banking and credits and investments, so that there will be an end to **speculation** *with other peo-*

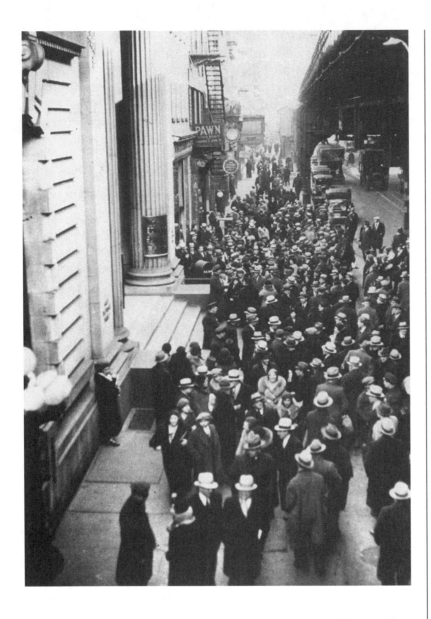

A crowd gathers in front of a bank as customers line up to withdraw all of their money. "Banks runs" were a common sight in early 1933. *UPI/Corbis-Bettmann. Reproduced by permission.*

*ple's money; and there must be **provision** for an adequate but sound **currency**.*

*These are the lines of attack. I shall presently **urge upon a new Congress**, in special session, detailed measures for their fulfillment, and I shall seek the immediate assistance of the several States.*

Through this program of action we address ourselves to putting our own national house in order and making income balance outgo....

Provision: A plan.

Currency: Monetary system.

Urge upon a new Congress: Present to a newly elected Congress.

*If I read the **temper** of our people correctly, we now realize as we have never realized before our interdependence on each other; that we cannot merely take but we must give as well; that if we are to go forward, we must move as a trained and loyal army willing to sacrifice for the good of a common discipline, because without such discipline no progress is made, no leadership becomes effective. We are, I know, ready and willing to submit our lives and property to such discipline, because it makes possible a leadership which aims at a larger good. This I propose to offer, pledging that the **larger purposes will bind upon us all as a sacred obligation with a unity of duty hitherto evoked only in time of armed strife.***

With this pledge taken, I assume unhesitatingly the leadership of this great army of our people dedicated to a disciplined attack upon our common problems.

*Action in this image and to this end is **feasible** under the form of government which we have inherited from our ancestors. Our Constitution is so simple and practical that it is possible always to meet extraordinary needs by changes in emphasis and arrangement without loss of essential form. That is why our constitutional system has proved itself the most superbly enduring political mechanism the modern world has produced. It has met every stress of vast expansion of territory, of foreign wars, of bitter internal strife, or world relations....*

... [If need be] I shall ask the Congress for the one remaining instrument to meet the crisis—broad Executive power to wage a war against the emergency, as great as the power that would be given to me if we were in fact invaded by a foreign foe.

*For the trust **reposed** in me I will return the courage and the devotion that befit the time. I can do no less.*

*We face the **arduous** days that lie before us in the warm courage of national unity; with the clear consciousness of seeking old and precious moral values; with the clean satisfaction that comes from the stern performance of duty by old and young alike. We aim at the assurance of a rounded and permanent national life.*

*We do not distrust the future of essential democracy. The people of the United States have not failed. In their need they have registered a **mandate** that they want direct, vigorous action. They have asked for discipline and direction under leadership. They have made me the present instrument of their wishes. In the spirit of the gift I take it.*

Temper: Thinking; attitude.

Larger purposes will bind upon us ...: Americans will work together to solve the economic problems much as they would unite to fight a war.

Feasible: Possible.

Reposed: Placed.

Arduous: Difficult.

Mandate: Demand.

In this dedication of a Nation we humbly ask the blessing of God. May He protect each and every one of us. May He guide me in the days to come. [Roosevelt, pp. 11–16]

What happened next...

Will Rogers (1879–1935), lecturer and humorist, was a master at capturing exactly how Americans felt at certain times, about certain happenings. According to Susan Winslow's 1976 book *Brother, Can You Spare a Dime?*, immediately following Roosevelt's inauguration speech, Rogers quipped, "America hasn't been as happy in three years as it is today. No money, no banks, no work, no nothing, but they know they got a man in there who is wise to Congress and wise to our so-called big men [wealthy men who had act dishonestly]. The whole country is with him, just so he does something. Even if what he does is wrong they are with him. Just so he does something. If he burned down the capitol, we would cheer and say, 'Well, we at least got a fire started anyhow.'"

Later on inauguration day, in an unprecedented action, Roosevelt called together the people he had chosen for his cabinet and had them sworn in. By evening they were at work. That evening Roosevelt called a special session of Congress to begin March 9. Congress would remain in session until June 16, one hundred days, and enact an amazing amount of legislation. Americans sorely needed help and hope. Their president and Congress did not disappoint.

Did you know...

- Roosevelt did not attend any of the inaugural balls held around Washington, D.C., on inauguration evening . Instead, Eleanor Roosevelt (1884–1962), his wife, went alone to represent the new president.

- By the 1932 election, Americans were ready for a change. Many Republican voters switched parties and voted for

the Democrats. Roosevelt, a Democrat, won the presidential election by a landslide, and the Democrats also claimed nearly a two-thirds majority in the Senate and three-fourths of the House of Representatives.

- Roosevelt had developed polio in 1921 and was paralyzed from the waist down. He could stand only with the help of heavy braces. He refused to let his physical handicap get in the way of his presidency, however, and served until his death in 1945.

Consider the following...

- When Roosevelt took office, do you think he had a clear vision of what needed to be done to save the nation from the Depression? Why or why not?

- Roosevelt said, "I shall ask the Congress for ... power to wage a war against the emergency." What does his choice of words indicate about his plan for future action?

For More Information

Books

McJimsey, George. *The Presidency of Franklin Delano Roosevelt*. Lawrence, KS: University of Kansas Press, 2000.

Roosevelt, Franklin D. *The Public Papers and Addresses of Franklin D. Roosevelt: Volume Two, 1933*. New York, NY: Random House, 1938.

Winslow, Susan. *Brother, Can You Spare a Dime? America from the Wall Street Crash to Pearl Harbor: An Illustrated Documentary*. New York, NY: Paddington Press, 1976.

A New Deal for Americans

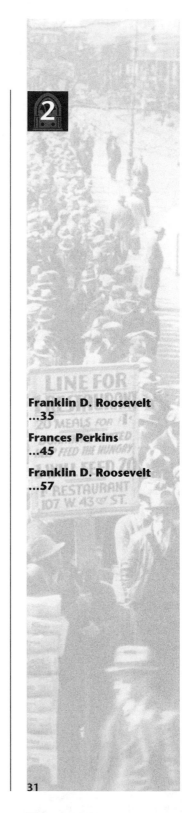

By the time Franklin D. Roosevelt (1882–1945) was inaugurated as the thirty-second president of the United States on March 4, 1933, the U.S. banking system had ceased to function. Roosevelt's first action as president was to take control of the banking system and stabilize the situation. Key actions included declaration of a nationwide bank holiday—a suspension of banking activities and closure of banks. The "holiday" allowed for the passage of the Emergency Banking Relief Act and Roosevelt's first "fireside chat," a radio broadcast to approximately sixty million worried Americans. These actions restored confidence in governmental leadership and in the banks. On March 13, only nine days after inauguration, banks began to reopen, Americans deposited more than they withdrew, and the U.S. banking system was saved.

The first few days of Roosevelt's presidency set the tone for the next eighteen months. Roosevelt (served 1933–45) and his advisers created political and economic programs, called the New Deal, to combat the Great Depression and return America to prosperity. (The Great Depression, America's worst economic downturn, was widely recog-

nized as beginning in October 1929, with the crash of the New York stock market, and not fully ending until the preparations for World War II were in full swing by 1941.) The New Deal programs were also referred to as the "three Rs": immediate Relief for the needy, longer-term plans for economic Recovery, and permanent Reform. Legislation rolled out of Washington at an unprecedented rate. The many measures passed during the sixteen-month period from March 1933 to June 1934 were known as the First New Deal. Although there were critics of the New Deal, Roosevelt clearly had the public on his side, and he could afford to ignore the critics. However, by later 1934 as the Depression dragged on, critics became more vocal. Many businessmen and conservatives, opposed to government involving itself in every aspect of American life, charged that the Roosevelt administration had exercised power far beyond what the U.S. Constitution allowed. Liberals, however, wanted the government to go much further. They called for government ownership of banks and industry.

One criticism Roosevelt did carefully listen to and respond to was that the First New Deal, after addressing the immediate problems of the needy, had concentrated too much on aiding business and large farm operators; it had unintentionally left out the everyday citizen and poorer people. With the 1936 election looming, Roosevelt made a clear shift to legislation addressing the needs of the common man and families, the working-class laborer, and the small farmer.

Legislation passed between April 1935 and June 1938 was known as the Second New Deal. Roosevelt's focus on the working man and small farmer resulted in intense opposition from the business community, who wanted the president to concentrate on protecting business interests. Roosevelt nevertheless continued on his course to help the unemployed, common laborers, young Americans, and the rural poor.

Through the "three Rs" of the First and Second New Deals, the federal government became involved in every aspect of people's lives—business activities, labor organizations, retirement and insurance programs, support of the arts (including literature, music, theater, and the visual arts), resource conservation, regulation of public utilities (such as electricity), stock market reform, and housing reform. For

many, the New Deal programs reestablished hope in the future and faith in the U.S. system of government.

The first excerpt in this chapter comes from **"The First 'Fireside Chat': An Intimate Talk with the People of the United States on Banking, March 12, 1933,"** published in 1938 in *The Public Papers and Addresses of Franklin D. Roosevelt: Volume Two, 1933.* With his confident, reassuring voice, Roosevelt seemed to come through the radio waves right into Americans' living rooms as he explained the banking crisis. The second excerpt, **"Labor under the New Deal and the New Frontier,"** comes from a 1965 publication by the Institute of Industrial Relations of UCLA, *Two Views of American Labor.* In the excerpt Frances Perkins, Roosevelt's secretary of labor, looks back at the beginning of the New Deal era and some of its legislation. The third excerpt, **"Second Inaugural Address of Franklin D. Roosevelt on January 20, 1937,"** was published in the 1941 edition of *The Public Papers and Addresses of Franklin D. Roosevelt: Volume 6.* In this speech, Roosevelt reviewed what the country had been through, and because he still saw "one-third of a nation ill-housed, ill-clad [poorly clothed], ill-nourished," he pledged to continue seeking "economic and political" progress.

Franklin D. Roosevelt

Excerpt from "The First 'Fireside Chat': An Intimate Talk with the People of the United States on Banking, March 12, 1933"

**Reprinted from *The Public Papers and Addresses of Franklin D. Roosevelt: Volume Two, 1933*
Published in 1938**

In 1933 Americans did not have televisions in their homes. Radio was the most powerful means to transmit ideas and information, so President Franklin Roosevelt instituted his "fireside chats" via radio broadcast, the first one airing on Sunday evening, March 12, 1933. In his comforting, reassuring voice, he clearly explained the bank crisis and the actions he had taken to relieve the crisis.

Roosevelt explained that when a person deposits money in a bank, all that money does not stay at that local bank. Instead it is used to make loans and other investments, which provide the bank with regular income. The bank keeps on hand only enough cash to take care of customers' needs on any normal day. Since the crash of the stock market in late 1929, banks had been forced to close when people could not make their regular loan payments—not enough cash was available to operate the banks. As a result, customers of the failed banks lost their savings—and their confidence in the banking system. On the mere rumor that a bank was in trouble, depositors lined up to take out all their money. This was known as a "bank run." Those at the end of the line did not

"I owe this [radio talk with the people] in particular because of the fortitude [bravery] and good temper with which everybody has accepted the inconvenience and hardships of the banking holiday."

Franklin D. Roosevelt

get all their money. Bank runs caused perfectly sound banks to collapse.

Believing that the banking system could not endure another day, Roosevelt had suspended all banking operations on March 6, 1933. In his "fireside chat" Roosevelt explained that banks across the country had undergone examinations by federal officials to ensure that only sound banks would re-open on March 13. Roosevelt then urged Americans to quit hoarding money in mattresses and redeposit it into banks, which he assured them were safe. Roosevelt was fully aware that the country's survival depended on the actions of its citizens on Monday, March 13, 1933.

Things to remember while reading the excerpt from "The First 'Fireside Chat': An Intimate Talk with the People of the United States on Banking, March 12, 1933":

- From the late 1920s to 1933 almost 40 percent of U.S. banks had failed or had to merge to stay in business. Most failed banks were local banks, often located in economically struggling rural areas. These banks had to stretch their resources to carry out an array of services because nationwide branch banking was prohibited.

- One city bank failure involved the Bank of the United States in New York City. The bank's failure on December 11, 1930, closed fifty-seven branches in the city, freezing $210 million in 440,000 accounts. Although it was a private bank, its name spawned fears that the whole U.S. banking system was failing.

- As the Depression wore on, businesses failed, workers lost their jobs, and as a result, bank loans were not repaid. This, in turn, caused more and more bank failures.

- With few retirement plans in existence, those who lost savings in bank failures often lost the only money they had set aside for their old-age living expenses.

- By March 5, 1933, the bankers themselves had come to no agreement on how to solve the bank crisis.

President Franklin D. Roosevelt preparing for his first "fireside chat" on March 12, 1933. *AP/Wide World Photo. Reproduced by permission.*

Excerpt from "The First 'Fireside Chat': An Intimate Talk with the People of the United States on Banking, March 12, 1933"

*I want to talk for a few minutes with the people of the United States about banking—with the comparatively few who understand the **mechanics** of banking but more particularly with the overwhelming majority who use banks for the making of deposits and the drawing of checks. I want to tell you what has been done in the last few days, why it was done, and what the next steps are going to be. I recognize that the many **proclamations** from State capitols and from Washington, the legislation, the Treasury regulations, etc., **couched** for the most part in banking and legal terms, should be explained for the benefit of the average citizen. I owe this in particular because of the **fortitude** and good temper with which everybody*

Mechanics: Business.

Proclamations: Statements.

Couched: Spoken of.

Fortitude: Bravery.

has accepted the inconvenience and hardships of the banking holiday. I know that when you understand what we in Washington have been about I shall continue to have your cooperation as fully as I have had your sympathy and help during the past week.

*First of all, let me state the simple fact that when you deposit money in a bank the bank does not put the money into a safe deposit vault. It invests your money in many different…kinds of loans. In other words, the bank puts your money to work to keep the wheels of industry and of agriculture turning around. A comparatively small part of the money you put into the bank is kept in **currency**—an amount which in normal times is wholly sufficient to cover the cash needs of the average citizen. In other words, the total amount of all the currency in the country is only a small fraction of the total deposits in all of the banks.*

*What, then, happened during the last few days of February and the first few days of March? Because of **undermined** confidence on the part of the public, there was a general rush by a large portion of our population to turn bank deposits into currency or gold—a rush so great that the soundest banks could not get enough currency to meet the demand. The reason for this was that on the spur of the moment it was, of course, impossible to sell perfectly sound **assets** of a bank and convert them into cash except at panic prices far below their real value.*

*By the afternoon of March 3 scarcely a bank in the country was open to do business. **Proclamations** temporarily closing them in whole or in part had been issued by the Governors in almost all the States.*

*It was then that I issued the proclamation providing for the nationwide **bank holiday**, and this was the first step in the Government's reconstruction of our **financial and economic fabric**.*

The second step was the legislation promptly and patriotically passed by the Congress confirming my proclamation and broadening my powers so that it became possible in view of the requirement of time to extend the holiday and lift the ban of that holiday gradually [the legislation made it legal for Roosevelt to call the bank holiday and allowed him to extend it, then lift it gradually]. *This law also gave authority to develop a program of **rehabilitation** of our banking facilities….*

*This bank holiday, while resulting in many cases in great inconvenience, is **affording** us the opportunity to supply the currency nec-*

Currency: Cash.

Undermined: Weakened.

Assets: Property or something of value.

Proclamations: Statements.

Bank holiday: Legal suspension of bank operations for a brief period of time.

Financial and economic fabric: The nation's monetary system.

Rehabilitation: To reform.

Affording: Allowing.

On the mere rumor that a bank was in trouble, depositors lined up to take out all their money. This was known as a "bank run." *Courtesy of the Franklin D. Roosevelt Library.*

essary to meet the situation. No sound bank is a dollar worse off than it was when it closed its doors last Monday....

A question you will ask is this: why are all the banks not to be reopened at the same time? The answer is simple. Your Government does not intend that the history of the past few years shall be repeated. We do not want and will not have another **epidemic** of bank failures.

As a result, we start tomorrow, Monday, with the opening of banks in the twelve **Federal Reserve Bank cities**—those banks which on first examination by the Treasury have already been found to be all right. This will be followed on Tuesday by the resumption of all their functions by banks already found to be sound in cities ... about 250 cities of the United States.

On Wednesday and succeeding days banks in smaller places all through the country will resume business, subject, of course, to the Government's physical ability to complete its survey [of soundness]. It is necessary that the reopening of banks be extended over a period in order to permit the banks to make applications for necessary

Epidemic: Outbreak or rapid spread.

Federal Reserve Bank cities: Twelve large cities across the United States that had a Federal Reserve Bank.

loans, to obtain currency needed to meet their requirements and to enable the Government to make common sense checkups.

Let me make it clear to you that if your bank does not open the first day you are by no means justified in believing that it will not open. A bank that opens on one of the subsequent days is in exactly the same status as the bank that opens tomorrow....

*It is possible that when the banks resume a very few people who have not recovered from their fear may again begin withdrawals. Let me make it clear that the banks will take care of all needs—and it is my belief that **hoarding** during the past week has become an exceedingly unfashionable pastime. It needs no prophet to tell you that when the people find that they can get their money—that they can get it when they want it for all legitimate purposes—the phantom of fear will soon be **laid**. People will again be glad to have their money where it will be safely taken care of and where they can use it conveniently at any time. I can assure you that it is safer to keep your money in a reopened bank than under the mattress.*

The success of our whole great national program depends, of course, upon the cooperation of the public—on its intelligent support and use of a reliable system....

One more point before I close. There will be, of course, some banks unable to reopen without being reorganized. The new law allows the Government to assist in making these reorganizations quickly and effectively....

*I hope you can see from this **elemental recital** of what your Government is doing that there is nothing complex, or radical, in the process.*

*We had a bad banking situation. Some of our bankers had shown themselves either incompetent or dishonest in their handling of the people's funds. They had used the money entrusted to them in **speculations** and unwise loans. This was, of course, not true in the vast majority of our banks, but it was true in enough of them to shock the people for a time into a sense of insecurity and to put them into a frame of mind where they **did not differentiate**, but seemed to assume that the acts of a comparative few had **tainted them all**. It was the Government's job to straighten out this situation and do it as quickly as possible. And the job is being performed.*

I do not promise you that every bank will be reopened or that individual losses will not be suffered, but there will be no losses that

Hoarding: Setting aside a supply for oneself.

Laid: Gone.

Elemental recital: Simple talk.

Speculations: High-risk investments in stocks of inflated value.

Did not differentiate: Could not tell the difference between a sound bank and an unsound bank.

Tainted them all: Made all banks unsound.

possibly could be avoided; and there would have been more and greater losses had we continued to drift.... We shall be engaged not merely in reopening sound banks but in the creation of sound banks through reorganization.

It has been wonderful to me to catch the note of confidence from all over the country. I can never be sufficiently grateful to the people for the loyal support they have given me in their acceptance of the judgment that has dictated our course, even though all our processes may not have seemed clear to them.

*After all, there is an element in the readjustment of our financial system more important than currency, more important than gold, and that is the confidence of the people. Confidence and courage are the essentials of success in carrying out our plan. You people must have faith; you must not be stampeded by rumors or guesses. Let us unite in **banishing** fear. We have provided the machinery to restore our financial system; it is up to you to support and make it work.*

It is your problem no less than it is mine. Together we cannot fail. [Roosevelt, pp. 61–62, 63, 64–65]

What happened next...

Lecturer and humorist Will Rogers (1879–1935) reviewed Roosevelt's first fireside chat the next day, March 13, 1933. His comments, reprinted here, appear in Susan Winslow's 1976 book titled *Brother, Can You Spare a Dime?*.

"Mr. Roosevelt stepped to the microphone last night and knocked another home run. His message was not only a great comfort to the people, but it pointed a lesson to all radio announcers and public speakers what to do with a big vocabulary—leave it at home in the dictionary.

"Some people spend a lifetime juggling with words, with not an idea in a carload.

"Our President took such a dry subject as banking (and when I say 'dry,' I mean dry, for if it had been liquid, he wouldn't have to speak on it at all) and made everybody understand it, even the bankers."

Banishing: Doing away with.

The United States National Bank was among the first to reopen, on March 13, after President Roosevelt had suspended all banking operations on March 6, 1933. *AP/Wide World Photo. Reproduced by permission.*

On Monday morning, March 13, as sound banks began reopening, Americans again lined up, but they deposited rather than withdrew money. The bank runs were over. Deposits exceeded withdrawals by $10 million in New York City alone. People had regained confidence in their political leadership and in the nation's banking system. Approximately 90 percent of the country's banking system had reopened for business by March 15.

Building on the actions of those first days of the Roosevelt administration, Congress passed the Banking Act of 1933 in June 1933 and the Banking Act of 1935 on August 23, 1935. Although the Emergency Banking Relief Act passed on March 9, 1933, had addressed the immediate crisis, the two subsequent banking acts laid the foundation for far-reaching changes in the U.S. banking system. The most enduring and influential agency to emerge from the banking acts was the Federal Deposit Insurance Corporation (FDIC), which insures depositor money against loss. The FDIC created such confidence that bank runs and failures were all but eliminated.

Did you know...

- On March 9, 1933, the entire process of enacting the Emergency Banking Act—the unanimous favorable vote in the House of Representatives, the Senate's favorable vote, and Roosevelt's signing—took less than eight hours.

- When all the banks closed on March 6, 1933, Americans responded to their common predicament with relief, not panic. They were thankful that, at least for the moment, the bank runs had stopped. For the most part people laughed, joked, and wrote lots of IOUs.

- The Banking Act of 1933 was commonly known as the Glass-Steagall Act. Under the guidance of Senator Carter Glass (1858–1946) of Virginia, this act separated commercial banks (banks that carry out regular operations of savings and checking accounts) from banks that carry out investment activities (such as investing in the stock market). Through the leadership of Representative Henry Steagall of Alabama, this act also created the Federal Deposit Insurance Corporation (FDIC) to insure depositors' money.

Consider the following...

- What do you think would have happened to the banking system if Roosevelt had not called the bank holiday? What might have happened to the United States?

- Imagine what would happen if all the banks today closed for one week. How would you live and get to and from

school or work? What alternative forms of payment might be created?

- Compared to banks with a single office location, why would it be easier for banks with regional, statewide, or nationwide branches to survive an economic crisis?

For More Information

Burns, Helen M. *The American Banking Community and New Deal Banking Reforms, 1933–1935.* Westport, CT: Greenwood Press, 1974.

Kennedy, Susan E. *The Banking Crisis of 1933.* Lexington, KY: University Press of Kentucky, 1975.

Roosevelt, Franklin D. *The Public Papers and Addresses of Franklin D. Roosevelt: Volume Two, 1933.* New York, NY: Random House, 1938.

Winslow, Susan. *Brother, Can You Spare a Dime? America from the Wall Street Crash to Pearl Harbor: An Illustrated Documentary.* New York, NY: Paddington Press, 1976.

Frances Perkins

Excerpt from "Labor under the New Deal"

**Reprinted from *Two Views of American Labor*
Published in 1965**

Frances Perkins served from 1933 to 1945 as secretary of labor under President Franklin D. Roosevelt. In the spring of 1963 Perkins was a guest lecturer at the University of California at Los Angeles (UCLA). There she gave a series of lectures titled "Labor under the New Deal and the New Frontier" [the New Frontier was a program under President John F. Kennedy's administration (1961–63)]. In the lectures Perkins discussed the New Deal, from the time it was little more than an "attitude" in 1932 through passage of several pieces of important legislation. Selections from these lectures were published in 1965 in *Two Views of American Labor.*

Perkins began by discussing a speech Franklin Roosevelt gave at the Democratic National Convention in Chicago on July 2, 1932. Roosevelt was accepting the nomination to be the Democratic candidate for the presidential election of 1932, but his speech was not particularly memorable until near the end. At that point Roosevelt spoke of the "forgotten man, the little man, at the bottom." He then declared, "I pledge you—I pledge myself—to a new deal for the American people." The phrase "new deal" caught on, and eventually it

"It [the New Deal] was, I think, basically an attitude. An attitude toward government, toward the people, toward labor. It was an attitude that found voice in expressions like 'the people are what matter to government.'…"

Frances Perkins

was used to label a large body of legislation that was passed during Roosevelt's term as president. The New Deal was designed to bring relief, reform, and recovery to the United States, whose citizens were mired in the worst economic crisis in U.S. history, the Great Depression.

In the following excerpt from "Labor under the New Deal," Perkins explains how the New Deal began as an attitude or "state of mind," a belief that people were what mattered to government and that government should aim to help people have the "best possible life." This was a rather radical idea at the time. Americans had traditionally looked only to themselves and their families for help in difficult times, but the economic depression had become so severe that many people could no longer help themselves. Perkins then speaks of "putting people to work" through New Deal government agencies such as the Works Progress Administration (WPA) and the Civilian Conservation Corps (CCC). She also describes passage of the Social Security Act of 1935, one of her proudest achievements. Finally, in her discussion of the New Deal legislation, Perkins covers the National Recovery Administration (NRA), which was created under the National Industrial Recovery Act (NIRA).

Things to remember while reading the excerpt from "Labor under the New Deal":

- Americans desperately needed help and hope when Roosevelt took office. They were attracted by the new president's warmth and charm. Public opinion gave Roosevelt an almost unlimited license to attack problems as he saw fit.

- The Civilian Conservation Corps (CCC) was established in April 1933. By that summer about 240,000 young men had settled into approximately 1,200 CCC camps, ready to begin work on projects such as planting trees, digging irrigation canals, and fighting wildfires.

- The Works Progress Administration (WPA), established in May 1935, was a unique program designed to get the unemployed working and pay them a minimal salary until they could find work in private (non-government) business.

- Up to 50 percent of elderly Americans were living in poverty in the early 1930s.

- Unlike previous administrations, Roosevelt and his key advisers, including Secretary of Labor Frances Perkins, supported the interests of labor.

Excerpt from Labor under the New Deal
A State of Mind

*I would first like to deal with questions that people ask me over and over again. What was the New Deal anyhow? Was it a political plot? Was it just a name for a period in history? Was it a revolution? To all of these questions I answer "no." It was something quite different. It was very real but it certainly was not a plot. It wasn't even a plan. It wasn't a platform put through by a **faction of the Democratic Party**, and certainly it wasn't the plan or program of the Democratic Party as a whole. If you had seen the Democrats assembled at their convention in 1932, you would have known they had no such thoughts in mind. No, it wasn't any of these things. It was, I think, basically an attitude. An attitude toward government, toward the people, toward labor. It was an attitude that found voice in expressions like "the people are what matter to government," and "a government should aim to give all the people under its **jurisdiction** the best possible life."*

I remember hearing the Irish Diplomatic Minister say just this in a speech he made in Canada. When he returned, I congratulated him for his statements and he said, "Why, there's nothing strange or new in that, is there?" And I said, "No, only strange and new in America because it hasn't *been the idea to require the government to provide the best possible life for* all *the people." Roosevelt wrote and talked about this, and an awareness developed that the working people had never received full recognition ... Roosevelt always said that the New Deal lasted from 1933 until war preparations in 1941, but actually the New Deal went right on and has been going on ever since.*

The New Deal was a state of mind. But how did it come about? It was born in 1932 at the Democratic National Convention at

Faction of the Democratic Party: Principles and policies of a small group of Democrats.

Jurisdiction: Legal authority.

Chicago. When the newly nominated candidate [Roosevelt] appeared on the platform at that convention … he delivered a speech on which he had worked very hard. It was a good speech, but with very little remarkable about it until the last phrases.… He began to describe the prosperous man at the top of the pyramid and the forgotten man, the little man, at the bottom. That was what made everyone sit up and listen. Then he said, "I pledge you—I pledge myself—to a new deal for the American people." No content, no specifics, no program. Nothing in particular mentioned—but the convention roared. We were going to have a new deal. It was a card playing term that every American understood. We get a new deal, the cards fall better, so we play better. We get a better hand, we play in luck. The audience got the idea at once. The reporters who had been following the speech with care had found nothing they could headline until that moment, but the "New Deal" would easily headline. (It was the right size. I don't think Roosevelt had that in mind when he used the words, but it was the right size.) It was a striking phrase and was headlined ROOSEVELT PROMISES NEW DEAL.

Everyone caught the phrase "New Deal." It became significant right away. And soon people began to ask just what the New Deal meant. At that time we didn't know. Because the man who had made the statement didn't know himself, I'm quite sure. He had no program. He had some vague ideas, but no real plan of what might be done.

*Nevertheless, as he campaigned you heard **reverberations of this same speech** over and over again. You heard promises to do something about the unemployed, but never specifically what he was going to do about them. On one occasion he said, "We're going to put the unemployed men and women to work." Not how, or where, or for whom. We were just going to put them to work. He hadn't thought of the Works Progress Administration; that was Harry Hopkins' contribution [Hopkins was an adviser to Roosevelt]. [Roosevelt] campaigned all those months before his election without a specific program in mind. But he knew something would have to be done so the unemployed could go back to work. I remember him saying, "I know men are eating out their hearts, walking up and down, doing nothing" ….*

People by instinct soon came to some conclusion about what he meant by a New Deal. Roosevelt liked people, he had a way with them. They could see he liked them and people began to warm up to him. They didn't know him very well but they began to feel a

Reverberations of this same speech: The same theme repeated.

*kind of warmth toward him, due, as the newspapers say today, to his charm. Gradually there came to be a sense that the New Deal would be something warm and comfortable. You would be getting dealt out of whatever terrible **predicament** you were in—and the whole country was in a terrible predicament. This was the period of the Great Depression, and an almost impenetrable fog of suffering and distress hung over the whole country.*

*I am one who is convinced that the Great Depression was the **proximal** cause of the New Deal. Not that there weren't other factors entering into the cause of the New Deal. There was the factor of long neglect, for example. If something had been done about the depression in the year it began, or the year after, it wouldn't have been so bad by the time Roosevelt came into office. Without that depression many of the things that were done and many of the bold stands that were taken ... would not have come about....*

*By the time [Roosevelt's] inauguration day came in 1933 the people of this country were almost exhausted. The last three months had been the worst in the depression. The banks were closing and long **runs** began on banks in every town. The banking examiners of the various states were in despair as to what they should do. They believed that the underlying support of the banks was sound, but no bank, no matter how strong, can stand a long run. And the small country banks, where many little people often have their life's savings, were the hardest hit of all because these banks did not have enough working **capital**.*

*All these patterns were working together to bring about a New Deal for the people of the United States. Now, how did it come about? The first thing the President did, of course, was to close the banks. However, the banks were closed not so much by presidential **proclamation** as by general **consent** of the community. This had to be done. The government had to put its strength behind the banks and help prepare a program by which they could be guided safely through the disaster. This may have been regarded as an economic matter but the President viewed it as a **humanitarian move**. The people's money was in the banks; therefore they [the banks] must be saved.*

*Once the bank situation was taken care of, we had to turn to the problem of more adequate relief. Traditionally all relief had been a local function, but relief funds had been exhausted in practically every state. Many of us were afraid that there would be some **hesitancy** to go ahead with a great relief program **financed by federal**

Predicament: Trying situation.

Proximal: Central.

Runs: Long lines of depositors demanding all their savings in cash.

Capital: Cash and things of value that can be converted into cash.

Proclamation: Declaration.

Consent: Approval.

Humanitarian move: An action promoting human well-being.

Hesitancy: Reluctance or unwillingness.

Financed by federal appropriation: Funded by the federal government rather than local governments.

Southern Sr. High Media Center
Harwood, Maryland 20776

Young men with the Civilian Conservation Corps putting up a fence in Greene County, Georgia, circa 1939.
Courtesy of the Library of Congress.

appropriation. Congress was not in the habit of making appropriations for the relief of poverty. I recall that after we had discussed the various aspects of this at some length John Garner, the Vice-President, turned to the President and said, "Mr. President, when we came into office we promised the poorer kind of people we were going to do something for them. I think we had better be about it." It was a simple, straightforward statement to which most of us agreed, and we subsequently petitioned Congress for relief money to be distributed to the states.

Putting People to Work

However, a few weeks of such distribution gave no real comfort to anyone and it made people feel restless. It's a horrid thing to have to take relief from the government. Harry Hopkins [an adviser to Roosevelt] *came up with the idea of the WPA—the idea of giving people something to do and paying them a flat rate of $15 a week, no matter what they did. Whether the person worked as an artist painting murals on the wall of a post office or as an ironmonger*

beating out iron bars for a public building, the rate was $15 a week. Now I suppose that many of you have been told the story of the leaf rakers. It is possible that someone saw some old men raking leaves and doing it very badly and the conclusion was drawn that they were doing make-believe work. The only leaf rakers I ever saw were those who were too sick and old to do anything else. These were men who wanted to do something rather than nothing to get their $15. For the most part, the WPA jobs were very well chosen. The program was run at the local level by social workers in every part of the country, and on the whole the WPA was a satisfying solution to an immediate problem. A great many people were put to work. They were not, of course, earning economic wages—they were earning relief wages—but if it had not been a relief operation no one would have had them working for $15 a week.

Another of the earliest projects was the Civilian Conservation Corps, which was a modern program designed to put young boys to work. The CCC was reserved for boys who could learn something from the experience. For the most part it was confined to young men between the ages of 15 and 19, until a little later when it took in some veterans. The project was a great success because the boys went into the woods and did healthful work and got some education at the same time. The Forestry Service supervised their work, the Labor Department ran them through the employment offices for their qualifications and general health, and the Army took care of the physical side while they were in camp. The Army called in reserve officers, most of whom were also out of work, and set them up in charge of the camps. The Army also supplied all of the housekeeping services: uniforms, camp kitchens, trucks, bedding, etc.

The CCC was no problem at all. Discipline turned out to be very easy although not because military rules were enforced. The reserve officers were carefully instructed that they were not under any circumstance to apply military discipline; CCC camp life was regulated by example and persuasion. Some of the officers said to me afterwards, "You know, it was one of the greatest experiences we reserve officers ever had, because later when we got into the European war and problems arose that could not possibly be settled by military discipline, we had already learned how to manage by persuasion and diplomacy." If a boy became too **obstreperous** or if he were absolutely **incorrigible**, he was just asked to go home; he was sent back to the relief family from which he came.

Obstreperous: Unruly.

Incorrigible: Not manageable.

*Each boy had come from a family on relief and he was paid a dollar a day for his work. He had his **board**, lodging, clothes, education, and all basic needs met. He sent all of what he earned except 25¢ a week to the head of his family, and the family relief allowance was reduced by that amount. Hardly a week goes by in my life that I don't meet someone who says to me, "You knew Roosevelt; he was a great fellow. I was in the CCC and it was the best experience I ever had." This, I think, is the memory that many men have of their period in the CCC camps. It was a form of relief but it was creative, constructive, imaginative relief. It was relief that did the government good, the Army good, and the forests good. It was a public service and it did enormous good for the people who did the work....*

*One of the tragic things about the whole situation was that, try as hard as we could and do as much as we could do, we never could put all of the unemployed to work. We never could put even a fair proportion of them to work until the **war orders** began to come in. This was a very disheartening thing. We were making progress; the people felt better and they were willing to try again. They could stand low wages and believe it would all come out right in the end. But we never did see a time when the 15 million unemployed were all back to work. There was a great deal of going in and out of the labor market: people got a few weeks' work, a few months' work, and then were idle again because the economy was not stable. It had not leveled off. In 1937 we thought we had it, we thought the economy was going to be all right, and then suddenly it began to fall again. Employment began to drop and we never got to the point where we could say: "See? We have done what we said we would do—we have cured unemployment."*

Rebuilding the Economy

*But we had other strings to our bow in the **unemployment insurance act** and the **old age insurance act**, which by then were already introduced into Congress and which passed through **concurrently**. (We would have had health insurance, too, if we had been able to get to it, but we couldn't get our information together quickly enough to get that part ready to present in the winter of 1935, so we let it go a year and by that time it was too late: the medical profession had found its voice and was not going to let it pass.)*

My project for Social Security was a little slow in coming into existence. It didn't come about as a true project for almost a year after the election, when in June 1934 the Wagner-Lewis bill for un-

Board: Daily ration of food.

War orders: Orders to increase production of war materials to prepare in case the United States entered World War II (1939–45).

Unemployment insurance act: Legislation that provided for cash payments to workers who lose their job but are able and willing to work.

Old age insurance act: Legislation that provided for cash payments, generally made monthly, to retired workers.

Concurrently: At the same time.

employment insurance failed to get committee agreement. The President then appointed a committee on economic security. (It was not economic at all but rather of a **social insurance** nature, but the President preferred to call it "economic security" to avoid the implication of a **dole**.) The committee, consisting of five cabinet members, faced a difficult operation because a bill had to be prepared quickly since we were confronted with the possibility of losing the good will of Congress if we let it go for another year. We had to bring to Washington a large number of professional people: economists, statisticians, and people knowledgeable in insurance matters in order to have our report ready by the deadline of January 1, 1935.

The passage of the Social Security bill was one of the extraordinary occasions of the New Deal. We had a bill that was really so unusual, so revolutionary, and so fundamentally controversial, and yet when the Social Security bill came before Congress it was passed on a broad tide of acceptance.

The National [Industrial] Recovery Act was a piece of economic planning that was fostered by the Roosevelt Administration. This program called for each industry to set up a code with standards for both business and labor that each firm would **abide by**. The NRA [National Recovery Administration] proved to be a really remarkable instrument, first, from an educational standpoint and, second, by terminating bad practices and **insuring compliance** with the hours and wages provided for in the Act. The NRA stimulated the economy; workers spent their money on the necessities. The outlook of the business community took on a tone of success rather than failure. The program went very well for the first five or six different industries but then began to run into trouble. If the NRA had covered only eight or ten or even twenty or thirty of the larger and more important industries, it might have lasted to this day. The principal cause of its failure was its attempt to spread its **jurisdiction** over too many and comparatively insignificant industries.

In spite of its relatively short life, the NRA did make a great contribution. This was the recognition given by the government to organized labor. The establishment of labor representatives in **prominent** advisory positions **gave impetus to** a good relationship between government and labor. This was the first time that the government had realized its right, and even its duty, to consult with labor in regard to wages, hours, and other working conditions, as well as general business conditions.

Social insurance: A broad term referring to government-sponsored social well-being programs such as old-age pensions, unemployment supports, workers' compensation for those injured on the job, and health care programs.

Dole: Welfare handout.

Abide by: Obey.

Insuring compliance: Making sure that rules were followed.

Jurisdiction: Authority or control.

Prominent: Important.

Gave impetus to: Helped to establish.

*However, the most important part of the Act as far as labor was concerned was Section 7(a). This section gave to labor the right to organize and **bargain collectively**. It is true that all through the New Deal period there ran an attitude toward the working people of the United States—that they must be recognized as our nation's most important resource—but those who wrote the NRA bill hardly anticipated the results of this particular section. The business community believed that Section 7(a) meant that those who were organized could remain so, and those who bargained collectively could continue to do so. But [labor leaders] John L. Lewis and Sidney Hillman used their entire treasuries to conduct extensive organizing drives [organizing unions]. They met with tremendous success and others followed their lead. Their right to do this was protected by the NRA and later by the Wagner Act.*

During the first year of the National Industrial Recovery Act, as I recall, William Green said that over a million people joined the labor movement. It was a period of great energy and activity in a group of people who had almost ceased to function as a movement. With this came a new spark of life in people who ought to have been organizing long before and who ought to have been taking the lead in expressing their views and opinions, but who had never had any political power or force. The self-propelling, self-directing activity began that made the modern labor unions of America so effective for their own people, and so persuasive to other people....

I have attempted to describe the background, and some of the causes and results, of the New Deal. [Perkins, pp. 2–4, 6–8, 9–12]

What happened next...

The CCC remained in operation until 1941 and provided work, food, shelter, and instruction in basic work skills to hundreds of thousands of young men. Likewise, the WPA provided millions of people with work from 1935 until 1943, when it was disbanded. The Social Security Act of 1935 was amended many times throughout the twentieth century and remained the century's premier piece of social legislation. The NRA was a bold experiment, but in May 1935 the U.S.

Bargain collectively:
Negotiate with an employer through representatives who work to reach agreement on working conditions, wages, and job benefits.

Supreme Court ruled that the act that created the NRA was unconstitutional. However, before it was disbanded, the NRA had laid important groundwork for modern labor unions.

Francis Perkins continued to teach until shortly before her death in New York City in 1965. In her last decade of life, much of it spent as a visiting professor at Cornell University, she constantly challenged young people to find ways to work for the betterment of humankind.

Did you know...

- Social insurance programs such as workers' compensation (cash payments to workers injured on the job) and old-age retirement payments were common in European countries by the early 1900s. However, Americans' firm belief in self-reliance kept such programs out of the United States for a long time. The Social Security Act of 1935 finally provided Americans with unemployment and retirement support.

- WPA projects provided jobs not only for construction workers but also for artists, musicians, writers, and students.

- Harry Hopkins (1890–1946), Roosevelt's close adviser and chief relief officer, was determined to fulfill Roosevelt's promise that no one would go hungry in the winter of 1933–34. Hopkins kept early relief efforts going despite the cost. He earned a reputation as an honest, hardworking professional administrator.

Consider the following...

- Do you think the American people would have approved of federal government involvement in so many aspects of American life if the Depression had been less severe?

- Why did the phrase "new deal" catch on as a name for the legislation of the 1930s? What images did the phrase create in the minds of people struggling through the Depression?

- What did Perkins say was the most "disheartening thing" about unemployment relief efforts in the 1930s?

• What do you think Perkins meant when she stated "Roosevelt always said that the New Deal lasted from 1933 until war preparations in 1941, but actually the New Deal went right on and has been going on ever since"? Remember, she was speaking in 1963.

For More Information

Books

Conkin, Paul Keith. *The New Deal.* Arlington Heights, IL: Harlan Davidson, 1992.

Perkins, Frances, and J. Paul St. Sure. *Two Views of American Labor.* Los Angeles, CA: Institute of Industrial Relations, 1965.

Reagan, Patrick D. *Designing a New America: The Origins of New Deal Planning, 1890–1943.* Amherst, MA: University of Massachusetts Press, 1999.

Roosevelt, Franklin D. *The Public Papers and Addresses of Franklin D. Roosevelt: Volume Two, 1933.* New York, NY: Random House, 1938.

Sternsher, Bernard. *Hope Restored: How the New Deal Worked in Town and Country.* Chicago, IL: Ivan R. Dee, 1999.

Web Sites

New Deal Network: A Guide to the Great Depression of the 1930s. http://newdeal.feri.org (accessed on August 27, 2002).

Franklin D. Roosevelt

Excerpt from "Second Inaugural Address of Franklin D. Roosevelt, Wednesday, January 20, 1937"

**Reprinted from *The Public Papers and Addresses of Franklin D. Roosevelt: Volume Two, 1937*
Published in 1941**

In his "Second Inaugural Address," delivered on January 20, 1937, Franklin D. Roosevelt reminded Americans how "a new chapter in our book of self-government" was written during his first term of office. Instead of leaving solutions for the economic crisis to the "winds of chance and the hurricanes of disaster," Roosevelt chose to put the federal government at the forefront of the war on the Depression. In his speech Roosevelt pointed out that the country had progressed a long way from the depths of the Depression in 1933. However, he also made this famous statement: "I see one-third of a nation ill-housed, ill-clad [poorly clothed], ill-nourished." Believing there was much still to be done, Roosevelt pledged to lead Americans forward in pursuit of full economic recovery.

"I see a great nation, upon a great continent, blessed with a great wealth of natural resources. Its ... people are at peace among themselves; they are making their country a good neighbor among the nations."

Franklin D. Roosevelt

Things to remember while reading the excerpt from "Second Inaugural Address of Franklin D. Roosevelt, Wednesday, January 20, 1937":

- The Second New Deal legislation and programs of 1935 and 1936, which focused on workers, small farmers,

artists, and young Americans, proved extremely popular with a majority of Americans.

- Roosevelt, a Democrat, won the 1936 election by the largest margin of victory ever in a U.S. presidential race. Democrats also continued to dominate the Senate and House of Representatives.

- Diverse groups of voters came together to support Roosevelt in the 1936 election. They included laborers, Catholics, Jews, big-city political organizations, Southerners, and a majority of black Americans. This was the first presidential election in which the Democratic candidate won a majority of black American votes. These various groups became known as the Democratic Coalition.

Excerpt from
"Second Inaugural Address of Franklin D. Roosevelt, Wednesday, January 20, 1937"

*When four years ago we met to **inaugurate** a President, the Republic, single-minded in anxiety, stood in spirit here. We dedicated ourselves to the fulfillment of a vision—to speed the time when there would be for all the people that security and peace essential to the pursuit of happiness. We of the Republic pledged ourselves to **drive from the temple of our ancient faith those who had profaned it**; to end by action, tireless and unafraid, the **stagnation** and despair of that day. We did those first things first.*

*Our **covenant** with ourselves did not stop there. Instinctively we recognized a deeper need—the need to find through government the instrument of our united purpose [to enlist the help of government] to solve for the individual the ever-rising problems of a complex civilization. Repeated attempts at their solution without the aid of government had left us **baffled** and bewildered ... We knew that we must find practical controls over blind economic forces and blindly selfish men.*

*We of the Republic sensed the truth that democratic government had **innate capacity** to protect its people against disasters*

Inaugurate: Swear into office.

Drive from the temple...: Remove dishonest persons from places of responsibility.

Stagnation: Lack of movement.

Covenant: Pledge or promise.

Baffled: Confused.

Innate capacity: The ability.

*once considered **inevitable**, to solve problems once considered unsolvable.... We refused to leave the problems of our common **welfare** to be solved by the winds of chance and the hurricanes of disaster.*

In this we Americans were discovering no wholly new truth; we were writing a new chapter in our book of self-government.

*This year marks the one hundred and fiftieth anniversary of the Constitutional Convention which made us a nation. At that Convention our forefathers found the way out of the **chaos** which followed the Revolutionary War; they created a strong government with powers of united action sufficient then and now to solve problems **utterly beyond individual or local solution**. A century and a half ago they established the Federal Government in order to promote the general welfare and secure the blessings of liberty to the American people.*

*Today we **invoke** those same powers of government to achieve the same objectives....*

Franklin D. Roosevelt making his inaugural speech after taking the oath of office for his second term, January 20, 1937. *©Corbis-Bettmann. Reproduced by permission.*

Inevitable: Unavoidable.

Welfare: Well-being.

Chaos: Utter confusion.

Utterly beyond individual or local solution: Too big for individuals or communities to figure out by themselves.

Invoke: Call upon.

*Government of the United States can do the things the times require, without yielding its democracy. Our tasks in the last four years **did not force democracy to take a holiday**....*

Our progress out of the depression is obvious. But that is not all that you and I mean by the new order of things. Our pledge was not merely to do a patchwork job with secondhand materials. By using the new materials of social justice [such as the ideas in the Social Security Act of 1935] *we have undertaken to erect on the old foundations a more enduring structure for the better use of future generations.*

In that purpose we have been helped by achievements of mind and spirit. Old truths have been relearned [Americans recognized more than ever that they had to work for what they earned]; *untruths have been unlearned* [the public realized that stock market profits would not continue forever]. *We have always known that heedless self-interest was bad morals; we know now that it is bad economics* [greed hurts people and the economy] ....

Shall we pause now and turn our back upon the road that lies ahead? Shall we call this the promised land? Or, shall we continue on our way? For "each age is a dream that is dying, or one that is coming to birth."

*Many voices are heard as we face a great decision. Comfort says, "**Tarry** a while." Opportunism says, "This is a good spot." Timidity asks, "How difficult is the road ahead?"*

Let us ask again: Have we reached the goal of our vision of that fourth day of March 1933? Have we found our happy valley?

*I see a great nation, upon a great continent, blessed with a great wealth of natural resources. Its hundred and thirty million people are at peace among themselves; they are making their country a good neighbor among the nations. I see a United States which can demonstrate that, under democratic methods of government, national wealth can be translated into a spreading volume of human comforts **hitherto unknown**, and the lowest standard of living can be raised far above the level of mere **subsistence**.*

But here is the challenge to our democracy: In this nation I see tens of millions of its citizens—a substantial part of its whole population—who at this very moment are denied the greater part of what the very lowest standards of today call the necessities of life.

*I see millions of families trying to live on incomes so meager that the **pall** of family disaster hangs over them day by day.*

Did not force democracy ...: U.S. leaders did not have to violate the principles of democracy to solve the country's problems.

Tarry: Stay.

Hitherto unknown: Never experienced before.

Subsistence: Survival.

Pall: Gloom.

I see millions whose daily lives in city and on farm continue under conditions labeled indecent by a so-called polite society half a century ago.

I see millions denied education, recreation, and the opportunity to better their lot and the lot of their children.

I see millions lacking the means to buy the products of farm and factory and by their poverty denying work and productiveness to many other millions.

Artist Conrad A. Albrizio titled his 1930s mural "The New Deal" and dedicated it to Franklin D. Roosevelt for his commitment to the people of the United States. *Courtesy of the Franklin D. Roosevelt Library.*

*I see one-third of a nation ill-housed, **ill-clad**, ill-nourished.*

*It is not in despair that I paint you that picture. I paint it for you in hope—because the Nation, seeing and understanding the injustice in it, proposes to paint it out. We are determined to make every American citizen the subject of his country's interest and concern; and we will never regard any faithful all-abiding group within our borders as **superfluous**. The test of our progress is not whether we add more to the abundance of those who have much; it is whether we provide enough for those who have too little.*

*If I know **aught** of the spirit and purpose of our Nation, we will not listen to Comfort, Opportunism, and Timidity. We will carry on.*

Overwhelmingly, we of the Republic are men and women of good will; men and women who have more than warm hearts of dedication; men and women who have cool heads and willing hands of practical purpose as well. They will insist that every agency of popular government use effective instruments to carry out their will.

*Government is **competent** when all who compose it work as **trustees** for the whole people. It can make constant progress when it keeps **abreast** of all the facts. It can obtain justified support and legitimate criticism when the people receive true information of all that government does.*

If I know aught of the will of our people, they will demand that these conditions of effective government shall be created and maintained. They will demand a nation uncorrupted by cancers of injustice and, therefore, strong among the nations in its example of the will to peace.

*Today we **reconsecrate** our country to long-cherished ideals in a suddenly changed civilization. In every land there are always at work forces that drive men apart and forces that draw men together. In our personal ambitions we are individualists. But in our seeking for economic and political progress as a nation, we all go up, or else we all go down, as one people.*

*To maintain a democracy of effort requires a vast amount of patience in dealing with differing methods, **a vast amount of humility**. But out of the confusion of many voices rises an understanding of **dominant public need**. Then political leadership can voice common ideals, and aid in their realization.*

In taking again the oath of office as President of the United States, I assume the solemn obligation of leading the American people forward along the road over which they have chosen to advance.

Ill-clad: Poorly clothed.

Superfluous: Not important.

Aught: Anything.

Competent: Adequate, effective.

Trustees: Representatives.

Abreast: Informed.

Reconsecrate: Rededicate.

A vast amount of humility: An attitude that is not overly prideful.

Dominant public need: The most important needs of the general public.

While this duty rests upon me I shall do my utmost to speak their purpose and to do their will, seeking Divine guidance to help us each and every one to give light to them that sit in darkness and to guide our feet into the way of peace. [Roosevelt, pp. 1–6]

What happened next...

After Roosevelt's reelection, Americans had anticipated with excitement more New Deal legislation. This excitement was short-lived. Riding the wave of public support, Roosevelt decided to introduce in 1937 bold new legislation to reform the U.S. Supreme Court. Roosevelt had been greatly angered when the sitting Court struck down two key pieces of New Deal legislation: the National Industrial Recovery Act (NIRA) in 1935 and the Agricultural Adjustment Act in 1936. Roosevelt proposed increasing the number of Supreme Court justices so he could appoint new judges who would be friendly to his programs. This bill was known as Roosevelt's "court-packing plan." The bill was debated in Congress for six months but failed to pass. Legislators and the general public both saw it as a power grab. As a result, momentum for more New Deal legislation was lost.

Another setback for Roosevelt was the economic downturn of 1937. In spring 1937 the economy had made substantial progress in recovering from the depths of the Depression, so Roosevelt and Congress began reducing funds for relief programs. By fall the recovery had stopped; industrial production fell, farm prices fell, and unemployment increased. Still, one new piece of New Deal legislation made it through Congress: The Wagner-Steagall Housing Act passed on September 1, 1937, and provided funds for housing for the needy. Two other important pieces of New Deal legislation, enacted in 1938, were the Food, Drug, and Cosmetic Act (a consumer protection bill) and the Fair Labor Standards Act. The Fair Labor Standards Act replaced some of the standards set by the no-longer-valid NIRA and added new ones. Most important, it set a minimum hourly wage and maximum weekly hours and banned most child labor. Under the

Food, Drug, and Cosmetic Act, the processing and labeling of foods, drugs, and cosmetics came under federal control.

The 1938 elections for the U.S. Senate and House marked the end of any new New Deal legislation. The public, increasingly concerned by the substantial growth of government, high government spending, and government regulation of business, elected a greater number of conservative politicians opposed to New Deal programs. Roosevelt, by necessity, turned his attention increasingly to the conflicts building in Europe. Although passage of new New Deal programs halted, many of the already established programs became cornerstones for government programs that lasted into the twenty-first century.

Did you know...

- Roosevelt's "Second Inaugural Address" was given on January 20, 1937, not in March as his first inaugural address was. The Twentieth Amendment to the U.S. Constitution had been ratified (approved) by the states so that a president-elect could take office in January rather than waiting until March.

- The economy had shown signs of recovery from the Depression, but it suffered setbacks in fall 1937. Roosevelt, trying to keep the public's morale up, coined a new term to describe the latest downturn: "recession." He desperately wanted to avoid the word "depression." Thus the period of reduced economic activity was labeled the Recession of 1937. By the start of the twenty-first century, the term "depression" had never again been used to describe an economic downturn.

Consider the following...

- In the "Second Inaugural Address," Roosevelt stated, "To maintain a democracy ... requires a vast amount of patience in dealing with differing methods, a vast amount of humility. But out of the confusion of many voices rises an understanding of dominant public need." Do you think these words still hold true? Give reasons why or why not.

- Why did Roosevelt's "court-packing plan" scare away many of his supporters and keep Congress from considering other New Deal initiatives?

For More Information

Books

Edsforth, Ronald. *The New Deal: America's Response to the Great Depression*. Malden, MA: Blackwell Publishers, 2000.

Leuchtenberg, William E. *Franklin D. Roosevelt and the New Deal, 1932–1940*. New York, NY: Harper &Row, 1963.

Roosevelt, Franklin D. *The Public Papers and Addresses of Franklin D. Roosevelt: Volume Two, 1937*. New York, NY: Macmillan, 1941.

Schlesinger, Arthur M., Jr. *The Coming of the New Deal: The Age of Roosevelt*. Boston, MA: Houghton Mifflin, 1988.

Sampling of Key New Deal Legislation

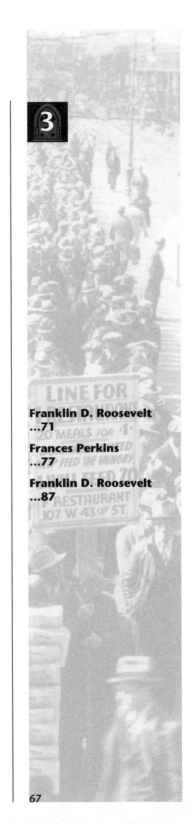

U pon his first inauguration in March 1933, President Franklin D. Roosevelt (1882–1945) and his close advisers and cabinet members immediately began to develop and write legislation designed to help bring the United States out of the Great Depression, the worst economic crisis ever experienced by the nation. The legislation and the relief and recovery programs it created became known as the New Deal. Once the most urgent needs of hunger and unemployment were addressed, the president turned his attention to establishing permanent programs of recovery, reform, and rebuilding. Included among these programs were the National Housing Act of 1934, the Social Security Act of 1935, and the Fair Labor Standards Act of 1938.

The Great Depression dealt blows to both the home owner and the construction industry. In 1932 between 250,000 and 275,000 homes were lost to foreclosure. (In comparison, 68,000 homes were foreclosed in 1926.) Foreclosure is a legal proceeding in which a bank that has loaned money for the purchase of a home takes the home back because the borrower has not kept up with payments on the

Electricity and the New Deal

Franklin D. Roosevelt supported electrical modernization of America on a broad basis. He believed that inexpensive electricity could greatly improve the quality of life for American families, especially in rural areas. To achieve the goal of affordable and plentiful electricity for all, Roosevelt sought to apply broad governmental planning to various regions of the nation. During Roosevelt's first one hundred days in office, Congress passed legislation establishing the Tennessee Valley Authority (TVA) on May 18, 1933. The TVA was an experiment in regional economic planning involving a large area that included portions of seven Southeastern states (Tennessee, Kentucky, Virginia, Mississippi, Alabama, Georgia, and North Carolina). The TVA built a series of dams and power plants to provide inexpensive electricity to farms and industry in the broad region. TVA also provided much more, including flood control, improvement of river navigability, and even reforesting nearby hills.

Associated with the TVA, the Rural Electrification Administration (REA) was created in May 1935. The REA provided loans

loan. By 1933 foreclosures reached a dismaying rate of a thousand per day. Between 1929 and 1933 construction of residential property fell 95 percent, and expenditures on repairs decreased from fifty million to one-half million dollars. Roosevelt knew that home loss and the construction downturn needed to be dealt with quickly if the U.S. economy was to be turned around. As a result, Congress passed the Home Owners' Refinancing Act of 1933 and the National Housing Act of 1934 to deal with these issues.

Roosevelt and Secretary of Labor Frances Perkins (1880–1965) considered the Social Security Act of 1935 a cornerstone of New Deal legislation. In the 1930s it was estimated that approximately 50 percent of the elderly lived in poverty. Anyone who was injured in an industrial accident, and who could no longer work, fell quickly into debt; injured workers' families became poverty-stricken. Those who were laid off because business was slow had the same difficulties. Roosevelt realized he could not protect all Americans from all hardships in life, but he wanted to institute some measure of social insurance or social security protection for U.S. citizens.

to local electrical cooperatives to build electrical transmission systems and purchase electricity from power companies. Originally focused on the TVA region, the REA eventually extended its activity nationwide. By 1939 the REA had assisted more than 400 cooperatives and 268,000 households.

By the end of the 1930s the TVA was generating and distributing large amounts of electric power for a huge territory. Ship traffic increased as new dams and navigation locks were completed. The New Deal experiment had a lasting effect on the economy and the lives of the people in the TVA region by providing power and navigatible waterways. Both of these measures provided for substantial industrial growth and linked agriculture to more distant markets. The TVA was the model of efficiency Roosevelt was seeking. In addition to providing electricity, massive dams served many purposes, including flood control, navigation, irrigation, and recreation. It was extremely popular with the public, employing many thousands of people and bringing electricity to the countryside. The TVA was one of the crowning achievements of the New Deal.

He had hoped to have everyone covered by the Social Security Act, but only about 50 percent of citizens ended up being covered through the act. Nevertheless, it was a start, a foundation to build upon. The act provided cash payments to those hurt on the job and to the unemployed. It also provided old-age retirement benefits and increased health services for children, mothers, and some disabled persons. The Social Security Act of 1935 was amended many times throughout the twentieth century to further improve social insurance programs for individuals and families.

The Fair Labor Standards Act, passed on June 25, 1938, proved to be the last New Deal measure. The act addressed vital issues such as minimum wage, maximum hours, overtime pay, and child labor. Like the Social Security Act, the Fair Labor Standards Act underwent numerous amendments during the twentieth century, and it remains a fundamental piece of labor legislation in the twenty-first century.

The first of the following excerpts is taken from "Recommendation for Legislation to Provide Assistance for Repairing and Construction of Homes, May 14, 1934," pub-

lished in *The Public Papers and Addresses of Franklin D. Roosevelt: Volume Three, 1934.* In this excerpt Roosevelt explains to Congress the need for action to aid the home construction industry. Then in his notes he describes the function of the Federal Housing Administration (FHA), which was established by the National Housing Act of 1934. The second excerpt is from **The Roosevelt I Knew,** a book published by Frances Perkins in 1946. Perkins gives an insider's view of the creation of the Social Security Act. The third excerpt is from Roosevelt's **"Annual Message to the Congress, January 3, 1938,"** published in *The Public Papers and Addresses of Franklin D. Roosevelt: 1938 Volume.* In this speech Roosevelt argues for a legal minimum wage to increase Americans' ability to purchase goods.

Franklin D. Roosevelt

Excerpt from "Recommendation for Legislation to Provide Assistance for Repairing and Construction of Homes, May 14, 1934"

Reprinted from *The Public Papers and Addresses of Franklin D. Roosevelt: Volume Three, 1934* Published in 1938

As part of President Franklin Roosevelt's New Deal economic policies, two pieces of legislation were passed by Congress to deal with the ailing home financing systems and the construction industry. On June 13, 1933, just three months after Roosevelt took office, Congress passed the Home Owners' Refinancing Act, which created the Home Owners' Loan Corporation (HOLC). The HOLC was an emergency agency whose goal was to stop the avalanche of foreclosures by refinancing home owners' loans. Refinancing means to set up new loan terms that are easier to pay back, such as a longer repayment period and lower interest rates.

To deal with the construction nosedive, Congress passed the National Housing Act on June 28, 1934; the act established the Federal Housing Administration (FHA). The National Housing Act was designed to stimulate construction without government spending, because Roosevelt wanted to rely on private enterprise: Home loans were to be made by private lending institutions, predominantly banks. The FHA made no loans but insured the home loans made by private lending institutions. If a borrower failed to make payment,

"The protection of the health and safety of the people demands that this renovizing [repairing] and building be done speedily."

Franklin D. Roosevelt

the FHA would pay the lending institution the amount owed on the failed loan. In response to this arrangement, bankers freed up a great deal of money for home loans, because they assumed almost no risk if borrowers could not repay them.

To help guarantee that the loans it insured would not go bad, the FHA helped lending institutions design loans that were more workable for the average American. Down payment requirements and interest rates were lowered and the repayment period was extended to twenty-five to thirty years, all translating into low, easily met monthly payments.

The first part of the following excerpt is from an address Roosevelt made to Congress, asking legislators to pass the National Housing Act. President Roosevelt wrote the second part of the excerpt beginning with "Note:" in December 1937. In his "note," Roosevelt explained the need for the 1934 act and related how successful the programs of the FHA had been.

Things to remember while reading the excerpt from "Recommendation for Legislation to Provide Assistance for Repairing and Construction of Homes, May 14, 1934":

- As more Americans lost their jobs or took salary cuts, they fell behind on house payments. No one was buying a new home. As a result, home construction stopped.

- By 1933, 40 to 50 percent of all home mortgages (loans) in the United States were in default (borrowers had not been able to make payments). The home financing system and the construction industry were near collapse.

- Because home owners could not afford regular maintenance repairs, houses became run-down and property values slid downward.

Excerpt from "Recommendation for Legislation to Provide Assistance for Repairing and Construction of Homes, May 14, 1934"

To the Congress:

May I draw your attention to some important suggestions for legislation which should tend to improve conditions for those who live in houses, those who repair and construct houses, and those who invest in houses?

*Many of our homes are **in decadent condition** and not fit for human habitation. They need repairing and modernizing to bring them up to the standard of the times. Many new homes now are needed to replace those not worth repairing.*

*The protection of the health and safety of the people demands that this **renovizing** and building be done speedily. The Federal Government should take the initiative immediately to cooperate with **private capital** and industry in this real-property conservation. We must lay the groundwork for this effort before Congress adjourns its present session.*

*The purpose of the program is twofold: first, to return many of the unemployed to useful and gainful occupation; second, to produce **tangible**, useful wealth in a form for which there is great social and economic need....*

*Note: ... **Pursuant to** the message, the Congress enacted a National Housing Act, approved June 28, 1934.... The declared purpose of the Act was to encourage improvement in housing standards and conditions and to create a sound system of **home financing**.*

*The Federal Housing Administration set up by the **statute** does not loan its own money or make any grant of Federal funds. What it does is to insure loans made by banks, building and loan associations, insurance companies and other private lending institutions for **refinancing** existing houses, for the construction of new homes and for the modernization and repair of all types of structures.*

*Owing to the continued depression, residential construction in America had sunk to a very low ebb. Not only was there a **cessation***

In decadent condition: Decaying.

Renovizing: Updating and repairing.

Private capital: Business.

Tangible: Material, real.

Pursuant to: In accord or agreement with.

Home financing: Methods to pay for a home.

Statute: Congressional act.

Refinancing: Setting up new terms under which it is easier for the borrower to pay back a loan.

Cessation: Halting.

*of new home construction, but because of general lack of funds, homes had been allowed to fall into disrepair. A program of construction of new homes and of repair and renovation would not only provide useful work for the unemployed, but would produce **tangible useful wealth in a form socially and economically desirable.***

The Federal Housing Administration has made much progress along the lines and objectives laid down by the statute. From the time of its creation to December 1, 1937 [when this note was written], *the gross business transacted by it totaled nearly $2,000,000,000. Over 250,000 **home mortgages**, valued at more than a billion dollars, were accepted by it for insurance. The homes securing these* [FHA-insured] *mortgages would provide for a city of nearly a million inhabitants; and it is estimated that, each week, over 2,000 additional families are acquiring their own homes under this program.*

*Modernization and repair **notes** amounting to over $560,000,000 were insured under the emergency provisions of the Act which have since expired. By this means the Housing Administration has raised the living standards of the millions of persons residing in the 1,250,000 urban dwellings and farm properties so improved; and it has enabled more than 100,000 small business concerns to modernize their plants and equipment.* [Roosevelt, pp. 232, 234–235]

What happened next...

The combined activities of the HOLC and the FHA enabled families to keep their homes and revived the construction industry. By February 1936 the HOLC had refinanced 992,531 home loans totaling more than $3 billion. The HOLC loans prevented countless foreclosures and allowed home owners to start paying their property taxes again. This permitted communities to pay for local schools, police, and other services, all of which depended on the regular collection of those taxes. Millions of loan dollars also went to repair and remodel homes. Thousands of jobs were created in the building trades, including jobs in the manufacture, transportation, and sale of construction materials. However, since the HOLC was set up only as an emergency

Tangible useful wealth...: Something real—houses—that people can either live in or sell, thereby improving their own situation and the economy

Home mortgages: Home loans.

Notes: Loans.

agency, it stopped offering loans in June 1935 and spent the next fifteen years collecting payments on its loans.

Unlike the HOLC, the FHA was established as a permanent agency. Between June 1934 and December 1937, the FHA insured more than 250,000 home mortgages valued at over a billion dollars. FHA loan terms made it possible for Americans to start purchasing new homes again, which stimulated the construction industry. Housing starts, or the number of new homes on which construction began, numbered only 93,000 in 1933 but had risen to 337,000 in 1937 and to 619,000 in 1941.

Did you know...

- No New Deal agencies had a more lasting or powerful impact on Americans over the rest of the twentieth century than the HOLC and the FHA. These agencies laid the foundation for low-risk, low-interest, equal-monthly-payment mortgages.

- The HOLC set standards for appraisal (evaluation) of a home's value, and the FHA set building construction standards.

- The FHA favored single-family homes in suburban areas. For example, in St. Louis, Missouri, between 1935 and 1939, 92 percent of new homes insured by the FHA were in the suburbs.

Consider the following...

- Use your math skills and figure out why it was easier to make loan repayments that were spread over thirty years than to pay back loans that demanded complete repayment in five years—the typical loan arrangement before the New Deal. Assume that the home cost $5,000, a typical selling price of a middle-class home in the late 1930s.

- New Deal support for suburban housing reflected Roosevelt's belief that people lived a better life in the country than in cities. The FHA discouraged loans for multi-family dwellings but encouraged loans for single-family

houses in the suburbs. What effect do you think the FHA loan practices had on inner-city residential areas?

For More Information

Gelfand, Mark I. *A Nation of Cities: The Federal Government and Urban America, 1933–1965.* New York, NY: Oxford University Press, 1975.

Jackson, Kenneth T. *Crabgrass Frontier: The Suburbanization of the United States.* New York, NY: Oxford University Press, 1985.

Roosevelt, Franklin D. *The Public Papers and Addresses of Franklin D. Roosevelt: Volume Three, 1934.* New York, NY: Random House, 1938.

Frances Perkins

Excerpt from **The Roosevelt I Knew**
Published in 1946

Historians consider the Social Security Act of 1935 the most important and revolutionary piece of social legislation ever passed by the U.S. Congress. The Social Security Act was revolutionary because before 1935 the U.S. federal government had never taken on the responsibility of social insurance for its people. Social insurance is a term referring to various government-sponsored programs designed to protect the living standards of a country's citizens, especially the aged, the very needy, and the disabled. Such programs include cash support known as unemployment insurance for those who have lost their jobs; old-age retirement income, often called an old-age pension; help for the very poor and the disabled; and certain health care benefits.

Social insurance answers a basic human need—the need to face the future with some measure of economic security. At one time or another all people endure the difficulties of illness, job loss, disability, or old age. Before the twentieth century, most Americans relied on the family farm and their extended family for economic security. Independent Americans, full of pride and determination to take care of their

"We must have a [social insurance] program by next winter and it must be in operation before many more months have passed."

Franklin D. Roosevelt

A poster advertises the benefits of Social Security for the elderly. *Courtesy of the Franklin D. Roosevelt Library.*

MORE SECURITY FOR THE AMERICAN FAMILY

THE SOCIAL SECURITY ACT AS AMENDED OFFERS GREATER OLD-AGE INSURANCE PROTECTION TO PEOPLE NOW NEARING RETIREMENT AGE.

FOR INFORMATION WRITE OR CALL AT THE NEAREST FIELD OFFICE OF THE

SOCIAL SECURITY BOARD

own, never thought of the government as a source of economic support. However, during the late nineteenth century many Americans left the land and the safety of their families to seek work in the cities, where factories were springing up. More and more individuals and their families became totally dependent on wages from industrial jobs; being injured, being laid off, becoming disabled, or merely growing too old to work frequently meant being penniless and helpless. The

Great Depression worsened the situation, especially for the elderly. Many lost their entire savings, intended for retirement, in bank failures. Frequently, the elderly had to move into the homes of their grown children who were already struggling to make ends meet. Poverty among the aged increased dramatically. By 1934 more than one-half of the elderly in the United States did not have enough income to support themselves.

By 1934 Roosevelt and Secretary of Labor Frances Perkins were convinced the nation needed some sort of long-term social insurance program to aid the unemployed, the elderly, and the very poor. On June 8, 1934, Roosevelt notified Congress of his intent to develop a plan of social insurance. On June 29, 1934, Roosevelt announced the formation of the Committee on Economic Security. He appointed Perkins as chairperson of the Committee, which was charged with the responsibility of creating the social insurance plan. Despite the complex issues that had to be considered, it took only thirteen and one-half months—from committee planning to passage by Congress— for the Social Security Act to arrive on Roosevelt's desk for signature on August 14, 1935.

"Cradle to the grave—from the cradle to the grave they [Americans] ought to be in a social insurance system." Roosevelt spoke these words to Perkins, as he turned the idea of social insurance over in his mind. Perkins recalled the president's statement in her book, *The Roosevelt I Knew*, as she described the period of time when she and others in Roosevelt's administration were developing the Social Security Act. Published in 1946, only a year after Roosevelt's death, Perkins's book provides a look into the inner circles of the White House during the New Deal era. The excerpt that follows ends with a description of the moment when Roosevelt signed the Social Security Act into law.

Things to remember while reading the excerpt from *The Roosevelt I Knew*:

- Two pieces of social legislation were already in Congress by early 1934: the Wagner-Lewis Bill, which concerned unemployment insurance, and the Dill-Connery Old Age Pension Bill.

- An elderly medical doctor named Francis Townsend (1867–1960) and Senator Huey P. Long (1893–1935) of Louisiana each promoted a plan for a nationwide old-age pension. These plans had great public support, but both plans were unworkable because they would have bankrupted the nation's treasury.

- Roosevelt wanted one act to cover social insurance issues for the whole nation, and he wanted everyone covered from birth to death.

- Roosevelt disapproved of funding the program from general taxes. He was afraid Congress would cut funds anytime they saw fit. Having citizens contribute from their own paychecks ensured that Congress could never take that money away from those who contributed it.

Excerpt from The Roosevelt I Knew
Chapter 23: Social Security

*Before his **Inauguration** in 1933 Roosevelt had agreed that we should explore at once methods for setting up unemployment and old-age insurance in the United States....*

*The President urged me to discuss the matter in as many groups as possible. I began in the **cabinet**. I made a point of bringing it up, at the least, at every second meeting. Gradually the other cabinet members became sincerely and honestly interested....*

I myself made over a hundred speeches in different parts of the country that year, always stressing social insurance as one of the methods for assisting the unemployed in times of depression and in preventing depressions. We stimulated others to talk and write about the subject....

*The Wagner-Lewis bill in the Congress covered only **unemployment insurance**, but there was a great demand for **old-age insurance** also. It was easy to add this feature—and politically almost essential. One hardly realizes nowadays how strong was the sentiment in favor of the **Townsend Plan** and other **exotic schemes** for giving the aged a weekly income. In some districts the Townsend*

Inauguration: Swearing-in ceremony.

Cabinet: A formal group of advisers to the president.

Unemployment insurance: Cash payments made for a limited period of time to those who lose their jobs.

Old-age insurance: Cash payments made monthly to retired workers; retirement pension pay.

Townsend Plan: A plan that proposed to pay $200 monthly to every sixty-year-old who was retired and not a criminal.

Exotic schemes: Imaginative but unworkable plans.

Plan was the chief political issue, and men supporting it were elected to Congress. The pressure from its **advocates** was intense. The President began telling people he was in favor of adding old-age insurance clauses to the bill and putting it through as one program....

By June 1934 the Wagner-Lewis bill had not reached committee agreement. There had been **divergences** of view in the **testimony** and recommendations. We began to see that there must be further study and a more complete plan before it could be presented to Congress for action.

The President had put the program on the must list. But the weather grew hot and the Congress was exhausted. Roosevelt was persuaded it might be better to say to Congress that he would be happy to agree to their **adjourning**, providing they understood that he would have a real study made during the summer and would present a full program on economic security on the first of January when they **reconvened**. Congress gladly agreed. Since members of the cabinet had developed great interest in the social security program, I suggested that it might be well to have the study made by a **cabinet committee**. The President readily **acquiesced**. He saw at once that a program developed by a committee of the cabinet would be under his control....

I asked him if he thought it best for me to be chairman, since the public knew I favored the general idea. Perhaps it would be better, from the point of view of Congress and the public, if the Attorney General were chairman.

He was quick in his response. "No, no. You [Perkins] care about this thing. You believe in it. Therefore I know you will **put your back to it** more than anyone else, and you will drive it through. You will see that something comes out, and we must not delay. I am convinced. We must have a program by next winter and it must be in operation before many more months have passed."

By the time the study was fully launched the President's imaginative mind had begun to **play over it**. At cabinet meetings and when he talked privately with a group of us, he would say, "You want to make it simple—very simple. So simple that everybody will understand it. And what's more, there is no reason why everybody in the United States should not be covered. I see no reason why every child, from the day he is born, shouldn't be a member of the social security system. When he begins to grow up, he should know he will have **old-age benefits** direct from the insurance system to

Advocates: Supporters.

Divergences: Differences or disagreements.

Testimony: Presentation of facts.

Adjourning: Closing the legislative session.

Reconvened: Assembled again.

Cabinet committee: A committee made up of members of the president's cabinet.

Acquiesced: Accepted.

Put your back to it: Get the job done with determination.

Play over it: Think about it.

Old-age benefits: Financial assistance during retirement.

President Franklin D. Roosevelt, with Frances Perkins behind him, signs the Social Security Act into law on August 14, 1935. *AP/Wide World Photo. Reproduced by permission.*

Rural free delivery carrier: Postal carrier.

Social insurance number: Social security number.

Industrial workers: Workers in factories.

which he will belong all his life. If he is out of work, he gets a benefit. If he is sick or crippled, he gets a benefit.

"The system ought to be operated," this country gentleman would go on, *"through the post offices. Just simple and natural—nothing elaborate or alarming about it. The **rural free delivery carrier** ought to bring papers to the door and pick them up after they are filled out. The rural free delivery carrier ought to give each child his **social insurance number** and his policy or whatever takes the place of a policy. The rural free delivery carrier ought to be the one who picks up the claim of the man who is unemployed, or of the old lady who wants old-age insurance benefits.*

*"And there is no reason why just the **industrial workers** should get the benefit of this. Everybody ought to be in on it—the farmer and his wife and his family.*

"I don't see why not," he would say, as, across the table, I began to shake my head [Perkins feared Roosevelt was proposing such a huge program that it would be impossible to carry out].

All Social Security applications and copies of numbers were filed by hand in the Social Security Bureau's headquarters in Baltimore, Maryland.
Courtesy of the Franklin D. Roosevelt Library.

*"I don't see why not. **Cradle to the grave**—from the cradle to the grave they ought to be in a social insurance system."*

That phrase, "cradle to the grave" insurance, on which he had sold himself, always remained with him as the desirable objective....

*When the law was signed by the President, we made a little ceremony in his office and he gave out the usual pen.... As he was signing the copies of the bill with pens that would be given to its **sponsors**, the President looked up at me. "Frances, where is your pen?" he asked.*

"I haven't got one," I replied.

"All right," he said to McIntyre, his secretary, "give me a first class pen for Frances." And he insisted on holding me responsible and thanking me personally in very appreciative terms. [Perkins, The Roosevelt I Knew, pp. 278–283, 299]

Cradle to the grave: Birth to death.

Sponsors: Senators and representatives who had introduced the bill to Congress.

What happened next...

Title VII of the Social Security Act established a three-member Social Security Board (SSB) to run all the programs. It quickly became apparent that the three board members would need a great deal of help to administer all parts of the act. To help with the challenging start-up, the U.S. Postal Service began delivering applications for social security numbers (SSN). As applications were mailed back, post office employees collected the completed applications, assigned numbers, typed the SSN cards, and returned the cards through the mail. With quiet efficiency the postal service assigned approximately thirty-five million numbers in 1936 and 1937, decades before the use of computers. All applications and copies of numbers were filed by hand in the SSB's headquarters in Baltimore, Maryland. Using workers' social security numbers, the Social Security Administration began paycheck withholding for the old-age retirement plan in early 1937. All other parts of the act became active in 1936 and 1937.

Very few Social Security benefits actually reached Americans in the 1930s. To allow time for the retirement fund to accumulate money, monthly retirement benefits were not scheduled to begin until 1942. However, the start year was eventually moved up to 1940. Only slightly more than 220,000 people received small monthly social security retirement payments in 1940. In fact, only 50 percent of American workers were covered by the retirement system in the 1940s.

The most significant benefit of the Social Security Act in the 1930s was peace of mind. Americans felt confident knowing that a federal government program was in place to guard against poverty in old age and to protect injured workers and disabled people who could not care for themselves. This New Deal program made it clear that people mattered to the government, and Americans eagerly supported the act. Congress continued to amend it as needs dictated throughout the twentieth century. By 2000, 98 percent of all workers were covered by the retirement plan. Approximately forty-five million people received Social Security benefits in 2000.

Did you know...

- The term "social security" was not used in the United States until early 1935; then a few experts testifying at the congressional hearings used it, and it caught on immediately. It replaced the term "social insurance."

- Roosevelt believed that the Social Security Act of 1935 represented a base of social insurance that could be improved upon and added to in future years.

- Social Security payments under the old-age retirement system were intended to supplement income, not to be the only support of retired individuals.

- In 2000 almost one-third of the beneficiaries (those persons receiving benefits) of the act were not retirees, but younger persons, including children, who received disability or survivors' benefits.

Consider the following...

- When he signed the Social Security Act, Roosevelt stated that no legislation could protect all people from all the "vicissitudes" (difficulties) of life. Do you agree?

- Explain the role that Francis Townsend and Senator Huey P. Long played in the passage of the Social Security Act.

- Why did Roosevelt want the Social Security retirement system funded by payroll contributions from workers?

For More Information

Books

Burns, James McGregor. *Roosevelt: The Lion and the Fox*. Norwalk, CT: Eaton Press, 1989.

Martin, George. *Madam Secretary: Frances Perkins*. 2nd ed. Boston, MA: Houghton Mifflin, 1976.

McElvaine, Robert S. *The Great Depression: America, 1929–1941*. New York, NY: Times Books, 1993.

Pasachoff, Naomi E. *Frances Perkins: Champion of the New Deal*. New York, NY: Oxford University Press, 1999.

Perkins, Frances. *The Roosevelt I Knew*. New York, NY: Viking Press, 1946.

Roosevelt, Franklin D. *The Public Papers and Addresses of Franklin D. Roosevelt: Volume Two, 1933.* New York, NY: Random House, 1938.

Schieber, Sylvester J., and John B. Shoven. *The Real Deal: The History and Future of Social Security.* New Haven, CT: Yale University Press, 1999.

Periodicals

Social Security Administration. "A Brief Description of the U.S. Social Security Program." SSA Publication No. 61-009, January 1997.

Social Security Administration. "A Brief History of Social Security." SSA Publication No. 21-059, August 2000.

Social Security Administration. "The Future of Social Security." SSA Publication No. 05-10055, July 1999.

Web Sites

Perkins, Frances. "The Roots of Social Security." *Social Security Administration.* http://www.ssa.gov/history/perkins5.html (accessed on August 28, 2002).

Social Security Administration. http://www.ssa.gov (accessed on August 28, 2002).

Franklin D. Roosevelt

Excerpt from "Annual Message to the Congress, January 3, 1938"

**Reprinted from *The Public Papers and Addresses
of Franklin D. Roosevelt: 1938 Volume*
Published in 1941**

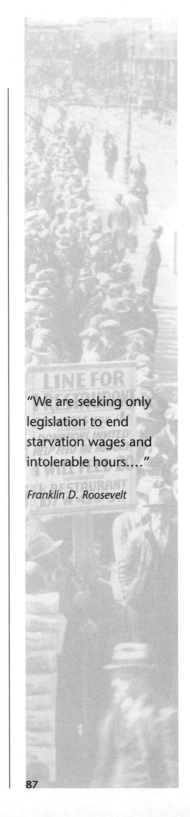

"We are seeking only
legislation to end
starvation wages and
intolerable hours...."

Franklin D. Roosevelt

In his annual message to Congress in January of each year President Franklin Roosevelt lobbied (tried to influence lawmakers) for important issues and pieces of legislation that would come before Congress during the next twelve months. In his speech on January 3, 1938, Roosevelt explained how the very low wages of factory jobs restricted the buying power of a large segment of the U.S. population. If their purchasing power could be raised, Roosevelt continued, they could buy their share of manufactured goods. With this line of reasoning, Roosevelt was making a case for passage of the Fair Labor Standards Act. Roosevelt analyzed the reasons for some groups' opposition to the act. He then stressed his view that businesses and "industries which bring permanent wealth will come more readily to those communities which insist on good pay and reasonable hours." Roosevelt believed that workers in such communities would be more content and efficient. And if their purchasing power increased, they could buy more goods, including farm goods. Therefore, farmers would also gain more purchasing power. This effect, Roosevelt said, would ripple through to "those who transport and distribute the products of farm and factory, and those of

the professions who serve all groups," from store keepers to dentists and medical doctors who had also seen their income plunge as people put off visits as long as they could.

Things to remember while reading the excerpt from "Annual Message to the Congress, January 3, 1938":

- No legally required minimum wage had ever existed in the United States.

- Pay special attention to Roosevelt's case for a minimum wage law.

- Many Americans believed that the federal government had no business regulating wages or the number of working hours.

Excerpt from "Annual Message to the Congress, January 3, 1938"

Mr. President, Mr. Speaker, Members of the Senate and of the House of Representatives: ....

To raise the purchasing power of the farmer is ... not enough. It will not stay raised if we do not also raise the purchasing power of that third of the Nation which receives its income from industrial employment. Millions of industrial workers receive pay so low that they have little buying power. Aside from the undoubted fact that they thereby suffer great human hardship, they are unable to buy adequate food and shelter, to maintain health or to buy their share of manufactured goods.

*We have not only seen minimum wage and maximum hour provisions prove their worth economically and socially under government **auspices** in 1933, 1934 and 1935, but the people of this country, by an overwhelming vote, are in favor of having the Congress—this Congress—put a floor below which industrial wages shall not fall, and a ceiling beyond which the hours of industrial labor shall not rise.*

Auspices: Oversight or guidance.

The Fair Labor Standards Act established a minimum wage and maximum working hours to protect miners, factory workers, and all workers against unfair labor practices. *Courtesy of the Library of Congress.*

Here again let us analyze the opposition. A part of it is sincere in believing that an effort thus to raise the purchasing power of lowest paid industrial workers is not the business of the Federal Government. Others **give "lip service" to a general objective, but do not like any specific measure that is proposed.** *In both cases it is worth our while to wonder whether some of these opponents are not at heart opposed to any program for raising the wages of the underpaid or reducing the hours of the overworked.*

Another group opposes legislation of this type on the ground that cheap labor will help their locality to acquire industries and outside capital, or to retain industries which today are surviving only because of existing low wages and long hours [the communities need to keep wages low to attract and keep industries]....

There are many communities in the United States where the average family income is pitifully low. It is in those communities that we find the poorest educational facilities and the worst conditions of health. Why? It is not because they are satisfied to live as they do.

Give "lip service"...: Others say they approve of a minimum wage but never agree to any actual measure.

It is because those communities have the lowest **per capita** wealth and income; therefore, the lowest ability to pay taxes; and, therefore, inadequate functioning of local government.

Such communities exist in the East, in the Middle West, in the Far West, and in the South. Those [political representatives] who represent such areas in every part of the country do their **constituents** ill-service by blocking efforts to raise their incomes, their property values and, therefore, their whole scale of living.... Indeed, new enterprises and new industries which bring permanent wealth will come more readily to those communities which insist on good pay and reasonable hours, for the simple reason that there they will find a greater industrial efficiency and happier workers.

No reasonable person seeks a complete uniformity in wages in every part of the United States; nor does any reasonable person seek an immediate and drastic

Among its directives, the Fair Labor Standards Act (FLSA) addressed child labor. Except in certain agricultural areas, the FLSA banned employment of children younger than fourteen years of age. *National Archives.*

change from the lowest pay to the highest pay. We are seeking, of course, only legislation to end starvation wages and intolerable hours; more desirable wages are and should continue to be the product of **collective bargaining**.

Many of those who represent great cities have shown their understanding of the necessity of helping the agricultural third of the Nation. I hope that those who represent constituencies primarily agricultural will not underestimate the importance of extending like aid to the industrial third.

Wage and hour legislation, therefore, is a problem which is definitely before this Congress for action. It is an essential part of economic recovery. It has the support of an overwhelming majority of our people in every walk of life....

Again I **revert** to the increase of national purchasing power as an underlying necessity of the day. If you increase that purchasing power for the farmers and for the industrial workers, especially for those in both groups who have least of it today, you will increase

*the purchasing power of the final third of our population—those who transport and distribute the products of farm and factory, and those of the professions who serve all groups. I have tried to make clear to you, and through you to the people of the United States, that this is **an urgency** which must be met by complete and not by partial action.*

If it is met, if the purchasing power of the Nation as a whole—in other words, the total of the nation's income—can be still further increased, other happy results will flow from such increase.

We have raised the Nation's income from thirty-eight billion dollars in the year 1932 to about sixty-eight billion dollars in the year 1937. Our goal, our objective is to raise it to ninety or one hundred billion dollars. [Roosevelt, pp. 1, 5–7]

What happened next...

On June 25, 1938, Congress passed the Fair Labor Standards Act (FLSA), also known as the Wages and Hours Law. The act applied to employees of businesses that operated in more than one state. The law mandated a minimum wage of 25 cents an hour and a workweek consisting of a maximum of 44 hours. By 1940 the act provided that the workweek be no longer than 40 hours. Any work over 40 hours would require "time and a half" pay. For example, if a minimum-wage worker labored 42 hours in a week, he would be paid 25 cents an hour for the first 40 hours and 38 cents an hour (roughly one and one-half times the minimum wage) for the 2 overtime hours.

The FLSA also addressed child labor. Except in certain agricultural areas, the FLSA banned employment of children younger than fourteen years of age. Fourteen- and fifteen-year-olds could not work in factories or during school hours. Individuals under eighteen years of age were banned from working in dangerous occupations such as mining.

The FLSA was amended many times during the rest of the twentieth century; the Equal Pay Act (equal pay for men and women doing equal work) was added in 1963, and a

Per capita: For each person.

Constituents: People who elect a political representative.

Collective bargaining: Negotiations between representatives of employers and workers to reach agreement on working conditions, wages, and job benefits.

Revert: Go back to a former condition or belief.

An urgency: An immediate and great need.

yearly increase amendment passed in 1977. The FLSA continues to serve as a foundation of labor standards at the beginning of the twenty-first century.

Did you know...

- The Fair Labor Standards Act (FLSA) replaced parts of the National Industrial Recovery Act (NIRA), which was ruled unconstitutional by the Supreme Court in 1936.

- Even after passage of the FLSA, it was still difficult to regulate some child labor, especially in agriculture.

- Frances Perkins, secretary of labor, had a lifelong interest in the issues that the FLSA addressed, and she played a key role in its passage.

Consider the following...

- If a family needs a child's income to live, should the family rather than the government be allowed to decide if, when, and for how long the child works?

- Do you think jobs were lost because some employers could not afford to pay workers the minimum wage? Does this same issue arise in the twenty-first century?

For More Information

Books

Bradley, Michael R. *On the Job: Safeguarding Workers' Rights*. Vero Beach, FL: Rourke Corporation, 1992.

Roosevelt, Franklin D. *The Public Papers and Addresses of Franklin D. Roosevelt: 1938 Volume*. New York, NY: Macmillan, 1941.

Schwartz, Alvin. *The Unions: What They Are, How They Came to Be, How They Affect Each of Us*. New York, NY: Viking Press, 1972.

Everyday Living

The Great Depression, the worst economic crisis in U.S. history, affected almost all Americans and their families to some degree. Only the very rich avoided having to make lifestyle changes. At least 25 percent of the American workforce was unemployed by late 1932. Those who managed to keep their jobs saw their salaries decline by 40 percent and their work hours cut back. Prices of goods had also dropped but not enough to offset unemployment and salary cuts. Frequently, a wage earner found himself supporting relatives who had lost their jobs or helping struggling friends.

Families did their best to carry on and keep their lives as close to normal as possible. They devised ways to "cut corners," "make do," and "keep up appearances." Cutting corners and making do meant reducing purchases of goods at stores and growing or making daily-use items at home. Families canned vegetables and fruit from their gardens. Clothing was sewn on a foot-operated (nonelectric) sewing machine or purchased at secondhand stores. A favorite way to "keep up appearances" was to paint the house; a fresh coat of paint on the outside said all was well inside.

The new game of miniature golf was an inexpensive form of entertainment during the Depression. ©*Minnesota Historical Society/Corbis Corporation. Reproduced by permission.*

With almost no extra money to budget for entertainment, Americans needed their leisure-time activities to be cheap or free. Popular at-home activities included card games, board games, puzzles, listening to the radio, reading, and having friends over. Children often spent after-school hours and summer days designing and building their own toys. Scrap lumber, orange crates, or discarded wheels from roller skates could be the raw materials for exciting construction projects. Away from home, entertainment included school and church socials, movies, dances, sporting events such as community baseball games, driving about, and a new source of fun rapidly growing in popularity—miniature golf.

The Depression caused changes in family structures: Marriages were postponed, fewer babies were born, and households combined to aid those out of work. Many teenagers stayed in school and lived at home longer because there were no jobs. On the other hand, some teens, feeling they were a burden to their families, left home and hit the road or the railways. Many Americans depended on strong family ties to see them through the hard times. For others the economic pressures were overwhelming and broke their families apart.

The first excerpts in this chapter portray family life during the Depression; they come from Volume Two of *Stories and Recipes of the Great Depression of the 1930s,* published in 1993 by Rita Van Amber of Menomonie, Wisconsin. Van Amber, who lived through the Depression, remembers how her family of ten children dealt positively with daily hardships: "We didn't know we were poor." With the help of her daughter, Janet, Van Amber has compiled three volumes of recipes and remembrances of the 1930s.

The second excerpt, taken from a 1935 pamphlet by Kingsley Davis titled *Youth in the Depression,* describes the

problems facing youths and the public education system during the Depression. Whereas twenty-first-century American students can count on attending public school from kindergarten through twelfth grade, consistency in public education was not a given in the United States during the 1930s. Public school funding came largely from property taxes, and schools experienced their bleakest years from 1932 to 1936, when a considerable number of Americans could no longer pay property taxes on their homes. The hardest hit were schools in poor districts and rural districts. School budgets were cut in most districts. The budget cuts resulted in shortened school years or school days, lower teacher salaries, teacher firings, inadequate funding for books and supplies, cuts in the number and variety of classes, and larger class sizes. A significant number of schools, particularly rural schools, closed altogether.

The third excerpt comes from **"Till the River Rises,"** a chapter in a book titled *These Are Our Lives,* compiled by writers of the Federal Writers' Project (FWP) and published in 1939. Americans who were barely making it economically before the Depression were the most severely affected in the 1930s. This group included factory workers, who were constantly susceptible to job loss; coal miners; poor farmers; black Americans; and the elderly. They sometimes became homeless and had nowhere to go except to a nearby Hooverville, a shantytown of temporary dwellings. There they constructed a crude shelter from scrap metal, cardboard, or lumber and survived as best they could. "Till the River Rises" is a fascinating look at life in a Hooverville.

Rita Van Amber

Excerpts from Stories and Recipes of the
Great Depression of the 1930s, *Volume Two*
Published in 1993

By 2001 Rita Van Amber of Menomonie, Wisconsin, had compiled three volumes of Great Depression cookbooks. These are not ordinary cookbooks, but rather a combination of Depression-era recipes and the personal stories and memories of individuals who lived through the Depression. The cookbooks include "heartwarming memories told in the words of those who survived those desperate times." In her introduction to Volume Two, Van Amber goes on to say, "Some stories are heartbreaking, some are hilarious, but all provide a rich historical account of the trials endured in homes across the country during the poorest time in the history of our nation.... My strong childhood impression of the Great Depression gave me a desire to document for all time the courage and grit displayed by families such as ours through collecting their own personal stories and memories." Five excerpts are taken from Volume Two: "Chicago, 1934," "The Annual School Picnic," "Chicago Kids Weren't Loafing," "Boys and How They Played," and "Excerpts."

In the first excerpt, "Chicago, 1934," families live happily together in very crowded conditions. Saving for a weekend

"Even then, you deprived yourself all summer, looking forward to Fair time with its big decisions. You had to decide which ride you'd enjoy the most and which treat would be the best and also the most for your dime or nickel. Money was tight. A quarter didn't go far with rides at 10¢ each."

at the Chicago World's Fair took months. The second excerpt, "The Annual School Picnic," tells of a fun event that costs nothing. It also shows how families solved problems using the few resources they had, such as making worn-out shoes last by putting cardboard in the soles. "Chicago Kids Weren't Loafing" tells rather humorously of some everyday activities of needy Chicago kids and ends on a surprisingly optimistic note. "Boys and How They Played" describes how homemade toys held the interest of children. The final excerpt reprinted from Van Amber's book features the memories of George Stockard of Eau Claire, Wisconsin. He recalls life as a sixteen-year-old at his family farm near Dallas, Texas, during the 1930s.

Things to remember while reading the excerpts from *Stories and Recipes of the Great Depression of the 1930s*:

- A frequently used term during the Depression was "making do." This meant using things already on hand to take care of basic family needs, such as fixing tasty meals with simple ingredients, sewing clothes at home instead of purchasing them, or making do-it-yourself car repairs.

- Finding themselves without income, young married couples often moved back into their parents' home. Elderly people sometimes had to move in with their grown children. One wage earner often supported an extended family.

Excerpts from Stories and Recipes of the Great Depression of the 1930s

"Chicago, 1934"

*The World's Fair was held in Chicago in 1934. Many who wished to go could only dream about it. You didn't even get to the State Fair and felt most fortunate if you were able to attend the County Fair. Even then, you **deprived yourself** all summer, looking forward to Fair time with its big decisions. You had to decide which*

Deprived yourself: Did not spend money on anything.

WORLD'S FAIR
CHICAGO
1934
Tour the World at the Fair

Families saved money for months leading up to the Chicago World's Fair just so they could enjoy themselves for a day or two. *Courtesy of the Library of Congress.*

ride you'd enjoy the most and which treat would be the best and also the most for your dime or nickel. Money was tight. A quarter didn't go far with rides at 10¢ each.

Herb and Rose Einerson, of Mt. Horeb, Wisconsin, had an unexpected **windfall**. Herb had worked very hard and had taken on a lot of responsibility at his father's dairy farm. He was paid a small wage and given a two-room apartment upstairs in the family home. He

Windfall: Sudden financial gain.

U.S. World's Fairs of the 1930s

The U.S. world's fairs of the 1930s offered an optimistic and promising vision of the future. The fairs were opportunities for American industries to showcase advances in science and technology. As the Great Depression lingered, these celebrations of the future gave hope for a better tomorrow. President Franklin Roosevelt's administration threw its support behind the fairs, hoping to boost civic and national pride. The president's New Deal programs shared a common goal with the fairs: to rebuild an economically healthy America.

Three world's fairs and one large state fair that gained nationwide attention were held during the 1930s. The world's fairs included (1) the Century of Progress Exposition in Chicago, Illinois, which ran from May 27, 1933, until November 12, 1933, and opened for a second season in 1934; (2) the Golden Gate International Exposition in San Francisco, California, which ran from February 1939 until October 29, 1939, and opened for a second season in 1940; and (3) the World of Tomorrow in New York City, which opened in April 1939 and closed October 29, 1939, reopening for another season in 1940. The Texas Centennial Exposition was held in Dallas during the summer of 1936 to celebrate the state's one hundred years of independence from Mexico. The Texas fair was a popular destination for young people across the country; many "rode the rails" (hitched rides on train cars) to get there. Each city that hosted a fair hoped the event would bring thousands of visitors to spur the local economy. The fairs also provided sorely needed employment. At the fairs Americans saw models of planned cities, labor-saving gadgets, and efficient transportation systems such as faster com-

and his family of four were quite comfortable. The dairy provided good food. They were very fortunate and they knew it. Even so, there was no money. Entertainment, if one had time for it, had to be free.

With the World's Fair being held in Chicago, Herb's father had been thinking for quite some time that there had to be a way for him to spare a few dollars to send the boy and his sweet little wife to the big event.

Even recalling it today, Rose Einerson still remembers it as an awesome occasion and a great surprise, saying, "Can you believe it? $15.00 for the World's Fair!"

... The adventuresome couple rode in the "rumble seat" of their cousin's Ford coupe. The wind was fierce back there, and it

Rumble seat: Folding backseat not covered by the car's top.

muter trains. Visitors to the fair were amazed by wonders such as color photographic film, nylon hose, and television. Millions of visitors were also introduced to the fine arts through exhibitions of murals, paintings, sculpture, and architectural design.

Chicago businessmen and politicians hoped the tourists their Century of Progress fair attracted would jump-start an economic recovery in their community. The Chicago fair emphasized technology, progress, and a utopian (perfect) country based on democracy and manufacturing. Fair-goers were greeted with a futuristic fantasyland far different from the unemployment and economic misery that was prevalent in Chicago at that time. Big businesses focused on scientific and industrial progress with exhibits such as radio-controlled tractors, assembly-line product packaging

demonstrations, and models of oil refineries. Ford Motor Company built a nine-hundred-foot-long building. Inside was an automobile assembly plant, a globe showing locations of Ford's worldwide plants, and models of historic highways. The "Drama of Agriculture" building celebrated advances in farming. Technology exhibits were always free. A pleasure area called a "midway" had games, rides such as a roller coaster, and shows.

Americans young and old carefully saved and planned so they could visit the fairs. The visions of the future presented at the fairs were not always realistic or practical, but nevertheless they were highly entertaining and full of hope for a better time. The world's fairs displayed the daydreams of those who created them, and they enticed hundreds of thousands of Americans to share in those dreams.

took quite a bit of combing to get the hair back into place. When they reached Chicago, they pulled into the parking lot of the Moody Bible Institute. They stayed there two nights at $1.00 a night. The bus the next morning cost them 10¢ each. Admission was free, and so were all the hundreds of exhibits. They had never walked so much in their lives! In between exhibits, they dined on big bowls of chili for 10¢ each and hamburgers for 25¢ each. 1934 was a memorable year for the Einersons....

"The Annual School Picnic"

For children during the Great Depression the school picnic was one of the most important occasions of the year, right in there with Christmas and the holiday school program.

As a little girl, Lorrayne N., of Menomonie, Wisconsin, remembers looking forward with the usual anticipation to the end of the school year picnic. It was always a family affair with fathers taking leave of their fields and jobs to take part in the fun with the neighbors and friends at this annual celebration finalizing the school year. The day would be filled with treats, ball games, races, prizes and the bountiful picnic dinner, such as the times provided. The adults would be there rooting for the winners of the games and consoling the losers.

On this day the Mothers, along with the children, would arrive early with their best dishes. There was potato salad, baked beans, cakes and pies, pickles, ham and deviled eggs, and, of course, the lemonade. Everything was prepared from scratch out of wholesome country produce; the food was delicious. It was almost impossible not to eat more than one needed before running races, but that was remedied by a custom of relaxing after a meal and enjoying pleasant newsy conversation. All the while the children were restlessly waiting for the games to begin.

Little Lorrayne of Menomonie was looking forward to this day for weeks. As the day came closer she realized she had a big problem. Her shoes were wearing out fast. In fact, the soles were gone. Her parents looked over the situation and agreed the shoes had to be replaced. The decision was made to order a pair from the catalog right away so their little girl would be sure to have them in time for the picnic. The big book was brought out and the pages were carefully examined for the best pair at the best price. The order was promptly sent in and Lorrayne began looking for the package to arrive....

Finally it was the day before the picnic and the shoes had not arrived....

*Her parents assured her there was an answer to this problem, as with all other problems, and they quickly went to work. Her Mother cut out a large piece of cardboard to fit the entire sole of Lorrayne's old shoes. But the cardboard wouldn't stay in; the soles were worn to the very edges. Her father had the answer to that when he got out the leather sewing **awl** and some twine. By crisscrossing the soles tightly all the way to the toe they could make the shoes last one more day....*

*The occasion is **indelibly etched** in Lorrayne's memory; it always will be. But as she thinks of it now she remembers lovingly how her parents together worked out the problem and came to her rescue in her **dilemma**....*

Awl: Needle.

Indelibly etched: Permanently marked.

Dilemma: Difficult situation.

"Chicago Kids Weren't Loafing"

From Twin Lakes, Wisconsin, Mrs. K. Russel recalls life being hard. Because of this, kids grew up knowing of responsibility and team work.

As children they went to the library a lot and she remembers as a very young child sounding out words in the 2 cent daily newspaper. She was absolutely elated when she could read some words and could take a book out on her own.

*After school they all took pails and **scoured** the railroad tracks for coal which fell from the train when the **stocker** was refueled. In the summer the ice man was followed for pieces dropped out of the truck as he made his deliveries.*

Kids were sent to the butcher shop for "dog bones." The butcher gave them nice meaty bones which made excellent soup. The meat was saved for hash the next day. Ground up and added to chopped potatoes and onions, it made a "heavenly" delicious meal....

Soon the "cat" needed food too, of course, and the children would be sent back to the butcher shop for liver. They'd come home with a lot of it, enough for several meals. Liver and onions with liver gravy and lots of potatoes were served a lot.

Because every bit of heat had to be conserved, "portiers" were in vogue. They hung in the doorways like a pair of drapes with a panel in the center. To keep it open one simply shoved the panel on the rod to one side and you had an open doorway. These were most often made out of heavy tapestry and were intended to be decorative as well as functional.

But of course, it got hot in the summer and one had to do something about that, too. The big boys solved the problem. They would take large wrenches and open the fire hydrants and all the neighbor kids would cool off by running through it. When anyone heard the fire trucks coming, the water would quickly be turned off and the kids disappeared.

Chicago wasn't a bad place for kids in the '30's. They grew up learning to fend for themselves....

"Boys and How They Played"

The little fellows in San Francisco, California had no problem with hard times. They were too busy to notice. Time after school and during the long summer days was spent creatively designing, building and playing with homemade toys.

Scoured: Searched.

Stocker: Train car carrying coal fuel.

Wedding Expenses in the 1930s

According to Rita Van Amber in Volume Two of *Stories and Recipes of the Great Depression of the 1930s,* the costs of a typical wedding did not usually exceed $100. Weddings were simple but beautiful. Van Amber records in her book the expenses of Cecilia Serio's 1930s wedding in Milwaukee, Wisconsin:

Dress	$30.00
Veil	$10.00
Reception where Chicken a la King in potato chip baskets with relishes was served	$19.95
Two-tiered wedding cake	$5.00
Groom's devils food cake	free
Total Expense	$64.95

Rustic: Rough.

Abusive: Harsh.

Improvise: Use what was on hand.

Dismantled: Taken apart.

Maneuver: Move.

Reprimands: Scolding.

Salvaged: Saved.

They built them sturdy and **rustic**. There were orange crates, pieces of old 2x4 lumber, scrap tires and inner tubes, wire, string, and whatever was needed or could be found. The finished product was always strong, well built and generally held up under the most **abusive** conditions. With few tools to work with the boys learned to **improvise**. They did not have drills to make holes in the wood, but it did not take them long to figure out that if one heated a nail over a gas fire, holding it with a pliers until it was red hot, one could make some nice holes. There was always a way to solve a problem if one put his mind to it.

The Scooters

All that was needed to build a well constructed scooter, which had to withstand wild rides down the big city hills, was a piece of scrap 2x4 lumber, part of an orange crate, and a **dismantled** roller skate (which would provide the front and rear wheels). The boys used their bodies to **maneuver** the machine around corners and past parked cars. After a few close calls they became very expert and daring in this skill. Scraped knees and ripped trousers brought severe **reprimands** at home and were dealt with according to the risks involved.

Whenever anything came loose or wore out, they simply hammered it together again using nails **salvaged** from scrap pieces of wood and in no time at all they were back on the streets again....

Kites

Generally made out of newspapers, kites were very popular with boys of all ages in the Springtime. Flour paste glue and string from the big ball Mom always had on hand was all that was needed to put a good kite together....

King of the Mountain

In this exciting and lively game, the boys would climb up the steepest mountain or hill, clawing to the very highest point. They would push each other off until there was only one left—"The King of the Mountain!"...

"Excerpts"

From the archives of the memories of the 1930's of George Stockard of Eau Claire, Wisconsin.

We were a large family; at times sixteen sat around the table. That included aunts and cousins brought in to Grandma's house when we learned they had no food or money. I was sixteen years old.

This was Texas, 80 miles east of Dallas. It was 1931 when the depression really hit. Oil wells had stopped operating because prices of **consumer goods** *had dropped out of sight.*

We lived on a farm and raised and sold cotton, peanuts, and all kinds of fruits and vegetables. We had our own cattle for beef and milk, plus hogs for butchering and to sell as well. There was lots of waste out there for the hogs to fatten up on. But we didn't have electricity then and ice had to be shipped in. It was a valued commodity, especially in the warm season which we had a lot of.

Dad had made arrangements for a farm loan but before it was finalized the banks were closed. There was no warning this would

Homegrown vegetables were stockpiled all summer to help feed the family during the winter months. *Courtesy of the Franklin D. Roosevelt Library.*

Consumer goods: Goods commonly purchased by the public to satisfy daily wants and needs.

Women learned to make clothes for their families rather than spend money on store-bought items.
Courtesy of the Franklin D. Roosevelt Library.

Make do: Find ways to cook with limited ingredients, repair home equipment, and make needed items rather than purchasing them.

Scrounge: Search.

Vogue: Style.

Transits: Transients; wandering men, boys, and occasionally girls.

happen in our area, and it was a shock to find out we had to live on what we had and that no money would be coming in....

Jobs were unheard of, and when the drought hit we were lucky to be able to raise some of our food for our accumulated family.

Women made everything out of flour sacks from the Hackers Best flour mills. Yukon flour was popular, but the ink didn't wash out well. When the girls strolled by with new skirts on we called them "Yukon Queens." They wore "prairie skirts," and when the wind blew it did all sorts of flirty things with them.

Our parents had to learn to be inventive and **make do**, and they passed these qualities on to their kids. We actually had a lot of fun. We'd work incredibly hard to figure out how to make a toy and then **scrounge** to find the scraps of material to build it. We made the Paddle & Wheel. A syrup-can lid provided the wheel and a stick and handle made a toy you never tired of playing with, going up and down the dusty roads and fields. The stick horse, of course, never went out of **vogue** especially for the smaller ones who couldn't keep up with some of our big toys. The Flying Jenny was something else. The biggest we ever made was a true to life merry-go-round. Crude and rough, but it went around and was made to last. Our wagons had wheels cut from logs. Big boys had to do the cutting, but we all had wagons for play and for our chores. And we had the swimming hole.... It was wonderful through all the hot weather. No electricity meant no air conditioning and no refrigeration. Ice was scarce.

Unfortunately it wasn't all fun. The **transits** came in from Pennsylvania, Maryland and Virginia to get to a warm climate because they didn't have a home. Illness was everywhere. The drifters lived under tarps or even right under the trees.... We had one doctor in town and he charged $1.00 a call or two live chickens. So we doctored ourselves. Generally with a bottle of 666 which was so unbelievably bitter tasting, one spoonful and no one except the dying would admit to not being cured....

Our family always had a big breakfast which consisted of meat, yams, cornbread, fruit and fresh milk just milked. It soured too fast to ever have any for long. Buttermilk kept a little longer and was the principal drink. The big meal had to be cooked in the morning before it got too hot. The evening meal always was bread and milk, bread meaning cornbread....

It was 1932 when the drought was a serious problem. We had no water whatsoever. None at all. We'd have to go to town and buy it for 5 cents a gallon. We took the wagon, not being able to afford the 7 cents a gallon for gasoline. Clothes were washed at a community ... well which was a dirty old place with filthy water. It made the clothes smell something awful.

About that time the government sent people out to pay us $1.00 each for our cattle. They shot and buried them right there in one big hole, but not before the drifters first got a roast cut out for their meal. The cattle were in bad shape. The hogs got **cholera** and it wiped them all out. Our stockpile of canned goods, dried fruits and vegetables, and salted things was going fast.

About this time **commodities** were sent in, and I'll always remember the stampede the people made for a little of the cheese, flour, raisins and whatever was brought. The drifters were starving and they couldn't be blamed. A father had swiped a sack of flour from the grocery. When the sheriff came for it the kids ran to it and stuffed their mouths full....

When Roosevelt came into power and started offering programs for the poor, people for the first time had hope. They came to **venerate** and worship our new president, and were glued to his Fireside Chats, absorbing all the confidence he displayed. When WPA and CCC camps became organized the drifters went back home because they qualified for help in their own states.

George Stockard joined the CCC camps and earned $25.00 a month, which went home for food. He was growing

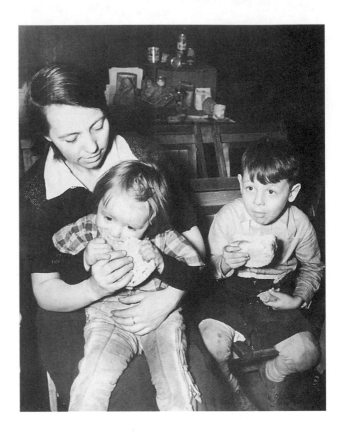

Hungry children eagerly consume ham sandwiches after a food relief shipment arrives in town. *AP/Wide World Photo. Reproduced by permission.*

Cholera: An intestinal disease caused by bacteria.

Commodities: Shipments of food products.

Venerate: Regard with great respect.

up and had started thinking about the army. He had heard if you could work yourself up to the proper sergeant rating you'd be eligible to volunteer for the Flying Tigers, which paid $90.00 a mission to fight in China. But the Japanese hit Pearl Harbor first and George was in.

George believes the Great Depression in his area was harder on people than the war was. He saw a lot of families suffer unbearably for years. He watched families of transits come in, hungry, living under tarps and trees, mothers having babies and both dying.... How can one ever forget. [Van Amber, pp. 6–9, 70–71, 87, 88, 89, 90–91, 93–94]

What happened next...

Even for families not devastated by the 1930s economic crisis, the pictures of the hungry and homeless left permanent impressions. There was a persistent fear that another depression would come, throwing more people out of work and onto the streets. Achieving and maintaining financial security became the most important goal of many Americans in the years following the Great Depression. People had developed habits of saving and thrift, which helped them cope with the rationing of food and other items during World War II (1939–45). During the war more married women went to work outside the home, in order to support the war effort. But after the war most returned to homemaking and raising children. Even though the United States experienced prosperity after World War II, those who had lived through the Depression years continued to save and reuse all possessions because they wanted to be prepared for any economic hard times in the future.

Did you know...

- Few clothes were store-bought. Most women were skilled in sewing and spent hours picking out patterns and fabric from catalogs.

- By 1930 most middle-class families, including those at the lower end of the middle class, owned a car. Even in

the worst years of the Depression, few were willing to give up driving. Instead, they saved expenses by taking care of repairs themselves.

- Unable to support a new household during economic hard times, young people put off marriage. Long engagements were common. During the Depression the birth rate declined from what it had been in previous decades.

- Although more women joined the workforce, only 15 percent of all married women worked by 1940.

- The only Americans to escape lifestyle adjustments in the 1930s were the very rich.

Consider the following…

- List several reasons why you think marriages and having children were postponed during the Depression.

- In "Chicago Kids Weren't Loafing" who were the "dog bones" and the liver for the "cat" really for?

For More Information

Reynolds, Edward B., and Michael Kennedy. *Whistleberries, Stirabout, and Depression Cake.* Helena, MT: Falcon Publishing, 2000.

Rogers, Agnes. *I Remember Distinctly: A Family Album of the American People 1918–1941.* New York, NY: Harper &Brothers Publishers, 1947.

Van Amber, Rita. *Stories and Recipes of the Great Depression of the 1930s.* Vols. 1 and 2. Menomonie, WI: Van Amber Publishers, 1986–93.

Winslow, Susan. *Brother, Can You Spare a Dime? America from the Wall Street Crash to Pearl Harbor: An Illustrated Documentary.* New York, NY: Paddington Press, 1976.

Kingsley Davis

Excerpt from **Youth in the Depression**
Published in 1935

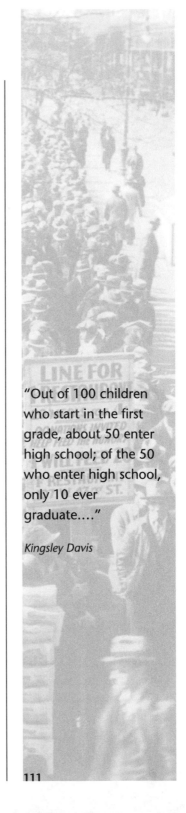

"Out of 100 children who start in the first grade, about 50 enter high school; of the 50 who enter high school, only 10 ever graduate...."

Kingsley Davis

In the 1930s the University of Chicago Press published a series of pamphlets designed to be used in high school classes and adult education programs and as educational resources for workers' groups. The series presented current issues in economics and government, and social issues such as crime and youth. One of these pamphlets was *Youth in the Depression* by Kingsley Davis, published in 1935. It covered a broad range of issues concerning youth in the 1930s, including young people who took to riding the rails (see Chapter 6); the public education system; youths in Germany and Russia; and various New Deal agencies helpful to young Americans. (The New Deal section refers to a series of programs established by President Roosevelt's administration in the 1930s. These programs were designed to lift the country out of the Depression and restore prosperity.)

When Davis discusses education, he likens it to a sieve. Think of the kitchen utensil that you sift flour with. It separates the finer grains from coarser ones. Davis explains that schools do the same thing. For example, one hundred children who enter first grade are sifted until only three of the

one hundred enter college. When they reach working age, they are also sifted into industrial, business, or professional jobs. Davis points out that the sieve got clogged during the Depression years. For those students who graduated, there were no jobs. Up to 25 percent of the American workforce was unemployed by 1932. People could no longer pay their property taxes, so school budgets (which relied on funding from those taxes) were cut. Therefore, many schools had to cut back on teachers and class offerings; some closed altogether. Older students could not find jobs, and many younger students no longer had schools to go to. Like other vital elements in American society, the public schools—and the students—suffered under the hardships of the Great Depression.

Things to remember while reading the excerpt from *Youth in the Depression*:

- The U.S. Constitution makes no provision for the funding of schools by the federal government. Instead, school funding is left to the states, which in turn have traditionally left the responsibility of funding to local communities. As a result, public schools are generally funded from local property taxes. Since poor communities have low property values and thus lower property taxes, they have always had poorly funded schools. During the Depression poor school districts were the hardest hit by the economic crisis.

- By 1930 elementary schools were available in almost all areas, but high school education in rural areas was spotty.

- The South had only a handful of high schools for black Americans. These schools taught only vocational education such as carpentry and laundry work. During the Depression jobs in these fields disappeared.

Excerpt from Youth in the Depression

Every young man and young woman wants to get somewhere in the world. Except for a few who are too lazy or too discouraged,

they are ambitious to become somebody. There are various ways of doing this, but most positions that are worthwhile nowadays require training. Before a boy can get a good job, he must learn something. He must attend some kind of school .....

Our schools act in much the same way as the **sieves**.... We may think of all the schools together, in all their branches, as a great sieve, or a series of sieves, by which young people are trained and sorted out for suitable positions in the business, industrial, and professional life of the nation. Many occupations, in fact, are closed to men who have not had a college training.

Of course, schools are just one of many kinds of training and grading places in which the younger generation proves its merits and qualifies for a place in social and business life.... But the schools show pretty well how the process works. Their selective action is shown partly by the number of boys and girls who drop out along the way. Out of 100 children who start in the first grade, about 50 enter high school; of the 50 who enter high school, only 10 ever

During the Depression years, many schools had to cut back on teachers and class offerings; some closed altogether. *Courtesy of the Library of Congress.*

Sieves: Devices that separate finer particles from coarser particles.

A few students manage to attend school at a small, rural schoolhouse in Alabama, circa 1935.
Courtesy of the Franklin D. Roosevelt Library.

graduate; of the 10, only about 3 enter college, and still fewer graduate from college.

Don't make the mistake of thinking that only the "dumbbells" drop out. Many good students drop out because of ill health or poverty. Intelligent boys and girls often dislike school work. Sometimes they leave school to take a job, or so that they can get married sooner.

Still, in the schools the sifting process is at work. It sorts out every year those who are ready for various kinds of employment....

But sometimes the machinery of our youth-sifting and youth-training system gets clogged. It clogs in a great crisis—a revolution, a famine, or some other disaster. It clogged badly in the Great Depression.

What happens to the sifting process in a business depression?

In the first place, millions of people are thrown out of work. Many who have proved their ability to do good work lose their jobs.

Young people looking forward to a business position find nothing open to them. Even if they pass all the tests and examinations in the world, they will not get the places they seem to deserve.

In the second place, the public schools get so little money that they lose teachers and equipment. Parents, also suffering reduced incomes, are not able to send their children to school [often parents could not provide adequate clothing and/or shoes; thus children could not attend school].

*Finally, to make matters worse, business firms can't promote their men. Skilled trades can't take on new **apprentices**. Thus the industrial system enlists no new recruits.*

*So, you see, the whole machinery of sifting, or selection, breaks down. Boys and girls all over the country find nothing but a blank wall in front of them. With their parents suffering, their own futures clouded, the ordinary roads to success closed, they blindly seek a way out. In such conditions youth movements spring up. If the older people do nothing to help the young, they may take matters in their own hands and do things, often strange things, for themselves. Crimes committed by young people increase; revolution is not improbable. Anything may happen in a country where the **normal selective processes** become clogged.*

Youth in America had a hard time during the Depression. [Davis, pp. 8, 9–10, 11–12]

What happened next...

Despite the public school system's struggles, high school enrollment kept increasing in the 1930s. With no jobs available, students chose to stay in school longer. The general public continued to have a desire for more public education. The economic crisis brought about lasting positive changes in public education:

- Teachers organized into professional groups to demand higher wages and more control of their workplace.

- State funding of schools increased to support local property tax funding.

Apprentices: Trainees.

Normal selective processes: The usual methods of selecting who is suitable for business, factory, or professional careers.

- Tiny rural school districts joined together to allow for more-efficient use of teachers, supplies, and building space. Combining white and black schools was another form of consolidation. A Philadelphia, Pennsylvania, suburb was the first to desegregate its schools, allowing black children and white children to attend school together.

Under President Franklin Roosevelt's New Deal education programs, new agencies that aided underprivileged young people were created. These agencies included the Civilian Conservation Corps (CCC) and the National Youth Administration (NYA).

Did you know...
- The years between 1932 and 1936 were the bleakest for U.S. public schools.

- Many teachers lost their jobs, and pay dropped an average of 13.6 percent—and in some cases, between 25 and 50 percent. Some schools closed altogether; others cut back school hours or cut months out of the school year.

- President Roosevelt did not include public schools in his New Deal legislation. Instead he created New Deal agencies to help the neediest students.

Consider the following...
- Why did students choose to stay in school longer during the Depression years?

- Why did so few students go on to college?

- Research why President Roosevelt did not put public schools under New Deal policy protection.

For More Information
Davis, Kingsley. *Youth in the Depression.* Chicago, IL: University of Chicago Press, 1935.

Krug, Edward A. *The Shaping of the American High School: Volume 2, 1920–1941.* Madison, WI: University of Wisconsin Press, 1972.

Tyack, David, Robert Lowe, and Elisabeth Hansot. *Public Schools in Hard Times: The Great Depression and Recent Years.* Cambridge, MA: Harvard University Press, 1984.

Federal Writers' Project

Excerpt from "Till the River Rises"

Reprinted in *These Are Our Lives*
Compiled by members of the Federal Writers' Project from
interviews with people in North Carolina, Tennessee, and Georgia
Published in 1939

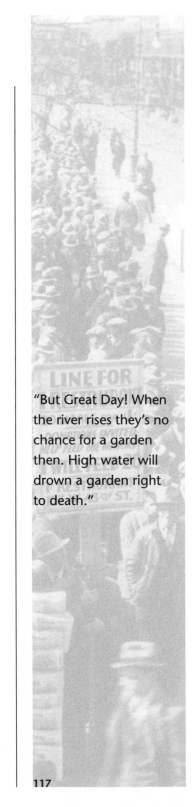

Thousands of makeshift dwellings appeared in towns and cities across the country by the early 1930s. Crude shacks were built with scrap boards, scrap metal, flattened boxes, and tar paper. These shacks went up on vacant lots, near railroad yards, on river bottomlands that were susceptible to flooding, and at the edge of towns. Unemployed and homeless people grouped together in these odd little communities known as shantytowns. The makeshift towns were also called "Hoover-villes," because many Americans blamed President Herbert Hoover (1874–1964), who served in the early years of the Great Depression (1929–33), for not doing enough to help people in need. Hoovervilles sprang up nationwide, from New York City and Washington, D.C., to Seattle, Washington.

The following excerpt, "Till the River Rises," was written by members of the Federal Writers' Project (FWP) and is taken from *These Are Our Lives,* a book published in 1939. When President Franklin D. Roosevelt (1882–1945; served 1933–45) took over the presidency in 1933, he established a series of relief and recovery programs, known as the New Deal, to pull the country out of the Depression. One of the

"But Great Day! When the river rises they's no chance for a garden then. High water will drown a garden right to death."

agencies created was the massive Works Progress Administration (WPA). The WPA put thousands of unemployed people to work on various public works projects, from constructing sidewalks, airports, and roads to building dams and hospitals. The WPA also created projects for out-of-work artists and writers. The FWP was the agency created to aid writers.

These Are Our Lives is a well-known publication written by members of the FWP from North Carolina, Tennessee, and Georgia. The writers interviewed a wide range of people, including sharecropping farmers, workers in cotton mills and brick-making plants, maids, truck drivers, small merchants, and country doctors and dentists. In "Till the River Rises" a resident of a Hooverville in Knoxville, Tennessee, is interviewed and relates a surprisingly homey picture of her tiny community.

Things to remember while reading the excerpt from "Till the River Rises":

- Hoovervilles often housed as many as a thousand residents, including entire families. In cities there were dozens of these communities, large and small.

- Hoovervilles of a more unusual nature were Pipe City in Oakland, California, where people lived in huge concrete sewer pipes that had been abandoned, and Carbarn City. Carbarn City was located south of San Francisco, California, in an area where dozens of old abandoned trolley cars were stored.

- In the 1930s rivers generally had no flood controls, so people living nearby had no protection against the whims of nature.

- The residents of Hoovervilles often had a better opinion of their makeshift homes than the general public did. In Seattle, Washington, a large Hooverville created within the view of downtown office buildings was burned to the ground twice by city officials. The residents rebuilt it each time.

Excerpt from "Till the River Rises"

*"As much sand and gravel as they is about here, you wouldn't hardly think nothing would grow. But it does. Every house down here, they's a spot for a garden near it if them that lives in it ain't too **trifling** to put it in. We have plenty of corn and 'taters and cucumbers and tomatoes in season. We shares with them that ain't got any if they's been down on their luck. I has flowers, too. Them seeds over there in the drying box is every one of them flower seeds. I save them from one year to the next."*

*Fan Flanigan sat against one of the crooked **sapling** poles which supported the driftwood **joists** of the porch. She was a small **wizened** woman, brown, **gnarled**, with thin gray hair. A washed-out shapeless house dress had not been pulled low enough to hide her large bony feet.*

An unemployed man uses bricks to try and repair the roof of his makeshift shack in a Seattle, Washington, Hooverville. *Corbis Corporation. Reproduced by permission.*

Trifling: Lazy.

Sapling: Young tree.

Joists: Beams supporting the ceiling.

Wizened: Shrunken and wrinkled.

Gnarled: Twisted in shape.

Children at a Washington, D.C., Hooverville in 1932.
Corbis Corporation. Reproduced by permission.

"It's all right here," she said, "and I like it pretty fair as long as the river don't start acting up. We don't have no rent to pay, jest sort of squat here **betwixt** the railroad tracks and the water and build our places out of what we can git off the dump and the wood we can ketch floating down the river. Me and mammy been here sence nineteen and thirty-two, that hard old year."

She **puckered** her eyes against the strong sunlight and glanced over the thirteen stilt-set shanties which straggled along the banks of the Tennessee River between the approaches to two of Knoxville's bridges. Most of them faced the railroad tracks where strings of coal cars and empty boxcars stood. Beyond the tracks was a high deeply eroded embankment criss-crossed by foot paths and littered with rusty cans, bottles, and other rubbish.

"You kind of grow to like this place," said Fan. "You'd like any place, though, if you live in it long enough, I reckon. A rich man up to Knoxville give this whole strip betwixt the bridges for poor folks to build they houses on. Them that come first taken the pick of what they was here. Ma done that. She come right after Pop died...."

Betwixt: Between.

Puckered: Squinted.

"When you git your claim that rich man don't care what you make your house of. But they's one thing about it, the outside, I mean the roof, is got to be tin. That's the law. No way to put out a fire in Shanty Town. So it's tin roofs here or you can't put up a house."

An old woman appeared at the door. She wore a broad-brimmed man's hat, full skirted brown calico dress, and a sweater with the elbows out. Toothless and **stooped**, she was as wrinkled as a dried apple....

Fan jerked her head toward the old woman.... "Don't you think Mammy looks awful old? She ain't, really. Just about seventy. I guess me and her both looks more age than we is. That's the way it is when you can't keep no meat to your bones. You just shrivel up.... Folks is always thinking I'm past the age I says I am. I don't **keer**, though....

"I may look bullhide strong, but I ain't. Mammy can outwork me two to one. My lands, she works out in that garden from sun-up till night come without stopping for more than a spitting spell. She's

This California family has only a primitive shelter to protect themselves from bad weather. *AP/Wide World Photo. Reproduced by permission.*

Stooped: Bent over.

Keer: Care.

*plumb stone **deef**. Couldn't hear you if you's to beller it right down her ear ..... She is got an old age **pension** and gits eleven dollars a month. It's what we live on. Besides that, we git supplies **off the relief**, stuff out of the garden when a **drouth** or a **rise** don't hit it.*

*"But Great Day! When the river rises they's no chance for a garden then. High water will drown a garden right to death. And we do git high water here off and on and the water **kivers** the whole place. This house is **sot** bout as high as any of them—ain't but one sot much higher. But you can't git away from high water. Git yourself, maybe, but not your house. The boy that's building that high one there has got hisself a city wife. He figgers he's smarter than the rest around here and he's perching his house a foot or two higher. Well, that bride ain't going to be no drier than the rest of us when the river rises up and starts flooding. Day of Judgment! She's going to be wetted down and mudified like anybody else.*

"Oh, I tell you I've see that old river come up. And the gov'ment never sent us no notice of what the water was going to do. We just set and see it come up. See it and know what we's in for. When it begins to git in the houses, we take and move everything up on the bank across the railroad tracks, and we camp there all on top of each other. Well, city folks come trotting up there gitting under our feets. Coming with soup kettles and knives and half of them wouldn't no more set foot in your house low water times than nothing at all. I ought not to say a word against them and I know it. I 'preciates what they does. But it's mighty hard for them that's had it easy all they lives to know what 'tis to be poor.

"They's always one saying to another, `Do you suppose them people's got little enough sense to go back to them shacks when the river goes down?' ... Yes Lord, we'll always go back to Shanty Town till the river rises some day and forgits to go down....

*"**Womern** is a big help to men more ways than one. Stretching a little money to go a long way and fixing up men's homes for them. I wish you could see that fern Jack Long's wife got off the undertaker. He had it left over from a funeral. It's so pretty. I jest like to go up there and set a spell to look at it all I want to. And Jack's got as much sense as she has about gitting the best that's to be got. He was a regular carpenter before hard times drug him down here to live. When it come to setting up his house, he know'd how. Got good lumber for doing it, too. The way he done it was to go down there to Henley Street where they's building the bridge. He picked up every stick of the wood they throwed away. Got enough*

Deef: Deaf.

Pension: Monthly cash payment to the aged.

Off the relief: Relief centers for the unemployed.

Drouth: Drought.

Rise: Increase in the river level.

Kivers: Covers.

Sot: Situated.

Womern: Women.

for everything but the walls and ceiling. That didn't stump Jack none. He jest went over to a dump heap in South Knoxville, and there he run into jest what he wanted. It was a lot of emptied out sheet-iron barrels. First he knocked the tops and bottoms out. He split the barrels open down the sides and flattened them out for the walls and roof. Right in that same dump he picked up two hundred paint buckets. They's supposed to be empty, but he scooped out about two gallons of paint. It was a plenty for spreading over his house. The colors ain't the same, but that don't matter. It's paint. See over there how he kind of worked the different kinds into stripes and wherly cues? Makes a right pretty sight, don't it? Well, then he tooled and nailed some great big split cardboard boxes for the inside walls and pasted paper over that. Then he tinned the top, for the roof has got to be tin down here in Shanty Town." [Federal Writers' Project, pp. 372–376, 377–378]

What happened next...

Hoovervilles continued to exist in various communities through the 1930s. In late 1941 preparations for the U.S. entry into World War II (1939–45) finally provided enough jobs for full employment, and shantytown residents were able to get jobs and homes. The FWP continued to write books and pamphlets on all aspects of American life. By 1942 the agency had produced 3.5 million copies of eight hundred different titles. The best-known series was the American Guide Series, illustrated guidebooks for all the states and many cities.

Did you know...

- Residents of Hoovervilles did their food shopping at the local dumps and in restaurant garbage cans. If soup kitchens were nearby, some people took a meal there.

- The FWP technique of compiling oral histories from interviews and then writing them down was a groundbreaking method of recording history. It came into common use by historians and social scientists in the following decades.

- The FWP employed almost seven thousand writers, researchers, and librarians at its peak in 1935. They documented many facets of American life, including cultural history of children, youth, and adults and American natural or landscape history.

Consider the following...

- Explain why shantytowns were called Hoovervilles.

- When the FWP was created and throughout the 1930s, a large controversy existed over the federal government spending money to employ out-of-work writers and artists. Do you think the federal government was justified in spending money in this way? Why or why not?

For More Information

Bustard, Bruce I. *A New Deal for the Arts*. Seattle, WA: University of Washington Press, 1997.

Federal Writers' Project. *These Are Our Lives*. Chapel Hill, NC: University of North Carolina Press, 1939.

Mangione, Jerre. *The Dream and the Deal: The Federal Writers' Project, 1935–1943*. Syracuse, NY: Syracuse University Press, 1996.

McElvaine, Robert S. *Down and Out in the Great Depression: Letters from the "Forgotten Man."* Chapel Hill, NC: University of North Carolina Press, 1983.

On the Farm

For much of U.S. history, farming had been the most important means of earning a living for Americans. A healthy agricultural economy was essential to the nation's overall economic health. Yet perhaps more than any other group of Americans, farmers experienced wide swings between prosperity and poverty during the early twentieth century. The years between 1909 and 1914 were frequently referred to as the "golden age of U.S. agriculture." Farm production and farm prices both rose steadily. During World War I (1914–18) food production in Europe was severely disrupted, and American agriculture further expanded to supply Europeans with food. However, with the end of the war Europeans resumed food production, and the market for American products declined by the early 1920s. Prices for farm products dropped dramatically. For example, wheat that sold for $2.94 a bushel in 1920 sold for $1.00 in 1929 and $0.30 by 1932. Nevertheless, farmers continued to produce large crops in an attempt to cover their costs. They took out loans on their land, houses, and equipment to meet living expenses and production costs such as the purchase of seed. By 1929 the overall state of American agriculture was very unhealthy. The large surpluses of farm prod-

ucts pushed prices ever downward. Still, 25 to 30 percent of Americans depended on farming for their livelihood.

In October 1929 the U.S. stock market crashed, signaling the start of the worst economic crisis ever experienced by the United States. Although almost all Americans were affected by the economic downturn, those who were already in the midst of economic hardship, such as the farmers, were devastated. By 1932 farmers' income was only one-third of what it had been in 1929, when farm income levels were already low. Farmers fell behind on their loan payments, and many were subjected to foreclosure. Foreclosure is a legal proceeding in which a bank takes over a property and sells it to recover the amount of the unpaid loan. Approximately four hundred thousand farms were lost through foreclosure between 1929 and 1932.

The federal government, under the leadership of President Herbert Hoover (1874–1964; served 1929–33), had no answer for the farmers' plight, so many farmers took matters into their own hands. Some destroyed their own products to lower availability and thereby raise prices. However, this action did not prove to be an effective solution. Not until 1933, when Franklin D. Roosevelt (1882–1945; served 1933–45) was inaugurated as president, did farmers see a glimmer of hope. Roosevelt (served 1933–45) placed government assistance to farmers at the highest priority level as he instituted his New Deal for Americans. The New Deal was a series of government programs and legislation designed to provide relief and recovery for the nation. For farmers the challenge was to decrease farm production in order to eliminate surpluses, yet maintain enough income to survive while they regrouped. In ***Hard Times: An Oral History of the Great Depression*** (1970), Studs Terkel records the memories of many individuals who lived through the Depression, including Oscar Heline, an Iowa farmer. Heline recounted for Terkel the desperate situation of farmers and the efforts of Henry Wallace (1888–1965), Roosevelt's secretary of agriculture, to offer farmers a share in the New Deal.

Some of the poorest farmers were sharecroppers and tenant farmers, who lived predominantly in the Southern states. Sharecroppers raised crops on property controlled by a landowner who generally provided shelter, fuel, farm tools,

Farmers in Spotsylvania, Virginia, listen intently as the auctioneer sells their land at a public auction for unpaid taxes.
©Bettmann/CORBIS.
Reproduced by permission.

and seed. Tenant farmers had basically the same arrangement except they provided their own tools. Both lived in extreme poverty and stayed in constant debt to the landowner. Katharine DuPre Lumpkin and Dorothy Wolff Douglas vividly relate the life of a sharecropper's son in Alabama in their 1937 book titled *Child Workers in America.* The book's purpose was to expose the extent to which child labor still existed in the United States, especially in agriculture. The excerpt reprinted in this chapter recounts twelve-year-old Tom's everyday existence and the hopeless situation of sharecropping families.

Farmers in the Dust Bowl region were another group in desperate need of relief. The region was experiencing a severe drought by late 1931. Between 1932 and 1939, a series of dust storms rolled over the Great Plains, from the Dakotas south to Texas. Plowed fields turned into sand dunes. **"Letters from the Dust Bowl,"** written in 1935 and 1936 by Caroline A. Henderson of Eva, Oklahoma, and published in a

condensed form in the July 1936 issue of *Reader's Digest,* clearly describes a family's struggle to maintain their farm. Henderson's letters allowed Americans who lived in other regions of the United States to better understand what it would be like to have clouds of dust envelop their homes and cover their land. Two of Henderson's letters are included in this chapter.

Unable to carry on with any farming activities, thousands of families living in the Dust Bowl packed their belongings into cars and headed west, primarily to the agricultural fields of California, in search of work. These migrants lived in their cars or makeshift shelters and rarely found any work. "Migrant Mother," a widely published photograph of a mother and her daughters living at a destitute pea pickers' camp in Nipomo Valley, California, is an indelible image of a displaced farming family. The picture is one of the extraordinary photographs from the files of the Farm Security Administration (FSA). The FSA photographers were charged with documenting the plight of the rural poor during the 1930s. In the final excerpt in this chapter, Dorothea Lange (1895–1965), the FSA photographer who took the famous picture, recalls the experience in an article titled **"The Assignment I'll Never Forget: Migrant Mother,"** originally published in the February 1960 issue of *Popular Photography.*

Oscar Heline

Excerpt from Hard Times:
An Oral History of the Great Depression

Edited by Studs Terkel
Published in 1970; excerpt taken from 1986 reprint

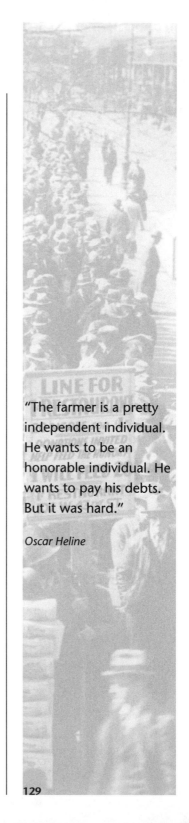

"The farmer is a pretty independent individual. He wants to be an honorable individual. He wants to pay his debts. But it was hard."

Oscar Heline

Between 1930 and 1932 more and more farmers faced losing their farms to foreclosure. In 1932 and 1933 approximately 150,000 farms a year were foreclosed. Farm families lived in constant dread that they would be next to have a bank agent come to their door. The agent would demand that they make their loan payments; if they couldn't, the farm would be auctioned off. Never had fear or anger run so deep in America's farming communities, from the Ohio and Mississippi River valleys to the wheat fields of the Great Plains. In protest and despair, farmers burned their corn and wheat and dumped milk on highways rather than sell it for a loss. In May 1932 farmers met in a national convention called by the Iowan Farmers' Union to decide how to pressure the government for change. They formed the Farmers Holiday Association and chose well-known farm advocate Milo Reno as its president. The association organized a farmers' strike or "farmers' holiday" in which farmers refused to sell their produce for a few weeks. By reducing the supply of farm produce available to markets, farmers hoped that they could raise produce prices. The action became so popular that it ended up lasting a few months. On August 25, twelve

129

hundred farmers separated into groups and blocked five highways leading to a large produce market in Omaha, Nebraska. Occasional violence erupted as some farmers tried to break through the blockades to get their products to the markets. In the excerpt from Studs Terkel's *Hard Times,* Oscar Heline points out that the poverty of the times led to such desperate actions and situations.

In late 1932 efforts turned from blocking highways to blocking farm foreclosures. "Penny auctions" occurred frequently. As related in T. H. Watkins's book titled *The Hungry Years,* published in 1999, a "penny auction" might proceed like this: A Nebraska farmer with a $400 mortgage (a bank loan on his property) could no longer make payments on the mortgage. The local bank allowed him to postpone payments, but the bank collapsed and a "receiver" bank took over the mortgages held by the local bank. This "receiver" bank sent out an agent to demand full payment of the $400 mortgage—$400 the farmer did not have. The agent set a date to auction off the farm. A group of local farmers came to the farm auction and bid only pennies for the farm animals and equipment. For example, they might bid 35 cents apiece for the cows, a few dollars for a horse, and 25 cents each for pieces of farm equipment. At the end of the auction perhaps $100 was collected. The $100 was given to the bank agent, who took it as full payment for the mortgage. The agent knew that it was all he could get and that demanding more would probably only get him a broken nose. The farmers who bid on the animals and equipment then gave everything back to the original owner and the farm was saved.

It was obvious that the government had to do something to aid farmers. When Franklin D. Roosevelt (1882–1945) was inaugurated as president of the United States on March 4, 1933, he appointed Iowan Henry Wallace (1888–1965) as secretary of agriculture. A few days later, on March 16, Wallace gathered farm leaders in Washington, D.C., to write a revolutionary farm bill to "adjust" farmer income. The resulting legislation, the Agricultural Adjustment Act of 1933, provided a voluntary production-control system. If a farmer agreed to reduce his crop production according to an established government plan, he received government payments to maintain his income. Another effort to lower sup-

ply and raise prices came in the summer of 1933, when the National Corn-Hog Committee, a group composed of farmers from around the country, decided to let the government purchase and slaughter six million hogs.

There were many critics of the crop and pig destruction policies, but these were desperate measures for desperate times. In *The Coming of the New Deal* (1988) historian Arthur M. Schlesinger Jr. relates an infamous statement made by Secretary of Agriculture Wallace on the pig-kill. Wallace said that the public seemed to believe that "every little pig has the right to attain before slaughter the full pigginess of his pigness. To hear them talk, you would have thought that pigs were raised for pets." Wallace responded to the uproar by giving millions of pounds of baby pork to the Federal Surplus Relief Corporation to feed the hungry people in relief programs.

In the following excerpt Oscar Heline recounts the farmers' holidays, the struggle for legislation, and his memories of Secretary of Agriculture Wallace.

A farm foreclosure sale in Iowa, circa 1933. *Courtesy of the Franklin D. Roosevelt Library.*

Things to remember while reading the excerpt from *Hard Times: An Oral History of the Great Depression*:

- Most farmers had not shared in the general economic prosperity of the 1920s. Instead, they struggled throughout the decade. As the Great Depression began, they had already endured economic difficulties for some time.

- Farmers traditionally were very independent individuals. Only with the increased levels of desperation reached by 1932—when 400,000 farms had been lost, farmers' income was one-third of what it was in 1929, and farm prices were at their lowest—did they finally accept government help.

- In addition to their economic problems, many farmers were affected by a drought that began in the East in 1931 and spread to the Midwest.

Excerpt from Hard Times: An Oral History of the Great Depression

The struggles people had to go through are almost unbelievable. A man lived all his life on a given farm, it was taken away from him. One after the other!...

The farmers became desperate....

First, they'd take your farm, then they took your livestock, then your farm machinery. Even your household goods. And they'd move you off. The farmers were almost united. We had penny auction sales. Some neighbor would bid a penny and give it [the auctioned property] back to the owner....

*We had lots of trouble on the highway. People were determined to withhold produce from the market—livestock, cream, butter, eggs, what not. If they would dump the produce, they would force the market to a higher level. The farmers would man the highways, and cream cans were emptied in ditches and eggs dumped out. They burned the trestle bridge, so the trains wouldn't be able to haul grain. **Conservatives** don't like this kind of rebel attitude and aren't very sympathetic. But something had to be done.*

Conservatives: Those who prefer to use established, traditional ways to accomplish goals.

*I spent most of my time in Des Moines [Iowa] as a **lobbyist** for the **state cooperatives**. Trying to get some legislation. I wasn't out on the highway fighting this battle. Some of the farmers probably didn't think I was friendly to their cause. They were so desperate. If you weren't out there with them, you weren't a friend, you must be a foe. I didn't know from day to day whether somebody might come along and cause harm to my family. When you have bridges burned, accidents, violence, there may have been killings, I don't know.*

*There were some pretty conservative ones, wouldn't join this group. I didn't want to particularly, because it wasn't the answer. It took that kind of action, but what I mean is it took more than that to solve it. You had to do **constructive things** at the same time. But I never spoke harshly about those who were on the highway.*

Some of the farmers with teams of horses, sometimes in trucks, tried to get through. He was trying to feed his family, trying to trade a few dozen eggs and a few pounds of cream for some groceries to feed his babies. He was desperate, too. One group tried to sell so

Striking farmers in Harvard, Illinois, dump fifty cans of milk in an attempt to stop the usual supply bound for Chicago on October 2, 1935. *AP/Wide World Photo. Reproduced by permission.*

Lobbyist: One who attempts to influence public officials and legislators.

State cooperatives: Organized farming groups.

Constructive things: Positive actions.

they could live and the other group tried to keep you from selling so they could live.

The farmer is a pretty independent individual. He wants to be a conservative individual. He wants to be an honorable individual. He wants to pay his debts. But it was hard. The rank-and-file people of this state—who were brought up as conservatives, which most of us were—would never act like this. Except in desperation....

There are always a few who make money out of other people's poverty. This was a struggle between the haves and the have-nots.

*The original bankers who came to this state, for instance. When my father would borrow $100, he'd get $80. And when it was due, he'd pay back the $100 and a **premium** besides that. Most of his early borrowings were on this basis. That's where we made some wealthy families in this country....*

*Through a federal program we got a farm loan. A committee of twenty-five of us drafted the first farm legislation of this kind thirty-five years ago. We drew it up with **Henry Wallace**. New money was put in the farmers' hands ... People could now see daylight and hope. It was a whole transformation of attitude. You can just imagine.... (He weeps.)*

*It was Wallace who saved us, put us back on our feet. He understood our problems. When we went to visit him, after he was appointed Secretary, he made it clear to us he didn't want to write the law. He wanted the farmers themselves to write it. "I will work with you," he said, "but you're the people who are suffering. It must be your program." He would always give his **counsel**, but he never directed us. The program came from the farmers themselves, you betcha.*

Another thing happened: we had twice too many hogs because corn'd been so cheap. And we set up what people called Wallace's Folly: killing the little pigs. Another farmer and I helped develop this. We couldn't afford to feed 45-cents corn to a $3 hog. So we had to figure a way of getting rid of the surplus pigs. We went out and bought 'em and killed 'em. This is how desperate it was. It was the only way to raise the price of pigs. Most of 'em were dumped down the river.

*The hard times put farmers' families closer together. My wife was working for the county Farm Bureau. We had lessons in home economics, how to make underwear out of gunny sacks, out of flour sacks. It was **cooperative labor**. So some good things came out of*

Premium: Additional fee.

Henry Wallace: Roosevelt's secretary of agriculture.

Counsel: Advice.

Cooperative labor: Working together.

Great Depression and New Deal: Primary Sources

*this. Sympathy toward one another was **manifest**. There were personal values as well as terrible hardships.* [Terkel, pp. 217–20]

In early 1933, Minnesota farmers march through the city of St. Paul to protest a lack of government relief funds. ©*Minnesota Historical Society/CORBIS. Reproduced by permission.*

What happened next...

      In late 1935, looking back at the first three years of the New Deal's effort to improve the economy, presidential adviser Raymond Moley (1886–1975) considered the Agricultural Adjustment Administration (AAA) programs some of the most successful and popular programs adopted. The desperation of farmers had helped ensure their acceptance of new programs and unusual solutions. Despite criticisms, the AAA and other farm programs, especially those providing easier repayment terms for farm loans, helped many farmers stay on their land.

Manifest: Evident, noticeable.

A group of Texas farmers stand in line to receive their Agricultural Adjustment Administration (AAA) benefit checks, circa 1934.
Corbis Corporation. Reproduced by permission.

While the U.S. economy as a whole still struggled in the mid-1930s, many farmers saw considerable recovery. Gross farm income rose from a low of $6.4 billion in 1932 to $8.5 billion in 1934. Between 1932 and 1936 farm income increased by 50 percent. Farm product prices rose by 67 percent. The AAA benefit payments to millions of farmers who followed AAA guidelines amounted to $577 million between 1933 and 1934. The federal government held 40 percent of farm mortgage debt by the end of the 1930s, replacing private banks as the key holder of farm mortgages. However, overproduction remained a problem through the rest of the 1930s. This would not be conquered until World War II (1939–45), when a high demand for farm products increased prices.

Oscar Heline was able to hold on to his farm. As Studs Terkel records in *Hard Times*, a neighbor once told Heline that they needed a war to solve their agricultural problems. When the United States entered World War II in late 1941, Heline's son joined the armed services. Sadly, Heline lost his son in the

war. He commented that his son's life was much too heavy a price to pay for the farms' economic stability.

Did you know...

- In 1931, when banks were foreclosing and selling so many farms, many defiant farmers put signs in front of their land that read "This Farm Is Not For Sale."

- Despite the Depression, more-efficient farm machinery continued to be developed. The new machinery meant that more acres could be planted and harvested by fewer people.

- In January 1936 the U.S. Supreme Court struck down the Agricultural Adjustment Act as unconstitutional because private companies were being taxed to fund the government's payments to farmers. However, new legislation soon took its place.

Consider the following...

- Why do you think farmers continued to overproduce during the 1920s and 1930s?

- Why did farmers, who were usually hardworking, law-abiding citizens, participate in the "farmers' holidays"?

- Why did the federal government pay farmers to kill livestock and reduce crop production when so many Americans were going hungry?

For More Information

Hamilton, David E. *From New Day to New Deal: American Farm Policy from Hoover to Roosevelt, 1928–1933*. Chapel Hill, NC: University of North Carolina Press, 1991.

Hurt, Douglas. *American Agriculture: A Brief History*. Ames, IA: Iowa State University Press, 1994.

Schlesinger, Arthur M., Jr. *The Coming of the New Deal: The Age of Roosevelt*. Boston, MA: Houghton Mifflin, 1988.

Terkel, Studs. *Hard Times: An Oral History of the Great Depression*. New York, NY: Pantheon Books, 1986. Reprint.

Watkins, T. H. *The Hungry Years: A Narrative History of the Great Depression in America*. New York, NY: Henry Holt, 1999.

Katharine DuPre Lumpkin and Dorothy Wolff Douglas

Excerpt from Child Workers in America
Published in 1937

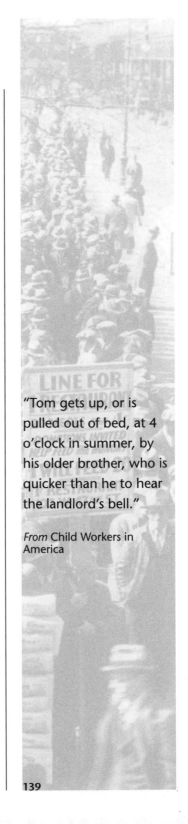

Before the American Civil War (1861–65), most black Americans worked and lived as slaves on plantations and farms in the Southern states. At the conclusion of the war, black Americans were freed from slavery but had no money to purchase their own farmland. White landowners still needed stable, low-cost laborers to work the land, so they devised a new farming system in which they divided their land into sections and assigned a family to work each section. These families were called sharecroppers because at harvest they had to share part of their crop, generally half, with the landowner. The shared crop was repayment for the use of the land and tools and for the cash advances that the landowner had given to the sharecropper for shelter, fuel, feed for livestock, seed, and fertilizer. Poor black Americans and poor white Americans worked as sharecroppers. Tenant farmers worked under the same arrangement as sharecroppers, but they usually owned their own tools.

Most sharecroppers and tenant farmers had, at best, minimal reading and math skills. This left them dependent on the honesty of the local store owner and landowner. They

"Tom gets up, or is pulled out of bed, at 4 o'clock in summer, by his older brother, who is quicker than he to hear the landlord's bell."

From Child Workers in America

In a sharecropper family, often children as young as six years old were expected to work in the fields. *Corbis Corporation. Reproduced by permission.*

had to buy their food, clothing, and other necessities from the store on credit because they had no money until their crop was harvested. Frequently the owner of the store would overcharge on goods and charge excessive rates of interest on the extended credit. Landowners might deliberately underestimate the value of the farmer's harvest and then demand a larger share of the crop, leaving the farmer with little crop to sell to pay back the store owner. This system kept the sharecropper and tenant families in constant debt. Sharecroppers and tenant farmers were legally bound to work for the landowners as long as their debt persisted.

Katharine DuPre Lumpkin and Dorothy Wolff Douglas's 1937 book, *Child Workers in America,* looks at the place of child labor in the nation's economic life. Arguments raged in the 1930s over the need for child labor regulation. In their first chapter Lumpkin and Douglas focus on children working in agriculture. They concentrate predominantly on the children of sharecroppers and tenant farmers working in the cotton fields of Southern states. The excerpt illustrates the poverty and hopelessness of a sharecropper family.

Things to remember while reading the excerpt from *Child Workers in America*:

- Sharecroppers and tenant farmers typically lived in crowded shacks, structures that failed to protect the inhabitants from rain and cold.

- Sharecroppers and tenant farmers ate poor diets of fatback (meat from the back of a hog carcass), corn bread, molasses, and potatoes.

- Black sharecroppers and tenant farmers suffered from racial discrimination and violence at the hands of the dominant white society.

- Children as young as six years old were expected to work in the fields.

Excerpt from Child Workers in America

*Tom is a sharecropper's child, black, in Alabama. His family (father, mother, and four children old enough to make "hands") all work for the landowner, are all **collectively** continually in debt to him (they get $75 worth of supplies for the growing season and he keeps the books), and all live in a two-room cabin furnished by the landowner.*

*The cabin sits close to the ground, with a single layer of boards for a floor; one window, or rather window hole, in each room (no glass, a wooden shutter instead); a roof that leaks so badly that when the last baby was born, the mother said, her bed had to be moved three times; walls without paper or plaster, of course—indeed you can see daylight through their cracks; no stove, only an open fireplace; no fence or garden outside (the landlord decrees that the cotton must be grown "up to the doorstep"); no well, because "the creek is so near"; and for outhouse a hole in the ground with **sacking** on poles rigged up by the family themselves.*

Here Tom lives and labors. He is now 12....

Tom gets up, or is pulled out of bed, at 4 o'clock in summer, by his older brother, who is quicker than he to hear the landlord's bell. Work for the entire plantation force is "from can see to can't see" (i.e., from daylight to dark), and the bell is their commanding timepiece....

*Little Jenny, aged 5, is being left at home today to care for the baby, because it is so hot; on cooler days the baby is carried along to the field and laid on a **pallet** under the tree, and Jenny can play among the cotton rows with the other children who are too young to work. (There are plantations where mothers of young infants are given fifteen minutes nursing time, no more, morning and after-*

Collectively: As a group.

Sacking: Empty flour or potato sacks, hung up like curtains around the outhouse.

Pallet: A straw-filled mattress.

Sharecropper's children picking string beans in New Madrid County, Missouri, May 1938. *Corbis Corporation. Reproduced by permission.*

"No-account": In debt.

He was a "prosperity" child: His schooling took place during the 1920s in better economic times.

noon. Then they must take the baby along: there is not enough time to go home.)

Tom is a good, steady chopper and can do over half a man's work. At picking he can do two-thirds. Peter, aged 9, does considerably less than that. In fact when his father asked to stay on at the beginning of the growing season, the landlord told him he didn't see how he could keep him on another year raising a crop on so many acres and living in such a good house, with his family so "no-account."

Tom has been to school part of three grades. The Negro school in his district runs four months "normally" (the white school runs six); but in the year 1932–33 it closed altogether, and since then it has been averaging less than three months. Besides, cotton-picking season in Alabama runs well into November, and after that it is often too cold to go to school without shoes. So from January on Tom and Peter have been taking turns in one pair.

The older brother did a little better. **He was a "prosperity" child,** and during several of the 1925–29 seasons he got the full

four-months school term. By the time he was 13, however, he had stopped going altogether, having finished the fifth grade (twenty months of education for a lifetime of work) and being, in the view of the **riding boss**, "plenty big for a man's work and likely to get uppity soon if he don't quit school."

In picking cotton Tom is not so much "smarter" than some of the younger children. At age 12 he can keep going longer, of course, at the end of a twelve-hour day with the thermometer still close to 100°, than he could when he was 7, but he can hardly pick faster. All the children pick with both hands, and by the end of the first season the lifetime rhythm of pluck, pluck, drop-in-the-bag is long since established. But now that Tom is taller he has to stoop so much, or move along on his knees, while the littlest fellows scramble by with "hardly a bend to them." The cotton plants often grow shoulder-high, to be sure, but the cotton bolls on them grow nearly all the way to the ground; so, for all but a tiny child, this means "stooping, stooping all day." But Tom can manage the big sack that he drags after him by a shoulder strap better now than when he was a little fellow. It grows so heavy dragging along after the smallest pickers all day that it nearly makes up for the "bends" of the older ones....

What is Tom—and what are all the hundreds of thousands of his fellows in the cotton belt of the South—getting for this investment of his childhood? An outlook for the future, a foundation for something better for him later on, an immediate financial return even in his own pocket, for his present **wretched and stultifying** toil? On the contrary, Tom is not only burying his own childhood in this cotton patch, he is drawing in return not a dollar of pay, from year's end to year's end. The landlord's account simply chalks up so many acres cultivated against the

Let Us Now Praise Famous Men (1941)

In the summer of 1936 James Agee (1909–1955), a writer for *Fortune* magazine, was assigned to write a story about an Alabama sharecropper and his family. He was to provide a portrait of poverty in the rural South. Agee hired Walker Evans (1903–1975), a photographer with the Farm Security Administration, to travel with him and take documentary photographs for the article. Although *Fortune* ended up not publishing the article, Agee and Evans continued their work together. In 1941 Houghton Mifflin published their five-hundred-page book *Let Us Now Praise Famous Men*. The book followed the lives of three rural families. Thirty-one striking photographs were included in the original edition, and another thirty-one were added in a 1960 edition. Close-up photos captured the desperation of rural America during the Depression. Although not a big seller when originally published, the book has become recognized as an American classic, providing one of the most famous visual and documentary accounts of the Great Depression.

Riding boss: Person who oversees the sharecroppers' work.

Wretched and stultifying: Miserable and dulling.

*family's debts for the coming year, and if Tom or his brothers did not work, their father would not get his farm for the next season. Tom's and his family's reward is that he continue shoeless and **abominably** fed, oppressed and **half-illiterate** from those first months in the fields when he was 6 until he shall be an old man.* [Lumpkin and Douglas, pp. 4–6]

What happened next...

The early New Deal agricultural policies such as those of the Agricultural Adjustment Administration (AAA) favored large landowners; small farmers like sharecroppers and tenant farmers had to fend for themselves. When the AAA paid large landowners to refrain from planting some crops and fields, the landowners no longer needed as many sharecroppers or tenant farmers. As a result, tens of thousands of sharecroppers and tenant farmers were forced off the land, and their families were suddenly homeless. In 1934 black and white sharecroppers in Arkansas, Oklahoma, Texas, and Mississippi joined together to try to put a stop to this trend. Calling themselves the Southern Tenant Farmers' Union, they gained twenty-five thousand members, but after the group achieved only limited success, membership declined by 1937.

A New Deal agency called the Resettlement Administration (RA) attempted to resettle sharecroppers and tenant farmers on good land and give them opportunities to buy the land. In reality, very few families were ever resettled. Instead, by 1937 the RA evolved into the Farm Security Administration (FSA), which concentrated on loaning money to the families (to buy food, clothing, feed, seed, and fertilizer) rather than trying to resettle them. Slowly many of the younger sharecroppers and tenant farmers managed to leave the farms and find jobs for wages in the industrialized Northern cities. This movement to industrial jobs accelerated with the start of World War II (1939–45), when U.S. factories needed to quickly manufacture war supplies, including bullets, tanks, and airplanes.

Abominably: Poorly.

Half-illiterate: Barely able to read and write.

Sharecroppers and tenant farmers who could not leave because they had nowhere else to go continued to live in poverty. For many the situation worsened, for two reasons: Increased mechanization (use of machinery) resulted in fewer people being needed to work the land. Secondly, in many small areas the land became so eroded—from continuous re-planting without replacing nutrients, and poor plowing practices—that the property was rendered useless for crop production. In both situations families were pushed off the land and had nowhere to resettle.

Did you know...

- In 1930 approximately 581,000 whites and 486,000 blacks were sharecroppers and tenant farmers.

- In the 1930s sharecroppers earned an average of $312 per year, and tenant farmers averaged $417 annually. The yearly median family income nationwide was $1,160 in 1935. The U.S. government estimated that a family of four needed at least $800 per year to survive in the mid-1930s.

Consider the following...

- How could the landowners routinely cheat sharecroppers and tenant farmers out of income? Consider the educational opportunities available to the children.

- The authors of the excerpt describe Tom's life and his family's situation in some detail. Judging from this description, what do you think their position is on unprotected child labor?

- Considering what you know about Tom's early life, do you think he was able to escape poverty and build a better life?

For More Information

Agee, James, and Walker Evans. *Let Us Now Praise Famous Men: Three Tenant Families*. Boston, MA: Houghton Mifflin, 2000. Reprint.

Conrad, David E. *The Forgotten Farmers: The Story of Sharecroppers in the New Deal*. Westport, CT: Greenwood Press, 1982.

Dregni, Michael, ed. *This Old Farm: A Treasury of Family Farm Memories.* Stillwater, MN: Voyageur Press, 1999.

Lumpkin, Katharine DuPre, and Dorothy Wolff Douglas. *Child Workers in America.* New York, NY: Robert M. McBride & Company, 1937.

Caroline A. Henderson

Excerpts from "Letters from the Dust Bowl"

**Originally published in *The Atlantic Monthly*, May 1936
Reprinted from *Reader's Digest*
Published in July 1936**

In 1930, the wheat farmers of the Great Plains, the vast middle space of the United States from North Dakota south to the Texas Panhandle, were relatively prosperous even as farmers struggled in other regions of the country. The spring of 1931 produced another record-breaking wheat crop. However, by summer of that year a drought that had begun in the eastern United States moved west to the Great Plains. The winter wheat crops planted in the fall of 1931 were unable to grow enough to protect the soil from furious windstorms that blew from the north every year. There were no native grasses to protect the soil, because farmers in the previous two decades had removed millions of acres of native sod to plant wheat. By January 1932, dust storms began to roll over the Great Plains. Winds of sixty miles per hour created huge clouds of thick dust reaching 10,000 feet into the air. The storms blew away valuable topsoil and covered farms in drifts of dust.

The drought persisted, and the dust storms steadily worsened over the next few years. Hardest hit were the southern plains in Kansas, Colorado, Oklahoma, the Texas Panhandle, and northeastern New Mexico. By 1935 and

> "We can't hold out indefinitely without some income, however small. But if we can keep the taxes paid, we can work and hope for a better day."
>
> *Caroline A. Henderson*

Dust storms often turned daylight into darkness for hours and days at a time.
Courtesy of the Library of Congress.

1936, horrific dust storms carrying millions of tons of black dirt swept across the Great Plains, plunging the daylight hours into total darkness and leaving days of half-light as dust remained suspended in the air. Businesses and schools were forced to close as people sought shelter in their homes. But the dust went anywhere air went. People would seal window frames with gummy tape, stuff rags into any cracks, and hang wet sheets in windows and doorways, but the dust—buckets of dust—still found its way inside. Dust got into people's eyes, noses, and mouths and into food and drinking water. Often people had to shovel their way out of the house following a storm. Families lost crops and livestock, and eventually they lost their farms to the banks when they could no longer make payments on their farm loans. People began to pack up their cars and drive away. The number of people leaving the Dust Bowl region grew from hundreds to thousands and then to hundreds of thousands. Many migrated to California, Oregon, and Washington to search for agricultural jobs.

The dust storms were not only an economic and social disaster but an environmental disaster as well. As early as 1930, the U.S. Department of Agriculture established a few soil erosion experimental stations, but by 1932 and 1933, when the dust storms became intense, still very little was known about preventing wind erosion. In 1933 the Soil Erosion Service (SES) was created under the U.S. Department of the Interior. Under Hugh Hammond Bennett, known as the "father of soil conservation," the SES encouraged new farming practices that conserved soil. For example, the stubble left after wheat harvests was no longer burned or used for grazing; leaving the stubble in the ground helped keep soil in place. Trees were planted in rows to serve as windbreaks.

The following excerpt from **"Letters from the Dust Bowl,"** written by Caroline A. Henderson of Eva, Oklahoma, and published in the July 1936 issue of *Reader's Digest,* describes life on a family farm in the Dust Bowl. The Hendersons believed that someday the rains would return so they struggled to stay on their farm.

Things to remember while reading "Letters from the Dust Bowl":

- Because of the great demand for wheat to feed Europeans during World War I (1914–18), U.S. wheat farmers extended cultivation deeper and deeper into the dry, short grass prairies of the western Great Plains.

- The native prairie grass sod that had anchored the topsoil was plowed up and planted in wheat. After harvest the land was bare for several months. Also, ranchers overgrazed their cattle on the remaining grasslands. The resulting bare soil was easily blown away by the strong winds that came from the north.

- In the 1920s, rains were constant and hid the damage to the land.

- At the beginning of the 1930s, little was known about farming techniques to prevent erosion of the land.

Excerpt from "Letters from the Dust Bowl"

Eva, Oklahoma
June 30, 1935

My dear Evelyn:

In the dust-covered desolation of our No Man's Land here, wearing our shade hats, with handkerchiefs tied over our faces and vaseline in our nostrils, we have been trying to rescue our home from the wind-blown dust which penetrates wherever air can go. It is an almost hopeless task, for there is rarely a day when at some time the dust clouds do not roll over. "Visibility" approaches zero and everything is covered again with a silt-like deposit which may vary in depth from a film to actual ripples on the kitchen floor. I keep oiled cloths on the window sills and between the upper and lower sashes. Some seal the windows with the gummed-paper strips used in wrapping parcels, but no method is fully effective.

*On a 60-mile trip yesterday to **procure** tractor repairs we saw many pitiful reminders of broken hopes. Little abandoned homes where people had drilled deep wells for the precious water, had set trees and vines, built **reservoirs**, and fenced in gardens—with everything now walled in or half buried by banks of drifted soil— told a painful story. I grieved especially over one lonely plum thicket buried to the tips of the twigs, and a garden with a fence closely built of boards for wind protection, now enclosing only a **hillock** of dust covered with the blue-flowered **nettles** which no sands discourage.*

Early in May, with no more grass or even weeds on our 640 acres than on your kitchen floor, and even the scanty remnants of dried grasses from last year cut off and blown away, we decided to ship our cattle to grass in the central part of the state. We sent 27 head.

*The next day, the long **drouth** was temporarily broken by the first effective moisture in many months—about one and one-quarter inches in two or three gentle rains. But all hope of a wheat crop had already been abandoned, and the helpful effects of the rains have been largely destroyed by the drifting soil from abandoned lands about us. It fills the air and our eyes and noses and throats, and worst of all, our furrows, where tender shoots are coming to the*

Procure: Obtain.

Reservoirs: Places to store water.

Hillock: Small hill or mound.

Nettles: A prickly weed.

Drouth: Drought.

*surface only to be buried by the smothering **silt** from the [abandoned] fields....*

*Naturally you will wonder why we stay here where conditions are so disheartening. Why not pick up and leave as so many others have done? Yet I cannot act or think as if the experiences of our 27 years of life had never been. To break all the closely knit ties of our continued and united efforts for the sake of a possibly greater comfort elsewhere seems like **defaulting on** our task. We may have to leave. We can't hold out indefinitely without some income, however small. But if we can keep the taxes paid, we can work and hope for a better day. We long for the garden and little chickens, the trees and birds and wild flowers of the years gone by. Perhaps if we do our part those good things may return some day, for others if not for ourselves.*

A great reddish-brown dust cloud is rising now from the southeast, so we must get out and do our night work before it arrives. Our thoughts go with you....

A South Dakota farm in the aftermath of a powerful dust storm, April 1935.
AP/Wide World Photo.
Reproduced by permission.

Silt: Deposits of blowing dirt.

Defaulting on: Failing to carry out.

March 8, 1936

Dear Evelyn:

*Since I wrote you, we have had several bad days of wind and dust. Old sheets, stretched over door and window openings, and sprayed with kerosene, quickly became black. Nothing that you hear or read will be likely to exaggerate the physical discomfort or material losses due to these storms. Less emphasis is usually given to the mental effect, the confusion resulting from the overthrow of all plans for normal farm work. To give just one example: the paint has been literally scoured from our buildings by the storms, but who knows when we might safely undertake to repaint, to "save the surface?" The pleasantest morning **may be a prelude** to an afternoon when the **"dust devils" unite in hideous onslaught**. The combination of fresh paint with a real dust storm is not pleasing to **contemplate**.*

*There has been no moisture of any kind since the light snow of early January. Still, there seems no doubt that improved methods of late, encouraged by the Soil Erosion Control Service, are already yielding some results in reduction of wind **erosion**. But rain must come soon to encourage growth even on the best fields if there is to be any wheat harvest. Interspersed with the more hopeful areas are other tracts apparently abandoned to their fate....*

*We have had only slight contact with the **Rehabilitation Service**. The man in charge stopped the other morning to see whether we really meant it when we promised the use of our tractor and other equipment to a young neighbor who is trying to make a new start for himself and wife and daughter through a rehabilitation loan. In spite of adverse conditions, this agent spoke of a surprising general spirit of optimism. I suppose there is something of the gambler in all of us. We instinctively feel that the longer we travel on a straight road, the nearer we must be coming to a turn. People here can't quite believe yet in a hopeless climatic change which would deprive them permanently of the gift of rain.*

*To me the most interesting government undertaking in the dust bowl centers about the group of erosion control experiments scattered over a wide area. The work includes such activities as **surveying contour lines, laying up terraces**, cleaning out fence rows piled high with drifted soil, filling **gullies** to prevent washing in that longed-for time of heavy rainfall, cutting down dead trees and brush, resetting trees in favorable locations, testing the **adaptability** of different types of grass to the difficult task of reseeding wind-*

May be a prelude: May lead.

"Dust devils" unite in hideous onslaught: Dust storms come together and form a frightening sight as they approach.

Contemplate: Think about.

Erosion: Deterioration of the soil.

Rehabilitation Service: Farm Security Administration, a government agency charged with helping farmers improve the land.

Surveying contour lines: Determining curving lines for plowing.

Laying up terraces: Building up raised areas.

Gullies: Trenches formed by water erosion.

Adaptability Suitability.

*blown spaces, and so on. Altogether it is just such work as a **provident** farmer would like to do if he had the means.* [Henderson, pp. 19–20, 21–22]

What happened next...

For those determined to stay on their land in the Dust Bowl, relief from the federal government was frequently the only way to survive. Federal plans were established to create easier repayment terms for farmers' loans. In addition, the Emergency Cattle Purchase Program was established in May 1934. Through this program starving cattle were purchased, often for above market value, and those still fit for consumption were slaughtered and given to the Federal Surplus Relief

A Farm Security Administration (FSA) supervisor develops a plan to get this farmer and his family back on their feet after suffering years of drought conditions.
Courtesy of the Franklin D. Roosevelt Library.

Provident: Wise in planning for the future.

Corporation, which distributed the meat to hungry families. The Taylor Grazing Act of June 1934 set up a program to limit the amount of grazing allowed; the goal was to allow some native grasses to return and prevent wind erosion. The Drought Relief Service (DRS) coordinated relief activities and designated certain counties as emergency areas. On April 8, 1935, Roosevelt signed another New Deal relief act, the Emergency Relief Appropriation Act, which provided $525 million for drought relief. On April 30, 1935, Roosevelt signed an executive order creating the Resettlement Administration (RA), which attempted to resettle sharecroppers and tenant farmers on good land and give them opportunities to buy the land. In reality, very few families were ever resettled. Instead, by 1937 the RA evolved into the Farm Security Administration (FSA), which concentrated on loaning money to the families (to buy food, clothing, feed, seed, and fertilizer) rather than trying to resettle them. The agency also designed an individualized farm management program for each farmer.

On April 27, 1935, Roosevelt signed the Soil Conservation Act, which shifted the Soil Erosion Service (SES) to the Department of Agriculture and renamed it the Soil Conservation Service (SCS). The SCS launched a much broader soil conservation program than the SES had offered. It featured a program to pay farmers approximately one dollar an acre for every acre that employed new conservation techniques. Under the SES, only 10,454 acres incorporated new methods. Under the SCS, which had help from workers in the Works Progress Administration (WPA) and the Civilian Conservation Corps (CCC), 600,000 acres were cultivated with contour plowing, strip-cropping, and terracing techniques. (Contour plowing is plowing across a hill rather than up and down; strip-cropping leaves unplowed strips between the plowed and planted land; terracing involves reshaping a sloping area into a series of flat, horizontal planting spaces. For example, in regard to strip-cropping, for every twenty planted rows a space for approximately five rows would be left unplowed and in natural vegetation such as grasses. This practice slowed runoff of water and helped hold topsoil in place.)

In February 1937, Roosevelt introduced a new program to encourage states to pass their own conservation laws and farmers to set up their own conservation districts. The efforts of the SCS and local programs began to take effect, and by 1938

it was estimated that 65 percent less soil was blowing across the land, even though the drought continued. Rain finally came in the fall of 1939 and continued through 1940. As the United States mobilized for World War II (1939–45), Europe again needed wheat in large amounts. By the early 1940s, golden wheat fields once again predominated across the Great Plains.

Did you know...

- One-fourth of the population of the southern Plains left the Dust Bowl in the 1930s. Approximately two hundred thousand went to California, and roughly half of them became migrant workers picking grapes and cotton in the San Joaquin valley.

- The Dust Bowl refugees were called "Okies," short for Oklahoma, whether they were from Oklahoma or another state.

- Californians did not welcome Dust Bowl refugees, fearing they would stretch relief resources to the limit.

- The Farm Security Administration built thirteen camps in California to improve the refugees' shelter and sanitation and to protect them from hostile local residents.

- Artists told the story of the migrants from the Dust Bowl. John Steinbeck's book *The Grapes of Wrath,* published in 1939, follows a fictional family, the Joads, to California. Woody Guthrie (1912–1967) produced an album in 1940 titled *Dust Bowl Ballads.*

- One of the most horrific dust storms of the 1930s descended on Kansas and Nebraska on April 14, 1935, which became known as "Black Sunday."

- Cooking and eating could be difficult in Dust Bowl homes because dust quickly found its way into food. Women kneaded bread in dresser drawers covered with a cloth, inserting their hands through two holes cut in the front of the drawer. Food was cooked in an oven, not on the stove top, and had to be eaten immediately.

- Many people were determined to stay on their land and endure the Dust Bowl hardships. John L. McCarty, a young editor of a Dalhart, Texas, newspaper, formed the

Last Man's Club. Each club member vowed that even if he were the last man on the plains, he would stay.

Consider the following...

- What personal traits do you think helped the Henderson family endure the hardships in the Dust Bowl?

- In a letter not included in this excerpt, Henderson questions whether they were courageous or foolish to stay on their land. What do you think and why?

- When the government began urging farmers to try new farming techniques, do you think the Hendersons welcomed or resented it?

For More Information

Books

De Angelis, Therese, and Gina DeAngelis. *The Dust Bowl.* Philadelphia, PA: Chelsea House Publishers, 2002.

Dyck, Mary K. *Waiting on the Bounty: The Dust Bowl Diary of Mary Knackstedt Dyck.* Iowa City, IA: University of Iowa Press, 1999.

Gregory, James N. *American Exodus: The Dust Bowl Migration and Okie Culture in California.* New York, NY: Oxford University Press, 1989.

McArthur, Debra. *The Dust Bowl and the Depression in American History.* Berkeley Heights, NJ: Enslow Publishers, 2002.

Meltzer, Milton. *Driven from the Land: The Story of the Dust Bowl.* New York, NY: Benchmark Books, 2000.

Periodicals

Henderson, Caroline A. "Letters from the Dust Bowl." *Reader's Digest* (July 1936): pp. 19-22.

Dorothea Lange

Excerpt from "The Assignment I'll Never Forget: Migrant Mother"

Published in *Popular Photography*, February 1960

By the mid-1930s, thousands of small farmers had lost their farms. Sharecroppers and tenant farmers, who did not own their land but rented from large landowners, continued living in poverty. Living in perhaps the most desperate condition were the migrant farm families. Migrant farmers, many of whom had abandoned their Dust Bowl farms, followed the seasonal crop harvest in the West, laboring in the fields for meager wages. Their families lived in destitute conditions, always on the brink of starvation.

Responding to the small farmers' difficulty, President Franklin D. Roosevelt (1882–1945; served 1933–45) established the Resettlement Administration (RA) in April 1935. One goal of the RA was to resettle the impoverished farm families on productive land with the opportunity to eventually buy the land. However, many Americans did not understand the plight of the rural poor. Rexford Tugwell (1891–1979), the chief of the RA, knew he must gain general public support if the RA was to be successful in its mission. To build support for his program, he established a photography branch, the Historical Section, within the agency and

> "I saw and approached the hungry and desperate mother, as if drawn by a magnet. I do not remember how I explained my presence or my camera to her, but I do remember she asked me no questions."
>
> *Dorothea Lange*

hired Roy Stryker to administer it. Both Tugwell and Stryker knew that photographs could communicate more powerfully than any written accounts.

Stryker hired a handful of highly professional and talented photographers who were able to compose and capture pictures with remarkable qualities. These photographers turned their cameras to the people who needed the RA's help: sharecroppers, tenant farmers, black American cotton pickers, and migrant families harvesting crops. The photos they took were black-and-white, simple, stark, and powerful. One of the photographers Stryker hired was Dorothea Lange (1895–1965). At the time she was hired, Lange was documenting the condition of migrant workers for the state of California. While working for Stryker she shot her most famous picture, "Migrant Mother." She encountered the subject of her photo and the woman's three daughters in California's Nipomo Valley at a pea pickers' migrant camp in March 1936. The moving picture illustrated the desperate situation of those in the camp. The following excerpt is Lange's account of how one of the greatest American documentary photographs came to be.

Things to remember while reading the excerpt from "The Assignment I'll Never Forget":

- Note that in 1937 Secretary of Agriculture Henry A. Wallace (1888–1965) established the Farm Security Administration (FSA), which absorbed the RA's Historical Section in its entirety. The RA photographers became known from that time on as FSA photographers.

- Before the 1930s most photography took place in a studio. Documentary photography, or photos of real-life situations, first became common in the 1930s during the Great Depression.

- The conditions under which "Migrant Mother" was made so impressed Lange that almost twenty-four years after taking the photo, she could recall her exact thoughts as she drove up to the camp.

Excerpt from "The Assignment I'll Never Forget: Migrant Mother"

When I began thinking of my most memorable assignments, instantly there flashed to mind the experience surrounding "Migrant Mother," an experience so vivid and well-remembered that I will attempt to pass it on to you....

"Migrant Mother" was made 23 years ago, in March 1936, when I was on the team of Farm Security Administration photographers (called "Resettlement Administration" in the early days). Their duties and the scope of their work is a story well known to students of contemporary photography. We had a unique job, and the results of our travels over the U.S.A. have proved of real value....

*To repeat, it was 23 years ago at the end of a cold, miserable winter. I had been traveling **in the field** alone for a month, photographing the **migratory farm labor** of California—the ways of life and the conditions of these people who serve and produce our great crops. My work was done, time was up, and I was worked out.*

It was raining, the camera bags were packed, and I had on the seat beside me in the car the results of my long trip, the box containing all those rolls and packs of exposed film ready to mail back to Washington [D.C.]. It was a time of relief. Sixty-five miles an hour for seven hours would get me home to my family that night, and my eyes were glued to the wet and gleaming highway that stretched out ahead. I felt freed, for I could lift my mind off my job and think of home.

I WAS ON MY WAY and barely saw a crude sign with pointing arrow which flashed by at the side of the road, saying, PEA-PICKERS CAMP. But out of the corner of my eye I did see it.

*I didn't want to stop, and didn't. I didn't want to remember that I had seen it, so I drove on and ignored the **summons**. Then, accompanied by the rhythmic hum of the windshield wipers, arose an inner argument:*

Dorothea, how about that camp back there?

What is the situation back there?

Are you going back?

In the field: Out on assignment as opposed to working in an office.

Migratory farm labor: Workers who move regularly to find work harvesting crops.

Summons: Calls in her mind to turn back.

Nobody could ask this of you, now could they?

To turn back certainly is not necessary. Haven't you plenty of negatives already on this subject? Isn't this just one more of the same? Besides, if you take a camera out in this rain, you're just asking for trouble. Now be reasonable, etc., etc., etc.

Having well convinced myself for 20 miles that I could continue on, I did the opposite. Almost without realizing what I was doing, I made a U-turn on the empty highway. I went back those 20 miles and turned off the highway at that sign, PEA-PICKERS CAMP.

*I was following **instinct**, not reason; I drove into that wet and soggy camp and parked my car like a homing pigeon.*

*I saw and approached the hungry and desperate mother, as if drawn by a magnet. I do not remember how I explained my presence or my camera to her, but I do remember she asked me no questions. I made five exposures, working closer and closer from the same direction. I did not ask her name or her history. She told me her age, that she was 32. She said that they had been living on frozen vegetables from the surrounding fields, and birds that the children killed. She had just sold the tires from her car to buy food. There she sat in that **lean-to** tent with her children huddled around her, and seemed to know that my pictures might help her, and so she helped me. There was a sort of equality about it.*

The pea crop at Nipomo had frozen and there was no work for anybody. But I did not approach the tents and shelters of other stranded pea-pickers. It was not necessary; I knew I had recorded the essence of my assignment.

*This, then, is the "Migrant Mother" photograph with which you are so familiar. It has, in a sense, lived a life of its own through these years; it goes on and on. The negative now belongs to the Library of Congress, which controls its use and prints it. Whenever I see this photograph reproduced, I give it a salute as to an old friend. I did not create it, but I was behind that big, old **Graflex**, using it as an instrument for recording something of importance. The woman in this picture has become a symbol to many people; until now it is her picture, not mine.*

*What I am trying to tell other photographers is that had I not been deeply involved in my undertaking on that field trip, I would not have had to turn back. What I am trying to say is that I believe this inner **compulsion** to be the vital ingredient in our work; that if*

Instinct: Natural impulse or calling.

Lean-to: Having only one slope or pitch.

Graflex: A type of camera.

Compulsion: Irresistible impulse.

Dorothea Lange's famous photo, "Migrant Mother." *Courtesy of the Library of Congress.*

our work is to carry force and meaning to our views, we must be willing to go "all-out."

"Migrant Mother" always reminds me of this, although I was in that camp for only ten minutes. Then I closed my camera, and did *go straight home.* [Lange, pp. 42, 126]

What Happened Next...

The RA/FSA nurtured a number of photojournalists and photo artists. Dorothea Lange, Arthur Rothstein (1915–1985), and Russell Lee (1903–1986) established their careers and went on to many photo-documentary projects. Others who served as RA/FSA photographers, such as Walker Evans (1903–1975) and Ben Shahn (1898–1969), went on to distinguished careers in the arts—Evans as a photographer and Shahn as a muralist.

By 1936, the government-sponsored photographs appeared in newspapers, magazines, and special exhibits. Roy Stryker carefully categorized and filed the pictures. Although the original intent of the photographs was to visually show the general public the extent of rural poverty in America, by the later 1930s Stryker broadened the projects' scope to include many aspects of more mainstream American life. Stryker had his photographers focus on such subjects as people at county fairs, multi-generational families, barber shops, road signs, and other scenes. Once he gave instructions to photograph "the smell" of apple pie in autumn in New England. The photos became a treasure trove of images that helped the nation understand the needs of those in poverty, make sense of Roosevelt's social welfare New Deal programs, including the RA/FSA, and see what life was like in the 1930s for middle class Americans.

The photographs—tens of thousands of images—spanned a six-year period, from 1935 to December 1941, the month when the United States entered World War II (1939–45). The Historical Section was transferred to the Office of War Information (OWI) in 1941. Stryker still headed the section, and a few of the FSA photographers followed

him. Their mission switched to documenting America's war preparation.

In 1943, Stryker left the OWI. The collection of prints and negatives, by then called the FSA/OWI collection, ended up in the Library of Congress. In 1944 the library received 277,000 negatives and 77,000 prints of the work done by Stryker's photographers in the RA, FSA, and OWI. For most

Dorothea Lange photographed this Texas family, penniless and hoping to find work picking cotton in Arkansas, in August 1936. *Courtesy of the Library of Congress.*

Americans at the start of the twenty-first century, images of America in the 1930s are based on the FSA/OWI collection.

Did you know...

- Roy Stryker asked the FSA photographers to take photos of specific subjects but always allowed them the artistic freedom to photograph anything that captured their eye, or as he put it, anything they "really saw."

- The photographers focused on the faces of people and on the land; they wanted their photos to tell a story.

- Two photojournalism magazines (magazines telling a story with photographs) began publication in the later 1930s: *Life* in 1936 and *Look* in 1938.

- Before the 1930s, photography was not generally considered part of the arts. Originally the RA and FSA photos were intended to serve as propaganda to build support for the two government aid agencies. But the outstanding work of the RA/FSA photographers elevated photography to an art form.

- At the beginning of the twenty-first century, the entire remarkable FSA/OWI collection can be viewed on the Internet at http://memory.loc.gov/ammem/fsowhome.html (the American Memory section of the Library of Congress Web site).

Consider the following...

- Some Americans thought it was a waste of money for the federal government to fund photography projects. Do you think government money should have been spent on photographs?

For More Information

Books

Garver, Thomas H. *Just Before the War: Urban America from 1935 to 1941 As Seen by Photographers of the Farm Security Administration.* New York, NY: October House, 1968.

O'Neal, Hank. *A Vision Shared: A Classic Portrait of America and Its People, 1935–1943*. New York, NY: St. Martin's Press, 1976.

Rothstein, Arthur. *The Depression Years*. New York, NY: Dover Publications, 1978.

Stryker, Roy E., and Nancy Wood. *In This Proud Land: America 1935–1943 As Seen in the FSA Photographs*. Greenwich, CT: New York Graphic Society, 1973.

Thompson, Kathleen, and Hilary MacAustin, eds. *Children of the Depression*. Bloomington, IN: Indiana University Press, 2001.

Periodicals

Lange, Dorothea. "The Assignment I'll Never Forget: Migrant Mother." *Popular Photography* (February 1960): pp. 42, 43, and 126.

Web Sites

"America from the Great Depression to World War II: Photographs from the FSA-OWI, 1935–1945." *Library of Congress*. http://memory.loc.gov/ammem/fsowhome.html (accessed on August 28, 2002).

Youth Riding the Rails

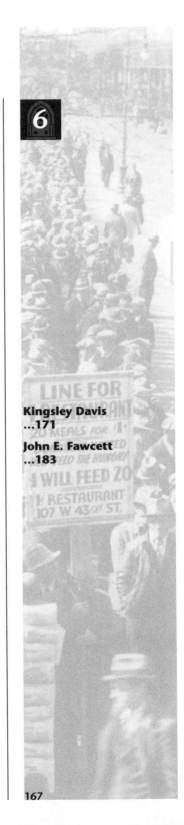

By 1932 an army of 250,000 boys and a scattering of girls were wandering about the United States on the railways. The hardships of the Great Depression pushed ever-increasing numbers of young people to join this vagabond army. The Depression, the worst economic crisis in U.S. history, was at its peak in 1932 and 1933. At least 25 percent of America's workforce was unemployed, and almost all families had experienced a significant decrease in income. For some Americans the only solution was to take to the road and search for work in another town or state. By 1933 the size of the transient population (people traveling around without work or homes) was estimated to be between two and three million, including hundreds of thousands riding the rails.

Before the Depression, in the prosperous 1920s, there were two types of transients on the rails: hoboes and seasonal workers. Hoboes were not in search of work, instead choosing to remain outside of mainstream American lifestyles. Seasonal workers, following the agricultural harvest, rode the trains from state to state in search of work on farms. On any given freight train, five or six transients would be on board. By 1932 train

agents reported up to ten thousand transients a month passing through the rail yards. Up to several hundred would be on a single freight train. It was estimated that at least 75 percent were between the ages of fifteen and twenty-five, and a considerable number were younger than fifteen. These young people often began their adventure with optimism and a thrill of freedom. But as the days turned into weeks and months—even years—the excitement gave way to hunger, boredom, despair, and the realization that danger lurked around each curve. Who were these wandering youths, and why had they left home?

Some of the most interesting accounts that answer this question can be found in magazines from the early 1930s. For example, in the September 1933 issue of *Ladies' Home Journal* an article by Maxine Davis, titled "200,000 Vagabond Children," describes three boys: Red, Mike, and Tom. Red was a freckled fifteen-year-old boy from Carthage, Missouri. He lived with relatives since both of his parents were dead. His relatives lost their jobs when hard times hit, and he lost his job delivering for a butcher. Knowing his relatives had no money, he felt he was no longer wanted, so he struck out on his own. Red had been on the road for seventeen months, was weary and frightened, and looked much older than his fifteen years. Mike, a bit older than Red, was from a small Southern town. His father, a police officer, had such a small salary that he could no longer afford to support Mike. The father gave Mike fifteen dollars and told him to try to find work somewhere else. Mike had not heard from his family in the last six months. Tom was the adventurer of the three. He had worked in a mill in Providence, Rhode Island, but when it closed, he decided it would be exciting to see the country. Tom was lucky—when he decided to return home, there would be a home to go back to. These three descriptions by Davis represent the type of young people who were riding the rails. Three out of four of America's wandering youths said the hard times of the Great Depression caused them to "hit the road." The first excerpt in this chapter is from **Youth in the Depression,** a pamphlet written by Kingsley Davis and published in 1935. It describes what life "on the bum" was like for youngsters who left home for economic reasons.

The second excerpt is taken from **"A Hobo Memoir, 1936"** by John E. Fawcett, published in the December 1994

issue of *Indiana Magazine of History.* Fawcett was part of the other one-fourth of wandering young people, who were merely seeking adventure and had homes to return to when they tired of life on the rails. The education Fawcett received while riding the rails for three weeks in June 1936 directed the course and philosophy of his adult life.

Kingsley Davis

Excerpt from Youth in the Depression
Published in 1935

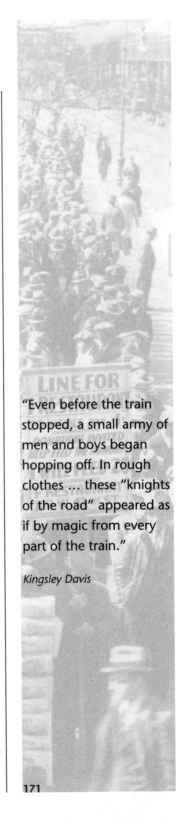

"Even before the train stopped, a small army of men and boys began hopping off. In rough clothes ... these "knights of the road" appeared as if by magic from every part of the train."

Kingsley Davis

The teenage hoboes on the rails in the early 1930s, the worst years of the Great Depression, left home for a variety of reasons, most of which related to economic difficulties. A great many left because they believed they were just one more mouth to feed and a burden to their struggling families. Others left families torn apart by the stresses of unemployment and poverty. Some fathers were forced to ask their sons to leave home to search for work in another location. There were also adventurers who could not resist the call of the steam locomotives as they pulled out of town bound for all regions of the United States.

The following excerpt from *Youth in the Depression* by Kingsley Davis was published in 1935 as part of a series of pamphlets used to educate Americans about current social issues. Davis focuses on the young people who left home under economic pressures. He explains the situation of youths on the rails through use of an imaginary dialogue between a railroad "bull" and an inspector from Washington, D.C., sent out to investigate the situation on the railroads. A "bull" was a railroad security guard whose job was to keep transients off

A wandering "stiff" carries his gear on his back as he moves from town to town. *AP/Wide World Photo. Reproduced by permission.*

the trains. The "bulls" pulled men and boys off trains while local police put them back on to get them out of their towns. Davis describes the wanderers' search for food in breadlines at town shelters, at housewives' back doors, and in the hobo "jungles" near the railroad tracks.

Few of the youths would have been classified as habitual transients (transients choosing to live life "on the bum"). In the May 1933 issue of the popular *Scribner's Magazine,* Lowell Ames Norris explains that, under normal economic conditions, most of them would have been in school or at work. Most had at least an eighth-grade education; many had attended and even graduated from high school. A few had been to college. But their situation grew more forlorn every day. There were no part-time jobs available; any job openings were saved for local citizens. The homeless boys learned to beg and became unkempt and dirty. They encountered criminals and fugitives from the law in the hobo "jungle" camps. In addition, the dangers of jumping on a moving train were great. As Norris relates, "Many were killed or seriously crippled while riding the freights."

In the following excerpt Davis calls for something to be done about the roaming thousands. He has the "bull" tell the investigator, "Somebody had better do something, and do it quick."

Things to remember while reading the excerpt from *Youth in the Depression*:

- In the 1930s American youths were not in revolt against the government, nor were they revolting against parents when they left home. They left because of economic reasons or to answer the call of adventure.

- Once a boy started to wander, he was kept constantly on the move. Local agencies no longer had the money to pay for the boys' return to their hometowns. At most, the agencies carried out a policy of one night's food and shelter, then moved the boys on to the next town. Among the hoboes, this experience was called "passing on."

- The initial excitement of riding the rails gradually gave way to hunger, despair, and hopelessness. Bands of shabby youths crisscrossed the country many times, arriving at each coast with no plans but to head back the other way.

Excerpt from Youth in the Depression

"The Road to Nowhere"

Wheezing and groaning to a slow halt, the long freight train of the Southern Pacific line pulled into the yards of El Paso, Texas. It was a bright April day back in 1932, and the long string of box cars gleamed warmly red in the afternoon sun.

Even before the train stopped, a small army of men and boys began hopping off. In rough clothes, many of them carrying small bundles, these "knights of the road" appeared as if by magic from every part of the train. All told, there were forty-four. Most of them had beaten their way from California. Now that the winter was over and the balmy climate of California was no longer necessary for the homeless, they were moving east.

Trains pointing west, however, were just as crowded. The nation's countless wanderers, half of them mere boys, did not know where they were going. Some were moving east, some were moving west. Victims of the depression, their greeting in every town was, "Keep moving!"

The travelers looked around to get their bearings. Then most of them scattered into the city to begin their long, weary search for a meal. Some visited back doors, but not the veterans of the road. They knew that boys and younger men appeal more successfully to motherly housewives.

Older wanderers tried the well-known ways of getting board and lodging—a mission, a Salvation Army ("Sally"), or a **municipal** shelter—any place where a man could eat and rest for the night. The food would probably be bad; the bed would have no sheets, no blanket to harbor lice or other **vermin**, not even a mattress—just a rubber pad or a piece of **linoleum** over some iron springs. Beggars can't be choosers.

As the price of this care and tenderness, the lodger would have to fill out a card giving his name, his home address, and so on. At a mission he might even have to sing a hymn, or at a city shelter chop wood, before being allowed to eat. Not an attractive prospect, but then—what was a man to do?

Just outside the town, along the main line of the railway, there was a "jungle," a village of tin cans, boxes, and crazily built shacks where **"stiffs"** could get together. Some of the men, upon leaving their **side-door Pullmans**, made immediately for this **hallowed** spot. Here there was at least a chance of cooking a **mulligan stew** over an open fire, without filling out a card or submitting to questions.

But, in one empty box car, there were three boys who went neither to the residential and business districts nor to the "jungle." They did not even get off. One of them was lying on the floor, groaning in misery. The other two were bending over him.

Some distance down the track, two men walking alongside the halted train were watching the crowd of "bums" and "tramps" as they scattered out of the freight yard. One, carrying a pistol, was a railroad policeman. The other, wearing thick glasses, was an investigator sent from Washington [D.C.] to find out, at first hand, about the floating population which was roaming through the country in ever greater numbers. The railroad **"bull"** was talking fast, waving his hands in the air.

"You see," he was saying, "there are so many of them we can't do anything about it. The railroad officials tell us to keep everybody who doesn't pay his fare off the trains. But we can't do it. In this town alone there are 200 bums coming in and going out every day. They do a lot of damage to the trains. They open the vents on the refrigerator cars and spoil the fruit. Our engineers can't always tell whether a man climbing up a car, swinging his arms, is a **transient** or a trainman trying to make a signal.

"… No town wants these men put off in its territory. If we put forty or fifty men off in a small town, the town has to feed them. It costs money, and the town officials bellyache and blame the railroad for it.

Municipal: Local city or town.

Vermin: Hard-to-control pests such as fleas.

Linoleum: A hard floor covering.

"Stiffs": Hoboes and wanderers.

Side-door Pullmans: Pullmans are railcars with sleeping quarters and parlors; "side-door Pullmans" is a sarcastic reference to a boxcar.

Hallowed: Sacred.

Mulligan stew: Scraps of any available food boiled together.

"Bull": Railroad policeman.

Transient: A person traveling around, usually in search of work.

A seventeen-year-old transient settles down for the night at a hobo "jungle," or camp along the rails where hoboes could stop to rest, wash, and cook. *AP/Wide World Photo. Reproduced by permission.*

"Sometimes a railroad bull and a town cop meet the same train. It is the bull's job to put the boys off the train and the cop's job to keep them on the train. To the fellows themselves it doesn't make much difference. Believe me, it's a hard nut to crack."

"Yes," said the man from Washington thoughtfully. "Most of them are only boys, too. It looks to me as if more than half of them were below twenty-five."

"Sure. Most of those on the road nowadays are young men. There used to be just two kinds, regular hoboes and seasonal workers; and most of them were older. Now there is a third kind, the unemployed. They make up 70 percent of the men on the road today, and the majority of them are young fellows, just boys who don't know where they are going, or why. Lots of them have been to high school. Some have been to college.

"They left home because their fathers didn't have jobs. They were just one more mouth around the house to be fed. Feeling they were a burden, and having nothing to do at home, no money to do anything with, they got restless and started on the road.

"It wasn't their fault. Most of them want to work, but they can't find it. No town, except the cities, will let them stop for long. The life is hard on them. Bad food, dirt, no sleep. Lots of them get hurt. Hundreds are killed or injured every year.

"But the worst thing is that the boys may turn into bums. This year, already, they are tougher than they were last year. If hard times last much longer and nothing is done for these boys, things will be pretty bad for them. They won't get an education. They'll form the habit of getting by without working. They'll get used to going for days without taking their clothes off, and they'll learn stealing and vice from the old bums that are always on the road. Take it from me, an awful lot of young people in America are growing up to be criminals."

At this point in their talk they walked past the open door of the box car in which the two boys were bending over their injured comrade. Stopping short and climbing into the car, they learned that the boy had hurt his foot. It was badly swollen. He had been standing with his leg wedged between two heavy packing boxes when somebody, accidentally, stepped on the "cutting lever," stopping the train. The sudden jolt threw him over and broke his ankle.

The railroad policeman left at once to find a doctor, sometimes a hard job when the patient is a homeless wanderer. In the meantime the investigator questioned the boys.

"Where are you fellows from?" he asked.

One proved to be from Oregon, another from Georgia, and the injured boy from Massachusetts.

When asked why they had taken to the road, one of the boys, nineteen years old, said, "There's nine in my family. Dad hasn't had work in over a year. He's a printer. I went to trade school and learned printing. If he can't find work, how can I? The charities was giving $3.20 a week for the nine of us. We were starved all the time. Finally I thought I better leave, so I hit the road."

At last the policeman came back, and they carried the injured boy to a car.

"When you get back to Washington," said the bull to the investigator, "you tell them that something has gone haywire when there are thousands and thousands of young men roaming over the country without a dime and without a place to sleep. Somebody had better do something, and do it quick."

Two young men walking the railroad tracks, looking to catch a ride to anywhere. *National Archives and Records Administration.*

The railroad policeman was right. Something had to be done. At that time, in 1932, there were a million and a quarter people in the bread lines and on the highways of America, more than lived in Arizona, Idaho, Wyoming, and Nevada combined. Over half of them were young men, between the ages of fifteen and twenty-five. One out of every twenty of the young men in the United States was wandering aimlessly around the country, often risking his life, leading a miserable existence.

The Civilian Conservation Corps (CCC) gave employment to thousands of wandering youths. Here, two young men survey a section of Black Hills National Forest, South Dakota, circa 1933.
Courtesy of the Franklin D. Roosevelt Library.

The newspapers often printed stories about the boys on the road. But these stories, by no means, showed the entire problem. Just as many young men, and probably more, were at home, idle. They needed only a little more want and suffering to push them, too, out on the road.

If we ask why so many men are hitch-hiking and riding the **rods** to nowhere, or fretting away their days idly in the home town, the answer is "the depression." The depression, which reached its low point in 1933, was **stifling** the industrial life of the country. It was also changing the outlook of young people. Youth was not in revolt against the government, nor against the old folks. Rather, the machinery by which young people are drawn into the work of the nation had broken down; and youth, bearing the burden of this breakdown, was seeking blindly for some way out. [Davis, pp. 1–2, 4–8]

Rods: Railroads.

Stifling: Shutting down.

What happened next...

Grace Abbott (1878–1939), chief of the Children's Bureau in the Department of Labor, called on president-elect Franklin D. Roosevelt to develop training and work centers for youths and to provide support for young people who were trying to stay in school. Roosevelt listened. He immediately addressed the "youth problem" after his inauguration in March 1933. The Federal Transient Relief Service was established in September 1933 under the Federal Emergency Relief Act, which passed in May 1933. The Transient Service set up centers in 250 communities, providing meals, beds, recreation, and study facilities. Also, 350 work camps were set up in rural areas. One of Roosevelt's favorite programs was the Civilian Conservation Corps (CCC), established in April 1933. Aimed at youths between ages eighteen and twenty-five, it provided food, shelter, and basic education including vocational work skills. Decades later, men who participated in the program often recalled fondly their time at CCC camps. At the beginning of the twenty-first century, a Web site existed for CCC alumni: www.cccalumni.org. Another highly successful program to keep young people in school and off the rails was the National Youth Administration (NYA). The NYA was established under the Works Progress Administration (WPA) in 1935.

Despite the efforts of the Transient Service, the CCC, and the NYA, only a portion of the hundreds of thousands of displaced young people could be reached. Many thousands continued riding the rails through the 1930s. The wandering stopped only when U.S. preparations for World War II (1939–45) began in 1940. Suddenly jobs were available as factories worked to produce war materials. When the United States entered the war in 1941, military service offered another form of employment.

Did you know...

- A favorite place to ride on the train was in the reefer, the space in a freight car where ice is kept during hot weather to preserve the goods inside. Boys would climb into the reefers and leave the door open. Perishable goods such as vegetables and fruit spoiled, costing the railroads a considerable amount of money.

- Empty boxcars were the safest place to ride. Sometimes trains added extra boxcars, so hoboes could ride these and be safe.

- The biggest worry of social workers and government workers was that the boys on the rails would eventually acquire a philosophy of shiftlessness, or laziness, and become permanent hoboes.

- Girls rode the rails in far fewer numbers than boys. For safety reasons, they often disguised themselves as boys and traveled with other companions. Of the estimated 256,000 transients on the rails in 1932, only about 11,000 were female. Of those, 35 to 40 percent were under twenty-one years of age.

- There were no estimates of black Americans on the rails, but they were few compared to whites. Racism was common throughout the nation, and lynchings were on the rise in the South during the Depression. For both reasons few black Americans rode the rails from town to town.

Consider the following...

- Imagine yourself the mayor of a small community along a railway. What kind of services would you offer the transients as they stopped over in your town? Where would you get the money to pay for the services?

- What would you do if you found yourself sitting at home with nothing to do, no job, no school, and no money? Would you perhaps choose the rails?

- Think of several reasons why railroads feared having transients on board the trains.

For More Information

Books

Davis, Maxine. *The Lost Generation: A Portrait of American Youth Today.* New York, NY: Macmillan, 1936.

Davis, Kingsley. *Youth in the Depression.* Chicago, IL: University of Chicago Press, 1935.

Merrill, Perry H. *Roosevelt's Forest Army: A History of the Civilian Conservation Corps, 1933–1942.* Montpelier, VT: Perry H. Merrill, 1981.

Reitman, Ben L. *Sister of the Road: The Autobiography of Box-Car Bertha.* New York, NY: Sheridan House, 1937.

Uys, Errol L. *Riding the Rails: Teenagers on the Move during the Great Depression.* New York, NY: TV Books, 1999.

Periodicals

Davis, Maxine. "200,000 Vagabond Children." *Ladies' Home Journal* (September 1933): pp. 8, 9, 46, 48, 50.

Norris, Lowell Ames. "America's Homeless Army." *Scribner's Magazine* (May 1933): pp. 316–318.

Web Sites

Civilian Conservation Corps Alumni. http://www.cccalumni.org (accessed on August 29, 2002).

Riding the Rails. http://www.pbs.org/wgbh/amex/rails/ (accessed on August 29, 2002).

John Fawcett

Excerpt from "A Hobo Memoir, 1936"

Published in *Indiana Magazine of History*, December 1994

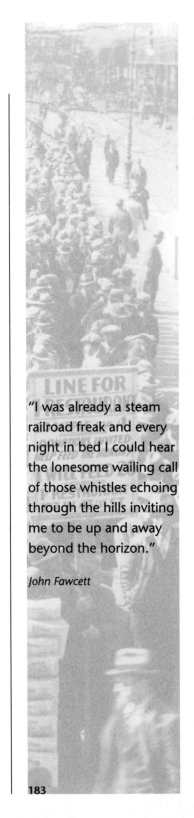

"I was already a steam railroad freak and every night in bed I could hear the lonesome wailing call of those whistles echoing through the hills inviting me to be up and away beyond the horizon."

John Fawcett

In 1936 John Fawcett knew little of the hardships many Americans were experiencing as the Great Depression lingered on. John's father was an ophthalmologist (medical doctor specializing in the eye) in Wheeling, West Virginia. His family lived a prosperous life, with two automobiles, summer vacations on the seashore of Maryland, and private schools for the children. John and his brother attended Linsly Military Institute as their father had. Feeling suffocated by the strict discipline of the school, John took to riding the rails on short jaunts near Wheeling. Then on June 6, 1936, sixteen-year-old John and his fifteen-year-old best friend, Mick McKinley, "caught out" on a Baltimore and Ohio Railroad, known as B&O, locomotive, hoping to reach the Texas Centennial Exposition in Dallas. They intended to become cowboys on a Texas ranch for the remainder of the summer.

Unlike the majority of youths, who were destitute and riding the rails in search of work, John and Mick were out for the thrill and excitement of traveling the country by way of steam locomotive. They both had comfortable homes to return to when they tired of their adventure. Nevertheless, for

the next three weeks John and Mick worked for food, begged for food, ate and slept in hobo "jungles" by the tracks, and even spent a few days in jail. John had been keeping a diary since he was thirteen years old, a practice he continued while he rode the rails. After three weeks of hard travel, John and Mick arrived in Dallas at the fair on June 28, 1936. The following excerpt comes from John Fawcett's unpublished memoir titled "Awakening of Conscience," compiled in 1991 and based on his hobo journal. Portions of the memoir were published in the December 1994 issue of the *Indiana Magazine of History* under the title "A Hobo Memoir, 1936."

Things to remember while reading the excerpt from "A Hobo Memoir, 1936":

- John Fawcett and Mick McKinley were accustomed to the niceties of life, but on the rails they had to wear the same clothes for days, even sleeping in them at night.

- They became acquainted with the ranks of starving youths and unemployed men, and they observed whole families wandering together in desperate search of work.

- Most youths on the rails had no home to return to.

Excerpt from "A Hobo Memoir, 1936"

*I was born and raised in Wheeling, W. Va. where I lived until my graduation from high school in June 1937, when I left home and went to sea. I had two brothers, one a year older and one a year younger than myself and I remember my childhood almost entirely with warmth and pleasure and satisfaction. My father was a doctor in the practice of **Ophthalmology**, and he and my mother were loving, caring parents who provided us with a secure and varied small town family life. As such we did not want for anything during the years of the nineteen thirties when the Great Depression brought so much poverty, suffering and **destitution** to our country....*

I had always been about an average student or maybe a little better, but in February 1936 I was full of anxiety and discontent. I

Ophthalmology: A branch of medical science dealing with the eye.

Destitution: Extreme want.

was a junior in high school and believed that I was flunking in Chemistry and Algebra, which were my hardest subjects. I think now that I was just using that as an excuse for revolting against the suffocating confines of the strictly disciplined military educational system which I was growing to detest more every day. So on the evening of February 7th, 1936, with the temperature down below zero, and the ground covered with snow, I ran away from home! Perhaps it would be more accurate to say I ran away from school, but I still shudder when thinking of that night [John rode the B&O train to Huntington, West Virginia, which is 180 miles from Wheeling, to visit a friend].

*One might guess that this act was not entirely **un-premeditated**! For over a year a couple of my non-conformist high school chums and I had been finding adventure in hopping freight trains on Saturdays. We would catch a train coming up out of the B&O freight yards and ride it thirty miles east to Washington, Pa. [Pennsylvania] and jump off. After waiting there for an hour or two we would catch another freight going back to Wheeling, arriving there by four or five in the afternoon, in time for me to duck into the house and take a shower with neither my brothers nor my parents being any the wiser. And they did not learn of it for over a year until our football coach (my Civics teacher) got wind of it from one of our classmates who we'd been bragging to in study hall about our exploits!...*

However, the damage was done. I was already a steam railroad freak and every night in bed I could hear the lonesome wailing call of those whistles echoing through the hills inviting me to be up and away beyond the horizon. All this is by way of saying that when I left home that frigid night in 1936, I did *know how to ride freight trains, and the blinds on passenger trains as well, ("riding the blind baggage," as it was called then).*

*The blinds were the spaces between baggage or passenger cars outside the accordion-like structure that surrounded the walkway between the cars. At the bottom of the car ends there was a narrow **transverse** platform or step that you could stand on. Then up the outer corner of the car there was a vertical railing or "grab-iron" as it was called, that you could hold on to. This put you in standing position looking out to the side enjoying the scenery as it flashed by. Riding the blinds was not all that dangerous so long as you stayed alert and did not loosen your hold. However it was very tiring over long distances, because you couldn't relax or sit down and have a cigarette as you might when riding the tops of freight cars, or inside an empty box car....*

Un-premeditated: Impulsive.

Transverse: Crosswise.

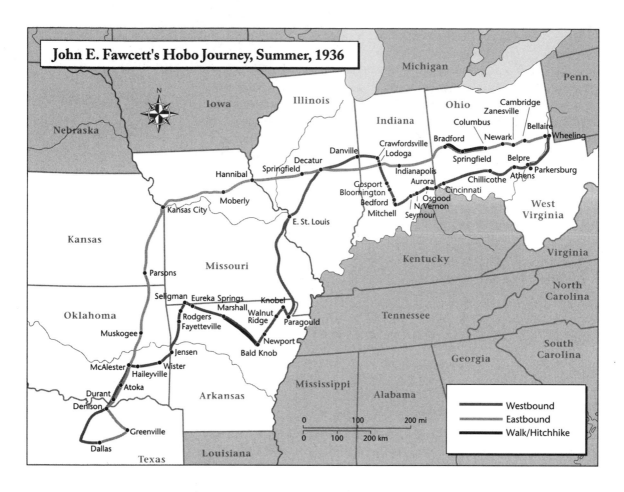

John Fawcett's travels by rail during the summer of 1936. *Gale Group.*

Gondola car: A railroad car with no top.

Meager: Lacking desirable qualities.

Hobo jungle: Place where hoboes stop to gather and eat, wash, and sleep.

[John's weekend escape to Huntington ended when his friend's parents called the Fawcetts, who arranged for John to ride home "on the cushions"—that is, in a passenger car. His next adventure began in June 1936, when he and a friend, Mick McKinley, rode the rails to the Texas Centennial Exposition. The next portion of the excerpt catches up with John and Mick in Cincinnati, Ohio.]

*We were at the west end of the railroad yard in Cincinnati munching on stale rolls when we heard the unmistakable sound of a big locomotive getting a long freight train under way. Within minutes my friend, Mick, and I were on a **gondola car** full of sand and reclining in the sunshine. It was a train of over a hundred cars carrying other freeloading "passengers". We passed through Aurora and Osgood, Indiana and after a couple of hours came to a ... stop in the town of North Vernon where we got off. A rather **meager hobo jungle** was located on the north side of the tracks just a few blocks from the residential part of town....*

| Leave Town | Safe Camp | Judge |

We learned that day, the **universal transient's rule** that, when possible, always enter from the alley and knock on the back door rather than the front. This way there was a much better chance of success. The reasons were self evident, especially in the South, where tradesmen, Negroes and other **unendowed** persons were expected to use the back door.

Another fascinating bit of **hobo-ology** ... was the habit of some old **Knights of the Road** of carrying a piece of chalk in their pockets. When one of those **worthies** received a handout, or especially a "sit down" (a plate of food brought out while sitting on the porch or back stairs), he would, when returning to the alley, write carefully with his chalk on the fence or garage door, the number eighteen. This was a secret code to **others of the brotherhood** that here is a house where "I ate."...

An hour after rolling out [of the boxcar in the train yard where they slept] in the morning, we were sitting on a grassy knoll beside the tracks having just heard the wail of steam whistles coming from down in the yards. There she came and what a sight to see! It was a long double headed freight train pulled by two huge steam locomotives spouting smoke and steam as they came roaring through the switches onto the main line. Nothing compares to that sight and sound and it raises my pulse and blood pressure to this day. No ... wonder kids run away from home!...

It was a truly hot day and we soon found the shady jungle on the banks of a creek not far from the yards. We all three splashed in

To pass information along to the next group of hoboes passing through town, many transients would leave chalk-written messages, using a variety of simple symbols, to communicate with one another. *Gale Group.*

Universal transient's rule: Something every hobo knew when looking for food.

Unendowed: Poor.

Hobo-ology: Information for or about hoboes.

Knights of the Road: Permanent hoboes.

Worthies: Hoboes.

Others of the brotherhood: Other hoboes.

the water and had a welcome wash up. Shorty [a hobo friend] *did not have a **"bindle"** instead carrying a worn old suit coat, the pockets of which held an impressive supply of basic possessions. These included a razor, bar of soap, small towel, jack knife, pair of socks and most surprising of all, a collapsible aluminum drinking cup such as I have not seen for many years. It consisted of four or five telescoping aluminum rings and when pressed flat was about the size of a snuff can....*

We all washed our socks and undershirts in the stream using Shorty's soap and hung them on a tree branch to dry....

[A difficulty on the road] *was the problem of drinking water. This was always so in the summer time when **"beating the road"** and especially in the South. One emergency source was the drain at the bottom of ice compartments on refrigerator cars. Only small amounts of water were accessible from this source. When the train was stopped it took a long while for the drip-drip to furnish enough water to satisfy a thirst. I have used this method when a freight train was stopped on a passing track awaiting a train from the opposite direction. Most times one would find a creek or pond and hoped the water wasn't **contaminated**.*

Toward evening the three of us walked the several blocks into downtown Bloomington [Indiana] *arriving by chance at the Salvation Army building. We entered just in time to take in the brief prayer service which was a prelude to their public feeding program. We were then led into a small dining room next to the kitchen with a dozen other guys and served a large bowl of chili, bread, coffee and canned applesauce. A real banquet for us and I have been partial to the Salvation Army ever since....*

In the morning I walked up to the main part of town and bummed my breakfast at a restaurant. It was here a trick that Shorty taught us came in handy. The way it worked was like this: You walked by the front of a café or restaurant a couple of times, peering in the window looking for a man that is eating his meal and has an empty stool next to him, or better yet, an empty stool between two men. You walk in and plop down on the empty stool and when the waiter or waitress comes to you, speak right up so you can be heard by the customers on both sides of you and make the pitch about "being hungry and doing any kind of work for something to eat." If it was the owner or a male waiter who'd spoken to you, then the chances were they would turn you down and tell you to "get outta here." If it was a waitress, then sometimes she would say

Bindle: Bundle of clothes and possessions.

Beating the road: On the road.

Contaminated: Polluted.

*"O.K. just a minute" and perhaps, putting her job right on the line, she would go get a coffee and a doughnut and slide it quickly in front of you without giving you a check. But usually the answer was "No" from the other side of the counter. However, the kicker here is that when the guys on either side of you heard your **plaintive pitch** there was a fair chance that one or the other of them would say something as follows, "It's O.K., miss, I'll buy the fellow a doughnut and coffee," or "That's alright waitress, give the man some breakfast and put it on my bill." Believe me there is no greater feeling when you are hungry and on the bum to have someone spring for your breakfast right there before God and everybody. I worked this **ruse** perhaps a dozen times on that trip, and **scored** maybe half the time, which is pretty good. [Fawcett, pp. 351, 352–353, 355, 356–357, 358, 359, 360, 363–364]*

What happened next...

John stayed at the Texas fair only one day, and instead of becoming a cowboy as planned, he headed home to West Virginia. His parents had sent money for the five-day ride home "on the cushions," that is, riding in a passenger car. John arrived home on July 4 and returned to school in the fall. However, he returned to school a changed boy. The destitution he had seen on his trip educated him on the hard life millions were facing during the Depression. Instead of going straight to college after high school graduation, John went to sea for a year or so on an old tramp steamer. After World War II (1939–45) broke out, John joined the army in 1942. Only a year later he was flying missions over North Africa, Sicily, and Italy and was awarded the Distinguished Flying Cross in 1944.

As reported in Errol Lincoln Uys's book *Riding the Rails,* published in 1999, Fawcett attended the University of Washington after the war and graduated with a degree in the transportation field. But Fawcett's trip in 1936 had forever altered his outlook, and he and his wife, Ellen, became staunch and active civil rights supporters. They both joined the American Civil Liberties Union (ACLU) in 1953. Fawcett re-

Plaintive pitch: Woeful, sad speech.

Ruse: Clever trick.

Scored: Succeeded.

signed his transportation job to go to Mississippi to organize voter registration. In 1965 Fawcett also participated in a civil rights march from Selma to Montgomery, Alabama; the march was led by Dr. Martin Luther King Jr. (1929–1968). Later that year Fawcett won Seattle's Community Brotherhood Award from the National Council of Christians and Jews for his work in the South.

In Uys's book Fawcett sums up the education he received on the rails in June 1936:

> My trip on the road in 1936 changed my life and the way I view the world I live in. I had a quick and fast education about how hard life was for millions of homeless and destitute people.... I didn't see the suffering until I ran away from home. It would be a cold and unfeeling person who wouldn't be stunned and angered at the squalor of the streets and migrant camps.... When I was forty years old [in 1960] I thought I had all the answers. I knew exactly what the word "love" meant and how the world was going to be saved. I don't know anymore.

Did you know…

- Some of the favorite destinations of adventuring youths were the exciting cities of New Orleans, Louisiana, and Los Angeles, California, as well as the 1933 Chicago World's Fair and the 1936 Texas Centennial Fair. Western teens looked east and had the Statue of Liberty as their goal. Eastern and Midwestern teens wanted to go to the Rocky Mountains and the cities along the West Coast.

- The economic hardships of the Depression caused many schools to shorten their school year; some closed altogether. For teenagers, riding the rails seemed better than sitting at home bored during the Depression days.

- A special hobo language developed along the rails; for example, "on the fly" meant catching hold of a moving train. Also, hoboes left symbols written in chalk around towns to let other hoboes know the best places to find food and other necessities.

Consider the following...

- It was unusual for a sixteen-year-old boy to keep a diary. John Fawcett had kept one since age thirteen. What personal characteristics or interests do you think John had that caused him to keep a diary?

- Local newspapers often ran stories on the adventures of local boys who were traveling about on trains. Do you think the articles told the whole truth about life on the rails?

- Do you think adventuresome youths realized what difficult conditions lay ahead of them?

- What do you think John Fawcett meant when he said his three weeks on the road changed his outlook on life?

- What kinds of difficult questions do you think Fawcett asked his high school teachers when he returned to school in the fall of 1936?

For More Information

Books

Uys, Errol L. *Riding the Rails: Teenagers on the Move during the Great Depression.* New York, NY: TV Books, 1999.

Periodicals

Fawcett, John E. "A Hobo Memoir, 1936." *Indiana Magazine of History* Vol 90, No. 4 (December 1994): pp. 346–364.

Web Sites

Riding the Rails. http://www.pbs.org/wgbh/amex/rails/ (accessed on August 29, 2002).

Women's Voices

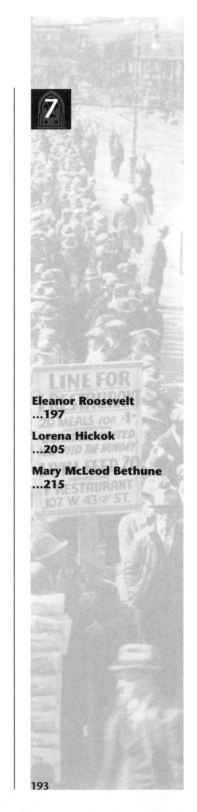

Franklin D. Roosevelt (1882–1945) was sworn in as president of the United States in March 1933. He and his advisers immediately began to introduce legislation designed to address the severe economic hardships brought on by the Great Depression, the worst economic downturn in U.S. history. Collectively, the "three Rs" legislation—providing for relief, recovery, and reform—was known as the New Deal. Under the New Deal, government agencies were established to carry out social and economic aid programs. The New Deal opened a wealth of opportunities for women. Many of the new programs required staff with training in social work, and women were the Americans who had the best training in that field. By the end of 1933 thirty-five women had been appointed to prominent federal government positions. Approximately fifty-five were in key positions in government by 1939. Even more important, the attitude that women belonged in government circles began to take root.

Women had gained the right to vote in 1920, and a few began to play active roles in government at that time. Beginning in 1921 Grace Abbott (1878–1939) served as chief

of the Children's Bureau within the Department of Labor. Mary Anderson (1872–1964) led the Women's Bureau in the Labor Department from 1920 until her retirement in 1944. Elected to Congress in 1924, Mary Norton (1875–1959) served in the U.S. House of Representatives until 1950. Molly Dewson (1874–1962) was active in women's reform groups in New York in the 1920s and became good friends with Eleanor Roosevelt (1884–1962), President Roosevelt's wife and a politically active person in her own right. Dewson was floor manager for women at the 1932 Democratic National Convention and served as chairperson of the Women's Division of the convention from 1932 to 1936. The influence of Eleanor Roosevelt and tireless lobbying by Dewson resulted in several government appointments for women. The most notable were Frances Perkins (1882–1965) as secretary of labor (the first woman ever appointed to a U.S. cabinet); Florence Allen (1884–1966) as a judge on the U.S. circuit court of appeals; and Ruth Owen (1885–1954) as ambassador to Denmark. Dewson never took on an appointment herself but was crucial in women's advancement in government. Both she and Eleanor Roosevelt believed that women's efficiency, energy, and idealism would bring out the humanitarian side of government—the side that cared about people. The idea of the federal government caring for its citizens was an entirely new concept that was pushed to the forefront of American political life by the hardships of the Great Depression.

Two prominent women appointed to New Deal positions were Ellen Sullivan Woodward (1887–1971) and Hallie Flanagan (1889–1969). Woodward served as head of the Women's and Professional Projects Division of the Works Progress Administration (WPA). Flanagan headed the Federal Theater Project (FTP) within the WPA. Several other women were prominent in the New Deal government, including Clara Mortenson Beyer (1892–1990), associate director of the Division of Labor Standards within the Department of Labor; Josephine Roche (1886–1976), the first woman to serve as assistant secretary of the Department of the Treasury, and the chairperson of the executive committee of the National Youth Administration (NYA); and Nellie Tayloe Ross (1876–1977), the first woman director of the U.S. Mint.

Along with Eleanor Roosevelt, who took an active role in explaining and promoting New Deal programs, two other women were especially adept at explaining the challenges of the Great Depression to others: Lorena Hickok (1893–1968) and Mary McLeod Bethune (1875–1955). Hickok served as chief investigator for the Federal Emergency Relief Administration (FERA), which was founded in May 1933 to bring immediate relief to the hungry. She had left her job as an Associated Press reporter to travel around the country and report back to Harry Hopkins (1890–1946), the head of the FERA, on the conditions she observed firsthand. Mary McLeod Bethune, a leader in education, was the first black American to be appointed as head of a federal agency—the Negro Affairs director for the National Youth Administration (NYA).

The excerpts in this chapter are taken from the writings of Eleanor Roosevelt, Hickok, and Bethune. In an article titled **"In Defense of Curiosity,"** published in the August 24, 1935, issue of *The Saturday Evening Post,* Eleanor Roosevelt urges women to be curious about and learn about the world beyond their immediate home environment. In **"The Unsung Heroes of the Depression"** Hickok describes her experiences as an investigator for Harry Hopkins of the FERA. She originally wrote the piece in 1937 as an introduction to a book she planned to write about her experiences as chief inspector for FERA; it ended up being published in the book *One Third of a Nation: Lorena Hickok Reports on the Great Depression* (1981), edited by Richard Lowitt and Maurine Beasley. In the third excerpt, taken from a 1936 speech titled **"National Youth Administration: Proceedings of the Second National Youth Administration Advisory Committee Meeting,"** Bethune speaks of the successes of the Negro Affairs Division of the NYA. The speech was published in the 1999 book *Mary McLeod Bethune: Building a Better World, Essays and Selected Documents,* edited by Audrey Thomas McCluskey and Elaine M. Smith.

Eleanor Roosevelt

Excerpt from "In Defense of Curiosity"

Published in *The Saturday Evening Post*, August 24, 1935

Eleanor Roosevelt (1884–1962), wife of President Franklin Roosevelt (served 1933–45), was a woman of boundless energy and curiosity. Her interests were wide-ranging. Throughout her adult life she supported relief and reform causes and related legislation. Immediately after her husband's election, she worked to open government doors and political appointments for women.

On March 6, 1933, only two days after President Roosevelt was sworn into office, Eleanor began weekly women-only press conferences. This caused newspapers to hire women journalists to cover the conferences, opening a new field of employment for women. The first lady's goal in holding these news conferences was to help women get a better understanding of legislative and political life. In 1935 Eleanor began writing her own daily news column titled "My Day."

Eleanor was a champion of women's rights and worked to improve the conditions under which women labored. She supported the Women's Trade Union League (WTUL), which established centers in New York City in 1932 and 1933 for unemployed women. She set up conferences in

"Few seem capable of realizing that the real reason that home is important is that it is so closely tied … to the rest of the world. That is what makes it an important factor in the life of every nation."

Eleanor Roosevelt

Eleanor Roosevelt, a champion for women's and children's rights, visits a Works Progress Administration-sponsored nursery school for black children in Des Moines, Iowa, in 1936. *Courtesy of the Franklin D. Roosevelt Library.*

Washington, D.C., to bring attention to the needs of women and children during the worst years of the Great Depression. Eleanor also fought for miners' rights and the rights of black Americans. She determinedly fought racial discrimination wherever she encountered it.

In its August 24, 1935, issue *The Saturday Evening Post* published an article written by Eleanor Roosevelt titled "In

Defense of Curiosity." In the article Eleanor urges all women to realize that individual homes are interconnected to one another and to the whole world. She suggests that curiosity and interest in the broader world may be the keys to solving problems such as the ones presented by the Great Depression.

Things to remember while reading "In Defense of Curiosity":

- Eleanor Roosevelt's own curiosity led her to tirelessly and fearlessly visit the most wretched areas in America. She reported her findings to the president, and her reports greatly influenced his courses of action.

- Believing that well-informed women could accomplish a great deal in government arenas, Eleanor worked to give women a broad understanding of their country and the problems it faced.

Excerpt from "In Defense of Curiosity"

A short time ago a cartoon appeared depicting two miners looking up in surprise and saying with undisguised horror, "Here comes Mrs. Roosevelt!"

*In strange and **subtle** ways, it was indicated to me that I should feel somewhat ashamed of that cartoon, and there certainly was something the matter with a woman who wanted to see so much and to know so much.*

*Somehow or other, most of the people who spoke to me, or wrote to me about it, seemed to feel that it was **unbecoming** in a woman to have a variety of interests. Perhaps that arose from the old **inherent** theory that woman's interests must lie only in her home. This is a kind of blindness which seems to make people feel that interest in the home stops within the four walls of the house in which you live. Few seem capable of realizing that the real reason that home is important is that it is so closely tied, by a million strings, to the rest of the world. That is what makes it an important factor in the life of every nation.*

Subtle: Through hints rather than direct statements.

Unbecoming: Not proper.

Inherent: Long held.

Eleanor Roosevelt rides in a coal car with miners at the Willow Grove Mine in Bellaire, Ohio, on May 22, 1935. She was there to gain firsthand information on the miners' working conditions.
©Bettmann/CORBIS. Reproduced by permission.

*Whether we recognize it or not, no home is an isolated object. We may not recognize it, and we may try to narrow ourselves so that our interest only extends to our immediate home circle, but if we have any understanding at all of what goes on around us, we soon see how outside influences affect our own existence. Take, for example, the money we have to spend. The economic conditions of the country affect our income whether it is earned or whether it is an income which comes to us from **invested capital**. What we are able to do in our home depends on the cost of the various things which we buy. All of us buy food, and food costs vary with conditions throughout the country and the world.*

The Interdependence of Individuals

It took us some time to realize that there was a relationship between the farm situation and the situation of the rest of our country, but eventually wage earners in the East did feel the results of the lack of buying power on the farms in the Middle West. To keep an even balance between the industrial worker and the agricultural worker is

Invested capital: Wealth that generates more wealth through investments.

an extremely difficult thing. Every housewife in this country should realize that if she lives in a city and has a husband who is either a wage earner or the owner of an industry, her wages or her profits will be dependent, not only upon the buying power of people like herself but upon the buying power of the great mass of agricultural people throughout the country. The farm housewife must realize, too, that her interests are tied up with those of the wage earner and his employer throughout the nation, for her husband's products can only find a ready market when the city dweller is prosperous....

To the city or suburban dweller, the price of a subway ride is of great importance, for if it costs ten cents a day to come and go from work, he may have enough left at the end of the week to take his wife to a movie, but twenty cents a day may mean that he has nothing left for entertainment. The city dweller could also do much for the price of milk, if he realized the dairy farmer's plight and how important the **consumption** of milk, and its price, is to general prosperity.

This **correlation** of interests is something that every woman would understand if she had the curiosity to find out the reason for certain conditions instead of merely accepting them, usually with rather bad grace....

It is man's **ceaseless** urge to know more and to do more which makes the world move, and so, when people say woman's place is in the home, I say, with enthusiasm, it certainly is, but if she really cares about her home, that caring will take her far and wide....

Rubbing Elbows With the Slums

A few years ago, when I was conducting a class in the study of city government, we took up one of the functions of the government—namely, public health. This is closely allied to housing, so I suggested that our group visit some of the different types of **tenements**. There was considerable concern among some of the mothers, for fear some illness might be contracted. It apparently never occurred to them that hundreds of young people lived in these tenements all the time, nor that, very likely, there entered into their sheltered homes daily people who served as delivery boys, servants and workmen, who spent much of their time in tenements; so, even if the **sheltered children** did not visit them, the tenement home **radiated out** all that was good in it and all that was bad in it and touched the home on **Park Avenue**. No home is isolated, remember, so why should we not have a curiosity about all the homes that must in one way or another affect our own?

Consumption: Buying.

Correlation: Relationship.

Ceaseless: Unending.

Tenements: Large housing structures containing apartments that barely meet minimum standards of sanitation, safety, and comfort.

Sheltered children: Children not raised in poverty conditions; that is, sheltered from poor living conditions.

Radiated out: Spread outward.

Park Avenue: A wealthy part of New York City; often used to describe wealthy people in general.

Traveled But Not Broadened

*On visiting the various types of tenements, I found again that the lack of curiosity makes a poor background for real understanding. To these children of the rich, I had to explain what it meant to sleep in a room which had no window, what it meant to pant on fire escapes in hot July with people **draped** on fire escapes all around you, what it meant for a woman with her husband and eight children to live in three rooms in the basement, and why a toilet with no outside **ventilation** could make a home unhealthy and **malodorous**.*

Lack of curiosity in these young people meant lack of imagination and complete inability to visualize any life but their own, and, therefore, they could not recognize their responsibility to their less-fortunate brothers and sisters.... [Roosevelt, pp. 8, 9, 65, 66.]

What happened next...

Eleanor continued her public work during World War II (1939–45). She traveled to England and the South Pacific, carrying messages from her husband to United States troops and government leaders. She worked for the Office of Civilian Defense. After the death of President Roosevelt in 1945, she continued to write and lecture to promote the causes she had long supported. President Harry Truman (1884–1972; served 1945–53) appointed her a delegate to the newly formed United Nations (UN). A skilled diplomat, she worked on the first international bill of rights as a member of the UN Commission on Human Rights. Eleanor remained a major force in the Democratic Party in the 1950s. In 1961 President John F. Kennedy (1917–1963; served 1961–63) sent her back to the UN as a delegate to the Commission on the Status of Women. Eleanor Roosevelt, perhaps America's most respected and loved first lady, died in 1962.

Draped: Stretched out.

Ventilation: Access to fresh air.

Malodorous: Having a bad odor.

Did you know...

• Eleanor Roosevelt's mother died when Eleanor was quite young, and Eleanor's father died when she was ten.

Eleanor and her brother were raised by their maternal grandmother.

- Both Eleanor and the president enjoyed a good laugh. Eleanor left the White House one morning very early to visit prisons in Baltimore, Maryland. When President Roosevelt asked where his wife was that particular day, his secretary informed him that Eleanor was in jail. Saying he was not surprised, he asked, "What is she in for?"

- Eleanor married Franklin D. Roosevelt in 1905 after several years of courtship. They were distant cousins.

- Eleanor Roosevelt promoted the rights of black Americans even though doing so meant that President Roosevelt might lose the support of Southern white voters.

- In 1939 Eleanor resigned from the Daughters of the American Revolution, an influential nationwide women's group, because the group had denied Marian Anderson (1897–1993), an internationally famous black American singer, permission to use their performance hall. Eleanor then helped set up a concert for Anderson at the Lincoln Memorial.

Consider the following...

- Why did Eleanor Roosevelt say that city and farm wives needed to understand the economic conditions of each other?

- Why did Eleanor think it necessary for wealthy people to visit the tenements?

For More Information

Books

Black, Allida M., ed. *"What I Hope to Leave Behind": The Essential Essays of Eleanor Roosevelt*. New York, NY: Carlson Publishing, 1995.

Black, Allida M., ed. *Courage in a Dangerous World: The Political Writings of Eleanor Roosevelt*. New York, NY: Columbia University Press, 1999.

Cook, Blanche W. *Eleanor Roosevelt, 1933–1938*. New York, NY: Viking, 1999.

Freedman, Russell. *Eleanor Roosevelt: A Life of Discovery*. New York, NY: Clarion, 1993.

Kingdon, Frank. *As FDR Said: A Treasury of His Speeches, Conversations, and Writings.* New York, NY: Duell, Sloan and Pearce, 1950.

Roosevelt, Eleanor. *This I Remember.* New York, NY: Harper, 1949.

Periodicals

Roosevelt, Eleanor. "In Defense of Curiosity." *Saturday Evening Post* (August 24, 1935): pp. 8, 9, 65, 66.

Lorena Hickok

Excerpt from "The Unsung Heroes of the Depression"

**Reprinted from *One Third of a Nation:
Lorena Hickok Reports on the Great Depression*
Edited by Richard Lowitt and Maurine Beasley
Published in 1981**

"**G**o talk with preachers and teachers, businessmen, workers, farmers. Go talk with the unemployed, those who are on relief and those who aren't. And when you talk with them don't ever forget that but for the grace of God you, I, any of our friends might be in their shoes. Tell me what you see and hear. All of it." These were the instructions Harry Hopkins (1890–1946), chief of the Federal Emergency Relief Administration, gave to Lorena Hickok (1893–1968) at the start of the summer of 1933. Hickok was to be his chief field representative—an investigator who would travel across the country to assess how New Deal relief programs were being carried out and accepted. Hopkins's humble recognition that anyone might have fallen on hard times during the Great Depression was typical of the entire Roosevelt administration.

Lorena Hickok began her career as a journalist in 1913. It soon became apparent that the talented, determined young woman had a "nose" for news. She practiced her investigative and writing skills, and in the mid-1920s the Associated Press hired her as a reporter. Very few women held

"People, with voices, faces, eyes. People with hope. People without hope. People still fighting. People with all courage squeezed out of them. People with stories."

Lorena Hickok

Women in the 1930s Workplace

Despite the many government positions women gained under the Roosevelt administration, American women as a whole did not enjoy much change in status. Almost 25 percent of American women worked outside their homes during the Great Depression, but they did not find a friendly work environment. The prevailing public attitude was that married women belonged at home, not in the workplace. In addition, considerably fewer single women worked in the 1930s than in the 1990s. One reason was that women married at a much younger age. Because they had to earn a living (that is, having no man to support them), widows and single women who worked outside the home were not as looked down upon. Many people in the 1930s believed that working women were taking much needed jobs away from men, who were unemployed and who held the responsibility of being the sole wage earners for their families.

Women worked long hours and received low wages. The average annual pay for women was $525, compared to $1,027 for men. Most Americans believed there was no economic reason for women to work; women who did work were thought to be seeking "pin money" (small amounts), merely a little extra spending cash. In many professions women—especially married women—faced strong discrimination against their right to work. For example, women in the teaching profession faced very restrictive policies. A National Education Association survey conducted in the 1930–31 school year revealed that 77 percent of the fifteen hundred school systems examined would not hire married women. Sixty-three percent made it a policy to dismiss female teachers if they became married. Other professions also had restrictive policies: In 1939, 84 percent of insurance companies, 65 percent of banks, and 63 percent of public utilities still had restrictions against hiring women.

such positions at that time, but Hickok had become the country's premier female "news hawk." She was a somewhat chubby woman with an imposing, husky voice and a self-assured manner. Most women at that time wore dresses or tailored, sophisticated jackets and skirts, but Hickok invariably wore rather baggy clothing. However, her unconventional appearance did not prevent her from succeeding in her career; her reporting was on the mark. Hickok was assigned to Albany, New York, to cover Franklin Roosevelt's activities as governor of the state (where he served from 1929 to 1933), and she would later cover Roosevelt's 1932 presidential cam-

paign. She and Eleanor Roosevelt (1884–1962) became fast friends, and the friendship was lifelong.

As soon as President Roosevelt took office in March 1933, he and his advisers, including Harry Hopkins, began introducing legislation that would bring relief to Americans devastated by the Depression. This legislation, along with subsequent reform and recovery programs, was known as the New Deal. On May 22, 1933, Hopkins was given the title of Federal Emergency Relief Administrator and $500 million to begin immediate relief services. He set up an aid organization in Washington, D.C., and in each of the states, determined the need in each state, and handed out half of the $500 million. He also set up work relief programs: If a man received $6 in relief money to pay for a week's groceries, for example, he would work on a road-building project or some other public works project long enough to earn the $6. The Civil Works Administration (CWA) was created in the fall of 1933, and Hopkins had four million men hired by Christmas.

Hopkins, a great admirer of both Eleanor Roosevelt and Lorena Hickok, hired Hickok away from the Associated Press in July 1933. Hopkins made her his chief investigator and sent her across the country to write reports on how the New Deal relief was being administered by local and state officials and how it was being received by the people.

Hickok's reports were secret, read only by Hopkins and a few select New Dealers. Hopkins had instructed Hickok not to bring him statistics but to interview people and report to him the conditions she found firsthand. Hickok met with Americans from across the country to find out whether help was getting to them and whether it made a difference. She also met with state and local government officials to determine whether they were carrying out their duties with fairness. She checked in on localities where Hopkins had gotten word that all was not running properly.

Hickok's reports were full of insight. Depending on the situation, they were angry or amusing in tone but always direct and to the point. Hickok had no patience with bureaucratic inefficiency; in her view, there was no excuse for it when people were starving. In the following excerpt from "The Unsung Heroes of the Depression," Hickok describes several of the people she encountered in her travels.

Things to remember while reading the excerpt from "The Unsung Heroes of the Depression":

- The push to get federal money out to the states for immediate relief resulted in some mishandling of funds.

- Hickok traveled to some of the most afflicted areas of the country, such as the mining communities in West Virginia, Eastern Kentucky, and Pennsylvania; the slum neighborhoods of New York City and Washington, D.C.; and the agricultural valleys of central California.

- Hickok had no idea of the extent of poverty in America before she began her travels. Gradually she came to understand the situation and provided those in Washington, D.C., with informative, precise reports.

Excerpt from "The Unsung Heroes of the Depression"

*It is their story, as they themselves told it—sometimes desperately, sometimes with quivering lips, sometimes only by the patient, **bewildered** expression in their eyes—to one who traveled up and down the country as **confidential observer** for the man [Harry Hopkins] who was charged by their Government with the job of seeing that they did not starve.*

*Four years ago, to the writer [Hickok], they were not really people at all. They had no faces. They were just "the unemployed." Muffled figures, backs curved against the wind, selling apples on the street corners of New York. One's friends made jokes about "unemployed apples." **Grimy hands thrusting needles and wilting gardenias** through your cab window when you were halted in cross-town traffic, while you wondered if you ought to buy them ....*

*"What I want you to do," said Harry Hopkins in July, 1933, "is to go out around the country and look this thing over. I don't want statistics from you. I don't want the **social-worker angle**. I just want your own reaction, as an ordinary citizen.*

"Go talk with preachers and teachers, businessmen, workers, farmers. Go talk with the unemployed, those who are on relief and

---

Bewildered: Confused.

Confidential observer: A trusted person who will discuss her observations only with Harry Hopkins.

Grimy hands...: The unemployed trying to sell flowers with pins to attach to clothes.

Social-worker angle: The view of a trained specialist using statistics.

*those who aren't. And when you talk with them don't ever forget that but for the grace of God you, I, any of our friends might be in their shoes. Tell me what you see and hear. All of it. Don't ever **pull your punches**."*

*First, a sickening trip on a blistering July morning through Washington's notorious slums, "the Alleys." Then, to Philadelphia. Down into West Virginia and Eastern Kentucky. A month in up-state New York and New England. Two weeks in New York City. Six weeks—and 7,000 miles in an old Chevrolet—in the Dakotas, Nebraska, Iowa, and Minnesota. Down through the Tennessee Valley. Two weeks among the beet sugar workers in Colorado. The Imperial Valley in California, where a thermometer in the car registered 126 degrees Fahrenheit. * * * Fayette county, Pennsylvania, during a coal strike. Aroostook County, Maine, during potato harvest. Bottineau County, North Dakota, just before the first blizzard * * * Wheeling, West Virginia, when smoke began pouring out of the stacks at the steel mills. Miami, Florida, when the tourists began to come back. * * * Pineville, Kentucky, when relief was cut off. Sioux City, Iowa, when **CWA** came in. Toledo, Ohio, as **WPA** was starting. * * * Back and forth, up and down the country. By motor, by train, by plane. A three-year **Odyssey** through every man's land—and no man's land.*

*One by one, sometimes bold, sometimes **hesitant**, sometimes demanding, sometimes **faltering**, they emerged—individuals. People, with voices, faces, eyes. People with hope. People without hope. People still fighting. People with all courage squeezed out of them. People with stories.*

There was the Negro woman in Philadelphia who used to walk eight miles every day over the scorching pavements just on the chance of getting, perhaps, a little cleaning to do, at 10 cents an hour.

There was the chauffeur in New York who, on the day before he reported for the first time to work as a laborer on a park project, stood about for hours watching how the other men handled their picks and shovels, so he would "get the hang of it and not feel so awkward."

There was the little Mexican girl, aged 6, in Colorado, who said, sure, she'd worked "in the beets" two Summers already and, yes, sometimes she did get pretty tired.

There was the young musician, who said: "For a few weeks it isn't so bad for a man and his wife and baby to get along on $4.80

Pull your punches: Withhold information.

CWA: The Civil Works Administration, a New Deal agency.

WPA: The Works Progress Administration, another New Deal agency.

Odyssey: Long trip.

Hesitant: Timid.

Faltering: Wavering or uncertain.

a week, paying $3 of it out for rent. But when it runs into months, and you can't see anything ahead, you get ... discouraged."

There was the WPA worker in Erie, Pa. [Pennsylvania], proud ... because he had developed into "a darned good asphalt man" while working on relief and WPA projects.

*There were those unemployed miners' wives in Scotts Run [West Virginia], who **instinctively** liked and trusted the tall, slender lady with the warming smile and soft, lovely voice who drove up to their homes in an old Ford one Summer day—and found out later that she was the President's wife [Eleanor Roosevelt].*

*There were those little boys who refused to go to school in Houston, Texas, wearing the trousers of terribly **conspicuous** black-and-white-striped ticking that had been given them, because everybody would know they were on relief.*

There were those two small boys, a year or so later, in Salt Lake City [Utah], who were overheard boasting about whose father had been on relief longer.

There was the small town woman in Iowa who spent part of her husband's first CWA check for oranges, because she hadn't tasted any for three years.

There was the architect who said he didn't mind working on a road as a day laborer because "at least my children can tell the teacher their father is working. They don't have to say what he's doing."

There was the farm woman in South Dakota who had a recipe for Russian thistle soup and said, "It don't taste so bad, only it ain't very filling."

There was the boy of 20 who limped wearily into his home in a Baltimore suburb one Autumn night in 1934 after having walked nearly 20 miles down into the center of the city and back, "just stopping at every place and asking if they didn't need somebody to work—at anything" ....

There was the unemployed fur-worker in Pittsburgh who said: "Lady, you just can't know what it's like to have to move your family out of the nice house you had in the suburbs, part paid for, down into an apartment, down into another apartment, smaller and in a worse neighborhood, down, down, down, until finally you end up in the slums."...

Instinctively: Immediately, without a conscious reason.

Conspicuous: Noticeable.

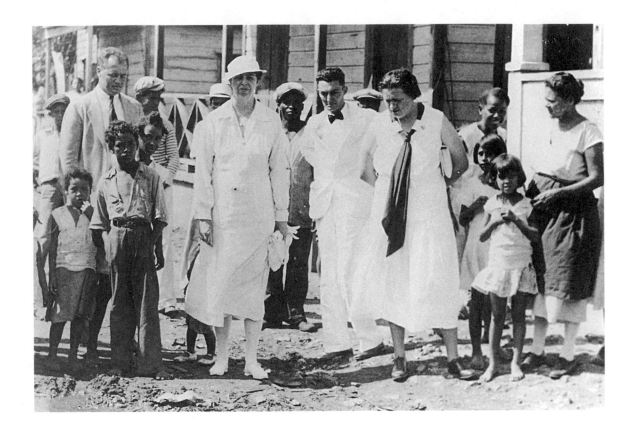

One by one, they come and go. Not all of them saints, by any means. And not all of them, by any means, dishonest or lazy or hopeless. Thousands of them in the last three years have "come back," have found jobs as industry revived, have moved out of the crowded flats where they were living with relatives, have paid up their debts. Perhaps—and it is to be hoped that this is so—many of them have even forgotten that there ever was a Depression! And thousands of them have not found jobs, perhaps never will. A reviving industry, with the best of intentions, cannot immediately absorb such a load as piled up in this country during the black years. The young, the physically fit, the mentally alert first are called and should be. The man over 40, the untrained, the weak, for many of these there may be no future at all. [Lowitt and Beasley, pp. ix, x–xi, xii]

Lorena Hickok (center-right) traveled to Puerto Rico with Eleanor Roosevelt in March 1934, to investigate labor conditions in large sugar companies, and housing and sanitation problems. *Courtesy of the Franklin D. Roosevelt Library.*

What happened next...

Lorena Hickok worked as the chief relief investigator for the Roosevelt administration until just after the presidential election in 1936. She left government service in late 1936 to take a public relations job and live quietly on Long Island, New York. But in 1940 the Roosevelts pressed her back into service. She lived at the White House and served as executive secretary of the Women's Division of the Democratic National Convention. From her retirement in 1945 to her death in 1968 she wrote a number of books on the Roosevelts.

Did you know...

- Lorena Hickok accompanied Eleanor Roosevelt on many of the first lady's travels around the country. She also traveled to Puerto Rico with Mrs. Roosevelt, in March 1934, to investigate labor conditions in large sugar companies, and housing and sanitation problems.

- In her reports Hickok exposed greedy politicians who were attempting to manipulate relief programs to benefit themselves and their friends.

- Racial discrimination greatly interfered with the proper administration of relief programs. Hickok reported back to Hopkins and President Roosevelt on this issue.

Consider the following...

- The phrase "one-third of a nation"—the title of the book that contains Hickok's excerpt—is taken from President Roosevelt's second inaugural address, given in January 1937. Refer to Chapter Two, "A New Deal for Americans," and find the "Second Inaugural Address" excerpt. According to President Roosevelt, what problems existed for one-third of Americans?

- What reporting skills would Hickok have had to possess to report back to Hopkins so clearly?

For More Information

Faber, Doris. *The Life of Lorena Hickok: E. R.'s Friend.* New York, NY: W. Morrow, 1980.

Lowitt, Richard, and Maurine Beasley, eds. *One Third of a Nation: Lorena Hickok Reports on the Great Depression.* Urbana, IL: University of Illinois Press, 1981.

Ware, Susan. *Beyond Suffrage: Women in the New Deal.* Cambridge, MA: Harvard University Press, 1981.

Ware, Susan. *Holding Their Own: American Women in the 1930s.* Boston, MA: Twayne Publishers, 1982.

Mary McLeod Bethune

Excerpt from "National Youth Administration: Proceedings of the Second National Youth Administration Advisory Committee Meeting"

Delivered by Mary McLeod Bethune in 1936
Reprinted from *Mary McLeod Bethune: Building a Better World, Essays and Selected Documents*
Edited by Audrey Thomas McCluskey and Elaine M. Smith
Published in 1999

"The Negro views with deep interest the national program for all youth and approves most highly its objectives."

Mary McLeod Bethune

The National Youth Administration (NYA), part of the massive Works Progress Administration (WPA) established in 1935, was designed to meet the educational and employment needs of young Americans between the ages of sixteen and twenty-five. To keep youths off the rails and in schools, the agency provided cash aid to high school, college, and graduate school students. Students worked part-time, generally on school-related jobs (such as custodial duties or maintenance of school grounds), in return for small monthly cash payments. Often the payments were just enough to allow the student to stay in school. For young people who had already left school, the NYA provided work relief programs that employed youths to build community and recreation centers. In cooperation with local communities, the NYA also provided an array of vocational training classes. Within the first year of the NYA's operation, in 1936, more than five hundred thousand students received cash aid, including nineteen thousand black American youths under the Negro Affairs branch of the agency. Mary McLeod Bethune (1875–1955) was appointed the first director of the NYA's Negro Affairs Division.

Sponsored by the National
Youth Administration, these
young black women
received training and
employment as assistants at
this Mississippi library, circa
1936. *Courtesy of the Franklin
D. Roosevelt Library.*

Bethune was already well known and respected by black Americans throughout the nation. Bethune was an educator, a social activist, and a leader in many organizations that promoted the rights and well-being of black Americans. She served as president of Bethune-Cookman College, a college that served black American women and men.

Gaining attention at the highest levels of the U.S. government, Bethune served at the Child Welfare Conference under President Calvin Coolidge (1872–1933; served 1923–29) and on the National Child Welfare Commission under President Herbert Hoover (1874–1964; served 1929–33). Bethune's leadership in education was matched by her leadership in many organizations, including the Florida Federation of Colored Women's Clubs, the Southeastern Federation of Colored Women's Clubs, and the National Association of Colored Women. In 1935 she founded and served as president of the National Council of Negro Women. That

same year the National Association for the Advancement of Colored People (NAACP) presented her with its highest award for advancing the cause of minorities.

Eleanor Roosevelt and Bethune became close friends. Bethune was a key adviser to the Roosevelts on minority issues. The NYA was the first government-sponsored agency to aid black American youths. As director of Negro Affairs within the NYA, Bethune sought cooperation from the black American public and from black American educators and leaders to develop NYA programs for black students. Bethune noted that the program was not only helpful to black students but was also instrumental in developing leaders among the black adult population. In the following excerpt from "National Youth Administration: Proceedings of the Second National Youth Administration Advisory Committee Meeting," Bethune conveys the message that the NYA was indeed successful in aiding black students and the entire black community.

Things to remember while reading the excerpt from "National Youth Administration: Proceedings of the Second National Youth Administration Advisory Committee Meeting":

- In the 1930s racism remained woven into every aspect of life in the United States and was freely expressed in public.

- Major New Deal programs established in 1933 and 1934 offered little opportunity for black Americans. Only when First Lady Eleanor Roosevelt openly committed to changing public attitudes toward black Americans and improving black Americans' economic condition did positive changes begin. With Eleanor Roosevelt's insistence, racial discrimination was weeded out of some federal programs, relief aid targeted more blacks, and several blacks were appointed to higher federal positions.

- Mary McLeod Bethune was the first black American to head a federal government agency.

Excerpt from "National Youth Administration: Proceedings of the Second National Youth Administration Advisory Committee Meeting"

*I want first of all to express on the part of the Negro people, our appreciation for the vision of our **illustrious** President, and his committee, in extending to the nation this NYA program. In my opinion and I think I am thinking in terms of thinking Negro people, I believe it to be one of the most stabilizing projects for the benefit of the American of tomorrow, than possibly any one thing that we have done.*

*It seems to me that the giving of opportunity to the youths of today to **round out** in training and in vision for the citizen[s] of tomorrow is vitally important.*

*The Negro views with deep interest the national program for all youth and approves most highly its objectives. More particularly is the Negro interested in those phases of the program, which for the first time in the history of the nation, affords to Negro youth through **Federal benefits**, larger opportunities for education, productive work and cultural and wholesome recreation. Among the most invaluable outcomes of the National Youth program as related to the Negro youth have been:*

1. His optimistic awakening to the responsibility of citizenship made possible through the channels of training provided through the program of the National Youth Administration.

*2. The fine spirit of cooperation of the general Negro public in **fostering** the objectives of the program of the NYA.*

3. The fine spirit of cooperation and healthy participation on the part of Negro educators and leaders, and state and local NYA Administrators.

*I think, Mr. Chairman, and members of this committee, this NYA program has afforded the finest opportunity for **interracial cooperation** and understanding in these local communities, than any one thing that we have had come among us, particularly in our own southern section.*

Through the program of the National Youth movement touching the humblest black boy of the South has come a realization on

Illustrious: Outstanding and honorable.

Round out: Be developed.

Federal benefits: Benefits provided through U.S. government programs.

Fostering: Helping to promote.

Interracial cooperation: Cooperation between black Americans and white Americans.

the part of thousands of untutored Negro parents that the government does care,—for 'even the least of these.'

In places where there is no need for a separate program, for Negro and white groups, we most heartily recommend the one program. And in fields where it is necessary for us to have a separate program, we most heartily recommend a separate program, **taking, of course, under advisement**, the necessity of the proper leadership and guidance [so] that we might be able to do the most effective work [good leaders are needed to ensure the programs' success].

It is recommended that this committee accept as a matter of policy the following: Continuing the policy adopted by the committee at its previous meeting regarding the appointment of qualified Negroes as members of staffs of state and local organizations; and the recognition of the value of Negro Supervision for strictly Negro work projects.

May I advise the committee that it does not matter how equipped your white supervision might be, or your white leadership, it is impossible for you to **enter** as sympathetically and understand-

Similar to the National Youth Administration, the Federal Art Program (FAP) also afforded opportunities to black students during the Depression. *Courtesy of the Franklin D. Roosevelt Library.*

Taking under advisement: Keeping in mind.

Enter: Participate.

After the Depression, Mary McLeod Bethune became assistant director of the Women's Army Auxiliary Corps and recruited black women for officer training during World War II. Here, Bethune greets a WAAC enlistee. ©Bettmann/CORBIS. Reproduced by permission.

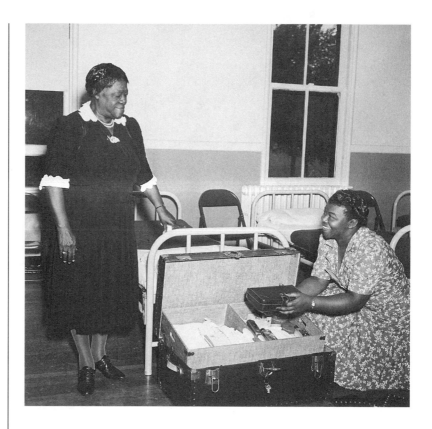

ingly, into the program of the Negro, as the Negro can do. Then it will give, also, the thing that we very much need nowadays, that opportunity for the development of leadership among the Negro people themselves, and it is becoming more important that the right type of leadership be produced. They can only become efficient by having the opportunity to develop and grow in participation in these programs ....

The committee must not permit itself to be turned aside from the **prosecution and realization** of the major objectives of the National Youth program, chief of which is the development of an appreciation of citizenship values in the minds of American youth regardless of race, creed or color.

Since in some states, particularly in the south where Negroes have not had the opportunities for preparation for college life, it is recommended that funds be **earmarked** to be used specifically for Negro youth in equalizing educational opportunities in certain states where the Negro has not been able to obtain equal educational opportunities.

Prosecution and realization: Pursuit and accomplishment.

Earmarked: Set aside.

*I beg this Committee, whose position is so sacred in administering this program as handed down by our illustrious President, to keep **eternal vigilance** to safeguard the interest and welfare of all the youth of America. I speak particularly in behalf of the Negro youth. (Applause.)....* [McCluskey and Smith, pp. 216–218]

What happened next...

The Negro Affairs Division of the NYA remained in operation until 1944. Bethune served as director throughout the division's existence. Because of Bethune's efforts, 10 to 12 percent of the young people who participated in the NYA were black. Overall, approximately three hundred thousand black youths benefited from NYA programs.

In response to the actions of the Roosevelt administration on behalf of black Americans, black voters switched from voting Republican to voting for Roosevelt, a Democrat, in the 1936 presidential election. Many black Americans voted for the first time. In the 1932 presidential election Herbert Hoover, a Republican, won 66 percent of the black vote; only four years later Roosevelt won 76 percent. This shift in black American voters' loyalty turned out to be a lasting trend: At the beginning of the twenty-first century, a majority of black American voters continue to support the Democratic Party.

In 1937 Bethune organized the National Conference on Problems of the Negro, which was held in Washington, D.C., and in 1939 she organized a second national conference on black American issues. Following the Depression, Bethune remained active in government, recruiting black women to the Women's Army Auxiliary Corps (WAAC) for officer training during World War II (1939–45); she also headed a black women's organization called the Women's Army for National Defense. Bethune participated in the organizational meetings of the United Nations after World War II. She continued to write and lecture until her death in 1955. Her work helped set the stage for the civil rights movement of the 1950s and 1960s.

Eternal vigilance: A careful watch.

Did you know...

- Mary McLeod Bethune was born in South Carolina in 1875, only a decade after the end of the American Civil War. She was the fifteenth child in a family of seventeen children and proved to be a gifted student at an early age.

- Confident and dignified, Bethune provided leadership and inspiration for many black Americans and for women in general.

- Bethune was the unofficial leader of Roosevelt's "Black Cabinet," a group of black federal officials who informally advised the president on issues of special importance to black Americans.

- In 1989 *Ebony,* an influential magazine for black Americans, listed Bethune—along with such prominent people as Frederick Douglass (1817–1895) and Martin Luther King Jr. (1929–1968)—as one of the fifty most important black Americans in U.S. history.

Consider the following...

- Why did Bethune call the NYA program "one of the most stabilizing projects for the benefit of the American of tomorrow, than possibly any one thing that we have done"?

- According to Bethune, whom did the NYA benefit in addition to black youths?

- What did Bethune say was the chief objective of the NYA?

For More Information

Books

Anderson, LaVere. *Mary McLeod Bethune: Teacher with a Dream.* Champaign, IL: Garrard, 1976.

McCluskey, Audrey Thomas, and Elaine M. Smith, eds. *Mary McLeod Bethune: Building a Better World, Essays and Selected Documents.* Bloomington, IN: Indiana University Press, 1999.

Ware, Susan. *Beyond Suffrage: Women in the New Deal.* Cambridge, MA: Harvard University Press, 1981.

Ware, Susan. *Holding Their Own: American Women in the 1930s.* Boston, MA: Twayne Publishers, 1982.

Web Sites

Bethune-Cookman College. http://www.bethune.cookman.edu (accessed on August 29, 2002).

Literature and Songs
of the Great Depression

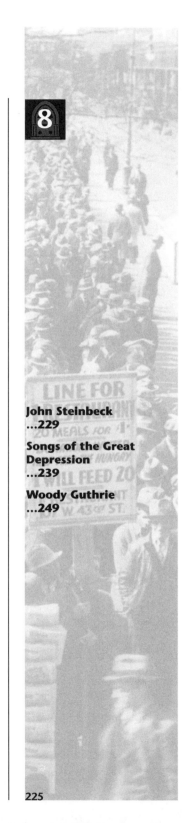

Every period of U.S. history has produced unique varieties of American literature. The Great Depression (1929–41), the most severe economic crisis the nation had ever experienced, was no exception. Talented writers produced an array of books. Some, following their own interests and passions, wrote without much regard to the conditions surrounding them in the 1930s. Others crafted books that revealed much about Americans caught in the economic devastation of the Depression; these socially aware books are known as proletarian (working-class) literature. Authors of such literature looked with disgust on the wealth that a few Americans had amassed at the expense of the majority of the people. The books they wrote had themes that supported working-class individuals and promoted the idea of economic cooperation rather than competition. Proletarian themes became a hallmark of Depression-era literature.

Several proletarian writers of the 1930s went on to fame, including John Dos Passos (1896–1970), James T. Farrell (1904–1979), Erskine Caldwell (1903–1987), Richard Wright (1908–1960), and John Steinbeck (1902–1968). Dos

Passos created *U.S.A.*, a trilogy (three novels) that tells of America's materialistic growth from the 1890s to the early Depression years. Farrell also wrote a trilogy, focusing on an imaginary young working-class Irish American named Studs Lonigan, who lives under harsh conditions in Chicago. Caldwell's *Tobacco Road* (1932) describes the poverty of a Southern tenant farming family whose lives become desperate as the Depression closes in. The story was made into a play that ran on Broadway in New York City for years. In 1933 Caldwell published *God's Little Acre,* which also tells the story of a poor family. Together with photographer Margaret Bourke-White (1906–1971), Caldwell published *You Have Seen Their Faces* (1937), a true story of rural poverty in the South. Richard Wright was a black author who wrote about the problems of black Americans in a white society. He published a collection of four short stories, *Uncle Tom's Children,* in 1938; his first novel, *Native Son,* appeared in 1940. He also published nonfiction, including *Twelve Million Black Voices* in 1941. John Steinbeck wrote a number of decidedly proletarian novels in the 1930s. This chapter includes an excerpt from one of Steinbeck's most famous novels, **The Grapes of Wrath,** published in 1939. An example of excellent proletarian literature, *The Grapes of Wrath* tells the story of the Joads, an Oklahoma family whose farm is destroyed by a severe drought. (Beginning in late 1931, a real drought had turned much of the Great Plains into a dust-covered wasteland that was impossible to farm.)

Next in the chapter are examples of 1930s songs that relate to the Great Depression. While big bands playing "swing," a form of jazz, were all the rage, songs of the Depression also caught the public's attention. No matter how miserable a situation seemed, some American songwriter always came up with lyrics and a melody to lighten the national mood. Uplifting tunes included **"Happy Days Are Here Again,"** a 1932 presidential campaign song; **"We're in the Money,"** from the musical *Gold Diggers of 1933;* and **"Over the Rainbow,"** from the 1939 movie *The Wizard of Oz.* Songs of protest also emerged, including **"Beans, Bacon, and Gravy"** and **"Soup Song." "Brother, Can You Spare A Dime?"** is another Depression-era protest song; it describes how a man could work hard, even serve his country in World War I (1914-18), but be forgotten and living in poverty by the

early 1930s. The lyrics of all these songs are included in this chapter under the heading **"Songs of the Depression."**

Woody Guthrie (1912–1967) was a folksinger and songwriter who wrote simple but powerful songs about conditions in the Dust Bowl during the Great Depression. He wrote about the people's migration westward, the same subject Steinbeck wrote about in *The Grapes of Wrath.* Guthrie also wrote a set of twenty-six songs about the Pacific Northwest in mid-1941. Several excerpts of Guthrie's lyrics are reprinted near the end of this chapter.

John Steinbeck

Excerpt from The Grapes of Wrath
Published in 1939; excerpt taken from 1955 reprint

"They streamed over the mountains, hungry and restless—restless as ants, scurrying to find work to do—to lift, to push, to pull, to pick, to cut—anything, any burden to bear, for food. The kids are hungry."

From The Grapes of Wrath

During the 1930s migrant workers poured into California in search of work. Most of them had been farmers in the Dust Bowl or sharecroppers or tenant farmers on cotton farms in the southern central states. John Steinbeck tells their story in his 1939 book *The Grapes of Wrath*. To describe the plight of migrants moving west into California, Steinbeck decided to concentrate on the story of one family, the Joads, and their struggles while traveling from the Dust Bowl region of Oklahoma to the promised land of California. Ultimately, the story is about the courage and passion of men and women who are able to overcome hardships and endure.

Born in Salinas, California, on February 27, 1902, John Steinbeck was the son of a farmer and a schoolteacher. His mother, the schoolteacher, read to John extensively from literature from around the world. His childhood days were spent in an intellectually stimulating environment—and outdoors in the beautiful Salinas valley. Steinbeck entered Stanford University in California in 1920 and remained at that school until 1925. Always committed to learning and to pursuing life on his own terms, Steinbeck left Stanford without

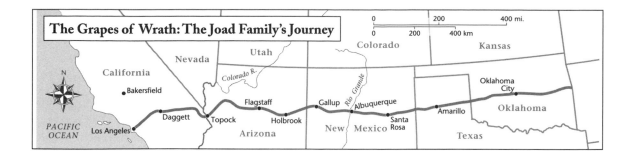

The Grapes of Wrath: The Joad Family's Journey

Though the Joad family from The Grapes of Wrath was fictional, their journey was typical of that taken by the many "Okie" families traveling to California to find a better life.
Gale Group.

earning a degree and moved to New York City. His stay there was short-lived; he felt more at home in the California countryside than on the streets of New York. Returning to California, he began to write. During the 1930s he produced a number of remarkable novels that portray the conditions that agricultural workers labored under in the Salinas valley—conditions Steinbeck had observed firsthand. His decidedly proletarian works (books about working-class conditions) include *Pastures of Heaven* (1932), *Tortilla Flat* (1935), *In Dubious Battle* (1936), and *The Grapes of Wrath* (1939). *The Grapes of Wrath* won a 1940 Pulitzer Prize for literature. Pulitzer Prizes, named for Joseph Pulitzer (1847–1911), are given each year for outstanding works in literature, journalism, drama, and music.

Steinbeck believed he could write best about the people he best knew. Therefore, before writing a novel, he would spend time observing firsthand the living and working conditions of the people he wanted to write about. In preparation for writing *The Grapes of Wrath,* Steinbeck spent eight weeks working in the fields as a pea picker.

In *The Grapes of Wrath* Steinbeck tells the story of the Joads in a straightforward narrative (direct storytelling) style. However, he intermixes the narrative chapters with chapters that are intended to inform the reader about the social and factual background against which the story is set. The following excerpt from *The Grapes of Wrath* is taken from one of these informational chapters.

Things to remember while reading the excerpt from *The Grapes of Wrath*:

• None of the main characters, the Joads, appear in the ex-

cerpt, but they are closely tied to the situations described in the excerpt.

- Writers of proletarian literature of the 1930s observed their fellow Americans struggling and suffering under an unequal social and economic order. In turn, they exposed the inequalities that they saw to the general public. In this spirit, Steinbeck wrote so the public could get to know a migrant family.

- *The Grapes of Wrath* was a call for California landowners to extend more tolerance and fairness to their workers.

Excerpt from Chapter 19 *of* The Grapes of Wrath

*And then the **dispossessed** were drawn west—from Kansas, Oklahoma, Texas, New Mexico; from Nevada and Arkansas families, tribes, dusted out, tractored out. Carloads, caravans, homeless and hungry; twenty thousand and fifty thousand and a hundred thousand and two hundred thousand. They streamed over the mountains, hungry and restless—restless as ants, scurrying to find work to do—to lift, to push, to pull, to pick, to cut—anything, any burden to bear, for food. The kids are hungry. We got no place to live. Like ants scurrying for work, for food, and most of all for land.*

We ain't foreign. Seven generations back Americans, and beyond that Irish, Scotch, English, German. One of our folks in the Revolution, an' they was lots of our folks in the Civil War—both sides. Americans.

*They were hungry, and they were fierce. And they had hoped to find a home, and they found only hatred. **Okies**—the **owners** hated them because the owners knew they were **soft** and the Okies strong, that they were fed and the Okies hungry; and perhaps the owners had heard from their grandfathers how easy it is to steal land from a soft man if you are fierce and hungry and armed. The owners hated them. And in the towns, the storekeepers hated them because they had no money to spend. There is no shorter path to a storekeeper's contempt, and all his admirations are exactly opposite. The town men, little bankers, hated Okies because there was nothing to*

Dispossessed: People who had lost their farms and homes.

Okies: The term "Okies" was originally short for the migrants from Oklahoma but soon came to refer to all impoverished migrants.

Owners: Established landowners in California.

Soft: Living well and not desperate for anything.

Driven from their Missouri farm by drought and dust storms, a family camps by the side of the road on their way to California.
©Bettmann/CORBIS. Reproduced by permission.

Intent: Determined.

Barbarians: The migrants.

Nebulous: Vague.

Beside the roads: Refers to the fields alongside the roads.

Coveted: Desired.

gain from them. They had nothing. And the laboring people hated Okies because a hungry man must work, and if he must work, if he has to work, the wage payer automatically gives him less for his work; and then no one can get more.

And the dispossessed, the migrants, flowed in California, two hundred and fifty thousand, and three hundred thousand. Behind them new tractors were going on the land and the tenants were being forced off. The new waves were on the way, new waves of the dispossessed and the homeless, hardened, **intent**, and dangerous.

And while the Californians wanted many things, accumulation, social success, amusement, luxury, and a curious banking security, the new **barbarians** wanted only two things - land and food; and to them the two were one. And whereas the wants of the Californians were **nebulous** and undefined, the wants of the Okies were **beside the roads**, lying there to be seen and **coveted**: the good fields with water to be dug for, the good green fields, earth to crumble experimentally in the hand, grass to smell, oaten stalks to chew until

*the sharp sweetness was in the throat. A man might look at a **fallow field** and known, and see in his mind that his own bending back and his own straining arms would bring the cabbages into the light, and the golden eating corn, the turnips and carrots.*

*And a homeless hungry man, driving the roads with his wife beside him and his thin children in the back seat, could look at the **fallow** fields which might produce food but not profit, and that man could know how **a fallow field is a sin and the unused land a crime against the thin children**. And such a man drove along the roads and knew temptation at every field, and knew the lust to take these fields and make them grow strength for his children and a little comfort for his wife. The temptation was before him always. The fields **goaded him**, and the company ditches with good water flowing were a goad to him.*

And in the south he saw the golden oranges hanging on the trees, the little golden oranges on the dark green trees; and guards with shotguns patrolling the lines so a man might not pick an orange for a thin child, oranges to be dumped if the price was low.

*He drove his old car into a town. He **scoured** the farms for work. Where can we sleep the night?*

*Well, there's **Hooverville** on the edge of the river. There's a whole raft of Okies there.*

He drove his old car to Hooverville. He never asked again, for there was a Hooverville on the edge of every town.

The rag town lay close to water; and the houses were tents, and weed-thatched enclosures, paper houses, a great junk pile. The man drove his family in and became a citizen of Hooverville—always they were called Hooverville. The man put up his own tent as near to water as he could get; or if he had no tent, he went to the city dump and brought back cartons and built a house of corrugated paper. And when the rains came the house melted and washed away. He settled in Hooverville and he scoured the countryside for work, and the little money he had went for gasoline to look for work. In the evening the men gathered and talked together. Squatting on their hams they talked on the land they had seen.

There's thirty thousan' acres, out west of here. Layin' there. Jesus, what I could do with that, with five acres of that! Why, hell, I'd have ever'thing to eat.

Notice one thing? They ain't no vegetables nor chickens nor pigs at the farms. They raise one thing - cotton, say, or peaches, or

Fallow field: Land that remained unplowed and unplanted.

A fallow field is a sin…: If the land were planted, it could produce food for his hungry children.

Goaded him: Urged him to find some way to grow food on the fields.

Scoured: Searched.

Hooverville: A community of makeshift shacks—made of cardboard boxes, scrap lumber, and scrap metal—that sheltered the homeless.

The Federal Writers' Project

Starting in 1935 the Federal Writers' Project (FWP) aided over six thousand novelists, journalists, poets, and other professionals such as lawyers, ministers, teachers, and anyone else willing to work in the publication field. The program was part of the Works Progress Administration (WPA), one of President Roosevelt's New Deal agencies, which were designed to rebuild America and return the nation to prosperity. Under the direction of Henry Alsberg (1881–1970), the FWP hired unemployed writers to produce a series of state and city guides, to write histories of immigrant groups, to identify and write about types of food in different regions of the country, and to record folklore stories from across the nation. Between 1935 and 1939 the FWP produced 378 books and pamphlets.

The FWP's American Guide Series included a guidebook for each state.

One of the FWP's most important publications was a collection of thirty-five stories about the lives of ordinary people from North Carolina, Tennessee, and Georgia; titled *These Are Our Lives,* the book was published in 1939. FWP writers who worked on the project used a new technique to research traditions and life histories: They collected their information through personal interviews, recording with pen and paper the personal experiences and memories of local citizens. This type of information is known as oral history. Richard Wright (1908–1960) and John Steinbeck (1902–1968), two authors who went on to fame, were supported by the FWP in the 1930s.

lettuce. 'Nother place'll be all chickens. They buy the stuff they could raise in the dooryard.

Jesus, what I could do with a couple pigs!

Well, it ain't yourn, an' it ain't gonna be yourn.

What we gonna do? The kids can't grow up this way.

In the camps the word would come whispering. There's work at Shafter. And the cars would be loaded in the night, the highways crowded—a gold rush for work. At Shafter the people would pile up, five times too many to do the work. A gold rush for work. They stole away in the night, frantic for work. And along the roads lay the temptations, the fields that could bear food.

That's owned. That ain't our'n.

Well, maybe we could get a little piece of her. Maybe—a little

piece. Right down there—a patch. Jimson weed now. [...] I could git enough potatoes off'n that little patch to feed my whole family!

It ain't our'n. It got to have Jimson weeds.

Now and then a man tried; crept on the land and cleared a piece, trying like a thief to steal a little richness from the earth. Secret gardens hidden in the weeds. A package of carrot seeds and a few turnips. Planted potato skins, crept out in the evening secretly to hoe in the stolen earth.

Leave the weeds around the edge—then nobody can see what we're a-doin'. Leave some weeds, big tall ones, in the middle.

Secret gardening in the evenings, and water carried in a rusty can.

And then one day a deputy sheriff: Well, what you think you're doin'?

I ain't doin' no harm.

Jane Darwell, Henry Fonda, and John Carradine (left to right) as the Joad family in the 1940 movie *The Grapes of Wrath.* *Corbis Corporation. Reproduced by permission.*

I had my eye on you. This ain't your land. You're trespassing.

The land ain't plowed, and I ain't hurtin' it none.

You [...] squatters. Pretty soon you'd think you owned it. You'd be sore as hell. Think you owned it. Get off now.

And the little green carrot tops were kicked off and the turnip greens trampled. And then the Jimson weed moved back in. But the cop was right. A crop raised—why, that makes ownership. Land hoed and the carrots eaten—a man might fight for land he's taken food from. Get him off quick! He'll think he owns it. He might even die fighting for the little plot among the Jimson weeds.

Did ya see his face when we kicked them turnips out? Why, he'd kill a fella soon's he'd look at him. We got to keep these here people down or they'll take the country. They'll take the country. [Steinbeck, pp. 207–210]

What happened next...

Few of the 1930s proletarian novels got very high on the best-seller lists, but *The Grapes of Wrath* was an exception. It topped the *New York Times* best-seller list in 1939 and remained eighth on the list in 1940. A film version of the book was made by Twentieth Century Fox in 1940 and directed by John Ford (1895–1973).

The novel and movie stirred up considerable controversy. Both in Oklahoma and California, citizens claimed that most of what Steinbeck had written was lies. Many of those citizens were ashamed that such conditions existed in their states. However, many government agents and sociologists confirmed Steinbeck's description of the horrid conditions. *Life,* a new photojournalism magazine, ran stories that also supported Steinbeck's portrayal of the migrant workers' existence.

Only about half of the migrants settled in the farming valleys of California. The rest went to San Francisco, Los Angeles, or San Diego. As the economy revived with the U.S. buildup for World War II in 1940 and 1941, most of the mi-

grants quickly acquired new skills and found regular jobs. Former migrants settled permanently in the California valleys as an increased demand for food created more jobs in farming.

The authors of 1930s proletarian literature began an American tradition: Since the 1930s, writers in the United States have continued to address class issues and political problems from all points of view. In 2000 *The Grapes of Wrath* was still considered one of the most important proletarian novels ever written.

Did you know...

- For years *The Grapes of Wrath* was spoken of only as a protest novel, and readers took sides over its message. Only after several decades was the book studied for its artistic literary qualities, such as superb character development.

- Steinbeck received support from the Federal Writers' Project (FWP), which was part of the Works Progress Administration (WPA), a New Deal agency established by President Roosevelt.

- In 1962 Steinbeck was honored with the Nobel Prize for literature. Nobel Prizes, named for Alfred Nobel (1833–1896), are awarded yearly to people who have made valuable contributions to humankind. Prizes are awarded in the fields of chemistry, economics, literature, medicine, physics, and world peace. Nobel Prizes include both a medal and a cash award.

Consider the following...

- Why did Californians not welcome the migrants into their state?

- What did Steinbeck mean when he said, "a fallow field is a sin and the unused land a crime against the thin children."?

- Reread the last portion of the excerpt. Side with either the deputy sheriff or the migrant who illegally planted the little patch of land. Defend your stance.

For More Information

Steinbeck, John. *The Grapes of Wrath.* New York, NY: Bantam Press, 1955. Reprint.

Swados, Harvey, ed. *The American Writer and the Great Depression.* New York, NY: Bobbs-Merrill, 1966.

Terkel, Studs. *Hard Times: An Oral History of the Great Depression.* New York, NY: Pantheon Books, 1986.

Worster, Donald. *Dust Bowl: The Southern Plains in the 1930s.* New York, NY: Oxford University Press, 1979.

Songs of the Depression

"Happy Days Are Here Again"

Written by Milton Ager and Jack Yellen
Copyrighted in 1929 by Warner Brothers
Excerpted from *Brother, Can You Spare a Dime? America from the*
Wall Street Crash to Pearl Harbor, An Illustrated Documentary

"We're in the Money"

Written by Harry Warren and Al Dubin
Copyrighted in 1933 by Warner Brothers
Excerpted from *Brother, Can You Spare a Dime? America from the*
Wall Street Crash to Pearl Harbor, An Illustrated Documentary

"Over the Rainbow"

Written by E. Y. Harburg and Harold Arlen
Copyrighted in 1939 by Leo Feist, Inc.

Excerpted from *Brother, Can You Spare a Dime? America from the*
Wall Street Crash to Pearl Harbor, An Illustrated Documentary

"Beans, Bacon, and Gravy"

Traditional
Excerpted from *Brother, Can You Spare a Dime?*
The Great Depression, 1929–1933.

"Soup Song"

Traditional
Reprinted by permission of Maurice Sugar
Excerpted from *Brother, Can You Spare a Dime?*
The Great Depression, 1929–1933.

"Brother, Can You Spare A Dime?"

Traditional
Copyrighted in 1932 by Harms, Inc.
Excerpted from *Brother, Can You Spare a Dime?*
The Great Depression, 1929–1933.

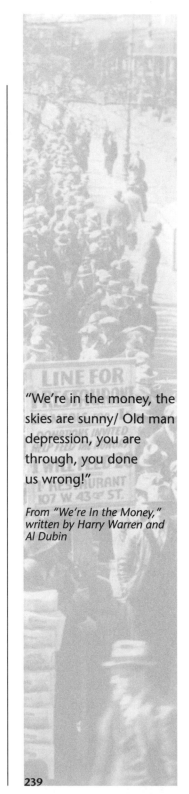

"We're in the money, the skies are sunny/ Old man depression, you are through, you done us wrong!"

From "We're In the Money," written by Harry Warren and Al Dubin

239

As Franklin D. Roosevelt ran for the presidency in 1932, "Happy Days Are Here Again" became his campaign song, symbolizing the belief that he would bring the United States out of the Depression. *AP/Wide World Photo. Reproduced by permission.*

In 1932 at the depth of the Great Depression, the most severe economic crisis in U.S. history, Franklin D. Roosevelt (1882–1945) accepted the nomination to run for president on the Democratic ticket in the November election. On the campaign trail Roosevelt's calm, reassuring manner quickly began to win over Americans desperate for new leadership. Soon the perky "Happy Days Are Here Again," a Roosevelt campaign song, was heard across the nation.

Another optimistic song that became well known nationwide was "We're in the Money," written by Harry Warren and Al Dubin in 1933. By 1933 big, splashy, squeaky-clean musicals were replacing the gangster movies that had been popular between 1930 and 1932. Three such musicals, all produced by Warner Brothers in 1933, proved wildly popular: *Gold Diggers of 1933, Forty-Second Street,* and *Footlight Parade.* In *Gold Diggers of 1933,* several dozen young women, holding giant coins, sing and dance along with actress,

singer, and dancer Ginger Rogers (1911–1995) as she sings the lively tune "We're in the Money." The words of the song expressed Americans' desire to be "through" with "old man depression." These three musicals lifted spirits and succeeded in putting Warner Brothers, a company that was struggling to survive in 1932, back "in the money."

The ultimate spirit-raising song appeared in 1939 in the movie *The Wizard of Oz*. The young lead actress, Judy Garland (1922–1969), sang "Over the Rainbow" with such conviction that most Americans soon learned and sang the hopeful lyrics to themselves. By 1939 everyone wanted to be at the end of the rainbow "where troubles melt like lemon drops, away."

However, before happy days, loads of money, or rainbows could be found, Americans would have to struggle through the Depression years. During the early 1930s hungry citizens waited in breadlines that extended for long city blocks. They waited for simple meals of coffee, bread, and beans or soup. Some unemployed and homeless people took to wandering on the railroads in search of work. They, too, would stand in breadlines in the towns they pulled into or fix food over campfires in hobo camps near the railroad tracks. From the unemployed and hungry came songs of protest. Two typical and popular protest songs sung throughout the country were "Beans, Bacon, and Gravy" and "Soup Song." Another such song, "Brother, Can You Spare A Dime?" recalls a man who had worked and had served his country in World War I (1914–18) only to be forgotten and left to live in poverty in the early 1930s.

Things to remember while reading the excerpts in this section, "Songs of the Depression":

• The popular movie musicals of the 1930s transported people away from hard times for a few hours and left them humming happy tunes to themselves.

• Songs of protest were sometimes very serious, but often they were funny. It seemed to be helpful for people to keep laughing instead of crying through their hard times.

Excerpt from "Happy Days Are Here Again"
Written by Milton Ager and Jack Yellen

Happy days are here again!
The skies above are clear again!
Let's all sing a song of cheer again—
Happy days are here again!
[Winslow, p. 51]

Excerpt from "We're in the Money"
Written by Harry Warren and Al Dubin

Gone are my blues, and gone are my tears;
I've got good news to shout in your ears.
The silver dollar has returned to the fold,
With silver you can turn your dreams to gold.

We're in the money, we're in the money,
We've got a lot of what it takes to get along!
We're in the money, the skies are sunny;
Old man depression, you are through, you done us wrong!

We never see a headline 'bout a breadline today,
And when we see the landlord,

We can look that guy right in the eye.
We're in the money, come on my honey,
Let's spend it, lend it, send it rolling along!
[Winslow, p. 55]

Excerpt from "Over the Rainbow"
Written by E. Y. Harburg and Harold Arlen

When all the world is a hopeless jumble,
And the rain drops tumble all around,
Heaven opens up a magic lane.
When all the clouds darken up the skyway,
There's a rainbow to be found
Leading from your windowpane.
To a place behind the sun,
Just a step beyond the rain.

Somewhere over the rainbow way
    up high,
There's a land that I dreamed of,
    once in a lullaby;
Somewhere over the rainbow, skies
    are blue,
And the dreams that you dare to
    dream really do come true.

Someday I'll wish upon a star
And wake up where the clouds are
    far behind me.
Where troubles melt like lemon
    drops, away,

Above the chimney-tops, that's
    where you'll find me.
Somewhere over the rainbow blue-
    birds fly,
Birds fly over the rainbow, why then,
Oh why can't I?
[Winslow, p. 103]

Excerpt from "Beans, Bacon, and Gravy"

Anonymous

I was born long ago, in 1894,
And I've seen many a panic, I will own;
I've been hungry, I've been cold,
And now I'm growing old.
But the worst I've seen is 1932.

REFRAIN:

Oh, those beans, bacon, and gravy,
They almost drive me crazy,
I eat them till I see them in my dreams,
    In my dreams;

When I wake up in the morning,
And another day is dawning,
Yes, I know I'll have another **mess** of beans.
We congregate each morning
At the country barn at dawning

A scene from the 1939
movie, *The Wizard of Oz,* in
which Dorothy, played by
Judy Garland, sang the
uplifting tune, "Over the
Rainbow." *The Kobal
Collection. Reproduced
by permission.*

Mess: Serving.

And everybody is happy, so it seems;
But when our work is done
We file in one by one,
And thank the Lord for one more mess of beans.

REFRAIN

*We have **Hooverized** on butter,*
For milk we've only water,
And I haven't seen a steak in many a day;
As for pies, cakes, and jellies,
We substitute sow-bellies,
For which we work the country road each day.

REFRAIN

If there ever comes a time
When I have more than a dime
They will have to put me under lock and key,
For they've had me broke so long
I can only sing this song,
Of the workers and their misery.

REFRAIN
[Meltzer, pp. 104–105]

Excerpt from "Soup Song"
Anonymous

*I'm spending my nights at the **flop-house**,*
I'm spending my days on the street.
I'm looking for work, and I find none,
I wish I had something to eat.

CHORUS:
Soo-oup,
Soo-oup,
They give me a bowl of Soo-oo-oup.
Soo-oup,
Soo-oup,

They give me a bowl of soup.
I spent twenty years in the factory,
I did everything I was told,
They said I was faithful and loyal,
Now even before I get old:

Hooverized: Skimped.

Flop-house: A cheap hotel or place to sleep.

(CHORUS)
I saved fifteen bucks with my banker
To buy me a car and a yacht,
I went down to draw out my fortune,
And this is the answer I got:

(CHORUS)
[Meltzer, pp. 84–85]

Excerpt from "Brother, Can You Spare A Dime?"
Anonymous

They used to tell me I was building
   a dream,
And so I followed the mob—
When there was earth to plough or
   guns to bear
I was always there—right there on
   the job.
They used to tell me I was building
   a dream
With peace and glory ahead—
Why should I be standing in line
Just waiting for bread?

Once I built a railroad, made it run,
Made it race against time.
Once I built a railroad,
Now it's done—
Brother, can you spare a dime?

Once I built a tower, to the sun.
Brick and rivet and lime,
Once I built a tower,
Now it's done—
Brother, can you spare a dime?
Once in **khaki suits**,
Gee, we looked swell,
Full of that Yankee Doodle-de-dum.
Half a billion boots went sloggin' thru Hell,
I was the kid with the drum.

Say, don't you remember, they called me Al—
It was Al all the time.

Many World War I veterans, considered heroes when they returned home from war in 1919, fell on hard times during the 1930s. *AP/Wide World Photo. Reproduced by permission.*

Khaki suits: World War I (1914–18) uniform.

Documentary Literature about Depression-Era America

Many American writers in the 1930s got their start as newspapermen. They left their offices and traveled through the United States to try to better understand the impact of the Depression on their fellow Americans. From these travels a group of documentary books emerged. Documentary literature provides an objective, factual, real-life description of people, places, historic moments, and other important events.

An early documentary work was *The American Jitters: A Year of the Slump*, written by Edmund Wilson (1895–1972) and published in 1932. The brilliantly perceptive and witty Sherwood Anderson (1876–1941), after a two-month trip around the country, produced *Puzzled America* in 1935. Nathan Asche (1902–)

also reported on his travels around the country in *The Road: In Search of America* (1937). *My America* (1938) by Louis Adamic (1899–1951) is one of the most famous of the 1930s documentary books. In the preface Adamic writes, "Since 1931 I have traveled perhaps 100,000 miles here in America, by train, by automobile, by plane, as well as afoot, pausing here and there to look and listen, to ask questions to get the feel of things; and I have developed, I think, a fairly steady feeling about this vast place. "*Let Us Now Praise Famous Men*, a documentary work by author James Agee (1909–1955) and photographer Walker Evans (1903–1975), examines the life of an Alabama sharecropper's family. Not published until 1941, the book became a classic of Depression-era literature.

Say, don't you remember I'm your pal—
Buddy, can you spare a dime?

[Meltzer, pp. 157–158]

What happened next...

When the United States entered World War II in late 1941, the country had to quickly mobilize all its industrial might to manufacture products needed for the war effort. The unemployed, including the migrant farmworkers, found jobs, and young men joined the armed services.

World War II effectively put an end to "old man depression." Songwriters turned their talents to writing stirring patriotic music.

Did you know...
- The 1930s protest songs were never part of large protest gatherings such as the ones that occurred from the 1950s to the 1970s in response to civil rights issues and the Vietnam War (1954–75). A different mind-set existed in the 1930s. Most Americans thought of their predicament as their own fault, and they believed they would have to work it out themselves. Few understood that the causes of the Depression were beyond the control of any individual.

- The most popular music during the Depression was swing, a type of jazz performed by big bands. Also popular were songs with a romantic theme. Examples include "Red Sails in the Sunset," "The Way You Look Tonight," "Whistle While You Work," "You Must Have Been a Beautiful Baby," "When You Wish upon a Star," and "A-Tisket, A-Tasket."

Consider the following...
- Music is said to be healing to the spirit. Do you believe this was the case in the Depression years? In what ways did music help Americans in the 1930s?

For More Information
Arnett, Hazel. *I Hear America Singing! Great Folk Songs from the Revolution to Rock.* New York, NY: Praeger Publishers, 1975.

Bergman, Andrew. *We're in the Money: Depression America and Its Films.* New York, NY: New York University Press, 1971.

Leyshon, Andrew, David Matless, and George Revill, eds. *The Place of Music.* New York, NY: Guilford Press, 1998.

Meltzer, Milton. *Brother, Can You Spare a Dime? The Great Depression, 1929–1933.* New York, NY: Alfred A. Knopf, 1969.

Winslow, Susan. *Brother, Can You Spare a Dime? America from the Wall Street Crash to Pearl Harbor, An Illustrated Documentary.* New York, NY: Paddington Press, 1976.

Woody Guthrie

"Dust Storm Disaster"

"I Ain't Got No Home"

"Pastures of Plenty"

"Roll On Columbia"

**Excerpted from *Woody Guthrie Songs*
Edited by Judy Bell and Nora Guthrie
Published in 1992**

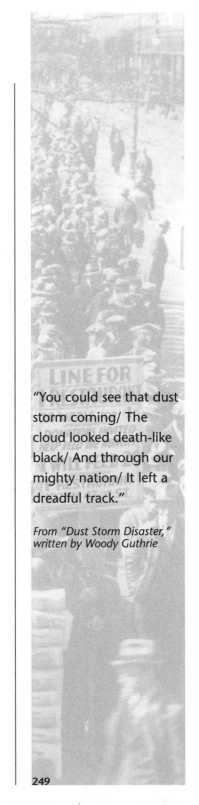

"You could see that dust storm coming/ The cloud looked death-like black/ And through our mighty nation/ It left a dreadful track."

From "Dust Storm Disaster," written by Woody Guthrie

The Dust Bowl refugees came to symbolize the extreme hardship of the Great Depression. Folk musician and songwriter Woody Guthrie (1912–1967) composed approximately twenty songs between 1936 and 1941 that together were known as the "Dust Bowl Ballads." These ballads were set against one of three backgrounds: (1) Dust Bowl farms with dry, barren land covered in drifts of topsoil dust; (2) the highway, which carried displaced farming families westward in overloaded old cars in search of work; and (3) the ideal vision of the "promised land" of California.

Guthrie was born and raised in the Oklahoma cotton-belt town of Okemah. He experienced his first dust storm in Pampa, Texas, a farming community in the Texas Panhandle, where he had moved in 1929. In 1935, as dust storms rolled over parts of Kansas, Oklahoma, Texas, New Mexico, and Colorado, Guthrie responded by writing "Dust Storm Disaster," the first excerpt in this chapter. The fourth verse reads:

> *It fell across our city*
> *Like a curtain of black rolled down*
> *We thought it was our judgment*

Woody Guthrie's songs gave a voice to the people about whom he was writing. *Courtesy of the Library of Congress.*

We thought it was our doom.

Guthrie's choice of words like "judgment" and "doom" bring to mind the many "judgment and doom" stories in the Old Testament of the Bible. In the final verse of "Dust Storm Disaster," the family moves out onto the highway:

We loaded our jalopies
And piled our families in,
We rattled down that highway
To never come back again.

The second ballad excerpt, "I Ain't Got No Home," is a classic Guthrie Dust Bowl ballad set on the highway. In the 1930s U.S. Routes 10, 66, and 90 to the western United States were filled with migrants who had lost their sense of self-pride and were "a-ramblin' 'round" in search of work. In the third verse, Guthrie refers to the sharecropping and tenant farmers of the cotton belt in southern and eastern Oklahoma and parts of Texas:

"I was farmin' on the shares
And always I was poor"

Sharecroppers and tenant farmers rented the land they worked, and a significant part of their crop went to the owners of the land. During the Depression these farm families took to the road, not because they were "dusted out" by the damaging dust storms but because they were told to leave by the landowners. The price of cotton had fallen so low by 1935 that there was no profit to be made in cotton; therefore, the landowners had no use for the sharecroppers and tenant farmers.

The third ballad excerpt, "Pastures of Plenty," describes what Dust Bowl refugees encountered in the promised land, the land at the end of the "hot dusty road." Guthrie tells of migrant pickers moving around the West, following the harvests of the "pastures of plenty." In 1937 Guthrie moved his own family to southern California where he continued to work on his Dust Bowl ballads.

Sharecropper families, now homeless, line the road after being told by landowners that their services were no longer needed, circa January 1939. ©Bettmann/CORBIS. Reproduced by permission.

The Guthrie family next moved to New York City, where Guthrie was offered a job on a nationwide radio program that paid a good wage. But, as his son Arlo (1947–), who also became a folk music writer and singer, explained years later, Woody Guthrie felt uncomfortable about making good money. He felt that by earning too much he was separating himself from hardworking but poor Americans. So the family went back to California. In May 1941 they moved to Portland, Oregon, where Guthrie took a job with the Bonneville Power Administration, an agency backed by the federal government. The job paid $266 for one month. Guthrie was to write a song a day about the Columbia River, the Bonneville Dam, and the Grand Coulee Dam, which was still under construction. The dams were federal government projects that brought jobs and hydroelectric power to the Pacific Northwest. Guthrie ended up writing twenty-six songs in thirty days, songs that caught the spirit of the region's people and river and called attention to the benefits that hydroelectric power brought to the Northwest. The fourth excerpt, "Roll On, Columbia," is one of the most famous of these songs.

The Dust Bowl

Beginning in late 1931 and continuing until the rains returned in 1939, an extreme drought afflicted the Great Plains, an area extending from North Dakota to the Texas Panhandle. Most of the area's native grasses had been plowed under, and the soil had been planted in wheat. When the rains failed to fall in late 1931, the wheat could not grow enough to anchor the topsoil. Then, strong winds blew down from the north, as they did every year, and the soil rose up into massive, threatening clouds of dust that traveled over the entire Plains region. The dust went everywhere, even into homes, covering everything. It piled up like deep snowdrifts around fences, barns, houses. Farming the land became impossible. The areas most affected by the devastating dust storms were southeast Colorado, western Kansas, the Oklahoma and Texas Panhandles, and northeastern New Mexico. One of the worst storms was recorded on April 14, 1935, over Kansas; it was known as the "Black Sunday" storm.

Many families put all their belongings and their children in the car and drove away from their farms; they were "dusted out." Most headed to the West Coast in search of work. They were no longer farmers but "migrants." Approximately two hundred thousand went to California. Some settled in cities, and others tried to make a living following the various West Coast harvests. These traveling farmworkers lived in desperate poverty and filthy conditions. Attempting to assist these workers, federal government agencies built a number of tent camps for the migrants in California. Nevertheless, the situation did not significantly improve until 1940 and 1941, when U.S. preparations to enter World War II (1939–45) created many new jobs.

A dust-covered farm in Texas, circa 1938.
©Bettmann/CORBIS. Reproduced by permission.

Things to remember while reading the excerpts from Woody Guthrie's original ballads and songs:

- Guthrie's songs reflected his experiences of the 1930s Great Depression, severe drought on the Great Plains, President Franklin D. Roosevelt's New Deal programs, and World War II.

- Through his music Guthrie became a spokesman for the oppressed and the victims of the Depression. His music focused on farmers, workers, unions, and the common people, and the injustices these groups experienced. His seemingly simple songs are about complex social and environmental issues that were affecting the nation at that time.

Excerpt from "Dust Storm Disaster"

On the fourteenth day of April
Of nineteen thirty-five,
There struck the worst of dust storms
That ever filled the sky.

You could see that dust storm coming
The cloud looked death-like black
And through our mighty nation
It left a dreadful track.

From Oklahoma City
To the Arizona line
Dakota and Nebraska
To the lazy Rio Grande.

It fell across our city
Like a curtain of black rolled down
We thought it was our judgment
We thought it was our doom.

The radio reported
We listened with alarm
The wild and windy actions
Of this great mysterious storm.

From Albuquerque and Clovis
And old New Mexico
They said it was the blackest
That ever they had saw.

In old Dodge City, Kansas,
The dust had rung their knell,
And a few more comrades sleeping
On top of old Boot Hill.

From Denver, Colorado,
They said it blew so strong,
They thought that they could hold out,
They did not know how long.

Our relatives were huddled
Into their oil-boom shacks,
And the children they were crying
As it whistled through the cracks.

And the family was crowded
Into their little room,
They thought the world had ended,
And they thought it was their doom.

The storm took place at sundown.
It lasted through the night.
When we looked out next morning
We saw a terrible sight.

We saw outside our window
Where wheatfields they had grown,
Was now a rippling ocean
Of dust the wind had blown.

It covered up our fences,
It covered up our barns,
It covered up our tractors
In this wild and dusty storm.

We loaded our jalopies
And piled our families in,
We rattled down that highway
To never come back again.
[Bell and Guthrie, p. 41]

A young South Dakota man takes to the road in 1936 to escape drought and search for work. *Courtesy of the Library of Congress.*

Excerpt from "I Ain't Got No Home"

I ain't got no home,
I'm just a-ramblin' 'round,
I'm just a-wand'rin' workin' man,
I go from town to town.
Police make it hard
Wherever I may go,
>*And I ain't got no home*
>*In this world anymore.*

My brothers and my sisters
Are stranded on this road;
It's a hot and dusty road
That a million feet have trod.
>*Rich man took my home and he drove me from*
>*my door*
>*And I ain't got no home in this world anymore.*

I was farmin' on the shares
And always I was poor;
My crops I lay
Into the banker's store.
My wife took down and died
Upon my cabin floor
>*And I ain't got no home in this world anymore.*

I mined in your mines
And I gather in your corn;
I been working, mister,
Since the day that I was born.
Now I worry all the time
Like I never did before
>*'Cause I ain't got no home in this world anymore.*

Now as I look around
It's might plain to see
This wide and wicked world
Is a funny place to be.
>*The gambling man is rich and the working man*
>*is not.*
>*And I ain't got no home in this world anymore.*
[Bell and Guthrie, p. 42]

Excerpt from "Pastures of Plenty"

It's a mighty hard row that my poor hands have hoed;
My poor feet have traveled a hot dusty road.
Out of your dust bowl and westward we rolled,
And your desert was hot and your mountains were cold.

I worked in your orchards of peaches and prunes,
Slept on the ground in the light of your moon,
On the edge of your city you've seen us and then,
We come with the dust and we go with the wind.

California and Arizona, I make all your crops,
*And it's north up to Oregon to gather your **hops**,*
Dig the beets from your ground, cut the grapes from your vines,
To set on your table your light sparkling wine.

Green pastures of plenty from dry desert ground,
From that Grand Coulee Dam where the water runs down,
Every state in this union us migrants have been,
We work in this fight, and we'll fight till we win.

Well, it's always we ramble, that river and I,
All along your green valley I'll work till I die,
My land I'll defend with my life, if it be,
'Cause my pastures of plenty must always be free.
[Bell and Guthrie, p. 8]

Excerpt from "Roll On, Columbia"

Roll on, Columbia, roll on.
Roll on, Columbia, roll on.
Your power is turning our darkness to dawn,
So, roll on, Columbia, roll on!

Green Douglas firs where the waters cut through.
Down her wild mountains and canyons she flew.
Canadian Northwest to the oceans so blue,
Roll on, Columbia, roll on!

Other great rivers add power to you,
Yakima, Snake and the Klickitat too,
Sandy Willamette and Hood River too,

Hops: Dried flowers of the hop vine, from which beer is made.

Roll on, Columbia, roll on.

Tom Jefferson's vision would not let him rest,
An empire he saw in the Pacific Northwest.
Sent Lewis and Clark and they did the rest,
Roll on, Columbia, roll on (Chorus)

It's there on your banks that we fought many a fight,
Sheridan's boys in the blockhouse that night,
They saw us in death but never in flight,
Roll on, Columbia, roll on (Chorus)

*At **Bonneville** now there are ships in the locks,*
The waters have risen and cleared all the rocks,
Shiploads of plenty will stream past the docks,
So roll on, Columbia, roll on.

And on up the river is Grand Coulee Dam,
The mightiest thing ever built by a man,
To run the great factories and water the land,
It's roll on, Columbia, roll on.

These mighty men labored by day and by night,
Matching their strength 'gainst the river's wild flight,
Through rapids and falls they won the hard fight,
Roll on, Columbia, roll on.
[Bell and Guthrie, p. 13]

What happened next...

Woody Guthrie worked and reworked the ballads he had composed between 1936 and 1941. The migrants he wrote about were largely absorbed into the Western population as jobs became available in the early 1940s. The "Dust Bowl Ballads" were never well known during the Depression. Instead, after World War II (1939–45), the "Dust Bowl Ballads" became more connected with worker protests than with the dust storms of the 1930s. This happened largely because by the late 1940s Guthrie switched his focus to labor struggles and the rights of workers. Guthrie's ballads were also popular during the folk song movement in the 1960s. In 1966 Secre-

Bonneville: A large dam located on the Columbia River in the Northwest.

tary of the Interior Stewart Udall presented Guthrie with a Conservation Service Award for his songs, officially recognizing that Guthrie's work had taught Americans about their country's history, the history of the people and of the land. In 2000, with over sixty years of hindsight, Guthrie's songs were still recognized as one of the most powerful records of social hardship found in American folk music.

Did you know...

- Woody Guthrie wrote for only seventeen years, but he produced over one thousand songs as well as several books and short writing exercises.

- Guthrie's prolific career was cut short when, at the age of thirty-nine, he developed Huntington's chorea, a hereditary disease that had killed his mother. Woody spent much of the rest of his life hospitalized at Creedmore State Hospital in Queens, New York. One symptom of his disease is loss of muscle, and Guthrie eventually lost the ability to write for he could no longer hold a pencil. He died in 1967 at the age of fifty-five.

Consider the following...

- Explain what Pete Seeger (1919–), songwriter and friend of Woody Guthrie, might have meant when he said "Pastures of Plenty" was a "complaint" and a "protest" but also an "affirmation."

For More Information

Books

Adamic, Louis. *My America, 1928–1938*. New York, NY: Harper & Brothers Publishers, 1938.

Arnett, Hazel. *I Hear America Singing! Great Folk Songs from the Revolution to Rock*. New York, NY: Praeger Publishers, 1975.

Bell, Judy, and Nora Guthrie, eds. *Woody Guthrie Songs*. New York, NY: TRO Ludlow Music, 1992.

Guthrie, Woody. *Bound for Glory*. New York, NY: New American Library, 1970.

Klein, Joe. *Woody Guthrie: A Life*. New York, NY: Ballantine Books, 1980.

Web Sites

Discographies: Woody Guthrie in Oregon. http://libweb.uoregon.edu/music/woody.html (accessed on August 30, 2002).

Where to Learn More

Books

Badger, Anthony J. *The New Deal: The Depression Years, 1933–1940.* New York: Hill and Wang, 1989.

Bowen, Ezra. *The Fabulous Century: 1930–1940.* New York: Time-Life Books, 1969.

Britton, Loretta, and Sarah Brash, eds. *Hard Times: The 30s.* Alexandria, VA: Time-Life Books, 1998.

Buhite, Russell D., and David W. Levy, eds. *FDR's Fireside Chats.* Norman: University of Oklahoma Press, 1992.

Burns, James McGregor. *Roosevelt: The Lion and the Fox.* Norwalk, CT: Eaton Press, 1989.

Cochran, Thomas C. *The Great Depression and World War II, 1929–1945.* Glenview, IL: Scott, Foresman, and Company, 1968.

Federal Writers Project. *These Are Our Lives.* New York: W.W. Norton & Company, Inc., 1939.

Horan, James D. *The Desperate Years: A Pictorial History of the Thirties.* New York: Bonanza Books, 1962.

Kennedy, David M. *Freedom From Fear: The American People in Depression and War, 1929–1945.* New York: Oxford University Press, 1999.

Leuchtenberg, William E. *Franklin D. Roosevelt and the New Deal, 1932–1940.* New York: Harper & Row, 1963.

Martin, George. *Madam Secretary: Frances Perkins*. Boston: Houghton Mifflin, 1976.

McElvaine, Robert S. *The Depression and the New Deal: A History in Documents*. New York: Oxford University Press, 2000.

McElvaine, Robert S. *The Great Depression: America, 1929–1941*. New York: Times Books, 1993.

Meltzer, Milton. *Brother, Can You Spare a Dime? The Great Depression, 1929–1933*. New York: New American Library, 1977.

Pasachoff, Naomi E. *Frances Perkins: Champion of the New Deal*. New York: Oxford University Press, 1999.

Perkins, Frances. *The Roosevelt I Knew*. New York: The Viking Press, 1946.

Phillips, Cabell. *From the Crash to the Blitz, 1929–1939*. New York: Macmillan, 1969.

Rogers, Agnes. *I Remember Distinctly: A Family Album of the American People, 1918–1941*. New York: Harper & Brothers Publishers, 1947.

Roosevelt, Eleanor. *The Autobiography of Eleanor Roosevelt*. New York: Da Capo Press, 2000.

Roosevelt, Franklin D. *The Public Papers and Addresses of Franklin D. Roosevelt*. 5 vols. New York: Random House, 1938–1950.

Schlesinger, Arthur M., Jr. *The Age of Roosevelt*. 3 volumes. Boston: Houghton Mifflin Company, 1957–1960.

Schlesinger, Arthur M., Jr. *The Coming of the New Deal: The Age of Roosevelt*. Boston: Houghton Mifflin Company, 1988.

Terkel, Studs. *Hard Times: An Oral History of the Great Depression*. New York: Pantheon Books, 1986.

Thompson, Kathleen, and Hilary MacAustin, eds. *Children of the Depression*. Bloomington: Indiana University Press, 2001.

Washburne, Carolyn Kott. *America in the 20th Century, 1930–1939*. North Bellmore, NY: Marshall Cavendish Corp., 1995.

Watkins, T. H. *The Great Depression: America in the 1930s*. Boston: Little, Brown, & Co., 1993.

Watkins, T. H. *The Hungry Years: A Narrative History of the Great Depression in America*. New York: Henry Holt and Company, 1999.

Winslow, Susan. *Brother, Can You Spare a Dime? America From the Wall Street Crash to Pearl Harbor: An Illustrated Documentary*. New York: Paddington Press, 1976.

Web Sites

Franklin D. Roosevelt Library and Museum. http://www.fdrlibrary.marist.edu

Library of Congress. American Memory. http://memory.loc.gov/ammem/fsowhome.html

New Deal Network. http://newdeal.feri.org

Index

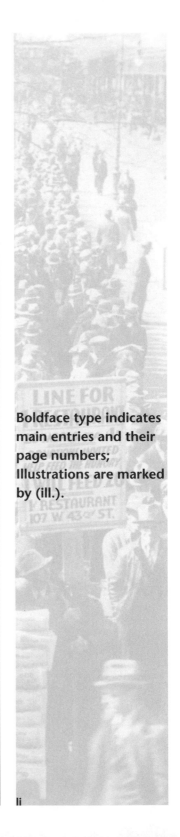

**Boldface type indicates
main entries and their
page numbers;
Illustrations are marked
by (ill.).**